A BIBLIOGRAPHY OF AFRICAN ART

A Bibliography of

AFRICAN ART

compiled at the International African Institute

by L. J. P. Gaskin, F.L.A.

under the direction of Guy Atkins, M.A., D.Phil.

School of Oriental and African Studies
University of London

International African Institute

10/11 FETTER LANE, LONDON, EC4

1965

The International African Institute
is grateful to the Ford Foundation for a generous
grant towards the cost of compiling and
publishing this bibliography

Printed in Great Britain by
W. & J. Mackay & Co. Ltd., Chatham, Kent

Contents-List

List of Countries

Introduction

For about half a century African sculpture has succeeded in holding its place in the eyes of the Western world as one of the most consistently admired art forms. The literature on every aspect of African art has grown so large, especially during the twenty years since the last war, that the time now seems ripe for publishing a list of titles, of which close on five thousand have come to light during the two years since work on the bibliography began. A companion volume entitled *A select Bibliography of Music in Africa* has recently appeared under the same auspices as this book.

The arrangement of the bibliography is geographical, with sub-headings to cover the main genres for every region. This method was thought to be the most serviceable for those readers who live in Africa and are interested mainly in the art of their own country, as well as for the specialist who will probably prefer to have the literature classified by areas rather than by topics. Cross-references and double entries have been avoided as far as possible, but the indexes are intended to help the reader to find those works which have had to be placed, sometimes rather arbitrarily, under one heading rather than another. The general reader will find that the first section of the bibliography contains a large choice of introductory studies which provide different approaches to the subject.

Some difficulty arose from the nomenclature of the new African states, but it is hoped that this has been overcome by the detailed geographical arrangement of African countries (p. vii), and, where necessary, by explanatory notes. Since ethnic and linguistic units do not always fit easily into political boundaries, classification by countries proved difficult at times. The literature on the Ewe, for instance, contains data collected in the former German Togo, the present-day Togo, or in Ghana or in Dahomey, while the art of the Tuareg might be described as from Niger or from Algeria: to analyse the entries in detail was impracticable.

Page references to the main headings and countries will be found in the contents and countries lists. References to the numbered entries have been made in the author, subject and geographical indexes. *See also* references in the text refer to the number of the entry. In the case of articles in periodical publications, reference is made in the entry to the actual pagination involved, but in the case of books the pagination of the whole work is recorded, and a note of the pages dealing with art is given at the end of the entry when the subject is not mentioned in the index or contents-list of the book.

The International African Institute's card index provided an initial basis for assembling entries, and working out the classification. This was extensively supplemented by further researches made in the libraries mentioned below to provide, it is hoped, an authoritative and useful survey of the literature on African art.

Grateful thanks are due to all those who, so kindly, supplied titles for inclusion in the bibliography. In this connection special mention should be made of Dr. Guy Atkins who supplied some 1,500 titles, Professor Westphal who contributed 100 titles, mainly on Bushman paintings, and Mrs. Norma Wolff, African specialist in the Michigan State University Library, who sent some 600 titles. The Ethnographical Museum at Antwerp sent a list of the catalogues of exhibitions on African art held in Belgium during the past few years, and Mr. Wassing of the Rotterdam

Museum sent a list of books on African art. Special mention too should be made of Mr. W. B. Fagg, Deputy-Keeper of the Ethnographical Department of the British Museum, who has given much valuable advice and help with the compilation of the bibliography.

Thanks are also due to the authorities of the under-mentioned institutions for the facilities granted to the Compiler for research in their libraries:

BRITISH MUSEUM: General Library

BRITISH MUSEUM: Department of Ethnography Library

COLONIAL OFFICE LIBRARY (London)

FROBENIUS INSTITUTE AND LIBRARY (Frankfurt a M)

MUSEE DE L'HOMME LIBRARY (Paris)

RAUTENSTRAUCH-JOEST-MUSEUM LIBRARY (Cologne)

ROYAL ANTHROPOLOGICAL INSTITUTE LIBRARY (London)

ROYAL COMMONWEALTH SOCIETY LIBRARY (London)

SCHOOL OF ORIENTAL AND AFRICAN STUDIES LIBRARY (London)

TERVUREN CONGO MUSEUM LIBRARY (Tervuren)

TROPEN MUSEUM LIBRARY (Amsterdam)

UNESCO LIBRARY (Paris)

VICTORIA AND ALBERT MUSEUM LIBRARY (London)

GENERAL

1. **Adama van Scheltema, Frederik.** 1950. *Die Kunst der Vorzeit.* Pp. 207, ill. Stuttgart: W. Kohlhammer.

2. **Africa Italiana.** 1927–41. *Revista di storia e d'Arte a cura del Ministero dell' Africa Italiana.* Bergamo: 8 vols. in 2, ill. Instituto Italiano d'Arte Grafiche.

3. **Alimen, H.** 1955. *Préhistoire de l'Afrique.* Pp. 579, ill., maps. Paris: Bonbée.

4. **Archer, W. G.** 1947. *The vertical man.* Pp. 122, ill. London: Geo. Allen.

5. **Bastide, R.** 1960. *Les religions africaines au Brésil.* Pp. 578. Paris: Presses univ. de France.

6. **Batten, T. R.** 1949. *Africa past and present.* Pp. 108. Oxford: Univ. Press.

7. **Beaver, P.** 1955. *L'Afrique vivante.* Pp. 253. Paris.

8. **Bernard, Augustin.** 1927–48. *Géographie universelle,* publié de P. Vidal de la Blache et L. Gallois. Tome, 11. Afrique septentrionale et occidentale par *A. Bernard.* Deuxième partie: Sahara, Afrique occidentale. Pp. 246, ill., map. Paris: Librairie Armand Colin.

9. **Bossert, H. Th.** 1959. *Janus und der Mann.* Pp. 26, ill., map. Leiden: Ned. Hist.-archeol. Inst., 1 (5).

10. **Bourel de la Roncière, Charles.** 1933. *Nègres et négriers.* PP. 121–30, ill. Paris: Editions des Portiques.

11. **Briault, Maurice.** 1943. *Les sauvages d'Afrique.* Pp. 311, ill. Paris: Payot.

12. **Conze, A.** *Über den Ursprung der bildenden Kunst.* SB. preuss. Akad. Wiss. zu Berlin, 1897, 98–109.

13. **Cornevin, Robert.** 1962. *Histoire de l'Afrique.* Pp. 453, bibl., maps. Paris: Payot.

14. **Crawley, Ernest.** 1931. *Dress, drink and drums.* Pp. x + 274, ill. London: Methuen.

15. **Danzel, Th-W.** 1947. *Magie et science secrète.* Pp. 198, ill. Paris.

16. **Dapper, Olfert.** 1668. *Nauwkeurige Beschrijvinge der Afrikaansche Gewesten.* Amsterdam.

17. —— 1686. *Description de l'Afrique.* Pp. 534. Amsterdam: Wolfgang, Waesberge, Boom et van Someren.

18. **Davidson, Basil.** *Archaeology in Africa.* Atlantic monthly, 203, 1959, 40–43, ill.

19. —— 1959. *Old Africa rediscovered.* Pp. 287, ill., maps. London: Gollancz.

20. —— *Lost cities of Africa* (review article). Archaeology, 13, 1960, 149–50.

21. —— 1961. *Urzeit und Geschichte Afrikas.* London.

22. **d'Azevedo, Warren.** *A structural approach to aesthetics: towards a definition of art in anthropology.* Amer. Anthrop., 60, 1958, 702–14.

23. **de Graft-Johnson, J. C.** 1954. *African glory: the story of vanished negro civilisations.* Pp. x + 209, ill., map. London: Watts.

24. **de Pedrals, D. P.** 1950. *L'archéologie de l'Afrique noire.* Pp. 234, bibl., ill. Paris: Payot.

25. **Diop, Ch.-A.** *Histoire primitive de l'humanité: Évolution du monde noir.* Bull. I.F.A.N., 24 (3–4), July Oct., 1962, 449–541, bibl., ill.

26. **Duyvendak, J. J. L.** 1949. *China's discovery of Africa: Lectures given at the University of London on Jan. 22 & 23, 1947.* Pp. 35, ill. London: A. Probsthain.

27. **Dvořak, Max.** 1928. *Kunstgeschichte als Geistesgeschichte.* Pp. xv + 276, ill. Munich: R. Piper.

28. **Forman, W.,** and **Poulik.** 1956. *Kunst der Vorzeit.* Pp. 189, ill. Prague: Artia.

29. **Frobenius, Leo,** and **Henri Breuil.** *L'Afrique.* Cahiers d'art. (Paris), nos. 8–9, 1930, bibl., 50 plates.

30. —— 1949. *Mythologie de l'Atlantide.* Pp. 260, ill. Paris: Payot.

31. **Fry, Roger.** 1928. *Vision and design.* Pp. 302, ill. London: Chatto & Windus. (Article on negro sculpture.)

32. —— 1939. *Last lectures.* Pp. xxix + 370. London: Cambridge Univ. Press.

33. **Gabus, J.** 1944. *L'Afrique aux trois visages.* Pp. 259. Lucerne: F. Rouge.

34. **Gamon, Gaspar.** 1958. *Las mascaras religiosas Africanos.* Pp. 13–16, ill. Africa (Madrid), 15 (202).

35. **Gatti, E. M. W.** 1943. *Here is Africa.* Pp. 166, ill., maps. New York: Scribner.

36. **Gibb, K. A. R.** 1958. *The travels of Ibn Battuta, A.D. 1325–54.* Pp. 269, ill., maps. Cambridge: Univ. Press.

37. **Glück, Heinrich,** and **Ernst Diez.** 1932. *Arte del Islam.* Pp. 776, ill. Madrid: Labor.

38. **Gosset, Pierre** et **Renée.** 1958–9. *L'Afrique, les africains.* 3 vols. Paris: René Julliard.

39. **Grosse, Ernst.** 1894. *Die Anfänge der Kunst.* Pp. vii + 301. Freiburg i.B.: Siebeck.

40. —— *The beginnings of art.* 1897. New York: Appleton.

41. **Haddon, A. C.** 1895. *Evolution in art.* Pp. xviii + 364, ill. London. Walter Scott.

42. **Hailey, Lord.** 1957. *An African survey. Revised to 1956.* Pp. xxvi + 1676, bibl., maps. (Art, pp. 72–78.) London: Oxford Univ. Press.

43. **Hamilton, R. A.** 1955. *History and archaeology in Africa: Report of a conference held in July 1953 at the School of Oriental and African Studies.* Pp. 99, maps. London: School of Oriental and African Studies.

44. **Herskovits, M. J.** 1941. *The myth of the negro past.* Pp. xiv + 374. New York: Harper.

45. —— *Some thoughts on American research in Africa.* Afr. stud. bull. (New York), 1 (2), 1958, 25.

46. **Hoefler, Paul L.** 193 . *Africa speaks.* Pp. xii + 469, ill., maps as end-papers. London: John Lane.

47. **Holm, Sverre.** *Gestalt-psychological interpretation of ornamental art,* Ethnos, 11, 1/2, 1946, 49–62, ill.

48. **Howlett, J.** *Présence africaine 1947–1958.* J. negro hist., 43 (2), 1958, 141–50.

49. **Huyghe, R.** 1957. *L'art et l'homme.* Pp. 463. Paris: Larousse.

50. —— 1959. *Discovery of art.* Pp. 400, ill. (From Prehistoric China to present day.)

51. **Junod, H. P.** 1938. *Bantu heritage.* Pp. (12) + 155, bibl., ill. Johannesburg: Horturs.

52. **Karutz, Richard.** 1927. *Das Rätsel des Janus.* Pp. iv + 171, ill. Basle: R. Geering.

53. **Kühnel, Ernst.** 1929. *Die islamische Kunst.* Anton Springer, Handbuch der Kunstgeschichte, Band VI, 373–550, ill. Leipzig: Kröner.

54. **Lange, J.** 1899. *Darstellung des Menschen in der älteren griechischen Kunst.* Pp. xxxi + 225. Strassburg.

55. **Lebeuf, A.** and **J. P.** *À la recherche des civilisations disparues.* France illustrée, 6, 1950, 578–9.

56. **Lebeuf, Jean-Paul,** and **A. Masson-Detourbet.** *L'archéologie. Afrique équatoriale française,* 1950, 40–46, bibl., ill.

57. **Leicht, H.** 1958. *History of world's art.* Pp. 300, ill. (Chap. on 'African Art'.)

58. **Lips, Julius E.** 1937. *The savage hits back.* Pp. 254, ill. New Haven: Yale Univ. Press.

59. **Luquet, G. H.** *Les origines de l'art figuré.* Ipek, 2, 1926, 3–28.

60. **McCall, Daniel F.** 1964. *Africa in time-perspective.* Pp. xvii + 175, bibl., ill. Boston: Univ. Press.

61. **Malinowski, B.** 1949. *The problem of meaning in primitive languages.* Ogden, C. K., and I. A. Richards, The meaning of meaning, pp. 296–336. (10th ed.)

62. **Marcais, Georges.** 1957. *Mélanges d'histoire et d'archéologie de l'occident musulman.* 2 vols. Alger: Imp. Officielle.

63. **Maringer, J.,** and **Bandi.** 1953. *Art in the ice age.* London: Allen & Unwin.

64. **Molema, S. M.** 1920. *The Bantu past and present.* Pp. xix + 398, bibl., map. Edinburgh: W. Green.

65. **Müller-Freienfels, R.** 1938. *Psychologie der Kunst.* Vol. 1, Pp. 160, ill. (Leipzig–Berlin.) Vol. 3, 2nd ed.

66. **Munro, Thomas.** 1949. *The arts and their interrelations.* Pp. xv + 559. New York: Liberal Arts Press.

67. —— *Evolution and progress in the arts; a reappraisal of Herbert Spencer's theory.* J. aesthetics, 1 (3), 1960.

68. —— *The psychology of art past, present and future.* J. aesthetics, 21, 1963, 263–82.

69. **Oliver, R.,** and **J. D. Fage.** 1962. *A short history of Africa.* Pp. 280, maps. London: Penguin African Library.

70. **Perham, M.,** and **J. Simmons.** 1947. *African discovery.* Pp. 280, ill., maps. London: Faber. (2nd ed.)

71. **Ratzel, F.** 1896–8. *The history of mankind.* (Translated from the 2nd German ed.) 3 vols. Ill., maps. London: Macmillan.

72. **Read, Sir Herbert.** 1951. *Art and the evolution of man.* Pp. 51. London: Freedom Press.

73. **Rimli, Eugen Th.,** and **Karl Fischer.** 1960. *Illustrierte Weltkunstgeschichte in 5 Bänden.* Band 5. Pp. 595, ill. Zürich: Stauffscher-Verlag.

74. **Schilde, W.** *Kulturen mit europäischem Einschlag.* Wiener Beitr. z. Kulturgesch., 5, 1943, 177–88.

75. **Schulthess, E.,** and **O. Lehmann.** 1958–9. *Afrika.* 2 vols. of photographs. Vol. 1, Vom Mittelmeer zum Äquator. Pp. 252, 162 photographs. Vol. 2, Vom Äquator zum Kap d. Guten Hoffnung. Ed. Egli, F. Morgenthaler.

76. **Schulthess, Emil.** 1960. *Africa.* Pp. 58, ill., maps. London: Manesse-Verlag. (Printed in Zürich.)

77. **Shaw, C. T.** 1946. *The study of Africa's past.* Pp. 23, ill. London: Oxford Univ. Press for Int. Afr. Inst. (Memorandum 21.)

78. **Snowden, F. M.** *The negro in ancient Greece.* Amer. Anthrop., 50, 1948, 31–44.

79. **Spearing, H. G.** 1913. *The childhood of art.* Pp. 482, ill.

80. **Suret-Canale, J.** 1958. *Afrique noire occidentale et centrale.* Tome 1, Géographie, Civilisation, Histoire. Pp. 288, bibl., ill. Paris: Éditions Sociales.

81. **Tempels, Placide.** 1959. *Bantu philosophy.* Pp. 123, ill. Paris: Présence Africaine. (English and latest ed.)

82. —— 1949. *La philosophie bantoue.* Pp. 129, ill. Paris: Présence Africaine.

83. **Van Gennep, A.** 1905. *Les divinités génératrices chez les anciens et modernes.*

84. **Verger, P.,** and **Others.** 1953. *Les Afro-Américains.* Pp. 268, ill. Dakar: I.F.A.N. Mém. 27.

85. **Verworn, M.** 1909. *Die Anfänge der Kunst.* Pp. 71, ill. Jena: G. Fischer.

86. —— *Zur Psychologie der primitiven Kunst.* Pp. 48. Jena: G. Fischer. (2nd ed. 1917.)

87. **Weltfisch, G.** 1953. *The origins of art.* Sp. Indianapolis New York.

88. **Westermann, Diedrich.** 1934. *The African to-day.* Pp. xv + 343, bibl. London: Oxford Univ. Press for Int. Afr. Inst.

88a.—— 1949. *The African to-day and to-morrow.* Pp. ix + 174, bibl. London: Oxford Univ. Press for Int. Afr. Inst. (3rd ed.)

89. —— *Cultural history of negro Africa.* J. world hist., 3 (4), 1957, 986–1004.

90. **Windels, F.** 1949. *The Lascaux cave paintings.* Pp. 139, ill. London: Faber. (Translated by C. F. C. Hawkes.)

91. **Woermann, K.** 1915. *Geschichte der Kunst aller Zeiten & Völker.* 3 vols, Vol. 1, Die Kunst der vor und ausserchristlichen Völker. Leipzig–Vienna.

Ia
Encyclopaedias

92. **Antonielli, Ugo.** *African art.* Enciclopedia Italiana, vol. 1, 1929, 765–74, ill.

93. **Bossert, H-Th.** 1937. *Encyclopédie de l'ornement.* Pp. 48, 120 plates. Paris: Calavas. (Objets conservés dans les musées d'ethnographie de Berlin et de Hambourg: plates 30–32, description, pp. 18–19.)

94. **Braunholtz, H. J.** *Ceramics (primitive cultures).* Encyclopaedia of world art, vol. 3, 1960, 206–21, ill.

95. **Les Carnets du Séminaire des Arts, Bruxelles.** 1951. *Les arts plastiques.* Pp. 80, ill. Brussels: Éditions des Arts Plastiques.

96. **Dimand, M. S.** 1944. *A handbook of Muhammadan art.* Pp. ix + 347, ill., maps. New York: Metropolitan Museum of Art. (2nd ed.)

97. **Encyclopédie Coloniale et Maritime, Paris.** 1949. *Afrique occidentale française.* (Ed. by E. Guernier.) 2 vols. *Vol. 1,* pp. ix + 390 (ii), bibl., ill., maps. *Vol. 2,* pp. 400 + (x), bibl., ill., maps. Paris: Encyclopédie Coloniale et Maritime. (Pp. 365–70, 'L'artisanat et les arts africains', by J. Le Gall.)

98. —— 1950. *Afrique équatoriale française.* (Ed. by E. Guernier.) Pp. 590 + vii, ill., maps. Paris: Encyclopédie Coloniale et Maritime.

99. —— 1951. *Cameroun-Togo.* (Ed. by E. Guernier.) Pp. 590 + vii, ill., maps. Paris: Encyclopédie Coloniale et Maritime.

100. **Encyclopédie du Congo Belge.** 1952–3. *Encyclopédie du Congo Belge.* Tom. 1–3: 1, 1952, 722; 2, 1952, 618; 3, 1953, 862, ill., maps. Brussels: Bieleveld.

100a. **Encyclopaedia of Islam.** 1960. New edn. Vol. 1. Leiden: Brill.

101. **Encyclopaedia of World Art.** 1958. Vol. 1, bibl., ill., maps. New York: McGraw-Hill. (Translation of Enciclopedia Universale dell' Arte.)

102. —— *Ivory and bone carving.* Vol. 8, 1963, 758–86, bibl.

103. **Encyclopaedia of Painting.** This work will comprise 15 vols. covering the visual arts of the entire world.

104. **Griaule, M.** *L'Afrique.* R. Huyghe (*ed.*), L'art et l'homme. Vol. I, fasc. 3, 57: 87–92. Paris: Larousse.

105. **Hornbostel, Erich von.** 1920. *Kunst der Eingeborenen.* Vol. 2, pp. 393–6. Schnee, H. (*ed.*), Deutsches Kolonial-Lexikon. 3 vols. (q.v.).

106. **Larousse.** 1959. *Larousse encyclopaedia of mythology.* Pp. x + 499, ill. London: Paul Hamlyn. (Africa: pp. 480–92, ill.)

107. **Laude, Jean.** *French equatorial Africa.* Encyclopaedia of world art, vol. 1, 1958, 51–55, maps.

108. —— *French West Africa.* Encyclopaedia of world art, vol. 1, 1958, 55–62, map.

109. **Olderogge, D.** 1949. *Encyclopaedia of art.* (Part of the great Soviet encyclopaedia.) Vol. 1, 1949. (Contains various articles of ethnographical interest. Russian text.)

110. **Schnee, Heinrich** (*ed.*). 1920. *Deutsches Kolonial-Lexikon.* 3 vols. Vol. 1, pp. xxx + 776, ill., maps. Vol. 2, pp. 698, ill., maps. Vol. 3, pp. 778, ill., maps. Leipzig: Quelle & Meyer.

111. **Schultz-Weidner, Willy.** *Gold and silverwork.* Encyclopaedia of world art, vol. 6, 1962, 453–4.

112. **Waage, Frederick O.** *African negro art.* Collier's encyclopedia (New York), vol. 1, 1962, 247–54, ill.

Ib
Ethnographical Works

113. **Adam, Leonhard.** 1958. *Bildende Kunst.* Adam, L., and H. Trimborn, Lehrbuch der Völkerkunde, 3rd edition, 1958,

pp. 111–38, bibl., ill., map ('Verbreitung der Plastik in Mittel- und Südafrika'). Anhang: 'Figuren- und Maskenkunst in Afrika'. Stuttgart: F. Enke Verlag.

114. —— 1958. *Lehrbuch der Völkerkunde.* Pp. iv + 303, bibl., ill., maps. Stuttgart: F. Enke Verlag. (3rd ed.)

115. **Adandé, A.** *Sur quelques noms du fusil en Afrique.* IRE Conférence Intern. des Africanistes de l'Ouest. CR. T.II, 1951, 166–92, maps. (Liste des noms du fusil en Afrique.)

116. **Ankermann, B.** *Kulturkreise und Kulturschichten in Afrika.* Z. f. Ethnol., **37**, 1905.

117. —— *Ueber den gegenwärtigen Stand der Ethnographie der Südhälfte Afrikas.* Archiv. f. Anthrop. N.F.4, 1906, 241–86.

118. —— *Totenkult und Seelenglaube bei afrikanischen Völkern.* Z. f. Ethnol., **50**, 1918, 89–153.

119. **Arts.** *Style regions of Africa; exhibition at Segy gallery.* Arts, **31**, Dec. 1956, 56.

120. **Bascom, William R.,** and **Melville J. Herskovits.** 1958. *Continuity and change in African cultures.* Pp. vii + 308, maps. Chicago: Univ. of Chicago Press. (See also Cordwell, Justine M.; Merriam, Alan P.)

121. **Battaglia, Raffaello.** 1954. *Africa; Genti i culture.* Pp. 102, bibl., ill., map. Rome: Instituto Italiano per l'Africa.

122. **Baumann, H.** 1955. *Das doppelte Geschlecht; Ethnologische Studien zur Bisexualität in Ritus und Mythus.* Pp. 420, map. Berlin: D. Reimer.

123. —— and **Others.** 1940. *Völkerkunde von Afrika.* Pp. xv + 665, ill., maps. Essen: Essener Verlagsanstalt.

124. —— and **D. Westermann.** 1957. *Les peuples et les civilisations de l'Afrique.* Pp. 605, bibl., ill., maps. Paris: Payot. (Translation of 'Völkerkunde von Afrika'.)

125. **Bernatzik, Hugo Adolf.** 1939. *Die Grosse Völkerkunde.* Band I, Europa-Afrika (225–371). Pp. xii + 371, ill., maps. Leipzig: Bibliographisches Institut.

126. —— 1947. *Afrika; Handbuch der angewandten Völkerkunde.* Pp. xvi + 703; xvii + 704–1429, bibl., ill., maps. Innsbruck: Schlüsselverlag.

127. **Buschan, Georg** (ed.). 1922. *Illustrierte Völkerkunde.* Band I, Amerika, Afrika. Pp. xvi + 686, ill. Stuttgart: Strecker u. Schröder. (Afrika by A. Haberlandt.)

128. **Cazaneuve, J.** 1958. *Les rites et la condition humaine d'après les documents ethnographiques.* Pp. 487, bibl.

129. **Cranstone, B. A. L.** 1958. *Ethnography handbook for museum curators.* Pp. 40. London: Museums Assoc.

130. **Cudjoe, Dzifanu.** *The social significance of African art.* W.A.R., **13**, 179, Aug. 1942, 11–12.

131. **Cunard, Nancy** (ed.). 1934. *Negro anthology.* Pp. viii + 855, ill., map. London: Wishard & Co. (Negro sculpture and ethnology, pp. 655–77, ill.)

132. **Corso, Raffaelo.** 1940. *Africa italiana; genti e costumi.* Pp. 188, bibl., ill. Naples: R. Pironti.

133. **Davis, S. A.** *Divining bowls; their uses and origin.* Man, **55**, no. 143, 1955, 132–5.

134. **de Beniparrall, C.** *Importance sociale de l'art nègre africain* (Importancia social del arte negro africano). Cuadernos africanos y orientales (Madrid), **33**, 1956, 63–76.

135. **Demaison, A.** 1956. *La vie des noirs d'Afrique.* Pp. 128, ill. Paris: Borrelier.

136. **de Pedrals, Denis-Pierre.** 1949. *Manuel scientifique de l'Afrique noire.* Anthropologie, préhistoire, archéologie, cultures et arts, etc. Pp. 202, bibl., ill., maps. Paris: Payot.

137. **de Rachewiltz, Boris.** 1964. *Black Eros; sexual customs of Africa from prehistory to the present day.* Pp. 329, bibl., ill. London: George Allen.

138. **Dias, A. Jorge.** 1961. *Portuguese contribution to cultural anthropology.* Pp. (vi) + 112, ill., map. Johannesburg: Witwatersrand Univ. Press.

139. **Diop, Cheikh Anta.** *Nations nègres et culture.* Pp. 390, ill. Paris: Présence Africaine.

140. **Dumoulin, John.** *The participative art of the Afrocuban religions.* Dresden, 1962. Pp. 63–77, ill. (Ex: Abhandlungen & Berichte des Staatlichen Museums für Völkerkunde, Dresden. Band 21.)

141. **Fagg, William B.** *African cultures.* Encyclopaedia of world art, vol. 1, 1958, 130–41, bibl.

142. **Forde, C. Daryll** (ed.). 1954. *African worlds.* Pp. xvii + 243. London: Oxford Univ. Press for Int. Afr. Inst.

143. —— 1956. *Habitat, economy and society.* Pp. xiv + 500, ill., maps. London: Methuen. New York, 1963 (reprint): Dutton & Co.

144. **Foucart, George.** 1919. *Introductory questions on African ethnology.* Pp. v + 159. Cairo: French Institute of Oriental Archaeology.

145. **Frazer, Sir James George.** 1938. *The native races of Africa and Madagascar.* Pp. xii + 578, ill., maps. London: Lund Humphries.

146. **Frobenius, Leo.** 1898. *Der Ursprung der Afrikanischen Kulturen.* Pp. xv + 368, ill., maps. Berlin: Gebr. Borntrager.

147. —— 1913. *The voice of Africa.* 2 vols. Vol. I, pp. xxiii + 349, ill., maps. Vol. 2, pp. 353–682, ill., maps. London: Hutchinson.

148. —— 1923. *Dokumente zur Kulturphysiognomik vom Kulturreich der Festländer.* Pp. 344, ill., maps. Berlin, Volksverband der Bücherfreunde.

149. —— 1923. *Das unbekannte Afrika.* Pp. xii + 185, ill., map. Munich: O. C. Recht.

150. —— 1928. *Das sterbende Afrika. Die Seele eines Erdteils.* Pp. 503. Frankfurt a M.: Sozietäts-Druckerei.

151. —— 1929. *Monumenta Africana; der Geist eines Erdteils.* Pp. 526, ill. Frankfurt a M.: Societats-Verlag.

152. —— 1954. *Kulturgeschichte Afrikas.* Pp. 656, ill., maps. Zürich: Phaidon Verlag.

153. **Fröhlich, Ed.** 1960. *Völkerkundliche Forschungen Martin Heydrich zum 70 Geburtsdag.* Pp. xx + 557, ill. Cologne: Brill. (Ethnologica N.S. 2.)

154. **Fuhrmann, Ernst** (ed.). 1923. *Afrika; Sakralkulte Vorgeschichte der Hieroglyphen.* Pp. 59, plates I–121. Hagen: Folkwang Verlag. (Part of 'Kulturen der Erde': Material zur Kultur- und Kunstgeschichte aller Völker, Band 6, Afrika.)

155. **Germann, Paul.** 1948. *Die Grundlagen der Afrikanischen Kultur.* Pp. 131, bibl., ill. Leipzig: Volk und Buch Verlag.

156. **Griaule, Marcel.** *Introduction méthodologique.* Minotaure (Paris), **II**, 1933, 7–12, ill.

157. —— 1948. *Dieu d'eau; Entretiens avec Ogotemmêli.* Pp. 269, ill. Paris: Éditions du Chêne.

158. —— *L'enquête orale en ethnologie.* Rev. philosophique, **142**, 1952, 737–53.

159. —— 1954. *Le problème de la culture noire.* U.N.E.S.C.O.: Unité et diversité culturelles: L'Originalité des cultures: Son rôle dans la compréhension internationale. Pp. 374–401. Paris: U.N.E.S.C.O. (2nd ed.)

160. —— 1957. *Méthode de l'ethnographie.* Pp. 107, ill. Paris: Presses Univ. de France.

161. **Haekel, J.** (ed.), and **Others.** 1957. *Die Wiener Schule der Völkerkunde. Festschrift.* Pp. viii + 568, ill., maps. Vienna: Berger.

162. **Herskovits, Melville Jean.** *A preliminary consideration of the culture areas of Africa.* Amer. Anthrop., **26**, 1924, 50–63.

163. —— *Adjiboto, an African game of the bush negroes of Dutch Guiana.* Man, **29**, no. 7, 1929, 122–7.

164. —— 1948. *Man and his works.* Pp. xviii + 678 (xxxvii), bibl., ill. New York: A. Knopf.

165. —— 1961. *The culture areas of Subsaharan Africa.* Pp. 381, map. Evanston, Ill.: Northwestern Univ.

166. **Hirschberg, W.** (ed.). 1962. *Monumenta-Ethnographica.* Vol. I, Schwarz-Afrika. Frühe völkerkundliche Bilddokumente. Pp. 269, Anhang, pp. 84, ill. Graz.

167. **Holas, B.** *L'Homme noir d'Afrique.* Initiations africaines, I.F.A.N., 8, 1951–3, 1–105, bibl., ill., maps.

168. —— *Sur la présence de la pensée totémique en Afrique noire.* Garcia de Orta (Lisbon), **III** (4), 1955, 427–43, ill., map.

169. **Holdsworth, M.** *African studies in the U.S.S.R.* West Afr., nos. 2130, 2131, Feb. 1958.

170. **Huggins, W. N.**, and **J. G. Jackson.** 1937. *An introduction to African civilisation.* Pp. 224, ill. New York: N.Y. Avon House.

171. **Humpidge, K. P.** *An African game (Mancala).* Nigeria, **16**, 1938, 300–2, ill.

172. **Immenroth, Wilhelm.** 1933. *Kultur und Umwelt der Klein-wüchsigen in Afrika.* Pp. xii + 380, bibl., maps. Leipzig: Verlag der Werkgemeinschaft.

173. **Jeffreys, M. D. W.** *Circumcision; its diffusion from Egypt among the Bantu.* Criteria (Witwatersrand), **I**, 1949, 73–84.

174. **Jensen, A. E.** 1949. *Das religiöse Weltbild einer frühen Kultur.* Pp. xii + 198. Stuttgart: A. Schröder. (2nd ed.)

175. —— 1954. *Mythes et cultes chez les peuples primitifs.* Pp. 381. Paris: Payot.

176. **Jünger, Alexander.** 1926. *Kleidung und Umwelt in Afrika. Eine anthropogeographische Studie.* Pp. viii + 165, ill., maps. Publikation der staatl. Forschungsinstitute in Leipzig. Inst. f. Völkerkunde, Reihe, **I**, 8. Leipzig: Voigtlander.

177. **Junger, E.** 1944. *Jeux africains.* Pp. 241. Paris: N.R.F.

178. **Junod, Henri A.** 1931. *Vier afrikanische Spiele.* Pp. 56, ill. Zürich: Wanderer Verlag.

179. **Lagercrantz, Sture.** *Schädeldeformation und ihre Verbreitung in Afrika.* Ethnos (Stockholm), **6**, 1941, 135–73, ill.

180. —— *Toe rings.* Ethnos, **10**, 1945, 39–43, ill.

181. —— 1950. *String figures.* Contribution to the Ethnography of Africa. Pp. 269–73, ill., map.

182. —— 1950. *Snake-pots; Face-pots; Ring-shaped vessels.* Contribution to the Ethnography of Africa. Pp. 274–86, ill., maps.

183. —— 1950. *Contribution to the ethnography of Africa.* Pp. 20 + 430, ill., maps. Lund: Hakan Ohlssons Boktryckeri. (Studia Ethnographica Upsaliensia 1.)

184. **Larteguy, Jean.** 1959. *Les clefs de l'Afrique; Femmes, confréries, fétiches.* Pp. 270, ill., map. Paris: Albin Michel.

185. **Leiris, M.** 1934. *L'Afrique fantôme (De Dakar à Djibouti, 1931–33).* Pp. 525, ill. Paris: Gallimard. (3rd ed.)

186. **Leroi-Gourhan,** and **Jean Poirier.** 1953. *Ethnologie de l'union française.* Vol. 1, Afrique. Pp. 482, bibl., ill., maps. Paris: Presses Univ. de France.

187. **Lima, Mesquitela.** *Origens do negro Banto.* Mensario Admin., **91–92**, 1955, 20 29, bibl.

188. **Lindblom, G.** 1927. *The use of stilts especially in Africa and America.* Pp. 40, ill., map. Stockholm: Ethnographical Museum.

189a. —— 1928. *Further notes on the use of stilts.* Pp. 3–19. Stockholm: Ethnographical Museum.

190. —— *Drinking tubes, especially in Africa.* Ethnos (Stockholm), **6**, 1941, 48–74, ill., map.

191. —— *Vessels with star-shaped lids.* Ethnos (Stockholm), **7**, 1942, 55–70, ill.

192. —— 1943. *African razors.* Pp. 59, ill. Stockholm: Statens Etnografiska Museum. (Smarre Meddelanden, no. 19.)

193. —— and **E. Manker.** *Knutar, flätningar och växtslinger i magikts bruk.* Ymer, **3**, 1927, 241–57, ill.

194. **Lindskog, Birger.** 1954. *African leopard men.* Pp. xii + 219, ill. Uppsala (Studia Ethnographica Upsaliensia, 7.)

195. **Little, K. L.** *The role of secret societies in cultural specialisation.* Amer. Anthrop., **51** (2), 1949, 199–212.

196. **Loeb, Edwin M.** 1962. *In feudal Africa.* Pp. xxii + 383, bibl., ill., maps. Bloomington (Indiana): Pubn. no. 23, Indiana Univ. Research Center in Anthropology, Folklore and Linguistics.

197. **Maggi, Emilio.** 1958. *Civilta Africane.* Pp. 604, bibl., ill. Milan: Zibetti.

198. **Malinowski, B.** 1944. *A scientific theory of culture and other essays.* Pp. 228. London: Oxford Univ. Press.

199. **Mauny, R.** *Enquête sur les noms de métaux dans les langues africaines.* Notes afr., I.F.A.N., **50**, avr. 1951, p. 61.

200. **Moeller, A.** 1936. *Les grandes lignes des migrations des Bantous.* Pp. 578, bibl., ill., maps. Brussels: Georges van Campenhout. (Inst. Royal Colonial Belge: Section des sciences morales et politiques. Mémoires in-8—VI—1936.)

201. **Muensterberger, Werner.** *Some elements of artistic creativity among primitive peoples.* Beitrag zur Gesellungs- und Völker-wissenschaft (Berlin), 1950, 313–17.

202. **Murdock, George P.** 1959. *Africa; its peoples and their culture history.* Pp. xii + 456, bibl., ill., maps. New York: McGraw-Hill. (List of tribes.)

203. **Ottenberg, Simon** and **Phoebe.** 1960. *Cultures and societies of Africa.* Pp. (10) 614, bibl., ill., maps as end-papers. New York: Random House.

204. **Pales, L.** *Les mutilations tégumentaires en Afrique noire.* J. soc. africanistes, **16**, 1946, 1–8, ill.

205. **Panetta, Ester.** 1959. *I pigmei e i pigmoidi Africani.* Pp. 169, ill. Parma: Ugo Guanda.

206. **Paulme, D.** *Systèmes pondéraux et monétaires en Afrique noire.* Rev. Sciences (Paris), **3208**, 1942, 219–26.

207. **Périer, G. D.** 1930. *Nègreries.* Paris: l'Églantine.

208. **Petri, H.** *Tiefenpsychologie und Ethnologie.* Studium generale, **3**, 1950, 348–58.

209. **Pinfold, G. F.** *Some notes on fork guards.* Man, **29**, no. 76, 1929, 97–98, ill.

210. **Pitt-Rivers, A. H.** 1906. *The evolution of cultures and other essays.* Ed. J. L. Myres. Oxford: Univ. Press.

211. **Powell-Cotton, P. H. G.** *A mancala board called 'Songo'.* Man, **31**, no. 132, 1931, 123.

212. **Preuss, K. R.** 1923. *Die geistige Kultur der Naturvölker.* Leipzig Berlin. (2nd ed.)

213. —— 1939. *Lehrbuch der Völkerkunde.* Pp. viii + 446, ill.

214. **Probst-Biraben, J. H.** *Main de Fatma et talismans.* En Terre Islam, Mar.–Apr., 1948, 91–97.

215. **Prother, R. M.** *African ethnographic maps, with a new example from Northern Nigeria.* Africa, **32**, 1962, 61–64, 71–72, map.

216. **Quiggin, A. Hingston.** 1949. *A survey of primitive money.* Pp. xxii + 344, bibl., ill., maps. London: Methuen.

217. **Royal Anthropological Institute, London.** 1951. *Notes and queries on anthropology.* Pp. xii + 403, bibl., ill. London: Routledge. (6th ed. Art, pp. 308–15.)

218. **Saint Petersburg; Academia Scientiarum Imperialis.** 1958. *Essays on African Ethnography.* Vol. 2 (Moscow). (Russian text.)

219. **Schneider, Oskar.** 1905. *Muschelgeld-Studien.* Pp. (4) + 190, ill. Dresden: Verein für Erdkunde.

220. **Scotti, Pietro.** 1955. *Africa; Lineamenti Etnologici.* Pp. 40, bibl., ill., maps. Genova: Liberia degli Studi.

221. —— 1958. *Le culture dell' Africa.* Pp. 26, ill. Genova: Lupa.

222. **Segy, Ladislas.** *African phallic symbolism.* Zaïre, **19**, 10, déc. 1955, 1039–65, ill.

223. —— *L'attitude de l'africain à l'égard de la maladie; ses rapports avec la sculpture.* Rev. de Psychol. des Peuples, **11**, 3, juil. 1956, 283–96.

224. —— *Plastic aspects of African sculpture.* Rev. of gen. Semantics (Chicago), **14**, 3, Spring 1957, 185–202, ill.

225. **Seligman, C. G.** 1957. *Races of Africa.* Pp. 236, bibl., maps. London: Oxford Univ. Press. (3rd ed.)

226. **Sigler, P. O.** *Primitive money of Africa.* Numismatist. 3 vols., 1952–1954, ill. Vol. 65, 567–73, 681–4, 781–4, 892–9. Vol. 66, 134–5, 695–706. Vol. 67, 238–45, 345–53.

227. **Smith, Edwin W.** (ed.). 1950. *African ideas of God.* Pp. 308, map. London: Edinburgh House Press.

228. **Sydow, E. von.** 1924. *Ahnenkult und Ahnenbild der Naturvölker.* Pp. 34 + 19 plates. Berlin: Furche-Kunstverlag.

229. **Turnbull, Colin M.** 1963. *The peoples of Africa.* Pp. 124, ill., maps. Leicester: Brockhampton Press.

230. **Tylor, E. B.** 1871. *Primitive culture.* 2 vols. London: J. Murray.

231. **United Africa Company.** *The manilla problem.* Statist. & econ. rev., 3, 1949, 44–56; 4, 1949, 59–60.

232. **Verger, Pierre.** 1954. *Dieux d'Afrique; culte des Orishas et Vodouns.* Pp. 194, ill., map. Paris: Paul Hartmann.

233. **Vreught, Aug. de.** 1894. *Afrikaansche Volken.* Pp. 137, ill., map. Gent: J. Vuylsteks. (Uitgeve van het Willems-Fond te Gent, 134.)

234. **Washington U.S. National Museum, Smithsonian Institution.** 1896. *Mancala; the national game of Africa.* Rep. Smithsonian Institution (U.S. National Museum), 1896.

235. **Welter, G.** 1960. *Les croyances primitives et leurs survivances.* Pp. 228. Paris: Collection Armand Colin.

236. **West Africa.** *Manchester's African trade (textiles).* West Afr., **1751**, Sept. 1950, 850–1, ill.

237. **Whitehouse, A. A.** *Note on the 'Mbari' Festival.* Man, 4, 1904, 162–3.

238. **Widstrand, Carl Gösta.** *Afrikas Folk.* Stockholm: Aldus Bonniers.

239. **Wouters, H.** 1958. *Volken en Volkenkunde.* Pp. 224, ill. Amsterdam: Querido. (Geillustreerde Salamander No. 16. Part 4, L'homme et l'art.)

240. **Zervos, C.** *L'Art nègre.* Cahiers d'Art, 2, 1927, 229–46.

Ic

African Art; Primitive Art

241. **Adam, Leonhard.** 1963. *Primitive art.* Pp. 250, ill. London: Cassell.

242. **Adandé, A.** *Artisanat africain et art sacré.* Notes afr. I.F.A.N., 48, Oct. 1950, 118–19.

243. **Adandé, A.** *Masques africains.* Notes afr. I.F.A.N., 51, 1951, 78–80.

244. —— *Les masques et leur rôle dans les sociétés africaines.* Brousse (Léopoldville), N.S. 5, 1954, 29–33.

245. —— *Fonctions et signification sociales des masques en Afrique noire.* Présence afr., N.S. 1–2, avr.–juil. 1955, 24–38.

246. **Agard, W. R.** *Cleveland's artistic appreciation of Africa.* Amer. Mag. of Art, 23, Sept. 1931, 201–9.

247. **Alvarez, H. R.** *Arte negro.* Africa (Madrid), 104, 1950, 19–22, 363–366, ill.

248. **Andrée, R.** *Die Masken in der Völkerkunde.* Archiv f. Anthrop., 16, 1886.

249. **Anti, Carlo.** *Scultura negra.* Dedalo (Milan, Rome), 1, 1921, 592–621.

250. —— *Sculpture of the African negroes.* Art in America, 12, 1923, 14–26.

251. **Apollinaire, G.,** and **P. Guillaume.** *Sculptures nègres.* Paris, 1917.

252. **Apollo.** *Bull market for negro art; important sale in Paris.* Apollo, 61, Apr. 1955, 95.

253. **Archaeology.** *African ivory at Minneapolis.* Archaeology, 11, March 1958, 58.

254. **Art Digest.** *Primitive or classic? African sculptures.* Art digest, 16, July 1942, 18.

255. —— *African masks at Boris Mirshi gallery, Boston.* Art digest, 27, Feb. 1953, 10.

256. **L'Art Nègre.** *Opinions sur l'art nègre par Apollinaire, Cocteau, Gris, Picasso, Vlaminck.* Action, 1920, 23–26, ill.

257. —— Paris: Éditions du Seuil, 1951. Pp. 254, ill.

258. **Art News.** *African sculpture and European reflections at the primitive art gallery.* Art news, 39, Oct. 1940, 9.

259. **Aupiais, F.** 1928. *L'art nègre.* Bull. des Missions, 2, pp. 77–85.

260. **Baer, Gérard.** *Le masque; expression du surnaturel.* Les Musées de Genève, no. 6, 1960, 16–18, ill.

261. **baNtu.** *Bantoekuns en-handewerk op drumpel van nuwe groei.* baNtu, 9, 5, May 1962, 306–14, ill.

262. **Barnes, Albert C.** 1925. *Die Negerkunst und Amerika.* Der Querschnitt, 5, S. 1–8.

263. —— *Negro art, past and present.* Opportunity. May 1926, 148–9: 168–9, ill.

264. —— *Primitive negro sculpture and its influence on modern civilisation.* Opportunity, May 1928.

265. **Barr, A. H.** *Antiquity of African Sculpture.* Museum of Modern Art Bulletin, 2, 1935, 3.

266. **Bascom, W. R.** *Art in ancient Africa.* African missionary (Cork, Ireland), 19 (4), 1941, 74–77, 87. (Reprint of 'Legacy of an unknown Nigerian Donatello'.)

267. **Basler, Adolphe.** *Opinions récentes sur l'art et la psychologie nègres.* Mercure de France, Nov. 1928, pp. 593–610.

268. —— 1929. *L'art chez les peuples primitifs.* Pp. 83, bibl., ill. Paris: Libr. de France. (African art, pp. 7–24.)

269. **Beaux Arts, Paris.** *Les arts sauvages d'Afrique et d'Océanie.* Beaux Arts, 8, 1930, ill.

270. **Beckmann, J.** *Die Stellung der katholischen Mission zur bildenden Kunst der Eingeborenen in den Tropen.* Acta tropica, 2, 3, 1945, 211–32, ill.

271. **Bedouin, Jean-Louis.** 1961. *Les masques.* Pp. 127, ill. Paris: ('Que sais-je' series.)

272. **Beier, U.** *Attitude of the educated African to his traditional art.* Phylon 18, July 1957, 162–5.

273. **Bell, Clive.** *Negro Sculpture.* Living Age, 306, 1920, 786–9.

274. —— *Negro Sculpture.* Arts and Decoration, 13, 1920, 178–202.

275. —— 1922. *Since Cézanne; negro sculpture.* London.

276. **Berthoud, Gerald.** 1962. *Magie, religion et art africains.* Pp. 23, ill. Geneva: Imp. populaires (Extrait de les Musées de Genève, 25, 28, 29, 1962).

277. **Bezombes, R.** 1953. *L'exotisme dans l'art et la pensée.* Pp. 200, ill. Paris: Elsevier.

278. **Biro de Stern, A.** *Sobre el arte de los primitivos.* Rev. geogr. Americana (Buenos Aires) (111), 5, 29, 135–42.

279. **Blaha, H. Haselberger.** *La peinture nègre s'éteint.* Les Musées de Genève, 14, 1957, 37, ill.

280. **Blossfeldt, Willy.** 1961. *Formen afrikanischer Plastik.* Pp. 77 (3), ill. (col.), maps as end-papers. Stuttgart: Schuler Verlagsgesellschaft.

281. **Boas, F.** 1955. *Primitive art.* Pp. 372, ill. New York: Dover Publ.

282. **Bossert, Helmuth Th.** 1955. *Folk art of primitive peoples.* Pp. 15. Col. plates 1–12 of Africana. London: Zwemmer.

283. **Breuil, Henri.** 1953. *Four hundred centuries of cave art.* (Montignac, Centre d'étude et de documentation préhistorique.)

284. —— and **Others.** 1960. *Die Steinzeit vierzig tausend Jahre Felsbilder.* Pp. 256, ill., maps. Baden-Baden: Holle.

285. **Brion, M.** *L'Art préhistorique africain et la magie.* Beaux Arts, Dec. 1933, pl.

286. **British Museum.** Calendar for 1963, 'African Art'. (12 coloured plates of African art treasures in the Museum.)

287. **Buraud, Georges.** *Les masques.* Paris: Éditions du Seuil. Pp. 238, ill.

288. **Burland, C.-A.** *Le portrait dans l'art africain.* Musée vivant, 21 (13-14-15), 57: 407.

289. **Bussi, K. H.** *Discussion after a lecture by M. Hoernes on Die Anfänge der bildenden Kunst.* Kongress f. Ästh. u. allg. Kunstwissenschaft, Berlin, 7–9 Oct. 1913. Bericht herausgegeben vom Orts-Anschluss, pp. 213–21. Stuttgart: 1917.

290. **Carline, R.** *Negro art in Africa.* African observer, 5 (3), 1936, 39–45.

291. —— *Dating and provenance of negro art.* Burlington magazine, 77, 451, 1940, 115–23, illus.

292. **Casson, S.** *Negro art.* Listener, May 1933, ill.

293. **Chalon, J.** 1920-21. *Fétiches, idoles et amulettes.* 2 vols.

294. **Charmet, R.** *Afrique noire; beaux-arts.* Grand Larousse Encyclopédique, Tome 1, 1960, 145-6, ill.

295. **Chauvet, Stephen.** *Objets d'or, de bronze et d'ivoire dans l'art nègre.* Cah. d'Art (Paris), **5**, 1930, 33-40, ill.

296. —— *Les arts indigènes d'Afrique et d'Océanie.* Variétés (Brussels), **2** (12), 1930, 849 55, ill.

297. **Chipp, Herschel B.** *Formal and symbolic factors in the art styles of primitive cultures.* J. aesthetics, **19**, 1960.

298. **Chlenov, A. M.** *Puti Afrikanskogo Izobrazitel'Nogo Iskusstva* (The paths of African pictorial art). Narody Azii i Afriki, no. 5, 1961, 201-12. (A review of W. Fagg's and E. Elisofin's 'The Sculpture of Africa'.)

299. **Christensen, E. O.** 1955. *Primitive art.* Pp. 384, ill. New York: Crowell.

300. **Christoffels, Hildegard.** *Über afrikanische Holzschnitzerei; eine Einführung.* Jb. Bern. hist. mus., **39 40**, 1959-60, 457-63, ill.

301. **Clement, Pierre.** *Sur les formes et les fondements de l'attitude du groupe vis-a-vis du forgeron en Afrique noire.* C.R. sommaires Séances inst. franç. anthrop. (Paris), **2**, janv. 1944-déc. 1946, 13-14.

302. **Clouzot, H.,** and **A. Level.** *L'Art nègre.* Gazette des beaux-arts, **15**, 1919, 311-24.

303. —— 1926. *Sculptures africaines et océaniennes.* Pp. 24, ill. Paris: Librairie de France.

304. **Cordwell, Justine M.** 1959. *African art.* Pp. 28-48. Bascom and Herskovits, Continuity and Change in African Cultures. Chicago: Univ. of Chicago Press.

305. **Craft Horizons.** *African wood at the museum of primitive art.* Craft horizons, **19**, 1959, 48.

306. —— *Antelopes and queens at the Museum of Primitive Art.* Craft horizons, **20**, 1960, 50.

307. **Cudjoe, S. D.** *Art in Africa.* W.A.R., **24**, 1953.

308. **Culin, S.** *Negro art.* Arts, **3**, 1923, 347-50, ill.

309. **Dark, Philip J. C.** 1954. *Bush negro art; an African art in the Americas.* Pp. vi + 48, bibl., ill., map. London: Tiranti.

310. **Davidson, B.** *Black arts* (review article). New Statesman, **60**, 1960, 893.

311. **de Amorim, Fernando Bayolo Pacheco.** *As artes dos negros africanos.* Garcia de Orta, **7** (3), 1959, 453-70, bibl.

312. **de Cleene, N.** *Symbolisme in de negerkunst.* Congo, **1**, 3, 1934, 348-56.

313. **de Oliveira, Antonio.** 1959. *Mahamba; tentativa de interpretaçao artistica e psicologica de documentos de arte dos negros africanos.* Pp. 150, ill., maps. Lisboa: Junta de Investigações do Ultramar: Centro estud. polit. e soc. (Estudos, ensaios e documentos, 57).

314. **de Rachewiltz, Boris.** 1960. *Afrikanische Kunst.* Pp. xix + 245, bibl., ill. Zürich: Artemis Verlag. (Translated from the Italian 'Incontro con l'arte africana'.)

315. **Design.** *Art of primitive peoples; (1) Bushmen; (2) African negro.* Design, **39**, 1937, 2-3: 4-14, ill.

316. **Dittmer, K.** 1952. *Die Kunst der Naturvölker.* Das Atlantisbuch der Kunst, 627-38.

317. **Dover, Cedric.** 1960. *American negro art.* Studio.

318. **Drost, Dietrich.** 1963. *Kunst aus Afrika.* Pp. 39. 24 plates, map. Leipzig: Museum für Völkerkunde.

319. **Duchartre, P. L.** *Poids et figurines nègres.* Art et décoration, **57**, May 1930, 145-52.

320. **Dunn, I.** *Principles of African art.* School arts magazine, **31**, Dec. 1931, 202-4.

321. **L'École des Arts et d'Artisanat en A.E.F.** *Chroniques d'Outre-Mer.*, **51**, Dec. 1958.

322. **Einstein, Carl.** 1920. *Negerplastik.* Pp. xxvii + 107, ill. Munich: Kurt Wolff.

323. —— 1921. *Afrikanische Plastik.* Pp. 29, ill. Berlin: Orbis Pictus, Weltkunstbücherei, 7.

324. —— 1922. *La sculpture africaine.* Pp. 32, ill. Paris: Crès.

325. **Elisofon, Eliot.** *African sculpture.* Atlantic monthly, **203**, no. 4, 1959, 48-60, ill.

326. —— and **Fagg, William.** 1958. *The sculpture of Africa* (Photos by E. Elisofon, text by W. Fagg). Pp. 256, bibl., ill. London: Thames & Hudson.

327. **Emerson, Ellen Russell.** 1892. *Masks, heads and faces.* Pp. 312, ill. London: A. & C. Black.

328. **Espérandieu, G.** 1957. *De l'art animalier dans l'Afrique antique.* Alger: Impr. Officielle.

329. **Esswein, H.** *Masken.* Frankfurter Zeit., 3 May, 1933.

330. **Fagg, William B.** *African negro art.* Archer, W. G., 40,000 Years of Modern Art, 1948 9, 13-21, ill.

331. —— *African art; the contrast with western tradition.* The Times, 1951, 6-8, ill. (From *The Times* review of British Colonies, no. 2.)

332. —— *On the nature of African art.* Mem. & proc. Manchester lit. & phil. soc. **94**, 1953, 12, ill.

333. —— *The study of African art.* Bull. of the Allen Memorial Art Museum, **12**, 1955-6, 44-61. Bull. Oberlin College, **13** (2), 1955, 44-61, bibl.

334. —— *Note on some African sculptures.* Bull. Oberlin Coll., **14**, no. 3, 1957, 98-105.

335. —— *The study of African art.* Ottenberg, S. and B., Cultures and societies of Africa, 1960, 458-73.

336. —— *On the nature of African art.* Legum, Colin. Africa: a handbook to the continent, 1961, 414-24, ill.

337. —— 1959. *Afro-Portuguese ivories.* Pp. xxiii + 86, bibl., ill. London: Batchworth.

338. —— 1959. *Vergessene Negerkunst. Afro-portugiesisches Elfenbein.* Pp. 24, ill. Prague: Artia.

339. —— See also: 1958. Elisofon, Eliot, and William Fagg. *The sculpture of Africa* (photos by E. Elisofon, text by W. Fagg). Pp. 256, ill. London: Thames & Hudson.

340. —— *Perspective from Africa.* Smith, Marian W., The artist in tribal society, 1961, 116-19, ill.

341. —— and **Plass, Margaret.** 1964. *African sculpture; an anthology.* Pp. 160, bibl., ill., map. London and New York: Dutton Vista.

342. **Fierens, P.** *L'Art nègre et l'art vivant.* Cahiers de Belgique (Brussels), **3**, 1930, 9.

343. **Forde, D.** *African art.* Apollo, **61**, 1955, 84-85.

344. **Forman, W.** and **B.** 1956. *Kunst ferner Länder; Ägypten, Afrika, Amerika, Ozeanien, Indonesien.* Pp. 323, ill. Prague: Artia.

345. —— 1957. *Exotic art.* Pp. xxi + 327, 218 plates (some col.). London: Zwemmer.

346. **France.** 1963. *Arts d'Afrique intertropicale.* Paris: Documentation française (La Docum. photographique, dossier no. 55-16, 1963, hors série).

347. **Fraser, Douglas.** *African masks from an unrecorded style province.* Man, **60**, 94, May 1960, p. 65, ill.

348. —— 1963. *Primitive art.* Pp. 320, ill. London: Thames & Hudson.

349. —— 1963. *L'Art primitif.* Pp. 320, ill. Paris: Somogy Editions d'Art.

350. **Friend, Donald.** *Masks.* Nigeria, **18**, 1939, 100-4, ill.

351. **Frobenius, Leo.** *Die Kunst der Naturvölker.* Westermanns Ill. Deutsche Monatshefte, 79, 1895 6: 1, Ornamentik, 329-40, ill.; 2, Plastik, 593-606, ill.

352. —— *Die bildende Kunst der Afrikaner.* Mitt. anthrop. gesell. Wien, **27** (17), 1897, 1-17, ill.

353. —— *Die Masken und Geheimbünde Afrikas.* Nova Acta. Abhandlungen der Kais. Leop.-Carol. Deutschen Akademie der Naturforscher (Halle), **74**, no. 1, 1898, 278, ill., map.

354. *Alte und junge afrikanische Kunst.* Die Kunstwelt, **2**, 1912, 97-114, ill.

355. —— *Die Kunst Afrikas.* Erdball, **5**, 3, 1931, 85-114.

356. —— *L'Art africain.* Cah. d'Art (Paris), **5**, 1930, 395-429, ill.

357. **Fröhlich, W.** *Beiträge zur afrikanischen Kunst.* Ethnologica, **III**, 1962, 300, ill.

358. **Fry, Roger.** *Negro sculpture and Bushmen paintings.* Vision and Design, 1920, 65–68, ill.

359. **Gamon, Gaspar.** *Las Mascaras religiosas africanos.* Africa (Madrid), **15** (202), 1958, 13–16, ill.

360. **Gerbrands, Adrianus A.** 1957. *Art as an element of culture, especially in Negro Africa.* Pp. vii + 158, ill., map. Leiden: E. J. Brill. (Mededelingen van het Rijksmuseum voor Volkenkunde, 12.)

361. —— 1956. *Kunst als cultuur-element in het bijzonder in Neger-Afrika.* (Diss.) Pp. 144, ill. 's-Gravenhage: Excelsior. (*Review*: Anthropos, **52**, 1 2, 1957, 341–2—P.S.)

362. **Germann, Paul.** *Die afrikanische Kunst.* Springer, Anton. Handbuch der Kunstgeschichte, Band 6, Die aussereuropäische Kunst, 1929, 549–88, ill.

363. **Germann, Paul.** *Afrikanische Kunst.* Beitr. z. Kol.-Forschung. Tagungsband, **1**, 1943, 71–78, 4 plates.

364. **Glück, J. F.,** and **M. Noske.** 1956. *Afrikanische Masken.* Pp. 16, 48 plates. Baden-Baden: W. Klein.

365. **Goldwater, R. U.** *Approach to African sculpture.* Parnassus, **7**, 1935, 25–27.

366. —— 1938. *Primitivism in modern painting.* Pp. xxiii + 210, ill. New York: Harper Bros.

367. —— 1957. *Museum of primitive art; selected works.* 2 vols. Vol. 1, 39 photographs. Vol. 2, 34 photographs. London: K. Paul.

368. **Goluber, Victor.** s.d. *L'art nègre.* Paris.

369. **Goodwin, A. J. H.,** and **Others.** *The art of Africa.* Afr. south (Cape Town), **2**, 4, July–Sept. 1958, 94–118, ill.

370. **Gorer, G.** *Black art.* Listener, 14 Aug. 1935.

371. **Gregor, J.** 1936–7. *Masks of the world.* ill. (some col.). London: Batsford.

372. **Griaule, Marcel.** *Mission Dakar-Djibouti; Rapport général.* J. soc. africanistes, 2(1) 1932, 113–22: 229–36.

373. —— 1947. *Arts de l'Afrique noire.* Pp. 127, ill. Paris: Éditions du Chêne.

374. —— 1950. *Arts of the African native.* Pp. 126, ill. London: Thames & Hudson.

375. —— 1950. *Folk art of black Africa.* Pp. 126, ill. New York: Tudor Publishing Co. (Also published under the name 'Arts of the African native', q.v.)

376. —— *Les symboles des arts africains.* Diop, A., l'Art nègre, 1951, pp. 12–24, ill.

377. —— *Art et symbole en Afrique noire.* Zodiaque, **5**, Oct. 1951, p. 35, ill.

378. **Guillaume, Paul.** 1917. *Sculptures nègres.* Paris.

379. —— *African art at the Barnes Foundation.* Opportunity, **2**, 17, May 1924, pp. 140–2.

380. —— *The triumph of ancient negro art.* Opportunity, **4**, 41, May 1926, pp. 146–7.

381. —— and **Th. Munro.** 1926. *Primitive negro sculpture.* Pp. 134, ill., map. New York: Harcourt, Brace & Co.

382. —— and **Th. Munro.** 1928. *La sculpture nègre primitive.* Pp. 150. Paris: G. Crès.

383. **Guillaume, H.** *La sculpture négro-africaine.* Probl. Afr. centr., **13**, 44, 1959, 97–109, ill.

384. **Grottanelli, Vinigi L.** *Sul significato della scultura africana* (Lugard lecture, 1961). Africa, **31**, 4, Oct. 1961, 324–43. (English summary.)

385. **Gris, Joan.** *Opinions sur l'art nègre.* Action, no. 3, Apr. 1920.

386. **Hall, H. U.** *Examples of African art.* Museum Journal, Univ. of Pennsylvania (Philadelphia, Pa.), **10**, 1919, 79–101, ill.

387. —— 1922. *Handbook of Africa and the South Seas. Primitive arts.* Pp. 62, ill.

388. 1920. *Handbook of Primitive Art of Africa and the South Seas.* Pp. 22, ill.

389. **Hardy, G.** 1927. *L'Art nègre. L'Art animiste des noirs de l'Afrique.* Pp. 168, 28 plates. Paris: Laurens.

390. **Haselberger, Herta.** *Die Wandmalerei der afrikanischen Neger.* Z. f. Ethnol. (Braunschweig), **82**, 2, 1957, 209–37, ill.

391. —— *Mural paintings of African negroes.* Z.f. Ethnol. (Braunschweig), **82**, 2, 1957, 209–37, ill., map.

392. —— *Method of studying ethnological art.* Current Anthrop., **2**, 4, Oct. 1961, 341–55, bibl. (Comments, pp. 355–81.)

393. —— *Quelques cas d'évolution du décor mural en Afrique occidentale.* Notes afr. I.F.A.N., **101**, Jan. 1964, 14–16, ill.

394. **Hausenstein, Wilhelm.** 1920. *Exoten, Skulpturen und Märchen.* Pp. 76, ill. Zurich.

395. —— 1922. *Barbaren und Klassiker.* Pp. 101, ill. Munich: R. Piper.

396. **Hautecoeur, L.** 1959(?). *Histoire de l'art.* 3 vols. Vol. 1, De la magie à la religion.

397. **Hazan, Fernand.** 1959. *La sculpture africaine.*

398. **Henderson, S. M. K.** *African masks and sculpture.* Glasgow art review, no. 2, 1946, 14–16.

399. **Hermann, Ferdinand.** 1951. *Die Bildnerei der Naturvölker als Forschungsgegenstand.* Studium Generale, 4, 8. Berlin: Springer Verlag.

400. —— *Die Bildnerei der Naturvölker und die Tiefenpsychologie.* Tribus, **2–3**, 1952–3, 125–39.

401. —— *Über Material, Gegenstand und Stil der afrikanischen Plastik.* Kunstwerk-Schriften, **17**, 1952, 1–22, ill. (Sonderausgabe der Zeitschrift 'Das Kunstwerk'.)

402. —— *Zur Interpretation der afrikanischen Plastik.* Kunstwerk-Schriften, Band 17 (Sonderausgabe der Zeitschrift 'Das Kunstwerk'), 1952, 49–50.

402a. —— *Um die Interpretation der Bildnerei der Naturvölker.* Studium Generale, 7 Jg.h7, 1954.

403. —— *Die afrikanische Negerplastik als Forschungsgegenstand* (African negro-sculpture as a subject of research). Veröff. Mus. Völkerk. Leipzig. **9**, 58, 3–29.

404. —— and **Paul Germann.** *Beiträge zur afrikanischen Kunst.* Veröff. Mus. Völkerk. Leipzig, Heft 9, 1958, vi, 1–59, bibl., ill., map.

405. **Herskovits, M. J.** *The nature of primitive art.* The arts, **14**, 1928, 47–50, ill.

406. —— *Afro-American art.* Encyclopedia of world art, **1**, 1958, 150–8, ill.

407. —— *Bush negro art.* Arts, **17**, 1930, 25–37.

408. **Heydrich, M.** *Stand und Aufgaben der afrikanischen Kunst-forschung.* Beitr. z. Kolonialforsch. Tagungsband, **1**, 1943.

409. **Hill, J. Newton.** *African sculpture.* Davis, John A. (ed.), Africa from the point of view of American negro scholars, 1958, 131–41, ill.

410. **Himmelheber, Hans.** 1960. *Negerkunst und Negerkünstler. Mit Ergebnissen von sechs Afrika-Expeditionen.* Pp. viii + 436, bibl., ill. Brunswick: Klinkhardt u. Biermann.

411. —— 1960. *Afrikanische Masken.* Pp. 46 + 20 plates (col.). Brunswick: Klinkhardt u. Biermann. (Translated into French as 'Les masques africains'. Pp. 47, ill. Paris: Presses Univ. de France.)

412. **Hooper, J. T.,** and **C. A. Burland.** 1954. *The art of primitive peoples.* Pp. 168, ill. New York: N.Y. Philosophical Library.

413. **Howlett, Jacques.** *L'Art nègre; Connais pas!* Présence afr., **10–11**, 1951, 85–90.

414. **Illustrated London News.** *Benin relics.* I.L.N., **176**, 1930, 531, ill.

415. —— *Art of ancient Benin.* I.L.N., **211**, 1947, 666–7, ill.

416. —— *Donatellos of mediaeval Africa; Ife bronze portrait heads.* I.L.N., **213**, 1948, 24, ill.

417. —— *Modern Nigerian artists' work.* I.L.N., **213**, 1948, 25, ill.

418. —— *Vital native Bantu genius; sacred and lay works by young artists.* I.L.N., **214**, 1949, 90–91, ill.

419. —— *Newly found terra-cotta heads from Ife; early African classical masterpieces.* I.L.N., **215**, 1949, 27, ill.

420. —— *Magnificent bronze leopard of Benin work.* I.L.N., **219**, 1951, 66, ill.

421. —— *Benin bronze head of a queen-mother.* I.L.N., **223**, 1953, 983, ill.

422. —— *As others see us . . . Europeans through the eyes of native artists.* I.L.N., **225**, 1954, 562, ill.

423. —— *Richest find of Ife bronzes since 1938.* I.L.N., **231**, 1957, 1097.

424. —— *Kneeling figure of Abuja of the neolithic Nok culture of northern Nigeria.* I.L.N., **237**, 1960, 563, ill.

425. —— *Artistic heritage of a newly independent nation.* I.L.N., **237**, 1960, 651.

427. **Inverarity, R. B.** 1955. *Anthropology in primitive art.* Yearbook of anthropology, 1955. Pp. 836, ill. New York: Wenner Gren Foundation.

428. **Jacovleff, Alexandre.** *Dessins et peintures d'Afrique.* Pp. 98, ill. Paris: Meynial.

429. **Jahn, Janheinz.** *Kuntu; l'impossibilité de la métamorphose du style.* Présence afr., N.S. 22, Oct.–Nov. 1958, 10–28.

430. —— 1961. *Muntu; an outline of neo-African culture.* Pp. 267, bibl., ill., map. London: Faber.

431. **Junod, Henri P.,** and **Others.** 1958. *The art of Africa.* Pietermaritzburg: Shuter & Shooter.

432. **Kahnweiler, D. H.** *Negro art and cubism.* Horizon, Dec. 1948. (French: Présence afr., no. 3, 1948, Paris Dakar.)

433. **Karutz, Richard.** 1901. *Die afrikanischen Hörnermasken.* Pp. 94. Lübeck: Mitt. Geog. Gesell. in Lübeck.

434. —— *Von Wesentlichem in der afrikanischen Kunst.* Ipek (Leipzig), **2**, 1927, 31–41, ill.

435. **Klingbeil, Waldemar.** 1932. *Kopf- und Maskenzauber in der Vorgeschichte und bei den Primitiven.* Pp. 144.

436. **Kochnitzky, L.** *Influence de la plastique nègre sur l'art contemporain.* Synthèses, 2e. ann., **121**, 1956, 292–9.

437. **Krause, F.** *Maske und Ahnenfigur; Das Motiv der Hülle und das Prinzip der Form.* Ethnol. Stud., **1** (4), 1931, 344–65.

438. **Kühn, Herbert.** 1923. *Die Kunst der Primitiven.* Munich. Pp. 246, ill. Delphin-Verlag.

439. **Küsters, M.** *Afrikanische Negerkunst und ihre Beziehungen zur Hoch-Kultur.* Ethnol. Anz., **3**, 1932–5, referate, 35–40.

440. **Kutscher, G.** 1953. *Exotische Masken.* Stuttgart.

441. **L.** *Aspects of the study of African art.* Phylon, **19** (4), Winter 1958, 372–87.

442. **Lagercrantz, S.** *Bildangst der Schwarzen.* Archiv f. Religionswissenschaft, **37** (2), 1942, 390–406.

443. **Lang, H.** *Famous ivory treasures of a negro king.* Nat. hist., **18**, 1918, 527–52.

444. **Laude, J.** *African art.* Rev. d'Esthétique, Oct.–Dec., 1951.

445. —— *African art.* Critique, no. 55, Dec. 1951, 1086–89.

446. —— 1953. *L'art nègre* 1. 6. No. 28, 28–29, ill. No. 29, 27–29, ill. Lausanne-Paris: Pour l'Art.

447. —— *African art.* Cah. d'Art, no. 1 (39e ann.), Oct. 1954, 122–3.

448. —— *Arts plastiques de l'Afrique noire et de l'Europe.* Thesis for Doctorate: in preparation 1959.

449. —— *En Afrique noire; arts plastiques et histoire.* Annales économies, sociétés, civilisations, **14** (4), 1959, 640–61, ill., map.

450. **Lavachery, Henri.** *L'art des noirs d'Afrique et son destin.* Diop, A., L'art nègre, 1951, pp. 38–57, ill.

451. —— *Beautés de l'art plastique africain.* Cah. Belgique (Brussels), **3**, 1930, 9.

452. —— 1954. *Statuaire de l'Afrique noire.* Pp. 151, ill., map. Brussels: Office de Publicité (Collections Lebègue et Nationale, N.S. no. III).

453. **Lebeuf, J.-P.,** and **A. Masson-Detourbet.** *Art d'Afrique; Une photographie commentée.* Rev. Géog. hum. Ethnol., **4**, 3, July–Sept. 1948, p. 25, ill.

454. **Le Gall, J.** *L'artisanat et les arts africains.* Encyclopédie Coloniale et Maritime, France, **2**, 1949, 365–70, ill.

455. **Leiris, M.** 1954. *Les nègres d'Afrique et les arts sculpturaux.* U.N.E.S.C.O.: Unité et diversité culturelles: L'Originalité des cultures: Son rôle dans la compréhension internationale. Pp. 336–73. Paris: U.N.E.S.C.O. (2nd ed.)

456. **Lem, F.-H.** *Musique et art nègres; Lettres adressées à M. Éboué.* Bull. rech. soudanaises, **3**, Sept. 1936, pp. 73–83.

457. —— *Réalité de l'art nègre.* Tropiques, 48e ann., **327**, 1950, 25–38, ill.

458. —— *Variété et unité des traditions plastiques de l'Afrique noire.* Présence afr., **10–11** (L'art nègre), 1951, 25–35, ill.

459. —— *L'Art d'Afrique noire.* Encyclop. mens. O.M., 1956, no. 67, 112–16, ill.

460. **Leuzinger, Elsy.** 1942. *Vom Wesen der Maske.* s.p. ill. Zürich: Sammlung für Völkerkunde, Universität Zürich.

461. —— *Africa; the art of negro peoples.* Pp. 247, bibl., ill., maps. London: Methuen.

462. **Levy-Bruhl, Lucien.** 1927. *L'âme primitive.* Paris. (3rd ed.)

463. —— 1951. *Les fonctions mentales dans les sociétés inférieures.* Pp. 475. Paris: Felix Alcan.

464. **Life.** *Mystic art of tribal Africa.* Life, **33**, 1952, 116–25, ill.

465. **Lind, Christer.** *Negerdikter och Negerkonst.* Konstrevy (Stockholm), 29 (I), 1953, 68–69, ill.

466. **Linné, S.,** and **G. Montell.** 1947. *Primitiv Konst.* Pp. 467, ill. Stockholm: Statens Ethnog. Museum.

467. **Liturgical Arts.** *Africa,* Part 1. Liturgical arts, **26**, 1958, 69–94. *Africa,* Part 2. Liturgical arts, **26**, no. 4, 1958, 105–44.

468. **Locke, Alain.** *A note on African art.* Opportunity, **2**, 17, May 1924, pp. 134–8.

469. —— *African art; classic style.* Amer. Mag. of Art, **28**, 1935, 270–8.

470. —— *Negro art, past and present.* U.S.A., 1936.

471. **Lommel, Andreas.** *Altafrikanische Kunst.* Afrika heute, Jb., 1957, 81–84, ill.

472. **Lopsiger-Dellenbach, M.** *Proverbes sculptés.* Les Musées de Genève, **16** (5), 1959, ill.

473. **Lucas, Heinz.** *Afrikanische Masken.* Kunstwerk-Schriften, **17**, 1952, 37–48, ill. (Sonderausgabe der Zeitschrift 'Das Kunstwerk'.)

474. **Luquet, G. H.** 1931. *L'Art primitif.* In-12., 142 fig. dans le texte. Paris: Gaston Doin.

475. **Mackay, M.** *African art in Paris.* W.A.R., **26**, 1955, 336, 805–7, ill. (See also under catalogues: France, Paris, Cercle Volney.)

476. **Mackenzie, H. F.** *Group of primitive carvings in wood and horn.* Bull. Chicago Art Inst., **24**, 1930, 8–9.

477. **Maigret, Julien.** 1931. *Afrique Occidentale et Afrique Équatoriale* (avec un avant-propos sur l'art nègre de M. Georges Hardy). Paris: Soc. d'Édit. géogr. marit. et col.

478. **Maquet, Jacques J.** 1962. *Afrique; les civilisations noires.* Pp. 288, bibl., ill., maps. Paris: Horizons de France.

479. **Marquetty, V.** *L'art des noirs d'Afrique.* Rev. des Voyages (Paris), Jan. 1939, 18–21.

480. **Marquez Nivanda, F.** 1958. *El arte primitivo.* Pp. 63, ill.

481. **Maurice, Albert.** *Union africaine des arts et des lettres.* Afr. affairs, **50**, 200, July 1951, 233–6.

482. —— 1951. *Afrikaanse kunsten en moderne wereld.* Pp. 62 (1). Brussels: Vissende Kat.

483. —— 1951. *Arts africains et monde moderne.* Pp. 62, ill. Paris, Brussels: A l'Enseigne du Chat qui Pêche.

484. **Medgyes, Ladislas.** *Art of the African negro.* Illus. Studio, **70**, 1922, 141–8, ill.

485. **Merriam, Alan P.** 1961. *A prologue to the study of the African arts.* Pp. 37, bibl. Yellow Springs, Ohio: Antioch Press. (Antioch College Founders Day Lecture no. 7.)

486. **Meyer, R. de.** *L'art nègre; Art véritable (Masques).* Rev. col. belge, **88**, June 1949, 341–3, ill.

487. **Muensterberger, W.** 1950. *Some elements of artistic creativity among primitive peoples.* Tonnier, L. (*ed.*), Beiträge zur Gesellungs- und Völkerwissenschaft. Pp. 313–17. Berlin: R. Thurnwalds Festschift.?

488. —— *Sculpture of primitive man.* 1955. Pp. xlvi + 136, ill. London: Thames & Hudson.

488a.—— and **W. L.** 1955. *Primitieve kunst uit West- en Midden-Afrika, Indonesie, Melanesie, Polynesie en Noordwest-Amerika.* Pp. 136, ill. Amsterdam: Contact. Ars Mundi, no. 3. (French edition, La sculptures des primitifs. Pp. 136, ill. Paris: Flammarion.)

489. **Munro, Eleanor C.** *Which way to see African sculpture.* Art news mag. (New York), May 1956.

490. **Munro, T.** *Primitive negro sculpture.* Opportunity, 1926, 150–2, ill.

491. **Munro, Thomas,** and **Paul Guillaume.** 1926. *Primitive negro sculpture.* Pp. 134, ill., map. New York: Harcourt. London: J. Cape.

492. **Musée Vivant.** *Essai de classification des styles de l'art nègre.* Musée vivant, **12** (1948), 30–31, 36–37, map.

493. **Mveng, Engelbert.** *Structures fondamentales de l'art négro-africain.* 1. La symbolique. Présence afr., **49**, 1964, 116–28.

494. **Newsweek.** *Segy's little people; African sculpture.* Newsweek, **45**, 1955, 90.

495. **Niessen, Carl.** *Vorformen der Maske.* Ethnologica, N.F., **2**, 1960, 274–84.

496. **Norbert, Mylius.** 1961. *Antlitz und Geheimnis der überseeischen Maske.* Pp. 53, ill. Vienna: Notring der wiss. Verbände Österreichs.

497. **Norlund, Mogeas Christian.** 1956. *Bag Afrikas Maske.* Pp. 196, ill. Copenhagen: Aschehoug.

498. **Noske, Margot.** *See no.* 364.

499. **Nuoffer, Oskar.** 1925. *Afrikanische Plastik in der Gestaltung von Mutter und Kind.* Pp. 45, ill. Dresden: Carl Reissner.

500. **Olbrechts, Frans M.** 1942. *Westersche invloed op de inheemsche kunst in Afrika?* Koninklijke Musea voor Schoone Kunsten van Belgie, Voordrachten 1940–1941. Pp. 24, ill. Brussels.

501. —— *Bijdrage tot de Kennis van de chronologie der Afrikaansche Plastiek.* I.R.C.B. (Sciences morales), **10** (2), 1941, 36, ill.

502. —— *Contribution to the study of the chronology of African plastic art.* Africa, **14**, 4 Oct. 1943-4, 183–93, ill.

503. **Osorio de Oliveira, José.** 1956. *El arte negro como expresión humana y como valor cultural.* Pp. 89, ill. Madrid: Coll. Goya.

504. **Palavecino, Enrique.** *La máscara y la cultura.* Pp. (142) + 22, bibl., plates (some col.), map. Buenos Aires: Ediciones de la Municipalidad.

505. **Panyella, A.** *Interpretacion etnologica del arte africano.* Africa (Madrid), **131**, 1952, 14–16, ill.

506. **Paulme, Denise.** 1956. *Les sculptures de l'Afrique noire.* Pp. 130, ill. Paris: Presses Univ. de France.

507. —— 1962. *African sculpture.* Pp. 160, ill. London: Elek Books.

508. —— 1962. *L'art sculptural nègre.* 2 vols. Paris.

509. **Pauvert, J. C.** *Approche de l'art africain noir.* Presénce afr., **10/11**, 1951, 72–84.

510. **Périer, Gaston Denys.** *Position de l'art nègre.* Rev. belge, **4**, 1930, 5.

511. —— *La valeur sociale de l'art nègre.* La vie économique et sociale, 1934, 282–9.

512. —— *Notre attitude devant l'art nègre.* Rev. de l'Aucam (Louvain), **9**, 1934, 242–6.

513. —— *Plastique nègre et statuaire religieuse.* Rev. de l'Aucam (Louvain), **13**, 1938, 285.

514. **Pittard, E.** *Statues à clous de l'Afrique noire.* Les Musées de Genève, **1** (2), 1944, ill.

515. **Plass, Margaret.** 1956. *African tribal sculpture.* Pp. 57 + 63 pl., map. Philadelphia, Pa.: Univ. Museum.

516. —— 1956. *The king's day.* Pp. 22, ill. Chicago: Chicago Natural History Museum.

517. —— *African negro sculpture.* Philadelphia: Univ. of Pennsylvania, Univ. mus. bull., **21** (4), 1957, 5–76, ill.

518. —— *Eye for beauty; African sculpture.* Liturgical arts, **26**, no. 4, 1958, 106–7.

519. **Pleasants, F. R.** *African sculpture in the Peabody Museum of Cambridge, Massachusetts.* Ipek, **11**, 1938, 117–24, ill.

520. **Porter, James Amon.** 1953. *The appreciation of African negro art.* Howard Univ., Washington, D.C., Gallery of Art.

521. **Portier, A.,** and **Fr. Poncetton.** 1936. *Les arts sauvages.* Tom. 1, Afrique—plates in a portfolio. Paris: A. Morancé.

522. **Preuss, K. Th.** *Der Ursprung der Religion und Kunst.* Globus. Vol. 86: 321–7; 355–63; 375–9; 388–92. Vol. 87: 333–7; 347–50; 380–4; 391–400; 413–19.

523. **Radin, Paul,** and **Others.** 1953. *African folktales and sculpture.* Pp. xxi + 355, ill. New York: Bollingen Series 32. (1954. London: Secker & Warburg.)

524. **Rasmussen, René.** 1951. *Art nègre; ou le salut par les sauvages.* Pp. 23 + 32 pl. Paris: Presses du Livre Francais (Le soleil noir, Sér. Art l).

525. **Ratton, Charles.** *Masques africains.* Paris, 1931, ill.

526. ——*L'or fétiche.* Diop, A., L'art nègre. 1951, pp. 136–55, ill.

527. **Redfield, Robert; Herskovits, Melville, J.,** and **Gordon F. Ekholm.** 1959. *Aspects of primitive art.* Pp. 100, ill. New York: Museum of Primitive Art.

528. **Redinha, J.** *Máscaras africanas.* Rev. Gabinete Est. Ultramar, **7–8,** July–Dec. 1952, 34–61, ill.

529. **Rhotert, H.** *Betrachtungen zur Frage der Felsbildforschung.* Paideuma, **1**, 4, July 1939, 159–67.

530. **Ridder, André de.** 1936. *Negerkunst; Vroeger nu en later.* Pp. 29. Antwerp: Koloniale Hoogeschool van Belgie.

531. **Rieser, H. F.** *African ivories.* Africa south, 4, 1961, 112–17, ill.

532. **Riley, Olive L.** 1955. *Masks and magic.* Pp. v + 122, bibl., ill. (col.). London: Thames & Hudson.

533. **Robert-Acarin, Germaine.** 1958. *Symbolisations, inspirées par l'Afrique; Peintures, bois brûlés, sculptures.* Pp. 6, ill. Brussels: Kumpo.

534. **Rothenberg, A.** *Primitive negro sculpture.* Craft horizons, **9**, no. 4, 1949, 6–11.

534a.**Rothenstein, William.** *The development of indigenous art.* Oversea education, **1**, 1, 1929.

535. **Rousseau, M.** *La signification sociale de l'art en Afrique noire.* Musée vivant (Paris), **19**, 1955, 92–104, ill.

536. **Routil, Robert.** *Über die Verbreitung des Nabelbruches in Afrika und seine plastische Darstellung in der Eingeborenenkunst.* Ann. naturhist. Mus. Wien, **55**, 1944–7, 185–206, map.

537. **Roy, Claude.** 1957. *Arts sauvages.* Pp. 103 (2), ill. Paris: Robert Delpire.

538. **Salisbury, Southern Rhodesia.** 1962. *First biennial International Congress of African culture , Rhodes National Gallery, August–September, 1962.* s.p. Ill. Salisbury: Rhodes National Gallery.

539. **Salles, G.** *Réflexions sur l'art nègre.* Cah. d'art, **2**, 1927, 247–58.

540. **Salmon, A.** *Negro art.* Burlington mag., **36**, 1920, 164–72.

541. ——*L'art nègre.* Propos d'Atelier, 1922, pp. 115–36.

542. **Santandrea, S.** *Artisti indigeni.* Africano fotografoto, 1938, 234–43.

543. **Sayce, R. U.** 1933. *Primitive arts and crafts.* Pp. xiii + 291, bibl., ill. Cambridge: Cambridge Univ. Press.

544. **Schlosser, K.** 1952. *Der Signalismus in der Kunst der Naturvölker.* Kiel.

545. **Schmalenbach, W.** 1953. *L'Art nègre.* Pp. 175, ill. Paris: Massim.

545a.—— 1954. *African art.* Pp. 175, ill. New York: Macmillan.

546. —— *Grundsätzliches zur primitiven Kunst.* Acta tropica (Basel), **15**, 4, 1958, 289–323.

547. —— 1959. *Primitive Kunst.* Pp. 48, ill. Munich: Ahrbeck, Knoor, & Hirth.

548. **Schneider, I. L.** 1951. *Masques primitifs.* Pp. 18, ill. Paris: Librairie Plon.

549. **Schneider-Lengyel, J. Ilse.** 1934. *Die Welt der Maske.* Munich.

550. **Schomburgk, Hans Hermann.** 1947. *Frauen, Masken und Dämonen.* Pp. 117, ill. Berlin: H. Wigankow.

551. **Schweeger-Hefel, Annemarie.** 1948. *Afrikanische Bronzen.* Pp. 34, ill. Wien: Wolfrum.

552. —— 1960. *Holzplastik in Afrika. Gestaltungsprinzipien.* Pp. (6) 148, bibl., ill., map. Vienna: Wilhelm Braumüller. (Veröff. z. Arch. f. Völkerkde., Band 5.)

553. **Sedlmayr, H.** 1959. *Kunst und Wahreit.* Hamburg.

554. **Segy, Ladislas.** *Negro sculpture in interior decoration.* Studio, 1934.

555. —— *The significance of African art.* Phylon (Atlanta Univ.), **12**, 1951, 371–7.

556. —— 1952. *African sculpture speaks.* Pp. 254, ill. New York: A. A. Wynn.

557. —— *Initiation ceremony and African sculptures.* Amer. Image, **10**, 1, 1953, 57–82.

558. —— *Sculptures africaines et animisme.* Psyché, **76**, Mar. 1953, 1–11.

559. —— *African sculpture and writing.* J. human relations (Wilberforce, Ohio), Winter 1953, 13–21.

560. —— *African names and sculpture.* Acta tropica, **10**, 4, 1953, 290–309, ill.

561. —— *The mask in African dance.* Negro hist. bull., **14**, 5, Feb. 1953, 6, ill. (Reprint.)

562. —— *Circle-dot symbolic sign on African ivory carvings.* Zaïre, **7**, 1, Jan. 1953, 35–54, ill.

563. —— *Cérémonie d'initiation et sculptures africaines.* Psyché (Paris), 88–89, Feb. and 89 Mar. 1954. (Reprint, pp. 23.)

564. —— *African snake symbolism.* Arch. f. Völkerkunde (Wien), **9**, 1954.

565. —— *Divers aspects de l'étude de l'art africain.* Rev. psychol. des peuples (Le Havre), **2**, 1954. (Reprint, pp. 19.)

566. —— *The artistic quality of African sculpture.* Tribus, N.F. 6, 1956 (1957), 83–101.

567. —— 1958. *African sculpture.* Pp. 34 + 163 pl., map. New York: Dover Publications.

568. —— *Aspects of the study of African art.* Phylon, **19**, 1958, 372–87.

569. —— *Aspects of African art for the museums.* Cah. d'ét. afr. (Paris), 1960, 125–8.

570. —— *The meaning of African sculpture.* J. human relations, **8**, 1960, 749–64, ill.

571. —— *African sculpture and cubism.* Criticism, **4**, 1962, 273–301, ill.

572. **Senghor, L. S.** *L'esthétique négro-africaine.* Diogène (Paris), **16**, 1956, 43–61.

573. **Sevier, M.** *Negro art.* Atelier, **11**, 1931, 116–21.

574. **Shadbolt, D.** *Our relation to primitive art.* Canadian art (Ottawa), 5 (1), 1947.

575. **Sieber, Roy.** *Masks as agents of social control.* Afr. stud. bull., **5**, 2, May 1962, 8–13.

576. —— MS. thesis: *African Tribal Sculpture.* Dept. of Fine Arts, State Univ. of Iowa.

577. **Smith, E.** 1952. *African symbolism.* Pp. 25. London: R. Anthrop. Institute.

578. **Snyder, N.** *Versatile traveler records the face of Africa—masks.* Interiors, **113**, 1954, 132.

579. **La Société Sécrete.** *Symbolisme in de Negerkunst.* Pp. 83, ill. Brussels: Congo Bib.

580. **Soyaux, Herman.** *Die Kunst beim Neger.* Illus. Deut. Monatshefte, 1877, 615–22, ill.

581. **Spinden, H. J.** *African masks and fetishes.* Brooklyn Mus. Q., **22**, 1935, 179–81.

582. **Springer, A.** (ed.). *Die aussereuropäische Kunst.* Leipzig, 1929. Handbuch der Kunstgeschichte, 6.

583. **Steinmann, Alfred.** *Masken und Krankheit.* Ciba-Z. 89, 1943, 3114–52, ill.

584. —— *Maske und Tod bei den primitiven Völkern.* Ciba-Z. 89, 1943, 3147–52, ill.

585. —— *Afrikanische Masken zur Behandlung von Krankheiten.* Ciba-Z., 89, 1943, 3120–4, 4 ill.

586. **Straube, Helmut.** *Thoughts on the colour symbolism of African native cultures.* Studium generale, **13**, 1960, 391–8.

587. **Strauss, Anselm L.** 1959. *Mirrors and masks. The search for identity.* Pp. 186.

588. **Sweeney, James J.** 1935. *African negro art.* New York: Museum of Modern Art. London: Allen & Unwin.

589. **Szecsi, L.** *Primitive negro art* (transl.). Art and archaeology, **34**, 1933, 130–6.

590. **Theile, Albert.** *Kunst in Afrika.* Pp. 320, ill. Brussels.

591. —— 1963. *Les arts de l'Afrique.* Pp. 320, bibl., ill., maps. Paris: Arthaud.

592. **Thienen, F. W. S. van.** 1951. *Exotische Kunst. De Kunst uit China, Japan, Islam, Afrika.* Utrecht: Antwerp.

593. **Thurnwald, R.** *Anfänge der Kunst. Verhandlungen des 6 Deutschen Soziologentages, 1928, in Zürich.* Schriften d. Deutschen Gesellschaft für Soziologie, Ser. 1, Band 6, 1929, 1076–9. Tübingen.

594. **Tong, Raymond.** 1958. *Figures in ebony.* Pp. (8), 131, ill. London: Cassell.

595. —— 1958. *Figures in ivory.* Pp. (8), 131, ill. London: Cassell.

596. **Trowell, Margaret.** *From negro sculpture to modern painting.* Uganda J., **6** (4), 1939, 169–75, ill.

597. —— 1954. *Classical African sculpture.* Pp. 103, ill. London: Faber. (2nd ed. (1964), pp. 103 + 68 pl. Faber.)

598. **Tzara, Tristan.** *La sculpture africaine et l'art moderne.* Konstrevy (Stockholm), no. 2, 1933, ill.

599. **Utzinger, Rudolf.** 1923. *Masken.* Pp. 26, bibl., ill. Berlin: E. Wasmuth. (Orbis Pictus, Band 13.)

600. **Van Bulck, G.** *Kunstgeschichte im Lichte der Kulturgeschichte.* Anthropos, **26**, 1931, 938–9.

601. **Van Overbergh, Cyrille.** 1913. *Les nègres d'Afrique; géographie humaine.* Pp. 276. Brussels: A. Dewit.

602. **Vatter, E.** 1926. *Religiöse Plastik der Naturvölker.* Pp. 192 (2), bibl. Frankfurt, a. M.: Frankfurter Verlags-Anstalt.

603. **Verité, P.** 1959/60. *Arts d'Afrique et d'Océanie.* Dictionnaire Larousse, 1959/60.

604. **Volmar, R.** 1956. *L'art psychopathologique.* (Bibliothèque de Psychiatrice.) Paris: Presses Univ. de France. (Chapter on primitive art and thought: Primitive symbols among Africans.)

605. **von Sydow, Eckart.** 1921. *Exotische Kunst; Afrika und Ozeanien.* Pp. 38, bibl., ill., map. Leipzig: Klinkhardt & Biermann.

606. —— *Afrikanische Holzbildwerke im Leipziger Museum.* Kunstchronik und Kunstmarkt, **59**, 1921, 625–39.

607. —— *Das Tier in der afrikanischen Plastik.* Der Ararat, **2**, 1921, 206–19.

608. —— 1923. *Die Kunst der Naturvölker und der Vorzeit.* Pp. (ix) + 569, ill. (many in col.). Berlin: Propyläen-Verlag.

609. —— 1926. *Kunst und Religion der Naturvölker.* Oldenburg.

610. —— 1927. *Primitive Kunst und Psychoanalyse.* Pp. 182, ill. Leipzig: Imago Bücher.

611. —— *African sculpture.* Africa, **1**, 2, Apr. 1928, 210–27.

612. —— 1939. *Handbuch der afrikanischen Plastik.* Bd. I. Die westafrikanische Plastik. Pp. 495, 10 Taf. Berlin: D. Reimer.

613. —— *The image of Janus in African sculpture.* Africa, 1932, **5**, 1, 14–27.

614. —— 1937. *Bildende Kunst der Naturvölker.* Preuss, K. Th., Lehrbuch der Völkerkunde.

615. —— 1954. *Afrikanische Plastik.* Pp. 177, 371 photos, maps. Berlin: Gebr. Mann.

616. **Weigert, H.** (*ed.*). 1957. *Kleine Kunstgeschichte d. aussereuropäischen Kulturen.* Pp. 420, ill.

617. **Weyns, J.** *Quelques remarques au sujet de nos sculptures africaines.* Les Arts Plastiques (Les carnets du Séminaire des Arts), 1949 (9–10), 373–81, ill.

618. **Whaite, H. C.** *African art.* J. soc. arts, **92** (4678), 1944, 660–9, ill.

619. **Wingert, Paul S.** 1948. *African Negro Sculpture.* Pp. v + 26, ill. San Francisco: M. H. de Young Memorial Museum.

620. —— 1950. *The sculpture of negro Africa.* Pp. x + 96, bibl., ill., map. New York: Columbia Univ. Press.

621. —— *Anatomical interpretations in African masks.* Man, **54**, no. 100, 1954, 69–71, ill.

622. —— 1962. *Primitive art; its traditions and styles.* Pp. xxii + 421, ill., maps. London: Oxford Univ. Press. (Africa, pp. 79–183.)

623. **Wissler, C.** 1950. *Masks.* New York: American Museum. (Science Guide no. 96.)

624. **Woelfel, Dominik.** *Die Kunst der Altvölker Afrikas.* Rimli, Eugen Th. Illustrierte Weltkunstgeschichte, vol. 5, 1960, 295–336, bibl., ill. Zürich: Stauffacher-Verlag.

625. **Zayas, M. de.** 1916. *African negro art.* (N.Y.) Ill.

626. —— *Negro Art.* The Arts, **3**, 1923, 199–205.

Id
Technology, Crafts, the Artist

627. **Achille, Louis-T.** *L'artiste noir et son peuple.* Présence afr., **16**, Oct.–Nov. 1957, 32–52.

628. **Andrée, R.** *Das Zeichnen bei den Naturvölkern.* Mitt. anthrop. gesell. Wien, **27**, 1887, 98–106.

629. **Anon.** *Tablet weaving.* Ciba rev., no. 117, **10**, 1956, 2–29, bibl., ill.

630. **Appia-Dabit, Beatrice.** *Quelques artisans noirs (teinturières, travailleurs du bois, potières).* Bull. I.F.A.N., **3**, 1–4, Jan.–Oct. 1941, 1–44, ill.

631. **Arkell, A. J.** *The distribution in Central Africa of one early neolithic ware (dotted wavy line pottery) and its possible connection with the beginning of pottery.* Actes 4. Congr. panafr. préhist. . . . (ed. G. Mortelmans and J. Nenquin), sect. 3, 1962, 283–7.

632. **Arriens, C.** *Die Schmuck- u. Handelsperlen Afrikas.* Kol. Runds. 1933, **25**, 5–7, 186–8 (vgl. auch Bd. 24, 7–8).

633. —— *Männer- und Frauenwebstühle in Afrika.* Umschau, **39**, Jg. 1935, h. 9.

634. **Balfet, Hélène.** *Problèmes relatifs à la position sociale de la potière.* CR. Séances Inst. franc. Anthrop., Fasc. 6, Jan.–Dec. 1952, 20–22.

635. **Balfour, Henry.** 1893. *The evolution of decorative art.* Pp. xv + 131, bibl., ill. London: Rivington, Percival & Co.

636. **Baumann, Hermann.** 1929. *Afrikanisches Kunstgewerbe.* H. Th. Bossert, Geschichte des Kunstgewerbes aller Zeiten und Völker, vol. 2, pp. 51–148, ill. Berlin: E. Wasmuth.

637. **Belcher, A.** *The future of pottery for African women.* Afr. women (London), **2**, 2, June 1957, 28–29.

638. **Belck, W.** *Die Erfinder der Eisentechnik.* Z. f. Ethnol. 39, 1907, 335–81; 40, 1908, 45–69; 42, 1910, 15–30. (Translated into English in Annual Report of the Smithsonian Institution, Washington, 1911, 507–27.)

639. **Blaha, Herta.** *Eine wenig beachtete Kunstfertigkeit der afrikanischen Neger; Skulpturen aus Lehm und Ton.* Wien. Völkerk. Mitt, **2**, 1, 1954, 13–15.

640. **Bloomhill, Greta.** *Africa's bead language; religious and social symbolism among primitive peoples.* Afr. world (London), Nov. 1957, 15–16, ill.

641. **Bohannan, Paul.** 1961. *Artist and critic in an African society,* pp. 85–94, ill. Smith, Marian W. (*ed.*), The artist in tribal society. Pp. xiii + 150, bibl., ill. London: Kegan Paul.

642. **Bossert, Helmuth Th.** 1955. *Ornamente der Völker.* Pp. 17, ill. Tübingen: Ernst Wasmuth.

643. **Bühler, A.** *Dyeing among primitive peoples.* Ciba rev., no. 68, 1948, 2478–512, ill.

644. —— *Färberei der Naturvölker.* Ciba-Rdsch., **75**, 1948, 2764–802, ill.

645. **Bühler, Kristin.** *Basic textile techniques.* Ciba rev., **63**, Jan. 1948, 2290–320, ill.

646. **Bühler-Oppenheim, Kristin.** *Primäre textile Techniken.* Ciba-Rdsch., **73**, Oct. 1947, 2688–720, ill.

647. **Cerulli, Ernesta.** *Sacralita della fucina e degli strumenti di lavoro del fabbro in Africa.* Ann. lat., **20**, 1956, 29–59.

648. —— *L'iniziazione al mestiere di fabbro in Africa.* Studi e Materiali Storia Relig. (Bologna), **27**, 1956, 87–101.

649. —— *Il fabbro africano eroe culturale.* Studi e Materiali Storia Relig. (Bologna), **28**, 11, 1957, 79–113.

650. **Clement, Pierre.** *Le forgeron en Afrique noire; Quelques attitudes du groupe à son égard.* Rev. géog. hum. ethnol. (Paris), **1**, 2, Apr.–June 1948, 35–58, ill., map.

651. **Cline, Walter.** 1937. *Mining and metallurgy in negro Africa.* Pp. 154, bibl., ill., map. Menasha (Wis.): Geo. Banta.

652. **Clouzot, Henri.** n.d. *Tissus nègres.* Pp. 6 + 48 pl. (some col.). Paris: Librairie des Arts Décoratifs.

653. **Cordezux, H.** 1943. *Fabrication de masque.* Pp. 55.

654. **Dark, Philip J. C.** *Cire-perdue casting; some technical and aesthetic considerations.* Ethnologica, 1964.

655. **Deloncle, Pierre.** 1945. *La parure féminine aux colonies.* Pp. 30. Paris: Agence des Colonies.

656. **Derry, T. K.,** and **T. I. Williams.** 1960. *A short history of technology from the earliest times to A.D. 1900.* Pp. 800. London: Clarendon Press.

657. **Dominjoud, M.** *La céramique africaine 1.* Les Musées de Genève, **11**, 1954 (3), ill.

658. **Drost, Dietrich.** *Mehrfüllige Tongefässe in Afrika und ihre Beziehungen zum Mittelmeergebiet. Eine völkerkundlich-vorgeschichtliche Studie.* Wiss. Z. Fr.-Schiller-Univ. Jena, **3**, 1, 1953–4, 61–79, ill., map.

659. —— *Tönerne Dachaufsätze in Afrika.* Jb. s. Mus. Völkerkunde. Leipzig, **15**, 1956 (1957), 83–105, ill.

659a. —— *Transportable Herde in Afrika.* Jb. s. Mus. Völkerkunde. Leipzig, **17**, 1958 (1960), 140–57, bibl., ill.

660. —— *Zur Technik der Holz- und Metallbearbeitung in Afrika.* Mitt. s. Mus. Völkerkunde Leipzig, **15**, 1963, 2–5, ill.

661. **Dubié, Paul.** *Industries de protection; vêtement.* C.R. 2. Conf. int. dos Africanistas ocidentais, Bissau, 1947 (1952), **5**, pp. 117–25.

662. **Fradier, G.** *The lesson of Abossolo Simion; African craftsman and artist.* Unesco courier, **4** (4), 1951, 6–7, ill.

663. **Fritze, G. A.** *Draht als Negerschmuck.* Afrika-Nachrichten, 1928, **9**, 20, S. 473–5.

664. **Frobenius, Leo.** *Das Hakenkreuz in Afrika.* Int. archiv. ethnog., **9**, 1896, 205–7.

665. —— *Beitrag zur afrikanischen Keramik.* Int. archiv. ethnog., **10**, 1897, 155, ill.

666. **Furlong, J. R.** *World outlets for African hides and skins.* Crown col., **15**, 162, May 1945, 309–11, ill.

667. **Gansser, A.** *The early history of tanning.* Ciba rev., no. 81, **7**, 1950, 2938–62, bibl., ill.

668. **George, M. F. A.** *Hides and skins from Africa.* Afr. world, July 1958, 15–16, ill.

669. **Germann, Paul.** *Afrikanische Puppen.* In Memoriam Karl Weule. Leipzig.

670. **Glück, Julius F.** *Die Kunst des Gelbgusses in Afrika.* Kunstwerk-Schriften, **17**, 1952, 27–36, ill. (Sonderausgabe der Zeitschrift 'Das Kunstwerk'.)

671. —— *Afrikanische Architektur* (African architecture), Tribus, **6**, 56, 65–82.

672. **Hambly, Wilfred Dyson.** 1925 *The history of tattooing and its significance; With some account of other forms of corporal marking.* Pp. 346, ill., maps. London: Witherby.

673. —— 1945. *Clever hands of the African negro.* Pp. xiii + 192, ill. Washington: Associated Publishers Inc.

674. **Hamlin, A. D. F.** 1916. *A history of ornament.* 2 vols.

675. **Harding, J. R.** *Conus shell disc ornaments (Vibangwa) in Africa.* J. roy. anthrop. inst., **91** (1), 1961, 52–66, ill., map.

676. **Heager, F.** 1899. *Alte Elfenbeinarbeiten aus Afrika in den Wiener Sammlungen.* Vienna.

677. **Hechter-Schulz, K.** *Wire bangles, a record of a Bantu craft.* S. Afr. J. sci., **59**, 2, Feb. 1963, 51–53, ill.

678. **Heese, C. H. T. D.** *Edged disks and armrings.* S. Afr. J. sci., **41**, 1945, 411–14.

679. **Hefel, Annemarie.** *Der afrikanische Gelbguss und seine Beziehungen zu den Mittelmeerländern (Diss. Wien).* Wiener Beitr. zur Kulturgeschichte u. Linguistik, **5**, 1943, 1–87, ill.

680. —— *Europäischer Einfluss auf alte und moderne afrikanische Metallkunst in verlorener Form.* Archiv f. Anthrop. N.F. 28, 3–4, 1943, 134-40.

681. **Henze, W.** 1958. *Ornament, Dekor und Zeichen.* Pp. 286, ill.

682. **Heydrich, Martin.** *Afrikanische Ornamentik.* Int. archiv ethnog., **22** (suppl.), 1914, 84, bibl., ill.

683. —— *Afrikanische Schnitzkunst.* Kunstblatt der Jugend (Berlin), **7**, 1928, 419–24, ill.

684. **Himmelheber, H.** 1935. *Negerkünstler.* Pp. 80, ill., map. Stuttgart: Strecker & Schröder.

685. **Inskeep, R. R.** *The march of iron across a continent.* Unesco courier, **12**, 1959, 20–23, ill.

686. **Jeffreys, M. D. W.** *The cowry shell.* Nigeria, **15**, 1938, 221–6, ill.

687. —— *The diffusion of cowries and Egyptian culture in Africa.* Amer. Anthrop., **50** (1), 1948, 45–53.

688. —— 1955. *The cowry shell and lozenge in African decorative art.* Samab., **6** (4), 1955, 83–95, ill.

689. **Jorrot, Jean.** *Coiffures d'enfants.* Réalisations, Mar.–Apr. 1935, 265–8, ill.

690. **Klusemann, Kurt.** *Die Entwicklung der Eisengewinnung in Afrika und Europa.* Mitt. anthrop. gesell. Wien, **54**, 1924, 120–40.

691. **Kramer, Augustin.** *Die Form neben der Zierkunst in ethnographischer Beleuchtung.* Ipek, **1**, 1925, 97–104, ill. (Behandelt u. a. Gegenstände der Ilerero, Zulu, Basiba, Bamum.)

692. **Krieger, Kurt.** *Studien über afrikanische Kunstperlen.* Baessler-Archiv, **25** (2), 1943, 54–103, bibl., ill., map.

693. **Lagercrantz, S.** *Becher aus Hörnern des Nashorns.* Ethnologica, N.F. **2**, 1960, 285–96, ill.

694. **Lane, S.** *African textile craftsmanship.* S. workman, **57**, 1927, 262–7, ill.

695. —— *African weapons and tools.* S. workman, **58**, 1929, 353–60, ill.

696. **Laufer, Berthold; Wilfrid D. Hambly** and **Ralph Linton.** 1930. *Tobacco and its uses in Africa.* Pp. 45, ill. Chicago: Field Museum of Natural History.

697. **Leakey, L. S. B.** *A new method of exhibiting prehistoric art.* Museums journal, 1954, 2, ill.

698. —— *Techniques of recording prehistoric art.* Third Pan-African Congress on Prehistory, Livingstone, 1955, 304–5.

699. **Lehmann, J.** 1920. *Die Ornamente der Natur- und Halbkultur-Völker.* Pp. 36 + 37 pl. (some col.). Frankfurt a M.: Joseph Baer.

700. **Lemaire, M. L. J.** *Techniken bei der Herstellung von Perlenarbeiten.* Baessler-Archiv, 8 (1), 1960, 215–33, ill.

701. **Le Page, P. C.** 1922. *La décoration primitive; Afrique.* 42 pl. with descriptive text. Paris: Librairie des arts décoratifs.

702. **Leroi-Gourhan, André.** 1943. *L'Homme et la Matière.* Pp. 367, ill. Paris: Albin Michel. 1945. *Milieu et techniques.* Pp. 512, ill. Paris: Albin Michel.

703. **Lester, Susan.** *The craft of 'cire perdue'.* W.A.R., **28**, 356, June 1957, 569–75, ill.

704. **Leuzinger, Elsy.** 1950. *Wesen und Form des Schmuckes afrikanischer Völker.* Pp. 139 (1), bibl., ill. Zürich: E. Lang.

705. **Lindblom, K. Gerhard.** *Läppsmycken i Afrika och särskilt sadena av sten.* Ymer., **45**, S. 457–66, ill., map.

706. —— 1947. *Tubular smoking pipes especially in Africa.* Ill. Stockholm: Statens Ethnog. Museum. (Smarre Meddelanden, no. 21.)

707. —— *Thread-crosses (Fadenkreuze) particularly in South America and Africa.* Ethnos, **5**, 1940, 89–111, bibl., ill.

708. —— 1945. *Nose ornaments in Africa.* Pp. 55, ill., map. Stockholm: Statens Etnografiska Museum. (Smarre Meddelanden, no. 20.)

709. **Maesen, A.** *La sculpture décorative.* Les arts plastiques (Brussels), 5e ser., 1951, 16–30, ill.

710. **Mancoba, Ernest.** sd. *Den afrikanske Kunstner* (The African Artist). Hvedekorn: Tidsskrift for litteratur og grafik (Copenhagen), **36** (4), 135–6.

711. **March, H. C.** *The meaning of ornament; or its archaeology and its psychology.* Trans. Lancs. & Cheshire antiq. soc., **7**, 160–92.

712. **Marie-André du Sacré Cœur, Sœur.** *Propos sur le vêtement en Afrique.* Rythmes du monde, **4**, 1946, 61–70, ill.

713. **Massion, Anne.** *Les bâtons africains décorés du Musée de l'Homme.* Objets et mondes, 4, 3, automne 1964, 157–86, bibl., ill.

714. **Mead, M.,** and **Others.** 1963. *Technique and personality in primitive art.* Pp. 110, ill. New York.

715. **Monod, Th.** *Sur quelques détails d'architecture africaine.* Acta tropica, **4**, 1947, 342–5, ill.

716. **Monteil, Charles.** 1927. *Le coton chez les noirs.* Pp. 100. (A reprint of the paper which appeared in Bull. com. études A. O. F., **2**, 1926, 585–684.)

717. **New York; Museum of Primitive Art.** 1963. *Lecture series 3. Technique and personality (of primitive art).* Personality and technique of African sculptors by H. Himmelheber. Pp. 79–110, ill. New York: Museum of Primitive Art.

718. **Nsiesie, T.** *Pipes indigènes de terre cuite.* Arts et métiers indig., **9**, 1938, 12–13.

719. **Panyella, A.** 1952. *Interpretacion etnologica del arte africano.* Africa (Madrid), **131**, 14–16, ill.

720. **Paulme, Denise.** *Les techniques.* Amis de l'art: Les arts africains, pp. 25–31.

721. —— and **Jacques Brosse.** 1956. *Parures africaines.* Pp. 91, ill. Paris: Hachette.

722. **Prost, A.** *Les ornements de nez en Afrique.* Notes Afr. I.F.A.N., **63**, 1954, 81–82. **72**, Oct. 1956, 110–12, ill.

723. **Racinet, A.** 1569–87. *L'ornement polychrome.* Ill. Paris.

724. **Rickard, T. A.** *The use of meteoric iron.* J. roy. anthrop. inst., **71**, 1–2, 1941, 55–66, and 2 pl.

725. **Rikli, M.** *Schmuck in Afrika.* Der Erdball, **4**, 1930, 1.

726. **Roth H. Ling.** *Studies in primitive looms.* 5. *African looms (West Coast, East Africa and Madagascar).* J. roy. anthrop. inst., **47**, 1917, 113–50, ill.

727. **Schebesta, R. P.,** and **G. Höltker.** *Der afrikanische Schild.* Anthropos, **18–19**, 1923–4, 1012–1062; **20**, 1925, 817–59, bibl., ill., map.

728. **Schmassow, A.** *Anfangsgründe jeder Ornamentik.* Z. f. Ästh. u. Allg. Kunstwissenschaft, **5**, 1910.

729. **Schmidl, Marianne.** *Das Verhältnis von Form und Technik bei der Übertragung afrikanischer Flechtarbeiten.* Mitt. anthrop. gesell. Wien (Sitzungsberichte). (49. Tagung d. Deutsch. Anthrop. Ges. Salzburg), **57**, pp. 101–4, ill.

730. **Schoffer, Rodin.** 1961. *African beadwork.* s.p., ill. Salisbury, S.A.: Rhodes National Gallery.

731. **Schurtz, Heinrich.** *Die geographische Verbreitung der Neger trachten.* Int. archiv. ethnog., **4**, 1891, 139–53, map.

732. —— *Das Augenornament und verwandte Probleme.* Abh. Sächs. Gesell. (Akad.) Wiss. (Leipzig), Bd. 15, no. 2, 1895, 1–96.

733. —— 1900. *Das Afrikanische Gewerbe von Heinrich Schurtz.* Pp. 146, ill., map. Leipzig: Teubner.

734. **Shaw, Thurstan.** *Early smoking pipes in Africa, Europe and America.* J. roy. anthrop. inst., **90** (2), 1960, 272–305, bibl., ill., map.

735. **Smith, Marian** (ed.). 1961. *The artist in tribal society* (pp. 85–120, Paul Bohannan, K. C. Murray and William Fagg on Nigeria). Proceedings of a symposium held at the Royal Anthropological Institute. Pp. xiii + 150, ill. London: Kegan Paul.

736. **Stolpe, Hjalmar.** 1927. *Collected essays in ornamental art.* (Part i, On evolution in the ornamental art of savage peoples.) Pp. 7 + 1 + 128, ill. Stockholm.

737. **Straube, Helmut.** 1955. *Die Tierverkleidungen der afrikanischen Naturvölker.* Pp. 234, bibl., map. Wiesbaden: Steiner. (Studien zur Kulturkunde, 13.)

738. **Teska, C.** *Afrikanische Tatuierungen und Körperbemalungen.* Der Erdball, 1928, **2**, 7, 264–5, ill.

739. **Thomas, T.** nd. *Artists, Africans and installation.* Parnassus, **12** (1), 32–36, part 1, and no. 4, 24–28, part 2.

740. **Thurnwald, R. C.** 1937. *Der soziologische und kulturelle Hintergrund der primitiven Kunstbetätigung.* Deuxième Congrès Internationale d'Esthétique et de Science de l'Art, **1**, pp. 271–4. Paris: Alcan.

741. **Trowell, K. M.** 1952. *Basket work.* (Art teaching in African Schools. Book 3.) Pp. 79, ill. London: Longmans.

742. **Tyrrell, Barbara Harcourt.** 1954. *African tribal dresses.* s.p. col. plates.

743. **van der Sleen, W. G. N.** *Trade wind beads.* Man, **56**, no. 27, 1956, 27–29, ill., map.

744. —— *Ancient glass beads, with special reference to the beads of East and Central Africa and the Indian ocean.* J. roy. anthrop. inst., **88**, 1958, 203–16, bibl., ill.

745. **Vaughan-Kirby, F.** *A description of the process of converting raw hides of game or domestic cattle into articles of native wearing apparel.* Man, **18**, 1918, 36–40.

746. **Verbeken, A.** *La signification de couleurs chez les Bantou.* Zaïre, 1947, 1139–44.

747. **von Luschan, F.** *Afrikanische Lehnstühle.* Globus, **77**, 1900, 259–61.

748. **Wainwright, G. A.** *Iron in the Napatan and Meroitic ages.* Sudan notes and records, **26**, 1, 1945, 3–36.

749. —— *The coming of iron to the Bantu; Summary of a communication to the Royal Anthropological Institute.* Man, **51**, 16, Feb. 1950, p. 19.

750. **Weule, Karl.** 1896. *Die Eidechse als Ornament in Afrika.* Bastian, Adolf (Festschrift) zu seinem 70 Geburtstage, 1896, 169–94, ill.

751. **Widstrand, Carl Gösta.** 1958. *African axes.* Pp. 164, ill., maps. Uppsala: Almquist & Wiksells Boktryckeri. (Studia Ethnographica Upsaliensia, 15.)

752. **Wilson, E.** 1914. *Das Ornament auf ethnologischer und prähistorischer Grundlage. Ein Abschnitt aus den Anfängen der Kunst.* Erfurt.

753. **Wolf, S.** *Afrikanische Elfenbeinlöffel des 16 Jarhunderts im Museum für Völkerkunde, Dresden.* Ethnologica, N.F., **2**, 1960, 410–25, bibl., ill.

754. **Zeltner, Fr. de.** *Tissus africains à dessins réservés ou décorés.* Bull. et mém. soc. anthrop. Paris. (1), ser. 6, 1910, 224–7, ill.

755. —— *Bijoux africains en test de coquillage.* Bull. et mém. soc. anthrop. Paris (1), ser. 6, 1910, 178–85, ill.

Ie
African Art Today

756. **Beier, Ulli.** *Contemporary Nigerian art.* Nigeria mag., **68**, 1961, 27–51, ill.

757. **Ben Enwonwu.** *Problems of the African artist to-day.* Présence afr., n.s., **8–10**, 1956, 147–78.

758. **Blaha, Herta.** *Bemalte Hausmauern in Negerafrika.* Wien. Völkerk. Mitt., **3** (1), 1955, 58–69, bibl. (Negro murals, wall paintings.)

759. —— *Moderne Negermalerei in Afrika.* Wien. völkerk. Mitt., **4** (1), 56, 13–19, bibl.

760. **Brausch, G. G. J-B.** *La crise de l'artisanat rural.* Brousse, **1–2**, 1949, 17–20.

761. **Duerden, Dennis.** *Black Orpheus.* W.A.R., **30** (385), 1959, 855–9, ill.

762. **Ema, A. J. Udo.** 1951. *African art teachers' handbook.* Pp. 95. London: Longmans.

763. **Fagg, William.** *The dilemma which faces African art.* Listener, 1951, 413–15, ill.

764. —— *African Christian art and the missionary's influence.* Liturgical arts, **20**, May 1952, 199.

765. **Fleming, Daniel Johnson.** 1938, 1952. *Each with his own brush; contemporary Christian art in Asia and Africa.* Pp. 85, ill. New York: Friendship Press.

766. **Grossert, J. W.** 1953. *Art and crafts for Africans.* Pp. 150. Pietermaritzburg: Shuter & Shooter.

767. **Hardy, G.** *La renaissance des métiers d'art indigène dans les colonies françaises.* Rev. économique française, 1930, 8–20.

768. **Illustrated London News.** *Modern Nigerian artists at work.* I.L.N., **213**, 1948, 25, ill.

769. —— *Vital native Bantu genius; sacred and lay works by young artists.* I.L.N., **214**, 1949, 90–91, ill.

770. **Italiaander, Rolf.** *Neue Kunst in Afrika.* Westermanns Monatshefte (Braunschweig), **7**, 1956. (Reprint, pp. 8, ill.)

771. —— 1957. *Neue Kunst in Afrika.* Pp. 32 + 39 pl. Mannheim: Bibliographisches Institut (Meyers Bildbändchen, N.F.6). (Liaison, 69, mars-avr. 1959, 36–40 (tr. of the above) by Th. David.)

772. —— *Introduction à l'art nouveau en Afrique.* Liaison, 64–66, juil.–déc. 1958; **67**, janv.–fev. 1959, 43–47.

773. **Lystad, Mary Hanemann.** *Paintings of Ghanaian children.* Africa, **30**, 1960, 238–42, ill.

774. **Olbrechts, Franz M.** *Centre pour l'étude de l'art africain à l'Université de Gand.* Bull. I.R.C.B., **12**, 2, 1941, 257–9.

775. **Paterson, Edward.** *The nature of Bantu art and some suggestions for its encouragement.* Nada, **19**, 1942, 41–50, ill.

776. **Pool, R. E.** *African renaissance (of art).* Phylon, **14**, Mar. 1953, 5–8.

777. **Segy, Ladislas.** *The future of African art.* Midwest J., **4**, 2, Summer 1952, 11–25, ill.

778. **Time.** *Wonderstone wonders, sculpture of Samuel Songo.* Time, **64**, 2 Aug. 1954, 58.

779. **U.N.E.S.C.O.** *The preservation and development of indigenous arts.* Pp. 45. Occasional papers in education, 8 Oct. 1950.

780. **von Sydow, Eckart.** *Die Zukunftsaussichten der negerischen Kunst.* Kol. Rund., **33**, 1, 1942, 26–31, ill.

REGIONAL CLASSIFICATION

NORTH AFRICA

781. **Ahlenstiegel-Engel, Elizabeth.** 1927. *Arte arabe.* Pp. 141, ill. Barcelona-Buenos Aires: Ed. Labor.

782. **Arriens, C.** 1930. *Urweltliche Künstler im Atlas.* Der Erdball, 4, 1.

783. **Barth, Heinrich.** 1859. 1890(?). *Travels and discoveries in north and central Africa . . . in . . . 1849–55.* Pp. xvii (1) + 548, ill., map. London: Ward Lock.

784. **Briggs, Lloyd Cabot.** 1955. *The stone-age races of northwest Africa.* Pp. vi + 98, ill. Cambridge, Mass.: American School of Prehistoric Research. Peabody Museum, Harvard Univ. Bull. 18.

785. **Delafosse, Maurice.** *North Africa.* Encyclopaedia of world art, 1, 1958, 62–130, maps.

786. **d'Ucel, Jeanne.** 1932. *Berber art; an introduction.* Pp. 227. Norman: Univ. of Oklahoma Press.

787. **Frend, W. H. C.** *The revival of Berber art.* Antiquity, 16, 64, Dec. 1942, pp. 342–52.

788. **Gallotti, Jean.** *L'art dans l'Afrique du nord.* Le Domaine colon. franc., 4, 1930, 303–318, ill. (See also France: Paris: Catalogues.)

789. **Herber, J.** *La main de Fathma.* Hespéris, 7 (2), 1927, ill.

790. **Joleaud, Leonce.** *Animaux totems nord-africains.* Rev. afr. 5, 1935, 325–48.

791. **Marcais, Georges.** *L'exposition d'art musulman.* Rev. afr., 49, 1905, 399–401.

792. —— and **G. Migeon.** 1926–7. *Manuel d'art musulman.* Vol. 1, L'architecture; Tunis, Algérie, Maroc, Espagne, Sicile, by G. Marcais. Vol. 2, Arts plastiques et industriels, by G. Migeon. Pp. 440: 460, ill. Paris: Picard. (2nd ed.)

793. —— *Art chrétien d'Afrique et art berbère.* Ann. 1st. univ. orient. Napoli, nuova ser. 3, 1949, 63–75, ill.

794. —— 1954–5. *L'art des berbères.* Pp. 19, ill. Alger: Gouverne-ment Générale de l'Algérie. (Gouvernement Générale de l'Algérie: Direction . . . des Beaux-Arts.)

795. **Mayer, L. A.** *Islamic wood carvers and their works.* Geneva.

796. **Paris-Teynac, E. J.** *Essai sur le koufique ancien dit koutique carré.* Bull. I.F.A.N., 21, 3 4, juil.–oct. 1959, 501–43, ill.

797. **Parry, R. E.** *The board game in north-west Africa.* Uganda J., 4 (2), 1936, 176–8, ill.

797a.**Precheur-Canonge, Thérèse.** 1961. *La vie rurale en Afrique romaine d'après les mosaïques.* Pp. 98, bibl., ill., map. Paris: Presses Universitaires de France. (Pubns. de l'Université de Tunis, Faculté des Lettres. 1re Série: Archéologie, Epigraphie, Vol. VI.)

798. **Ricard, P.** *Les arts tripolitains.* Riv. della Tripolitania (Rome), no. 4, 1926.

799. **van Gennep, Arnold.** *Etudes d'ethnographie Algérienne.* Avant-propos—Les soufflets algériens, 270–6. Les poteries kabyles, 277–331, ill. Le Tissage aux cartons, 332–46, ill. L'art décoratif Rev. Ethnog., Tome 2, 1911.

800. —— 1914. *En Algérie.* Pp. 217. Paris: Mercure de France.

801. —— *Etudes d'ethnographie algérienne.* Rev. études ethnog. sociol., 1911, 1–103, ill.

802. —— *L'art ornemental,* 1–21, ill. Rev. études ethnog. sociol., Tome III. *Études 2e series (decoration of flutes).* Rev. ethnog., Tome III, 349–69. La gravure sur corne, 4, 1913, 187–210, ill.

803. **Wulsin, Frederick R.** 1941. *The prehistoric archaeology of northwest Africa.* Pp. xii + 173, bibl., ill., maps. Cambridge, Mass.: Peabody Museum. (Papers of the Peabody Museum of American archaeology and ethnology, Vol. 19 (1).)
See also 809.

BUILDINGS AND FURNITURE

804. **Bernard, Augustin.** 1951. *L'habitation indigène dans les possessions françaises (Afrique du nord).* Pp. 112, ill. Paris: Société de Géographie Maritime et Coloniale.

805. **Despois, Jean.** *Les greniers fortifiés de l'Afrique du Nord.* Cah. de Tunisie, no. 1, 1953, 38–60, ill.

806. **Feilberg, C. G.** 1944. *La tente noire.* Pp. xi + 254, ill. Copen-hagen: National Museets Skrifter Etnografiske Raekke, 2.

807. **Rackow, Ernst,** and **Werner Caskel.** *Das Beduinenzelt.* Teil 1. Baessler-Archiv, 21 (4), 1938, 151–84, ill.

CLOTHING AND ADORNMENT

808. **Anon.** *La femme et la parure en Afrique du nord.* Afr. du N. ill., 21 Mar. 1936, 24, ill.

809. **Bertholon, L.,** and **E. Chantre.** 1913. *Recherches anthropolo-giques dans la berbérie orientale. Tripolitaine, Tunisie, Algérie.* 2 vols. Lyon: A. Rey. (Chap. VI, la musique et la danse.)

810. **Besancenot, Jean.** *Bijoux berbères.* Art de l'industrie, 11, Mar. 1948, s.p., ill.

811. —— *Costumes berbères.* Rev. française de l'élite, 26, 1951, 28–32, ill.

812. —— *Parures féminines nord-africaines.* Le magazin de l'Afrique du Nord, 7, 1949, 10, ill.

813. **Chabelard, R.** 1940. *Le tatouage des indigènes en Afrique du Nord.* Alger: Imp. Nord-afr.

814. **Clouzot, Henri.** *Les bijoux indigènes au Maroc, en Algérie et en Tunisie.* La Géog., 45, 1906, 153–8.

815. **des Villettes, Jacqueline.** *La collection de bijoux de la région de Taza au Musée de l'Homme.* Hespéris Tamuda, 1 (2), 1960, 295–309, ill.

816. **El Bekri.** *Bijoux en 'or feint' de Mopti.* Notes afr., I.F.A.N. 25, 1945, 7–8.

817. **Eudel, Paul.** 1902. *L'orfèvrerie algérienne et tunisienne.* Pp. xx + 544, ill. Alger: A. Jourdan.

818. —— 1906. *Dictionnaire des bijoux de l'Afrique du Nord; Maroc, Algérie, Tunisie, Tripolitaine.* Pp. 242, ill. Paris: Leroux.

819. **Fievet, Maurice.** *Salt caravan.* Nigeria, 41, 1953, 4–21, ill., map.

820. **Gobert, F. G.** *Remarques sur les tatouages nord-africains.* Rev. afr. (Alger), 100, 1956, 501–22, ill.

821. **Maitrot de la Motte-Capron, A.** *Essai sur les tatouages nord-africains.* Bull. soc. géog. Alger et Afrique nord, 32, 1927, Pp. 275–90, ill.

822. —— and **Probst-Biraben.** *Les tatouages des indigènes de l'Afrique du nord. Classement et hypothèse.* Rev. ethnog. trad. pop., 10, 1929, pp. 114–27.

823. **Rackow, Ernst.** *Sattel und Zaum in Nordwestafrika.* Baessler-Archiv, 17 (4), 1934, 172–85, ill.

824. —— *Das Beduinenkostüm in Tripolitanien.* Baessler-Archiv, 25 (1), 1943, 24–50, ill.

825. —— 1953. *El traje musulman feminino en Africa del Norte.* Madrid.

826. —— 1958. *Beiträge zur Kenntnis der materiellen Kultur Nordwest-Marokkos. Wohnraum, Hausrat, Kostüm.* Pp. 54 + 72 pl. Wiesbaden: Harrassowitz.

ROCK ART

827. **Arkell, W. J.** *Rock paintings and drawings in northern Africa,* 1933–34. Geog. rev. (New York), 26, 1936, 153–5, ill.

828. **Bernard, Augustin.** *Les gravures rupestres de l'Afrique du Nord.* La G., 37, 1922, 252–7.

829. **Carl, L.,** and **J. Petit,** tr. from the French by **K. Wagenseil.** 1955. *Geheimnisvoller Tefedest. Auf den Spuren einer alten Kultur.* Pp. 272, ill., map. Hamburg: Hoffmann und Campe Verlag.

830. **Espérandieu, G.** *Domestication et élevage dans le nord de l'Afrique au néolithique et dans la protohistoire d'après les figurations rupestres.* Congr. panafr. préhist., 2. Session, Alger, 1952. Commun., no. 53, 1955, 551–73, ill.

831. **Flamand, G. B. M.** 1921. *Les pierres écrites (Hadjrat-Mektoubat) gravures et inscriptions rupestres du nord africain.* Pp. 434, ill. Paris: Masson.

832. **Frobenius, Leo,** and **Hugo Obermaier.** 1925. *Hadschra Maktuba; Urzeitliche Felsbilder Kleinafrikas.* Pp. 8, 61 ill., maps. Munich: Kurt Wolff Verlag.

833. **Joleaux, L.** *Gravures rupestres et rites de l'eau en Afrique du nord.* I, Rôle des Bovins, des Ovins, et des Caprins dans la magie berbère préhistorique et actuelle. J. soc. africanistes, **3**, 1, 1933, 197–282. II, Rôle de l'éléphant dans la magie préhistorique et dans les légendes populaires historiques de la Berbérie. J. soc. africanistes **4**, 2, 1934, 285–302, ill.

834. **Kühn, Herbert.** *Alter und Bedeutung der nordafrikanischen Felszeichnungen.* Ipek, **I**, 1927, 13–30, ill.

835. —— *Das Alter der Felsbilder in Nordafrika.* Ipek, **II**, 132–3

835a.—— *Neue Felsbilder in Nordafrika.* Ipek, **II**, 131–2. 1938.

836. —— 1928. *Die nordafrikanischen u. ägyptischen Felsbilder der Eiszeit.* Tagungsberichte d. Dtsch. Anthrop. Ges. 49. Versammlung in Köln. Pp. 68–79, ill.

837. **Masson, P.** *L'art rupestre nord-africain.* Arch. I. paleontol. hum. mém., **20**, 1939, 1–125.

838. **Obermaier, Hugo.** *L'âge de l'art rupestre nord-africain.* L'Anthropologie, **41**, 1931, 1 2, 65–74.

839. —— *Das Alter der vorgeschichtlichen Felskunst Nordafrikas.* Forsch. u. Fortschritte, Jahrg. **8**, 1932, 1, 1–3.

840. —— *Das Alter der nordafrikanischen Felskunst.* Forsch. u. Fortschritte, **8**, 1932, 35–36.

841. —— *La Antigüedad del arte rupestre del norte de Africa.* Boletim de la Academia de la Historia; Tomo C. Guaderno I, Madrid, 1932.

842. **Pierret, Robert.** *Une carte des gravures rupestres et des peintures à l'ocre de l'Afrique du nord.* J. soc. africanistes, **8**, 1938, 107–23.

843. **Schultz, W.** *Felsbilder Skandinaviens und Nordafrikas.* Mitt. anthrop. gesell. Wien., **61**, 1931, 5.

844. **Vaufrey, R.** *L'âge des spirales de l'art rupestre nord-africain.* Bull. soc. préhist. fr., **33**, 1936, 624–38.

845. —— *L'âge de l'art rupestre nord-africain.* Cah. d'art, 1937, 63–77, 181–92, ill., map. 1938, 197–211, ill., map. Ipek, **12**, 1938, 8–27, ill.

TECHNIQUES

846. **Anon.** *Poterie, motifs décoratifs de portes.* Fichier de documentation berbère, 1950, 15, ill. (Texte kabyle et traduction.)

847. **Basset, Henri.** *Les influences puniques sur les berbères.* Rev. afr. **62**, 1921, 340–74.

848. **Gallotti, Jean.** *Weaving and dyeing in North Africa.* Ciba rev., no. 21, **2**, 1939, 734–64, ill., map.

849. **Geslin, Leopold.** *Le moulin à main en Afrique du Nord.* Bull. Soc. géog. d'Oran, Mar. June 1941, 29–44.

850. **Golvin, Lucien.** 1957. *Aspects de l'artisanat en Afrique du Nord.* Pp. 235, ill. Paris: P.U.F. (Publications de l'Institut des Hautes Études de Tunis.)

851. **Haberland, Eike.** *Eisen und Schmiede in Nordost-Afrika.* Veröff. Mus. Völkerk. (Leipzig), no. 11, 1961, 191–210.

852. **Koechlin, R.,** and **G. Migeon.** 1929. *Cent planches en couleurs d'art musulman céramique, tissus, tapis.* Pp. 20. Paris: Édit. Albert Lévy.

853. **van Gennep, Arnold.** *L'ornamentation du cuir.* Rev. études ethnog. sociol. (Paris), **4**, 1913, 200–10.

854. —— *Recherches sur les poteries peintes de l'Afrique du Nord.* Harvard African studies, **2**, 1918, pp. 235–97.

ALGERIA

855. **Gaudry, Mathéa.** 1929. *La femme Chaouia de l'Aurès.* Pp. xvi + 316, bibl., ill. Paris: Geuthner.

856. **Lhote, Henri.** 1944. *Les Touaregs du Hoggar (Ahaggar).* Pp. 415, bibl., ill. Paris: Payot.
See also 932–40.

FIGURES AND MASKS

857. **Champault, Dominique.** *Un coffre sculpté kabyle (donation Berliet).* Objets et mondes, **3**, 1, printemps 1963, 35–40, ill.

858. **Marchand, Henri-François.** 1951. *Masques carnavalesques et carnaval en Kabylie.* Bull. soc. hist. algérienne, 1938. Reprinted in Mélange d'anthropologie et de sociologie nord-Africaine. Pp. 113–23. Alger: Vollot.

BUILDINGS AND FURNITURE

859. **Barlette, L.** *Notice sur la mode d'habitation des indigènes dans la commune mixte de Dra-el-Mizan.* Bull. soc géog d'Alger et d'Afrique du nord, **17 & 18**, 1912–13, 101–13: 433–96.

860. **Bernard, Augustin.** 1921. *Enquête sur l'habitation rurale des indigènes de l'Algérie.* Pp. 150, ill. Alger: Imp. Orientale Fontana.

861. **Genevois, R. P. Le.** *L'habitation Kabyle.* Fichier documentation berbère, no. 46, 1er trim., 1955.

862. **Maunier, René.** *Les rites de la construction en Kabylie.* Rev. hist. rel., 1925, 18. (Also in Mélanges de sociologie nord-Africaine, 1930, pp. 153–77. Paris: Alcan.)

863. —— 1926. *La construction collective de la maison en Kabylie.* Pp. 83, ill. Paris: Institut d'Ethnologie. (Travaux et mémoires de l'institut d'ethnologie, III.)

CLOTHING AND ADORNMENT

864. **Champault, Dominique.** *La donation Jean-Philippe Crouzet (Algerian costume).* Objets et mondes, **1**, 3–4, 1961, 33–38, ill.

865. **Goichon, A. M.** 1927. *La vie feminine au Mzab.* Pp. xiv + 348. Paris: Paul Geuthner.

866. **Grange, E.** *Les bijoux de l'Aurès et leur symbolique.* Algeria (Alger), 1961, 24–28, ill.

867. **Jacquot, Lucien.** *Etude sur les tatouages des indigènes de l'Algérie.* L'Anthropologie, **10**, 1899, 430–8, ill.

868. **Lacoste, Camille.** *Sabres kabyles.* J. soc. africanistes, **28**, 1958, 111–91, ill.

869. **Lefebre, L.** *La toilette féminine dans deux villages de Petite Kabylie.* Libyca, **11**, 1963, 199–220, ill.

870. **Magasin Pittoresque.** *La bijouterie chez les Kabyles.* Le magasin pittoresque, **45**, 1877, 180. (After Hanoteau and Letourneux.)

871. **Rivière, T.,** and **J. Faublée.** *Les tatouages des Chaouia de l'Aurès.* J. soc. africanistes, **12**, 1942, 67–80, ill., map.

872. **Sadouillet, Alberte.** *Bijoutiers et bijoux kabyles d'aujourd'hui.* Algeria, 1952, 18–22, ill.

ROCK ART

873. **Balout, Lionel.** *La gazelle sculptée de l'Imakassen (Tassili n'Ajjer).* Trav. inst. rech. sahariennes (Alger), **9**, 1, 1953, 125–9, ill.

874. **Chasseloup-Laubat, F. de.** 1938. *Art rupestre au Hoggar (Haut Mertoutek).* Pp. iii + 62, ill. Paris: Librairie Plon.

875. —— *Le sens du Haut-Mertoutek.* J. soc. africanistes, **12**, 1942, 139–47, ill.

876. **Chavaux, G.** *Fresque gravée dans le Tanget (Tassilides Ajjer).* Bull. liaison saharienne, no. 40, déc. 1960, p. 298.

877. **Durand, P.,** and **L. Lavauden.** *Les peintures rupestres de la grotte d'In-Ezzan.* L'Anthropologie, **36**, 1926, 409–27, ill.

878. **Huxley, Francis.** *The lost people of the Green Sahara.* Sunday Times, Mar. 24, 1963, 14–21, ill. (Tassili: first colour photographs.)

879. **Lajoux, Jean Dominique.** 1962. *Merveilles du Tassili n'Ajjer.* Pp. 195, ill., maps. Paris: Éditions du Chêne.

880. **Lhote, Henri.** *Peintures rupestres de l'Oued Takéchérouet (Ahaggar).* Bull. I.F.A.N., **15**, 1, janv. 1953, 283–91, ill.

881. —— *Les gravures rupestres d'Aouineght (Sahara occidental); nouvelle contribution à l'étude des chars rupestres du Sahara.* Bull. I.F.A.N., **19** (B), 3 4, juil.–oct. 1957, 617–58, ill.

882. —— *Les nouvelles découvertes des peintures pré-historiques du Tassili.* C.R. Acad. Sci. O.-M., **17**, 7, nov. 1957, 341–7.

883. —— *Le ultime scoperte di arte rupestre nel Tasili degli Azger.* Riv. sci. preist., **12**, 1957, 110–15.

884. —— 1958. *A la découverte des fresques du Tassili.* Pp. 270, ill., map. Paris: Arthaud.

885. —— 1958. *Die Felsbilder der Sahara.* Pp. 368, ill., maps. Würzburg-Wien: Andreas Zettner.

886. —— and **Alan H. Broderick.** 1959. *The search for the Tassili frescoes.* Pp. 236, ill. London: Hutchinson.

887. —— *Nouvelle contribution à l'étude des gravures et peintures rupestres au Sahara central; la station de Tit (Ahaggar).* J. soc. africanistes, **29**, 2, 1959, 147–92.

888. —— *Gravures et inscriptions rupestres de 'Téhi-n-tr'atimt' (Ahaggar Sahara central).* Bull. liaison saharienne, **12**, 42, 1961, 113–21.

889. —— *Nouvelle mission au Tassili des Ajjers.* Objets et mondes, **3**, 3, automne 1963, 237–46, ill.

890. **Monod, Théodore.** *Sur les inscriptions arabes peintes de Ti-M-Missao Sahara central.* J. soc. africanistes, **8**, 1938, 83–95, bibl., ill., maps.

891. —— *Peintures rupestres du Zemmour français (Sahara occidental).* Bull. I.F.A.N., **13**, i, janv. 1951, 198–213, ill.

892. **Perret, Robert.** *Recherches archéologiques et ethnographiques au Tassili des Ajjers (Sahara central); Les gravures rupestres de l'Oued Djaret, La population et les ruines d'Iherir.* J. soc. africanistes, **6** (1), 1936, 41–64, ill.

893. **Reygasse, Maurice.** *Gravures et peintures rupestres du Tassili des Ajjers.* L'Anthropologie, **45**, 5–6, 1935, 533–71, ill.

894. **Rouch, Jean.** *Contribution à l'étude du site rupestre de Tessalit.* Notes afr. I.F.A.N., **79**, juil. 1958, 72–77, ill.

895. **Tschudi, Jolande.** 1955. *Pitture rupestri del Tassili degli Azger.* Firenze: Sansoni. (*C.R.:* Bull. I.F.A.N., **18**, 3 4, juil.–oct. 1956, 520–1—H.L.)

896. —— 1955. *Nordafrikanische Felsmalereien (Tassili n' Ajjer).* Pp. 106, bibl., ill. Studien und Zeugnisse Veröff. vom Istituto Italiano di Preistoria e Protostoria.

897. —— 1956. *Les peintures rupestres du Tassili n' Ajjer.* Pp. 103, bibl., ill., map. Neuchâtel: À. la Baconnière.

TECHNIQUES

898. **Alexandre, Arsène.** 1907. *Réflexions sur les arts et les industries d'art en Algérie.* Pp. (4), 42, ill. Alger: Edition de l'Akhbar.

899. **Algérie.** *Algérie; Direction de l'intérieur et des beaux-arts.* 1948. Note sur l'ethnographie, la préhistoire, l'archéologie, l'art musulman, les beaux-arts en Algérie. Pp. 112, ill.

900. **Balfet, Hélène.** *La poterie des Ait Smail du Djurdjura.* Rev. afr., **99**, 1955, 289–340, ill.

901. —— *Les poteries modelées d'Algérie dans les collections du musée du Bardo.* Pp. 61, 1957, ill., map. Alger: Imp. officielle. (Centre algérien de recherches anthropologiques, préhistoriques, et ethnographiques.)

902. **Bel, A.** 1918. *Les industries de la céramique à Fès.* Pp. 319, ill. Alger-Paris: .

903. —— and **P. Ricard.** 1913. *Le travail de la laine à Tlemcen.* Pp. 359, ill. Alger: Adolphe Jourdan.

904. **Bel, Marguerite A.** 1947. *Les arts indigènes féminins en Algérie.* Pp. 24, ill. Alger: Gouvernement de l'Algérie.

905. **Bergue, A.** 1930. *Art antique et art musulman en Algérie.* Pp. 144. Orléans: A. Pigelet. (Cahiers du centenaire de l'Algérie. Publ. du comité national métropolitain du centenaire de l'Algérie, **6**.)

906. **Calvet, Léon.** *Les poteries fines d'Ait Mesbah.* Algeria, fév. 1953, 29–36, ill.

907. **Carl L.,** and **J. Petit.** *Une technique archaïque de la fabrication du fer dans Le Mourdi (Sahara oriental).* L'Ethnographie (Paris), no. 50, n.s., 1955, 60–81, ill.

908. **Chalumeau, P.** *Les nattes d'alfa du Bou-Taleb; Technique de fabrication, décor.* I.B.L.A., **16**, 61, 1953, 75–94, ill.

909. **Champault, Dominique.** *Un coffre sculpté kabyle.* Objets et mondes, **3** (1), 1963, 35–40, bibl., ill. (La revue du Musée de l'Homme.)

910. **Godon, R.** *Les formes du batik dans l'Aurès.* Rev. afr., **1/2**, 1944, 116–23, ill.

911. **Great Britain; Admiralty; Naval Intelligence Division.** 1943. *Algeria.* Vol. 1, pp. xi + 313, ill., maps.

912. **Hilton-Simpson, M. W.** 1921. *Among the hill folk of Algeria.* Pp. 248, ill., map. London: T. Fisher Unwin.

913. **Jacquot, Lucien.** *Les M'Rahane; étude sur certaines poteries d'un caractère religieux en usage dans la Petite-Kabylie.* L'Anthropologie, **10**, 1899, 47–53, ill.

914. **Konrad, Walter.** *Herstellung und Funktionsweise eines Zierschlosses (Tanast). Beobachtungen bei den Tuareg-Schmieden von Tamanrasset im Hoggar.* Baessler-Archiv., N.F. **4**, 1, 1956, 13–24.

915. **Laforgue, Pierre et Saucin, F.** *Nouvelles recherches sur les objets anciens de l'Aouker.* Bull. com. études. A.O.F., no. 1, 1923, 105–19, ill.

916. **Marcais, Georges.** 1913. *Les poteries et faïences de la Qal'a des Beni Hammâd (XIe siècle). Contribution à l'étude de la céramique musulmane.* Pp. 31 (3), ill. Constantine: D. Braham.

917. —— *Notice sur deux vases kabyles trouvés à Constantine.* Rec. not. et mém. sté. arch. et hist. const., **48**, 1914, 175–83.

918. —— *Notice sur deux poteries trouvées dans la grotte des pigeons.* Rec. not. et mém. sté. arch. et hist. const., **50**, 1916, 37–47.

919. —— *Matériaux pour un catalogue du musée de Mustapha. Notes sur un coffre kabyle.* Rev. afr., **68**, 1927, 330–1.

920. —— 1931. *L'art musulman en Algérie.* Alazard, Albertini, Histoire et historiens de l'Algérie. Pp. 426. Paris: Alcan.

921. **Mauny, Raymond.** *Une tortue sculptée néolithique de l'Aouker.* Notes afr. I.F.A.N., **45**, 1950, 2–3, bibl.

922. **Myres, Sir John Linton.** *Notes on the history of the Kabyle pottery.* J. anthrop. inst., **32**, 1902, 248–62, ill.

923. **Nougier, L. R.** *Poterie préhistorique de l'Ouan Bender dans le Tassili des Ajjers.* Riv. sci. preist., **8**, 1953, 152–70.

924. **Randall-MacIver, D.** *On a rare fabric of Kabyle pottery.* J. anthrop. inst., **32**, 1902, 245–7, ill.

925. **Ricard, P.** 1924. *Pour comprendre l'art musulman dans l'Afrique du Nord et enl 'Espagne.* Paris: Hachette. (Les bois, pp. 65–66. Une figuration de coffre Kabyle des Beni Oughlis.)

926. —— *Tissage berbère des Ait Aissi (Grande Kabylie).* Hespéris, **5**, 1925, 219–25.

927. —— *Techniques et rites du travail de la laine en Algérie.* Paris: Paul Geuthner. (Extrait du Mémorial Henri Basset, publications de l'Institut des Hautes Etudes Marocaines, XVIII, 1928, 207–27.)

928. **Rio, Cap.** *L'artisanat à Tamentit.* Trav. inst. rech. sahariennes, **20**, 1/2, 1961, 135–83.

929. **Van Gennep, A.** *On R. MacIver's and J. L. Myres's 'Toudja' series of Kabyle pottery.* Man, **12**, no. 63, 1912, 121–2, ill.

930. **Violard, E.** 1897. *De la céramique berbère. Mission en Kabylie.* Pp. 34. Alger.

931. **Wilkin, Anthony.** 1900. *Among the Berbers of Algeria.* Pp. 263. London: Fisher Unwin.

ADDENDA TO GENERAL

932. **Algeria.** *Algeria in Encyclopaedia of Islam.* Vol. 1, 1960, fasc. 6, pp. 364–79.

933. **Bel, A.** *La population musulmane de Tlemcen.* Rev. étud. ethnog. sociol., **1**, 1908, 416–30.

934. **Certeux, Alphonse,** and **E.-Henry Carnoy.** 1884. *L'Algérie tradionelle, légendes, contes, chansons, musique, moeurs, coutumes, fêtes, croyances, superstitions . . . (Contribution au folklore des arabes.)* 2 vols. Paris: Maisonneuve et Leclerc et Challamel.

935. **Hanoteau, A.,** and **A. Letourneux.** 1872–3. *La Kabylie et les coutumes kabyles.* 3 vols. Paris. (Another edition Paris: Challamel, 1893.)

936. **Hilton-Simpson, M. W.** 1906. *Algiers and beyond.* Pp. xii + 294, ill., map. London: Hutchinson.

937. **Mercier, Marcel.** 1932. *La civilisation urbaine au Mzab.* Pp. 391, ill., maps. Alger, Paris: P. & G. Soubiron. (2nd ed.)

938. **Soustelle, Jacques.** 1955. *Deuxième note sur l'ethnographie, la préhistoire, l'archéologie, l'art musulman, les beaux-arts en Algérie.* Pp. 118. Alger: Govt. Printer. (Imprimerie officielle.)

939. **Stuhlmann, Franz.** 1912. *Ein kulturgeschichtlicher Ausflug in den Aures (Atlas von Süd-Algerien).* Pp. xii + 205, bibl., ill., maps. Hamburg: L. Friederichsen. (Abhandlungen des Hamburgischen Kolonialinstituts, Band 10.)

940. **Villot, C.** 1875. *Moeurs, coutumes et institutions des indigènes de l'Algérie.* Constantine. (2nd ed.)

CANARY ISLANDS

941. **Abercromby, John.** *Plastic art in the Grand Canary.* Man, **15**, no. 64, 1915, 113–16, ill.

942. **Bannerman, D. A.** 1922. *The Canary Islands.* Pp. 380, ill., maps. London: Gurney.

943. **Hooton, E. A.** 1925. *The ancient inhabitants of the Canary Islands.* (Harvard African Studies, Vol. 7.)

944. **Krämer, A.** *Ein Besuch von Gran Canaria.* Globus, **78**, 1900, 365, ill.

945. **Pinto de la Rosa, José Maria.** 1954. *Canarias prehispanica y Africa occidental española.* Pp. 272, bibl., ill., maps. Madrid: Consejo Superior de Investigaciones Cientifica.

946. **Sanchez, S. T.** 1946. *Excavaciones arqueologicas en Gran Canaria . . . 1942–44.* Pp. 153 + lxxvi, ill. Madrid: Comisaria General de Excavaciones Arqueologicas, Informationes y Memorias, 11.

947. **Stone, Olivia M.** 1887. *Tenerife and its six satellites.* Pp. 459, ill. London: Marcus Ward.

LIBYA

948. **Abd Allah, H.** *Siwan customs.* Harvard African studies, Vol. 1, 1917, Varia Africana, 1.

949. **Bates, Oric.** 1914. *The eastern Libyans.* Pp. xviii + 298, bibl., ill., maps. London: Macmillan.

950. **Cline, W.** 1936. *Notes on the people of Siwah and El Garah in the Libyan desert.* Pp. 64. Menasha, Wis.: G. Banta.

951. **King, W. J. Harding.** 1925. *Mysteries of the Libyan desert.* Pp. 348, ill., maps. London: Seeley Service.

952. **Randall MacIver, David,** and **Anthony Wilkin.** 1901. *Libyan notes (a study of the Kabyles and the Chawia).* Pp. viii + 113, ill. London: Macmillan.

953. **White, Arthur Silva.** 1889. *From sphinx to oracle; through the Libyan desert to the oasis of Jupiter Ammon.*

ROCK ART

954. **Battaglia, R.** *Iscrizioni e graffiti rupestri della Libia.* Rev. col. Ital. (Rome), **11**, no. 3, 1928, 407–21, ill.

955. **Bellini, E.,** and **S. Ariè.** *Segnalazione di pitture rupestri in localita Carcur Dris nel Gebel Auenat (Libia) (English and French summaries).* Riv. sci. preist., **17**, 1 4, 1962, 261–7, ill.

956. **Breuil, Henri.** *Gravures rupestres du désert Libyque identiques à celles des anciens Bushmen.* L'Anthropologie, **36**, 1–2, 1926, 125–7, ill.

957. ——— and **V. Paques.** *Gravures rupestres préhistoriques du Fezzan (déscription par H. Breuil, gravures relevées par V. Paques).* J. soc. africanistes, **28**, 1–2, 1958, 25–32, ill.

958. **Camps-Fabrar, H.** *Figurations animales dans l'art mobilier préhistorique d'Afrique du nord.* Libyca, **9–10**, 1961–2, 101–13, ill., map.

959. **di Caporiacco, L.,** and **Paolo Graziozi.** 1934. *Le pitture rupestri di Àin Dòua (El-Auenàt).* Pp. 29, ill., maps. Florence: Centro di Studi Coloniali.

960. **Frobenius, L.** 1922. *Einführung in die Felsbilderwerke von Fezzan.* 22–35. Manufaktenforschung in der Wüste. Forschg. u. Fortschr., **10**, 12, 149–50.

961. ——— 1937. *Ekade Ektab; die Felsbilder Fezzans.* Pp. xxix + 74, ill. Leipzig: Otto Harrassowitz.

962. **Graziosi, Paolo.** *Le pitture della Grotta di In Elegghi presso Gat.* Bol. soc. geog. Ital., ser. 7, no. 2, 1937, 408–11, ill.

963. ——— *Graffiti rupestri e stazioni prehistoriche del Fezzan.* Ann. Afr. Ital., **1**, 1938, 973–8, ill.

964. ——— 1942. *L'arte rupestre della Libia.* 2 vols. Vol. 1, pp. 326, bibl., map. Vol. 2, pl. 1–160. Naples: Edizioni della mostra d'Oltremare.

965. ——— *Le incisioni rupestri dell'Ushi el Cher, in Tripolitania.* Riv. sci. preist., **11**, 1956, 234–8.

966. **Haseltine, Nigel.** 1962. *From Libyan sands to Chad.* Pp. 208, bibl., ill., maps. London: Museum Press.

966a. **Mori, F.** *Nuove scoperte d'arte rupestre nell'Acacus (Fezzan).* Riv. sci. preist., 1957, 251–62.

967. **Murphy, J.** *Rock paintings at Owenat in Libya.* I.L.N., 1934, 796–9, ill.

968. **Newbold, D.** *Rock-pictures and archaeology in the Libyan desert.* Antiquity, **2**, 1928, 261–91, ill.

969. **Paradisi, U.** *I recenti ritrovamenti d'arte preistorica nel margine orientale della Hameda-el-Hamra.* Libia, **3**, 1, 1955, 55–63, ill.

970. **Pauli, Elisabeth.** *Felsbilder in der libyschen Wüste.* Passat (Hamburg), **2**, 3, 1950, 16–22, ill.

970a. **Pauphilet, D.** *Gravures rupestres de Maknusa (Fezzan).* Trav. inst. rech. sahariennes, **10**, 2, 1953, 107–22, ill.

971. **Peel, R. F.** *Rock-painting from the Libyan desert.* Antiquity, **13**, 1939, pp. 389–402.

972. **Rhotert, Hans.** 1952. *Libysche Felsbilder. Ergebnisse der XI und XII deutschen inner-afrikanischen Forschungs-Expedition, D.I.A.F.E. 1933–34–35.* Pp. 146, bibl., ill., maps. Darmstadt: L. C. Wittich Verlag.

973. ——— *Forschungsreise nach Südwest-Libyen.* Tribus, **12**, Dec. 1963, 12–31, ill., map.

974. **Sattin, F.** *Arte rupestre fezzanese.* Riv. sci. preist., **14**, 1959, 295–305, ill.

975. **Shaw, W. B. K.** *Rock paintings in the Libyan desert.* Antiquity, **10**, 1936, 175–8, ill.

976. ——— *Rock drawings in the South Libyan desert.* Kush, **1**, 1953, 35–39, ill.

TECHNIQUES

977. **Lapanne-Joinville, J.** *Les métiers à tisser de Fès.* Hespéris, **27**, 1, 1940, 21–65, ill.

UTENSILS, TOOLS, WEAPONS; MISCELLANEOUS

978. **Cline, Walter.** *An antique pipe-bowl from the Siwa depression.* Man, **29**, no. 149, 1929, 194, ill.

MOROCCO

979. **Alazard, Jean.** *Les arts au Maroc et l'artisanat.* Le monde colonial, 1929, 289, ill.

980. **Bourilly, J.** 1932. *Éléments d'ethnographie marocaine.* Pp. viii + 264, ill., maps. Paris: Larose.

981. **Colin, Georges S.** *La Noria marocaine.* Hespéris, **14** (1), 1932 22–49, bibl., ill.

982. **Garcia Figueras, Tomas.** 1944. *Marruecos.* Madrid.

983. —— and **Juan L. Fernandez-Llebrez.** 1955. *Manuales del África Española;* (2) *La zona española del protectorado de Marruecos.* Pp. 210 + (10), ill., maps. Madrid: Instituto de estudios africanos. (Art, pp. 79–97.)

984. **Koller, Ange.** 1952. *Los Berbères marroquies; estudio etnografico.* Pp. xxii + 315, map. Tetuan: Editora Marroqui.

985. **Ossendowski, F.** 1926. *The fire of desert folk . . . a journey through Morocco.* Pp. 312, ill. London: Allen & Unwin.

986. **Rousseau, Gabriel.** 1921. *Les arts marocains.* Pp. 24. Rabat: Cours de perfectionnement du Service des Renseignements.

987. —— *Les notions d'art du Maroc. Les bijoux berbères.* Art et décoration, 1922, 60–64, ill.

988. **Séguy, René.** *L'art marocain.* La renaissance, Apr. 1922, 193–207, ill.

989. **Terrasse, Henri.** *Le sens artistique des marocains.* Bull. enseign. pub. Maroc., May 1924, 274–85.

990. —— *Les limites de l'art chez les berbères du Maroc.* Outre-Mer, **1**, 4, 1929, 447–76, ill.

991. —— 1932. *L'art Hispano-Mauresque des origines au 13e siècle.* Rabat: Publications de l'Institut des Hautes Études Marocaines, tome 25.

992. —— and **Jean Hainaut.** 1925. *Les arts décoratifs au Maroc.* Pp. xii + 120, ill. Paris: H. Laurens.

993. **Vidalenc, G.** 1935. *L'art marocain.* Pp. 130, ill. Paris: Alcan.

994. **Weisgerber, F.** 1935. *Casablanca et les Chaouia en 1900.* Pp. 136, ill., map. Paris: Geuthner.

BUILDINGS AND FURNITURE

995. **Adam, André.** *La maison et le village dans quelques tribus de l'Anti-Atlas.* Hespéris, **37**, 1950, 289–353, ill.

996. **du Puigaudeau, O.** *Contribution à l'étude du symbolisme dans le décor mural et l'artisanat de Walata.* Bull. I.F.A.N., **19** (B), 1–2, janv.–avr. 1957, 137–83, ill.

997. **Jacques-Meunié, D.** *Les greniers collectifs au Maroc.* J. soc. africanistes, **14**, 1944, 1–16, ill., map. Hespéris, **36**, 1949, 97–137, ill., maps.

998. —— 1951. *Greniers-citadelles au Maroc.* (1) Texte et plans; (2) Photographies. Pp. 249: 109, bibl., ill., maps. Rabat: Pubns. de l'Institut des Hautes Études Marocaines, T.52. Paris: Arts et métiers graphiques.

999. —— 1962. *Architectures et habitats du Dades, Maroc Présaharien.* Pp. 128, bibl., ill., map. Paris: Librairie C. Klincksieck.

1000. **Laoust, E.** 1930–4. *L'habitation chez les transhumants du Maroc central.* Hespéris, 1930, **10** (2), 151–253, ill.; **14** (2), 1932, 1–115, ill.; **18** (2), 1934, 1–196, ill. Paris: Larode.

CLOTHING AND ADORNMENT

1001. **Adam, André.** *Le costume dans quelques tribus de l'Anti-Atlas.* Hespéris, **39**, 3 4, 1952, 459–85, ill.

1002. **Besancenot, Jean.** 1940. *Costumes et types du Maroc.* Paris.

1003. —— 1953. *Bijoux arabes et berbères du Maroc.* Pp. xv (1), 18 (6), ill. (loose sheets in portfolio). Casablanca: Jacques Klein: Éditions de la Cigogne.

1004. **Cola Alberich, Julio.** *El tatuaje en Marruecos.* Africa (Madrid), **75–76**, 1948, 129–30, ill.

1005. —— 1949. *Amuletos y tatuajes marroquies.* Pp. 142 (8), ill. Madrid: Instituto de Estudios Africanos.

1006. **de Hen, F. J.** *Quelques notes ethnographiques sur les Ihansalen.* Jb. s. Mus. Völkerkunde (Leipzig), **20**, 1964, 282–318, bibl.

1007. **Goudard, Lieut.** *Bijoux d'argent de la Tache de Taza.* Hespéris, 8, 1928, 285–332.

1007a. **Herber, Jean.** *Tatouages du pubis au Maroc.* Rev. ethnog. trad. pop., **3**, no. 9, 1922, 37–47, ill.

1008. —— *Les tatouages du pieds au Maroc.* L'Anthropologie, **33**, 1923, 87–102, ill.

1009. —— *Origine et signification des tatouages marocains.* L'Anthropologie, **37**, 5 6, 1927, 517–25.

1010. —— *Tatouages curatifs au Maroc.* Rev. ethnog. trad. pop., **9**, nos. 34–36, 1928, 179–87, ill.

1011. —— *Tatouages curatifs au Maroc.* Maroc méd., **15**, déc. 1929, 621–4.

1012. —— *Peintures corporelles au Maroc. Les peintures au harqûs.* Hespéris, **9**, 1, 1929, 59–77, ill.

1013. —— *Tatouages marocaines; tatouages crapuleux.* Maroc méd., mai 1929, 381–4, ill.

1014. —— *Les tatouages nord-africains sont-ils bleus ou verts?* Rev. afr. (Alger), **72**, 1931, 66–77.

1015. —— *L'origine du décor des tatouages marocains.* 4e congr. de la fédérat. des soc. sav. de l'Afrique du Nord, Rabat, 18–20 Apr. 1938 (Tom. 2), 763–82, ill.

1016. —— *La boucle d'oreille et les 'lobes percés' chez les marocains.* Hespéris, **32**, 1945, 89–93.

1017. —— *Les tatouages de la face chez la marocaine.* Hespéris, **33**, 1946, 323–51, ill.

1018. —— *Le tatouage du dos au Maroc.* Rev. afr., **91**, 1 2, 1947, 118–22.

1019. —— *Onomastique des tatouages marocains.* Hespéris, **35**, 1948, 31–56, ill.

1020. —— *Tatoueuses marocaines.* Hespéris, **35**, 3 4, 1948, 289–97.

1021. —— *Notes sur les tatouages au Maroc.* Hespéris, **36**, 1949, 11–46, ill.

1022. —— *Les tatouages du cou, de la poitrine et du genou chez la marocaine.* Hespéris, **36**, 3 4, 1949, 333–45, ill.

1023. —— *Influence de la bijouterie soudanaise sur la bijouterie marocaine.* Hespéris, 37, 1950, 5–10, ill.

1024. —— *Note sur l'influence de la bijouterie soudanaise sur la bijouterie marocaine.* Ann. ist. univ. orient. (Napoli), N.S. 3, 1949, 93–97, ill.

1025. —— *Tatouage et états mentaux.* Albums du crocodile (Lyon), 1950, 28.

1026. —— *Les tatouages des bras de la marocaine.* Hespéris, **38**, 3 4, 1951, 299–325, ill.

1027. **Jouin, J.** *Le costume de la femme israélite au Maroc.* J. soc. africanistes, **6**, 1936, 167–86, ill.

1028. **Rousseau, Gabriel.** 1938. *Le costume au Maroc.* Pp. 36, ill. Paris: E. de Bocard.

1029. **Terrasse, Henri.** *Note sur l'origine des bijoux du sud marocain.* Hespéris, **11**, 1930, 125–30, ill.

ROCK ART

1030. **Cola Alberich, Julio.** 1954. *Cultos primitivos de Marruecos.* Pp. 138, bibl. Madrid: Instituto de Estudios Africanos.

1031. **du Puigaudeau, O.,** and **M. Senones.** *Gravures rupestres de l'Oued Tamanart (sud-marocain).* Bull. I.F.A.N., **15** (3), 1953, 1242–61, ill.

1032. **Jacques-Meunier, D.** and **Allain, Charles.** *Quelques gravures et monuments funéraires de l'extrème sud-est marocain.* Hespéris, **43**, 1 2, 1956, 51–85, ill., map.

1033. **Malhomme, Jean.** *Aperçu sur les gravures rupestres de la région de Marrakech.* Hespéris, **40**, 1 2, 1953, 255–63.

1034. —— 1959. *Corpus des gravures rupestres du Grand Atlas (1e partie).* Pp. lx + 156 (3), ill., map. Rabat: Publ. service des antiquités du Maroc, 13.

1035. —— 1961. *Corpus des gravures rupestres du Grand Atlas* (2e partie). Pp. 164, ill. Rabat: Publ. Service des Antiquités du Maroc, 14.

1036. —— *Deux tables gravées du Grand Atlas (Maroc).* Notes afr. I.F.A.N., **67**, juil. 1955, 79–82, ill.

1037–1038. See 966a and 970a.

1039. **Ruhlmann, A.** *Deux gravures rupestres de style géométrique trouvées aux Ait Saadane (Maroc saharien).* I. Conf. int. africanistes de l'ouest, C.R., **2**, 1951, 450–6.

1040. **Senones, M.,** and **du Puigaudeau, O.** *Gravures rupestres de la Montagne d'Icht (sud-marocain).* J. soc. africanistes, **11**, 1941, 147–55, ill.

1041. —— —— *Gravures rupestres de la Vallée Moyenne du Draa (sud-marocain).* J. soc. africanistes, **11**, 1941, 157–67, ill.

TECHNIQUES

1042. **Beckett, T. H.** *Two pottery techniques in Morocco.* Man, **58**, 251, Dec. 1958, 185–8, ill.

1043. **Benitez Cantero, V.** *Industrias marroquies; 'Dar Degab'.* Africa (Madrid), **7**, 106, Oct. 1950, 445–8.

1044. **Brunot, Louis.** *La cordonnerie indigène à Rabat.* Hespéris, **33**, 1946, 227–321, ill.

1045. **Brunot-David, Christiane.** 1943. *Les Broderies de Rabat.* 2 vols. Vol. 1, Text, pp. xvi + 101. Vol. 2, Plates. Rabat: École du Livre. (Collection Hespéris, Tom. 9.)

1046. **Chantreaux, Germaine.** *Le tissage sur métier de haute-lisse à Ait Hichem et dans le Haut-Sebaou.* Rev. afr., **85–86**, 1941–2, 78–116, 212–29, 261–313, ill.

1047. —— *Les tissages décorés chez les Beni-Mguild.* Hespéris, **32**, 1945, 19–34, ill.

1048. —— *Notes sur un procédé de tissage torsadé.* Hespéris, **33**, 1946, 65–81, ill.

1049. **Gauthier, Maximilien.** *La céramique marocaine.* Sphere, 1930, 15–16, ill.

1050. **Goichon, A. M.** *La broderie au fil d'or à Fès.* Hespéris, **26**, 1939, 49–85, ill.

1051. **Guyot, R., R. le Tourneau,** and **L. Paye.** *La corporation des tanneurs et l'industrie de la tannerie à Fès.* Hespéris, **21**, 1935, 167–240, ill.

1052. —— —— —— *Les cordonniers de Fès.* Hespéris, **23**, 1936, 9–54, ill.

1053. **Herber, J.** 1928. *Technique des potiers. Beni Mtir et Beni Mgild.* Mémorial Henri Basset, pp. 18, 3 pl. Paris: Geuthner.

1054. —— *Contribution à l'étude des poteries Zaer (Poteries à la tournette, poteries au moule).* Hespéris, **13**, 1, 1931, 1–34, ill.

1055. —— *Notes sur les poteries de Karia (Cheraga).* Hespéris, **15** (2), 1932, 157–61, ill.

1056. —— *Les potiers de Mazagan.* Hespéris, **17** (1), 1933, 49–57, ill.

1057. —— *Les poteries de Bhalil.* Hespéris, **33**, 1 2, 1946, 83–92, ill.

1058. **Jouin, Jeanne.** *Les thèmes décoratifs des broderies marocaines.* Hespéris, **15**, 1932, 11–30, ill.; **21**, 1935, 149–66, ill.

1059. **Kiewe, Heinz E.** 1952. *Catalogue; Ancient Berber tapestries and rugs and ancient Moroccan embroideries.* Pp. 40, ill., map. Oxford: Maison Française.

1060. **Miège, Jean Louis.** 1961. *Le Maroc et l'Europe, 1830–1894.* Tome 1, pp. 234. Paris: Presses Univ. de France.

1061. **Moriaz, J.** *Feu l'artisanat du Mzab.* Bull. liaison saharienne, no. 40, déc. 1960, 365–6.

1062. **Ricard, Prosper.** *Corpus des tapis marocains.* 3 vols. Tom. 1, Tapis de Rabat. 1925. Pp. xiv + 31, ill. Tom. 2, Tapis du Moyen-Atlas. 1926. Pp. 74, ill. Tom. 3, Tapis du Haut-Atlas et du Haouz de Marrakech. 1927. Pp. 25, ill. Paris: Geuthner.

1063. —— 1928. *Dentelles algériennes et marocaines.* Pp. (6) 48. 66 pl. (loose sheets). Paris: Éditions Larose.

1064. —— *Les arts marocains et leur rénovation.* Rev. d'Afrique, **3**, 6, jan.–fév. 1930, 10–22; **7**, avr.–mai. 1930, 20–31.

1065. —— *Les arts indigènes du Maroc et l'Amérique.* Afr. franç. Rens. col., **7**, juil. 1933, 382–4.

1066. **Vicaire, Marcel.** *L'artisanat marocain.* Bull. soc. neuchâteloise géog., **51**, 4, 1952–3, 147–62.

1067. —— and **Roger le Tourneau.** *La fabrication du fil d'or à Fès.* Hespéris, **24**, 1937, 67–88, ill.

UTENSILS, TOOLS, WEAPONS AND MISCELLANEOUS

1068. **Buttin, Ch.** *Les poignards et les sabres marocains.* Hespéris, **26**, 1939, 1–48, ill.

SAHARA

including: SPANISH SAHARA, IFNI and RIO DE ORO

1069. **Almonte, E. d.** *Ensayo de una breva descripcion del Sahara español.* Bol. soc. géog. (Madrid), **56**, 1914, 129–347, ill., map.

1070. **Bovill, E. W.** 1933. *Caravans of the Old Sahara.* Pp. 300. maps. Oxford: Oxford Univ. Press for the International African Institute.

1071. **Briggs, Lloyd Cabot.** 1958. *The living races of the Sahara desert.* Pp. xii + 217, bibl., ill., maps. Cambridge, Mass.: Peabody Museum. (Papers of the Peabody Museum of Archaeology and Ethnology, 28 (2).)

1072. —— 1960. *Tribes of the Sahara.* Pp. xx + 295, bibl., ill., maps. London: Oxford Univ. Press.

1073. **Busch-Zautner, Richard.** *Die spanische West Sahara.* Geographische Zeitung, **40**, 1934, 321–32, bibl.

1074. **Campbell, Dugald.** 1928. *On the trail of the veiled Tuareg.* Pp. 282, ill., map. London: Seeley Service.

1075. **Caro Baroja, Julio.** 1955. *Estudios saharianos.* Pp. xvii + 502, bibl., ill., maps. Madrid: Instituto de Estudios Africanos.

1076. **Coon, C. S.** 1931. *Tribes of the Rif.* Harvard Afr. Studies, 9. Pp. 417 + 617, bibl., ill., maps. Cambridge, Mass.: Harvard Univ.

1077. **De Gironcourt, G.** *L'art chez les Touareg.* Rev. ethnog., **5**, 1914–19, 42–56, ill.

1078. **Dermenghem, Émile.** 1960. *Le pays d'Abel; Le Sahara des Ouled-Naîl, des Larbaâ et des Amour.* Pp. 217, ill. Paris: Gallimard.

1079. **Diaz, Galo Bullon.** 1944–5. *Notas sobre geografia humana de los territorios de Ifni y del Sahara.* Pp. 56, ill. Madrid: Direccion general de marruecos y colonias.

1080. **Dupuis, Auguste, dit Yakouba.** *Notes sur Tombouctou.* Rev. étud. ethnog. sociol., **5**, 1914–19, 248–63, ill.

1081. **Gabus, Jean.** 1958. *Au Sahara; arts et symboles.* Pp. 407, ill. Neuchâtel: À la Baconnière. (Vol. 2 of the series 'Au Sahara'.)

1082. **Garcia Figueras, T.** *Santa Cruz de Mar Pequeña-Ifni-Sahara.* Madrid.

1083. **Guinea Lopez, Emilio.** 1945. *España y el Desierto.* Pp. 279, ill., maps. Madrid: Instituto de Estudios Politicos. Coleccion España ante el Mundo.

1084. **Haardt, G. M.,** and **L. Audouin-Dubreuil.** *Expedition Citroën Centre Afrique.* La G., **45**, 1926, 121–57; 295–331.

1085. **Hernandez, Pacheco,** and **Others.** 1947. *El Sahara Español.* Pp. 178, ill., maps. Madrid: Inst. de Estudios Africanos.

1086. **Kachkarov, D. N.,** and **E. P. Korovine.** 1942. *La vie dans les déserts.* Pp. 350. Paris: Bibliothèque Scientifique.

1087. **Kilian, C.** *L'art des Touareg.* La renaissance, 1944, 7–9.

1088. **Lhote, Henri.** *Jouets en pierre des enfants touaregs.* Bull. soc. préhist. fr., **49**, 1953, 278–82. *Jouets touaregs; note complémentaire.* Bull. soc. préhist. fr., **49**, 1952, 349–51.

1089. **Montagne, Robert.** 1947. *La civilisation du désert.* Pp. 267, ill., map. Paris: Hachette.

1090. **Monteil, V.** *Notes sur Ifni et les Ait Ba-Amram.* Notes et documents, Inst. des hautes études marocaines, **2**, 1948, 6–8.

1091. **Mulero Clemente, Manuel.** 1945. *Los territorios españoles del Sahara y sus grupos nómadas.* Pp. 442, ill., maps. Sahara.

1092. **Norris, H. T.** *Tuareg drawings on crashed bomber.* Antiquity, **24,** 93, Mar. 1950, 41–42.

1093. **Santa-Olalla, Julio Martinez.** 1944. *El Sahara Español ante Islamico.* Vol. 2. Pl. 1–235 only. Madrid: Publicaciones de las Expediciones paletnologicas al Sahara Español.

1094. **Steinilber-Oberlin, E.** 1934. *Les touareg tels que je les ai vus.* S.p. Paris: Roger.

1095. **Zeltner, Fr. de.** *Les touareg du sud.* J. roy. anthrop. inst., **44,** 1914, 351–75, ill.

BUILDINGS AND FURNITURE

1096. **Chapelle, Jean.** *Nomades noirs du Sahara.* Pp. 449, bibl., ill., maps. Paris: Plon.

1097. **Lhote, Henri.** 1947. *Dans les campements touaregs.* Pp. 413. Paris: Oeuvres Francaises.

1098. —— 1947. *Comment campent les touaregs.* Pp. 164, ill., maps. Paris: J. Susse.

CLOTHING AND ADORNMENT

1099. **Fuchs, Peter.** 1955. *The land of veiled men (The Touaregs of North Africa).* Pp. x + 168, ill. London: Weidenfeld & Nicholson.

1100. **Howe, S. E.** *Touareg women and their veiled men.* Muslim world, **18,** 1928, 34–44.

1101. **King, W. J. Harding.** 1903. *A search for the masked Tawareks.* Pp. viii + 334, ill. London.

1102. **Laugel, A. M. M.,** and **Ph. Marcais.** *Les coiffures à Tindouf (Sahara occidental).* Trav. inst. rech. sahariennes, **12,** 2, 1954, 113–21, ill.

1103. **Lhote, Henri.** *L'anneau de bras des touareg, ses techniques, et ses rapports avec la préhistoire.* Bull. I.F.A.N., **12** (2), 1950, 456–87, bibl., ill.

1104. —— *Au sujet du port du voile chez les touareg et les teda.* Notes afr. I.F.A.N., **52,** oct. 1951, 108–11.

1105. —— *'Varia' sur les sandales et la marche chez les Touareg.* Bull. I.F.A.N., **14,** 1952, 596–622.

1106. **Palmer, H. R.** *The tuareg veil.* Geog. J., **68,** 1926, 412–18.

1107. **Rodd, Francis Rennell.** 1926. *The people of the veil.* Pp. xvi + 504, bibl., ill., maps. London: Macmillan.

ROCK ART

1108. **Almagro, Martin.** *El arte prehistórico del Sahara español.* Ampurias (Barcelona), **6,** 1944, 273–84, ill.

1109. **Clark, J. Desmond.** 1954. *Prehistoric cultures of the Horn of Africa.* Pp. 386, ill. Cambridge: Museum of Archaeology and Ethnology.

1110. **Davidson, B.** *Saharan painting.* New Statesman, **55,** 1958, 162–4.

1111. **Demoulin, F.** *Gravures et inscriptions rupestres sahariennes.* La Nature (Paris), no. 2726, 1926, 1–8, ill., maps.

1111a. **Gautier, E. E. F.** *Gravures rupestres sud-oranaises et sahariennes.* L'Anthropologie, **15,** 1904, 497–517, ill.

1112. **Huard, Paul.** *Répertoire des stations rupestres du Sahara oriental français (confins Nigéro-Tchadiens, Tibesti, Borku, Ennedi.)* J. soc. africanistes, **23,** 1953, 43–76, maps. (Contains an index bibliographique, pp. 74–76.)

1113. —— *Les figurations d'animaux à disques frontaux et attributs rituels au Sahara oriental.* Bull. I.F.A.N., **23** (B), 3–4, juil.–oct. 1961, 476–517, bibl., ill., map.

1114. **Lelong, M.** 1945. *Le Sahara aux cent visages.* Pp. 306, ill., maps. Paris: Éd. Alsatia.

1115. **Lhote, H.** *Nouvelle contribution à l'étude des gravures et peintures rupestres du Sahara central.* Riv. sci. preist. (Florence), **6,** 1–2, 1951, 34–48.

1116. —— *Interprétations indigènes de quelques gravures et peintures rupestres géométriques du Sahara occidental.* Notes afr. I.F.A.N., **53,** janv. 1952, 5–6, ill.

1117. —— *Gravures, peintures et inscriptions rupestres du Kaouar, de l'Aïr et de l'Adrar des Iforas.* Bull. I.F.A.N., **14,** 4, oct. 1952, 1268–1340, ill., map.

1118. —— *Le cheval et le chameau dans les peintures et gravures rupestres du Sahara.* Bull. I.F.A.N., **15,** 3, juil. 1953, 1138–1228, ill., map.

1119. —— *Nouvelles stations de gravures rupestres.* Trav. inst. rech. sahariennes, **9,** 1, 1953, 143–57, ill.

1120. —— 1957. *Peintures préhistoriques du Sahara; Mission H. Lhote au Tasili.* Pp. 66, ill. Paris: Musée des Arts Décoratifs.

1121. —— 1958. *Die Felsbilder der Sahara.* Pp. 368, ill., maps. Würzburg-Wien: Andreas Zettner.

1122. —— *Klippmälningar i Sahara.* Konstrevy (Stockholm), **35** (5–6), 1959, 189–95, ill. (Rock paintings in the Sahara.)

1123. —— *Saharan rock art.* Nat. hist. **69,** 6, June–July 1960, 28–43, ill.

1124. —— *Le problème de la datation des peintures rupestres en Espagne et en Afrique.* Ipek, **20,** 1960–3, 62–67.

1125. —— *L'art préhistorique saharien.* Objets et mondes, **2,** 4, 1962, 201–14, ill.

1126. **Mauny, Raymond.** *Un âge du cuivre au Sahara occidental?* Bull. I.F.A.N., Jan. 1951, 168–80, ill., map.

1127. —— *Encore les chars rupestres sahariens.* Notes afr. I.F.A.N., **55,** juil. 1952, 70–71, ill.

1128. —— *autour de la répartition des chars rupestres du Nord-Ouest Africain.* Congr. panafr. préhist., 2e Session, Alger, 1952. Commun., no. 80, 1955, 741–6, ill.

1129. **Monod, Théodore.** *Gravures et inscriptions rupestres du Sahara occidental.* Bull. com. études, A.O.F., **20,** 1–2, 1937, 155–78.

1130. —— 1938. *Contributions à l'étude du Sahara occidental.* Fascicule I. *Gravures, peintures et inscriptions rupestres.* Pp. 158, ill., map. Paris: Larose. Publications du comité d'études historiques et scientifiques de l'Afrique occidentale française. Sér. A, no. 7.

1131. —— and **R. Mauny.** *Nouveaux chars rupestres sahariens.* Notes afr. I.F.A.N., **44,** oct. 1949, 112–14, ill.

1132. —— and **Capt. Cauneille.** *Nouvelles figurations rupestres de chars du Sahara occidental.* Bull. I.F.A.N., **13,** 1, janv. 1951, 181–95, ill.

1133. **Mordini, Antonio.** *Les inscriptions rupestres tifinagh du Sahara et leur signification ethnologique.* Ethnos, **2,** 1937, 333–7, bibl., ill.

1134. **Regnier, J.,** and **F. Lesbra.** *Peintures rupestres énigmatiques du Sahara central.* Bull. liaison saharienne, **12,** 42, 1961, 156–8.

1135. **Reygasse, Maurice.** 1932. *Contribution à l'étude des gravures rupestres et inscriptions tifinar du Sahara central.* Pp. 98, ill. Alger: J. Carbonel.

1136. **Russo, Dr.** *Les inscriptions rupestres du Nord-Saharien et leur rapports avec les caractères glozéliens.* Le monde colon. ill., **6,** 56, 1928, 80, ill.

1137. **Voinot, L.** *Quelques dessins et inscriptions rupestres du Sahara.* Rev. afr. **3–4,** 1929, 345–57, ill.

TECHNIQUES

1138. **Gabus, Jean.** *Techniques artisanales des régions sahariennes.* Bull. schweiz. Ges. Anthrop. u. Ethnol., **26,** 1949–50, 8–9.

1139. **Jest, Corneille.** *La poterie dans le Sahara oriental (Souf, Touggourt, Ouargla).* Trav. inst. rech. sahariennes, **19,** 1960, 105–18, ill.

1140. **Monod, Théodore.** *Une exploration scientifique au Sahara occidental.* Sci. et voyages, no. 12, 1936, 329–42, ill.

1141. **Zöhrer, L.** *Die Metallarbeiten der Tuareg der Sahara.* Beitr. z. Kolonialforsch., **4,** 1943.

UTENSILS, TOOLS, WEAPONS AND MISCELLANEOUS

1142. **Gabus, Jean.** 1954. *Les hommes et leurs outils.* Pp. 102, ill. Neuchâtel: À la Baconnière. (Vol. 1 of the series "Au Sahara".)

1143. **Huard, Paul.** *Contribution à l'étude du cheval, du fer et du chameau au Sahara oriental.* Bull. I.F.A.N., **22** (B), 1–2, janv.–avr. 1960, 134–78, bibl., ill., maps.

1144. **Hugot, H. J.** *Un vase de bronze d'origine inconnue.* Notes afr. I.F.A.N., **87**, 1960, 71–72, ill.

1145. **Lhote, Henri.** *Nouvelles statuettes néolithiques du Sahara.* Objets et mondes, **1**, 3–4, 1961, ill.

TUNISIA

1146. **Balout, L.** 1959. *Collections ethnographiques.* Album No. 1, 'Touareg Ahaggar'. s.p. 76 pl. with descriptive text. Tunis: Musée d'Ethnographie et de Préhistoire du Bardo (Tunis).

1147. **Great Britain; Admiralty; Naval Intelligence Division (Reports).** 1945. *Tunisia.* Pp. xix + 532, bibl., ill., map.

1148. **Nachtigall, Horst.** *Beiträge zur Ethnographie der tunesischen Nomaden.* Baessler-Archiv, **9** (1), 1961, 151–85, bibl., ill.

1149. **Stuhlmann, Franz.** 1914. *Die Mazigh-Völker.* Pp. 6 + 59, ill. Hamburg: Friederichsen. (Ab. Hamburg. Kolonialinst., Band 27. Sec. B. Völkerkunde, etc. Band 16.)

BUILDINGS AND FURNITURE

1150. **Bruun, Daniel.** 1898. *Cave dwellers of Southern Tunisia.* Pp. xii + 335, ill., map. London: W. Thacker & Co.

1151. **Letourneux, M. A.** 1887. *Les troglodytes de Tunisie.* (Mission scientifique de 1884.) Alger.

1152. **Nachtigall, Horst.** *Zum Problem der Höhlenwohnungen in Süd-Tunesien.* Ethnos (Sweden), **27**, 1962, 129–49, bibl., ill.

1153. **Norris, H. T.** *Cave habitations and granaries in Tripolitania and Tunisia.* Man, **53**, no. 125, 1953, 82–85, ill.

1154. **Prost, Gérard.** *Habitat et habitation chez les Ouderna et les Matmata.* Cah. de Tunisie, nos. 7–8, 1954, 239–53, ill.

CLOTHING AND ADORNMENT

1155. **Aumont, Gérard.** *Grandeur et décadence des tatouages.* Tunisie, 1942, ill.

1156. **Ginestous, Lucienne et Paul.** *Le vêtement féminin usuel à Bizerte.* Cah. de Tunisie, no. 28, 1959, 519–35, ill.

1157. **Gobert, E.** *Notes sur les tatouages des indigènes tunisiens.* L'Anthropologie, **34**, 1924, 57–90, ill.

1158. **Karutz, R.** *Tatauiermuster aus Tunis.* Archiv. f. Anthrop., **7**, 1908, 51–61, ill.

1159. **Zawadowski, G.** *Le costume traditionnel tunisien et son évolution actuelle.* En Terre d'Islam, **19**, 1944, 96–115, ill.

TECHNIQUES

1160. **Balfet, Hélène.** *Poterie artisanale en Tunisie.* Cah. de Tunisie, 6, 23–24, 1958, 317–47.

1161. **Bertholon, L.,** and **J. L. Myres.** *Note on the modern pot fabrics of Tunisia.* Man, **3**, 47, 1903, 86–88, ill.

1162. **Combès, Mme.,** and **J. L.** 1946. *Les femmes et la laine à Djerba.* Pp. 81, ill. Tunis: I.B.L.A., **10**.

1163. **Coustillac, Lucien.** *Note sur la teinture végétale à Oudref.* Cah. des arts et techniques d'Afrique du Nord, no. 1, 1951–2, 24–40, ill.

1164. —— *Note sur la teinture végétale dans le Sud-Tunisien.* Cah. de Tunisie, nos. 23–24, 1958, 353–63, ill.

1165. **Dawkins, R. M.** *A beam oil-press in Tunisia.* Man, **38**, no. 173, 1938, 150–3, ill.

1166. **Golvin, Lucien.** 1949. *Les tissages d'El-Djem et de Djebeniana.* Pp. vii + 186, ill., map. Tunis, Basconi and Muscat: I.B.L.A.

1167. **Lisse, P.,** and **Louis, A.** *À Nabeul, les nattiers et les nattes, étude technique et sociale d'artisanat tunisien.* I.B.L.A., **17**, 65, 1954, 49–92, ill.

1168. **Lobsiger-Dellenbach, M.** *Les poteries de Nabeul (Tunisie) du Musée d'Ethnographie de Genève.* Mélanges Pittard, 1957, 207–28.

1169. **Massabie, Guy.** *La vannerie de roseau à Chenini de Gabès.* Cah. de Tunisie, nos. 23 24, 1958, 365–71, ill.

1170. **Poinssot, Louis,** and **J. Revault.** 1950–7. *Tapis tunisiens.* (1) 'Kairouan' et imitations. (2) Tapis bédouins à haute laine. (3) Tissus décorés de Gafsa et imitations. (4) Tissus Ras décorés de Kairouan, du Sahel et du Sud-Tunisien. Paris: Les Horizons de France. (4 vols.)

1171. **Revault, Jacques.** *Arts traditionnels en Tunisie.* Encycl. mens. d'O.-M. (Paris), **76**, déc. 1956, 489–96.

1172. —— *Tapis tunisiens à haute laine et à poil ras.* Cah. de Tunisie, nos. 21 22, 1958, 119–38, ill., map.

1173. —— *Broderies tunisiennes.* Cah. de Tunisie, nos. 29, 30, 1960, 137–57, bibl., ill.

NORTH-EAST AFRICA

1174. **Palmer, Sir Richmond.** 1936. *The Bornu Sahara and Sudan.* Pp. viii + 296, ill. London: John Murray.

EGYPT

In view of the extensive literature on the arts of Ancient Egypt, only bibliographical works have been entered here.

1175. **Al-Funun (the Fine Arts).** A periodical published annually by the Arts Section of the Technical Institute, Khartoum (in English and Arabic). 1958– .

1176. **Cairo; Dar al-Kutab al Misriyah.** Egypt subject-catalogue, 2 vols. Cairo: Egyptian National Library Publications.

1177. **Cambridge Ancient History.** 1924. Vol. 1, Egypt and Babylonia. Vol. 2, Egyptian and Hittite Empires. Cambridge: Cambridge Univ. Press. (Both volumes contain valuable bibliographies. Numerous fascicules to this work have been issued to keep it up to date.)

1178. **Coult, L. H.** n.d. *An annotation research bibliography of the Egyptian fellah, 1788–1955.* Pp. vi + 144. London.

1179. **Creswell, K. A. C.** 1961. *A bibliography of archaeology, arts and crafts of Islam.* Pp. 480, ill. London.

1180. **de Heusch, Luc.** *Le rayonnement de l'Egypte antique dans l'art et la mythologie de l'Afrique occidentale.* J. soc. africanistes,, **28** 1-2, 1958, 91–100.

1181. **Encyclopaedia of World Art.** 1958. Vol. 4, 706–10. Bibliography by Hans Wolfgang Müller. (1) General. (2) Prehistory and protohistory. (3) Thinite period: (*a*) Architecture; (*b*) Relief painting and sculpture. (4) *Old Kingdom:* (*a*) Royal tombs; (*b*) Palaces and temples; (*c*) Tombs of court officials. (5) First intermediate period and eleventh dynasty. (6) Middle Kingdom. (7) New Kingdom. (8) Transition from the New Kingdom to the late period. (9) Late period.

1182. **Janssen, Jozef M. A.** (comp.). *Annual egyptological bibliography.* 1947– . In progress. Leiden: Brill. (International Association of Egyptologists.)

1183. **Lorin, Henri.** 1928–9. *Bibliographie géographique de l'Égypte.* 2 vols. Vol. 1, Géographie physique et géographie humaine. Pp. xvi + 472. Vol. 2. Pp. iv + 272. Cairo: Société royale de géographie d'Égypte.

1184. **Mayer, L. A.** *Annual bibliography of Islamic art and archaeology.* Vol. 1, 1935. Vol. 2, 1936. Jerusalem: Divan Publishing House.

1185. **Munier, Henri.** *Catalogue de la bibliothèque du musée égyptien du Caire.* 2 vols. Pp. 1010. Paris: Leroux.

1186. **New York; Public Library.** *Ancient Egypt; sources of information.* 1925–51.

1187. **Santandrea, P. Stefano.** 1948. *Bibliografia di Studi Africani della Missione dell'Africa Centrale.* Pp. xxviii + 167, map. Verona: Missioni Africane. (Museum Combonianum, no. 1.)

1188. **Bibliographies-Sudan.** 1962. Abdel Rahman El Nasri. A bibliography of the Sudan, 1938–1958. Pp. x + 171. Oxford: Oxford Univ. Press. 1939. Hill, R. L. A bibliography of the Anglo-Egyptian Sudan to 1937. Pp. xi + 213. Oxford: Oxford Univ. Press.

SUDAN

1189. **Addison, F.** *Archaeological discoveries on the Blue Nile.* Antiquity, **24**, 1950, 12–24, ill., map.

1190. **Anon.** *Nubia before the flood.* Sunday Times (colour magazine), 14 June 1964, 22–29, ill.

1191. **Bernatzik, Hugo Adolf.** 1936. *Gari-Gari.* Pp. xv + 138, ill., map. London: Constable.

1192. **Bieber, Friedrich J.** 1920–3. *Kaffa; ein altkuschitisches Volkstum in Inner-Afrika.* 2 vols. Pp. xxiv + 500; x + 560, bibl., ill. Vienna: Luzac.

1193. **Cheesman, Robert Ernest.** 1936. *Lake Tana and the Blue Nile.* Pp. xiv + 400, ill., map. London: Macmillan.

1194. **Cummins, S. L.** *Sub-tribes of the Bahr-el-Ghazal Dinkas.* J. anthrop. inst., **34**, 1904, 149–66, ill.

1195. **Domville Fife, C. W.** 1927. *Savage life in the black Sudan.* Pp. 284, ill., maps. London: Seeley Service.

1196. **Evans-Pritchard, E. E.** 1937. *Witchcraft, oracles and magic among the Azande.* Pp. 558, ill., map. Oxford: Univ. Press.

1197. **Hilberth, John.** 1962. *Les Gbaya.* Pp. viii + 143, ill. Lund: Hakan Ohlssons Boktryckeri. (Studia Ethnographica Upsaliensia, XIX.)

1198. **Hofmayr, Wilhelm.** 1925. *Die Schilluk.* Pp. xvi + 521, ill., map. Vienna: Verlag Administration Anthropos.

1199. **Kitching, A. L.** 1912. *On the backwaters of the Nile.* Pp. xxvli + 295, ill., map. London: Unwin.

1200. **Kumm, Hermann W.** 1910. *From Hausaland to Egypt through the Sudan.* Pp. xi + 324, ill., maps. London: Constable.

1200a. **Lagal, C. R.** *Les Azande ou Niam-Niam.* Brussels, 1926.

1201. **Junker, Wilhelm.** 1889–91. *Reisen in Afrika, 1875–86.* 3 vols. Vol. 1 (1875–8), pp. xvi + 585, ill., maps. Vol. 2 (1879–82), pp. xvi + 560, ill., maps. Vol. 3 (1882–6), pp. xvi + 741, ill., maps. Vienna and Olmütz: Eduard Hölzel.

1202. —— 1890. *Travels in Africa.* 3 vols. Vol. 1 (1875–8), pp. viii + 582, ill., map. Vol. 2 (1879–83), pp. viii + 477, ill., map. Vol. 3 (1882–6), pp. viii + 573, ill., map. London: Chapman & Hall.

1203. **Meinhof, Carl.** 1916. *Eine Studienfahrt nach Kordofan.* Pp. xii + 134, bibl., ill., map. (Abh. Hamburg. Kolonialinstituts, Band XXXV.)

1204. **Negri, A.** *Le arti belle dei Nilotici.* Strenna, *Missioni Africane,* 1927, 46–47.

1205. **Paulitschke, Philipp.** 1885. *Die Sûdanländer.* Pp. xi + 311, bibl., ill., map. Freiburg im Breisgau: Herdersche Verlagshandlung.

1206. —— 1893–6. *Ethnographie Nordost-Afrikas.* 2 vols. Vol. 1, Die materielle Cultur der Danâkil, Galla und Somâl. Pp. xvi + 338, ill., maps. Berlin: D. Reimer. Vol. 2, Die geistige Cultur der Danâkil, Galla und Somâl. Pp. xvii + 312. Berlin: D. Reimer.

1207. **Powell-Cotton, Mrs.** *Village handicrafts in the Sudan.* Man, **34**, no. 112, 1934, 90–91.

1208. **Savage-Landor, A. Henry.** 1907. *Across widest Africa.* 2 vols. Vol. 1, pp. xv + 396, ill., map. Vol. 2, pp. xii + 511, ill. London: Hurst & Blackett.

1209. **Schweinfurth, Georg August.** 1875. *Artes Africanae; illustrations and descriptions of productions of the industrial arts of Central African tribes.* Pp. xii + 42, ill. Leipzig: F. A. Brockhaus. London: Sampson Low. (Text in English and German.)

1210. —— 1878. *The heart of Africa.* 2 vols. Vol. 1, pp. xvi + 559, ill., map. Vol. 2, pp. x + 521, ill., map. London: Sampson Low.

1211. —— 1922. *Im Herzen von Afrika.* Pp. xviii + 578, ill., map. Leipzig: Brockhaus. (4th ed.)

1212. **Seligman, Charles Gabriel,** and **Brenda Z. Seligman.** *The social organisation of the Lotuko.* Sudan notes and records, **8**, 1925, 12–14.

1213. —— 1932. *Pagan tribes of the Nilotic Sudan.* Pp. xxiv + 565, ill., maps. London: Routledge.

1214. **Tangye, H. L.** 1910. *In the torrid Sudan.* Pp. xii + 300, ill., map. Boston: R. G. Badger.

1215. **Zaloscer, Hilde.** *Coptic art; its nature and origin.* Apollo, July 1963, 6–11, ill.

FIGURES AND MASKS

1216. **Kronenberg, Andreas,** and **W.** *Wooden carvings in the southwestern Sudan.* Kush, **8**, 1960, 274–81, ill.

1217. **Olderogge, D.** *Figuri nredkov plementi bari* (Ancestral figures of the Bari tribe). Sbornik Museia Antropologii i Etnografii, **10**, 1949.

1218. **Paulme, Denise.** *Carved figures from the White Nile in the Musée de l'Homme.* Man (London), **53**, 172, Aug. 1953, 113–14, ill.

1219. **Seligman, C. G.** *A Bongo funerary figure.* Man, **17**, no. 67, 1917, 97–98, ill.

1220. **von Luschan, Felix.** *Schnitzwerke aus dem westlichen Sudan.* Z. f. Ethnol., **35**, 1903.

1221. **Whitehead, G. O.,** and **Trevor Thomas.** 1939. *Carved wooden figures from the White Nile.* CR. 2e session du Congrès intern. des sciences anthropologiques et ethnologiques. Pp. 265–6. Copenhagen: Einar Munksgaard.

BUILDINGS AND FURNITURE

1222. **Emery, Walter B.** 1948. *Nubian treasure.* Pp. 72, ill. London: Methuen.

CLOTHING AND ADORNMENT

1223. **Arkell, Anthony John.** *Kohl pins (Khartoum).* Sudan notes and records, **19**, 1936, 150–1, ill.

1224. —— *Cambay and the bead trade.* Antiquity, **10**, 1936, 292–305, ill.

1225. —— *'T'Alhakimt and Tanaghilt; some North African finger-rings illustrating the connexion of the Tuareg with the 'Ankh' of ancient Egypt.* Man, **39**, 184, 1939, 185–7, ill.

1226. —— *Beads made in Darfur and Wadai.* Sudan notes and records, **26**, 2, 1945, 305–10, ill.

1227. **Arriens, C.** *Kostümkundliches aus dem West Sudan.* Kol. Rundschau u. Mitt. Schutz, **8**, 1929, 255–60.

1228. **Fischer, H. T.** *The clothes of the naked Nuer.* Int. archiv. ethnog., **50** (1), 1964, 60–71, bibl.

1229. **Herzog, Rolf.** *Der Rahat, eine fast verschwundene Mädchentracht im Ost Sudan.* Baessler-Archiv, **4**, N.F. 1956, 1–12, ill.

1230. **Nigrizia.** *Il tatuaggio fra i Nuer.* Nigrizia, 1941, 44–46, 59–61.

1231. **Robinson, A. E.** *Some notes on the regalia of the Fung Sultans of Sennar.* J. afr. soc., **30**, 1931, 361–76, ill.

1232. **Tessitore, R.** *Il gor-nom tra i Denka (Dinka).* Nigrizia (Verona), **68**, 6, June 1949, 109–12.

ROCK ART

1233. **Arkell, A. J.** *Rock pictures in northern Darfur.* Sudan notes and records, **20** (2), 1937, 281–8, ill.

1234. **Dunbar, J. H.** *Some Nubian rock pictures.* Sudan notes and records, **17**, 1934, 139–67, ill., map; **18**, 1935, 303–7, ill.

1235. —— *The rock pictures of lower Nubia.* Pp. xxv + 100, ill., map. Cairo: Govt. Press, Bulaq. (Service des Antiquités de l'Égypte).

1236. **Herzog, Rolf.** 1957. *Die Nubier.* Pp. 218, bibl., ill., map. Berlin: Akademie-Verlag. (Deutsche Akad. Wiss., Berlin: Völkerkundliche Forschungen, Bd. 2.)

1237. **Jungraithmayr, Herrmann.** *Felsbilder von Süd-Darfur.* Afr. u. Übersee, **44**, 3, Mar. 1961, 193–207, ill.

1238. —— *Rock paintings in the Sudan.* Current anthrop., **2**, 4, Oct. 1961, 388–9, ill.

1239. **Köster, A.** *Schiffsdarstellungen aus der Nubischen Wüste.* Erdball, **5**, 11, 1931, 419–23.

1240. **MacMichael, H. A., Sir.** *Rock pictures in north Kordofán.* J. anthrop. inst., **39**, 1909.

1241. **Meyers, O. H.** *Drawings by the Sudanese artists of seven thousand years ago.* I.L.N., **213**, 1948, 556–7, ill.

1242. **Parker, O. F.,** and **M. C. Burkitt.** *Nubia; rock engravings— rock engravings from Onib, Wadi Allaki, Nubia.* Man, **32**, no. 297, 1932, 249–50, ill.

1243. **von Luschan, F.** *Über Petroglyphen bei Assuan und bei Demir-Kapu.* Z. f. Ethnol., **54**, 1922, 177–92, ill.

TECHNIQUES

1244. **Arkell, A. J.** *Darfur pottery.* Sudan notes and records, **22**, 1, 1939, 79–88, illus.

1245. —— *The making of mail at Omdurman.* Kush, **3**, 1955, 83–84, ill.

1246. **Ben Sai, S.** *Plantes à tannins. Tannage et teinture des cuirs au Soudan.* Notes afr. I.F.A.N., **24**, Oct. 1944, 20–22.

1247. **Bentley, Oswald,** and **Crowfoot, W.** *Nuba pots in the Gordon College.* Sudan notes and records, **7**, 2, Dec. 1924, 18–28, ill.

1248. **Crawhall, T. C.** *Iron working in the Sudan.* Man, **33**, no. 48, 1933, 41–43, ill.

1249. **Crowfoot, Grace M.** *Weaving and spinning in the Sudan.* Sudan notes and records, **4** (1), 1921, 20–38, ill.

1250. —— *The handspinning of cotton in the Sudan.* Sudan notes and records, **7** (2), 82–89, ill.

1251. —— *The Sudanese camel girth in double weave.* Sudan notes and records, **32**, 1, June 1951, 71–76, ill.

1252. —— *The Sudanese camel girth.* Kush, **4**, 1956, 34–38, ill.

1253. **Crowfoot, J. W.** *Further notes on pottery.* Sudan notes and records, **8**, 1925, 125–36, ill.

1254. —— *Pot making in Dongala Province, Sudan.* Man, **33**, no. 6, 1933, 11–12, ill.

1255. **Howell, P. P.** *On the value of iron among the Nuer.* Man, **47**, 144, Oct. 1947, 131–3.

1256. **Kirchhoff, Alfred.** *Über Farbensinn und Farbenzeichnung der Nubier.* Z. f. Ethnol., **11**, 1879, 397–402.

1257. **MacMichael, H. A.** *Pottery making on the Blue Nile.* Sudan notes and records, **5**, 1922, 33–38.

1258. **Nur, Sadik.** *Some basketwork and gourd receptacles in the Sudan Museum, Khartoum.* Man, **61**, 51, Mar. 1961, 45–55, ill.

1259. **Paul, H. G. Balfour.** *Decorated pipes of the Fung kingdom.* Sudan notes and records, **32**, 2, Dec. 1951, 325.

1260. **Sterns, F. H.** *Some Bisharin baskets in the Peabody Museum.* Harvard African studies, **2**, 1918, 194–6, ill.

UTENSILS, TOOLS AND WEAPONS; MISCELLANEOUS

1261. **Beaton, A. C.** *A Bari game.* Sudan notes and records, **22** (1), 1939, 133–43, ill.

1262. **Davies, R.** *Some Arab games and puzzles.* Sudan notes and records, **8**, 1925, 137–52, ill.

1263. **Gates, E. A.** *Sudanese dolls.* Man, **3**, 22, 1903, 41–42, ill.

1264. **Owen, T. R. H.** *A Bega game 'Andot'.* Sudan notes and records, **21** (1), 1938, 201–5.

1265. **Sterns, F. H.** *Darfur gourds.* Harvard African studies, **1**: Varia Africana, **1**, 1917, 193–6, ill.

AFRICAN ART TODAY

1266. **Comte, M. P.** *Les peintures zandes.* Connaissance du monde, juin-juil. 1957, 21–26, ill.

1267. —— *Zande popular art; with German and French texts.* Graphic, **13**, 1957, 136–7.

1268. *Taj el Anbia el Dawi. Omdurman craftsmen; a preliminary report.* Sudan soc., **2**, 1963, 43–53.

ETHIOPIA

1269. **Annaratore, Carlo.** 1914. *In Abissinia.* Rome.

1270. **Baker, Sir Samuel.** 1871. *The Nile tributaries of Abyssinia.* Pp. xix + 568, ill. London: Macmillan.

1271. **Baum, James E.** 1928. *Savage Abyssinia.* Pp. xix + 271, maps as end-papers. London: Cassell.

1272. **Bent, J. Theodore.** 1893. *The sacred city of the Ethiopians.* Pp. xv + 309, ill. London: Longmans Green.

1273. **Borelli, J.** 1890. *Éthiopie méridionale; Journal de mon voyage aux pays Amhara, Oromo, et Sidama, 1885–1888.* Pp. 520, ill., maps. Paris: Ancienne Maison Quantin.

1274. **Conti Rossini, Carlo.** 1928. *Storia d'Etiopia.* Pp. 330. Bergamo.

1275. **Da Offeio, Francesco.** *Proverbi Abissini in Lingua Tigray.* Anthropos, **1**, 1906, 296–301, ill. (Fig. 3, Tamburini per il canto sacro.)

1276. **Doresse, Jean.** *The greatness of Ethiopia; its legends and realities.* Unesco courier, **12**, 1959, 30–32, ill.

1277. —— 1959. *Ethiopia.* Pp. 239, bibl., ill., maps. London: Elek Books.

1278. **Frobenius, Leo.** 1922–30. *Atlas Africanus.* Heft 8.48 Blatt. 'Die äthiopische Kultur'. Berlin: de Gruyter.

1279. **Grant, John Cameron.** 1900. *The Ethiopian.* Pp. xv + 288, ill. Paris.

1280. **Griaule, Marcel.** *Dessins et peintures abyssines.* L'Anthropologie, **40**, 1930, 287–8.

1281. —— *Peintures Abyssines.* Minotaure (Paris), **11**, 1933, 83–88, ill.

1282. —— *Moules et tour à travailler la corne (Abyssinie).* J. soc. africanistes, **11**, 1941, 201–7, ill.

1283. **Haberland, Eike.** 1963. *Galla Süd-Äthiopiens (with English summary).* Pp. xix + 815 + 82, bibl., ill., maps. Stuttgart: Kohlhammer. (Frobenius-Institut, Frankfurt a.M. (Völker Süd-Äthiopiens: Ergebnisse d. Frobenius Expeditionen, 1950–2: 54–56: Band 2.)

1284. **Hoskins, G. A.** 1835. *Travels in Ethiopia.* Pp. xix + 367, ill., map. London: Longmans.

1285. **Jensen, A. E.** (ed.). 1959. *Altvölker Süd-Äthiopiens.* Pp. 14 + 455, bibl., ill., maps. Stuttgart: W. Kohlhammer. (Band 1 of Völker Süd-Äthiopiens: Ergebnisse der Frobenius-Expedition, 1950–52 & 1954–56. With an English summary.)

1286. **Kuls, Wolfgang.** 1958. *Beiträge zur Kulturgeographie der Südäthiopischen Seen-Region.* Pp. 179, ill., maps. Frankfurt a.M.: W. Kramer.

1287. **Lifszyc, Deborah.** *Amulettes Éthiopiennes.* Minotaure (Paris), **11**, 1933, 71–74, ill.

1288. **Lipsky, George A.,** and **Others.** 1962. *Ethiopia.* Pp. 376, bibl., map. New Haven: H.R.A.F. Press.

1289. **Massari, C.** *Appunti di Arte Etiopici (Notes on Ethiopian Art).* Archivio antrop. e etnol. (Florence), **82**, 1952, 109–15, bibl., ill.

1290. **Montandon, George.** *Au pays Ghimirra . . . voyage à travers le massif Éthiopien (1909–1911).* Bull. soc. neuchâteloise. géog., **22**, 1913, 463, ill., maps.

1290a. **Pankhurst, Sylvia.** 1955. *Ethiopia, a cultural history.* Pp. xxxviii + 747, ill. Woodford Green: Lalibela House.

1291. **Pittard, Eugène.** *Les arts populaires de l'Afrique; Quelques peintures d'Abyssinie.* Arch. suisses anthrop. générale, **5**, 1928–31, 87–103, ill.

1292. —— *Une exposition temporaire de peintures d'Abyssinie.* Les Musées de Genève, **4**, 1947, 3, ill.

1293. **Playne, Beatrice.** 1954. *St. George for Ethiopia.* Pp. 200. London: Constable.

1294. **Rein, G. K.** 1918–20. *Abessinien.* 3 vols. Vol. 1, pp. xii + 495, bibl., ill. Vol. 2, pp. xix + 358, ill., map. Vol. 3, pp. xxxii + 395, bibl., ill. Berlin: Reimer. (Special bibliographies 'Kunst', 'Anthropologie' and 'Ethnographie' in vol. 3.)

1295. **Rey, Charles E.** 1923. *Unconquered Abyssinia as it is to-day.* Pp. 312, ill., map. London: Seeley Service.

1296. **Rohlfs, G.** 1883. *Meine Mission nach Abessinien.* Pp. xx + 348, ill. Leipzig.

1297. **Rohrer, Ernst Friedrich.** *Beiträge zur Kenntnis der Materiellen Kultur des Amhara.* Jahresbericht der Geographischen Gesellschaft in Bern, **29**, 1929–30, xi + 174, bibl., ill. Bern: Geographischen Gesellschaft. Buchdruckerei: W. P. Wälchli.

1298. —— 1949. *Lendenschürzen, Hüte und Wurfhölzer aus West und Südabessinien.* Jb. Bern. hist. mus., **29**, 1949, 79–89, ill.

1299. **Rothemund, H. J.** 1956. *Aethiopische Malerei.* Munich.

1300. **Staude, W.** *Die Profilregel in der christlichen Malerei Äthiopiens und die Furcht vor dem 'Bösen Blick'.* Arch. f. Völkerkunde, **9**, 1954, 116–61, ill.

1301. **Tubiana, Joseph.** *Le frère de Saint Lâlibalâ* (peinture éthiopienne). Objets et mondes, **3**, 3, automne 1963, 221–8, ill.

1302. **Ullendorff, Edward.** 1960. *The Ethiopians.* Pp. xiv (2) 232, bibl., ill., map. London: Oxford Univ. Press.

BUILDINGS AND FURNITURE

1303. **Berlin: Koenigliche Museen.** 1913. *Deutsche Aksum-Expedition.* 3 vols., ill., maps. Berlin: Reimer.

1304. **Mordini, Antonio.** *L'église rupestre de Woqro-Maryâm (Amba Seneiti) au Tigré.* Éthiopie d'aujourd'hui, **6/7**, nov.–déc. 1962, 27–34, ill.

1305. **Staude, Wilhelm.** *Étude sur la décoration picturale des Églises Abbâ Antonios de Gonder et Dabra Sinâ de Gorgora.* Ann. d'Éthiopie, **3**, 1959, 185–250, ill.

CLOTHING AND ADORNMENT

1306. **Messing, Simon D.** *The non-verbal language of the Ethiopian toga.* Anthropos, **55**, 3/4, 1960, 558–60, ill.

ROCK ART

1307. **Conti Rossini, Carlo.** *Incisioni rupestri all'Haghèr.* Rass. studi etiopici., **3**, 1943, 102–6.

1308. **Graziosi, P.** *Le pitture rupestri nell'Amba Focadà.* Rass. studi etiopici., **1**, 1941, 61–70.

1309. —— *New discoveries of rock paintings in Ethiopia,* 1. Antiquity, **38**, 150, 1964, 91–98, ill., map.

1310. **Griaule, Marcel.** 1933. *Silhouettes et graffiti abyssins.* Pp. 36, ill. Paris: Larose.

1311. **Mordini, A.** *Un riparo sotto roccia con pitture rupestri nell'Amba Focadà.* Rass. studi etiopici., **1**, 1941, 54–60.

TECHNIQUES

1312. **Haberland, Eike.** *Äthiopische Dachaufsätze.* Jb. S. Mus. Völkerkunde (Leipzig), **17**, 1958 (1960), 158–76, ill.

1313. **Mordini, Antonio.** *Un vasetto con figurazioni votive proveniente da Daroda.* Boll. ist. studi etiopici, **1**, 1, 1953, 17–20.

1314. **Olderogge, D.** *Einige bisher unveröffentlichte Tonfiguren aus S.W.—Abyssinien.* Acad. des sci. de l'union des republiques soviétiques socialistes publ. du musée d'anthrop. et d'ethnogr., **8**, 1928, 324–9.

1315. **Rohrer, E. F.** 1928. *Die Flechterei der Amhara.* Sonderabdruck Jb. Bern. hist. mus., 1927, 31, ill.

1316. **Sanguineti Poggi, N.** *L'espressione e il colore nella pittura popolare dell'Eritrea* (Expression and colour in the popular painting of Eritrea). Boll. ist. studi etiopici, **2**, 57, 22–26.

1317. **Wainwright, G. A.** *Early records of iron in Abyssinia.* Man, **42**, 43, July–Aug. 1942, 84–88.

UTENSILS, TOOLS AND WEAPONS; MISCELLANEOUS

1318. **Pankhurst, R.** *'Primitive money' in Ethiopia.* J. soc. africanistes, **32**, 1962, 213–47.

AFRICAN ART TODAY

1319. **Vollbach, F.** *Moderne abessinische Malerei.* Die Woche (Berlin), **29**, 14, 1927, 375–8, ill.

SOMALIA

1320. **Corni, Guido.** 1937. *Somalia Italiana.* 2 vols. Milan: Editoriale Ante E Storia.

1321. **Drake-Brockman, Ralph E.** 1912. *British Somaliland.* Pp. xvi + 334, bibl., ill., map. London: Hurst & Blackett.

1322. **Francolini, Bruno.** *Arte indigena Somala.* Riv. col. Ital. ('Oltremare') (Bologna), **11**, 1933, 891–4.

1323. —— *Migiurtina.* Riv. col. Ital. ('Oltremare'), Jan. 1936, 31–44.

1324. —— *Manifestazioni e applicazioni dell'arte indigena Somala.* Centro di studi colon. ist. colon. Fascista: Atti del 3 congresso di studi colon., **6**, 5, Apr. 1937, 136–45.

1325. **Grottanelli, Vinigi L.** *Asiatic influences on Somali culture.* Ethnos, **12**, 1947, 153–81, ill.

1326. —— 1955. *Pescatori dell'Oceano Indiano; Saggio etnologico preliminaire sui Bagiuni Bantu costieri dell'Oltregiuba.* Pp. xxi + 409, ill., map. Rome: Cremonese.

1327. **Lewis, I. M.** 1955. *North Eastern Africa.* Part 1, Peoples of the Horn of Africa: Somali, Afar and Saho. Pp. ix + 200, bibl., map. London: International African Institute. (Ethnographic Survey of Africa: North Eastern Africa, Part 1.)

1328. **Mordini, Antonio.** *Stato attuale delle ricerche etnografiche (Cultura Materiale) nell'A.O.I.* Atti del III congresso di studi coloniale, **6**, 1937, 149–59.

1329. **Powell-Cotton, Miss D.** 1935. *Somali notes,* MS. Pp. 85. (In British Museum (Ethnographical Dept.).) 1935. *Notes on Italian Somaliland,* MS. Pp. 74. (In British Museum Ethnographical Dept.)

1330. **Robecchi-Bricchetti, L.** 1902. *Somalia e Benadir.* Milan.

1331. **Smith, A. Donaldson.** 1897. *Through unknown African countries . . . from Somaliland to Lake Lamu.* Pp. xvi + 471, ill., maps. London: Arnold. (Appendix G. Catalogue of ethnographical objects, pp. 430–43 (described by) S. Culin.)

FIGURES AND MASKS

1332. **Clark, J. Desmond.** *Dancing masks from Somaliland (Eile tribe).* Man, **53**, 72, Apr. 1953, 49–51, ill.

1333. **Massari, C.** *Maschere di danza degli Uaboni.* Archivio antrop. e etnol. (Florence), **80/81**, 1950–1, 143–6, ill.

1334. **Pirone, M.** *Le maschere di Bur Eybi.* Somali d'oggi (Mogadiscio), **2**, 2, Giu. 1957, 37–39, ill.

BUILDINGS AND FURNITURE

1335. **Cipriani, Lidio.** 1940. *Abitazioni indigene dell'Africa orientale Italiana.* Pp. 181, bibl., ill., map. Naples: Edizioni della Mostra D'Oltremare.

CLOTHING AND ADORNMENT

1336. **Chailley, M.** *Sandale dankalie (Somalie).* Notes afr. I.F.A.N., **71**, juil. 1956, 69–71, ill.
1337. **James, F. L.** 1888. *The unknown horn of Africa.* Pp. xiv + 344, ill., maps. London: George Philip & Son. (Notes: p. 324, Somali weapons; pp. 325–6, dress; p. 326, ornaments; p. 326, tent equipments; p. 327, horse equipment.)

ROCK ART

1338. **Drew, Sannie.** *Two Eritrean rock sculptures probably of Coptic origin.* Man, **51**, 155, July 1951, 89–90, ill.
1339. —— *Mysterious rock carvings of the Eritrean highlands; modernistic sculpture and enigmatic inscriptions.* I.L.N., **221**, 1952, 225–7, ill.
1340. —— 1954. *Rock paintings and engravings of Eritrea.* M.S. typescript in British Museum (Ethnographical Dept.).
1341. **Duncanson, D. J.** *Eritrean rock sculptures.* Man, **52**, 117, May 1952, 78–79, ill.
1342. **Franchini, Vincenzo.** *Pitture rupestri a Sullum Baatti.* Rass. studi etiopici, **10**, Gen.–Dic. 1951, 122–3, ill.
1343. —— *Altre pitture rupestri nell' Akkelè Guzay.* Boll. ist. studi etiopici (Asmara), **2**, 1957 (1958), 1–12, ill., map.
1344. —— *Pitture rupestri e antichi resti architettonici dell'Acchelè Guzài (Eritrea).* Rass. studi etiopici, **17**, 1961, 5–10, ill.
1345. —— *Nuovi ritrovamenti di pitture rupestri e graffiti in Eritrea.* Rass. studi etiopici, **20**, 1964, 97–102.
1346. **Frobenius, Leo.** 1931. *Erythräa; Länder und Zeiten des heiligen Königsmordes.* Pp. 368 (vii), ill., maps. Berlin: Atlantis-Verlag.
1347. **Graziosi, Paolo.** *Graffiti rupestri in Migiurtinia, Somalia.* Archivio antrop. e etnol., **91**, 1961, 153–63.
1348. **Lewis, I. M.** *The Godhardunneh cave decorations of north-eastern Somaliland.* Man, **58**, 234, 1958, 178–9, ill.
1349. **Micheli, A. Vigliardi.** *Le pitture rupestri di Karora (Nord-Eritrea).* Riv. sci. preist., **11**, 1956, 193–209.
1350. **Mordini, A.** *Incisioni rupestri di Gazièn (Medrì Senafè) nell' Endertà.* Riv. sci. preist., **2**, 1947, 212–13.
1351. **Mori, Fabrizio.** *Un singolare esempio di scultura rupestre nell' Acacus; i 'fori Accoppiati'.* Riv. sci. preist., **16**, 1961, 231–7.

TECHNIQUES

1352. **Chailley, M.** *Nattes de Tadjourah (Somalie).* Notes afr. I.F.A.N., **70**, avr. 1956, 46, ill.
1353. **Haberland, Eike.** *Nachträge zu Äthiopischen Dachaufsätzen.* Jb. S. Mus. Völkerkunde (Leipzig), **19**, 1962, 167–70, ill.

WEST AFRICA

See also 2847.

1354. **Andrée, Richard.** *Seltene Ethnographica des städtischen Gewerbe-Museums zu Ulm, 11 Objekte aus Afrika,* p. 34. Baessler-Archiv, **4** (1), 1913, 29–38, ill.
1354a. **Arkell, A. J.** *Archaeological research in West Africa.* Antiquity, **71**, 1944, 147–50.
1355. **Armattoe, R. E. G.** 1946. *The Golden Age of West African civilization.* Pp. 97, bibl., ill. Londonderry: Londonderry Sentinel.
1356. **Balandier, G.** 1957. *Afrique ambiguë.* Pp. 293, ill. Paris: Plon.
1357. **Bascom, W. R.** *About West African art.* The Art League news, **3**, 1956: no. 6, pp. 4–7; no. 7, pp. 3–6. (Reprint of section of handbook on West African art.)
1358. **Brasseur, G.** *L'A.O.F.* Initiations africaines, **13**, 1954, Pp. 74, ill., tribal map. Dakar: I.F.A.N.
1359. **Cole of Shaingay, J. A.** 1886. *A revelation of the secret orders of Western Africa.* Dayton, Ohio.
1359a. **Congresses.** *Conf. Int. des Africanistes de l'Ouest.* Every two years in W. Africa; Dakar, 1945. Bissau, 1947. Ibadan, 1949; Fernando Po, 1951; Ibidjan, 1953. (Reports published.)
1360. **Davidson, B.,** and **A. Ademola** (ed.). 1953. *The new West Africa.* Pp. 187. London: Allen & Unwin.
1361. **Delafosse, Maurice.** 1927. *Les nègres.* Pp. 80, 59 pl. Paris: Les Editions Rieder.
1362. —— *The negroes of Africa* (tr. by F. Flegelman). Washington, 1931.
1363. **Ellis, G. W.** 1914. *Negro culture in West Africa.* Pp. 290, ill., map. New York: Neale Publishing Co.
1364. **Fage, J. D.** 1955. *An introduction to the history of West Africa.* Pp. xl + 210. Cambridge: Univ. Press.
1365. **Friend, D.** *Art of the West Coast of Africa.* London Studio, **24**, 1942, 128–9.
1366. **Ghislain, Marc.** 1961. *Tropiques enchantées.* Pp. 381, ill., map. Paris: Ligel.
1367. **Harden, D. B.** *The Phoenicians on the West Coast of Africa.* Antiquity, **87**, 1948, 141–50.
1368. **Hardy, Georges.** 1937. *L'Afrique occidentale française.* Pp. 244, bibl., ill., maps. Paris: Laurens. (Music and art, pp. 74–77.)
1369. —— See Maigret, Julien. *Afrique occidentale et Afrique équatoriale.* (477). (Avec un avant-propos sur l'art nègre de M. Georges Hardy.)
1370. **Helfritz, Hans.** 1958. *Schwarze Ritter zwischen Niger und Tschad.* Pp. 357, bibl., ill., map. Berlin: Safari-Verlag.
1371. **Hodgkin, T.** *Journeys of discovery; ancient chronicles of West Africa's past.* Unesco courier, **12**, 1959, 26–27, ill.
1372. **International West African Congress.** No. 1, 1950. *Première conférence des africanistes de l'ouest.* Dakar. C.R. Tome I, pp. 531. Dakar: I.F.A.N.
1373. **Jacques, V.,** and **E. Storms.** 1886. *Notes sur l'ethnographie de la partie orientale de l'Afrique équatoriale.* Pp. 112. Brussels: Hayez.
1374. **Jeanes, G. F.** *Art in West Africa.* U. empire, **20**, 8, 1929, 441.
1375. **Karsten, Paula.** 1903. *Wer ist mein Nächster; Negertypen aus Deutschwestafrika.* Berlin: Gose.
1376. **Lebedev, Yu.** 1962. *Isskustvo zapadnoy tropicheskoy Afriki* (The art of western tropical Africa). Pp. 14 + 48, ill. Moscow: Izdat. Iss. (Art Publ. House).
1377. **Mauny, Raymond.** 1961. *Tableau géographique de l'ouest africain au moyen âge.* Pp. 587, bibl., ill., maps. Dakar: I.F.A.N. Mém. no. 61.
1378. **Migeod, F. W. H.** 1923. *Across Equatorial Africa.* Pp. (8) + 397, ill., map. London: Heath Cranton.
1379. **Mohammed Ebn-Omar El-Tounsy.** 1845. *Voyage au Darfour.* Pp. lxxxviii + 491, ill., map. Paris: Benjamin Duprat.
1380. **Monod, Th.** *The Atlantic and Africa.* Report of a lecture delivered at Duala on the influence of the Atlantic upon Africa. Africa, **15**, 1945, 161–2.
1381. **Oberländer, Richard.** 1874. *Westafrika vom Senegal bis Benguela.* Pp. xvi + 464, ill., maps. Leipzig: O. Spamer.
1382. **Park, Mungo.** 1816. *Travels in the interior districts of Africa . . . in . . . 1795–1797 and 1805.* 2 vols. Vol. 1, Travels in 1795, 1796 and 1797, pp. xx + 551. Vol. 2, Last journey and life, pp. ccviii + 301, map. London: John Murray.
1383. **Raffenel, Anne.** 1846. *Voyage dans l'Afrique occidentale . . . en 1843 and 1844.* Paris: Bertrand. (P.A., pp. 151–2.)
1384. **Rivet, Paul,** and **Georges-Henri Rivière.** *La mission ethnographique et linguistique Dakar-Djibouti, 1931–1933.* Minotaure (Paris), **11**, 1933, 3–6 (3–61), ill., maps.

1385. **Sadler, Sir Michael E.** (*ed.*). 1935. *Arts of West Africa (excluding Music)*. Pp. xi + 96 + 5, ill. London: Oxford Univ. Press for International African Institute.

1386. **Schweeger-Exeli, Annemarie.** *Probleme mediterraner Kultureinflüsse in Westafrika*. Tribus, **9**, 1960, 81–89, ill.

1387. **Soyaux, Herman.** 1879. *Aus West-Afrika*. 2 vols. Vol. 2, pp. 174–9. Leipzig: Brockhaus.

1388. **Steinmann, A.** *Das chamäleon in der Kunst von Westafrika*. Atlantis, Jg. 23, 1951, 439–41.

1389. **von Sydow, E.** 1943. *Im Reiche Gottähnlicher Herrscher. Streifzüge durch Westafrika*. Pp. 148, ill., map. Brunswick: Wenzel & Sohn.

FIGURES AND MASKS

1390. **Andrée, R.** *Alte westafrikanische Elfenbeinschnitzwerke im Herzogl. Museum zu Braunschweig*. Globus, **79**, 10, 1901, 156–9.

1391. **Bascom, William R.,** and **Paul Gebauer.** 1954. *Handbook of West African art*. Pp. 83, ill., maps. Milwaukee: Milwaukee Public Museum. (Popular Science Handbook Series, no. 5.)

1392. **Bernatzik, Hugo Adolphe.** 1935. *L'Afrique équatoriale*. Pp. xxvi + 256 pl. Paris: Librairie des Arts Décoratifs.

1393. **Boulton, L. C.** *Bronze artists of West Africa*. Nat. hist., **36**, 1935, 16–28, ill.

1394. **Butt-Thompson, F. W.** 1929. *West African secret societies*. Pp. 320, bibl., ill., map. London: Witherby.

1395. **Carline, R.** *West African art and its tradition*. Studio, **109**, 1935, 186–93.

1396. **Clarke, Dora.** *Negro art; sculpture from West Africa*. J. Afr. soc., **34**, no. 135, 1935, 129–37.

1397. **Davies, O.** *West African sculpture is perishing*. Universitas (Accra), **2** (6), June 1957, 183–4.

1398. **de Beauchêne, Guy.** *Une statuette en pierre ouest-africaine*. Objets et mondes, **3**, 4, hiver 1963, 267–72, bibl., ill.

1399. **Decker, Vincent de,** and **Others.** *Dans la boucle du Congo; La sculpture africaine et son destin*. Pp. 64, ill., map. Namur: Éditions Grands Lacs.

1400. **Eberl-Elber, Ralph.** 1936. *Westafrikas letztes Rätsel*. Pp. 386, ill., maps. Salzburg: Das Bergland-Buch.

1401. **Frölich, Willy.** *Das Westafrikanische Elfenbeinhorn aus dem 16 Jarhunderts im Rautenstrauch-Joest-Museum, Cologne*. Ethnologica, N.F. vol. 2, 1960, 426–32, bibl., ill.

1402. **Haitz, Linn.** 1961. *Juju gods of West Africa*. Pp. 113, ill. St. Louis: Concordia Publishing House.

1403. **Hall, H. U.** *Dwarfs and divinity in West Africa*. Museum journal (Univ. of Pennsylvania, Philadelphia, Pa.), **18**, 1927, 5, ill.

1404. —— *Two new West African sculptures*. Museum journal (University of Pennsylvania, Philadelphia, Pa.), 1930, 60–63, ill.

1405. —— *West African masks*. Connoisseur, **93**, 1934, 380–3.

1406. **Himmelheber, Hans.** *Einige Eigentümlichkeiten westafrikanischer Plastiken*. Ethnologica, N.F. 2, 1960, 407–9, ill. (Some characteristic features of West African plastic art.)

1407. **International West African Congress.** No. 5, 1953. *Report of the 5th International Congress, Abidjan (French Ivory Coast)*. Ethnol. Section. Plastic art in West Africa, pp. 135–6. Abidjan.

1408. **Karutz, R.** *Zur westafrikanischen Maskenkunde*. Globus, **79**, 1901, 361–8, ill.

1409. **Kjersmeier, Carl.** *Negerskulptur*. Epoke, **3**, 3, 1933, 1–4, ill.

1410. —— *Habbe-Kunst*. Ymer, 1934, H. 1, 2, 58–68.

1411. —— 1935–8. *Centres de style de la sculpture nègre africaine*. Vol. 1, Afrique occidentale française. Pp. 46, bibl., pl. 1–64.

1412. —— Vol. 2, Guinée Portugaise, Sierra-Leone, Libéria, Côte d'Or, Togo, Dahomey & Nigéria. Pp. (39), bibl., pl. 1–58.

1413. —— Vol. 3, Congo Belge. Pp. (43), bibl., pl. 1–56.

1414. —— Vol. 4, Cameroun, Afrique équatoriale française, Angola, Tanganyika, Rhodésie. Pp. (34), pl. 1–42. Paris: Éditions Albert Morancé. Copenhagen: Fischers Forlag.

1415. —— 1947. *Afrikanske Negerskulpturer (African Negro sculptures) (with brief notes on the tribes represented)*. Pp. 88, ill. London: A. Zwemmer.

1416. —— 1948. *Afrikanske Negerskulpturer (African negro sculptures)*. Pp. 86, ill. New York: Wittenborn, Schultz.

1417. —— 1959. *Scultura Africana*. Pp. 75, ill. Milan: All'Insegna del Pesce D'Oro.

1418. **Joyce, T. A.** *Steatite figures from West Africa in the British Museum*. Man, **5**, 1905, 97–100.

1419. **Krieger, Kurt,** and **Kutscher, Gerdt.** 1960. Westafrikanische Masken. Pp. 93, bibl., ill., map. Berlin: Museum für Völkerkunde.

1420. **Nassau, P. H.** *Fetishism in West Africa*. London, 1904.

1421. **Néel, H.** *Statuettes en pierre et en argile de l'Afrique occidentale*. L'Anthropologie, **24**, 1913, 419–43, ill.

1422. **Rütimeyer, L.** *Über westafrikanische Steinidole*. Int. archiv. Ethnog., **14**, 1901, 195–215, ill. *See also* Globus, **80**, 1, 1901, 14–15, ill.

1423. —— *Weitere Mitteilungen über westafrikanische Steinidole*. Int. archiv. Ethnog., **18**, 1908, 167–87, ill.

1424. **Schnell, R.** *Sur deux statuettes à double visage provenant de la région forestière d'Afrique occidentale*. Notes afr. I.F.A.N., 38, 1948, 9, ill.

1425. —— *Note sur le tatouage de quelques masques et d'une statuette d'Afrique occidentale*. Notes afr. I.F.A.N., 74, 1957, 49–52, ill.

1426. **Sydow, J.** 1941. *Steinkult in Westafrika und Parallelen in anderen Gebieten*. Pp. 373, ill. Berlin: Typescript of Dissertation.

1427. **Underwood, Leon.** 1947. *Figures in wood of West Africa (in English and French)*. Pp. xlix + 45, ill., map. London: John Tiranti.

1428. —— 1948. *Masks of West Africa*. Pp. 49, ill., map. London: Alec Tiranti.

BUILDINGS AND FURNITURE

1428a.**Foyle, A. M.** *Architecture in West Africa*. Afr. south, **3**, 1959, 97–105, ill.

1429. **Fry, E. M.** *West Africa (architecture)*. Arch. rev., **128**, 1960, 7–20, ill., map.

1430. **Haselberger, Herta.** *Le décor mural chez les noirs de l'ouest africain*. Africa-Tervuren, **9**, 3, 1963, 57–61, ill.

1431. —— *Die Wandzierkunst der Neger in Savanne und Waldland Westafrikas*. 6e Congr. int. sci. anthrop. et ethnol. (Paris, 1960), **2**, 1, 1963, 123–9.

1432. —— *Quelques Cas d'évolution du décor mural en Afrique occidentale*. Notes afr. I.F.A.N., 101, 1964, 14–16, ill.

1433. **Haselberger-Blaha, Herta.** *La peinture murale africaine en A.O.F.* Notes afr. I.F.A.N., **74**, 1957, 61–62, ill.

1434. —— *Afrikanische Freskokunst*. Ipek, **19**, 1954–9, 85–98, bibl., ill.

CLOTHING AND ADORNMENT

1435. **Kouaovi, B. M.** *La coiffure chez les noirs de l'Afrique occidentale et ses rapports avec l'art, l'occultisme et la médecine*. Encyclop. mens. O.M., **5** (59), juil. 1955, 334–6, ill.

1436. **Le Gal, J. R.** *La parure de la femme en Afrique équatoriale*. Sci. et voyage, **29**, 22, sept. 1947, 283–4.

1437. **Mauny, Raymond.** *Le costume en damier dans les rites funéraires*. Notes afr. I.F.A.N., **53**, janv. 1952, 22–23, ill.

1438. —— *Perles ouest-africaines en amazonite*. Bull. I.F.A.N., **18** (B-), 1–2, janv.-avr. 1956, 140–7, ill., map.

1439. —— *Note sur l'âge et l'origine des perles à chevrons*. Notes afr. I.F.A.N., **74**, avr. 1957, 46–48, ill.

1440. —— *Akori beads*. J. hist. soc. Nigeria (Ibadan), **1**, 3, Dec. 1958, 210–14.

1441. **Read, C. H.** *A necklace of glass beads from West Africa*. Man, **5**, 1, 1905, 1–2.

1442. **Zeltner, Fr. de.** *La bijouterie indigène en Afrique occidentale.* J. soc. africanistes, **1**, 1931, 43–48, ill.

ROCK ART

1443. **Mauny, R.** *Gravures, peintures et inscriptions rupestres de l'ouest Africain.* Initiations et études africaines I.F.A.N., **11**, 1954, 1–91, bibl., ill., map.

TECHNIQUES

1444. **Africa.** *Africa South*, 2:4. Murray: West African wood-carving. Goodwin: The art of Africa. Nov. 1959.
1445. **Balfour, Henry.** *Modern brass-casting in West Africa.* J. roy. anthrop. inst., **40**, July–Dec. 1910, 525–8, ill.
1446. **Bellamy, C. V.** 1905. *A West African smelting house (near Lagos).* J. of the iron and steel institute, no. 2, for 1904, 99–126.
1447. **Francis-Bœuf, Claude.** *L'industrie autochtone du fer en Afrique occidentale française.* Bull. com. études A.O.F., **20**, 4, oct.–déc. 1937; 403–64.
1448. **Hambly, W. D.,** and **A. E. Hambly.** *Weavers of West Africa; mats and basketry in Nigeria and Angola.* Craft horizons, **14**, 1954, 29–31.
1449. **Knops, P.** *Fer météorique; sacralité du fer minéral et du forgeron en Afrique occidentale.* Bull. soc. roy. belge anthrop., **72**, 1961, 70–75.
1450. **Krucker, H.** *Westafrikanische Mattengeflechte.* Mitt. Ostschweiz. Geogr.—Kom. Gesellsch., s. d., pp. 20, ill. C. R. Anthropos, 1940–1, XXXV–XXXVI, 996.
1451. **Lhote, Henri.** *La connaissance du fer en Afrique occidentale.* Encycl. mens. O.-M. (Paris), **1**, 25, 3e année, sept. 1952, 269–72, ill.
1452. **Lippmann, M.** 1940. *Westafrikanische Bronzen.* Frankfurt-a-M: Breidenstein, pp. 79, ill., map.
1453. **Malzy, P.** *Les calebasses.* Notes afr. I.F.A.N., **73**, 1957, 10–12, ill.
1454. **Mauny, Raymond.** *Essai sur l'histoire des métaux en Afrique occidentale.* Bull. I.F.A.N., **14**, 1952, 545–95, bibl., ill., map.
1455. —— *Autour de l'historique de l'introduction du fer en Afrique occidentale.* Encycl. mens. O.-M., **1**, 32, avr. 1953, 109–10, map.
1456. **Meyerowitz, E. L. R.** *Sacred twinned vessels from West Africa.* Man, **40**, no. 22, 1940, 16, ill.
1457. **Stopford, R. W.** *The institute of West African arts, industries and social science (at Achimota).* J. roy. Afr. soc., **42**, 169, Oct. 1943, 183–90.
1458. —— *Some problems in the development of secondary industries in West Africa.* Africa, **14**, 4, Oct. 1943, 165–9.
1459. **Underwood, Leon.** 1949. *Bronzes of West Africa.* Pp. 32, ill. London: J. Tiranti.
1460. —— *Bronzes of West Africa.* Artibus Asiae, **13**, nos. 1–2, 1950, 137.
1461. **West Africa.** *Town of royal weavers.* West Afr., 14 July 1956, p. 483, ill.
1462. —— *Pottery for posterity (Mrs. Leith-Ross and the Jos Museum collection).* West Afr., **2373**, 24 Nov. 1962, 1293, ill.

UTENSILS, TOOLS AND WEAPONS; MISCELLANEOUS

1463. **Béart, Ch.** 1955. *Jeux et jouets de l'ouest africain.* 2 vols. Pp. 438; 443–889, bibl., ill. Dakar: I.F.A.N. (Mém. I.F.A.N., 42.)
1464. **Bell, A. S.** *Manilla token; currency of the West African slave trade.* Numismatist, **63**, 1950, 518–23.
1465. **Mauny, R.** *Monnaies anciennes d'Afrique occidentale.* Notes afr. I.F.A.N., **42**, 1949, 60–61.
1466. **Palmer, H. R.** *'Trident' sceptres from West Africa.* Man, **32**, no. 47, 1932, 41–43, ill.
1467. **Rodd, Francis.** *Tridents and triliths in West Africa.* Man, **32**, no. 162, 1932, 139–40, ill.

1468. **Siegel, Morris.** 1940. *The Mackenzie collection; a study of West African gambling chips.* Pp. 81, ill. Menasha, Wis.: American Anthrop. Assoc. Vol. 42.

AFRICAN ART TODAY

1469. **Appia, Beatrice.** *La représentation humaine dans les dessins d'enfants noirs.* Bull. I.F.A.N., **1** (2–3), 1939, 405–8, ill.
1470. **West Africa.** *The potter of Abuja (Michael Cardew).* West Afr., no. 2134, 1958, 221, ill.

GAMBIA

1471. **Béart, Ch.** *Sur les Bassaris de Haute-Gambie.* Notes afr. I.F.A.N., 35, 1947, 1–7, ill.
1472. **Park, Mungo.** 1924. *Vom Gambia zum Niger (1795–97).* Paul Germann. Pp. 158, ill. Leipzig: Brockhaus.
1473. **Parker, H.** *Stone circles in the Gambia.* J. roy. anthrop. inst., **53**, 1923, 173–228, ill.
1474. **Rancon, André.** 1894. *Dans la haute Gambie, voyage d'exploration, 1891–92.* Pp. 592, ill., maps. Paris: Soc. d'éditions scientifiques. (Art, pp. 324–32.)

SIERRA LEONE

1475. **Lewis, Roy.** 1954. *Sierra Leone.* Pp. ix + 263, bibl., ill., maps. London: H.M.S.O.
1476. **Little, K. L.** *The Poro society as an arbiter of culture.* (Sierra Leone.) Afr. stud., **7**, 1948, 1–15.
1476a. —— 1951. *The Mende of Sierra Leone.* Pp. 307, bibl., ill., maps. London: Kegan Paul.
1477. **McCulloch, M.** 1950. *Peoples of Sierra Leone Protectorate.* Pp. 102, bibl., map. London. Int. Afr. Inst. (Ethnographic Survey of Africa: Western Africa, Part 2.)
1478. **Poole, Thomas Eyre.** 1850. *Life, scenery and customs in Sierra Leone and the Gambia.* 2 vols.
1479. **Staub, Jules.** 1936. *Beiträge zur Kenntnis der materiellen Kultur der Mendi in der Sierra Leone.* Pp. iv + 63, ill., map. Solothurn: Vogt-Schild. (Jb. Bern. hist. mus.)
1480. **Zeller, R.** *Die Bundugesellschaft. Ein Geheimbund der Sierra Leone.* Wiss. Beiläger 2 Jb. Bern. hist. mus. (Ethnog. Abt.), 1912.

FIGURES AND MASKS

1481. **Addison, W.** *Steatite figures from Moyamba District, Central Province, Sierra Leone, West Africa.* Man, **23**, 109, 1923, 176–7.
1482. —— *The Nomori of Sierra Leone.* Antiquity, **8**, 1934, 335–8.
1483. **Alldridge, T. J.** 1910. *A transformed colony—Sierra Leone.* Pp. xvi + 368, ill., map. London: Seeley Service.
1484. **Brown, Stanley.** *The nomoli of Mende country (a stone figurine).* Africa, **18**, 1, Jan. 1948, 18–20, ill.
1485. **Eberl, Elber.** *Die Masken der Männerbünde in Sierra Leone.* Ethnos, **2**, 1937, 38–46, ill.
1485a. **Joyce, T. A.** *Steatite figures from Sierra Leone.* Man, **9**, 40, 1909, 65–68, ill.
1486. **Mauny, R.** *Masques Mende de la société Bundu (Sierra Leone).* Notes afr. I.F.A.N., **81**, janv. 1959, 8–13, ill.
1487. **N'Diaye, Samba.** *Masques d'ancêtres de la société Poro de Sierra Leone.* Notes afr. I.F.A.N., **103**, juil. 1964, 73–81, bibl., ill., map.
1488. **Notes Africaines I.F.A.N.** *Femmes de la société Bundu portant leur masque et recouvertes de fibres.* Notes afr. I.F.A.N., 81, 1959 (cover ill.).
1489. **Zeller, R.** *Jahresbericht über die ethnographische Sammlung in Bern. Beilage; über ein interessantes Steinidol aus der Sierra Leone.* Jb. Bern. hist. mus., **6**, 1926, 20–26, ill.

TECHNIQUES

1490. **Adandé, A.,** and **G. Savonnet.** *Un métier à tisser en pays Kono (Sierra Leone).* Notes afr. I.F.A.N., **61**, janv. 1954, 21–22, ill.

1491. **Easmon, M. C. F.** 1924. *Sierra Leone country cloths.* Pp. 34, ill. London: British Empire Exhibition Publications.

1492. **Hall, H. U.** 1938. *The Sherbro of Sierra Leone.* (A preliminary report on the work of the University Museum's Expedition to West Africa, 1937.) Pp. v + 51, ill., map. Philadelphia: Univ. of Pennsylvania.

1493. **Hambly, W. D.** *A trident from Sierra Leone in the collections of the Field Museum of Natural History, Chicago.* Man, **31**, no. 44, 1931, 42, ill.

1495. **Thomas, W. T.** *The industrial pursuits of the Yalunka.* Sierra Leone studies, **1**, 1918.

AFRICAN ART TODAY

1496. **Massie-Taylor.** 1961. *Traditional carvings and craft work from Sierra Leone.* London.

1496a. —— *Making ritual masks; revival in Sierra Leone.* Times, 12 Aug. 1961.

GHANA

1497. **Antubam, Kofi.** 1963. *Ghana's heritage of culture.* Pp. 222, ill. Leipzig: Koehler & Amelang.

1498. *Art and anthropology among the Akan.* West Africa, **2017**, 39, 1955, 987, ill.

1499. **Balfour, Henry.** *A collection of stone implements from Ejura, Ashanti.* J. afr. soc., **12**, 1912, 1–16.

1500. **Béart, Ch.** *Les poupées Akua ba du Ghana.* Notes afr. I.F.A.N., no. 78, 1958, 37–38, ill.

1501. **Beecham, John.** 1841. *Ashantee and the Gold Coast.* Pp. xix + 376, map. London: John Mason.

1502. **Bennet-Clark, M. C.** *Ghana.* Encyclopaedia of world art, **6**, 1962, 297–300, ill.

1503. **Cardinall, A. W.** 1927. *In Ashanti and beyond.* Pp. 279, ill., map. London: Seeley Service.

1504. **Fagg, W. B.** *Art in the Gold Coast.* W.A.R., July 1951.

1505. **Freeman, Richard Austin.** 1898. *Travels and life in Ashanti and Jaman.* Pp. xx + 559, ill., maps. Westminster: Archibald Constable.

1506. **Great Britain: Admiralty: Naval Staff Intelligence Reports.** 1919. *The Gold Coast.* Pp. 27. London: Admiralty.

1507. **Grottanelli, Vinigi L.** *Asonu worship among the Nzema; a study in Akan art and religion.* Africa, **31**, 1, Jan. 1961, 46–60, ill.

1508. **Kyerematen, A. A. Y.** 1964. *Panoply of Ghana.* Pp. viii + 120, ill. London: Longmans.

1509. **Meyerowitz, E. L. R.** 1960. *The divine kingship in Ghana and ancient Egypt.* Pp. 260, ill., map. London: Faber.

1510. **Nunoo, R. B.** *A report on the excavations at Nsuta Hill, Gold Coast.* Man, **48**, no. 90, 1948, 73–76, ill.

1511. **Rattray, R. S.** 1927. *Religion and art in Ashanti.* Pp. xviii + 414, ill. Oxford: Clarendon Press.

1512. —— 1932. *The tribes of the Ashanti hinterland.* 2 vols., ill. Oxford: Univ. Press.

1513. **Shaw, C. T.** *Archaeology in the Gold Coast.* Afr. Stud., **2**, 1943, 139–47.

1514. —— *Report on excavations carried out in the cave known as 'Bosumpra' at Abetifi, Kwahu, Gold Coast Colony.* Proc. prehist. soc., n.s., **10**, 1944, 1–67, ill.
See also 1558, 1559.

FIGURES AND MASKS

1515. **Agbley, Seth.** *The origins of idols (Ewe beliefs).* Ghana bull. theol. (Achimota), **1**, 1959, 3–11.

1516. **Bowdich, T. Edward.** 1819. *Mission from Cape Coast Castle to Ashantee.* Pp. 10, 512, ill., maps. London: John Murray. (Coloured plates of the yam customs and the decoration of houses.)

1517. **Braunholtz, H. J.** *Notes on two pottery heads from near Fomena, Ashanti.* Man, **34**, no. 2, 1934.

1518. **Davies, O.** *Human representation in terracotta from the Gold Coast.* S. Afr. J. sci., **52**, 6, janv. 1956, 147–51, ill., map.

1519. **Hinderling, Paul.** *Three human figures from near Kumasi, Ghana.* Man, **61**, no. 245, 1961, 207–8, ill.

1520. **Kerr, R.** 1924. *Clay heads from Sekondi, Gold Coast.* Man, **24**, 27, 1924, 33, ill.

1521. **Man.** *The gold mask of King Kofi of Ashanti.* Man, **51**, Jan. 1951, plate A (with description).

1522. **Segy, Ladislas.** *The Ashanti Akua'ba statues as archetype, and the Egyptian Ankh; a theory of morphological assumptions.* Anthropos, **58**, 5/6, 1963, 839–67, bibl., ill.

1523. **Sutherland, D. A.** 1954. *State emblems of the Gold Coast.* Pp. 70, ill. Accra: Govt. Printer. (1956 (2nd ed.). Pp. 80.)

1524. **Wild, R. P.,** and **H. J. Braunholtz.** *Baked clay heads from graves near Fomena, Ashanti.* Man, **34**, 1, 1934, 1–4, ill.

1525. **Wolf, S.** *Zwei Gelbguss-Masken aus Kete Kratschi.* Ann. Náprstek Museum (Prague), **1**, 1962, 173–86.

1526. **Wolfson, Freda.** 1958. *Pageant of Ghana.* Pp. xvi + 266, ill., maps. London: Oxford Univ. Press.

1527. **Zwernemann, Jürgen.** *Eine Maske aus Mittel-Ghana.* Tribus, **11**, 1962, 143–8, bibl., ill.

BUILDINGS AND FURNITURE

1528. **Griffith, Brandford W.** *Native stools on the Gold Coast* (ill.). J. afr. soc., **4**, 15, Apr. 1905, 290–4.

1529. **Mauny, R.** *Niches murales de la maison fouillée à Koumbi Saleh (Ghana).* Notes afr. I.F.A.N., **46**, 1950, 34–35, ill.

CLOTHING AND ADORNMENT

1530. **Armitage, Sir Cecil Hamilton.** 1924. *The tribal markings and marks of adornment of the natives of the Northern Territories of the Gold Coast Colony.* Pp. viii + 23, ill., map. London: Royal Anthropological Institute.

1531. **Cardinall, A. W.** *Stone armlets on the Gold Coast.* Man, 1923, no. 106.

1532. —— *Aggrey beads of the Gold Coast.* J. afr. soc., **24**, 96, July 1925, 287–98.

1533. **Delange, Jacqueline.** *The El Dorado of the Ashantis.* Unesco courier, **12**, 1959, 33–34, ill.

1534. **Fagg, W.** *Little-known examples of native art (Gold Coast).* W.A.R., **22**, 286, July 1951, 761–5, ill.

1535. **Foote, H. S.** *Gold ornaments from Ashanti.* Cleveland mus. bull., **31**, 1944, 180–1.

TECHNIQUES

1536. **Burton, William.** *A note on the black pottery from the Gold Coast and Ashanti.* Mem. and proc. Manchester lit. and phil. soc., 1912–13, 4.

1537. **Fagg, William.** *A golden ram head from Ashanti.* Man, **54**, 20, Feb. 1954, 17, ill.

1538. **Huber, Hugo.** *Traditional crafts in a Nigo village (Ghana).* Anthropos, **54**, 3/4, 1959, 574–6.

1539. **Meyerowitz, Eva L. R.** *Snake-vessels of the Gold Coast.* Man, **40**, no. 59, 1940, 48.

1540. —— *Some gold, bronze, and brass objects from Ashanti.* Burlington magazine, **139**, 526, Jan. 1947, 18–21.

1541. —— *Gold and the art of the Akan.* Africa south, **3** (1), Oct.–Dec. 1958, 103–8. (Ghana.)

1542. **Meyerowitz, H. V.** *Pottery research work at Achimota* (a broadcast talk). Gold Coast Information Department Bulletin, no. 41, May 1941.

1542a.—— *West African creative arts in the service of local industries* (four broadcast talks). Gold Coast Information Department bulletin, nos. 74, 75, 81, 82, Sept.–Oct. 1941.

1543. —— *Progress for Africans.* I.R.M., **32**, 26, Apr. 1943, 165–71.

1544. **Rattray, R. S.** *The iron-workers of Akpafu.* J. roy. anthrop. inst., **46**, 1916, 431–5, ill.

1545. —— *Arts and crafts of Ashanti.* J. afr. soc., **23**, 92, July 1924, 265–70, ill.

1546. **Shaw, C. T.** *Bead-making with a bow-drill in the Gold Coast.* J. roy. anthrop. inst., **75**, 1/2, 1945, 45–50, ill., map.

1547. **Sinclair, G. E.** *A method of bead-making in Ashanti.* Man, **39**, no. 111, 1939, 128, ill.

1548. **Wild, R. P.** *Cuttlefish bone mould casting as practised in the Gold Coast.* Gold Coast rev., **5**, 1, 1930, 144–50.

1549. —— *Unusual type of primitive iron smelting furnace at Abomposu, Ashanti.* Gold Coast rev., **5**, 1, 1930, 184–92, ill.

1550. —— *Stone Age pottery from the Cold Coast and Ashanti.* J. roy. anthrop. inst., **64**, 1934, 203–15.

1551. —— *A method of bead-making practised in the Gold Coast.* Man, **37**, no. 115, 1937, 96–97, ill.

1552. —— *The manufacture of a 'Ntiriba' hairpin at Ohuasi, Ashanti.* Man, **39**, 1939, no. 17, ill.

UTENSILS, TOOLS AND WEAPONS; MISCELLANEOUS

1552a.**Arkell, A. J.** *Gold Coast copies of 5th–7th century bronze lamps.* Antiquity, **24**, 93, Mar. 1950, 38–40, ill.

1553. **Ehsanullah, Lilian.** *Ashanti gold weights.* Nigerian field, **29**, 2, Apr. 1964, 82–88, ill.

1554. **Holas, B.** *Les poids à peser l'or.* Notes afr. I.F.A.N., 104, Oct. 1964, 113–16, ill.

1555. **Kjersmeier, Carl.** 1941. *Ashanti gold weights in the National Museum.* Pp. 99–106, ill. Copenhagen: Ethnographical Studies. Nationalmuseets Skrifter. Etnografisk Raekke 1.

1556. —— *Vaegtlodderne fra Ashanti.* Konstrevy (Stockholm), **25** (1), 1949, 33–35, ill.

1557. —— 1948. *Ashanti (gold) weights.* Pp. 24, ill. Copenhagen: Jul. Gjellerups Forlag.

1558. **Meyerowitz, Eva L. R.** 1958. *The Akan of Ghana.* Pp. 164, ill. London: Faber.

1559. —— 1951. *The sacred state of the Akan.* Pp. 222, bibl., ill., maps. London: Faber.

1560. **Paulme, Denise.** *À propos des kuduo Ashanti.* Diop, A., L'art nègre, 1951, pp. 156–62, ill.

1561. **Perregaux, Edmond.** *Chez les Achanti.* Bull. soc. neuchâteloise géog., **17**, 1906, ill., maps.

1562. **Plass, Margaret Webster.** *Poids à Or des Ashanti.* Présence africaine, **10/11**, 1951, 163–6, ill.

1563. **Rattray, R. S.** 1923. *Ashanti.* Pp. 348, ill., map. Oxford: Clarendon Press. (Goldsmiths and gold weights, p. 300.)

1564. **Rohrer, E.** *Tabakpfeifenköpfe und Sprichwörter der Asante.* Jb. Bern. hist. mus., 26 Jg., 1947, 104–21.

1565. **Schulze, L.** *Ashanti figures for weighing gold.* Bull. Transvaal Mus., **9**, July 1962, pp. 2–3, ill.

1566. **Shaw, Thurstan.** 1961. *Excavation at Dawu; report on an excavation in a mound at Dawu, Akuapim, Ghana.* Pp. viii + 124, 55 pl., bibl. Edinburgh: Nelson for University College of Ghana.

1567. **Thomas, N. W.** *Ashanti and Baule gold weights.* J. roy. anthrop. inst., **50**, 1920, 52–68, bibl.

1568. **Thomassey, P.** *Autour des poids d'or Ashanti-Baoulé.* Tom. 2, C.R. conf. intern. africanistes de l'ouest, 1951, 281–9.

1569. **Zeller, Rudolf.** *Die Goldgewichte von Asante.* Baessler-Archiv, Beiheft III, 1912, 1–77, ill.

AFRICAN ART TODAY

1570. **Antubam, Kofi.** *Arts of Ghana.* United Asia, **9** (1), 1957, 61–70.

1571. —— 1962. *Ein ghanesischer Künstler.* Berlin.

1572. **Kutscher, G.** 1947. *West-Afrika und die Moderne Kunst.* Berlin.

1573. **Lystad, Mary H.** *Paintings of Ghanaian children.* Africa, **30**, 3, July 1960, 238–42, ill.

1574. **West African Review.** *Records in wood and stone; African artists create works of art for Accra Community Centre.* W.A.R., 1951, 1042–3, ill.

1574a.—— *Portrait of an artist (Ben Enwonwu).* W.A.R., **28**, no. 352, 1957, 2–7, ill.

NIGERIA

1575. **Abraham, R. C.** 1940. *The Tiv people.* Pp. x + 177, ill., maps. London: Crown Agents. (2nd ed.)

1576. **Akenzua, E.** *Benin; 1897—a Bini's view.* Nigeria, no. 65, 1960, 177–90, ill.

1577. **Alexander, Boyd.** 1907. *From the Niger to the Nile.* 2 vols. Vol. 1, pp. xv + 358, ill., map. Vol. 2, pp. xi + 420, ill., map. London: Edward Arnold.

1578. **Alldridge, Thomas Joshua.** 1901. *The Sherbro and its hinterland.* Pp. xvi + 356, ill., maps. London: Macmillan.

1579. **Bacon, Sir R. H. S.** 1897. *Benin, the city of blood.* Pp. 151, ill., map. London: Edward Arnold.

1580. **Barth, Heinrich.** 1962. *Barth's travels in Nigeria; extracts from the journal of Heinrich Barth's travels in Nigeria, 1850–55.* A. H. M. Kirk-Greene. Pp. 312, ill., map. London. O.U.P.

1581. **Bascom, William R.** *The Yoruba in Cuba.* Nigeria, **37**, 1951, 14–20, ill.

1582. **Basden, G. T.** 1921. *Among the Ibos of Nigeria.* Pp. 306, ill., maps. London: Seeley Service.

1583. —— 1938. *Niger Ibos.* Pp. xxxii + 448, ill., map. London: Seeley Service.

1584. **Bauer, Fritz.** 1904. *Die Deutsche-Niger-Benue-Tsadsee-Expedition, 1902–1903.* Part 5, Ethnographisches. Pp. viii + 182, ill., map. Berlin: Reimer.

1585. **Baumann, H.** *Bénin.* Cah. d'Art, **7** (nos. 3–5), 1932, 197–203.

1586. **Benson, E. M.** *Benin, a dead people and a living art.* Amer. mag. of art, **29**, 1936, cover, 36–38.

1587. **Biobaku, S. O.** *The problem of traditional history with special reference to Yoruba traditions.* J. hist. soc. Nigeria, **1**, 1956, 43–47.

1588. —— *The Yoruba historical research scheme.* J. hist. soc. Nigeria, **1**, 1956, 59–60.

1589. —— 1957. *The Egba and their neighbours, 1842–1872.* Pp. 128, maps. Oxford: Clarendon Press.

1590. **Boisragon, Alan.** 1897. *The Benin massacre.* Pp. 190, ill., map. London. Methuen.

1591. **Corbeau, J.** *L'Empire du Bénin.* Écho missions afr. (Lyon), **49** (3), 1950, 10–12; **51** (6), 1952, 90–94, ill.

1592. **Court, J. W.** *Pictures in Northern Nigeria.* Oversea education, **31** (3), 1959, 120–4.

1593. **Damm, Hans.** 1961. *Beiträge zur Völkerforschung Hans Damm zum 65 Geburtstag.* Pp. 752, bibl., ill., maps. (Verzeichnis der Schriften und Vorlesungen von Hans Damm.) Berlin: Akademie-Verlag.

1594. **Da Mota (Avelino Teixeira).** *Novos elementos sobre a acção dos portugueses e franceses em Benin na primeira metade do século XVI.* Bol. cultural Guiné Portug., **7** (27), 1952, 525–31.

1595. **D'Avezac, K.** 1844. *Notice sur le pays et peuple des Yébous (Yoruba) en Afrique.* Pp. 203, map. Paris: Dondey-Dupré.

1596. **Davidson, Basil.** *Yoruba achievement; art flourished when Old Oyo held sway (Empires of old Africa, 3).* W.A.R., **33**, 414, June 1962, 17–21 and 43, ill.

1597. **Dayrell, E.** *Further notes on 'Nsibidi' signs with their meanings from the Ikom district, Southern Nigeria.* J. roy. anthrop. inst., **41**, 1911, 521–40, ill.

1598. **Denham, Dixon.** 1831. *Travels and discoveries in Northern and Central Africa in 1822–24.* 4 vols., ill., maps. London: John Murray.

1599. **Dennett, R. E.** *At the back of the black man's mind.* Pp. xv + 288, ill. London: Macmillan.

1600. —— 1910. *Nigerian studies.* Pp. xiii + 232, ill., map. London: Macmillan.

1601. **Desplagnes, Louis.** 1907. *Le plateau central Nigérien.* Pp. 504, ill., map. Paris: Larose.

1602. **Eisner, A.** *(Nigeria) Letter from Africa.* Art digest, **21**, 1947, 23.

1603. **Ekandem, M. J.** *The use of plants as symbols in Ibibio and Ibo country.* Nigerian field, **20**, 1955, 53–64, ill.

1604. **Ellis, Alfred Burdon.** 1894. *The Yoruba-speaking peoples of the Slave Coast of West Africa.* Pp. 402. London: Chapman & Hall.

1605. **Forde, Daryll,** and **G. I. Jones.** 1950. *The Ibo and Ibibio-speaking peoples of South-Eastern Nigeria.* Pp. 94, bibl., map. London: International African Institute. (Ethnographic Survey of Africa: Western Africa, part 3.)

1606. —— 1951. *The Yoruba-speaking peoples of South-Western Nigeria.* Pp. (6), 102, bibl., map. London: International African Institute. (Ethnographic Survey of Africa: Western Africa, part 4.)

1607. —— and **Others.** 1955. *Peoples of the Niger-Benue confluence. The Nupe,* by Daryll Forde. *The Igbira,* by Paula Brown. *The Igala,* by Robert G. Armstrong. *The Idoma-speaking peoples,* by Robert G. Armstrong. Pp. xiv + 160, bibl., map. London: International African Institute. (Ethnographic Survey of Africa: Western Africa, part 10.)

1608. —— 1956. *Efik traders of Old Calabar.* Pp. xiii + 166, bibl. London: International African Institute: Oxford Univ. Press.

1609. **Gunn, Harold D.** 1953. *Peoples of the plateau area of Northern Nigeria.* Pp. viii + 110, bibl., map. London: International African Institute. (Ethnographic Survey of Africa: Western Africa, part 7.)

1610. **Hambly, Wilfrid D.** 1935. *Culture areas of Nigeria.* Pp. 365–502, bibl., ill., maps. Chicago: Field Museum. (Field Museum of Natural History: Anthropological Series, vol. 21, no. 3.)

1611. **Jeffreys, M. D. W.** *The burial bird for an Okuku.* Afr. stud., **14** (3), 1955, 134–7, ill.

1612. **Jensen, Ad.** *Les orbes culturels de l'Afrique.* Cah. d'art, **5**, 8/9, 1930, 444–8.

1613. *Katsina.* Nigeria, **51**, 1956, 299–317, ill.

1614. **Kingsley, Mary H.** 1897. *Travels in West Africa, Congo français, Corisco and Cameroons.* Pp. xvi + 743, ill. London: Macmillan.

1615. —— 1901. *West African studies.* Pp. xxxii + 507, ill., map. London: Macmillan. (2nd ed.)

1616. **Johnson, S.** 1937. *The history of the Yoruba.* Pp. 684. London: Routledge.

1617. **Jones, G. I.** *Art of South-Eastern Nigeria.* Pp. 60 (approx). Museum of Archaeology and Ethnology, Cambridge. MS. (typescript).

1618. **Joset, Paul Ernest.** 1955. *Les sociétés secrètes des hommes-léopards en Afrique Noire.* Pp. 276, bibl., ill. Paris: Payot.

1619. **Lander, Richard** and **John.** 1832. *Journal of an expedition to explore the course and termination of the Niger.* 3 vols. London: John Murray.

1620. **Manoukian, M.** 1950. *The Akan and Ga-Adangwe peoples of the Gold Coast.* Pp. 108, map. 1952. *The Ewe-speaking people of Togoland and the Gold Coast.* Pp. 61, map. 1952. *Tribes of the Northern Territories of the Gold Coast.* Pp. 102, map. London. Int. Afr. Inst. (Ethnographic Survey of Africa: Western Africa, parts 1, 5 and 6.)

1621. **Mattei, Le Commandant.** 1890. *Bas-Niger, Bénoué Dahomey.* Pp. xv + 196, ill., map. Grenoble: Baratier Frères.

1622. **Meek, C. K.** 1931. *Tribal studies in Northern Nigeria.* Vol. 1, pp. viii + 633. Vol. 2, ill., maps. London: Oxford Univ. Press.

1623. —— 1931. *A Sudanese kingdom.* Pp. xxxiii + 548, ill., maps. London: Kegan Paul.

1624. **Morton-Williams, Peter.** *Yoruba responses to the fear of death.* Africa, **30**, 1960, 34–40, ill.

1625. **Murray, K. C.** *Our art treasures.* Lagos, Nigeria. Pp. 16. Public Relations Dept.

1626. —— *Art in Nigeria; need for a museum.* J. afr. soc., **41**, 165, Oct. 1942, 241–9.

1627. —— *Oloku (Yoruba god).* Nigeria, **35**, 1950, 364–5, ill.

1628. **Nadel, S. F.** 1942. *A black Byzantium.* Pp. xiv + 420, bibl., ill., maps. London: Oxford Univ. Press. (Published for the International Institute of African Languages and Cultures.)

1629. **Nicol, D.** *Twins in Yorubaland.* W.A.R., **28**, 360, 1957, 845–7, ill.

1630. **Rattray, R. S.** 1913. *Hausa folk-lore, customs, proverbs, etc.* 2 vols. Vol. 1, pp. xxiv + 326, ill. Vol. 2, pp. 315, ill. Oxford: Univ. Press.

1631. **Robinson, Charles Henry.** 1896. *Hausaland or fifteen hundred miles through the central Sudan.* Pp. xv + 304, ill., maps. London: Sampson Low.

1632. —— 1900. *Nigeria; our latest protectorate.* Pp. xii + 223, ill., map. London: Horace Marshall.

1633. **Singer, Caroline,** and **Cyrus Le Roy Baldridge.** 1929. *White Africans and black.* Pp. 120, ill., map. New York: W. W. Norton.

1634. **Slye, Jonathan.** *Gwari people and their art; traditional skills and affinity with nature.* African world, Nov. 1964, 6–8, ill.

1635. **Staschewski, F.** *Die Banyangi.* Baessler Archiv, **7**, 1917 (Beihefte 8), 66, ill.

1636. **Talbot, P. Amaury.** *The land of the Ekoi.* Geog. J., **36**, no. 6, 637–57.

1637. —— 1912. *In the shadow of the bush.* Pp. xiv + 500, ill., map. London: Heinemann.

1638. —— 1915. *Woman's mysteries of a primitive people; the Ibibios of Southern Nigeria.* Pp. 252, ill. London: Cassell.

1639. —— 1932. *Tribes of the Niger Delta.* Pp. xi + 350, ill., map. London: Sheldon Press.

1640. **Thomas, Northcote W.** 1913. *Anthropological report on the Ibo-speaking peoples of Nigeria.* Part 1, Law and custom of the Ibo of the Awka neighbourhood, S. Nigeria. Pp. 161, ill., maps. London: Harrison.

1641. **Tremearne, Arthur John Newman.** *Some Nigerian head-hunters.* J. roy. anthrop. inst., **42**, 1912, 136–99, ill.

1642. —— 1912. *The tailed head-hunters of Nigeria.* Pp. xvi + 342, ill., map. London: Seeley Service.

1643. —— 1913. *Hausa superstitions and customs.* Pp. xv + 548, ill., map. London: John Bale & Danielsson.

1644. —— 1914. *The Ban of the Bori; demons and demon-dancing in West and North Africa.* Pp. 497, ill. London: Heath, Cranton & Ouseley.

1645. **Tschudi, Jolantha.** *Aus dem sozialen Leben der Afo, Hügelland von Nasarawa, Nigeria.* Baessler-Archiv, **4** (2), 1956, 147–71, ill.

1646. **Watson, C. B. G.** *Death and burial among the Yakoro and Yache peoples of Ogoja Division, Southern Nigeria.* Man, **30**, no. 66, 1930, 81–84, ill.

1647. **Wescott, Joan.** 1958. *Yoruba art in German and Swiss Museums.* Pp. 38, ill. Ibadan: Yoruba Historical Research Scheme.

1648. —— *Tradition and the Yoruba artist.* Athene, **2** (1), 1963, 9–16, ill.

1649. —— and **P. Morton-Williams.** *The festival of Iya Mapo.* Nigeria, **58**, 1958, 212–24, ill.

1650. **Wescott, Roger W.** *Did the Yoruba come from Egypt?* Odù, **4** (1958), 10–15.

FIGURES AND MASKS

1651. **Ademakinwa, J. A.** 1958. *Ife, cradle of the Yoruba, parts 1 and 2; a handbook on the history of the origin of the Yorubas.* Pp. 88, 56. Lagos: Pacific Printing Works.

1652. **Aderemi, Oni of Ife.** *Notes on the city of Ife.* Nigeria, **12,** 1937, 3–7, ill.

1653. **Akeredolu, J. D.** *Thorn figure carving.* Nigeria, **14,** 1938, 134–6, ill.

1654. —— *Thorn carvings by native Nigerian artist.* Design, **47,** 1945, 8, ill.

1655. —— *Ife bronzes.* Nigeria magazine, no. 59, 1958, 341–53, ill.

1656. **Akpata, Akitola.** *Benin; notes on altars and bronze heads.* Ethnologia Cranmorensis, **1,** 1937, 1–10, ill.

1657. **Aldred, Cyril.** *A bronze cult object from Southern Nigeria.* Man, **49,** 47, April 1949, 38–39, ill.

1658. **Allison, Philip A.** *Newly discovered stone figures from the Yoruba village of Ijara, Northern Nigeria.* Man, **63,** 115, June 1963, 93–94, ill.

1659. —— *A terra-cotta head in the Ife style from Ikirun, Western Nigeria.* Man, **63,** no. 194, 1963, 156–7, ill.

1660. —— *A carved stone figure of Eshu from Igbajo, Western Nigeria.* Man, **64,** 131, July–Aug. 1964, 104–5, ill.

1661. **Anon.** *Bamenda brass.* Nigeria, **55,** 1957, 344–55, ill.

1662. **Armstrong, R. G.** *The religions of the Idoma.* Ibadan, **13,** 1961, 5–9.

1663. **Arriens, C.** *Die heiligen Steinfiguren von Ife.* Erdball, **4,** 9, 1930, 333–41, ill.

1664. **Art News.** *Benin art seen in Paris show.* Art news, **30,** 1932, 6.

1665. —— *Benin bronze panthers from the Ratton Collection.* Art news, **34,** 1935, 11.

1666. **Balfour, Henry.** *Ceremonial paddle of the Kalabari of Southern Nigeria.* Man, **17,** no. 44, 1917, 57–58, ill.

1667. **Bascom, William R.** *Brass portrait heads from Ile-Ife, Nigeria.* Man, **38,** 1938, 176.

1668. —— *The legacy of an unknown Nigerian 'Donatello'; The simple beauty of the mysterious bronze heads recently discovered at Ife.* I.L.N., Apr. 1939, 592–4, ill.

1669. —— *Odu Ifa; The names of the figures of Ifa.* (Submitted to Odu 1959.)

1669a. —— *Odu Ifa; The order of the figures of Ifa.* (Submitted to Odu 1959.)

1670. **Basden, G. T.** 1938. *Niger Ibos.* Pp. xxxii + 448, ill., map. London: Seeley Service.

1671. **Baumann, H.,** and **Others.** *Bronzes et ivories du Benin au Musée d'Ethnographie, Palais du Trocadéro.* Cah. d'art, **7,** 1932.

1672. **Beier, H. Ulli.** *Festival of the images.* Nigeria, **45,** 1954, 14–20, ill.

1673. —— *Yoruba cement sculpture.* Nigeria, **46,** 1955, 144–53.

1674. —— *The Oba's festival, Ondo.* Nigeria magazine, no. 50, 1956, 238–59, ill.

1675. —— *Ibibio monuments.* Nigerian magazine, no. 51, 1956, 318–36, ill.

1675a. —— *The Egungun cult.* Nigerian magazine, no. 51, 1956, 380–92, ill.

1676. —— *Oshun festival.* Nigeria magazine, no. 53, 1957, 170–87, ill.

1677. —— 1957. *The story of sacred woodcarvings from one small Yoruba town.* Ed. by D. W. Macrow. Pp. 13 + 37 pl. + 3 f. Marina, Lagos, Nigeria: Nigeria magazine.

1678. —— *The bochio, a little-known type of African carving.* Black Orpheus (Ibadan), **3,** May 1958, 28–31, ill.

1679. —— *Shango shrine.* Black Orpheus (Ibadan), **4,** 1958, 30–35, ill.

1680. —— *Ori-oke festival, Iragbiji.* Nigeria magazine, no. 56, 1958, 65–83, ill.

1681. —— *Gelede masks.* Odù (Ibadan), 6, June 1958, 5–23, ill.

1682. —— 1960. *Art in Nigeria.* Pp. 24, ill. London: Cambridge Univ. Press.

1683. —— 1963. *African mud sculpture.* Pp. 96, ill. London: Cambridge Univ. Press.

1684. **Bertho, J.,** and **Mauny, R.** *Archéologie du pays Yoruba et du Bas-Niger.* Notes afr. I.F.A.N., 56, Oct. 1952, 97–115, bibl., ill., map.

1685. **Blauensteiner, Kurt.** *Bildwerke aus Benin im Wiener Museum für Völkerkunde.* Belvedere, **10,** 1931, 63–67, ill.

1686. **Boston, D.** *An early Benin bronze.* Liverpool Libraries, Museums and Arts Committee bull., **7,** no. 1, 1958, 3, ill. (on front cover).

1687. **Boston, John Shipway.** *Alosi shrines in Udi Division.* Nigeria, **61,** 1959, 157–65, ill.

1688. —— *Some Northern Ibo masquerades.* J. roy. anthrop. inst., **90,** 1960, 54–65, bibl., ill.

1689. **Bouchaud, J. R. P.** *Les Portugais dans la Baie de Biafra au XVIeme siècle.* Africa, **16,** 1946, 217–27, ill., map. (Four Benin plaques from B.M.)

1690. **Bradbury, R. E.,** and **P. C. Lloyd.** 1957. *The Benin kingdom and the Edo-speaking peoples of South-Western Nigeria . . . together with a section on the Itsekiri* (by P. C. Lloyd). Pp. xii + 210, bibl., map. London: Int. Afr. Inst. (Ethnographic Survey of Africa: Western Africa, part 13.)

1691. —— *Divine kingship in Benin.* Nigeria magazine, no. 62, 1959, 186–207, ill.

1692. —— *Chronological problems in the study of Benin history.* J. hist. soc. Nigeria, **1,** 4, 1959, 263–87.

1693. —— *Ezomo's ikegobo and the Benin cult of the hand.* Man, **61,** no. 165, 1961, 129–38, ill.

1694. **Braunholtz, H. J.** *Two bronze plaques from Benin.* Man, **22,** no. 91, 1922, 161–2.

1695. —— *Bronze head from Ife, Nigeria.* B.M.Q., **14** (4), 1940.

1696. —— *The bronze heads of Ife, Nigeria.* Congr. int. sci. anthrop. et ethnol., 3e Session, Bruxelles, 1948 (1960), 22–24.

1697. **Brinkmann, J.** *Die Bronzen von Benin.* Korrespondenzblatt der deutschen gesellschaft f. anthropologie, **29,** 1898, 62.

1698. **Brinkworth, Ian.** *Benin 'city of blood' and bronze.* Geog. mag., **27,** 1954–5, 248–55, ill., map.

1699. —— *Nigeria's cultural heritage.* Geog. mag., **31** (9), 1959, 425–38, ill., map.

1700. —— *Mud sculpture of Benin.* W.A.R., **31,** 390, 1960, 30–31, ill.

1701. **Bunt, C. G. E.** *Two examples of Nigerian wood-carving.* Burlington magazine, **82,** 483, June 1943, 146–9, pl.

1702. **Butler, Vincent F.** *Cement funeral sculpture in Eastern Nigeria.* Nigeria magazine, **77,** June 1963, 117–24, ill.

1703. **Carré, L.** *Benin, city of bronzes.* Parnassus, **8,** 1953, 13–15.

1704. **Carroll, K.** *Yoruba masks (North-East Yoruba country).* Odù, **3,** 1956, 3–15, ill.

1705. —— *Ekiti Yoruba wood-carving.* Odù, **4,** 1958, 3–9, ill.

1706. **Caturla, Eduardo del Val.** *Benin.* Africa (Madrid), **49–50,** 1946, 28–30, ill.; **51,** 1946, 80–82, ill.

1707. —— *Busto de bronce de Benin.* Cuadernos de hist. primitiva (Madrid), **1,** 2, 1946, 102–3, ill.

1708. —— *Benin la ciudad cruenta.* Africa (Madrid), **49–50,** 1946, 28–30, ill.

1709. **Chukuegga, Aggu.** *History of the Kemalu Juju.* Nigeria, no. 39, 1952, 252–3, ill.

1710. **Clarke, J. D.** *Carved posts at Old Oyo.* Nigeria, **15,** 1938, 248–9, ill.

1711. —— *Yoruba wood-carving.* Nigeria, **14,** 1938, 140–53.

1712. —— *The stone figures of Esie.* Nigeria, **14,** 1938, 106–8.

1713. **Connoisseur** (Am. ed.). *Benin ivory.* Connoisseur, **128,** 1951, 143.

1714. **Cordwell, T. M.** 1952. *Some aesthetic aspects of Yoruba and Benin cultures.* (MS. thesis: Dept. of Anthropology, Northwestern University, Evanston, Ill.)

1715. **Correia, Miguel Pupo.** *Por Terras de Benim . . . Dahomé—O Reino da Serpente.* Mensário admin., **61/62,** 1952, 5–12, ill.

1716. **Crocker, H. E.** *The bronzes of Ife.* J. afr. soc., **42,** 1943, 38–39.

1717. **Dalton, O. M.** *Works of art from Benin-City.* J. anthrop. inst., **27,** 1898, 362–82, ill.

1718. —— *Note on an unusually fine bronze figure from Benin.* Man, **3,** no. 105, 1903, 185, ill.

1719. **Daniel, F.** *Note on a gong of bronze from Katsina, Nigeria.* Man, **29**, Sept. 1929, 157–8.

1720. —— *The stone figures of Esie, Ilorin Province, Nigeria.* J. roy. anthrop. inst., **67**, 1937, 43–50, ill.

1721. —— *Stone sculpture in Nigeria. Stone figures at Ofaro.* Nigeria, **18**, 1939, 107–9, ill.

1722. —— *Figures at Jebba and Tada.* Nigeria, **20**, 1940, 282–4.

1723. **Dark, Philip John Crossley.** *Benin; a West African kingdom.* Discovery (London), May 1957, 199–206, ill.

1724. —— *A preliminary catalogue of Benin art and technology; some problems of material culture analysis.* J. roy. anthrop. inst., **87**, 1957, 175–89.

1725. —— *West African bronzes.* Afr. South, **3**, 1959, 109–16, ill.

1726. —— (introd.). 1961. *Benin art.* (Photographs by W. and B. Forman.) Pp. 59 + 94 pl., map. London: Hamlyn. (Rev.: Nigeria mag., **71**, Dec. 1961, 373–8, ill. K. C. Murray.)

1727. —— *Two bronze heads from Benin.* Scottish art rev., **8**, 1, 1961, 5–11.

1728. **Della Santa, E.** *Deux remarquables ivoires nigériens de la collection de . . . le Prince et Princesse de Ligne au Château de Beloeil.* Bull. mus. roy. belge, d'art et d'hist., 30e ann. 4e serie, 1958, 111–32, ill.

1729. **Dike, K. O.** *The Benin scheme begins.* Corona, **9**, 1957, 325–8.

1730. —— *The kingdom of Benin.* Unesco courier, **12**, 1959, 12–14, ill.

1731. **Dresler, A.** *Die Siegener Taufschüssel, ein Zeugnis der sogenannten 'Benin-Kultur'.* Deutsche Kolon. Ztg., 1940, 52, Jg., 9, 176–7.

1732. **Drayer, Walter.** 1962. *Nigeria; 2000 Jahre afrikanischer Plastik.* Pp. 64, ill. München: Piper-Bücherei.

1733. **Duckworth, E. H.** *Recent archaeological discoveries in the ancient city of Ife.* Nigeria, no. 14, 1938, 101–4.

1734. —— *The bronze heads of Ife.* Nigeria, no. 21, 1940, 341–2, ill.

1735. **Eccles, Polly.** *Nupe bronzes.* Nigeria magazine, no. 73, June 1962, 13–25, ill., map.

1736. **Egharevba, Jacob U.** *Art and craft work in the city of Benin.* Nigeria, **18**, 1939, 105–6, ill.

1737. —— 1951. *Some tribal gods of Southern Nigeria.* Pp. 59, ill. Benin City: Author.

1738. —— 1960. *A short history of Benin.* Pp. xvi + 102, ill. Ibadan: Ibadan Univ. Press.

1739. **Einstein, C.** *Masque de danse rituelle Ekoi.* Documents, **7**, 1927, 396.

1740. **Elgee, C. H.** *The Ife stone carvings.* J. afr. soc., **7**, 1907–8, 338–43, ill.

1741. **Ema, A. J. Udo.** *The Ekpe society.* Nigeria, no. 16, 1938, 314–16, ill.

1742. **Fagg, Bernard.** *A preliminary note on a new series of pottery figures from Northern Nigeria.* Africa, **15**, 1, Jan. 1945, 21–22.

1743. —— *Figures from Northern Nigeria.* Nigeria digest, **1**, 5, May 1945, 5–6, ill.

1744. —— *Primitive art of problematic age; North Nigerian heads now at the British Museum.* I.L.N., Apr. 1947, 442–3, ill.

1745. —— *New discoveries from Ife on exhibition at the Royal Anthropological Institute.* Man, **49**, 79, June 1949, 61, ill.

1746. —— *A life-size terra-cotta head from Nok.* Man, **46**, 95, July 1956, 89, ill.

1747. —— *A fertility figure of unrecorded style from Northern Nigeria.* Man, **48**, 140, Nov. 1948, 125, ill.

1748. —— *The Nok culture.* W.A.R., **27**, 351, Dec. 1956, 1083–7, ill.

1749. —— *The Nok culture in prehistory.* J. hist. soc. Nigeria, **1**, 4, Dec. 1959, 288–93, ill.

1750. —— *Masterpieces of early Nigerian art; recently discovered figurines of a primitive culture in the Nok valley.* I.L.N., **213**, 1948, 586–7.

1751. —— *The Nok terra-cottas in West African art history.* Actes 4e congrès panafricain de préhistoire. . . . (ed. G. Mortelmans, and J. Nenquin), sect. 3, 1962, 445–50.

1752. —— and **William.** *Remarkable new finds at Ife, Western Nigeria.* Man, **58**, Jan. 1958, pl. A.

1753. —— and **William.** *The ritual stools of ancient Ife.* Man, **60**, no. 155, 1960, 113–15, ill.

1754. **Fagg, William B.** *A mask from Jaman, Western Gold Coast.* B.M.Q., **15**, 1941–50, 108–9, ill.

1755. —— *An Epa mask from North-East Yorubaland.* B.M.Q., **15**, 1941–50, 109–11.

1756. —— *Art without age (mostly Nigeria).* Corona, **2**, 1, Jan. 1950, 24–26, ill.

1757. —— *Un art sans âge.* Jeune afr. (Elizabethville), 1950, 4–11, ill.

1758. —— *A bronze figure in Ife style at Benin.* Man, **50**, 98, June 1950, 69–70, ill.

1759. —— *Antiquities of Ife.* Magazine of art, **43**, 1950, 129–33.

1760. —— tr. by Arnaud, Marthe. *L'art nigérien avant Jésus-Christ.* Diop, A., L'art nègre, 1951, 91–95.

1761. —— *Tribal sculpture and the festival of Britain—the art style of Owo.* Man, **51**, 124, June 1951, 73–76, ill.

1762. —— *Nigerian antiquities in the Oldman collection.* B.M.Q., **16**, 1951, 106–9, ill.

1763. —— *De l'art des Yoruba.* Présence afr., **10–11**, 1951, 103–33, ill.

1764. —— *The sibylline books of tribal art.* Blackfriars (Oxford), **33**, 382, Jan. 1952, 38–44, ill.

1765. —— *A Nigerian bronze figure from the Benin expedition.* Man, **52**, 210, Oct. 1952, 145, ill.

1766. —— *The Allman collection of Benin antiquities.* Man, **53**, no. 261, 1953, 165–9, bibl., ill.

1767. —— *The Seligman ivory mask from Benin.* Man, **57**, 143, Aug. 1957, 113, ill.

1768. —— *On a Benin bronze plaque representing a girl.* Man, **58**, 154, July 1958, 105, ill.

1769. —— 1958. *The latest Ife finds, with a note by William Fagg.* Pp. 12, ill. New York: Museum of Primitive Art.

1770. —— *Ife and Benin; two pinnacles of African art.* Unesco courier, **12**, 10, Oct. 1959, 15–19, ill.

1771. —— *Cire-Perdue casting. 7 metals of Africa,* by Plass, Margaret, and Others. 1959. Pp. 5, ill.

1772. —— *On a stone head of variant style at Esie, Nigeria.* Man, **59**, 60, Mar. 1959, 41, ill.

1773. —— *Mysterious bronzes of Jebba and Tada, Northern Nigeria.* I.L.N., **236**, Feb. 1920, 297–9.

1774. —— *Another Yoruba hunter's shrine.* Man, **59**, no. 335, 1959, 216–17.

1775. —— (photographs by Herbert List). 1963. *Nigerian images.* Pp. 1–40 + 117–24 text, 144 pl, bibl., map. London: Lund Humphries.

1776. —— and **H. List.** 1963. *Bildwerke aus Nigeria.* Pp. 124, ill. Munich.

1777. —— and **Leon Underwood.** *An examination of the so-called 'Olokun' head of Ife, Nigeria.* Man, **49**, 1, Jan. 1949, 1–7, ill.

1778. —— and **F. Willett.** *Ancient Ife; an ethnographical summary.* Actes du IVe congrès panafricain de préhistoire, 1962. Pp. 357–73, bibl., ill. (First published in Odù, No. 8, 1960.)

1779. **Farrow, Stephen S.** 1924. *Faith, fancies and fetich or Yoruba paganism.* Pp. xi + 180, ill. London: S.P.C.K.

1780. **Filesi, Teobaldo.** *L'arte misteriosa e sorprendente di Ife.* Universo, no. 2, Apr. 1960, 315–28, ill.

1781. **Forbes, H. O.** *On a collection of cast metalwork from Benin.* Bull. Liverpool museum, **1**, 1897, 49; **2**, 1899, 13.

1781a. **Forman, W.,** and **B.** 1961. *Benin art.* Pp. 59, ill., map. London: Hamlyn.

1782. **Friend, D.** *Stone sculpture in Nigeria. Carved stones at Effon.* Nigeria, **18**, 1939, 108.

1783. —— *Masks.* Nigeria, **18**, 1939, 100–4, ill.

1784. **Frobenius, Leo.** *Terrakotten aus Ife.* Feuer (Weimar), **3**, 1921, 26, ill.

1785. **Galway, Sir Henry,** and **G. P. L. Miles.** *Benin.* (Additional notes by G. P. L. Miles.) Ethnologia Cranmorensis, **3**, 1938, 3–8, ill.

1786. **Garlanda, Ugo.** *Areopago di idoli in Nigeria.* Africa (Milan), **13** (1), 1958, 27–31, ill. (Ancient soapstone of Esie.)

1787. **Gaskell, W.** *The influence of Europe on early Benin art.* Connoisseur, June 1902.

1788. **Goodwin, A. J. H.** (*ed.* W. Fagg). *A bronze snake head and other recent finds in the old palace at Benin.* Man, **63**, 174, Sept. 1963, 142–5, ill.

1789. **Hagen, Karl.** 1900–18. *Altertümer von Benin im Hamburgischen Museum für Völkerkunde.* Teil 1 (1900), pp. 26, ill. Teil 2 (1918), pp. 90, bibl., ill. Hamburg: Lütcke u. Wulff. (Mitt. Mus. Völkerk., Hamburg, 6.)

1790. **Hall, H. U.** *Some Gods of the Yoruba.* Museum journal (Univ. of Pennsylvania, Philadelphia, Pa.), **8** (1), 1917, 5, ill.

1791. —— *Great Benin royal altar.* Museum journal (Univ. of Pennsylvania, Philadelphia, Pa.), **13**, 1922, 105–67, ill.

1792. —— *An ivory standing cup from Benin.* Museum journal (Univ. of Pennsylvania, Philadelphia, Pa.), **17** (4), 1926, 414–32, ill.

1793. —— *A large drum from Benin.* Museum journal (Univ. of Pennsylvania, Philadelphia, Pa.), **19**, 1928, 130–43, ill.

1794. **Harris, Rosemary L.** *A note on sculptured stones in the Mid-Cross river.* Man, **59**, no. 177, 1959, 113–14.

1795. **Hau, Kathleen.** *A royal title on a palace tusk from Benin.* Bull. I.F.A.N., **26** (B), 1/2, janv.–avr. 1964, 21–39, ill.

1796. **Heger, Franz.** *Benin und seine Alterthümer.* Mitt. anthrop. gesell. (Wien.), **29**, 1899, Sitzungsb. 2–6.

1797. —— *Die Altertümer von Benin.* Mitt. geog. gesell. (Wien), **44**, Heft 1 and 2, 1901, 9–28, ill.

1798. —— *Drei Merkwürdige Bronze Figuren von Benin; mit einem Anhange—Die Benin-Sammlung des Naturhistorischen Hofmuseums in Wien.* Mitt. anthrop. gesell. (Wien), **46**, 1916, 132–82, ill.

1799. —— *Merkwürdige Altertümer aus Benin in West-Afrika. Anlässlich der Herausgabe des Werkes F. v. Luschan 'Die Altertümer von Benin'.* Mitt. geog. gesell. (Wien), Heft 4–9, 1921, 1–16.

1800. —— *Nigeria—Archaeology.* Ymer, 1921, 25–46, ill.

1801. **Hooton, E. A.** *Benin antiquities in the Peabody Museum.* Harvard African studies, **1**, 1917, 130–46, ill.

1802. **Ingham, K.** 1955. *An introduction to the art of Ife.* Pp. 28, ill. Lagos: The Nigerian Museum.

1803. **Jeffreys, M. D. W.** *Awka wood carvers, by 'Ntokon'.* Nigerian field, **2**, Dec. 1931, 35–39, ill.

1804. —— *Sacred twinned vessels (from Awka and Agu).* Man, **39**, 129, Sept. 1939, 137–8, ill.

1805. —— *Some notes on the Ekoi.* J. roy. anthrop. inst., **69**, 1939, 95–108, ill.

1806. —— *The Oreri mask.* Nigerian field, **10**, Oct. 1941, 140–2.

1807. —— *The origins of the Benin bronzes.* Afr. stud., **10**, 1951, 87–91.

1808. —— *Those Benin bronzes; An explanation of the puzzle offered.* W.A.R., **23**, 292, Jan. 1952, 5–8, ill.

1809. —— *Ikenyga; the Ibo ram-headed God.* Afr. stud., **13** (1), 1954, 25–40, ill.

1810. —— *Altars or sacred stools; the Ibo 'Tazza' or 'Ada'.* Man, **55**, no. 46, 1955, 42–44, ill.

1811. —— *Ibo club heads.* Man, **57**, no. 63, 1957, 57–58, ill.

1812. —— *A wood-carver's sample (Banso).* Man, **62**, 261, Nov. 1962, 169–70, ill.

1813. **Jensen, A.** *De la technique à employer pour recueillir les poésies africaines (Ife heads).* Cah. d'art, 5, 1930, 431–43.

1814. **Jones, G. I.** *The distribution of negro sculpture in S. Nigeria.* Nigerian field, **7**, 3, 1938, 102–8, ill., map.

1815. —— *On the identity of two masks from S.E. Nigeria in the British Museum.* Man, **39**, 35, 1939, 33–34, pl. (Identifies the two masks as being from the Ada area of the Eastern Ibo.)

1816. —— *Masked plays of South-Eastern Nigeria.* Geog. mag., **18**, 5, Sept. 1945, 190–9. (Ibo, Ibibio and Ijaw plays.)

1817. —— *Some Nigerian masks.* Geog. mag., **18**, 5, Sept. 1945, 200, pl. (Ibo, Ijaw and Ibibio masks.)

1818. **Jones, R. W.** *Orisa Oko; the Yoruba goddess of the farm and agriculture.* Nigeria, **23**, 1946, 118–21, ill.

1819. **Joyce, T. A.** *Note on a carved door and three fetish staves from Northern Nigeria.* Man, **3**, 100, 1903, 177–9, ill.

1820. —— *Note on the relation of the bronze heads to the carved tusks, Benin City.* Man, **8**, 2, 1908, 2–4, ill. (Further note on above by C. Punch, Man, **8**, 44, 1908, 84, ill.)

1821. —— *An ivory ewer from Benin in the British Museum.* Man, **31**, 1931, 1–2, ill.

1822. **Kiéner, L.** *Notices sur les fétiches des populations Bassoundi (Yoruba) . . . de Pangala.* Bull. soc. rech. congol., **1**, 1, 1922, 21–27.

1823. **Kiewe, Heinz E.** *Nigerian sculpture of a Jewish trader.* Jewish quart. rev. (Philadelphia, Penn., U.S.A.), **44**, 2, Oct. 1953, 162–8, ill.

1824. **Krieger, Kurt.** *Terrakotten und Steinplastiken aus Ife, Nigeria.* Berliner Museen, N.F. **5**, 3, 4, 1955, 32–39, bibl., ill.

1825. —— *Das Schicksal der Benin-Sammlung des Berliner Museums für Völkerkunde.* Baessler-Arch., N.F. **5**, 2, 1957, 225–32.

1826. **Kus-Nikolajev, Mirko.** 1931. *Beninska Plastika i Problem Migracije (Crtezi Zdenke Sertic).* Pp. 32, ill., map. Zagreb: Etnoloska Biblioteka, 13.

1827. **Küsters, M.** *Die figürlichen Darstellungen auf den Beninzähnen des Linden Museums Stuttgart.* 50. Jahresber. des Württ. Ver. f. Handelsgeogr., 1932, 116–20 (mit Tafel V).

1828. **Labouret, Henri.** *Les arts du Bénin.* Le monde colon. ill., no. 108, Août 1932, no. 150–2.

1829. —— *Les bronzes de cire-perdue du Bénin.* Cah. d'art, **7**, 1932, 204–8.

1830. **Lagos; Nigerian Museum.** 1955. *The art of Ife.* Pp. 28, ill. Lagos: Nigerian Museum.

1831. **Lallemand, Jacqueline.** *Ivoires et bronzes du Bénin.* Art et décoration, **61**, 1932, 257–64, ill.

1832. **Lannert, E.** *Ekwechi-Anokehi festival.* Nigeria magazine, no. 80, 1964, 44–56, ill.

1833. **Leith-Ross, S.** *Une figurine à coupe.* Man, **30**, 1930, 16.

1834. **Lindblom, K. G.** *Einige Benin-Bronzen im Staatl. Ethnographischen Museum in Stockholm.* Z. f. Ethnol., **70**, 3–5, 1939, 193–8.

1835. **Linné, S.** *Masterpiece of primitive art.* Ethnos, **29** (2–4), 58, 172–4. (Seligman ivory mask from Benin.)

1836. **Lloyd, Peter.** *Craft organization in Yoruba towns.* Africa, **23**, 1, Jan. 1953, 30–44.

1837. **Lombard, J.** *À propos des pierres sculptées d'Ifé.* Notes afr. I.F.A.N., **68**, Oct. 1955, 97.

1838. **Lucas, J. Olumide.** 1948. *The religion of the Yorubas.* Pp. xii + 420, bibl., ill., map. Lagos: C.M.S. Bookshop.

1839. *See* 1939.

1840. **Mackenzie, H. F.** *Bronze plaque from Benin.* Chicago art institute bulletin, **28**, 1934, 19–20.

1841. **Malmsten, Karl.** *A Benin bench.* Part 1, Description. Ethnos, **2**, 1937, 199–207, ill.

1841a. **Marquart, Jos.** 1913. *Die Benin-Sammlung des Reichsmuseums für Völkerkunde in Leiden. Beschrieben und mit ausführlichen Prolegomena zur Geschichte der Handelswege und Völkerbewegungen in Nordafrika.* Pp. 16 + ccclxvii + 132 + 14 pl., maps. Leiden: Brill (Veröff. d. Reichsmus. f. Völkerkde. Ser. 2, no. 7).

1842. **Mauny, R.** *A possible source of copper for the oldest brass heads of Ife.* J. hist. soc. Nigeria, **2**, 3, Dec. 1963, 393–5.

1843. **Messenger, John C.** *Anang art, drama and social control.* Afr. stud. bull., **5**, no. 2, 1962, 29–35.

1844. **Meyer, H.** *Die Altertümer von Benin.* Kol. Rund., 1920, 60–68.

1845. **Meyerowitz, H.** and **V.** *Bronzes and terra-cottas from Ile-Ife.* Burlington magazine, **75**, 439, Oct. 1939, 151–5, ill.

1846. **Meyerowitz, Eva L. R.** *Four pre-portuguese bronze castings from Benin.* Man, **40**, no. 155, 1940, 129–32, ill.

1847. —— *Ancient Nigerian bronzes.* Burlington magazine, **79**, 462–3, Sept. and Oct. 1941, 89–93; 121–6, ill.

1848. —— *Ancient bronzes in the royal palace at Benin.* Burlington magazine, **83**, 1943, 248–53, bibl., f., 2 pl.

1849. —— *The stone figures of Esie in Nigeria.* Burlington magazine, **82**, 479, Feb. 1943, 31–36, ill.

1850. —— *Ibeji statuettes from Yoruba, Nigeria.* Man, **44**, 94, Sept.–Oct. 1944, 105–7, ill.

1851. —— *Notes on the King-God Shango and his temple at Ibadan, Southern Nigeria.* Man, **46**, no. 27, 1946, 25–31, ill.

1852. **Milburn, S.** *These disgusting images.* Nigerian teacher, **1** (4), 1935, 14–17, ill.

1853. —— *Stone sculptures at Esie.* Nigerian teacher, **2**, no. 8, 1936, 2–7, ill.

1854. —— *A Yoruba household altar.* Nigerian field, **17**, 1952, 43–44, ill.

1855. **Miles, G. P. L.** *Benin; ring and bronze head.* Ethnologia Cranmorensis, **1**, 1937, 2.

1856. **Milliken, W. M.** *Treasure of ivories and bronzes from the ancient kingdom of Benin.* Cleveland museum bull., **24**, 1937, 34–36.

1857. **Morton-Williams, P.** *The Egungun society in South-Western Yoruba kingdoms.* Proc. Third (1954) Annual Conf. of the West African Institute of Social and Economic Research, 90–103. Ibadan: Univ. College.

1858. —— *The Yoruba Ogboni cult in Oyo.* Africa, **30**, 1960, 362–74, ill.

1859. **Murray, K. C.** *Ogbom.* (*Ibo carvings.*) Nigerian field, **10**, Oct. 1941, 127–31, ill.

1860. —— *Nigerian bronzes; work from Ife.* Antiquity, **15**, 1941, 71–80, ill.

1861. —— *Arts and crafts of Nigeria; their past and future.* Africa, **14**, 4, Oct. 1943, 155–64.

1862. —— *Frobenius and Ile Ife.* Nigerian field, **11**, 1943, 200–3.

1863. —— *The art of Ife.* Nigeria digest, **1**, 4, Apr. 1945, 11–16, ill.

1864. —— *The wood carvings of Oron (Calabar).* Nigeria, **23**, 1946, 113–14, ill.

1865. —— *Ancestor figures of Oron clan, Ibibio, near Calabar, Nigeria.* Burlington magazine, **89**, 1947, 310–14.

1866. —— *Idah masks.* Nigerian field, **14**, 3, July 1949, 85–92, ill.

1867. —— *The stone images of Esie and their yearly festival.* Nigeria, **37**, 1951, 45–63, ill.

1868. —— and **B. E. B. Fagg.** 1955. *An introduction to the art of Ife.* Pp. 28, ill. Lagos: Nigerian Antiquities Service. London: Crown Agents.

1869. —— *West African wood carving.* Afr. south, **2** (4), 1958, 102–5.

1870. —— *Benin art.* Nigeria magazine, no. 71, 1961, 370–8, ill.

1871. —— and **Frank Willett.** *The Ore grove at Ife, Western Nigeria.* Man, **58**, 187, Sept. 1958, 137–41, ill.

1872. **Murry, J. M.** *Negro sculpture.* Nation (London), **27**, 1920, 69–70, ill.

1873. **Museck, J. B.** *Group of seven African sculptures in wood.* Bull. St. Louis museum, **27**, 1942, 45–49.

1874. **New York; Museum of Primitive Art.** 1961. *Sculpture of Northern Nigeria,* by Roy Sieber. Pp. 32, ill., map. New York: Museum of Primitive Art.

1875. **Nigeria.** (*Ed.* E. H. Duckworth.) *The bronze heads of Ife.* Nigeria, **21**, 1940, 341–3, ill.

1876. —— *The recovery of Benin antiquities.* Nigeria, 32, 1949, 63–71, ill.

1877. —— (*Ed.* E. H. Duckworth.) *Ife Bronzes.* Nigeria, **37**, 1951, 20–24, ill.

1878. —— (*Ed.* D. W. MacRow.) *Idanre.* Nigeria, no. 46, 1955, 154–80, ill.

1879. **Nigeria Magazine.** (*Ed.* D. W. MacRow.) *God of iron.* Nigeria magazine, no. 49, 1956, 118–37, ill.

1880. —— (*Ed.* D. W. MacRow.) *The Nupe of Pategi.* Nigeria magazine, no. 50, 1956, 260–79, ill.

1881. —— (*Ed.* D. W. MacRow.) *Mud shrines of Olokun.* Nigeria magazine, no. 50, 1956, 280–95, ill.

1882. —— (*Ed.* D. W. MacRow.) *Inside Arochuku.* Nigeria magazine, no. 53, 1957, 100–18, ill.

1883. —— (*Ed.* D. W. MacRow.) *Asaba.* Nigeria magazine, no. 54, 1957, 226–42, ill.

1884. **Nigerian Antiquities Service.** *The art of Ife.*

1885. **Nsugba, P. O.** *Oron ekpu figures.* Nigeria magazine, **71**, Dec. 1961, 357–65, ill.

1886. **Nzekwu, Onuora.** *Gloria Ibo.* Nigeria magazine, no. 64, 1960, 72–88, ill.

1887. **Olbrechts, Frans M.** *Notre ivoire sculpté du Benin.* Bull. mus. roy (belge) d'art et d'histoire, **3**, no. 2, 1931, 51–55.

1888. **Olderogge, D. A.** *Die Altertümer Benins.* II. Sbornik Museia Antropologii i Etnografii, **16**, 1955.

1889. —— *Drevnosti Benina,* I–3 (Benin Antiquities). Izd. Ak. Nauk SSR Sbornik Museia Antropologii i Etnografii. (Proc. Mus. Anthrop. and Ethnol, Moscow–Leningrad, 1954, 358–410; 1957, 346–61.)

1890. **Palau-Marti, M.** *A propos de quelques monuments d'Ifé.* Notes afr. I.F.A.N., **78**, 1958, 35–36.

1891. **Palmer, H. R.** *Gabi figures from Jebba Island.* Man, **31**, no. 261, 1931, 261–2, ill.

1892. **Palmer, Sir Richmond.** *Ancient Nigerian bronzes.* Burlington magazine, **81**, 1943, 252–4.

1893. **Paulme, Denise.** 1944–6. *Un problème d'histoire de l'ait en Afrique; des bronzes du Benin.* C.R. sommaires séances inst. franç. anthrop., **2**, janv. 1944, déc. 1946, 4–5.

1894. **Peake, H. J. E.,** and **H. J. Braunholtz.** *Earthenware figure from Nigeria in Newbury museum.* Man, **29**, no. 87, 1929, 117–18, ill.

1895. **Petri, H.** *Religion and art in ancient Nigeria.* West Afr., no. 1774, 1951, 155, ill.

1896. **Pettazzoni, Raffaele.** 1912. *Avori scolpiti Africani in collezioni Italiane; contributo allo studio dell'Arte 'Di Benin'.* Pp. iv + 44, ill. Rome: E. Calzone.

1897. —— 1948. *Miti e Legende.* I *Africa, Australia.* Pp. xxviii + 480, ill., maps. Turin: Unione Tipografico-Editrice Torinese.

1898. **Pinnock, James.** 1897. *Benin; the surrounding country, inhabitants, customs and trade.* Pp. 54, ill., map. Liverpool: Journal of Commerce Printing Works.

1899. **Pittard, Eugène.** *L'Art du Benin.* Les Musées de Genève, 7 ann., no. 10, 1950, 3, ill.

1900. **Pitt-Rivers, A. H. Lane Fox.** 1900. *Antique works of art from Benin.* Pp. 100, ill. London: privately printed.

1901. **Plass, M.** *Art of Benin.* Expedition—Pennsylvania University (University Museum Bulletin), **1**, no. 4, 1959, ill., map.

1902. **Ratton, Charles.** *Les Bronzes du Benin.* Cah. d'art, **7**, 1932, 209–16.

1903. —— *The ancient bronzes of black Africa.* Cunard, Nancy (*ed.*), Negro anthology, 1934, 684–6, ill.

1904. **Read, Sir Charles Hercules.** *Notes on certain ivory carvings from Benin.* Man, **10**, 1910, 49–51.

1905. —— *On a carved ivory object from Benin in the British Museum.* Man, **18**, no. 72, 1918, 129–30, ill.

1906. —— and **Ormonde Maddock Dalton.** *Works of art from Benin City.* J. anthrop. inst., **27**, 1898, 362–78, ill.

1907. —— —— 1899. *Antiquities from the city of Benin and from other parts of West Africa.* Pp. vi + 61, ill. London: British Museum.

1908. **Rogers, M. R.** *Bronze head of a youth, Benin A.D. 1360–1500.* St. Louis museum bull., **22**, 1937, 9–11.

1909. **Roth, F. N.** 1897. *A diary of a surgeon with the Benin punitive expedition.* Pp. 14.

1910. **Roth, Henry Ling.** *Notes on Benin art.* Reliquary and ill. archaeol., 1898, 14, ill.

1911. —— *Personal ornaments from Benin.* Bull. museum of sci. and art, Philadelphia, **2**, no. 1, 1899, ill.

1912. —— *Primitive art from Benin.* Studio (London), **15**, 174, ill.

1913. —— Stray articles from Benin. Int. archiv. ethnog., **13**, 1900, 194–7, ill.

1914. —— 1903. Great Benin; its customs, arts and horrors. Pp. 234. Halifax, England: F. King & Sons, Ltd.

1915. **Rousseau, Madeleine.** Les fouilles archéologiques en Nigéria. Musée vivant, **12**, 1948, 84–86.

1916. —— L'art ancien de l'Afrique noire. Rech. et débats centre cath. des intellectuels franç., **24**, sept. 1958, 44–60.

1917. —— Benin-Königreich der klassischen afrikanischen Kunst. Afrika, **2**, 1960, 399–402, ill.

1918. **Schweeger-Hefel, Annemarie.** Zur Thematik und Ikonographie der geschnitzten Elfenbeinzähne aus Benin im Museum für Völkerkunde in Wien. Arch. f. Völkerkunde, **12**, 1957, 182–229, bibl., ill.

1919. **Schweeger-Exeli, Annemarie.** Ein Elfenbein blashorn aus Benin. (An ivory horn from Benin.) Arch. f. Völkerkunde (Wien), **13**, 1958, 227–35, ill.

1920. **Shaw, Thurston.** Nigeria's past unearthed and finds at Igbo-Ukwu. W.A.R., **31**, 397, 1960, 30–37, ill.

1921. **Simmons, D. C.** The depiction of Gangosa on Efik-Ibibio masks. Man, **57**, no. 18, 1957, 17–20, ill.

1922. **Smith, H. F. C.** The Benin study. J. hist. soc. Nigeria, **1**, 1956, 60–61.

1923. **Sölken, Heinz.** Innerafrikanische Wege nach Benin. Anthropos, **49**, 5/6, 1954, 809–933, map.

1924. **Stoll, O.** Zur frage d. Benin-Altertümer (u. andere Beiträge). Int. archiv. ethnog., **15** (5), 1902, 5.

1925. **Strieder, Jakob.** Negerkunst von Benin und deutsches Metall-exportgewerbe im 15 und 16 Jahrhundert. Z. f. Ethnol., **64**, 1932, ill.

1926. **Struck, B.** Zur chronologie der Benin-Altertümer. Z. f. Ethnol., **55**, 1923, 113–66.

1927. **Talbot, P. Amaury.** 1923. Life in Southern Nigeria. Pp. xv + 356, ill., map. London: Macmillan.

1928. —— 1926. The peoples of Southern Nigeria. 4 vols. Vol. 1, Historical notes, pp. xii + 365, map. Vol. 2, Ethnology, pp. xx + 423, ill., map. Vol. 3, . Vol. 4, Linguistics and statistics, pp. 234, maps. London: Oxford Univ. Press.

1929. 1927. Some Nigerian fertility cults. Pp. xi + 140, ill. Oxford: Univ. Press.

1930. **Thomas, N. W.** Some Ibo burial customs. J. roy. anthrop. inst., **47**, 1917, 160–212.

1931. —— Note on an object from Benin. Man, **20**, no. 53, 1920, 109–10.

1932. **Thorburn, J. W. A.** The city of Benin. Nigeria, no. 10, 1937, 65–69, ill.

1933. **Times, The.** Benin's past glories. Times British colonies, rev., **21**, 1956, 23, ill.

1933a.—— The brassmakers of Benin. Times British colonies, rev., **28**, 1957, 20, ill.

1934. **Tong, R.** The ancient city of Benin. Corona, **3**, 1951, 30–32.

1935. **Tremearne, A. J. N.** Notes on Nigerian tribal masks. J. roy. anthrop. inst., **41**, 1911, 162–78.

1936. **Tremlett, Mrs. Horace.** 1915. With the tin gods. Pp. x + 308, ill. London: Lane. (First mention of the figures from Jebba.)

1936a. **Underwood, Leon.** Nigerian art. Nigeria, **24**, 1946, 215–20, ill.

1937. —— Abstraction in African and European art. Studio, **136**, Dec. 1948, 182–5.

1938. **Vaughan, M.** Exceptional Benin ivory at Brooklyn Museum. Connoisseur (Am. ed.), **144**, Sept. 1959, 67–68.

1939. **von Luschan, Felix.** 1901. Die Karl Knorr'sche Sammlung von Benin-Altertümern im Museum für Länder-und Völkerkunde in Stuttgart. Pp. 95 (14). Stuttgart: W. Kohlhammer.

1940. —— 1919. Die Altertümer von Benin. Veröff. Mus. f. Völkerkunde, Berlin, VIII–X (3 vols.), 1919. Berlin/Leipzig.

1941. **von Sydow, Eckart.** Masques-Janus du Cross River. Documents, no. 6, 1930, 321–8, ill.

1942. —— Panther-Ornament auf d. Panzern von Benin. Ethnol. Anz., **3** (5), 1934, 231–8, ill.

1943. —— Zur chronologie von Benin Ornamenten. Ethnol. Anz., **4**, 1935, 31–38.

1944. —— Kunst und Kultur von Benin. Atlantis, **10**, 1938, 46–56, ill.

1945. —— Ancient and modern art in Benin City. Africa, **11**, 1938, 55–62.

1946. **Walker, S. W.** Gabi figures and Edegi, first king of the Nupé. Man, **34**, no. 193, 1934, 169–72, ill.

1947. **Wescott, Joan.** The sculpture and myths of Eshu-Elegba, the Yoruba trickster. Definition and interpretation in Yoruba iconography. Africa, **32** (4), 1962, 336–54, ill.

1948. **West Africa.** Benin's own antiquarian (Chief Jacob Egharevba). West Africa, **1725**, 1950, 221.

1949. —— Carver from Benin (F. O. Idubor). West Afr., 2 Feb. 1957, 102, ill.

1950. **Willett, Frank.** The discovery of new brass figures at Ife. Odù, 6, June 1958, 29–34, ill.

1951. —— Excavations at Old Oyo and Ife. West Afr., **2153**, 19 July 1958, 675.

1952. —— Recent excavations at Old Oyo and Ife, Nigeria. Man, **59**, no. 135, 1959, 99–100.

1953. —— Bronze and terra-cotta sculptures from Ita Yemoo, Ife. S. Afr. archaeol. bull., **14**, no. 56, 1959, 135–7, ill.

1954. —— Bronze figures from Ita Yemoo, Ife, Nigeria. Man, **59**, 308, Nov. 1959, 189–93.

1955. —— A terra-cotta head from Old Oyo, Western Nigeria. Man, **59**, 286, Oct. 1959, 180–1.

1956. —— A hunter's shrine in Yorubaland, Western Nigeria. Man, **59**, no. 334, 1959, 215–16, ill.

1957. —— Recent archaeological discoveries at Ilesha. Odù, no. 8, 1960, 3–20, ill.

1958. —— L'art d'Ifé; sa nature et son origine. 6e congr. int. sci. anthrop. et ethnol. (Paris, 1960), **2**, 1, 1963, 487–9, bibl.

1959. —— and **A. Dempster.** Stone carvings in an Ife style from Eshure, Ekiti, Western Nigeria. Man, **62** (1), 1962, ill.

1960. **Williams, Denis.** The iconology of the Yoruba edan Ogboni. Africa, **34**, 2, Apr. 1964, 139–66, ill.

1961. **Wolf, Siegfried.** Die Gelbguss-Köpfe der Dresdener Benin-Sammlung; Beschreibung und Vergleich. Abh. u. Ber. staatl. Mus. Völkerkde. (Dresden), **21**, 1962, 91–121, bibl., ill.

1962. —— Vogelgestaltiges Benin-Zeremonialgerät aus Elfenbein. Abh. u. Ber. staatl. Mus. Völkerkde. (Dresden), **22**, 1963, 135–42, bibl., ill.

1963. —— Bemerkungen zu drei Benin-Gelbgussköpfen des Museums für Völkerkunde Leipzig. Abh. u. Ber. staatl. Mus. Völkerkde. (Dresden), **22**, 1963, 109–34, bibl., ill.

BUILDINGS AND FURNITURE

1964. **Beier, H. Ulli.** The palace of the Ogogas in Ikerre. Nigeria, no. 44, 1954, 303–14, ill.

1965. —— Changing face of a Yoruba town. Nigeria magazine, **59**, 1958, 373–82, ill.

1966. —— Carvers in modern architecture. Nigeria magazine, no. 60, 1959, 60–75, ill.

1967. —— Yoruba wall paintings. Odù, 8, Oct. 1960, 36–39, ill.

1968. —— Sacred Yoruba architecture. Nigeria, **64**, 1960, 93–104, ill.

1969. —— Oshogbo; portrait of a Yoruba town. Nigeria magazine, **64**, Oct. 1960, 95–102, ill.

1970. **Campbell, M. J.** The walls of a city. Nigeria magazine, no. 60, 1959, 39–59, ill.

1971. **Chadwick, E. R.** Wall decorations of Ibo houses. Nigerian field, **6**, 1937, 134–5, ill.

1972. **Crowder, M.** The decorative architecture of Northern Nigeria; indigenous culture expressed in Hausa craftmanship. African world, 1956, 9–10, ill.

1973. **Denfield, Joseph.** *The practical pagan.* Geog. mag., **20**, 1947–8, 74–79, ill.

1974. **Elliot, M. P.** *Mud-building in Kano.* Nigeria, **20**, 1940, 275–8, ill.

1975. **Feilberg, C. C.** *Remarks on some Nigerian house types.* Folk, **1**, 1959, 15–26, ill., map.

1976. **Foyle, Arthur M.** *Nigerian architecture.* Geog. mag., **23**, 1950–1, 173–80, ill.

1977. —— *Houses in Benin.* Nigeria, **42**, 1953, 132–9, ill.

1978. —— *Some aspects of Nigerian architecture.* Man, **53**, no. 1, 1953, 1–3, ill.

1979. **Goodwin, A. J. H.** *Archaeology and Benin architecture.* J. hist. soc. Nigeria, **1** (2), 1957, 65–85.

1980. —— *Walls, paving, water-paths and landmarks.* Odù, **6**, 1958, 45–53.

1981. **Jeffries, W. F.** *Mud building in Northern Nigeria.* Nigeria, **14**, 1938, 110, ill.

1982. **Jeffreys, M. D. W.** *West African night commodes.* Man, **57**, no. 121, 1957, 103, ill.

1983. **Jones, G. I.** *Mbari houses.* Nigerian field, **6** (2), 1937, 77–79, ill.

1984. —— *Ohaffia Obu houses.* Nigerian field, **6** (4), 1937, 169–71, ill.

1985. **Kirk-Greene, Anthony.** *Decorated houses in Zaria.* Nigeria magazine, **68**, Mar. 1961, 53–78, ill.

1986. **Kirkman, James.** 1963. *Gedi the palace.* Pp. 80, bibl., ill. The Hague: Mouton & Co. (Includes catalogue of beads.)

1987. **Large, W. H.** *The red walls of Bida.* Nigeria, **30**, 1949, 271–315, ill.

1988. **Mbanefo, Frank.** *The Iba house in Onitsha.* Nigeria magazine, no. 72, 1962, 18–25, ill.

1989. **Moore, G.,** and **H. U. Beier.** *Mbari houses.* Nigeria magazine, no. 49, 1956, 184–98, ill.

1990. **Murray, K. C.** *The Okwu wall, near Umuahia (Ibo art).* Nigeria, **27**, 1947, 19–24, ill.

1991. **Nigeria.** *The painted court house of Inre.* Nigeria, **16**, 4, 1938, 288–9.

1992. **Nigeria; Architecture.** *Yoruba architecture.* Nigeria, **37**, 1951, 39–44, ill.

1993. **Nzekwu, Onuora.** *Omo Ukwu temple.* Nigeria magazine, **81**, June 1964, 117–26, ill.

1994. **Talbot, P. Amaury.** *Note on Ibo houses.* Man, **16**, no. 79, 1916, 129, ill.

1995. **Thomas, N. W.** *Decorative art among the Edo-speaking peoples of Nigeria.* (1) Decoration of buildings. Man, **10**, no. 37, 1910, 65–66, ill.

1996. **Tremearne, A. J. N.** *Hausa houses.* Man, **10**, no. 99, 1910, 177–80, ill.

CLOTHING AND ADORNMENT

1997. **Alexander, D.** *Notes on ornaments of the Womdeo pagans, who are a section of the Marghi pagans (females only).* Man, **11**, 1, 1911, 1, ill.

1998. **Arnot, Mrs. A. S.** *Uri body painting and Aro embroidery.* Nigerian field, **15**, 3, July 1950, 133–7, ill.

1999. **Beier, H. U.** *The Egungun cult.* Nigeria, **51**, 1956, 380–92, ill.

2000. —— *Oloko festival.* Nigeria magazine, no. 49, 1956, 168–83, ill.

2001. —— *Obatala festival.* Nigeria magazine, no. 52, 1956, 10–28, ill.

2002. **Bertho, Jacques.** *Coiffures-masques à franges de perles chez les rois yoruba de Nigéria et du Dahomey.* Notes afr. I.F.A.N., **47**, juil. 1950, 71–74, ill.

2003. **Bohannan, Laura** and **Paul.** 1953. *The Tiv of central Nigeria.* Pp. viii + 98, bibl., map. London: Int. Afr. Inst. (Ethnographic Survey of Africa: Western Africa, part 8.)

2004. **Bohannan, P. J.** *Beauty and scarification amongst the Tiv.* Man, **56**, no. 129, 1956, 117–30, ill.

2005. **Boyle, V.** *The marking of girls at Ga-Anda.* J. Afr. soc., **15**, 1915–16, 361–6, ill.

2006. **Brice-Bennett, F. O.** 1959. *Festival of Kano.* Pp. 20. London: Brown, Knight & Truscott for Festival of Kano Committee.

2007. **Campbell, M. J.** *People in trust.* Nigeria magazine, no. 62, 1959, 208–29, ill.

2008. **de Negri, Eve.** *Hairstyles of Southern Nigeria.* Nigeria, no. 65, 1960, 191–8, ill.

2009. —— *Yoruba women's costume.* Nigeria magazine, no. 72, 1962, 4–12, ill.

2010. —— *Yoruba man's costume.* Nigeria magazine, no. 73, 1962, 4–12, ill.

2011. —— *. . . the King's Beads (Benin).* Nigeria magazine, no. 82, 1964, 210–16, ill.

2012. —— *Nigerian jewellery.* Nigeria magazine, no. 74, 1962, 43–54, ill.

2013. **Elias, T. O.** *Hausa marriage.* Nigeria magazine, no. 53, 1957, 135–49, ill.

2014. **Heath, D. F.** *Bussa regalia.* Man, **37**, no. 91, 1937, 77–80, ill.

2015. **Jeffreys, M. D. W.** *Ichi scarification among the Ibo.* Man, **48**, June 1948, p. 89.

2016. —— *The winged solar disk or Ibo itΣi facial scarification.* Africa, **21**, 2, Apr. 1951, 93–111, ill.

2017. —— *Some beads from Awka.* Nigerian field, **19**, 1, Jan. 1954, 37–44, ill.

2018. —— *Negro abstract art or Ibo body patterns.* SAMAB, **6**, 9, Mar. 1957, 218–29, ill.

2019. —— *Aggrey beads.* Afr. stud., **20**, 1961, 97–113, bibl.

2020. **Macfie, J. W. Scott.** *A Yoruba tattooer.* Man, **13**, no. 68, 1913, 121–2.

2021. **Moore, Gerald.** *The Ila Oso festival at Ozuakoli.* Nigeria magazine, no. 52, 1956, 60–69, ill.

2022. **Murray, K. C.** *Body paintings from Umuahia.* Nigerian teacher, **1**, 4, 1935, 3–4, photos.

2023. —— *Ibo headdresses combining human and animal features.* Man, **48**, 1, Jan. 1948, 1–2, ill.

2024. **Nigeria.** *(Yoruba) hairdressing.* Nigeria, **18**, 1939, 163–5, ill.

2025. —— *Ibo body painting design from Arochuku.* Nigeria, **25**, 1946, 321.

2026. **Nigeria Magazine** (ed. by D. W. MacRow). *Niri traditions.* Nigeria magazine, no. 54, 1957, 273–88, ill.

2027. —— *Su; Argungu fishing festival.* Nigeria magazine, no. 55, 1957, 294–316, ill.

2028. **Nzekwu, J. O.** *Ofala festival.* Nigeria magazine, no. 61, 1959, 104–22, ill.

2029. **Nzekwu, Onuora.** *Carnival at Opobo.* Nigeria magazine, no. 63, 1959, 302–19, ill.

2030. —— *Iria ceremony.* Nigeria magazine, no. 63, 1959, 340–52, ill.

2031. —— *Ibo people's costumes.* Nigeria magazine, no. 78, 1963, 164–75, ill.

2032. **Pinfold, G. F.** *Some notes on 'fork guards'.* Man, **29**, no. 76, 1929, 97–98, ill.

2033. **Rowe, C. F.** *Abdominal cicatrisations of the Munshi tribe, Nigeria.* Man, **28**, no. 131, 1928, 179–80, ill.

2034. **Shell Company of Nigeria.** 1960. *Nigeria in costume.* Pp. 102: col. plates with descriptive text. Amsterdam and London: L. van Leer & Co.

2035. **Verger, Pierre.** *Ejigbo festival.* Nigeria magazine, no. 70, 1961, 206–17, ill.

2036. **Wainwright, G. A.** *The Egyptian origin of a ram-headed breastplate from Lagos.* Man, **51**, no. 231, 1951, 133–4, ill.

2037. **Wilson-Haffenden, J. R.** *Notes on the Kwottos of Toto District.* J. Afr. soc., **26**, 1926–7, 368–79. (Anklets, p. 378.)

2038. —— *Some notes on fork guards in Nigeria.* Man, **29**, no. 132, 1929, 172–4.

ROCK ART

2039. *See* 3663a.

2040. **Fagg, W. B.** *Grooved rocks at Apoje near Ijebu-Igbo, Western Nigeria.* Man, **59**, no. 330, 1959, 205, ill.

2041. **Morton-Williams, P.** *A cave painting, rock gong and rock slide in Yorubaland.* Man, **57**, no. 213, 1957, 170–1, ill.

2042. **Sassoon, Hamo.** *Cave paintings recently discovered near Bauchi, Northern Nigeria.* Man, **60**, no. 70, 1960, 50–53, ill.

2043. **Vaughan, James H., Jr.** *Rock paintings and rock gongs among the Marghi of Nigeria.* Man, **62**, 83, Apr. 1962, 49–52, ill.

TECHNIQUES

2044. **Ahmed, S. Gimba.** *Grass weaving.* Nigeria magazine, **74**, Sept. 1962, 10–15, ill.

2045. **Ankermann, Bernhard.** *Gemusterte Raphiagewebe vom unteren Niger.* Baessler-Arch., **6**, 1922, 204–6. (Description of two raffia cloths in the Berlin Museum, probably of Ibo or Edo origin.)

2046. **Arriens, C.** 1929. *Die Epigonen von Benin.* Kol. Rund., **12** (Dez.), 377–81. Darstellung der heutigen Gusstechnik in Oberguinea.

2047. **Balfour, Henry.** *The tandu industry in Northern Nigeria and its affinities elsewhere.* Evans-Pritchard, and others (*ed.*), Essays presented to C. G. Seligman, 1934, pp. 5–18. (Skin flasks, boxes, etc.)

2048. **Birkett, John D.** *Northern Nigeria's hides and skins industry.* W.A.R., **23**, 296, May 1952, 434–7, ill.

2049. **Braunholtz, H. J.** *Wooden roulettes for impressing patterns on pottery.* Man, **34**, no. 107, 1934, 81, ill.

2050. —— *Pottery in Nigeria.* Congr. int. sci. anthrop. et ethnol., 3ᵉ Session, Bruxelles, 1948 (1960), 24–25.

2051. **Brinkworth, Ian.** *The crown makers of Effon Alaye.* W.A.R., **29**, 372, Sept. 1959, 728–32, ill.

2052. **Cardew, Michael.** *Nigerian traditional pottery.* Nigeria, **39**, 1952, 189–201, ill.

2053. —— *West African pottery.* Africa south, **3**, 1, Oct.–Dec. 1958, 109–13, ill.

2054. —— *Firing the big pot at Kwali.* Nigeria magazine, no. 70, Sept. 1961, 199–205, ill.

2055. **Clarke, J. D.** *Ilorin weaving.* Nigeria, **14**, 1938, 121–4.

2056. —— *Ilorin stone bead making.* Nigeria, **14**, 1938, 156–7. (Notes illustrées sur la fabrication des perles en pierre, par les Yoruba.)

2057. **Cordwell, Justine M.** 1952. *Some aesthetic aspects of Yoruba and Benin cultures.* Evanston, Ill.: Northwestern Univ. (Unpublished dissertation). (Contains a description of the *cire perdu* method of brass casting together with a still picture, step by step, pictorial sequence of that art as practised at Ibadan.)

2058. **Daniel, F.** *Bead-workers of Ilorin, Nigeria.* Man, **37**, no. 2, 1937, 7–8, ill.

2059. **Daniel, Mrs. F.** *Yoruba pattern dyeing.* Nigeria, **14**, June 1938, 125–9, ill.

2060. **Dodwell, C. B.** *The tim-tim makers of Oyo.* Nigeria, **42**, 1953, 126–31, ill.

2061. —— *Iseyin; The town of weavers.* Nigeria, **46**, 1955, 118–43, ill.

2062. **Fagg, William.** *Ironworking with a stone hammer among the Tula of Northern Nigeria.* Man, **52**, 76, Apr. 1952, 51–53, diagr.

2063. **Field, J. O.** *Bronze castings found at Igbe, Southern Nigeria.* Man, **40**, 1940, 1.

2064. **Fitzgerald, R. T. D.** *Dakakari grave pottery.* J. roy. anthrop. inst., **74**, 1/2, 1944, 43–57, ill., maps.

2065. —— *Dakakari grave pottery.* Nigerian field, **23**, 2, Apr. 1958, 76–84, ill.

2066. **Harris, P. G.** (the late). *Notes on tanning in Argungu Emirate (Jima), Nigeria; Notes on dyeing in Argungu Emirate.* Farm and forest, **10**, 1950, 32–35.

2067. **Hollis, Rosemary.** *Dakakari grave pottery.* Nigerian field, **23**, 1, Jan. 1958, 23–26, ill.

2068. **Jeffreys, M. D. W.** *Ogoni pottery.* Man, **47**, no. 84, 1947, 81–83, ill.

2069. —— *A pot from Oyo, S. Nigeria.* Man, **48**, 24, Feb. 1948, 24.

2070. —— *Cordage among the Ibo.* Nigerian field, **25**, 1, Jan. 1960, 42–44.

2071. —— *Oku blacksmiths.* Nigerian field, **26**, 3, July 1961, 137–44.

2072. **Jeffries, W. F.** *Leatherwork in Northern Nigeria.* Nigeria, **14**, 1938, 160–3.

2073. **Jest, C.** *Décoration des calebasses foulbées.* Notes afr. I.F.A.N., **72**, oct. 1956, 113–16, ill.

2074. **Kangiwa, Mallam Shehu M.,** and **Alhaji A. K. Mattedan.** *Leatherwork in Northern Nigeria.* Nigeria magazine, **74**, Sept. 1962, 2–9, ill.

2075. **Kiewe, H. E.** *Can migration of man be traced by African textile designs? (Nigerian designs at Oxford exhibition.)* West Afr., 25 June 1955, 579, ill.

2076. **Krieger, Kurt.** *Terrakotten und Steinplastiken aus Ife, Nigeria.* Berliner Museen, N.F. **5**, 3, 4, 1955, 32–39, bibl., ill.

2077. —— *Töpferei der Hausa.* Veröff. Mus. f. Völkerkunde (Leipzig), no. 11, 1961, 362–8, ill.

2078. **Lantz, S. P.** (Miss). *Jebba island embroidery.* Nigeria, **14**, 1928, 130–3.

2079. **Macfie, J. W. S.** 1913. *Pottery of Ilorin, Northern Nigeria.* Pp. 11, ill. (Offprint from Memoirs and Proceedings of the Manchester Literary and Philosophical Society.)

2080. **Mellor, W. F.** *Bead embroiderers of Remo.* Nigeria, **14**, 1938, 154–5.

2081. **Murray, K. C.** *Women's weaving among the Yorubas at Omuaran in Ilorin Province.* Nigerian field, **5**, 4, 1936, 182–91, ill.

2082. —— *Basket making.* Nigeria, **14**, 1938, 158–9.

2083. —— *Wood carving; its place in the cultural life of the African.* Nigeria, **14**, 1938, 138–9.

2084. —— *Weaving in Nigeria.* Nigeria, **14**, 1938, 118–20.

2085. —— *Tiv pattern dyeing.* Nigeria, **32**, 1949, 41–46, ill.

2086. **Museums Journal.** *Nigerian pottery shown at the Berkeley Galleries; new techniques based on traditional West African methods.* Museums journal, **57**, 1958, 291.

2087. **Nadel, S. F.** *Glass-making in Nupe.* Man, **40**, no. 107, 1940, 85–86.

2088. **Neher, Gerald.** *Brass casting in North-East Nigeria.* Nigerian field, **29**, 1, Jan. 1964, 16–27, ill.

2089. **Nicholson, W. E.** *The potters of Sokoto, Northern Nigeria.* Man, **29**, no. 34, 1929, 45–50, ill.

2090. —— *The potters of Sokoto; B. Zorumawa; C. Rumbukawa.* Man, **31**, no. 186, 1931, 187–90, ill.

2090a. —— *1. Brief notes on pottery at Abujuan Kuta, Niger Province. 2. Bida (nupe) pottery.* Man, **34**, nos. 88/89, 1934, 70–71; 71–73, ill.

2091. **Nigeria.** *Ibo village crafts.* Nigeria, **28**, 1948, 118–35.

2092. —— (Ed. E. H. Duckworth.) *Art on the drying field. (Yoruba dyeing.)* Nigeria, **30**, 1949, 325–9, ill.

2093. **Nigeria Magazine.** *Crafts issue.* Nigeria magazine, **74**, Sept. 1962, 1–99, ill.

2094. **Nigerian Field Society.** *Tiv pottery; an account of making pots, Gloko district, Benue Province.* Nigerian field, **11**, 1943, 147–55, ill.

2095. **Nyabongo, A. K.** *Leather industries.* Negro history bull., **8**, Nov. 1944, 34–35.

2096. **Nzekwu, J. O.** *Awka—town of smiths.* Nigeria magazine, no. 61, 1959, 136–56, ill.

2097. **Ogbodobri, A. A.** *The mat making industry in Warri.* Nigeria, **23**, 1946, 122–3, ill.

2098. **Robertson, K. A.** *The mat and hat industry.* Nigeria, **14**, 1938, 165–8.

2099. —— *Brass work.* Nigeria, **14**, 1938, 169–70.

2100. **Roth, Henry Ling.** *Unglazed pottery from Abeokuta.* Man, **31**, no. 246, 1931, 248–50, ill.

2101. **Sassoon, Hamo.** *Birom blacksmithing.* Nigeria magazine, **74**, Sept. 1962, 25–31, ill.

2102. **Saulawa, Mallam Ibo.** *Thread making and weaving in Katsina Province.* Nigeria, **23**, 1946, 115–16, ill.

2103. **Scott Macfee, J. W.** *The pottery industry of Ilorin, Northern Nigeria.* Pp. 110–21, ill.

2104. **Simmons, Donald C.** *Efik knots.* Nigerian field, **21**, 3, July 1956, 127–34, ill.

2105. **Slye, Jonathan.** *Ceramics in N. Nigeria; fame of traditional Abuja stoneware pottery.* African world, Apr. 1964, 6–7, ill.

2106. **Southern, A. E.** *Cloth making in Nigeria.* Nigeria, **32**, 1949, 35–40, ill.

2107. **Staudinger, Paul.** *Zinnschmelzen afrikanischer Eingeborener (Bauchi).* Z. f. Ethnol., **43**, 1911, 147–8, ill.

2108. **Stevens, R. A.** *Ikot Ekpene raffia.* Farm and forest, **6**, 1, Jan.–Mar. 1945, 42–46, photos.

2109. **Thomas, N. W.** *Pottery-making of the Edo-speaking peoples, Southern Nigeria.* Man, **10**, no. 53, 1910, 97–98, ill.

2110. —— *Nigerian notes; I. Agricultural rites. II. Metal work.* Man, **18**, nos. 75 and 100, 1918, 138–42, 184–6.

2111. **Tremearne, A. J. N.** *Pottery in Northern Nigeria.* Man, **10**, no. 57, 1910, 102–3, ill.

2112. **Ukeje, L. O.** *Weaving in Akwete.* Nigeria magazine, **74**, Sept. 1962, 32–40, ill.

2113. **Vernon-Jackson, Hugh.** *Craft work in Bida.* Africa, **30**, 1960, 51–61.

2114. **Wenger, S.,** and **H. U. Beier.** *Adire—Yoruba pattern dyeing.* Nigeria magazine, no. 54, 1957, 208–25, ill.

2115. **Wills, Colin.** *Nigerian hides and skins.* Progress (London), **46**, 260, autumn 1958, 258–65, ill.

UTENSILS, TOOLS AND WEAPONS; MISCELLANEOUS

2116. **Amogu, O. O.** *The introduction into and withdrawal of 'Manillas' from the 'Oil Rivers' as seen in Ndoki District.* Nigeria, **38**, 1952, 135–9, ill.

2117. **Balfour, Henry.** *'Thunderbolt celts' from Benin.* Man, **3**, 102, 1903, 182–3, ill.

2118. **Beasley, Harry G.** *'Thunderbolt celts' from Benin.* Man, **37**, no. 175, 1937, 137, ill.

2118a. **Brewster, P. G.** *Some Nigerian games with their parallels and analogues.* J. soc. africanistes, **24**, 1954, 25–48.

2119. **Grey, R. F. A.** *Manillas.* Nigerian field, **16**, 2, Apr. 1951, 52–66, ill.

2120. **Jeffreys, M. D. W.** *Some negro currencies in Nigeria.* SAMAB (Durban), **5**, Dec. 1954, 405–16, ill.

2121. —— *Multiple-stem pipe bowls.* Man, **55**, no. 6, 1955, 8–9, ill.

2122. **Jones, G. I.** *Native and trade currencies in Southern Nigeria during the 18th and 19th centuries.* Africa, **28**, 1958, 43–54.

2123. **Meek, C. K.** *Chess in Bornu, Nigeria.* Man, **34**, no. 48, 1934, 33, ill.

2124. **Nigeria** (Ed. E. H. Duckworth). *Snuff-making in Nigeria.* Nigeria, **19**, 1939, 190–3, ill.

2125. **Nigeria Magazine** (Ed. D. W. MacRow). *Uburu and the Salt Lake.* Nigeria magazine, no. 56, 1958, 84–96, ill.

AFRICAN ART TODAY

2126. **Abosede, A.** *A Nigerian at the Eisteddfod. Art festivals in Wales and West Africa; some comparisons.* W.A.R., **26** (339), 1955, 1066–9.

2127. **Allison, P. A.** *A Yoruba carver.* Nigeria, **22**, 1944, 49–50, ill.

2128. **Arnot, A. S.** *Art and an industry in Arochuku.* Nigeria, **12**, 1937, 10–14.

2129. **Bascom, W. R.** *Modern African figurines; satirical or just stylistic?* Lore, **7** (4), 1957, cover and 118–26.

2130. **Beier, H. Ulli.** *Two Yoruba painters.* Black Orpheus, **6**, 1959, 29–32, ill.

2131. —— *Complicated carver; Lamidi Fakeye exhibition in Ibadan.* W.A.R., **31**, 391, June 1960, 30–31, ill.

2132. —— *Three Zaria artists.* W.A.R., **31**, 395, 1960, 37–41, ill.

2133. —— *Ibrahim Salahi.* Black Orpheus, no. 10, 48–50, ill.

2134. —— *Contemporary Nigerian art.* Nigeria magazine, **68**, Mar. 1961, 27–51, ill.

2135. —— *Idah; an original Bini artist.* Nigeria magazine, no. 80, 1964, 5–16, ill.

2136. **Cardew, Michael.** *Pioneer pottery at Abuja.* Nigeria, **52**, 1956, 38–59, ill.

2137. **Carroll, K.** *Yoruba craft work at Oye-Ekiti, Ondo Province.* Nigeria, **35**, 1950, 345–54, ill.

2138. —— *Ekiti Yoruba wood carving.* Odù, **4**, 57, 3–10.

2139. —— *Christian art in Nigeria.* Liturgical arts, **26**, May 1958, 91–94.

2140. **Cordwell, Justine Mayer.** *Naturalism and stylization in Yoruba art.* Magazine of art, **46**, 1953, 220–5.

2141. —— *The problem of process and form in West African art.* 3rd Int. W. Afr. Conf. 1949 (1956), 53–60.

2142. **Crownover, David.** *Pink people; Europeans in the tribal art of Nigeria.* Univ. mus. bull., **2**, no. 3, 1960, 33–35. (Pennsylvania University Expedition.)

2143. **Danford, J. A.** *Art in Nigeria.* Afr. Affairs, **48**, 190, Jan. 1949, 37–47.

2144. —— *Nigerian art.* Nigeria, **33**, 1950, 153–74, ill.

2145. **Duckworth, E. H.** (Ed.). *Arts and crafts number.* Nigeria, **14**, 1938, 90–182, ill., map.

2146. —— *Return of Ife antiquities from America.* Nigeria, **35**, 1950, 362–3, ill.

2147. **Duerden, Dennis G.** *Is there a Nigerian style of painting?* Nigeria, **41**, 1953, 51–59, ill.

2148. —— *Low visibility in Nigerian art.* The arts review, **16** (6), 1964, 2, ill.

2149. **Enwonwu, Ben.** *Modern Nigerian artists' work.* I.L.N., **213**, 1948, 12, ill.

2150. —— *Out of Africa.* Time, **56**, 1950, 49–50, ill.

2151. **Ezekwe, P. V. N.** *Native art and industry in Awka.* Nigerian teacher, **1**, 2, 1934, 28–33, ill.

2152. **Illustrated London News.** *Vital native Bantu genius; sacred and lay works by young artists.* I.L.N., Jan. 1949.

2153. **Jeffries, W. F.** *Experimental art work in Northern Nigeria.* Oversea education, **15**, 2, Jan. 1944, 62–65, ill.

2154. —— *Bauchi training centre, Northern Nigeria.* Studio, **128**, 144–8.

2155. **King, John B.** *A commentary on contemporary Nigerian pottery.* Nigeria magazine, **74**, Sept. 1962, 16–24, ill.

2156. **MacRow, Donald.** *Art club (Lagos).* Nigeria, **43**, 1954, 250–7, ill.

2157. **Meyerowitz, H. V.** 1942. *The making of things.* (African Home Library, 22.) Pp. 16. London: Sheldon Press.

2158. **Meyerowitz, Eva L. R.** *Woodcarving in the Yoruba country today.* Africa, **14**, 1943, 66–70, ill.

2159. **Murray, K. C.** *The condition of arts and crafts in West Africa.* Oversea education, **4**, 4, 1932, 173–80.

2160. —— *The condition of arts and crafts in W. Africa (2).* Oversea education, **5**, 1, Oct. 1933, 1–8.

2161. —— *Painting in Nigeria.* Nigeria, **14**, 1938, 112–13.

2162. —— *The progress of art in Nigeria.* Nigeria review, **3**, 88, Jan. 29, Feb. 5, 1944.

2163. —— *Art courses for Africans.* Oversea education, **21**, 2, Jan. 1950, 1020–1.

2164. —— *The decoration of calabashes by Tiv (Benue Province).* Nigeria, **36**, 1951, 469–74, ill.

2165. —— *The chief art styles of Nigeria.* Tom. 2. C.R.Ie. conf. intern. africanistes de l'ouest, 1951, 318–30, ill., map.

2166. —— 1961. *The artist in Nigerian tribal society.* Pp. 95–100, ill. Smith, Marian W. (ed.). The artist in tribal society. Pp. xiii + 150, bibl., ill. London: Kegan Paul.

2167. **Mveng, Engelbert.** *Die afrikanische Kunst von gestern und das Afrika von heute.* Neues Afr., **3**, 12, Dec. 1961, 475–9, ill.

2168. **Nigeria.** *A new carver (Felix Idubor of Nigeria).* Nigeria, **41**, 1953, 22–27, ill.

2169. **Nigeria Magazine** (*Ed. D. W. MacRow*). *Crafts of Bida.* Nigeria magazine, no. 49, 1956, 138–47, ill.

2170. **Nigeria, Western Region: Ministry of Education.** *Benin crafts.* Teachers' monthly, **6**, 6, June 1960 (*summary* Oversea quart., **2**, 4, Dec. 1960, 118).

2171. **Nnadozie, M. A.** *Floor-rug making in Umulogho school; Nsu Parish, Okigwi District.* Nigeria, **30**, 1949, 330–1, ill.

2171a. **Nsugbe, P. O.** *Cane and raffia work.* Nigeria magazine, **74**, Sept. 1962, 61–66, ill.

2172. **Osula, A. O.** *Nigerian art.* Nigeria, no. 39, 1952, 245–51, ill.

2173. **Page, P. R.** *Benin arts and crafts today.* Farm and forest, **5** (4), 1944, 166–9.

2174. **Saville, A. G.** *The Okigwi local craft and industries exhibition.* Nigeria, **36**, 1951, 443–68, ill.

2175. **Vernon-Jackson, Hugh.** *Craft work in Bida.* Africa, **30**, 1, Jan. 1960, 51–61.

2176. **Wenger, S.** *Drawings of pagan ceremonies by a Christian boy from Ora.* Odù, **2** (1955), 3–13, ill.

2177. **Williams, Denis.** *Second experimental art school (Oshogbo), 27 April to 4 May 1963.* Ibadan, **17**, Nov. 1963, 22–26, ill.

FORMER FRENCH WEST AFRICA

Note: Nos. 2178–9, 2184, 2188–9, 2196–7, 2839, 2848, 2856 should appear under West Central Africa, page 51.

2178. **Bruel, Georges.** 1918. *La France équatoriale africaine.* Pp. ix + 558, ill., maps. Paris: Larose.

2179. **Cahiers Charles de Foucauld.** 1952. *L'Afrique équatoriale française.* Pp. 155, ill., map. Paris: Cahiers Charles de Foucauld. (P. 78, Un aspect de l'art en A.E.F., by Marcel Lucain.)

2180. **Cederschiold, Gunnar.** 1917. *Negrer, Studier och Muentyr i Franska Västafrika.* Pp. 154. Stockholm: P. A. Norstedt.

2181. **Chailley, Ct.** 1953. *Les grandes missions françaises en Afrique occidentale.* Pp. 145, ill., maps. Dakar: I.F.A.N. (I.F.A.N. Initiations et Études Africaines, no. 10.)

2182. **Chauvet, Stephen.** 1924. *Les arts indigènes des colonies françaises.* Cah. d'art, **2**, 1927, and **5**, 1927.

2183. —— *Musique et arts nègres en A.O.F.* Apollon (Paris), 1931, 39.

2184. **Chauvet, W.** *L'Effort français en Afrique équatoriale.* Bordeaux, 1930. (Bon résumé de la situation actuelle de l'A.E.F., intéressant article sur l'art indigène par le Dr. W. Chauvet.)

2185. **Clouzot, H.**, and **A. Level.** *Afrique occidentale française.* La Renaissance, **5** (1922), 216–27.

2186. **Costantini, Mgr.** *Arte Christiana negra.* A.F.E.R., **14**, 1938, 1–16.

2187. **Cureau, Adolphe Louis.** 1915. *Savage man in Central Africa.* Pp. 351, ill., map. London: T. F. Unwin. (See chap. X, pp. 87–93.)

2188. **Delavignette, R.** 1957. *Afrique équatoriale française.* Pp. 127, ill. Paris: Hachette. (Les Albums des Guides Bleus.)

2189. —— 1957. *French equatorial Africa.* Pp. 127 of plates and text. Paris: Librarie Hachette. (Hachette World Albums.)

2190. **de Pedrals, Denis-Pierre.** 1952. *Les peuples de l'A.E.F.* Cahiers Charles de Foucauld.

2191. **Great Britain: Admiralty—Naval Intelligence Division.** 1939–45. *French equatorial Africa and Cameroons.* Pp. xi + 524, ill., maps. London: Admiralty. (Pp. 220–1 Art.)

2192. **Hanel, Karl.** 1958. *Französisch Äquatorial-Afrika.* Pp. 78, map. Bonn: Kurt Schroeder.

2193. **New York: Museum of Primitive Art.** 1959. *Sculpture from three African tribes; Senufo, Baga, Dogon.* Pp. 32, ill. New York: Museum of Primitive Art. (Introduction by Robert Goldwater.)

2194. **Olbrechts, Frans-M.** *Notre mission ethnographique en Afrique occidentale française.* Bull. mus. roy belge, d'art et d'hist., Ser. 3 (5), 1933, 98–107, ill.

2195. **Sonolet, L.** *L'Art dans l'Afrique occidentale française.* Gazette des beaux arts (Paris), 1923.

2196. **Trézenem, E.** 1955. *L'Afrique équatoriale française.* Pp. 203, ill., map. Paris: Éd. Maritime et Colon. (3rd ed.)

2197. **Zièglè, Henri.** 1952. *Afrique équatoriale française.* Pp. 199. Paris: Berger-Levrault.

FIGURES AND MASKS

2198. **Hall, H. U.** *Fetish figures of equatorial Africa.* Museum journal (Univ. of Pennsylvania, Philadelphia, Pa.), **11**, 1920, 27–55, ill.

2199. —— *Two wooden statuettes from French West Africa.* Museum journal (University of Pennsylvania, Philadelphia, Pa.), **18**, 1927, 175–87, ill. (West Sudan and Baga.)

2200. **Moreau, Réne.** 1931. *Afrique équatoriale; images du Cameroun et de l'Afrique équatoriale française (Oubangi-Chari, Tchad, Congo, Gabon).* Pp. 88, ill. Brussels: Éditions Duchartre.

2201. **von Sydow, Eckart.** *Ahnenfiguren aus Französisch-Äquatorial-Afrika.* Cicerone, **22**, 8, 1930, 214–18, ill.

2202. —— *Zum Problem der sogenannten 'Kopffüssler Figuren' aus Französisch- Äquatorial-Afrika.* Ethnol. Anz., **3**, 2, 1933, 99–100, 1 Tafel.

TECHNIQUES

2203. **Lhote, Henri.** *Instructions pour une enquête sur la poterie en Afrique noire française.* Notes afr. I.F.A.N., **39**, juil. 1948, 11–14.

AFRICAN ART TODAY

2204. **Italiaander, Rolf.** *Experiments in modern African art; etchings in French equatorial Africa.* Africa, **30**, 1, Jan. 1960, 46–50, ill.

2205. **Lebeuf, Jean-Paul.** *L'École des peintres de Poto-Poto.* Africa, **26**, 1956, 277–80, ill.

MAURITANIA

2206. **Dubie, P.** 1953. *La vie materielle des Maures.* Mélanges ethnologiques, 111–252, ill., maps. (In Mém. de l'I.F.A.N., no. 23.)

2207. **Gabus, Jean.** *Les sources magico-religieuses de l'art Maure.* Rapport des musées et bibliothèques de la ville de Neuchâtel, 1951, 21, ill.

2208. —— *Contribution à l'étude des Nemadi.* Bull. Schweiz. Ges. Anthrop. u. Ethnol., **28**, 1951–2, 49–83.

2209. **Kühnel, Ernest.** 1924. *Maurische Kunst.* Pp. viii + 76, ill. Berlin: Cassirer. (Die Kunst des Ostens, 9.)

2210. **Martin, H.** *Les tribus du Sahel mauritanien et du Rio de Oro (Les Oulad Bou Sba).* Bull. I.F.A.N., **1**, 1939, 587–629, ill.

BUILDINGS AND FURNITURE

2211. **Duchemin, G. J.** *A propos des décorations murales des habitations de Oualata (Mauritanie).* Bull. I.F.A.N., **12**, 4, oct. 1950, 1095–110, ill.

2212. **Engeström, Tor.** *Wall decorations of the Oualata type at Bamaka.* Ethnos (Mauritania), **21** (3–4), 56, 216–19.

CLOTHING AND ADORNMENT

2213. **Cheneveau, R.** *Sur un anneau de pierre polie de l'Ile de Ngor.* Notes afr. I.F.A.N., **80**, 1958, 97–98, ill.

ROCK ART

2214. **Bessac, H.** *Découverte d'un site rupestre près de Kaédi (Mauritanie).* Notes afr. I.F.A.N., 66, avr. 1955, 34–37, ill.

2215. **Favotti, Jean.** *Découverte de peintures rupestres anciennes à Tenses (Adrar mauritanien).* Notes afr. I.F.A.N., 88, oct. 1960, 103–6, ill.

2216. **Jacques-Meunié, D.** *Quelques gravures et peintures rupestres de la Mauritanie sahélienne. Une pierre taillée de Tinigar.* J. soc. africanistes, **29**, 1, 1959, 19–31, ill., map.

2217. **Laforgue, Pierre.** *Les gravures et peintures rupestres en Mauritanie.* Bull. trim. géog. d'archéol. d'Oran, **46**, 174, 1926, 205–10, ill.

2218. **Mauny, R.** *Peintures rupestres d'Hamdoun (Adrar mauritanien).* Notes afr. I.F.A.N., **51**, juil. 1951, 70–72, ill.

2219. **Senones, M.,** and **O. du Puigaudeau.** *Peintures rupestres du Tagant (Mauritanie).* J. soc. africanistes, **9** (1), 1939, 43–70, ill.

TECHNIQUES

2220. **Balandier, Georges,** and **Paul Mercier.** *Les Outils du Forgeron Maure.* Notes afr. I.F.A.N., no. 33, 1947, 8–11, ill.

2221. **Leriche, A.** *Notes pour servir à l'histoire maure; Notes sur les forgerons, les Kunta et les Maures du Hodh.* Bull. I.F.A.N., **15**, 2, avr. 1953, 737–50.

SENEGAL

2222. **Béranger-Féraud, Laurent Jean Baptiste.** 1879. *Les peuplades de la Sénégambie.* Pp. xvi + 420. Paris: Leroux.

2223. **Fernandes (Valentim),** 1506–10. (*See* Monod, Th., and others.) 1951. *Description de la côte occidentale d'Afrique.* Pp. 97, 105. Bissau (ed.).

2224. **Gamble, David P.** 1957. *The Wolof of Senegambia.* Pp. x + 110, bibl., maps. London: Int. Afr. Inst. (*Ethnographic Survey of Africa: Western Africa, part 14.*)

2225. **Joire, J.** *Découvertes archéologiques dans la région de Rao (Bas-Sénégal).* Bull. I.F.A.N., **17** (3–4), 1955, 249–333, ill.

2226. **Lasnet, Dr.,** and **Others.** 1900. *Une mission au Sénégal.* Pp. (vi) + 348, bibl., ill. Paris: A. Challamel.

2227. **Mauny, R.** *Les Murs Tatas de Dakar.* Notes afr. I.F.A.N., **17**, 1943, 1–3, ill.

2228. **Mollien, G.** 1820. *Travels in the interior of Africa to the sources of the Senegal and Gambia in . . . 1818.* Pp. xii + 378, ill., map. London: Henry Colburn.

2229. **Monod, Th., Teixeira da Mota, A.,** and **R. Mauny.** 1951. *Description de la Côte occidentale d'Afrique (Sénégal au Cap de Monte, Archipels par V. Fernandes (1506–10).* Pp. 225, ill. Bissau: Mém. no. 11, Centro de Estud. da Guiné Port.

2230. **Thomas, Louis-Vincent.** 1959. *Les Diola; essai d'analyse fonctionnelle sur une population de Basse-Casamance.* Pp. 344 + 345–821, bibl., ill., maps. Dakar: I.F.A.N.

FIGURES AND MASKS

2231. **Bardon, P.** 1949. *La collection des masques d'or de l'I.F.A.N.* Pp. 22, ill. Dakar: I.F.A.N. (Catalogue no. 4.)

2232. **Gessain, Robert.** *Sénégal oriental 1963.* Objets et mondes, **3** (4), 1963, 317–28, ill.

2233. **Notes Africaines, I.F.A.N.** *Jeunes circoncis en pays sérère. Diohine cercle de Kaolack (Sénégal).* Notes afr. I.F.A.N., 73, 1957 (cover ill.).

BUILDINGS AND FURNITURE

2234. **Thomas, L. V.** *Pour une systématique de l'habitat diola.* Bull. I.F.A.N., **26**, 1964, 78–118, ill.

CLOTHING AND ADORNMENT

2235. **Appia-Dabit, Beatrice.** *Note sur quelques bijoux sénégalais.* Bull. I.F.A.N., 1943, 27–32, ill.

2236. **Bodiel, Thiam.** *Le tengue ou bijoutier ouolof.* Notes afr. I.F.A.N., **61**, 1954, 22–25, ill.

2237. **Lafon, Suzanne.** *La parure chez les femmes Peul du Bas-Sénégal.* Notes afr. I.F.A.N., **46**, avr. 1950, 37–41, ill.

2238. **Lèques, R.** *La mode actuelle chez les Dakaroises (étude de psychologie sociale).* Bull. I.F.A.N., **19** (B), 3/4, juil.–oct. 1957, 431–42, ill.

2239. **Schweeger-Hefel, A.** *Einige Bemerkungen zu Wolof Schmucksachen.* Arch. f. Völkerkunde (Wien), **9**, 1954, 95–102, ill.

2240. **Thiam, N'diaga.** *L'apprentissage du bijoutier Wolof.* Notes afr. I.F.A.N., **42**, 1949, 53–54.

ROCK ART

2241. **Jouenne.** *Les roches gravées du Sénégal.* Bull. com. études A.O.F., 1920, 1–42, ill., maps.

TECHNIQUES

2242. **Adandé, A.** *Gargoulette inusitée.* Notes afr. I.F.A.N., **78**, avr. 1958, 36–37.

2243. **Mauny, Raymond.** *Du nouveau sur les poteries minuscules du Cap-Vert.* Notes afr. I.F.A.N., **32**, oct. 1946, 16–18, ill.

2244. —— *Poteries néolithiques du Cap Vert (Sénégal).* Bull. I.F.A.N., **13**, 1, janv. 1951, 155–67, ill.

See also 2228.

UTENSILS, TOOLS AND WEAPONS; MISCELLANEOUS

2245. **Ames, D. W.** *The use of a transitional cloth-money token among the Wolof.* Amer. Anthrop., **57**, 1955, 1016–24.

MALI

(Formerly Soudan Français)

2246. **Bâ, A. H.** *Un événement culturel; création à Bamako du cercle soudanais d'études traditionelles. (C.S.E.T.)* Afrique en marche, 3/4/57, 2.

2247. **Boyer, G.** 1953. *Un peuple de l'ouest soudanais: les Diawara. L'Histoire des Songhay, par J. Rouch.* Pp. 259, bibl., ill., maps. Dakar: I.F.A.N. Mém. 29.

2247a. **Champigneulle, B.** *Sculpture du Soudan.* France illustrée, **6**, 1950, 646.

2248. **Daget, J.,** and **M. Konipo.** *La pince-amulette chez les Bozo.* Notes afr. I.F.A.N., **51**, 1951, 80–81, ill.

2249. **Daveau, Suzanne.** 1959. *Recherches morphologiques sur la région de Bandiagara.* Pp. 120, ill., maps. Dakar: I.F.A.N. Mém. no. 56.

2250. **de Ganay, Solange.** 1941. *Les devises des Dogons.* Pp. 192, bibl., ill. Paris: Institut d'Ethnologie. (Travaux et Mémoires de l'Institut d'Ethnologie, 41.)

2251. —— *Aspects de mythologie et de symbolique bambara.* J. psychol. norm. path. (Paris), **42**, 1949, 181–201.

2252. —— *Graphies bambara des nombres.* J. soc. africanistes, **20** (2), 1950, 295–305, ill.

2253. **Daget, J.** *Vases de nuit soudanais (Marka).* Notes afr. I.F.A.N., **72**, oct. 1956, 116–18, ill.

2253a. **Dedien, F.** *Voici le film des funérailles dogons du Professor Griaule.* Afrique en marche, 2/2/1957, 12–14, ill.

2254. **Delafosse, Maurice.** 1912. *Haut-Sénégal-Niger (Soudan Français).* 3 vols. Pp. 428: 428: 316, bibl., ill., maps. Paris:

E. Larose. (Vol. 1: Le pays, les peuples, les langues. Vol. 2: L'Histoire. Vol. 3: Les civilisations-bibliographie-index.)

2257. **Delange, Jacqueline.** *Une pièce Dogon de la collection Tristan Tzara.* Objets et mondes, 4, 1, printemps 1964, 39–41, ill.

2258. **Dieterlen, G.** *Note sur le génie des eaux chez les Bozo.* J. soc. africanistes, 12, 1942, 149–55.

2259. —— *L'arme et l'outil chez les anciens Bambara.* Africa, 18, 1948, 105–11, ill.

2260. —— 1951. *Essai sur la religion Bambara.* Pp. xviii + 240, bibl., ill. Paris: Presses Univ. de France.

2261. —— *Les résultats des missions Griaule au Soudan français (1931– 1956).* Arch. sociol. relig. (Paris), 3, 1957, 137–42.

2262. —— and **F. Ligers.** *Un objet rituel bozo; le maniyalo.* J. soc. africanistes, 28, 1/2, 1958, 33–42.

2263. —— and **Z. Ligers.** *Note sur un talisman bambara.* Notes afr. I.F.A.N., 83, 1959, 89–91, bibl.

2264. **Gabus, J.** *Organisation et premiers resultats de la mission ethnographique chez les Touaregs soudanais (1947).* African transcripts (Univ. Museum, Univ. of Pennsylvania, Pa.), vol. 5, 1948, 1–56, ill., maps.

2265. **Griaule, Marcel.** *Blasons totémiques des Dogon.* J. soc. africanistes, 7 (1), 1937, 69–78, ill.

2266. —— and **Germaine Dieterlen.** *Signes graphiques soudanais.* L'Homme (Paris), 3, 1951, 1–85, ill.

2267. **Henry, Abbé Jos.** 1910. *L'Ame d'un peuple africain; les Bambara.* Pp. v + 238, ill. Münster: Bibliothèque Anthropos.

2268. **Kjersmeier, Carl.** *Bambara-Kunst.* Ymer, 4, 1932, 321–6, ill.

2269. —— *Bambara sculpture.* Cunard, Nancy (ed.), Negro anthology, 1934, 682–3, ill.

2270. **Langlois, P.** 1954. *Art soudanais, tribus Dogons.* (Texte et notice—'Les arts plastiques'.) Pp. 62, ill. Brussels: Marcel Evrier.

2271. **Lanrezac, Lt.** 1905. *L'Art et les croyances chez les noirs du Soudan français (Mali), musique, et sculpture, legendes, etc.* C.R. 26e Congrès nat. soc. franc. géogr. et soc. assimilées, 453–65. Saint-Étienne.

2272. **Laude, J.** *Culturi Soudanaise.* Enciclopedia dell'Arte, Rome.

2273. **Lem, F. H.** *L'Art décoratif des peuples du Soudan.* Art et décoration, no. 20, 1951, 17–24.

2274. **Lugard, Lady** (formerly Flora Shaw). 1905. *A tropical dependency.* Pp. viii + 508, maps. London: Nisbet.

2275. **Macleod, Olive.** 1912. *Chiefs and cities of Central Africa.* Pp. xiv + 322, ill., maps. Edinburgh: William Blackwood.

2276. **Monteil, Charles.** 1915. *Les Khassonké . . . du Soudan français.* Pp. 528, bibl., ill., maps. Paris: E. Leroux. (Collection de la revue du Monde Musulman.)

2277. —— 1924. *Les Bambara du Ségou et du Kaarta.* Pp. 403, ill., map. Paris: Larose.

2278. **Palau Marti, Montserrat.** 1957. *Les Dogon.* Pp. 122, bibl., maps. Paris: Presses Univ. de France. (Monographies Ethnologiques Africaines de l'Institut International Africain.)

2279. **Pâques, Viviana.** 1954. *Les Bambara.* Pp. viii + 123, bibl., map. Paris: Presses Univ. de France. (Monographies Ethnologiques Africaines de l'Institut International Africain.)

2280. **Rouch, Jean.** *Aperçu sur l'animisme Sonrai.* Notes afr. I.F.A.N., 20, 1943, 4–8, ill.

2281. —— 1954. *Les Songhay.* Pp. viii + 100, bibl., map. Paris: Presses Univ. de France. (Monographies Ethnologiques Africaines de l'Institut International Africain.)

2282. **Saint Père, J. H.** 1925. *Les Sarakollé du Guidimaka.* Pp. 188, ill. Paris: Larose.

2283. **Spitz, Georges.** 1955. *Le Soudan français.* Pp. 111, bibl., ill., maps. Paris: Éditions Maritimes et Coloniales. (Pays Africains, 5.)

2284. **Szumowski, G.** *Notes sur la grotte préhistorique de Bamako.* Notes afr. I.F.A.N., 58, 1953, 35–40, ill.

2285. —— *Fouilles de l'Abri sous roche de Kourounkorokalé (Soudan français).* Bull. I.F.A.N., 18, 1956, 462–8, ill.

2286. —— *Fouilles au nord du Macina et dans la région de Ségou.* Bull. I.F.A.N., 19, 1957, 224–58, ill., maps.

2287. **Zahan, Dominique.** 1960. *Sociétés d'initiation Bambara.* Pp. 438, bibl., ill., map. Paris: Mouton & Co.

2288. —— *Les couleurs chez les Bambara du Soudan français.* Notes afr. I.F.A.N., 50, 1951, 52–56.
See also 2295.

FIGURES AND MASKS

2288a. **Ankermann, B.** *Figürliche Darstellungen aus dem westlichen Sudan.* Baessler archiv., 5, 1915, 63–74, ill.

2289. **Anon.** *Casques et masques de danse au Soudan français.* Minotaure, 2, 1933, 20–21.

2290. —— 1961. *Mythen, maskers, magie bij het volk van de Dogon.* Pp. 36, ill. Rotterdam: Museum voor Land- en Volkenkunde.

2291. **Arnaud, Robert.** *Notes sur les Montagnards Habé des cercles de Bandiagara et de Hombori (Soudan français).* Rev. ethnog. trad. pop., 2, no. 8, 1921, 241–314, ill.

2292. **Arts.** *Bambara sculpture at the Museum of Primitive Art.* Arts, 34, Apr. 1960, 57.

2293. **Dermenghem, Emile.** *Les masques et les danses rituelles des Bambaras.* Sci. et voyages (Paris), N.S., août 1939, 50–53.

2294. **Desplagnes, L.** 1907. *Le plateau central nigérien; Une mission archéologique et ethnographique au Soudan français.* Pp. 504, ill., map. Paris: Larose.

2295. **Dieterlen, Germaine.** 1941. *Les âmes des Dogons.* Pp. viii + 268, ill. Paris: Institut d'Ethnologie. (Travaux et Mémoires de l'Institut d'Ethnologie, 40.)

2296. —— *Symbolisme du masque en Afrique occidentale.* Le masque, 1959, 49–55.

2297. **Goldwater, Robert.** 1960. *Bambara sculpture from the Western Sudan.* Pp. 64, bibl., ill., map. New York: Museum of Primitive Art.

2298. **Griaule, Marcel.** 1958. *Masques Dogons.* Pp. xi + 896, ill., maps. Paris: Institut d'Ethnologie. (Travaux et Mémoires d'Institut d'Ethnologie, no. 33.)

2299. —— *Notes complémentaires sur les masques dogons.* J. soc. africanistes, 10, 1940, 79–85.

2300. —— *Un masque du Mont Tabi.* J. soc. africanistes, 14, 1944, 25–32, ill.

2301. **Leiris, Michel.** *Objets rituels dogon. Masques dogon.* Minotaure (Paris), 2, 1933, 26–30: 45–51, ill.

2302. —— 1948. *La langue secrète des Dogons de Sanga (Soudan français).* Pp. xxxii + 530, bibl. Paris: Institut d'Ethnologie. (Travaux et Mémoires de l'Institut d'Ethnologie, 50.)

2303. **Lem, F. H.** 1948. *Sculptures soudanaises.* Pp. 110, ill. Paris: Arts et Metièrs Graphiques.

2304. —— *The art of the Sudan.* Masterpieces of African art. (Catalogue of an exhibition held at the Brooklyn Museum, 21 Oct. 1954–2 Jan. 1955.)

2305. **Ligers, Zacharie.** *Têtes sculptées en terre cuite trouvées au Soudan sur les bords du Niger.* Notes afr. I.F.A.N., 74, 1957, 43–46, ill.

2306. **L'Universo.** *Le maschere presso i Dogons.* L'Universo (Florence), dec. 1939, 967–8.

2307. **Maesen, A.** *Une acquisition du Musée du Congo Belge.* Brousse, 1/2, 1951, 5–6.

2308. **Mauny, Raymond.** *Statuettes de terre cuite de Mopti.* Notes afr. I.F.A.N., 43, juil. 1949, 70–72, ill., map.

2309. **Notes Africaines I.F.A.N.** *Statuette ancienne de terre cuite trouvée à Kaniana-Djenné (Bas-Bani, Soudan).* Notes afr. I.F.A.N., 43, 1949 (cover ill.).

2310. **Paulme, Denise.** *La divination par les chacals chez les Dogon de Sanga.* J. soc. africanistes, 7 (1), 1937, 1–13, bibl., ill.

BUILDINGS AND FURNITURE

2311. **Hugot, P.** *Note sur la construction et l'ornementation des cases Daguerra.* Notes afr., I.F.A.N. **20**, oct. 1943, 10–11.

2312. **Miner, Horace.** 1953. *The primitive city of Timbuctoo.* Princeton, N.J.: Princeton Univ. Press.

CLOTHING AND ADORNMENT

2313. **Binger, Le Capitaine.** 1892. *Du Niger au Golfe de Guinée par le pays de Kong et le Mossi, 1887–89.* 2 vols. Vol. 1, pp. 506, ill. Vol. 2, pp. 416, ill., map. Paris: Hachette.

2314. **Bodiel, Thiam.** *La coiffure 'gossi' et les bijoux qui lui sont asortis.* Notes afr. I.F.A.N., **45**, 1950, 9–11, ill.

2315. **Decorse, J.** *Le tatouage; les mutilations ethniques et la parure chez les populations du Soudan.* L'Anthropologie, **16**, 1905, 129–47, ill.

2316. **de Ganay, Solange.** *Symbolisme de quelques scarifications au Soudan français en rapport avec l'excision.* C.R. Sommaires séances inst. franc. anthrop., Jan. 1947–Dec. 1949, 7–8.

2317. —— *On a form of cicatrization among the Bambara.* Man, **49**, 65, May 1949, 53–55, ill.

2318. **Griaule, Geneviève.** *Le vêtement dogon, confection et usage.* J. soc. africanistes, **21**, 2, 1951, 151–62, ill.

2319. **Griaule, Marcel.** *Réflexions sur la parure et le vêtement au Soudan.* Éduc. ménagère, **10**, 1/2, oct.–nov. 1947, 29–31.

2320. —— and **Émile Gallois.** 1947. *Costumes de l'union française.* Pp. 8. Paris: Éd. Arc-en-Ciel.

2321. **Lhote, H.** *Coiffures soudanaises.* L'Illustration, **95**, no. 4904, 1937, 233–4, ill.

2322. —— *Bijoux en paille de Tombouctou.* Notes afr. I.F.A.N., **32**, 1946, 4–8, ill.

2323. **Muraz, Gaston,** and **Sophie Getzowa.** *Les lèvres des femmes 'Djingés' dites 'Femmes à Plateaux'.* L'Anthropologie, **33**, 1923, 103–25, ill.

2324. **Nicolas, François-J.** *Le bouracan ou bougran, tissu soudanais du moyen age.* Anthropos, **53**, 1/2, 1958, 265–8, bibl.

2325. **Paris, E.** *Bijoux en paille et poupées de cire sonrai de Tombouctou.* Notes afr. I.F.A.N., **51**, 1951, 84–88, ill.

2326. **Siguino, Sanogho.** *Les ornementations tégumentaires des Sénoufo du Kénédougou (Soudan français).* Notes afr. I.F.A.N., **58**, janv. 1953, 22–23, ill.

ROCK ART

2327. **de Ganay, S.** *Rôle protecteur de certaines peintures rupestres du Soudan français.* J. soc. africanistes, **10**, 1940, 87–98, ill.

2328. **Griaule, Marcel.** *Rites relatifs aux peintures rupestres dans le Soudan français.* C.R. séances soc. de biogéog., **95**, 1934, 65–68.

2329. —— *Peintures rupestres du Soudan français et leur sens religieux.* Int. congr. anthrop. & ethnol. sci., roy. anthrop. inst. London, 1934, 256.

2330. **Henninger, J.** *Abris sous roche de la région de Bobo-Dioulasso.* Notes afr. I.F.A.N., **64**, 1954, 97–99, ill.

2331. **Jaeger, Paul,** and **Duong-Huu-Thoi.** *Grottes à dessins rupestres de la région de Kita (Soudan français).* 1e Conf. int. africanistes de l'ouest, C.R., **2**, 1951, 313–17, ill.

2332. **Pérois, Lieut.** *Les dessins rupestres du Point G à Bamako (Grotte de Médina Koura).* Notes afr. I.F.A.N., 27, 1945, 1, ill.

2333. **Perrot-Desnoix.** *Découverte d'un nouveau site rupestre; Tessalit-Amachach (Mali).* Notes afr., 93, 1962, 5–7, bibl., ill.

2334. **Schaeffner, André.** *Peintures rupestres de Songo.* Minotaure (Paris), **11**, 1933, 52–55, ill. (Mission Dakar-Djibouti.)

2335. **Urvoy, Y.** *Peintures rupestres de Takoutala (Soudan français).* J. soc. africanistes, **8** (2), 1938, 97–101, ill.

2336. —— *Gravures rupestres dans l'Aribinda (Boucle du Niger).* J. soc. africanistes, **11**, 1941, 1–5, ill.

2337. **de Zeltner, Fr.** *Les grottes à peinture du Soudan français.* L'Anthropologie, **22**, 1911, 1.

TECHNIQUES

2338. **Athié, Y.** *La teinture chez les Sarakolés.* Notes afr. I.F.A.N., 18, 1943, 7.

2339. **Barlet, P.** *Jarres funéraires au Soudan.* Notes afr. I.F.A.N., **44**, 1949, 107–8, ill.

2340. **Daget, J.,** and **Z. Ligers.** *Une ancienne industrie malienne; les pipes en terre.* Bull. I.F.A.N., **24** (B), 1/2, janv.–avr. 1962, 12–53, bibl., ill.

2341. **Dakar: Bulletin Information et Renseignement.** *Le tissage à la maison des artisans soudanais.* Bull. information et renseignement, **215**, 1939, 155.

2342. **Doumbia, Paul Émile Namoussa.** *Étude du clan des forgerons.* Bull. com. études A.O.F., **19**, 2–3, 1936, 334–60.

2343. **Dupuis, Auguste-Victor, dit Yakouba.** 1921. *Industries et principales professions des habitants de la région de Tombouctou.* Pp. viii + 196, ill. Paris: Larose.

2344. **Gaillard, J.** *Niani, ancienne capitale de l'Empire Mandingue.* Bull. com. études A.O.F., no. 4, 1923, 618–36, ill.

2345. **Heuzey, J. A.** *Note sur le tissage au Soudan.* Bull. I.F.A.N., **3**, 1941, 145–50.

2346. **Lhote, Henri.** *Les boîtes moulées en peau du Soudan, dites 'Bata'.* Bull. I.F.A.N., **14**, 1952, 919–55, ill.

2347. **Mauny, R.** *Une hache polie à bandes peintes du Soudan.* Notes afr. I.F.A.N., **46**, 1950, 33, ill.

2348. **Monteil, Charles.** 1932. *Une cité soudanaise; Djénné; métropole du delta central du Niger.* Pp. vii + 301, bibl., ill., maps. Paris: Société d'éditions géographiques, maritimes et coloniales.

2349. **Prost, A.** *La vannerie chez les Songay.* Notes afr. I.F.A.N., **60**, oct. 1953, 115–16.

2350. **Vieillard, Gilbert.** *Sur quelques objets en terre cuite de Dienné.* Bull. I.F.A.N., **2**, 3–4, juil.–oct. 1940, 347–9, ill.

2351. **Zeltner, Fr. de.** *Notes sur quelques industries du Soudan français.* L'Anthropologie, **26**, 1915, 219–34, ill.

2352. —— *Les boites en cuir moulé du Soudan.* J. soc. africanistes, T2, fasc. 1, 1932, 23–34, ill.

UTENSILS, TOOLS AND WEAPONS; MISCELLANEOUS

2353. **Griaule, Marcel.** 1938. *Jeux dogons.* Pp. 291, ill. Paris: Institut d'Ethnologie. (Travaux et Mémoires de l'Institut d'Ethnologie, no. 32.)

AFRICAN ART TODAY

2354. **Notes Africaines I.F.A.N.** *Atelier du sculpteur Fangolo Coulibaly près de San. Cet artisan a participé à l'Exposition Coloniale de 1931. Près de son pied, une statuette ébauchée (Bambara).* Notes afr. I.F.A.N., 35, 1947 (cover ill.).

NIGER

2355. **Abadie, Maurice.** 1927. *La colonie du Niger.* Pp. 466, ill., map. Paris: Soc. d'Édit. Géogr., Marit. et Col.

2356. **Ardant du Picq, Colonel.** *Une population africaine—les Dyerma.* Bull. com. études A.O.F., **14**, 4, 1931, 477–704, ill., maps.

2357. **Hama, Boubou.** *Le culte des ancêtres. Quelques tableaux de la vie d'un prêtre de la terre (Téra, cercle de Tillabéry, Niger).* Notes afr., I.F.A.N., **31**, 1946, 22–23.

2358. **Lhote, Henri.** *Quelques coutumes en usage chez les Kel Oui.* Contribution à l'étude de l'Air, 1950, 504–7, ill., map. Paris: Larose. (Mém. I.F.A.N., 10.)

2359. **Mauny, Raymond.** *Découverte d'un atelier de fonte de cuivre à Marandet (Niger).* Notes afr. I.F.A.N., 58, avr. 1953, 33–35, ill.

2360. **Nicolas, Francis.** *Les industries de protection chez les Twareg de l'Azawagh.* Hespéris, **25**, 1938, 43–84, ill.

2361. **Robin, J.** *Description de la province de Dosso.* Bull. I.F.A.N., **9**, 1947, 56–98, ill., map.

2362. **Urvoy, Y.** *L'Art dans la colonie du Niger.* Études nigériennes, **2**, 195.

CLOTHING AND ADORNMENT

2363. **de Gironcourt, G.** *La coiffure féminine chez les Sonraïs de Gao (Niger).* Missions de Gironcourt: Documents scientifiques, 261–8, ill.

2364. **Lhote, Henri.** *Un bijou anthropomorphe chez les Touareg de l'Aïr.* Notes afr. I.F.A.N., **44**, 1949, 114–16.

2365. —— *Les Sandales.* Contribution à l'étude de l'Aïr, 1950, 512–33, bibl., ill., map. Paris: Larose. (Mém. I.F.A.N., 10.)

2366. **Nicolas, F.** *Le voilement des Twareg.* Contribution à l'étude de l'Aïr, 1950, 497–503, ill., map. Paris: Larose. (Mém. I.F.A.N., 10.)

ROCK ART

2367. **Bouesnard, L.,** and **R. Mauny.** *Gravures rupestres et sites néolithiques des abords de l'Aïr.* Bull. I.F.A.N., **24** (B), 1/2, janv.–avr. 1962, 1–11, ill.

2368. **Nicolas, F.** *Inscriptions et gravures rupestres.* Contribution à l'étude de l'Aïr, 1950, 562, bibl., ill., map. Paris: Larose. (Mém. I.F.A.N., 10.)

2369. **Rodd, Francis.** *Some rock drawings from Aïr in the Southern Sahara.* J. roy. anthrop. inst., **68**, 1938, 99–111, ill.

2370. **Rouch, Jean.** *Gravures rupestres de Kourki (Niger).* Bull. I.F.A.N., **11**, 3/4, juil.–oct. 1949, 341–53, ill.

2371. **Védy, Jean.** *La station rupestre de Ziri-Betidai (Niger).* Bull. I.F.A.N., **23** (B), 3/4, juil.–oct. 1961, 456–75, ill.

2372. —— *Contribution à l'inventaire de la station rupestre de Dao Timni-Woro-Yat (Niger).* Bull. I.F.A.N., **24** (B), 3/4, juil.–oct. 1962, 325–82, ill., tables.

2373. **Zeltner, Fr. de.** *Des dessins sur des rochers à Aïr qui appartient au territoire des Touareg.* L'Anthropologie, **23**, 1912, 101–4; **24**, 1913, 171–84.

TECHNIQUES

2374. **Lhote, Henri.** *La technique de la poterie à Agadez.* Contribution à l'étude de l'Aïr, 1950, 507–12, ill., map. Paris: Larose. (Mém. I.F.A.N., 10.)

GUINEA

2375. **Bowald, Fred.** 1939. *In den Sümpfen des Rio Nunez.* Pp. 309, ill., map. Zürich: Büchergilde Gutenberg.

2376. **Chauvet, S.** 1930. *Art de la Nile. Guinée. Les arts indigènes en Nile. Guinée.* Pp. 350, ill. Paris.

2377. **Delacour, A.** *Les Tenda (Koniagui, Bassari, Badyaranké) de la Guinée française.* Rev. Étud. Ethnog. Sociol., Paris, 1912–13: 1912, pp. 287–96, 370–81; 1913, pp. 31–52, 105–53, ill., maps.

2378. **Delange, Jacqueline.** *L'Art peul.* Cah. d'ét. afr., **13** (4, 1), 1963, 5–13, ill.

2379. **Frölich, Gerd.** 1961. *Guinea nach der Regenzeit.* Pp. 135, ill. (some col.), maps as end-papers. Leipzig: Brockhaus.

2380. **Gaisseau, Pierre-Dominique.** *The sacred forest.* Pp. 199, ill., map. London: Weidenfeld & Nicolson.

2381. **Gessain, M.** *Pantalon de lutteur Fulakunda.* Notes afr. I.F.A.N., 73, janv. 1957, 13–15, ill.

2382. **Guinean Cultures.** *Guinean cultures.* By E. Cerulli. Encyclopaedia of world art, vol. 7, 1963, 216–48, ill., map.

2383. **Hall, H. U.** *Twins in Upper Guinea.* Museum journal (Univ. of Pennsylvania, Philadelphia, Pa.), **19**, 1928, 403–27.

2384. **Haselberger, Herta.** *Wandzierrate in Guinea, Dahomey, Togo und Obervolta.* (To be published in Int. Archiv Ethnog.)

2385. —— *Wandmalereien und plastischer Bauschmuck in Guinea.* Jb. S. Mus. Völkerkunde (Leipzig), **19**, 1962, 138–66.

2386. **Holas, B.** 1962. *Guineane culture.* Pp. 22–56, bibl., ill., map. Venezia, Rome. (Reprint from Enciclopedia Universale dell' Arte, 7.)

2387. **Houis, M.** 1953. *Guinée française.* Pp. 95, ill., maps. Paris: Éd. Maritimes et Coloniales.

2388. **Jaeger, P.** *La case Kouranko (Guinée française et Sierra Leone).* Notes afr. I.F.A.N., 1946, 16–19, ill.

2389. **Lestrange, Monique de.** 1955. *Les Coniagui et les Bassari (Guinée française).* Pp. vi + 86, bibl., map. Paris: Presses Univ. de France. (Monographies Ethnologiques Africaines de l'Institut International Africain.)

2390. **Lobsiger-Dellenbach, M.** *Au XXe siècle dans la Guinée de Sékou Touré; croyances moribondes.* Les Musées de Genève, **10**, 1960, 9–10, ill.

2391. **Mauny, Raymond.** *Rayonnement d'Ifé; Capitale artistique et religieuse ancienne du Golfe de Guinée.* Présence africaine, N.S. 4, oct.–nov. 1955, 80–82.

2392. **Paulme, D.** *Utilisation moderne d'objets préhistoriques à des fins rituelles en pays Kissi.* Notes afr. I.F.A.N., **44**, 1949, 119.

2393. **Schnell, R.** *Sur quelques utilisations actuelles d'objets lithiques anciens par les indigènes de Guinée française et de côte d'Ivoire.* Bull. soc. préhist. fr., **44** (5–6), 1949, 215–17.

2394. **Techer, H.** *Coutumes des Tendas.* Bull. Com. Études A.O.F., **16**, 4, 1933, 630–66, ill., map.

FIGURES AND MASKS

2395. **Appia, Beatrice.** *Masques de Guinée française et de Casamance.* J. soc. africanistes, **13**, 1943, 153–82, ill.

2396. **Delange, Jacqueline.** *Le bansonyi du pays Baga.* Objets et mondes, **2**, 1, printemps 1962, 3–12, ill.

2397. **Delafosse, M.** *Au sujet des statuettes en pierre du Kissi.* Rev. étud. ethnog. sociol. (Paris), **5**, 1914, 143–4.

2398. **Fagg, William B.** *A colossal mask from the Baga of Guinea.* B.M.Q., **24**, 1961, 61–65, ill.

2399. **Holas, Bohumil.** *Le masque Komo de Korodou.* Notes afr. I.F.A.N., **38**, 1948, 24–25.

2400. —— 1952. *Les masques Kono (Haute-Guinée française).* Pp. 200, bibl., ill., map. Paris: Paul Geuthner.

2401. **Itier, G.** *Notice au sujet de deux statuettes funéraires kissiennes.* Bull. com. études A.O.F., **9**, 1, 1926, 126–30.

2402. **Jeanneret, A.** *Elek, une sculpture rituelle des Baga.* Les Musées de Genève, **35**, mai 1963, 14–15, bibl., ill.

2403. **Jéremine, E.** *Étude des statuettes kissiennes au point de vue minéralogique et pétrographique.* J. soc. africanistes, **15**, 1945, 3–14, ill., map.

2404. **Mengrelis, Thanos.** *La sortie des inities en pays guerze.* Notes afr. I.F.A.N., **50**, 1951, 44–46, ill.

2405. —— *Le sens des masques dans l'initiation chez les Guerzé de la Guinée française.* Africa, **22**, 3, July 1952, 257–62, ill., map.

2406. **Notes Africaines I.F.A.N.** *Danseur masqué guerzé-conon N'Zérékoré (Guinée).* Notes afr. I.F.A.N., 41, 1949 (cover ill.).

2407. **Olderogge, D.** *Zhenskaya statuetka Plemens Baga (Female Baga statuette).* Izvestia Akad. Nauk, 1934.

2408. **Paulme, Denise.** *Deux statuettes en pierre de Guinée française.* Bull. et méin. soc. d'anthrop., Paris, **3**, sér. 9, 1942, 38–43.

2409. —— 1954. *Les Gens du Riz.* Pp. 225, bibl., ill., map. Paris: Librairie Plon.

2410. —— *'Elek', a ritual sculpture of the Baga of French Guinea.* Trans. William Fagg. Man, **59**, no. 28, 1959, 28, ill.

2411. **Person, Y.** *Les Kissi et leurs statuettes de pierre dans le cadre de l'histoire ouest-africaine.* Bull. I.F.A.N., **23** (B), 1/2, janv.–avr. 1961, 1–59, ill., maps.

2412. **Schaeffner, A.** *Les rites de circoncision en pays Kissi.* (Haute Guinée française). Études Guin., **12**, 1954, 3–56, ill.

2413. **Simõe, Landerset.** (1937.) *Babel negra* (*Etnografia arte, e cultura dos indigenas de Guiné*). Pp. 184, ill. Porto: O Comacio do Porto.

2414. **Wixom, William D.** *Two African tribal sculptures.* Bull. Cleveland museum of art, **48**, 1961, 39–45, ill.

BUILDINGS AND FURNITURE

2415. **Creac'h, Paul.** *Notes sur l'art décoratif architectural foula du Haut Fouta-Djallon.* Iᵉ Conf. int. Africanistes de l'Ouest, C.R., **2**, 1951, 300–12, ill.

2416. **Notes Africaines I.F.A.N.** *Cases peules à Labé* (*Fouta-Djallon*). Notes afr. I.F.A.N., 60, 1953 (cover ill.).

2417. **Poujade, J.** 1948. *Les cases décorées d'un chef du Fouta-Djallon.* Pp. 40, ill. Paris: Gauthier-Villars.

CLOTHING AND ADORNMENT

2418. **Fourneau, J.,** and **L. Kravetz.** *Le pagne sur la Côte de Guinée et au Congo du XV siècle à nos jours.* Bull. inst. ét. centrafricaines (Brazzaville), N.S. 7/8, 1954, 5–22.

2419. **Notes Africaines I.F.A.N.** *Coiffure des femmes peules du Fouta-Djalon, Guinée.* Notes afr. I.F.A.N., 30, 1946 (cover ill.).

2420. —— *Fileuse 'Peul' Mali. Mali-Labe* (*Guinée Française*). Notes afr. I.F.A.N., 38, 1948 (cover ill.).

2421. —— *Jeune fille peul.* Notes afr. I.F.A.N., 48, 1950 (cover ill.).

2422. —— *Chapeau-parapluie de Macenta* (*Guinée*). Notes afr. I.F.A.N., 70, 1956 (cover ill.).

TECHNIQUES

2423. **Balandier, Georges.** *L'or de la Guinée française.* Présence africaine, 4, 1948, 539–48.

2424. **Burland, C. A.** *Lost wax, metal casting on the Guinea coast.* Studio, 154, 18–21.

2425. **Baldé-Saikhou.** *Les forgerons du Fouta-Djallon.* Educ. afr., **24**, 1935.

2426. **Corbeil, R.** *Quelques détails sur la fabrication des poteries indigènes à Siguiri* (*Guinée Française*). Notes afr. I.F.A.N., **32**, Oct. 1946, 29–30.

2427. **Earthy, E. D.** *Short note on a Kissi smith.* Man, **34**, 180, Oct. 1934, 159–61.

2428. **Fagg, William.** *Two woodcarvings from the Baga of French Guinea.* Man, **47**, no. 113, Aug. 1947, 105–6, ill.

2429. **Glück, J.** 1937. *Die Goldgewichte von Oberguinea.* Pp. 132, ill. Heidelberg: Heidelberger Akten. Porth. Stift. Vol. 21.

2430. **Holas, B.** *Qui connait l'origine de ces statuettes de poterie.* Notes afr. I.F.A.N., 53, 1952, 18–20, ill.

2431. **Rutz, Werner.** *Keramik bei Bagas und Balantas.* Baessler-Arch., **7**, 1, Aug. 1959, 201–8, ill.

IVORY COAST

2432. **Clamens, G.** *Le serpent en pays Sénoufo.* Notes afr. I.F.A.N., **56**, 1952, 119–20.

2433. —— *Notes d'ethnologie Sénoufo.* Notes afr. I.F.A.N., **59**, 1953, 76–80, ill.

2434. —— *Dieux d'eau en pays Sénoufo.* Notes afr. I.F.A.N., **60**, 1953, 106–8.

2435. **Clozel, F. J.,** and **Roger Villamur.** 1902. *Les coutumes indigènes de la Côte d'Ivoire.* Pp. xx + 539, map. Paris: Challamel.

2436. **Crosson-Duplessis, Capt.** *L'Ethnographie de la Côte d'Ivoire.* Afr. Franc. Rens. Col., **10**, 1900, 93–99: 111–18.

2437. **Delafosse, M.** *Les Agni.* L'Anthropogie, 4, 1893, 402–45.

2438. **Germain, J.** *Extrait d'une monographie des habitants du Cercle de* N'Zerékoré (*Guerzé, Kono, Manon*). *Les artisans, les techniques et les arts.* Études Guin., **13**, 1955, 3–54, ill.

2439. **Holas, Bohumil.** *Teinturiers Mossi à Dimbokro* (*Côte d'Ivoire*). Notes afr. I.F.A.N., **38**, 1948, 18–21, ill.

2440. —— *Les monstres du Cavally; En marge des légendes du lamantin.* Notes afr. I.F.A.N., **41**, janv. 1949, 1–3, ill.

2441. —— *Motif à face double et multiple dans les arts plastiques éburnéens.* Acta tropica, **10**, 2, 1953, 97–112, ill., map.

2442. —— 1960. *Cultures matérielles de la Côte d'Ivoire.* Pp. 96, bibl., ill. Paris: Presses Univ. de France.

2443. **Knops, P.,** and **J. Weyns.** *Bijdragen over kunst en kultuur van de Senufo* (*Ivoor kust, Frans-West-Afrika*). 1. Twee kenschetsende beelden der Senufo. Bull. mus. roy. belge (d'art et d'hist.), 25e ann., 40 sér., 1953, 60–65, ill.

2444. —— *Bijdragen over kunst en kultuur van de Senufo* (*Ivoorkust, Frans-West-Afrika*). 2. Notes sur une lampe Sénoufo et ses artisans. Bull. mus. roy. belge (d'art et d'hist.), 25e ann. 40 sér., 1953, 66–71, ill.

2445. **Lindholm, Britt.** 1957. *Les portraits Baoulé et leur base sociale.* Pp. 40–53, ill. Gothenburg: Ethnographical Museum. (Ex. Etnografiska Museet, Arstryck, 1955.)

2446. **Maesen, A. E.** MS. thesis. University of Ghent. 'De plastiek in de Kultuur van der Senufo van de Troor kunst.' 1946.

2447. **New York; Museum of Primitive Art.** 1963. *Senoufo sculpture from West Africa.* Pp. 80 + 125, ill. New York: Museum of Primitive Art.

2448. **Olbrechts, Frans M.** *Ivoorkust-expeditie der Rijksuniversiteit de Gent en van het Vleeschhuis-Museum te Antwerpen.* Kongo-Overzee, **5**, 4, Oct. 1939, 177–87.

2449. **Paulme, Denise.** 1962. *Les Bété; une société de Côte d'Ivoire hier et aujourd'hui.* Pp. 197, bibl., ill., maps. Paris: Mouton & Co.

2450. **Proteaux, M.** *Divertissements de Kong* (*Diula*). Bull. com. études A.O.F., **8**, 1925, 606–50, ill.

2451. **Rahm, U.** *Über einige Säugetierfallen der Basse Côte d'Ivoire.* Acta tropica, **11** (1), 1954, 63–68, ill.

2452. **Rougerie, Gabriel.** *Les pays Agni du Sud-Est de la Côte d'Ivoire forestière.* Pp. 211, ill. (Abidjan) I.F.A.N. Centre de Côte d'Ivoire.

2453. **Szecsi, Ladislaus.** *Stilgebiete der Elfenbeinküste.* Ethnol. Anz., **3**, 3, 1933, 140–2, 3 Taf. m. 14 Abb.

2454. **Viard, Rene.** 1934. *Les Guérés; peuple de la forêt.* Pp. 142, ill., maps. Paris: Société d'Éditions géographiques, maritimes et coloniales.

2455. **Villamur, Roger.** 1904. *Les coutumes Agni.* Pp. 174. Paris: Challamel.

2456. —— and **Richaud.** 1903. *Notre colonie de la Côte d'Ivoire.* Pp. 400. Paris: Challamel.

2457. **Weyns, J.** *Een muizenorahel van de Baule, Ivoorkust, Frans West-Afrika.* Bull., mus. roy. belge d'art et d'hist., 54, **24**, 35–38.

2458. —— and **P. Knops.** *Bijdragen over kunst en kultuur van de Senufo.* Bull., mus. roy. belge d'art et d'hist., 54, **25**, 60–71.
See also 2463, 2472–3, 2475, 2485–7.

FIGURES AND MASKS

2459. **Bodiel, Th.** *Canne coutumière Sénoufo.* Notes afr. I.F.A.N., **88**, 1960, 122–3, ill.

2460. **Clamens, Gabriel.** *Curieuse statue de cuivre sénoufo.* Notes afr. I.F.A.N., **58**, janv. 1953, p. 14, ill.

2461. —— *Les Nyi-kar-yi de Watyene.* Notes afr. I.F.A.N., **60**, oct. 1953, 108–10, ill.

2462. **Fagg, William.** *Two early masks from the Dan tribe in the British Museum.* Man, **55**, Nov. 1955, 175, 161–2, ill.

2463. **Hallouin, C.** *Géographie humaine de la subdivision de Daloa.* Bull. I.F.A.N., **9**, 1947, 18–55, ill., map.

2464. **Himmelheber, Hans.** *Massa—Fetisch der Rechtschaffenheit bei den Senufo und Baoulé.* Tribus, 4–5, 1954–5, 56–62, ill.

2465. —— *Die Masken der Guéré, im Rahmen der Kunst des oberen Cavally-Gebietes.* Z. f. Ethnol., **88**, 2, 1963, 216–33, bibl., ill.

2466. **Holas, Bohumil.** *Le masque do des Baoulé Aitou d'Akoué Koidiokro.* Notes afr. I.F.A.N., **38**, 1948, 5–6, ill.

2467. —— *Sur l'utilisation rituelle des statuettes funérairies au Royaune de Krinjako (Côte d'Ivoire).* Acta tropica, **8**, 1, 1951, 1–17, ill., maps.

2468. —— *Une 'génitrix' baoulé.* Acta tropica, **9**, 3, 1952, 193–203, ill.

2469. —— *Sur quelques divinités Baoulé de rang inférieur; leurs figurations, leur rôle liturgique.* Bull. I.F.A.N., **18** (3–4), 1956, 408–32, ill.

2470. —— *Note sur la fonction rituelle de deux catégories de statues Sénoufo.* Artibus Asiae, **20**, 1957, 29–35.

2471. —— *Senufo sculpture.* Black Orpheus (Ibadan), **5**, 1959, 30–32, ill.

2472. —— 1961. *Changements sociaux en Côte d'Ivoire.* Pp. 117 + 3, bibl., ill. Paris: Presses Univ. de France.

2473. —— 1962. *Les Toura.* Pp. 234, ill. Paris: Presses Univ. de France.

2474. —— 1964. *Sculpture Sénoufo.* Pp. 24 + 45 pl., bibl. Abidjan: Centre des Sciences Humaines de la Côte d'Ivoire.

2475. **Kerharo, J.**, and **A. Bouquet.** *La chasse en Côte-d'Ivoire et en Haute-Volta.* Acta tropica, **6**, no. 3, 1949, 193–220, bibl., ill.

2476. —— —— 1950. *Sorciers, féticheurs et guérisseurs de la Côte-d'Ivoire-Haute-Volta.* Pp. 144, ill., map. Paris: Vigot Frères.

2477. **Lavachéry, H.** *Apparente évolution des masques de la région de Man (Côte d'Ivoire).* Bull. mus. roy. belge d'art et d'hist., **6**, 1939, 137–41.

2478. **Lem, F. H.** *Au sujet d'une statuette Sénoufo.* Bull. I.F.A.N., **4**, 1942, 175–80, ill.

2479. —— *Statuettes funéraïres (à Krinjabo, Côte d'Ivoire).* Encycl. mens. d'O.-M. (Paris), **1**, 20, avr. 1952, 110–14.

2480. **Lobsiger-Dellenbach, M.** *Les masques dans le monde. 11: La fabrication des masques à la Côte d'Ivoire.* Les Musées de Genève, **1** (4), 1944, 3, ill.

2481. **Michelet, Raymond**, and **L. Szecsi.** *The different styles of masks of the Ivory Coast.* Cunard, Nancy (ed.), Negro Anthology, 1934, 680–1, ill.

2482. **Neveux, Maurice.** 1923. *Fétiches de la Côte d'Ivoire.* Pp. 33, ill. Alencon: Imp. Laverdure.

2483. **Siroto, Leon.** *A note on Guro statues.* Man, **53**, 24, Feb. 1953, 17–18, ill.

2484. —— *Baule and Guro sculpture of the Ivory Coast, and notes on the Bakota, Pangwe and Balumbwe sculpture of the Gabon and the Middle Congo.* Masterpieces of African Art. Catalogue of an exhibition held at the Brooklyn Museum, 21 Oct. 1954–2 Jan. 1955.

2485. **Tauxier, L.** 1921. *Le noir de Bondoukou.* Pp. xii + 770, bibl., ill. Paris: Geuthner.

2486. —— 1924. *Nègres Gouro et Gagou (Centre de la Côte d'Ivoire).* Pp. 374, bibl., ill. Paris: Geuthner.

2487. —— 1932. *Religion, moeurs et coutumes des Agnis de la Côte-d'Ivoire (Indénié et Sanwi).* Pp. 256, ill. Paris: Geuthner.

2488. **Vandenhoute, P. J. L.** 1945. 'Het Masker in de cultuur en kunst van het Boven-Cavally Gebied.' MS. thesis, University of Ghent.

2489. —— *Classification stylistique du masque Dan et Guéré de la Côte d'Ivoire occidentale (A.O.F.).* Meded. Rijksmus. Volkenkunde (Leiden), **4**, 1948.

2490. —— *Het ontstaan en de betekenis van maskernamen in het Boven-Cevalley-gebied (Ivoorkust).* Handelingen van het 19th Vlaamse Filologen-Congres (Brussels), 1951, 261–4.

2491. —— 1963. *Masks of the Dan-Ivory Coast.* (Art in its context series: Studies in Ethno-Aesthetics.)

2492. **Verneau, R.** 1924. *Le cavenerment dans l'art nègre.* L'Anthropologie, **34**, 189–.

2493. **Wirz, P.** *Ein neuer Fetischkult im Gebiet der Elfenbeinküste.* Ethnol. Anz., **3**, 1934, 280–2.

2494. **Zemp, Hugo.** *Eine esoterische Überlieferung über den Ursprung der maskierten Stelzentänzer bei den Dan (Elfenbeinküste).* Festschrift Alfred Bühler, 1965, 451–66, bibl., ill.

CLOTHING AND ADORNMENT

2495. **Ake Assi, L.**, and **J. Bouton-Martin.** *Bracelet ébrié ancien.* Notes afr. I.F.A.N., no. 89, 1961, 4, ill.

2496. **Bertho, J.** *Le Labret des femmes Bobo-Fing, en Haute Côte d'Ivoire.* Notes afr. I.F.A.N., 29, 1946, 21, ill.

2497. **Holas, Bohumil.** *Vêtements d'écorce (Côte d'Ivoire).* Notes afr. I.F.A.N., 43, juil. 1949, 77–80, ill., map.

2498. —— *Note sur le vêtement et la parure baoulé (Côte d'Ivoire).* Bull. I.F.A.N., **11**, 3/4, juil.–oct. 1949, 438–57, ill.

2499. **Notes Africaines I.F.A.N.** *Coiffures de danse Sénoufo-Korhogo.* Notes afr. I.F.A.N., 55, 1952 (cover ill.).

ROCK ART

2500. **Clamens, Gabriel.** *Gravures rupestres en Côte d'Ivoire.* Notes afr. I.F.A.N., 49, janv. 1951, 1, ill.

2501. **Mockers, P.**, and **G. Clamens.** *Hauts lieux et gravures rupestres en pays djimini (Côte-d'Ivoire).* Notes afr. I.F.A.N., 46, avr. 1950, 35–36, ill.

TECHNIQUES

2502. **Bertho, Jacques.** *Note sur le haut-fourneau et la forge des Bobo-Oulé (Bobo rouges), de Dédougou (Haute Côte d'Ivoire).* Notes afr. I.F.A.N., 30, avr. 1946, 10–12, ill.

2503. **Bouys, P.** *Samory et les forgerons de Dabakala.* Notes afr. I.F.A.N., 18, avr. 1943, 11–12.

2504. **Fischer, Eberhard.** *Die Töpferei bei den westlichen Dan. Eine Darstellung auf Grund einer Reise ins Hinterland von Liberia (8. Expedition Dr. Hans Himmelheber, 1960).* Z. f. Ethnol., **88**, 1, 1963, 100–15, ill.

2506. —— *Zur Technik des Gelbgusses bei den westlichen Dan.* Festschrift Alfred Bühler, 1965, 93–115, ill.

2507. **Foote, H. S.** *Gold ornaments from the Ivory Coast.* Cleveland museum bull., **29**, 1942, 104.

2508. **Knops, P.** *L'artisan sénoufo dans son cadre ouest-africain.* Bull. soc. roy. belge anthrop., **70**, 1959, 83–111.

2509. **Labouret, Henri.** *Notes contributives à l'étude du peuple Baoulé.* Rev. étud. ethnog. sociol. Paris, 5, 1914–19, 73–91: 181–94, ill. (Describes the making of brass weights on the Ivory Coast.)

2510. **Lobsiger-Dellenbach, M.** *Documents pour l'ethnographie de la Côte d'Ivoire; poids pour peser la poudre d'Or.* Arch. Suisses anthrop. générale, **7**, no. 1, 1934, 58–72.

2511. **Maesen, A.** *La fonte à la cire perdue en Haute-Côte d'Ivoire.* Congr. int. sci. anthrop. et ethnol., 3e Session, Bruxelles, 1948 (1960), 136–8.

2512. **Kulaseli.** *Esotérisme africain. Une phase de l'initiation à un 'poro forgeron' Senoufo.* Eurafrique, 28e ann., 3, 1955, 47–56, ill.

UTENSILS, TOOLS AND WEAPONS; MISCELLANEOUS

2513. **Abel, H.** *Déchiffrement des poids à peser l'or en Côte d'Ivoire.* J. soc. africanistes, **22**, 1952, 95–114, ill.; **24**, 1954, 7–23, ill.; **29**, 1959, 273–86, ill.

2514. **Clamens, Gabriel**, and **A. Adandé.** *Poignard et haches de parade en cuivre sénoufo ancien.* Notes afr. I.F.A.N., **58**, avr. 1953, 49–51, ill.

2515. **Durville, Gaston.** *Symboles divins monothéistes sur les plus anciens poids de bronze à peser l'or en Côte d'Ivoire et en Gold Coast.* Bull. soc. préhist. fr., **47**, 1950, 172–81.

2516. **Paulme, D.** *Les poids-proverbes de la Côte d'Ivoire au Musée de l'Homme.* J. soc. africanistes, **11**, 1941, 228–9.

2517. **Rahm, U.** *La Côte d'Ivoire; Centre de recherches tropicales.* Acta tropica, **11**, no. 3., 1954, 283–95, bibl., ill.

AFRICAN ART TODAY

2518. **Fischer, Eberhard.** *Künstler der Dan; die Bildhauer Tame, Si, Tompieme und Sön—ihr Wesen und ihr Werk.* Baessler-Arch., n.f., **10**, 2, June 1963, 161–263, bibl., ill.

2519. **Himmelheber, Hans.** *Sculptors and sculptures of the Dan.* First Int. Congress of Africanists (Accra, 1962, *eds.* L. Brown and M. Crowder), 1964, 243–55.

2520. **Maesen, A.** *Le sculpteur dans la vie sociale chez les Sénoufo de la Côte d'Ivoire.* Congr. int. sci. anthrop. et ethnol. 3e Session, Bruxelles, 1948 (1960), 138–9.

DAHOMEY

2521. **Adandé, Alexandre.** 1962. *Les récades des rois du Dahomey.* Pp. 104, bibl., ill., map. Dakar: I.F.A.N.

2522. —— *Protection et développement de l'artisanat d'art au Dahomey.* Études dah., N.S. 2, 1964, 93–100.

2523. **Akindele, Adolphe,** and **Cyrille Aguessy.** 1955. *Le Dahomey.* Pp. 126, bibl., ill. Paris: Éditions Maritimes et Coloniales.

2524. **Bertho, J.** *Les sièges des rois d'Abomey.* Notes afr. I.F.A.N., 1946, 7–9, ill.

2525. **Brunet, L.,** and **L. Giethlen.** 1900. *Dahomey et dépendances.* Pp. xi + 544, ill. Paris: Challamel.

2526. **Chaudoin, E.** 1891. *Trois mois de captivité au Dahomey.* Pp. xi + 409, ill. Paris: Hachette.

2527. **Cornevin, Robert.** 1962. *Histoire du Dahomey.* Pp. 568, bibl., ill., maps. Paris: Berger-Levrault. (Note chap. 6 (5 and 6), pp. 230–5.)

2528. **Cornevin, G.** *Le Canton de l'Akebou.* Études dah., 7, 1952, 114–32, bibl., ill., map.

2529. **Corpel, Kid et René.** 1961. *Terre dahoméenne.* S.P. (A series of plates with descriptive text.) Porto-Novo: Arts et Métiers Graphiques.

2530. **de Pedrals, Denis Pierre.** 1946. *Dans la brousse africaine au Dahomey-Borghou.* Pp. 245, ill., map. Paris: La Nouvelle Edition.

2531. **France d'Outre-Mer.** *Le passé vivant au Dahomey.* Chron. d'outre-mer (Paris), 1953, 15–18, ill.

2532. **Griaule, Marcel.** *Fragments sur le Dahomey.* Minotaure (Paris), 11, 1933, 57–61, ill.

2633. **Herisse, A. le.** *L'Ancienne Royaume de Dahomey.* Paris, 1911.

2534. **Herskovits, Melville J.** *Some aspects of Dahomean ethnology.* Africa, 5, 1932, 266–96, ill.

2535. —— 1938. *Dahomey; an ancient West African kingdom.* 2 vols. Vol. 1, pp. xxi + 402, ill. Vol. 2, pp. xiv + 407, bibl., ill. New York: J. J. Augustin. (Vol. 2, pp. 311 72, art and art forms.)

2536. —— *Symbolism in Dahomean art.* Man, 41, no. 84, 1941, 117.

2537. —— 1945. *Backgrounds of African art.* Pp. 64, ill., map. Denver: Denver Art Museum. (The Cooke-Daniels Lecture Foundation in conjunction with an exhibition of African Art assembled by the Denver Art Museum, January and February 1945.)

2538. —— and **F. S.** 1958. *Dahomean narrative; a cross-cultural analysis.* Pp. xvi + 490. Chicago: North Western Univ. Press.

2539. **Lombard, J.** *Aperçu sur la technologie et l'artisanat Bariba.* Études dah., 18, 19–57, 759, ill.

2540. **Marin, J.** *Étude des moyens de pêche dans la Basse et moyenne vallée de l'Ouémé.* Études dah., 16, 1956, 7–20, ill.

2541. **Mauny, R.** *État actuel de nos connaissances sur la préhistoire du Dahomey et du Togo.* Études dah., 4, 1950, 5–11, ill.

2542. **Mercier, Paul.** *Évolution de l'art dahoméen.* Diop, A., L'art nègre, 1951, 185–93, ill.

2543. **Quénum, Maximilien.** *Au pays des Fons.* Bull. com. études A.O.F., 18, nos. 2–3, 1936, 141–379, ill.

2544. **Réal, Daniel.** *Note sur l'art dahoméen.* L'Anthropologie, 30, 1920, 369–92, ill.

2545. **Skertchly, J. A.** 1874. *Dahomey as it is.* Pp. xx + 524, ill., map. London: Chapman & Hall.

2546. **Turnbull, C. M.** *Tribal art from Africa; Dahomean sculptors.* Nat. Hist., 73, 3, 1964, 46–53, ill.

2547. **Vellut, Jeanne.** 1928. *Art nègre; l'art dahoméen.* Rev. missionnaire des Jésuites belges, 2, 5, 199–202.

2548. **Weyns, J.,** and **F. van Trigt.** *Gietwerkgroepen uit Dahomey, West-Afrika* (with French summary). Bull. mus. roy. belge. d'art et d'hist., s4, v.27, 77–83.

FIGURES AND MASKS

2549. **Baudin, Noel.** 1885. *Fetishism and fetish worshippers by Baudin, missionary on the Slave Coast.* Pp. 127. New York.

2550. **Bertho, Jacques.** *L'Habitation des Somba (Dahomey).* Conferencia International dos Africanistas Occidentais. 2a Bissau, 1947. Trabalhos, vol. 5. 3a Secção 2a Parte. (Meio Humano), 1952, 95 104, ill. Lisbon: Junta de Investigações Coloniais.

2551. —— *La case des morts chez les Yoabou de la région de Natitengou (Dahomey).* Notes afr. I.F.A.N., 36, 1947, 28–29.

2552. **Delange, Jacqueline.** *Sur un oshe Shango.* Objets et mondes, 3, 3, automne 1963, 205–10, ill.

2553. **Frazer, J. G.** *Statues of three kings of Dahomey.* Man, 8, 73, 1908, 130–2, ill.

2554. **Fuchs, P.** *Les figurines en métal d'Ouagadougou.* Notes afr. I.F.A.N., 87, juil. 1960, 76–82, ill.

2555. **Gaillard, Dr.** *Étude sur les lacustres du Bas-Dahomey.* L'Anthropologie, 18, 1907, 103–4, ill.

2556. **Liturgical Arts.** *Religious sculpture; work of Dahomey artists.* Liturgical arts, 26, no. 4, 1958, 104a–b, ill.

2557. **Lobsiger-Dellenbach, Marguerite.** *Figurines en terre modelée du Dahomey.* Arch. suisses anthrop. générale, 11, 2, 1945, 215, ill.

2558. **Macfie, J. W. Scott.** *Shongo staffs.* Man, 13, no. 96, 1913, 169–71, ill.

2559. **Mercier, P.** *Images de l'art animalier au Dahomey.* Études dah., 5, 1951, 93–103, ill.

BUILDINGS AND FURNITURE

2560. **Haselberger, Herta.** *Gemalter, gravierter und modellierter Bauschmuck in Dahomey.* Tribus, no. 10, Sept. 1961, 33–56, ill.

2561. **Mercier, P.** *L'Habitation à étage dans l'Atakora.* Études dah., 11, 1954, 29–77, ill., map.

2562. **Valogne, C.** *L'Histoire du Dahomey sculptée sur les murs du palais royal d'Abomey.* Arts, 2 avr. 1948, 1.

2563. **Verger, Pierre.** *Note on the bas-reliefs in the royal palaces of Abomey.* Odù, 5, 1958, 3–13, ill.

2564. **Waterlot, Em. G.** 1926. *Les bas-reliefs des batiments royaux d'Abomey (Dahomey).* Pp. vi + 10, ill. Paris: Institut d'Ethnologie. (Travaux et mémoires de l'Institut d'Ethnologie, 1.)

CLOTHING AND ADORNMENT

2565. **Bernolles, J.** *Note sur l'ornementation d'un chapeau peul en usage dans la région de Djougou (Dahomey Septentrional).* Notes afr. I.F.A.N., 98, 1963, 47–50, ill.

2566. **Dunglas, E.** *Perles anciennes trouvées au Dahomey.* 1er Conf. Int. Africanistes de l'Ouest. Compte rendu, 2, 1951, 431–4.

2567. **Notes Africaines I.F.A.N.** *Coiffure dit doka d'une femme du collège royal d'Abomey (Dahomey).* Notes afr. I.F.A.N., 44, 1949 (cover ill.).

2568. **Dakar: I.F.A.N.** 1953. No. 23. *Mélanges Ethnologiques.* Pp. 408, ill., maps. Dakar: I.F.A.N. (Mémoires de I.F.A.N., no. 23. Contains: P. Dubie, La vie materielle des Maures, 111–252. J. C. Froelich, Cat. des scarifications en usage chez certaines populations du Dahomey et du Nord-Togo, 253–64, ill.)

TECHNIQUES

2569. **Griaule, M.,** and **G. Dieterlen.** *Calebasses dahoméennes.* J. soc. africanistes, 5, 1935, 203–46, ill.

2570. **Herskovits, M. J.,** and **F. S. Herskovits.** *The art of Dahomey;* (1) Brass casting and appliqué cloths. Amer. mag. of art, 27

(2), 1934, 67–76. (2) Wood-carving. Amer. mag. of art, **27** (3), 1934, 124–31.

2571. **Hunt-Cooke, A.,** and **K. C. Murray.** *Dahomeyan crafts.* Nigeria, **10**, 1937, 23–26, ill.

VOLTAIC REPUBLIC

2572. **Charles, Léon.** *Les Lobí.* Rev. étud. ethnog. sociol. (Paris), **2**, 1911, 202–20, ill.

2573. **Crémer, Jean.** *Matériaux d'ethnographie et de linguistique soudanaises.* 1924. Tome 3, Les Bobo (La vie sociale). Pp. 175, ill. Paris: Geuthner. 1928. Tome 4, Les Bobo (La mentalité mystique). Pp. viii + 212. Paris: Geuthner.

2574. **Dim Delobson, A. A.** 1932. *L'Empire du Mogho-Naba. Coutumes des Mossi de la Haute-Volta.* Pp. (4), vii + 303, ill. Paris: Domat-Montchrestien, Loviton.

2575. **Dittmer, K.** *Afrika-Expedition des Hamburgischen Museums für Völkerkunde.* Z. f. Ethnol. (Brunswick), **80**, 1955, 138–40.

2576. **Labouret, Henri.** *Le mystère des ruines du Lobi.* Rev. Ethnog. Trad. Pop., 1920.

2577. **Le Moal, G.** *Note sur les populations 'Bobo'.* Bull. I.F.A.N., **19** (B), 3/4, juil.–oct. 1957, 418–30, map.

2578. **Lilley, E. S.** *Notes on the Chamba tribe.* MS. Ethnog. Doc. 226, Dept. of Ethnography, British Museum.

2579. **Mangin, Eugène.** *Les Mossi.* Pp. xi + 116, ill. Paris: A. Challamel. (Ex: Anthropos, 1916.)

2580. **Marc, Lucien.** 1909. *Le pays Mossi.* Pp. (2), viii + 189, ill., map. Paris: Larose.

2581. **Mauny, R.** *État actuel de nos connaissances sur la préhistoire et archéologie de la Haute-Volta.* Notes afr. I.F.A.N., **73**, 1957, 16–24, ill., map.

2582. **Schweeger-Hefel, Annemarie.** *Die Kunst der Kurumba (Haute-Volta, Westafrika).* Arch. f. Völkerkunde (Wien), **17–18**, 1962/1963, 194–260, bibl., ill.

2583. —— *Les insignes royaux des Kouroumba (Haute-Volta).* J. soc. africanistes, **32**, 1962, 275–323, bibl., ill.

2584. **Tauxier, L.** *Les Gouin et les Tourouka.* J. soc. Africanistes, **3** (1), 1933, 52, ill.

FIGURES AND MASKS

2585. **Griaule, Marcel.** *Notes sur les masques des Kouroumba.* J. soc. africanistes, **11**, 1941, 224–5.

2586. **Zwernemann, Jürgen.** *Zur figürlichen Plastik der Bwa.* Tribus, **11**, 1962, 149–52, bibl., ill.

BUILDINGS AND FURNITURE

2587. **Zahan, D.** *L'habitation Mossi.* Bull. I.F.A.N., **12**, 1950, 223–9, ill.

CLOTHING AND ADORNMENT

2588. **Labouret, H.** *A propos des labrets en verre de quelques populations voltaïques.* Bull. I.F.A.N., **14**, 4, oct. 1952, 1385–1401, ill., map.

2589. **Mercier, P.** *Marques du statut individuel chez les Somba.* Bissau, Conferência international dos Africanistas ocidentais. 2. Conferência Bissau, 1947. Vol. V. 3ª secção, 2ª párte, 1952, 219–40.

2590. **Tauxier, Louis.** *Les Ouara ou Guala, et les Natioro.* J. soc. africanistes, **9** (2), 1939, 159–95, ill., map.

ROCK ART

2591. **Henninger, Jean.** *Signification des gravures rupestres d'une grotte de Borodougou (Haute-Volta).* Notes afr. I.F.A.N., **88**, oct. 1960, 106–10, ill.

AFRICAN ART TODAY

2592. **Fortes, M.** *Children's drawings among the Tallensi.* Africa, **13**, 3, 1940, 293–4.

TOGO

2593. **Ahyi, Paul.** *Die schweigende Welt der togolesischen Kunst und das Motiv der Schildkröte.* Afrika (München), **2**, 2, Apr. 1960, 157–60, ill.

2594. **Cornevin, Robert.** 1962. *Les Bassari du Nord-Togo.* Pp. 156, bibl., ill., maps. Paris: Berger-Levrault.

2595. **Froelich, Jean-Claude.** *Généralités sur les Kabrè du Nord-Togo.* Bull. I.F.A.N., **11** (1–2), 1949, 77–105, ill., maps.

2596. —— *Les Konkomba du Nord-Togo.* Bull. I.F.A.N., **11** (3–4), 1949, 409–37, ill., maps.

2597. —— *Notes sur les Naoudeba du Nord-Togo.* Bull. I.F.A.N., **12** (1), 1950, 102–21, ill., map.

2598. —— 1954. *La tribu Konkomba du Nord-Togo.* Pp. 253, bibl., ill., maps. Dakar: I.F.A.N. (Mém. I.F.A.N., 37.)

2599. **Garnier, Christina,** and **Jean Fralon.** 1951. *Le fétichisme en Afrique noire (Togo-Cameroun).* Pp. 213, bibl., ill., maps. Paris: Payot.

2600. **Haselberger, Hérta.** *Wandmalerei, gravierter und modellierter Wandschmuck in den Savannen von Togo und Obervolta.* Int. archiv. ethnog., **49**, 2, 1960, 201–24.

2601. **M. et S.** *Les Arts au Togo.* Togo Cameroun, 1931, mars–avr., 147–55.

2602. **Schönhärl, Josef.** 1909. *Volkskundliches aus Togo.* Pp. x + 204, ill. Dresden: Koch.

FIGURES AND MASKS

2603. **Chermette, A.** *À propos de pierres sculptées trouvées au Togo.* Notes afr. I.F.A.N., **15**, 1942, 5.

2604. **Cornevin, Robert.** *Masques de laiton de type Yorouba provenant du Nord Togo.* Notes afr. I.F.A.N., **84**, oct. 1959, 101–2, ill.

2605. —— *A propos des masques de laiton du Nord-Togo.* Notes afr. I.F.A.N., no. 101, 1964, 7–11, ill., map.

2606. **Zwernemann, Jurgen.** *Un masque de Laiton provenant du Togo au Linden-Museum à Stuttgart.* Notes afr. I.F.A.N., 101, 1964, 11–13, bibl., ill.

CLOTHING AND ADORNMENT

2607. **Froelich, J. C.** 1953. *Catalogue des scarifications en usage chez certaines populations du Dahomey et du Nord-Togo.* Mém. I.F.A.N., 23, 'Mélanges ethnologiques', 253–64, ill.

2608. **Gessain, Monique.** *Ceinture Bassari en feuille de ronier pyrogravée.* Notes afr. I.F.A.N., **72**, oct. 1956, 112–13, ill.

TECHNIQUES

2609. **Bérard, M.** *La métallurgie bassari au Togo français.* Iᵉ conf. int. africanistes de l'ouest, C.R. (Dakar), **2**, 1951, 231–5, diagr.

2610. **de Lestrange, Monique.** *A propos de petites poteries; Petite poterie percée de devins coniagui et bassari.* Notes afr. I.F.A.N., **54**, avr. 1952, 48–49, ill.

2611. —— *À propos d'une terre cuite bassari.* Notes afr. I.F.A.N., **36**, oct. 1947, 4–5, ill.

2612. **Mann, O.** 1925. *Die Eisengewinnung in Togo und Kamerun.* Afrika-Nachrichten, **3**, S. 150.

2613. **Staudinger, P.** *Über Bronzeguss in Togo.* Z. f. Ethnol., **41**, 1909, 855–62, ill.

2614. **Damascus.** *Die Weberei in Togo.* Steyler Missions Bote, 1911–12.

CAMEROONS

2615. **Adrianov, B. V.** *Etnicheskii sostav soviemennogo Kameruna (The ethnic composition of contemporary Cameroons).* Sovetskaya Etnog. (Moscow), **5**, 1959, 52–62, maps.

2616. **Anon.** *The Cameroon highlands.* Nigeria, **31**, 1949, 355–422, ill., maps.

2617. **Ardener, Edwin.** 1956. *Coastal Bantu of the Cameroons.* Pp. viii + 116, bibl., map. London: Int. Afr. Inst. (Ethnographic Survey of Africa: Western Africa, part 11.)

2618. **Baumann, H.,** and **L. Vajda** (*Ed.*). *Bernhard Ankermanns Völkerkundliche Aufzeichnungen im Grasland von Kamerun, 1907–1909.* Baessler-Archiv, **7**, N.F., 1959, 217–317, ill.

2619. **Bouchaud, J.** 1944. *Histoire et géographie du Cameroun.* Pp. 48, ill., maps. Duala: Vicariat Apostolique.

2620. —— 1953. *La côte du Cameroun dans l'histoire et la cartographie des origines à l'annexion allemande.* Pp. 217, ill., maps. Duala: I.F.A.N.: Centre du Cameroun, Mém. 5.

2621. **Buisson, E. M.** 1934. *L'Art chez les Bamiléké.* Truitard, S., et Autres, Arts du Cameroun à l'exposition d'art colonial de Naples, 20–23.

2622. **Cottes, Capt. Antony.** 1911. *La mission Cottes au Sud-Cameroun, 1905–1908.* Pp. xv + 254, ill., maps. Paris: Leroux.

2623. **Dark, Philip.** *Notes on the Eton of the Southern French Cameroons.* Man, **56**, no. 132, 1956, 124–5, ill.

2624. **Delarozière, Simone,** and **Gertrude Luc.** *Une forme peu connue de l'expression artistique africaine; 'l'Abbia', jeu de dés des populations forestières du Sud-Cameroun.* Études Cam., 49–50, 1955, 1 52, ill.

2625. **de Lyée de Belleau, M.** 1945. *Du Cameroun au Hoggar.* Pp. 172, ill. Paris: Éditions Alsatia.

2626. **Dugast, Idelette.** 1949. *Inventaire ethnique du Sud-Cameroun.* Pp. xii + 159, bibl., maps. Dakar: Mém. I.F.A.N. (Centre du Cameroun), Série: Populations, no. 1.

2627. —— *Monographie de la tribu des Ndiki (Banen du Cameroun).* 1955. Tome 1, pp. xxiv + 823, bibl., ill., maps. 1960. Tome 2, Vie sociale et familiale, pp. xx + 633, bibl. Paris: Travaux et Mémoires de l'Institut d'Ethnologie, 58 and 63.

2628. **Egerton, F. Clement C.** *African majesty.* Pp. xx + 348, ill., maps. London: Routledge.

2629. **Emonts, P. I.** 1922. *Ins Steppen und Bergland Inner-Kameruns.* Aix-la-Chapelle.

2630. **Frobenius, Leo.** 1897. *Der Kameruner Schiffsschnabel und seine Motive.* Pp. 95, ill. Halle a.s.: E. Karras. (Leopoldinisch-Carolinische Deutsche Akademie der Naturforscher, Nova Acta, Band 70 (1).)

2631. **Froelich, Jean-Claude.** 1956. *Cameroun-Togo; territoires sous tutelle (L'Union française).* Pp. ix + 217, ill. Paris: Editions Berger-Levrault.

2632. **Gardi, R.** 1956. *Mandara; Unbekanntes Bergland in Kamerun.* Pp. 231, ill., map. Zürich: Orell Füssli Verlag. (2nd ed.)

2633. —— 1957. *Kirdi; Parmi les peuplades païennes des monts et des marais nord-Cameroun.* Pp. 28, ill., map. Paris: Albin Michel.

2634. **Gebauer, Paul.** *Art of the British Cameroons.* Bascom, W., and Paul Gebauer, Handbook of West African art, 1954, 83, ill.

2635. **Hagen, Günther von.** *Die Bana.* Baessler Archiv, Band 2, Heft 2, 1911, 77–116, ill.

2636. —— *Einige Notizen über die Müsgu.* Baessler-Archiv, **11** (2), 1911, 117–22, ill.

2637. **Hambly, Wilfrid D.** *Notes on objects from Cameroon.* Man, **30**, no. 45, 1930, 57–58, ill. (Beaded gourds, snake and drum: costume of medicine man.)

2638. **Harttmann, Hermann.** *Ethnographische Studie über die Baja.* Z. f. Ethnol., **59** (1–2), 1927, 1–61, ill. (Art, pp. 37–45.)

2639. **Hoesemann, Dr.** *Aus dem Schutzgebiete Kamerun; Ethnologisches aus Kamerun.* Mitt. Schutz., **16**, 1903, 150–82, ill.

2640. **Hutter, Franz.** 1902. *Wanderungen und Forschungen im Nord-Hinterland von Kamerun.* Pp. xiii + 578, ill., maps. Brunswick: F. Vieweg.

2641. **Hurault, J.** 1956. *Notes sur la structure sociale des Bamiléké.* Pp. 108, ill., map. Paris. (Ronéo.)

2642. **Janze, J. B.** *Contribution à l'étude de l'archéologie du Cameroun.* Bull. soc. des études camerounaises, 8, 1944, 105–22, ill., map. (See also Études Camerounaises (Études cam.).)

2643. **Jeffreys, M. D. W.** *Notes on twins; Bamenda.* Afr. stud., **6**, 1947, 189–95.

2644. **Labouret, Henri.** 1935. *Études et observations Cameroun, 1934–35.* S.P., plates. Paris: Togo-Cameroun.

2645. —— *Les populations dites Bamiléké.* Togo-Cameroun, 1935, 135–66, ill.

2646. —— *L'Art au Cameroun.* Togo-Cameroun, avr.–juil., 1935, 167, ill.

2647. —— 1937. *Le Cameroun.* Pp. viii + 200, maps. Paris: Hartmann.

2648. **Laude, Jean.** *Cameroons.* Encyclopaedia of world art, vol. 3, 1960, 35–38, bibl., map.

2649. **Lebeuf, Jean-Paul.** *Poupées et bâtons Fali.* J. soc. africanistes, **11**, 1941, 225–7, ill.

2650. —— 1954. *Du Cameroun au Tchad.* Pp. 88, ill., map. Paris: Nathan.

2651. **Lecoq, Raymond.** *L'Art au Cameroun.* Tropiques, **327**, 48e ann., 1950, 39–46, ill.

2652. —— 1953. *Les Bamiléké; Une civilisation africaine.* Pp. 213, ill., map. Paris: Présence africaine (Aux Éditions Africaines).

2653. —— *Quelques aspects de l'art bamoun.* Diop, A., L'Art nègre, 1951, 175–81, ill.

2654. **Lem, F. H.** *L'Art du Cameroun; les caractères généraux.* Encyclopédie de l'Afrique Française, Cameroun-Togo, 1951, 362–74, bibl., ill.

2655. **Lembezat, B.** 1950. *Kirdi; Les populations paiennes du Nord-Cameroun.* Pp. 93, bibl., ill., maps. Cahors (Lot): A. Coueslant.

2656. —— 1952. *Mukulehe; un clan montagnard du Nord-Cameroun.* Paris: Editions Berger-Levrault.

2657. **Letouzey, Yvonne.** *Propos et suggestions tirés d'expériences relatives à l'enseignement du dessin au Cameroun.* Bull. I.F.A.N., **15**, 4, oct. 1953, 1710–15.

2658. **McCulloch, M., Margaret Littlewood,** and **I. Dugast.** 1954. *Peoples of the Central Cameroons. Tikar* by Merran McCulloch: *Bamum and Bamiléké* by Margaret Littlewood: *Banen, Bafia and Balom* by I. Dugast. Pp. vii + 172, bibl., map. London: Int. Afr. Inst. (Ethnographic Survey of Africa: Western Africa, part 9.)

2659. **Maclean, E.** *Kunst in Kamerun.* Deutsche Kolon. Ztg., 1940, 52, Jg., 11, 209–12.

2660. **Macleod, Olive.** 1912. *Chiefs and cities of Central Africa.* Pp. xiv + 322, ill., maps. Edinburgh: William Blackwood.

2661. **MacRow, D.** *Bamenda art.* Nigeria, **57**, 1958, 132–53, ill.

2662. **Malcolm, L. W. G.** 1924. *Short note on native drawings from the Bagam area, Central Cameroon, West Africa.* Man, **24**, 53, 70, ill.

2663. —— *The tribes of the Grassland area, Central Cameroon.* Mitt. anthrop. gesell. (Wien), **55**, 1925, 7–45.

2664. **Mansfeld, Alfred.** 1908. *Urwald-Dokumente; Vier Jahre unter den Crossflussnegern Kameruns.* Pp. xvi + 309, ill., map. Berlin: Reimer.

2665. —— 1924. *Westafrika; Urwald und Steppenbilder.* Pp. viii + 144, ill., maps. Berlin: Auriga-Verlag. (Kulturen der Völker: Material zur Kulturgeschichte der Menschen: Abteilung: Bildwerke.)

2666. —— and **H. Reck.** 1928. *Westafrika; aus Urwald und Steppe zwischen Crossfluss und Benue.* Pp. viii + 76, ill., maps. Munich: Georg Müller.

2667. **Martin, H.** *Le pays de Bamum et le Sultan Njoya.* Études cam., 4 (33–34), 1951, 5–40.

2668. **Mveng, Engelbert.** *L'Art Camerounais.* Abbia, no. 3, 1963, 3–24, ill.

2669. **Nicol, Y.** 1930. *La tribu des Bakoko.* Pp. 240, ill., maps. Paris: Larose.

2670. **Oldenburg, Richard.** 1930. *Bamum; ein Negerreich im Innern Kameruns.* Atlantis, **11** and **111**, 1930, 161–5, ill.

2671. **Passarge, Siegfried.** 1895. *Adamaua; Bericht über die Expedition des Deutschen-Kamerun-Komitees . . . 1893–4.* Pp. xvi + 573, ill., maps. Berlin: Reimer.

2672. **Rein-Wuhrmann, A.** 1925. *Mein Bamumvolk.* Stuttgart: Basle.

2673. **Routil, R.** 1941. *Kamerun; Land und Leute.* Pp. 54, ill., map. Vienna: Veröffentlichungen der wissenschaftlichen Staatsmuseen in Wien.

2674. **Schmidt, A.** 1955. *Die Rote Lendenschnur als Frau im Grasland Kameruns.* Pp. 197, ill. Berlin: Dietrich Reimer.

2675. **Schrieke, B.** (*Ed.*). 1940–1. *Primitieve Kunst en Cultuur; 3, Kameroen en Kongo; Kunst en Cultuur in Afrika.* Pp. 63, ill. Arnhem: Van Loghum Slaterus (under the auspices of the Koloniaal Instituut).

2676. **Seidel, August.** 1906. *Deutsch-Kamerun.* Pp. 227–8. Berlin: Meidinger.

2677. **Sieber, J.** 1925. *Die Wute.* Pp. xi + 114, ill. Berlin: Reimer.

2678. **Sydow, Eckard von.** *Die Abstrakte Ornamentik der Gebrauchskunst im Grasland von Kamerun.* Baessler-Archiv, **15**, 1932, 160–80, ill.

2679. **Thorbecke, Franz.** 1914–19. *Im Hochland von Mittel-Kamerun.* 3 vols. Teil 1, Die Reise. Teil 2, Anthropogeographie des Ost-Mbamlandes. Teil 3, Beiträge zür Völkerkunde des Ost-Mbamlandes. Hamburg: L. Friederichsen. (Abh. Hamburg. Kolonialinst, **21**, 36, 41.)

2680. **Trézenem, Edouard,** and **Bertrand Lembezat.** 1947. *La France Équatoriale. L'Afrique équatoriale française par E. Trézenem . . . Le Cameroun par Bertrand Lembezat.* Pp. 1250, ill. Paris: Société d'études Géographiques Maritimes et Coloniales. (2nd ed.)

2681. **Truitard, Suzanne.** *L'Art chez les Bamouns.* Truitard, S., et Autres, Arts du Cameroun à l'Exposition d'art colonial de Naples, 1934, 2–7.

2682. **Volz, Walter.** *Reise durch das Hinterland von Liberia.* Jahresber. Geog. Gesells. (Bern), **22**, 1908–10.

FIGURES AND MASKS

2683. **Delarozière, R.** *Les institutions politiques et sociales des populations dites Bamiléké.* Études. cam. **25–26**, 1949, 5–68, ill.; **27–28**, 1949, 127–75, bibl., ill. (Illustrations of masks and wooden figures.)

2684. **Drost, Dietrich.** *Eine Reiterdarstellung aus dem Kameruner Grasland (Tabakspfeifen).* Veröff. Mus. Völkerk. (Leipzig), no. 11, 1961, 104–13, ill.

2685. **Dugast, Mme René.** *Les figurines humaines du pays Babimbi (Cameroun).* Conf. Intern. dos Africanistas Ocidentais, 2a Bissau, 1947. Trabalhis, vol. 5, 3a Seccão, 2a Parte (Meio Humano), 1952, 205–17, ill. Lisbon: Junta de Investigacões Coloniais.

2686. **Germann, Paul.** *Das plastisch-figürliche Kunstgewerbe im Grasland von Kamerun.* Jb. s. Mus. Völkerkunde (Leipzig), **4**, 1910, 1–37, ill.

2687. —— *Verzierter Monolith aus dem Kameruner-Grasland.* Jb. Mus. Völkerkunde (Leipzig), **11**, 1952 (1953), 100.

2688. **Jeffreys, M. D. W.** *Carved clay tobacco pipes from Bamenda, British Cameroons.* Man, **50**, no. 29, Mar. 1950, 25, ill.

2689. —— and **G. Tischhauser.** *Carved figures from Bali, Cameroons.* Man, **38**, nos. 186–7, 1938, 160.

2690. —— *Le serpent à deux têtes Bamoun.* BSEC, 9/3/45, 7–16. *See also* 5008.

2691. **Lecoq, Raymond.** *Introduction à la sculpture Bamiléké.* Jeune afr., **13**, 4e ann., 1950, 5–6.

2692. **Lobsiger-Dellenbach, Marguerite.** *Une calabasse-trophée utilisée dans la magie guerrière chez les Bamouns (Cameroun).* L'Ethnographie, **23**, 1931, 97–100, ill.

2693. **Rusillon, J.** *A propos d'une nouvelle acquisition de notre musée.* (Cameroon bronze masks.) Les Musées de Genève, **8**, 1951, 3, ill.

2694. **Tardits, Claude.** *Panneaux sculptés bamoun.* Objets et mondes, **2**, 4, hiver 1962, 249–60, bibl., ill., map.

2695. **Thomas, Trevor.** *Variation on a theme; analysis of small carved figures from Bali, Cameroons, Africa.* Man, **38**, no. 32, 1938, 33–37, ill.

BUILDINGS AND FURNITURE

2696. **Béguin, J. P.** (*Ed.*). 1952. *L'Habitat au Cameroun.* Pp. 151, ill., maps. Paris: Office de la recherche Scientifique Outre-Mer.

2697. **Lebeuf, A.** and **J. P.** *Monuments symboliques du palais royal de Logone-Birni (Nord-Cameroun).* J. soc. africanistes, **25** (1 and 2), 1955, 25–34, ill.

2698. **Lebeuf, Jean-Paul.** 1961. *L'Habitation des Fali, montagnards du Cameroun Septentrional.* Pp. 608, bibl., ill. Paris: Hachette.

2699. **Malcolm, L. W. G.** *Huts and villages in the Cameroons.* Scottish geographical magazine, **38**, 1923, 21–27.

CLOTHING AND ADORNMENT

2700. **Buisson, E. M.** *Les tatouages Bamiléké.* Togo-Cameroun (Paris), 2 Feb. 1931, , ill.

2701. —— *De la signification de certains tatouages en relief chez quelques tribus nègres du Cameroun.* Revue anthropologique, **64**, 1934, 1/3.

2702. **Kisob, J. A.** *An appreciation of Bamenda traditional costume.* Abbia, **3**, Sept. 1963, 55–65, ill.

2703. **Kunike, H.** *Narbentätauierung eines Banso-Mädchens.* Der Erdball, **2** (11), 1928, 423, ill.

2704. **Lagrave, R.** *Quelques remarques sur les dessins spontanés d'écoliers du Nord-Cameroun.* Études cam., **55**, mars 1957, 16–33, ill.

2705. **Lebeuf, Jean-Paul.** 1946. *Vêtements et parures du Cameroun français.* Pp. 47, ill. Paris: Arc-en-Ciel.

2706. —— *Labrets et greniers des Fali (Nord-Cameroun).* Bull. I.F.A.N., **15**, 3, juil. 1953, 1321–8, ill.

2707. **Noël, P.** *Tatouages et leur technique au Cameroun central.* Rev. ethnog. trad. pop., **3**, no. 11, 1922, 241–4, ill.

ROCK ART

2708. **Buisson, E. M.** *La préhistoire en pays Kirdi; les gravures rupestres de Bidzar.* Bull. soc. préhist. fr., 1933.

TECHNIQUES

2709. **Braunholtz, H. J.** *Wooden throne from the Cameroons.* B.M.Q., **12**, 1938, 6–7.

2710. **Buisson, E. M.** *La céramique bamiléké.* Bull. soc. préhist. fr., **27**, 1930, 522–36.

2710a.—— *La céramique Bamiléké; quelques réalisations animales chez les Bamiléké.* Togo-Cameroun, Feb. 1931, 117–21.

2711. **Cozens, A. B.** *A village smithy in the Cameroons.* Nigerian field, **20**, 1, Jan. 1955, 25–34, ill.

2712. **de Lauwe, Paul-Henry.** *Pierres et poteries sacrées du Mandara, Cameroun Nord (Mission Sahara-Cameroun).* J. soc. africanistes, **7**, 1937, 53–67.

2713. **Gardi, René.** 1954. *Der schwarze Hephästus.* Pp. 22, ill. Bern: Büchler & Co.

2714. —— *Plangi und Tritik von Farben mit Indigo in Nordkamerun.* Atlantis (Zurich), **29** (8), Aug. 1957, 369–73.

2715. **Guillou** (Administrateur). *L'industrie du fer dans la subdivision de Babimbi.* Études cam., **3**, 31/32, sept.–déc. 1950, 207–9.

2716. **Hinderling, Paul.** *Schmelzöfen und Eisenverarbeitung in Nord-Kamerun (Bericht Nr. 9 des Geschichtsausschusses des Vereins Deutscher Eisenhüttenleute).* Stahl und Eisen (Düsseldorf), **75**, 19, 1955, 1263–6, ill.

2717. **Jeffreys, M. D. W.** *Stone-age smiths (Fungom tribe, Bamenda, Cameroons).* Arch. f. Völkerkunde (Wien), **3**, 1948, 1–23.

2718. —— *Some notes on the Bikom blacksmiths.* Man, **52**, 75, Apr. 1952, 49–51, ill.

2719. **Jest, C.** *Notes sur les poteries kapsiki (pays kirdi).* Notes afr. I.F.A.N., **70**, avr. 1956, 47–52, ill.

2720. **Lebeuf, J. P.** *Les rites funéraires chez les Fali.* J. soc. africanistes, **8**, 1938, 103–22, ill.

2721. **MacRow, D. W.** (*Ed.*). *Bamenda brass.* Nigeria magazine, no. 55, 1957, 344–55, ill.

2722. **Malcolm, L. W. G.** *A note on brass-casting in the Central Cameroon.* Man, **23**, 1, 1923, 1–4.

2723. —— 1924. *Iron-working in the Central Cameroon.* Man, **24**, 102, 136–8.

AFRICAN ART TODAY

2724. **Hirschberg, Walter.** *Die Künstlerstrasse in Foumban (Kamerun).* Tribus, **9**, Sept. 1960, 90–106, ill.

2725. **Kunzfeld, Alois.** 1925. *Kinderzeichnungen aus Kamerun.* Völkerkunde (Wien), **1**, S. 157–67, ill.

2726. **Njoya, Arouna M.** *Rapport sur l'art indigène au Cameroun.* (MS. report (French) of a meeting on 18th October 1956 on 'Conservation of old and maintenance of tradition in modern times'.)

2727. **Pare, Isaac.** *Un artiste camerounais peu connu; Ikrahim Njoya.* Abbia, **6**, août 1964, 173–85, ill.

LIBERIA

2728. **Büttikofer, Johann.** 1890. *Reisebilder aus Liberia.* 2 vols. 1879–82 and 1886–7. Vol. 1, Reise und Charakterbilder, Pp. xv + 440, ill., maps. Vol. 2, Die Bewohner Liberia's Thierwelt, pp. viii + 510, ill. Leiden: Brill.

2729. **Frobenius, Leo.** 1911. *Auf dem Wege nach Atlantis.* Pp. xv + 410, ill., maps. Berlin-Charlottenburg: Vita, Dt. Verlagshaus.

2730. **Gamory-Dubourdeau, P. M.** *Notice sur les coutumes des Toma.* Bull. com., études, A.O.F., **9**, 1926, 288–350, ill.

2731. **Germann, Paul.** 1933. *Die Völkerstämme im Norden von Liberia.* Pp. 8 + 141, bibl., ill., map. Leipzig: Voigtlander. (Veröff. Staat. Sächsischen Forschungs-Institutes f. Völkerkunde in Leipzig, Band 1.)

2732. **Holas, B.** 1952. *Mission dans l'Est Libérien (P.-L Dekeyser— B. Holas, 1948).* Pp. xiii + 566, bibl., ill., maps. Dakar: I.F.A.N. (Mém. I.F.A.N., no. 14.)

2733. **Migeod, F. W. H.** *The Poro society.* Man, **16**, 1916, 102–8.

2734. **Schwab, George,** and **George W. Harley.** 1947. *Tribes of the Liberian hinterland.* Pp. 19 + 526, ill., maps. Cambridge, Mass.: Peabody Museum of American Archaeology and Ethnology. (Papers of the Peabody Museum, vol. 31.)

2735. **Segy, Ladislas.** *Liberian art; A documentation for a cultural heritage of the Liberian people.* Liberia today, **4**, 8, Aug. 1955.

2736. **Shattuck, George C.** *Liberia and the Belgian Congo.* J. Roy. Geog. S., **46**, 1929, 229.

2737. **Sibley, James L.** 1928. *Liberia old and new.* Pp. xviii + 317, ill., map. New York: Doubleday, Doran & Co.

2738. **Strong, Richard Pearson** (*Ed.*). 1930. *The African republic of Liberia and the Belgian Congo.* 2 vols. Vol. 1, pp. xxvi + 568, ill. Vol. 2, pp. ix + 1064, ill. Cambridge, Mass.: Harvard Univ. Press.

2739. **Westermann, Diedrich.** 1921. *Die Kpelle; ein Negerstamm in Liberia.* Pp. 16 + 552, bibl., map. Göttingen: Vandenhoeck & Ruprecht.
See also 2740–1, 2744–5.

FIGURES AND MASKS

2740. **Donner, Etta.** 1939. *Hinterland Liberia.* Pp. xiv + 302, ill., maps as end-papers. Glasgow: Blackie.

2741. —— *Kunst und Handwerk in No-Liberia.* Baessler Archiv, **23** (2–3), 1940, 45–113, ill.

2742. **Harley, George W.** 1941. *Notes on the Poro in Liberia.* Pp. 36, ill., map. Cambridge, Mass.: Peabody Museum. (Papers of the Peabody Museum of American Archaeology and Ethnology, vol. 19 (2).)

2743. —— 1950. *Masks as agents of social control in Northeast Liberia.* Pp. xiv + 44 + 15 pl. Cambridge, Mass.: Peabody Museum. (Papers of the Peabody Museum, vol. 32 (2).)

2744. **Himmelheber, Hans u. Ulrike.** 1958. *Die Dan; ein Bauernvolk im Westafrikanischen Urwald.* Pp. 256, bibl., ill., maps. Kohlhammer. (Bildende Kunst, pp. 248–9.)

2745. **Johnston, Sir Harry.** 1906. *Liberia.* 2 vols. Vol. 1, pp. xxviii + 520, bibl., ill., maps. Vol. 2, pp. xvi + 521–1183, ill., maps. London: Hutchinson.

2746. **Segy, Ladislas.** *Masks from Liberia.* Liberia today (Washington, D.C.), **3**, 7, July 1954.

2747. —— *Liberian masks and modern art.* Liberia today, **3**, 10, Nov. 1954.

2748. **Vandenhoute, P. J.** *Poro en masker; Enkele beschouwingen over 'Masks as agents of social control in Northeast Liberia' door G. W. Harley.* Kongo-Overzee, **18**, 2/3, 1952, 153–94, ill. (English summary.)

AFRICAN ART TODAY

2749. **Germann, P.,** and **E. Franke.** 1929. *Zeichnungen von Kindern und Jugendlichen aus dem Waldlande von Nord-Liberia.* 21 S. 10 Tafeln. Ethnolog. Studien, her. v. F. Krause. Leipzig: Asia Major. 1. Entstehung u. Inhalt der Zeichnungen. 2. Form und Psychologie d. Zeichnungen.

PORTUGUESE GUINEA

2750. **Bernatzik, Emmy.** 1936. *Afrikafahrt.* Pp. 240, ill. Vienna: Seidel & Sohn.

2751. **Bernatzik, Hugo Adolf.** 1933. *Aethiopien des Westens.* 2 vols. Band 1, pp. xii + 303, ill. Band 2, plates. Vienna: Seidel & Sohn.

2752. —— *Meine Expedition nach Portugiesisch-Guinea.* Atlantis, **4**, 1932, 197–211.

2753. —— 1944. *Im Reich der Bidyogo; Geheimnisvolle Inseln in Westafrika.* Pp. 200, ill., map. Innsbruck: Osterreichische Verlagsanstalt. (5th ed.)

2754. **Caroco, Jorge Vellez.** 1948. *Monjur O Gabú e a sua História.* Pp. 269, ill. Bissau: Centro de Estudos da Guiné Portuguesa.

2755. **Carreira, António.** 1936. *Costumes mandingas.* (Cadernos coloniais, no. 29.) Pp. 28. Lisbon: Cosmos.

2756. —— 1947. *Mandingas da Guiné Portuguesa.* (Pp. 12), 326 (3), ill., map. Bissau: (Printed in Lisbon). (Centro de Estudos da Guiné Portuguesa, no. 4.)

2756a. —— 1947. *Vida social dos Manjacos.* Pp. 188, ill., map. Bissau: Centro de Estudos da Guiné Portuguesa.

2757. **Claridge, G. Cyril.** 1922. *Wild bush tribes of tropical Africa.* Pp. 314, ill., map. London: Seeley Service.

2758. **Corrêa, António Mendes.** 1943. *Raças do Império.* Pp. 625, bibl., ill., maps. Pôrto: Portucalense Editora.

2759. —— 1949–54. *Ultramar Português.* 1, Síntese de África. 2, Ilhas de Cabo Verde. Pp. xxxii + 400, 261 (24), ill., maps. Lisbon: Agência geral das colónias, Divisâo de Publicações e Bibliotheca. (Vol. 1, Art. pp. 290–9.)

2760. **Cunha Taborda, Antonio da.** *Apontamentos etnograficos sobre os Felupes de Susana.* 2nd part. Bol. cultural Guiné portug., **5**, no. 20, 1950, 511–61, ill.

2761. **da Mota, Avelino Teixeira.** 1947. *Inquérito Etnogrâfico (Guiné Portuguesa).* Pp. 164 (2). Bissau: Publicação comemorativa do V Centenario da descoberta da Guiné.

2762. ——— *Centro de Estudos da Guiné Portuguesa.* Garcia de Orta, **1** (1), 1953, 107–37.

2763. ——— 1954. *Guiné Portuguesa.* 2 vols. Pp. xxxvi + 394, 297, ill., maps. Lisbon: Agência Geral do Ultramar.

2764. **de Albuquerque, Orlando.** *Para uma introdução ao estudo do arte quioca.* Est. ultramar (Lisboa), **3**, 1959, 179–85.

2765. **Moreira, José Mondes.** 1948. *Fulas do Gabu.* Pp. 328, ill., map. Bissau: Centro de Estudos da Guiné Portuguesa.

2766. **Santos Lima, Augusto J.** 1947. *Organização económica e social dos Bijagos.* Pp. 154, ill., map. Lisbon: Centro de Estudos da Guiné Portuguesa, no. 2.

2767. *See* 2756a.

2768. **da Mota, Avelino Teixeira.** *Descoberta de Bronzes Antigos na Guiné Portuguesa.* Bol. cultural Guiné portug., **15**, 1960, 625–32, ill.

2769. **da Silva, Artur Augusto.** *Arte Nalú.* Bol. cultural Guiné portug., **11**, 44, Out. 1956, 27–42.

2770. ——— *Essay of comprehnsion of Nalu sculpture.* Conferencia Internaçional dos Africanistas Ocidentais, 6th Session, vol. 5, 1956, 431–41, ill.

2771. ——— *Ensai de compreensão da escultura Nalu.* 6ª Conf. int. Africanistas ocid., S. Tomé, 1956 (1959), vol. 5, 431–41, ill.

2772. **Gonçalves, J. J.** *Escultura dos negros da Guiné Portuguesa.* Rev. Gabinete Est. Ultramar., **11/12**, 1956, 40–65, ill.

BUILDINGS AND FURNITURE

2772a. **da Mota, Avelino Teixeira,** and **Mário G. Ventim Neves.** *A Habitaçdo Indígena na Guiné Portuguesa.* Pp. 538 (30), ill., maps. Bissau: Centro de Estudos da Guiné Portuguesa, no. 7. (Ethnographic map.)

CLOTHING AND ADORNMENT

2773. **Bernatzik, H. Adolf.** *Von den Kleidermoden der schwarzen Völker in portugiesisch Guinéa.* Atlantis, **6**, 7, 1934.

2774. **Carreira, António.** 1950. *Mutilações corporais e pinturas cutâneas rituais dos negros da Guiné Portuguesa; Questionário de inquérito.* Pp. 51. Bissau: Centro de Estudos da Guiné Portuguesa.

2775. ——— *Mutiliações étnicas dos manjacos.* Bol. cultural Guiné portug., **16**, 61, Jan. 1961, 83–101, ill.

2776. **Martins de Meireles, Artur.** 1960. *Mutilações étnicas dos Manjacos.* Pp. 172, bibl., ill. Bissau. (Centro de Estudos da Guiné Portuguesa, no. 22.)

2777. **Quintino, Fernando Rogado.** *Como se trajam e se adornam os Povos da Guiné Portuguesa.* Bol. cultural Guiné portug., **19**, no. 73, 1964, 37–47, ill.

2778. *See* 2772a.

TECHNIQUES

2779. **Correia, Bento.** *A cerâmica na vida dos Balantas e Manjacos.* Bol. cultural Guiné portug., **13**, 50, 1958, 133–48, ill.

CAPE VERDE ISLANDS

2780. **Le Maire.** 1696. *A voyage . . . to the Canary Islands, Cape-Verd, Senegal and Gamby.* Pp. 135 (2). London: F. Mills.

2781. **Mendes Corrêa, Antonio.** 1954. *Ultramar Português.* (2) Ilhas do Cabo Verde. Pp. 261, ill., maps. Lisbon: Agência Geral do Ultramar.

WEST CENTRAL AFRICA

See 2178–9, 2184, 2188–9, 2196–7, 2839, 2848, 2856.

CHAD

2782. **Boulnois, J.** *La migration des Sâo au Tchad.* Bull. I.F.A.N., **5**, 14, 1943, 80–120, ill., map.

2783. **Brunache, P.** 1894. *Le centre de l'Afrique autour du Tchad.* Pp. 340, ill., map. Paris: Felix Alcan.

2784. **Cline, Walter.** 1950. *The Teda of Tibesti, Borku and Kawar in the Eastern Sahara.* Pp. 52, bibl. Menasha, Wis.: G. Banta.

2785. **Fuchs, P.** 1961. *Die Völker der Südost-Sahara (Tibesti, Ennedi.)* Pp. 254, ill. Vienna: Braumüller.

2786. **Garcia, T.** *Moeurs et coutumes des Tedâ du Tou.* Bull. inst. ét. centrafricaines, **10**, 1955, 167–209, map.

2787. **Griaule, Marcel,** and **Jean-Paul Lebeuf.** *Fouilles dans la région du Tchad.* (1) J. soc. africanistes, **18** (1), 1948, 1–116, ill. (2) J. soc. africanistes, **20** (1), 1950, 1–51, ill. (3) J. soc. africanistes, **21** (1), 1951, 1–95, ill.

2788. **Huard, P.** *Préhistoire et archéologie au Tchad.* Bull. inst. ét centrafricaines (Brazzaville), **17–18**, 1959, 5–20, map.

2789. **Konrad, Walter.** 1955. Zad: Geheimnis. Zwischen Niger und Nil: ein ethnographischer Beitrag zur kenntnis der Tschadsee-Insulaner. Pp. 84, ill. Hildesheim: Gebr. Gerstenberg. (Zeit. des Museums zu Hildesheim, N.F., Heft 9.)

2790. **Lebeuf, Annie M.-D.** 1959. *Les populations du Tchad.* Pp. 130, bibl., maps. Paris: Presses Univ. de France.

2791. **Lebeuf, Jean-Paul.** *La plaine du Tchad et ses arts.* Paris, 1946.

2792. ——— *Petits objets en terre cuite du Tchad.* Notes afr. I.F.A.N., **55**, 1952, 69.

2793. ——— *Fouilles archéologiques dans la région du Tchad.* Zaïre, 1947, 543–55, ill.

2794. ——— *L'Archéologie de la region du Tchad.* Actes du IVe congrès panafricain de préhistoire, 1962, 427–36, ill.

2795. ——— 1962. *Archéologie tchadienne; Les Sao du Cameroun et du Tchad.* Pp. 147, bibl., ill., maps. Paris: Hermann.

2796. ——— and **A. Masson-Detourbet.** *Le site de Tago (Tchad); Mission Logone-Lac-Fitri.* Préhistoire (Paris), **11**, 1950, 143–92, ill., map.

2796a. ——— ——— *Nouvelles découvertes archéologiques chez les Sao du Tchad.* France illustrée, **5**, 516–17.

2797. **van Kretschmar, J. A.** *Tibesti; Een bergwoestijn in de Sahara.* Meded. Afr. Inst. (Leiden), **4**, 1950, 282–7, ill.

2798. **Wainwright, G. A.** *Pharaonic survivals between Lake Chad and the West Coast.* J. Egypt archaeol., 1949.

FIGURES AND MASKS

2799. **Lebeuf, Jean-Paul,** and **Detourbet, A. M.** *Sculptures on Lake Chad; new light on the cryptic Sao.* I.L.N., **215**, 1952–3.

BUILDINGS AND FURNITURE

2800. **Akester, Roger.** *Tibesti—land of the Tebu.* Geog. mag., **31** (1), 1958, 12–26, ill., map.

ROCK ART

2801. **d'Alverny, F.** *Vestiges d'art rupestre au Tibesti oriental.* J. soc. africanistes, **20**, 1950, 239–72, ill.

2802. **Arkell, A. J.** *The petroglyphs of Wadi Zirmei in North-Eastern Tibesti.* Actes du IVe congrès panafricain de préhistoire, 1962, 391–4, ill.

2803. **Desio, A.** *Sculture rupestri in nuova localita del Tibesti settentrionale e del Deserto Libico.* R. Univ. Milano. Ser. G. Pub., no. 2, 1941, 203–6, ill., map.

2804. ——— *Una ricognizione nel Tibesti settentrionale.* Bol. R. soc. geogr. Ital., 1941, 401–8, ill.

2805. **Fuchs, Peter.** *Felsmalereien und Felsgravuren in Tibesti, Borku und Ennedi.* Arch. f. Völkerkunde (Wien), **12**, 1957, 110–35, ill., maps.

2806. **Huard, Paul.** *État des recherches rupestres au Tchad.* Tropiques, 1952.

2807. —— *L'art rupestre au Tchad.* Encycl. mens. d'O.-M., **39**, nov. 1953, 313–17.

2808. —— *Gravures rupestres des confins nigérotchadiens.* Bull. I.F.A.N., **15**, 4, oct. 1953, 1569–81, ill.

2809. —— *Gravures rupestres de la lisière nord-occidentale du Tibesti.* Trav. inst. rech. sahariennes (Alger), **10**, 2, 1953, 75–106, ill.

2810. —— *Gravures et peintures rupestres du Borkou.* Bull. inst. ét. centrafricaines, no. 6, 1953, 149–60, bibl., ill.

2811. —— *Nouvelles gravures rupestres du Djado, de l'Afafi et du Tibesti.* Bull. I.F.A.N., **19** (B), 1/2, janv.–avr. 1957, 184–223, ill., map.

2812. **Hugot, Henri J.** 1962. *Missions Berliet Ténéré—Tchad.* 9 Nov. 1959–7 Jan. 1960. 23 Oct. 1960–9 Dec. 1960. Pp. 375, bibl., ill., maps. Paris: Arts et Métiers Graphiques.

2813. **Kronenberg, Andreas.** 1958. *Die Teda von Tibesti.* Pp. xiv + 160, ill. Horn-Wien (Vienna): Berger.

2814. **Lebeuf, Jean-Paul.** *Les Sao du Tchad; la renaissance d'une civilisation disparue.* C.R. Acad. sci. colon. Séance 5, May 1944, 257–67.

2815. —— and **A. Masson-Detourbet.** *L'Art ancien du Tchad.* Cah. d'art, **26**, 1951, 7–28, bibl., ill., map.

2816. **Le Coeur, Charles.** 1950. *Dictionnaire ethnographique Teda.* Pp. 211, ill., maps. Paris: Larose. (Mém. I.F.A.N., 9.)

2817. **Monod, Theodore.** *Sur quelques gravures rupestres de la région d'Aozou (Tibesti).* Riv. sci. preist., **2**, 1947, 30–47, ill.

2818. —— *Note préliminaire sur quelques gravures rupestres de la région d'Aozou (Tibesti).* Iᵉ conf. int. africanistes de l'ouest, C.R., **2**, 1951, 443–6, ill.

2819. **Passemard, E.,** and **H. de Saint-Floris.** *Les peintures rupestres de l'Ennedi.* J. soc. africanistes, **5**, 1, 1935, 97–112, ill., maps.

TECHNIQUES

2820. **Derendinger, Le Général.** *Les curieuses mines de Fer de Télé-Nugar (Tchad).* J. soc. africanistes, **6** (2), 1936, 197–204, ill., map.

2821. **Hamelin, Pierre.** *Les bronzes du Tchad.* Tribus, N.F., **2–3**, 1952–3, 379–99, ill.

2822. **Hottot, R.** 1934. *Sara-Kabba-Jingé Pottery.* C.R. congr. int. sci. anthrop.-ethnol., no. 1, London, 254–5.

2823. **Lebeuf, Jean-Paul.** 1945. *Quand l'or était vivant; aventures au Tchad.* Pp. 218, ill., maps. Paris: Susse.

2824. —— and **A. Masson-Detourbet.** 1950. *La civilisation du Tchad suivi d'une étude sur les bronzes Sao.* Pp. 198, bibl., ill., maps. Paris: Payot.

2825. —— *Signification de la céramique Sao.* C.R. séances acad. inscriptions et belles-lettres, 1960, 393–404.

2826. **Pales, Leon.** *Découverte d'un important gisement préhistorique à Fort-Lamy (Tchad).* J. soc. africanistes, **7**, 1937, 125–72, ill.

AFRICAN ART TODAY

2826a.**Tubiana, Marie-José,** and **Joseph Tubiana.** 1962. *Contes Zaghawa.* Pp. 206, ill. Paris: Les quatres jeudis. (Coloured drawings by children in Chad.)

CENTRAL AFRICAN REPUBLIC

(Formerly Oubangui–Shari)

2827. **Bobichon, Henri.** *Les peuplades de l'Oubangui chari M'Bomou à l'époque des missions Liotard et Marchand (1891–1901).* L'Ethnographie, 1932.

2828. **Bruel, Georges.** *Les M'Bakas Mambe (famille Mandjia).* L'Ethnographie, N.S., nos. 29/28, 1934, 15–4, 15–12.

2829. **Darrè, E. L.** *De l'organisation familiale chez les peuples N' Zakaras.* Bull. soc. rech. congol., no. 21, 1935, 61–92.

2830. **Daigre, R. P.** *Les Banda de l'Oubangui-Chari (Afrique équatoriale française).* Anthropos, **26**, 1931, 647–95, ill.; **27**, 1932, 153–81, ill.

2831. **Dubosc, Taret.** *Moeurs et coutumes Bayas. Le Labi.* Bull. soc. rech. congol., no. 6, 1925, 39–45.

2832. **Éboue, Felix,** and **Simonin.** *Les Bayas de l'Ouham-Pende.* Bull. soc. rech. congol., no. 9, 1928, 32–38.

2833. —— *Les sociétés d'initiés au pays banda.* Bull. soc. rech. congol, no. 13, 1931, 3–15.

2834. —— 1933. *Les peuples de l'Oubangui-Chari.* Pp. 111, ill. Paris: Comité de l'Afrique française.

2835. **Gaud, Fernand.** 1911. *Les Mandjia.* Pp. xxiv + 574, ill., map. Brussels: Institut Intern. de Bibliographie. (Coll. Monographies Ethnographiques, 8.)

2836. **Gillier, Commandant.** *L'Industrie et les arts chez les indigènes du Haut Oubangui.* Le monde, colonial ill., 1925, 292–4.

2837. **Kalck, Pierre.** 1959. *Réalités Oubanguinnes (Mondes d'Outre-Mer série).* Pp. 356, ill. Paris: Éditions Berger-Levrault.

2838. **Lebeuf, Jean-Paul.** *L'Art du delta du Chari.* Diop, A., L'Art nègre, 1951, 96–102, ill.

2839. **Lem, F.** *L'Art de l'Afrique centrale.* Encyclopédie coloniale et maritime (direction d'Eugène Guernier), 1950, 537–52, ill.

2840. **Vivier, P.** *Essai sur une optique neuve de l'art centre-africain.* Lovania, **13**, 35, 1955, 53–57.

FIGURES AND MASKS

2840a.**Fortier, J.** *Le masque de l'initiation chez les Mbaye-Moissala.* Notes afr. I.F.A.N., **87**, 1960, 82–85, ill.

2841. **Harttmann, Herman.** *Ethnographische studie über die Baja.* Z.f. Ethnol., **59**, 1927, 1–61, ill.

2842. **Vergiat, A. M.** 1937. *Moeurs et coutumes des Manjas.* Pp. 323, ill. Paris: Payot.

2843. —— 1951. *Les rites secrets des primitifs de L'Oubangui.* Pp. 158, ill., map. Paris: Payot.

CONGO

(Formerly Middle Congo)

2844. **Ballif, Noël.** 1955. *Dancers of God.* Trans. from the French. Pp. 213, ill. London: Sidgwick & Jackson. (Ogowe-Congo Mission to French Equatorial Africa.)

2845. **Blondet, R.** *Au mysterieux pays des noirs de Loango (Vili).* Bull. inform et docum. (Brazzaville), **65**, 1950, 1–6.

2846. **Chevalia, F.** 1908. *L'Afrique centrale française.* Paris.

2846a.**Darré, E.** *Notes sur la tribu des Bomitaba (Moyen Congo).* Rev. ethnog. trad. pop., **3**, no. 12, 1922, 304–25.

2847. *See* 1359a.

2848. **Cureau, Dr. Adolphel.** 1912. *Les sociétés primitives de l'Afrique équatoriale.* Pp. xii + 420, ill., map. Paris: A. Colin.

2849. **Dennett, R. E.** 1887. *Seven years among the Fjort.* Pp. xvi + 240, ill., map. London: Sampson, Low.

2850. —— 1898. *Notes on the folklore of the Fjort.* Pp. 32 + 169. London: Folklore Society.

2851. —— *The religion of the Fjort.* J. Afr. soc., **1**, 4, 452–4.

2852. **Johnston, Sir Harry Hamilton.** 1884. *The river Congo, from its mouth to Bólóbó.* Pp. xviii + 458, ill., maps. London: Sampson, Low.

2853. *See* 3043a.

2854. **Poupon, M. A.** *Étude ethnographique de la tribu Kouyou.* L'Anthropologie, **29**, 1919, 53–88: 297–335, ill.

2855. **Poutrin, Dr.** *Notes ethnographiques sur les populations M'Bwaka du Congo français.* L'Anthropologie, **21**, 1910, 35–54, ill.

2856. —— 1914. *Esquisse ethnologique des principales populations de l'Afrique équatoriale française.* Pp. 129, ill., map. Paris: Masson.

2857. **Vassal, Gabrielle M.** 1925. *Life in French Congo.* Pp. (2), 192, ill. London: Fisher, Unwin.

2858. **Voulore, Joseph Denis Antoine André.** 1897. *Le Congo français. Le Loango et la vallée du Louilou.* Pp. 207, maps. Paris: Joseph André.

FIGURES AND MASKS

2859. **Hottot, Robert.** *Teke fetishes.* J. roy. anthrop. inst., **86**, 1956, 25–36, ill., map.

2860. **Peissi, P.** *Les masques blancs des tribus de l'Ogoué.* Diop, A., L'Art nègre, 1951, 182–4.

2861. **Siroto, Leon.** *A mask style from the French Congo.* Man, **54**, 232, Oct. 1954, 149–50, ill.

BUILDINGS AND FURNITURE

2862. **Jung, Renée.** *Notes sur la case des Bembé.* J. soc. africanistes, **16**, 1946, 9–21, ill.

CLOTHING AND ADORNMENT

2863. **Fourneau, J.** *Sur des perles anciennes de pâte de verre provenant de Zanaga (Moyen Congo).* Bull. I.F.A.N., **14**, 3, juil. 1952, 956–69, ill. (Ancient glass-paste beads from Zanaga . . . (Engl. tr. of the above), S. Afr. archaeol. bull., **10**, 37, Mar. 1955, 15–19.)

2864. —— *Recherches sur l'origine des perles de Zanaga.* Bull. I.F.A.N., sér. B, **16**, 1/2, janv.–avr. 1954, 1–21, ill.

2865. —— *Les verroteries de l'époque coloniale en Afrique centrale.* Notes afr. I.F.A.N., **64**, oct. 1954, 110–13.

2865a. **Muraz, G.** *Les cache-sexe du centre africain.* J. soc. africanistes, **2**, 1, 1932, 103–11.

TECHNIQUES

2866. **Demetz, H.** *Les poteries des peuplades Batéké du Moyen-Congo.* Tom. 2, C.R. conf. intern. africanistes de l'ouest, 1951, 260–71, ill.

2867. **Géo-Fourrier, G.** *Les bourmas du Bahr Sara.* Art et décoration (Paris), **61**, mai 1932, 157–60, ill.

2868. **Lalouel, Médecin-Lieut.** *Les forgerons Mondjombo.* Bull. inst. ét centrafricaines. (Brazzaville), **2**, 1, 1947, 106–14.

2869. **Masson-Detourbet, A.** *Le tissage du raphia chez les Batéké (Moyen-Congo).* J. soc. africanistes, **27**, 1, 1957, 67–79, ill.

2870. **Möller, M.** *Einige Korbtypen bei den Buende.* Ethnos, **2**, 4, 1938, 219–29.

AFRICAN ART TODAY

2871. **Italiaander, Rolf.** *Les graveurs de Poto-Poto (résumé).* J. soc. africanistes, **30**, 2, 1960, 229–31.

2872. —— *Experiments in modern African art; etchings in French Equatorial Africa.* Africa, **30**, 1960, 46–50, ill.

2873. **Lebeuf, Jean-Paul.** *L'école des peintres de Poto-Poto.* Africa, **26**, 3, July 1956, 277–80, ill.

2874. **Lhote, H.** *L'école des arts et de l'artisanat de Poto-Poto.* Tropiques, **55**, 401, déc. 1957, 74–79, ill.

2875. **Pepper, M.** *Visite à l'Atelier de Céramique de Brazzaville.* Le Mois, **3**, mars 1945, 11–18.

GABON

2876. **Allégret, E.** *Les idées religieuses des Fan.* Rev. hist. rel., **50**, 1904, 214–33.

2877. **Barret, Paul.** 1888. *Sénégambia et Guinée—La région Gabonaise. L'Afrique occidentale.* 2 vols. Vol. 1, pp. xiii + 402, map. Vol. 2, pp. 438, map. Paris: Challamel.

2878. **Bautista Velarde, German.** *Una antigua moneda Pamue; La 'Viguela'.* Africa (Madrid), **11**, 147, 1954, 8–9, ill.

2879. **Bennett, A. L.** *Ethnological notes on the Fang.* J. Anthrop. Inst., **2**, no. 5, 1899, 66–98, ill.

2880. **Chauvet, Stéphen.** 1933. *L'Art funéraire au Gabon.* Paris.

2881. **du Chaillu, Paul Bertoni.** 1861. *Exploration and adventures in Equatorial Africa.* Pp. xviii + 479, ill., map. London: John Murray.

2882. **Diego, G.** *Etnologia Pamue.* Arch. Inst. Estudios Africanos, Ano 10, **40**, 1957, 35–42.

2883. **Ferves, M.** *Parmi les Fang de la forêt equatoriale; le jeu de l'abbia.* Rev. géog. hum. ethnol., no. 3, 1948, 26–41.

2884. **Frey, Roger.** *Une évolution de l'art nègre—Les pierres taillées de Mbigou.* Bull. inst. ét. centrafricaines, **1**, 1, 1945, 97–104, ill.

2885. **Guinea, Emilio.** 1947. *En el Pais de los Pamues.* Pp. 156, ill. Madrid: Instituto de Estudios Africanos.

2886. **Hée, R. P. A.** *Le Ngo, société secret du Haut-Ogowe (Gabon).* Africa, **10**, 1937, 472–80.

2887. **Howe, R. W.** *Art of dying jungle tribes; travel notes on some primitive Gabonese cannibal races.* Apollo, **61**, 1955, 110–12.

2888. **Tessmann, Günter.** *Die Kinderspiele der Pangwe.* Baessler-Archiv, **11** (2), 1912, 250–80, ill.

2889. —— 1913. *Die Pangwe; Völkerkundliche Monographie eines westafrikanischen Negerstammes.* 2 vols. Vol. 1, pp. xxi + 275, ill. (some col.), maps. Vol. 2, pp. 402, ill. (some col.). Berlin: Wasmuth. (Ergebnisse der Lübecker Pangwe-Expedition, 1907–9 and 1904–7.)

2890. **Trezenem, E.** *Notes ethnographiques sur les tribes Fan du Moyen Ogooué (Gabon).* J. soc. africanistes, **6**, 1936, 65–93.

FIGURES AND MASKS

2891. **Hall, H. U.** *Two masks from French Equatorial Africa.* Museum journal (Univ. of Pennsylvania, Philadelphia, Pa.), **18**, 1927, 381–409, ill. (Ngunie, Gabun.)

BUILDINGS AND FURNITURE

2892. **Balandier, G.,** and **J-Cl. Pauvert.** 1952. *Les villages Gabonais.* PP. 86 (6), bibl., ill. Montpellier: Imprimerie Charité. (Mémoires de l'Institut d'Études Centrafricaines, no. 5.)

2893. **Martrow, L.** *Les 'Eki' du Fang.* Anthropos, **1**, 1906, 745–61.

CLOTHING AND ADORNMENT

2894. **Walker, A.** *Les tatouages au Gabon.* Liaison (Brazzaville), **65**, sept.–oct. 1958, 34–39, ill.

TECHNIQUES

2895. **Waissenborn, B.** *Die Eisenbereitung bei den Jaunde-Leuten.* Mitt. Schutz., **1**, 1888.

AFRICAN ART TODAY

2896. **Grébert, F.** *Arts en voie de disparition au Gabon.* Africa, **7**, 1, Jan. 1934, 82–88.

CONGOLESE REPUBLIC

(Formerly Belgian Congo)

2897. **Adolf Friedrich, Duke of Mecklenburg.** 1913. *From the Congo to the Niger and the Nile.* 2 vols. Vol. 1, pp. xvi + 241, ill., map. Vol. 2, pp. xii + 285, ill. London: Duckworth.

2898. **Andersson, Efraim.** 1953. *Contribution à l'ethnographie des Kuta*, 1. Pp. xxiii + 363, ill. Uppsala: Almqvist & Wiksells. (Studia Ethnographica Upsaliensia, VI.)

2899. **Annales du Musée du Congo Belge (Tervuren).** *Les arts.* Religion, Ethnographie et Anthropologie (Brussels), **3**, 1902–6.

2900. **Balandier, G.** *Messianisme des Ba-Kongo.* Encyclopédie coloniale et maritime, **1** (12), 1951, 216–20, ill.

2901. —— *Naissance d'un mouvement politico-réligieux chez les Ba-Kongo du Moyen Kongo.* 3rd Intern. W. African Conf., 1949 (1951), 324–6.

2902. **Baumann, H.** *Die Materielle Kultur der Azande und Mangbetu.* Baessler-archiv, **11**, 1927, 1–131.

2903. **Bequaert, M.** *Présentation de pièces.* Bull. soc. roy. belge d'anthrop. et préhist., **55**, 1940, 114–15.

2904. **Bernatzik, Hugo Adolf.** 1929. *Zwischen Weissen Nil und Belgisch-Kongo.* Pp. 140, ill., maps. Vienna: L. W. Seidel.

2905. **Bevel, M. L.** *L'Art de la décoration chez les Basonge.* Conseiller Congolaise, **10**, 1937, 1, 10.

2906. **Biebuyck, D.** *Some remarks on Segy's 'Warega Ivories'.* Zaïre, **7**, 1953, 1076–82.

2907. —— *De verwording der kunst bij de Balega.* Zaïre, **8**, 3, mars 1954, 273–8.

2908. —— *L'Art des Balega. Sa signification sociale.* Jeune afr., **25**, 1957, 15–17.

2909. **Bittremieux, Leo.** 1922–7. *Mayombsch Idioticon.* 3 vols. in one. Brussels: Essorial.

2910. —— 1924. *Mayombsche Volkskunst.* Pp. 227. Gent. Mechelen en Veurne: De Vlaamsche Bockenhalle S.V.

2911. —— *Symbolisme in de negerkunst.* Congo, **2**, 5, 1930, 662–80.

2912. —— *Symbolisme in de Negerkunst of beeldspreuken der Bawoyo's (tweede reeks).* Congo, **2**, 2, 1934, 168–204. 8 T. 112 Abb.

2913. —— 1936. *La société secrète des Bakhimba au Mayombe.* Pp. 326, ill., map. Brussels: Hayez.

2914. —— 1937. *Symbolisme in de negerkunst.* Pp. 83, ill. Brussels: Vromant.

2915. —— *De 'Goden' van Kakongo en Ngoyo.* Kongo Overzee, **12–13**, 1946–7, 1–10.

2916. **Boelaert, E.,** and **G. Hulstaert.** *Les manifestations artistiques des Nkundo (Tshuapa).* Brousse, **2**, 1939, 18–21, ill.

2917. **Brandt, L.** *Note sur les mambela des Babali.* Congo, **1**, 1923, 344–8.

2918. **Burrows, Guy.** 1898. *The land of the pigmies.* Pp. xxx + 299, ill. London: C. Arthur Pearson.

2919. **Burssens, Herman.** *The so-called 'Bangala' and a few problems of art-historical and ethnographical order.* Kongo-Overzee (Antwerpen), **20**, 3, 1954, 221–36, ill.

2920. —— 1958. *Les peuplades de l'entre Congo-Ubangi (Ngbandi, Ngbaka, Mbandja, Ngombe et Gens d'Eau).* Pp. xi + 219, bibl., ill., map. London: Int. Afr. Inst. (Ethnographic Survey of Africa: Congo, part 4.)

2921. —— *Congo Belga.* Enciclopedia Universale dell'Arte, **3**, 1960, 774–82, map.

2922. —— 1963. *Yanda-beelden en Mani-sekte bij de Azande, Centraal-Afrika.* (Yanda sculptures and Mani-sect among the Azande: a study in ethno-aesthetics.) Ann. Kon. Mus. Midd. Afr. sér. in 4°, N.S. 4. (Brussels): 2 vols, 231, ill., maps.

2923. **Burton, W. F. P.** *The country of the Baluba in Central Katanga.* Geog. J., **70**, 1927, 321–42.

2924. —— *The secret societies of Lubaland, Congo Belge.* Bantu studies, **4**, 1930, 217–50.

2925. **Césard, Le R. P. Edmond.** *Le Muhaya (l'Afrique orientale).* Anthropos, **30**, 1935, 75–106, 451–62, ill.; **31**, 1936, 97–114, 821–49, ill.; **32**, 1937, 15–60.

2926. **Christen, Le R. P.** 1935. *Mambela et Anyoto; Initiation tribale des Babali et hommes-léopards.* Pp. 54, ill. Brussels: .

2927. **Clits, H. L.** *Moeurs et coutumes du Bas-Congo.* Bull. militaire (Léopoldville), **50**, 1951, 723–36.

2928. **Clouzot, H.** *Les arts appliqués Mangbetu.* La Renaissance, **9**, 1926, 569–72.

2929. **Colle, R. P.** 1913. *Les Baluba. Congo Belge.* Tome 1. Pp. lxxx + 422. Brussels: Institut Intern. de Bibliographie. (Collection de monographies ethnographiques, no. 10.)

2930. **Costermans, B. J.** *Relevé de stations préhistoriques dans les territoires de Watsa-Gombari et de Dungu.* Zaïre, **3** (2), 1949, 153–74.

2931. —— 1953. *Mosaïque Bangba. Notes pour servir à l'étude des peuplades de l'Uele.* Pp. 175, maps. Brussels: (I.R.C.B. Sciences morales. Mém. Tom. 28, fasc. 3.)

2932. **Cuvelier, J.** 1946. *L'Ancien royaume de Congo.* Pp. 361, ill. Bruges: Desclée de Brouwer.

2933. —— and **L. Jadin.** *L'Ancien Congo d'après les archives romaines (1518–1640).* Mém. in 8e, A.R.S.C., **36** (2), 1954, 1–600, ill., maps.

2934. **Daize, L.** 1938. *Les Boules de Pierre et les Pierres perforées des collections de préhistoire du musée du Congo.* Pp. 89–140, Planche XIV. Tervuren: Annales du Musée du Congo Belge.

2935. **Daye, Pierre,** and **Jacque Crockaert.** 1929. *Le miroir du Congo Belge.* Pp. 284. Bruxelles: Aux Editions.

2936. **de Beaucorps, R.** 1933. *Les Bayansi du Bas-Kwilu.* Pp. 136, ill., map. Louvain: Editions de l'Aucam.

2937. —— 1941. *Les Basongo de la Luniungu et de la Gobari.* Pp. 172, ill., maps. Brussels: (I.R.C.B., 10, fasc. 3.)

2938. **de Beauplan, R.** *La documentation artistique de M. Alexandre Jacovleff.* L'Illustration, **83** (2), 1925, 433–7, ill.

2939. **de Bouveignes, O.** *Les anciens rois du Congo.* Pp. 176. Grands Lacs.

2940. **de Calonne-Beaufaict, Adolphe de.** *Les Ababua.* Mouvement sociologique internationale, **10** (2), 1909, 285–431.

2941. —— 1912. *Études Bakongo; Notes de sociologie coloniale.* Pp. 152, ill. Liege: M. Thorne.

2942. —— 1921. *Azande; Introduction à une ethnographie générale des bassins de l'Ubangui-Uele et de l'Aruwimi.* Pp. xxxi + 280, map. Brussels: Maurice Lamerton.

2943. **de Cleene, N.** 1957. *Introduction à l'ethnographie du Congo belge et du Rwanda-Burundi.* Pp. viii + 159, bibl., ill., map. Anvers: Editions de Sikkel.

2944. **de Jonghe, E.** 1907. *Les sociétés secrètes du Bas-Congo.* Pp. 74. Brussels: Polleunis.

2945. **de Josselin de Jong, J. P. Schmelz,** and **J. D. E. Marquart.** 1904–16. *Ethnographisch Album van het stroomgebied van den Congo.* Pp. 242, plates. The Hague: Rijks Ethnog. Museum. (Rijks Ethnographisch Museum, Publicaties, Serie 2, no. 2.)

2946. **De Kesel, C.** *De kunst bij de Bashi.* Nieuw Afrika, **55**, 6, 1938–9, 232–5.

2947. **Delcourt, L.,** and **A. Dallons.** *Les Mongo du Sankuru.* Bull. jurid. indig., no. 6 (7), 1949, 180–6, ill.

2948. **Deleval, Hector.** 1913. *Les tribus Kavati du Mayombe; notes ethnographiques.* Pp. 53, ill. Brussels: Vromant.

2949. **Delhaise, Charles Godefroid Felix François.** 1908. *Chez les Wabemba.* Pp. 81, ill., map. Brussels: Soc. R. Belge de Géog.

2950. —— 1908. *Chez les Warundi et les Wahorohoro.* Pp. 64, ill. Brussels: Soc. R. Belge de Géog.

2951. —— 1909. *Les Warega.* Pp. xx + 376, ill., maps. Brussels: Institut Intern. de Bibliographie. (Collection de monographies ethnographiques, no. 5.)

2952. **De Rop, A.** *Lilwa-beeldjes bij de Boyela.* Zaïre, **9**, 2, fév. 1955, 115–20, ill.

2953. **de Ryck, F. D.** 1937. *Les Lalia-Ngolu.* (Extrait de 'Le Trait d'Union: organe de l'Association des étudiants de l'Université Coloniale de Belgique'.) Pp. 167, map. Anvers: Université Coloniale.

2954. **de Sousberghe, León.** *Découverte de 'tours' construites par les Pende sur le Haut-Kwango.* Bull. A.R.S.C., **4** (7), 1958, 1334–45.

2955. —— 1958. *L'Art Pende*. Pp. ix + 165, ill., map. Brussels: Académie Royale de Belgique: Beaux-Arts, Tome 9, Fasc. 2.

2956. **Dijkman, B.** *De kunst bij de Azanden*. Kruis en Wereld, **30**, 1, 1950–1, 7–13, ill.

2957. **Engels, Lieutenant.** 1912. *Les Wangata (tribu du Congo Belge); étude ethnographique*. Pp. (8) + 101, ill., map. Brussels and Paris: Vromant.

2958. **Faure, H.** *Contribution à l'étude des races de la région de Carnot*. Bull. soc. rech. congol., no. 21, 1935, 99–109.

2958a.—— *Notes sur l'exploration de la Haute Sangha*. Bull. soc. rech. congol., no. 24, 1937, 113–23.

2959. **Franck, Louis.** 1930. *Le Congo Belge*. 2 vols. Vol. 1, pp. 380, ill. Vol. 2, pp. 490, ill., map. Brussels: La Renaissance du Livre.

2960. **Franssen, J.** 1943. *Dioramas Congolais, vie matérielle du Noir*. Pp. 124, ill. Liége: Soledi.

2960a.—— 1943. *La vie du Noir*. Pp. 121, ill. Liége: Soledi.

2961. **Fraser, Douglas.** 1927. *Through the Congo basin*. Pp. xii + 283, ill., maps. London: Herbert Jenkins.

2962. **Frobenius, Leo.** 1907. *Im Schatten des Kongostaates*. Pp. 468, ill., maps. Berlin: G. Reimer.

2963. **Grands Lacs.** *L'art nègre au Congo Belge*. Pp. 64, ill., map. Namur: Grands Lacs. (*C.R.*: Rev. colon. belge, **11**, 261, nov. 1956, 843.)

2964. **Great Britain: Admiralty: Naval Intelligence Division.** 1944. *The Belgian Congo*. Pp. xiii + 558, ill., maps. London: H.M.S.O. (Art, pp. 178–80, ill.)

2965. **Grigsby, J. E.** *Bakuba art*. Davis, John A. (*ed.*), Africa from the point of view of American Negro Scholars, 1958, 143–61, ill.

2966. **Haene, J. de.** *Découvertes préhistoriques en Haut-Ituri*. Zaïre, **3** (9), 1949, 1003–10.

2967. **Haveaux, G. L.** *La tradition historique des Bapende orientaux*. Pp. 55, maps. Brussels: Mém. in 8e, I.R.C.B., Sect. Sci. Mor. and Pol., 27.

2968. **Hazard, Lieut.** *Les Boffis de Boda*. Bull. soc. rech. congol., no. 20, 1935.

2969. **Hulstaert, G.** *Grafbeelden en standbeelden*. Aequatoria, **4**, 1938, 8; *also* Congo, **2**, 1, 1938, 94–100.

2970. —— *Les cercueils des Eleku*. Aequatoria, 22e. ann, **1**, 1959, 10–15, ill.

2971. **Ihle, Alexander.** 1929. *Das alte Königreich Kongo*. Pp. 285, maps. Leipzig: Vogel. (Studien zur Völkerkunde, 1.)

2972. —— *Das alte Königreich Kongo*. Afrika (Berlin), **3** (2), 1944, 49–72.

2973. **Iyeky, J. F.** *L'Art congolais*. Brousse, **10**, 1957, 25–29.

2974. —— 1956. *Essai de psychologie du primitif*. Pp. 53, ill. Leopold-ville: La Voix du Congolais. (Published from articles in La Voix du Congolais, q.v.)

2975. —— *Essai de psychologie du primitif*. La voix du congolais, 1956, 12 ann., no. 118, 15–20; 119, 89–93; 121, 251–5; 122, 323–6, ill.

2976. **Jadot, Joseph-Marie.** *Les arts et les métiers congolais à l'Exposition de Paris, 1937*. Beaux-Arts, 7e ann., no. 250, 28–29.

2977. —— *L'Art nègre au Congo Belge (1886–1946)*. Rev. col. belge, **19**, 15 juillet 1946, 41–45, ill. (Grands lacs, no. 185, 1956, 5–10, ill.)

2978. —— *Le miracle Bushongo; Contribution à la philosophie et à l'histoire de l'art mélanien au Congo Belge*. Vét. col., **19**, 9, sept. 1947, 3–11, ill. (Idem in Le graphisme et l'expression graphique au Congo belge (Bruxelles), 1950, 39–47.)

2979. —— *Les arts populaires au Congo Belge, au Ruanda et dans l'Urundi*. Zaïre, **4**, 2, fév. 1950, 181–8.

2980. —— *Popular arts in the Belgian Congo and in Ruanda-Urundi*. Unesco occasional papers in educ. (Paris), **8**, Oct. 1950, 7–13.

2981. —— *L'Art nègre au Congo Belge*. Grands lacs, no. 185, 1956, 5–10.

2982. —— *Les lettres et les arts en Belgique. Coloniale et au Congo belge en 1957*. Zaïre, **12**, 1958, 179–90.

2983. —— *Les métiers d'art au Congo Belge*. Extrait des Annales des Classes Moyennes fr. Belgique, no. 4, 1958, 5, ill.

2984. —— and **Others.** *L'art et les métiers d'art au Congo Belge*. Belgique d'Outremer, no. 275, fév. 1958, 85–95, ill.

2985. **Jameson, James S.** 1890. *Story of the rear column of the Emin Pasha Relief Expedition*. Pp. xxxii + 455, ill., maps. London: R. H. Porter.

2986. **Kane, Aboud Salam.** 1936. *Arts et métiers indigènes dans la province de Léopoldville*. Pp. 24. Léopoldville: Le Courrier d'Afrique.

2987. **Kerels, H.** *L'Art chez les Mangbwetu*. Beaux-arts, **7**, Brussels, 1936, 22–23, ill.

2988. —— 1937. *Arts et métiers congolais*. 12 pl. Brussels: Les édit. de Belgique.

2989. **Kochnitzky, Léon.** 1948. *Negro art in the Belgian Congo*. Pp. 82, ill. New York: Belgian Govt. Information Center. (3rd ed.)

2989a.—— 1958. *Negro art in the Belgian Congo*. Pp. 88, ill., map. New York: Belgian Govt. Information Center. (4th ed.)

2990. **Kócsvay, Marzit.** *Kongoi irodalom és Müvészet*. Nagyvilág, 1960, 1742–3, ill. (Literature and the fine arts in the Congo.)

2991. **Laman, Karl.** 1953. *The Kongo*, I. Pp. viii + 155, ill. Uppsala: Afrikainstitutet vid Uppsala Universitet. (Studia Ethnographica Upsaliensia, 4.)

2992. —— 1957. *The Kongo*, II. Pp. 164, ill. Uppsala: Afrikainstitutet vid Uppsala Universitet. (Studia Ethnographica Upsaliensia, 8.)

2993. **Latouche, John Treville,** and **André Cauvin.** 1945. *Congo* (written by John Latouche, photographed by A. Cauvin). Pp. 197, ill. New York: Willow, White.

2994. **Johnston, Harry.** 1908. *George Grenfell and the Congo*. 2 vols. Vol. 1, pp. xxiii + 496, ill., maps. Vol. 2, pp. xx + 494 (497–990), ill., map. London: Hutchinson.

2995. **Jonghe, E. de.** *Formations récentes de sociétés secrètes au Congo Belge*. Africa, **9**, 1936, 55–63.

2996. **Leyder, Jean.** 1935. *L'Information chez les primitifs du Congo Belge*. Pp. 22. Brussels: Remy.

2997. —— *Symbolisme et art mélanien au Congo Belge*. Vét. col., **11**, 1947, 3–6, ill.

2998. —— and **Others.** 1950. *Le graphisme et l'expression graphique au Congo Belge*. Pp. 155 (pp. 70–154, bibl.), ill. Bruxelles: Société Royal Belge de Géographie.

2999. **Lelong, M. H.** 1946. *Mes frères du Congo* (1). Pp. 481 (2), 484, ill., maps. Alger: Éditions Baconnier.

3000. **Locke, Alain.** *A collection of Congo art*. The arts, **11**, 1927, 60–70, ill.

3001. **Lombard, Jean.** *Matériaux préhistoriques du Congo français*. J. soc. africanistes, **1** (1930), 49–59, ill.

3002. **Loukou, J.** *Quelques croyances et superstitions du Bas-Congo*. Liaison (Brazzaville), **67**, 1959, 71–74.

3003. **Lutter, E.** *Les Wasamba et leur usage dans la circoncision*. Minotaure, **11**, 1933.

3004. **Maes, J.** *Notes sur le matériel du feticheur Baluba*. Man, **11**, 1911, 181–5.

3005. —— 1924. *Notes sur les populations des bassins du Kasaï et de la Lukenie et du Lac Léopold II*. Pp. 210, ill., map. Tervueren: Musée royal de l'Afrique Centrale. (Annales du Musée Royal du Congo Belge, I, 1.)

3006. —— *La psychologie de l'art nègre*. Ipek, **2**, 1926, 275–83, ill.

3007. —— *L'Artiste nègre*. Cah. Belgique, **9**, 1930, 287–98.

3008. —— *Les sources de l'art nègre*. Cah. d'art, **6**, 1930, 307–13.

3009. —— *L'Ethnologie de l'Afrique centrale et le Musée du Congo Belge*. Africa, **7**, 1934, 174–90.

3010. —— *Symbolismus in de Negerkunst en beeldenschrift in Neder-Kongo*. Kunst, 2/3, 1934, 39–43.

3011. —— and **Olga Boone.** 1935. *Les peuplades du Congo Belge*. Pp. iv + 379, maps. Brussels: Musée du Congo Belge. (List of names of tribes, places and rivers of the Congo.)

3012. —— 1936. *Symbolisme en Negerkunst. Bij de Baluba*. Pp. 24, ill. Brussels. (Artes Africanae, 2.)

3013. —— *Beeldhouwkunst en Symbolisme in Kongo*. Rev. artes africanae (Brussels), no. 11, 1937.

3014. —— 1938. *Kabila—en grafbeelden uit Kongo*. Pp. 65–146 + xxi–xxx pl. Tervueren: Annalen van het Museum van Belgisch Congo.

3015. —— 1939. 1. *Kabila—en grafbeelden uit Kongo* (Addenda). 2. *Moedereerebeelden uit Kongo*. Pp. 149–219 + xxxi–xxxvii pl. Tervueren: Annales du Musée du Congo Belge.

3016. —— *L'art nègre au service de l'industrie belge*. Illustr. congol., 1940, 222, 116–18.

3017. **Manker, Ernst.** '*Niombo*'; '*Die Totenbestattung der Babwende*'. Z.f. Ethnol., **64**, 1932, 159–72, ill.

3018. —— 1929. *Bland Kristallburgens Folk*. Stockholm. (Tribes of the Congo.)

3019. **Maquet-Tombu, J.** *L'avenir de l'art nègre*. Le Courrier d'Afrique, 1935, 148, 1; 155, 1; 163, 1.

3020. —— *Notes de route. Encore le symbolisme*. Arts et métiers indig., **9**, 1938, 14–15.

3021. —— *Les motifs décoratifs du Mayumbe et leurs noms*. Brousse, **1**, 1939, 8–9.

3022. **Mbali, J.** *Croyance au Ndoki; obstacle au progrès*. Voix du congolais, **3**, 13/1/47, 544–50, ill.

3023. **Maurice, Le P. Henri.** *A propos d'art Ba-Luba*. Rev. ethnog. trad. pop., **1**, no. 3, 1920, 161–8, ill.

3024. **Merriam, A. P.** *The concept of culture clusters applied to the Belgian Congo*. South-western journal of anthropology, **15** (4), 1959, 373–95, map.

3025. **Mertens, J.** *Comment les Bakongo recherchent les responsables d'une mort*. Band, 20 Jg. (6), 1943, 192–5.

3026. **Meylemans, M.** *Kongoleesche Kunst en hare aanpassing aan de missie*. Zaïre, **2**, 1947, 141–57.

3027. **Minne, Georges.** *L'art bantou à Kansenia*. Cah. de St. André (St.-André-lez-Bruges), **17**, 3, mai–juin 1960, 2–14.

3028. **Moeller de Laddersous, A. J.** 1949. *Guide du voyageur au Congo Belge et au Ruanda-Urundi*. Pp. 757, bibl., ill., maps. Brussels: Editeur R. Dupriez. (Pp. 87–94, 'Les arts et la Litterature'.)

3029. **Moorsell, R. F. van.** 1959. *Esquisse préhistorique de Leopoldville; Musée de la vie indigène*.

3030. **Mortelmans, G.** *La préhistoire du Congo Belge et de l'Afrique Sud-Saharienne*. Probl. afr. centr., 1952, 233–63, ill.

3031. **Nairn, M.** *Congo art*. Studio, **130**, 1945, 88–89.

3032. **Nauwelaert, P.** *L'état actuel de l'art indigène au Mayumbe*. Arts et métiers indig., **1**, 1936, 17–19.

3033. **Olbrechts, Frans M.** 1935. *Het Roode Land der zwarte kariatieden*. Pp. 209 (+ 16), ill., maps. Tervueren: Museum van Belgisch Congo. (Davidsfonds: Keurboeken, no. 14.)

3034. —— *De 'Kabila'-beelden van Dr. J. Maes*. Kongo-Overzee, **6**, 1, Feb. 1940, 38–48.

3035. —— *Kongolese kunst en haar aanpassing aan de missie*. De Standaard (Anvers), 1946.

3036. —— and **Others.** 1958. *Art in the Congo*. Pp. 33 + 43, ill. Brussels Universal Exhibition, Belgian Congo and Ruanda-Urundi Section.

3037. **Peeraer, S.,** and **J. Manoly.** *Au sujet du dessin chez les Baluba Shankadi*. Bull. amis art indig. Katanga, **4**, 1938, 4 pp.

3038. **Périer, Gaston Denys.** *L'art nègre du Congo*. L'Universitaire colonial, **1**, mai 1928, 8.

3039. —— *L'Art nègre*. Franck, Louis, Le Congo Belge, **2**, 1930, 405–15, ill.

3040. —— *L'Art indigène au Congo Belge*. Beaux-arts, Brussels, **8**, 1930, 33–36.

3041. —— *Un edifice d'art Mangbetu*. Beaux-arts, Brussels, **7**, 250, 1937, 25–27.

3042. —— 1948. *Les arts populaires du Congo Belge*. Pp. 77, ill. Brussels: Editions de l'Office de Publicité.

3043. —— *L'évolution de l'art du Congo Belge et du Ruanda-Urundi sous l'influence de la colonisation belge*. Les arts au Congo Belge et au Ruanda-Urundi 1950 (Brussels), 1950, 55–62.

3043a. **Philippart, L.** 1947. *Le Bas Congo*. Pp. 247. Louvain: Impr. St. Alphonse.

3044. **Pierpont, J. de.** *Les Bambala*. Congo, **I**, 1932, 22–37, 185–205.

3045. **Pintassilgo, A. R.** *Seitas secretas no Congo*. Portugal em Afr. (Lisbon), **10**, 60, 1953, 361–71.

3046. **Plancquaert, M.** 1932. *Les Jaga et les Bayaka du Kwango*. Pp. 184, ill. Brussels: Institut Col. Belge.

3047. **Polome, E.** *Rapport sur les récherches ethnographiques et linguistiques au Congo Belge et au Ruanda-Urundi*. Bull. int. ctee. urgent anthrop. research, **2**, 1959, 103–9.

3048. **Régamey, O. P.** *Les arts congolaises au service du Culte*. L'Art sacré (Lille), **2**, 1937, 27.

3049. **Regnault, M.** *Les Babenga*. L'Anthropologie, **22**, 1911, 261–88, ill.

3050. **Rome: De Luca Editore.** 1959. *Arte del Congo*. Pp. 86 (2), ill. Rome: De Luca Editore.

3051. **Schebesta, Pater.** *Die Bambuti Pygmäen von Ituri*. I.R.C.B., 1941.

3052. **Schmitz, Robert.** 1912. *Les Baholoholo (Congo Belge)*. Pp. xxxii + 605, ill., maps. Inst. Intern. Bibliog. Brussels: A. Dewit. (Collection de monographies ethnographiques, 9.)

3053. **Scohy, André.** *Réflexions sur l'évolution de l'art congolais*. Brousse (Léopoldville), 1/2, 1948, 18–20.

3054. —— *Les tailleurs de chaises de Bengamisa*. Messager de St. Joseph, **22**, 1, 1951, 19–22.

3055. —— 1952. *Étapes au soleil*. Pp. ix + 255, ill., maps. Brussels: Aux editions du Chat qui pêche.

3056. —— 1955. *L'Uele secret*. Pp. 178 (4), ill., map. Brussels: Office Int. de Librairie: Léopoldville-Librairie Congolaise.

3057. **Six, J.** *De geheime Mani-Sekte te Boma*. Congo, **2** (1), 1921, 226–41.

3058. **Soupault, P.** *L'Art nègre au Congo*. Miroir du Congo Belge, **2**, 1929, 203–50.

3059. **Stanley, H. M.** 1955. *Sur le Bas-Congo*. Pp. 296, ill., map. Namur: Van Stockum.

3060. **Starr, F.** 1912. *Congo natives*. Pp. 38, ill. Chicago: Lakeside Press.

3061. **Stechow, E.** *Reichte die Erdkenntnis der alten Ägypter bis zu den Kongo Urwäldern*. Petermanns Geogr. Mitt. (Gotha), **92**, 1948, 181–3.

3062. **Stillman, E. C.** *The traditional art of the Belgian Congo*. Masterpieces of African Art. Catalogue of an exhibition held at the Brooklyn Museum 21 Oct. 1954–2 Jan. 1955. Pp. 54, ill.

3063. **Storms, Arnold.** *Aux sources de l'art congolais*. Grands lacs, no. 185, juin-juil. 1956, 51–60.

3064. **Struyf, Ivor.** *Le Kindoki*. Revue missionnaire, Nov. 1933, 400–2.

3065. **Tanghe, P. Basile.** 1926. *Le culte du serpent chez les Ngbandi*. Pp. 284, ill. Bruges and Mons: L'Etendard Franciscain.

3066. **Torday, Emil.** 1913. *Camp and tramp in African wilds*. Pp. 314, ill., map. London: Seeley Service.

3067. —— 1925. *On the trail of the Bushongo*. Pp. 286, ill. London: Seeley Service. (Bushongo arts and crafts, 202–21.)

3068. —— *Arts et métiers Bushongo*. Nervie, 9/10, 1926, 12–22.

3069. —— *Nzambi Mpungu; the god of the Bakongo*. Man, **30**, no. 3, 1930, 3.

3070. —— and **Thomas Athol Joyce.** *Notes on the ethnography of the Bayaka*. J. anthrop. inst., **36**, 1906, 39–59.

3071. —— —— *Notes on the ethnography of the Bambala*. J. anthrop. inst., **35**, 1905, 398–426, ill., map.

3072. —— —— *Note on the Southern Bambala*. Man, **7**, no. 52, 1907, 81–84, ill.

3073. —— —— *On the ethnology of the South-Western Congo Free State*. J. anthrop. inst., **37**, 1907, 133–56, bibl., ill., map.

3074. —— —— 1911. *Notes ethnographiques sur les peuples communément appelés Bakuba ainsi que sur les peuplades apparentées. Les*

Bushongo. Pp. 292, ill. Brussels: Musée Royal de l'Afrique Centrale. (Annales du Musée Royal de l'Afrique Centrale: Ethnographie-Anthropologie, Série III, Tome 2, fasc. 1.)

3075. —— —— 1922. *Notes ethnographiques sur les peuplades habitant les bassins du Kasai et du Kwango oriental peuplades de la forêt; peuplades des prairies.* Pp. (4) 359, ill. Brussels: Musée Royal de l'Afrique Centrale. (Annales du Musée Royal de l'Afrique Centrale: Ethnographie-Anthropologie, Série III, Tome 2, fasc. 1.)

3076. **Toura Gaba, M. J.** *Traditionele kunst van Belgisch Kongo; de beeldhouwkunst.* Esso magazine, 1956, 44–51, ill.

3077. **van Caeneghem, R.** *Hekserij bij de Baluba van Kasai.* Mém. in-8e., A.R.S.C., Classe Sci. Mor. and Pol. (N.S.) III, 1 (Ethnog.), 1955, 280.

3078. **van Coillie, G.** *Recueil de signaux claniques ou Kumbu des tribus Mbagani et du Kasai (Congo Belge).* Afr. stud., 8 (1), 1949, 35–45; 8 (2), 1949, 80–100, ill., map.

3079. **van den Bossche, Adr.** *Art Bakuba.* Brousse, 1, 1952, 11–26, ill.

3080. **van den Bulcke, A.** *Geestenverering.* Nieuw Afrika, 71jg. 4, 1955, 159–63, ill.

3081. —— *Totems en Totemismus.* Nieuw Afrika, 2, 1955, 67–69, ill.

3082. **Vandenhoudt, Niko.** *Inlandsche kunst.* Missions de Scheut, mars 1939, 85–88.

3083. —— *Aangepaste christelijke Kunst in Kongo.* Zaïre, 3, 1949, 279–84.

3084. **van den Plas, J.** 1910. *Les Kuku.* Pp. xlii + 407, bibl., ill., map. Brussels: Institut Intern. de Bibliographie. (Collection de Monographies Ethnographiques, 6.)

3085. **van der Kerken, Georges.** 1933. *Notes sur les Mangbetu.* Pp. 28. Anvers: Univ. Coloniale.

3086. —— 1952. *De Afrikaanse bevolking van Belgisch-Kongo en van Ruanda-Urundi. Haar verleden en haar toekomst.* Pp. 194, ill., maps. Gent: Boekhandel Fecheyr. (Consult especially Part 4, La culture matérielle, intellectuelle, artistique.)

3087. **van Geluwe, H.** 1956. *Les Bira et les peuplades limitrophes.* Pp. 9 + 165. Tervueren: Musée Royal de l'Afrique Centrale. Sci. de l'Homme, Monogr. Ethn., vol. II.

3088. —— 1960. *Les Bali et les peuplades apparentées (Ndaka, Mbo, Beke, Like, Budu, Nyari).* Pp. ix + 130, map. Tervueren: Musée Royal de l'Afrique Centrale. Monogr. Ethnogr., no. 5.

3089. **van Overbergh, Cyr.,** and **de Jonghe** (*Ed.*). 1907. *Les Bangala.* Pp. xv + 458, bibl., map. Brussels: Institut Intern. de Bibliographie. (Collection de Monographies Ethnographiques, 1.)

3090. —— —— 1907. *Les Mayombe.* Pp. xvi + 470, bibl., map. Brussels: Institut Intern. de Bibliographie. (Collection de Monographies Ethnographiques, 2.)

3091. —— 1908. *Les Basonge.* Pp. xvi + 564, bibl., ill., map. Brussels: Institut Intern. de Bibliographie. (Collection de Monographies Ethnographiques, 3.)

3092. —— —— 1909. *Les Mangbetu.* Pp. xvi + 594, bibl., ill., map. Brussels: Institut Intern. de Bibliographie. (Collection de Monographies Ethnographiques, 4.)

3093. **Vansina, J.** *Réflexions sur le rôle de l'art dans la société kuba.* Folia scientifica africaen centralis, 3, 4, 1957, 77–79.

3094. **van Wing, J.** *Ndoki.* Jezuieten missies, 11, 1937, 551–6.

3095. —— *Nkisi-kapiangoe.* Jezuieten missies, 15, 1937, 904–20.

3096. —— *Études Bakongo,* 11: Religion et magie. Brussels, I.R.C.B., Mém. 9 (1), 1938, 301.

3097. —— *Bakongo magic.* J. roy. anthrop. inst., 71, 1941, 85–97, ill.

3098. **Verner, Samuel P.** 1903. *Pioneering in Central Africa.* Pp. ix + 500, ill., maps. Richmond, Va.: Presbyterian Committee of Publication. (Ch. xxiii, pp. 292–298, ill. Native African arts and industries.)

3099. **Vervaecke, R. P.** *Les Bena Lulua.* Revue Congo, 1910.

3100. **Wannijn, R. L.** 1950. *Ancient religious insignia in the Bas-Congo.* Vatican Exhibition catalogue, pp. 41–55.

3101. **Ward, Herbert.** 1910. *A voice from the Congo.* Pp. xv + 299, ill. London: W. Heinemann.

3102. **Wauters, A. J.** *Les Bapoto.* Congo illus., 1, no. 27, 1892, 210–11, ill.

3103. **Weeks, John H.** *Notes on some customs of the Lower Kongo people.* Folklore (London), 19, 1908, 4.

3104. —— *Anthropological notes on the Bangala of the Upper Congo river.* J. roy. anthrop. inst., 39, 1909, 97–136.

3105. —— 1914. *Among the primitive Bakongo.* Pp. xvi + 318, ill., map. London: Seeley Service. (Ch. 12, pp. 121–40, Native amusements.)

3106. **Weghsteen, R. P. Joseph.** *Art décoratif dans la region de Baudouinville (Haut-Congo).* Ann. Lat., 27, 1963, 193–205, ill.

3107. **Wingert, Paul S.** *Congo art.* Trans. New York acad. sci., ser. 2, 9, 8, 1947, 320–37.

3108. **Wolfe, Alvin W.** *Art and the supernatural in the Ubangi District.* Man, 55, 76, May 1955, 65–67, ill.

3109. —— 1961. *In the Ngombe tradition.* Pp. viii + 167, bibl., ill., map. Chicago: Northwestern Univ. Press. (Northwestern University African Studies, no. 7.)

3110. **Zangrie, Luc.** *Les institutions, la religion et l'art des Ba Buye; Groupes Ba Sumba du Ma Nyéme (Congo belge).* L'Ethnographie, N.S. no. 45, 1947–50: 54–80, ill.

3111. **Zwernemann, Jürgen.** *Spiegel- und Nagel-plastiken vom unteren Kongo im Linden-Museum.* Tribus, no. 10, Sept. 1961, 15–32, ill.

FIGURES AND MASKS

3112. **Adé, B.** *Art spontané ou réminiscences d'une tradition inconnue. Les plastiques d'argile cuite de Takuboyo (Congo Belge).* Les Musées de Genève, 10, 1953, 37, ill.

3113. **Anon.** *Dans la boucle du Congo; La sculpture africaine et son destin.* Pp. 64, ill. Namur.

3114. —— *Skulptur från Kongo.* Konstrevy (Stockholm), 36 (5–6), 1960, 202–3, ill. (Photos of five Congo figures, with captions: no other text.)

3115. **Belgian Congo of Today.** *Batshoko Mask (Upper Kasai region of Dilolo).* Belgian Congo of today, 7 (4), 1958, facing p. 12.

3116. —— *Styles in Congolese sculpture.* Belgian Congo of today, 8 (2), 1959, 33–37.

3117. **Belgium.** Theses: Burssens, 'La sculpture chez les Zande'. Cuypers, 'Sculpture des Bembe'. Vierin, 'Crucifixes des Bas-Congo'.

3118. **Biebuyck, D.** *Signification d'une statuette Lega.* Rev. col. belge, 8, 195, 1953, 866–7, ill.

3119. —— *Function of a Lega mask.* Int. archiv. ethnog., 47 (1), 1954, 108–20, ill.

3120. **Borchgrave d'Altena, Comte J. de.** *Christs de l'ancien Congo.* Rev. artisan. et arts liturgiques (Bruges), 1949, 177.

3121. **Bourdarie, P.** *Un coffre sculpté de la forêt du Mayumbé.* C.R. acad. sci. colon., 4, 1924–5, 259–63.

3122. **Burssens, Herman.** *Sculptuur in Ngbandi-stijl; een bijdrage tot de studie van de Plastiek van Noord-Kongo.* Kongo-Overzee, 24, 1/2, 1958, 1–50, ill., map.

3123. —— *La fonction de la sculpture traditionelle chez les Ngbaka.* Brousse, 11, 1958, 10–28, ill. (Printed by 'Courrier d'Afrique, Léopoldville'.)

3124. —— *Enkele Zande-maskers uit Uele.* Congo-Tervueren, 6, 4, 1960, 101–8, ill.

3125. **Butaye, R.** *Les fétiches et les maléfices.* Missions belges. Cie. Jesus, 8, 1899, 309–15.

3126. —— *De la mentalité des Bakongo.* Missions belges. Cie. Jesus, 1908, 155–60, 187–92, 210–19.

3127. **Cazet, T.,** and **C. Denart.** N.D. *Images du Congo.*

3128. **Clouzot, H.**, and **A. Level.** *L'Art du Congo Belge.* Art et décoration, **40**, 1921, 149–60.

3129. **Colle, Le R. P.** 1913. *Les Baluba. Congo Belge.* 2 vols. Vol. 1, pp. lxxxiii + 422, ill. Vol. 2, pp. lvii + 429–918, ill., map. Brussels: Institut Intern. de Bibliographie.

3130. **Daniel, G.** *L'Art nègre au Congo Belge.* La Nature, **51**, 1, 1923, 37–40. (Sculptures des Luba.)

3131. **Dartevelle, E.** *Note sur une main sculptée d'origine Kabinda.* Bull. soc. anthrop. (Bruxelles), **49**, 1934, 212–13.

3132. **Delange, Jacqueline.** *A Bushongo cup in the Musée de l'Homme.* Man, **56**, no. 194, 1956, 170–1, ill.

3133. **De Rop, A.** *Les statuettes Lilwâ chez les Boyela (Lilwâ-beeldjes bij de Boyela).* Zaïre, **9**, 2, fev. 1955, 115–20.

3134. **de Sousberghe, L.** *De la signification de quelques masques Pende; shave des Shona et mbuya des Pende.* Zaïre, **14**, 5/6, 1960, 505–31, ill.

3135. —— *Un masque Tshokwe de Cucumbi (Haut-Kwango, Angola).* Africa-Tervueren, **7**, 3, 1961, 85–87, ill.

3136. —— *Quelques pièces sculptées de la région de Kingandu (Kwenge).* Africa-Tervueren, **8**, 1/2, 1962, 54–55, ill.

3137. **Einstein, C.** *Masques Bapendé.* Documents, **1**, 1930, 48–54.

3138. **Fagg, William B.** *A master sculptor of the Eastern Congo.* Man, **48**, 42, Apr. 1948, 37–38, ill.

3139. —— *Congo sculptures in the Oldman collection.* B.M.Q., **16**, 1951, 109–10.

3140. **Faider-Thomas, T.** *Katatora; objet divinatoire sculpté chez les Luba.* Africa-Tervueren, **7** (1), 1961, 18–20, ill.

3141. **Feilberg, C. G.** *En Kongo-Statuette fra Bakuba-Folket.* Fra Nationalmuseets Arbejdsmark, 1934, 70–80.

3142. **Gaffe, René.** 1945. *La sculpture au Congo Belge.* Pp. 69, ill. Paris: Editions du Cercle D'Art.

3143. —— 1945. *La sculpture nègre.* Pp. 66 (32 pl.). Bibliothèque Française.

3144. **Gregoire, G. F.** *Tombeaux et monuments funéraires chez les Songo de la rive gauche de la Maringa.* Rev. cong., **4**, 1913–14, 178–83, ill.

3145. **Hall, H. U.** *Baluba chieftain's staff.* Museum journal (Univ. of Pennsylvania, Philadelphia, Pa.), **14** (3), 1923, 8, 2, ill.

3146. —— *Notes on some Congo and West African woodcarvings.* Museum journal (Univ. of Pennsylvania, Philadelphia, Pa.), **14**, 1923, 47–84, 101–34, ill.

3147. —— *A Congo fetish and divining image from the coast region.* Museum journal (Univ. of Pennsylvania, Philadelphia, Pa.), **15** (1), 1924, 58–69, ill.

3148. —— *African cups embodying human forms.* Museum journal (Univ. of Pennsylvania, Philadelphia, Pa.), **15** (3), 1924, 190–227, ill.

3149. —— *Two wooden statuettes from the Lower Congo.* Museum journal (Univ. of Pennsylvania, Philadelphia, Pa.), **18**, 1927, 99–110, ill.

3150. —— *Batetela image.* Museum journal (Univ. of Pennsylvania, Philadelphia, Pa.), **2**, 1931, 155–7.

3151. **Himmelheber, Hans.** *Les masques Bayaka et leurs sculpteurs.* Brousse, **1**, 1939, 19–39, ill.

3152. —— *Art et artistes 'Bakuba'.* Brousse, **1**, 1940, 17–30.

3153. **Holz, P.** *Traditional art of the Congo; religious beliefs expressed in wood-carving.* African world, Aug. 1958, 10–11, ill.

3154. **Huber, Hugo.** *Magical statuettes and their accessories among the Eastern Bayaka.* Anthropos, **51**, 1956, 265–90, ill.

3155. **Huet, M., Jeanson, S.,** and **R. Delmarcelle.** 1958. *Congo.* Pp. 164, ill., map. Brussels: Office International de Librairie: Léopoldville: La Librairie Congolaise. (Album of photographs including masks.)

3156. **Johnson, M.** *Congolese and Romanesque sculpture—a comparison.* Studio, **143**, 1952, 10–15.

3157. **Joyce, T. A.** *On a carved wooden cup from the Bakuba, Kasai District.* Man, **9**, 1, 1909, 1–3, ill.

3158. —— *On a wooden portrait-statue from the Bushongo people, Kasai District, Congo State.* Man, **10**, no. 1, 1910, 1–2, ill.

3159. —— *The portrait-statue of Mikope Mbula, 110th paramount chief of the Bushongo.* Man, **25**, 115, 1925, 185f., ill.

3160. **Katanga: Images du Congo.** 1954. *Katanga: Images du Congo.* Pp. 147, ill. Brussels: Ch. Dessart.

3161. **Kochnitzky, Léon.** 1952. *Shrines of wonders.* Ill. New York: Clark & Fritts.

3162. —— *Masques géants, masques en miniature.* Rev. col. belge (Bruxelles), **8**, 175, janv. 1953, 53–55, ill.

3163. **Lavachery, Henri.** *Essay on styles in the statuary of the Congo.* Cunard, Nancy (*ed.*), Negro anthology, 1934, 687–93, ill.

3164. **le Paige, G.** *L'art et la statuaire au Congo.* Revue missionnaire, juin 1935, 245–8.

3165. **Madaus, Ludwig.** 1929. *Die Holzfiguren des Kongo-Kassai-Gebietes.* (Dissertation.) Pp. v (1), 43, ill. Bad Segeberg: C. H. Wäsers Druckerei.

3166. **Maes, Joseph.** 1924. *Aniota-Kifwebe. Les masques des populations du Congo Belge, et le matériel des rites de circoncision.* Pp. 64, ill. Anvers: De Sikkel.

3167. —— *Beschouwingen over negerplastiek.* Nederl.-Indies oud en nieuw (Haag), **11**, 1926, 194–207, ill.

3168. —— *Figurines Na Mogonga ou de guérison des populations du Bas-Congo.* Pro medico (Paris), **7**, 1927, 68–73, ill.

3169. —— *Figurines commémoratives et allégoriques du Congo Belge.* Ipek, **3**, 1928, 76–91, ill.

3170. —— *La sculpture Bashilele.* Cahiers de Belgique, **6**, 1928, 238.

3171. —— *Les figurines pezo des populations du Bas-Congo.* Pro medico, **2**, 1929, 48–52.

3172. —— *Une figurine à coupe provenant du Katanga.* Man, **29**, no. 39, 1929, 56–57, ill.

3173. —— *Les trépieds et appuis-dos du Congo Belge.* Annales du musée du Congo Belge, ethnogr., Ser. VI, **1**, 1930, 45–78, ill.

3174. —— *Les appuis-tête du Congo-Belge.* Annales du musée du Congo Belge, Tervueren, Ethnographie, Sér. VI. Catalogues illustrés des collections ethnographiques du musée du Congo Belge. T.I, fasc. 1, mai 1929. Pp. viii + 40, 1 map, 8 pl. h.t.

3175. —— *Les figurines sculptées du Bas-Congo.* Africa, **3**, 1930, 347–59.

3176. —— 1930. *Figurines à clous ou fétiches 'Konde' des populations du Bas-Congo.* Pro medico (Paris), **7**, 1, 4–7.

3177. —— *Le Katotora, figurine divinatoire des Baluba.* Pro medico, **1**, 1933, 27–31.

3178. —— 1935. *Fetischen of Tooverbeelden uit Kongo.* Pp. 62, ill., map. Tervueren: Annales du Musée (Royal) du Congo Belge. Ser. VI, **11**, 1.

3179. —— *Les statues de rois Bakuba.* Beaux-arts, **7**, 1936, 18–21.

3180. —— *Musique et sculpture congolaises.* Illustr. congol., **192**, 1937, 6533–4, 6539–42.

3181. —— 1937. *Sculpture décorative ou symbolique des instruments de musique du Congo Belge.* Pp. 43, ill. Brussels. (Artes Africanae, 8.)

3182. —— *Les Kabila ou figures mendiantes.* Annales du musée du Congo Belge, Tervueren, Ser. 6, 1938, 65–148.

3183. —— *Figurines mendiantes dites 'Kabila' des Baluba.* Brousse no. 2, 1939, 10–17, ill.

3184. —— *Figurines commémoratives et allégoriques du Kwango (Congo Belge).* Pro medico (Bruxelles), **15**, 4, 1938, 119–22. Pro medico (Paris), **15**, 3, 1938, 87–90.

3185. —— *Figurines phemba dites maternité des Bena Lulua.* Illustr. congol., **220**, 1940, 29–31.

3186. —— *'Kabila' - beelden en 'Kabila'-stijl.* Wetensch. Tijdingen, Jg. 5, 6, 1940, 239–43.

3187. —— tr. by A. Schulz. *Die soziale und kulturelle Bedeutung der Kabila-Figuren aus Belgisch-Kongo.* Paideuma, **2**, 6/7, März 1943, 249–67, xiii pl.

3188. **Maesen, Albert.** *Styles et expérience esthétique dans la plastique congolaise.* Probl. Afr. centr., **13**, 44, 1959, 85–93.

3189. —— and **Others.** *Les arts plastiques africains.* Probl. Afr. centr. (Bruxelles), **13**, 44, 1959, 79–159, ill.

3190. —— 1960. *Umbangu; art du Congo au musée royal du Congo Belge.* Pp. 27 + 50 pl. Bruxelles: Éd. Cultura (l'Art en Belgique, 3).

3191. **Manoly, J.** *Les arts traditionnels de quelques chefferies Katangaises.* Bull. amis art indig. (Katanga), 1937, 3–6, ill.

3192. —— *Notules sur les manifestations artistiques des Baluba de la région de Mwanza.* Bull. amis art indig. (Katanga), 1937, 1–3, ill.

3193. **Mertens, Joseph.** 1935. *Les Ba Dzing de la Kamtsha. Première partie-Ethnographie.* Pp. 381, ill., maps. Brussels: G. van Campenhout. (I.R.C.B. (Sciences Morales): Mém. no. 4.)

3194. **Michelet, Raymond.** *Different types of Congo masks and fetish figures in Tervueren Museum, Belgium.* Cunard, Nancy (ed.), Negro anthology, 1934, 693–731, ill.

3195. **Milou.** *Les masques.* Illustr. congol., **194**, 1937, 6627–8, ill.

3196. **Notes Africaines I.F.A.N.** *Statuette mendiante (Baluba, Congo belge).* Notes afr. I.F.A.N., 95, 1962 (cover ill.).

3197. **Olbrechts, Frans M.** 1940. *Maskers en Dansers in de Ivoorkust.* Pp. 183, ill. (Davidsfonds Völksboek no. 290.)

3198. —— *Stijl en sub-stijl in de plastiek der Ba-Luba (Belgisch Kongo) 'De Kabila stijl'.* Wetensch. Tijdingen, **5** (2), 1940, 22–30.

3199. —— 1946. *Plastiek van Congo.* Pp. 165 + xliv, ill. Antwerp: Standaard-Boekhandel.

3200. —— *Le statuaire du Congo Belge.* Les arts plastiques (Brussels), **5** (I), 1951, 5–15.

3201. —— *Le Congo au XVIe siècle.* Les arts plastiques (Brussels), **5**, 1951, 31–36, ill.

3202. —— *Découverte de deux statuettes d'un grand sous-style Ba-Luba.* I.R.C.B. bull. séances, **22**, 1, 1951, 130–40, ill.

3203. —— 1952. *Some masterpieces of African art from the collections of the Royal Museum of Belgian Congo, Tervueren.* XXIV pl. Tervueren.

3204. —— and **Others.** *Invitation au voyage congolais (nombreux photographies de sculptures, masques, etc., du Musée Royal du Congo Belge).* Sabena rev. (Bruxelles), hiver 1954, 24–79, ill.

3205. —— *Une curieuse statuette en laiton des Ba-Teke.* Congo-Tervueren, **1**, 3, juil. 1955, 103–4, ill.

3206. —— 1959. *Les arts plastiques du Congo Belge.* Pp. 161 + 44, ill. Bruxelles: Érasme. (Transl. from Flemish ed. of 1940.)

3207. **'Oost en West', Amsterdam.** *Styles in Congolese sculpture.* Belgian Congo today, **8** (2), 1959, 33–37.

3208. **Olsen-Manke, E.** *Santu der Kreuzförmige Jagdfetisch der Bakongo.* Völkerkunde, **4**, 10/12, 217–23.

3209. **Périer, G. D.** 1928. *Regardons l'art nègre en face.* (Masques.) Arts et métiers congolais, 27–29, ill.

3210. —— 1928. *Introduction aux masques congolais.* Cahiers de Belgique, févr., 16–21.

3211. **Plancquaert, M. Le R. P.** 1930. *Les sociétés secrétes chez les Bayaka.* Pp. 131, ill., map. Brussels: Falk.

3212. **Scohy, A.** *Un sculpteur tchécoslovaque devant les tailleurs d'images congolais.* Jeune Afr., 40 ann., **11**, 1950, 39–40.

3213. **Segy, Ladislas.** *Bakuba cups; an essay on style-classification.* Midwest J. (Jefferson, Ohio), **4**, 1, Winter 1951–2, 26–49, ill.

3214. —— *Bakota funerary figures.* Zaïre, **6**, 5, mai 1952, 451–60, ill.

3215. —— *Sculptures shango.* Acta tropica, **12**, 2, 1955, 136–73.

3216. **Söderberg, Bertil.** *Ancestor guardian figures and ancestral baskets among the Bakuta.* Ethnos, **21**, 1956, 105–17, bibl., ill.

3217. **Tata Nsiesie.** *Notes sur les Christs et statues de l'ancien Congo.* Brousse, **3**, 1959, 32.

3218. **Thomas, T.** *Les itombwa; objets divinatoires sculptés conservés au Musée du Congo-Belge.* Congo-Tervueren, **6** (3), 1960, 78–83, ill.

3219. **Timmermans, P.** *Les Sapo Sapo près de Luluabourg.* Africa-Tervueren, **8**, 1/2, 1962, 29–53, ill., maps.

3220. **Torday, E.** 1924. *Note on certain figurines of forged iron formerly made by the Bushongo of the Belgian Congo.* Man, **24**, 13, 17 ill.

3221. —— *Le fetichisme, l'idolatrie et le sorcellerie des Bantous occidentaux.* L'Anthropologie, **39**, 1929, 431–54.

3222. **Vanden Bossche, Adr.** *La sculpture de masques Bapende.* Brousse, **1**, 1950, 11–15, ill.

3223. **Vanden Bossche, Jean.** *L'Art plastique chez les Bapende.* Brousse **2**, 1950, 7–16, ill.

3224. —— *L'Art plastique indigène.* La revue française, de l'élite, **47**, 1953, 5 + 4 pp., 10 + 11, ill.

3225. —— *De dieren als onderwerp in de negerkunst.* Band (Léopoldville), **13**, 3, mars 1954, 109–10, ill.

3226. **van Geluwe, H.** *Préliminaires sur les origines de l'intérêt pour l'art africain et considérations sur le thème de la femme dans la sculpture congolaise.* Africa-Tervueren, **7**, 3, 1961, 71–81, bibl., ill.

3227. **Vansina, J.** *Initiation rituals of the Bushong.* Africa, **25** (2), 1955, 138–53.

3228. **van Wing, J.** *Fetichisme bij de Bakongo.* Congo, **2** (I), 1931, 1–25.

3229. **Verheyleweghen, J.** and **F.** *Objets du culte yakouba associant la corne 'fetiche' au masque ancestral.* Bull. soc. roy. belge d'anthrop. et préhist., 1934.

3230. **Verly, R.** *La statuaire de pierre du Bas-Congo (Bamboma-Mussurongo).* Zaïre, **9**, 5, mai 1955, 451–528, ill. (Also reprint.)

3231. **Verwilghen, T.** *Maskers.* Jezuietenmissies, **10**, 76, 1951, 43–45, ill.

3232. **Wauters, A. J.** *Les fétiches (wooden figures).* Congo illus., **1**, no. 3, 1892, S.P., ill.

3233. **Weyns, J. A.** *Drie merkwaardige Scheptere nit Neder-Kongo.* Bull. mus. roy. (belge), d'art et d'hist., **3**, 1943, 44–48.

3234. —— *Un chef-d'œuvre de la sculpture africaine provenant des Bakongo occidentaux.* Bull. Mus. roy. (Belge) d'art et d'histoire, **3**, 1944, 71–82.

3235. —— *Een afrikaansch Beeld van een Buktenaar.* Bull. mus roy. (belge) d'art et d'hist., **3**, 1945, 76–80.

3236. —— *Contribution à l'étude du complexe stylistique Ba-Yaka—Ba-Suku (Kwango, Congo Belge) (statuettes et masques).* Congr. int. sci. anthrop. et ethnol. (3e Session, Bruxelles), 1948 (1960), 275.

3237. **Wingert, Paul S.** *Congo art.* Trans. New York acad. sci., **9** (1947), 330–7.

3238. *See 4369.*

3239. —— *From darkest Africa; fetishism and secret ritual have inspired the sophisticated Belgian Congo sculptors.* Art digest, **28**, 1954, 15 +.

3240. **Zaal, C.** *Bij de Nzakara.* Bendo, een fetisj voor de vrouwen. Kongo-Overzee, **24** (I–2), 1958, 80–89.

BUILDINGS AND FURNITURE

3241. **Annaert, Jean.** 1960. *Contribution à l'étude géographique de l'habitat et de l'habitation indigènes . . . dans les provinces orientale et du Kivu.* Pp. 162, ill., map. Brussels: Académie Royale des Sciences d'Outre-Mer, Classe des Sciences Naturelles et Médicales. Mém. in 8, N.S., Tome 10, fasc. 3.

3242. **Comhaire-Sylvain, Jean.** *L'Habitation chez les Nkundu du territoire d'Oshwe, Congo Belge.* Afr. stud., **8**, 1949, 66–69, ill.

3243. **Costermans, B.** *De gebouwen bij de Mamvu-Mangutu-Walese.* Zaïre, 1947, 281–95, ill.

3244. **Decorse, J.** *L'Habitation et le village au Congo et au Chari.* L'Anthropologie, **16**, 1905, 639–56, ill.

3245. **de Sousberghe, L.** *Cases cheffales sculptées des Ba-Pende.* Bull. soc. roy. belge anthrop. et préhist., **65**, 1954, 75–81, ill.

3246. —— *Cases cheffales du Kwango.* Congo-Tervueren, **6**, 1, 1960, 10–16, ill.

3247. **Devulder, Le Père M.** *Peintures murales et pratiques magiques dans la tribu de Ouadhias.* Rev. Afr., **95**, 1951, 63–102.

3248. **du Plessis, J.** 1917. *Thrice through the Dark Continent . . . during the years 1913–1916.* Pp. viii + 350, ill., map. London: Longmans, Green.

3249. **Elisabethville; C.E.P.S.I., 1950.** 1950. Bull. no. 12. *Numéro consacré aux maisons indigènes au Congo.* Pp. 204, ill., plans. Elisabethville.

3250. **Périer, G. D.** *Formes congolaises et architecture.* Bull. missions, **18** (3), 1939, 211–20, ill.

3251. **Scohy, André.** *Ekibondo . . . ou les murs veulent parler* (*Les cases peintes d'un village de l'Uélé*). Brousse, 1/2, 1951, 17–34, ill.

3252. **Verhulpen, Edmond.** 1936. *Baluba et Balubaisés du Katanga.* Pp. 534, bibl., ill., maps. Anvers: Les éditions de l'Avenir Belge.

CLOTHING AND ADORNMENT

3253. **Bayer, L.** *Ventouses sèches et scarifications chez les Balese* (*entre Kwese et Irumu*). Rev. congl., **2**, 1911–12, 391–2, ill.

3254. **Bazin, I.** *Comment s'habillent nos Noirs.* Grands lacs, **67**, 146, 1951–2, 23–26. (Région des lacs Albert et Edouard.)

3255. **Birnbaum, M.** *The long-headed Mangbetus.* Nat. hist., **43**, 2, 1939, 73–83, ill.

3256. **Bräuning, P. H.** 1929. *Kleidung und Schmuck unserer Neger.* Echo aus den Missionen, **5**, mai.

3257. **Chapoix, Lucienne.** *Les anneaux en cuivre jaune au Bas-Congo.* Congo (Tervueren), **5**, 3, 1959, 74–75, ill.

3258. **Dernoncourt, J.** *Quelques tatouages de l'Equateur.* Bull. nat. Mons and Borinage, **15** and **16**, 1932–3, 1933–4, 198–202.

3259. **Lemaire, Ch.** *De la toilette.* Congo illus., **2**, no. 1, 1893, 8, ill.

3260. **Manoly, Jorj.** *Coiffure Muluba.* Bull. amis art indig. (Elisabethville), **1**, 1937.

3261. **Matton, Arsène.** *Tatouages.* Arts et métiers congolais, 24–25, ill.

3262. **Milou.** *Tatouages.* Illustr. congol., **190**, 1937, 6468–55, ill.

3263. **Pienard, G. A.** *Contribution à l'étude des costumes de Chasse chez les Babira.* Kongo-Overzee, **21** (5), 1955, 1389–1419.

3264. **Segy, Ladislas.** *Warega ivories.* Zaïre, **5**, 10, déc. 1951, 1041–5, ill.

3265. **Soupart, J.** *Les tatouages chez les Budja.* Bull. jurid. indig., **6**, 12, nov.–déc. 1938, 317–25.

3266. **Torday, E.** *Note on unusual form of tatu.* Man, **13**, 2, 1913, 3.

3267. **van den Brande, Fr.,** and **M. Appelmans.** *De cheloïden bij de inboorlingen van Belgisch-Congo.* I.R.C.B., bull. séances, **11**, 2, 1940, 374–87.

3268. **van den Plas, J.** *L'opération du tatouage chez les Mobali.* Rev. cong., **1**, 1910–11, 226–7, ill.

3269. **Van Roy, P.** *La mode au Lac Albert.* Grands lacs, **51**, 11/12, 1935, 615–16.

3270. **Wannijn, J.** *Porter de lourds bracelets n'a pas toujours été coquetterie.* Rev. cong., **26**, 2, 1954, 27–29, ill.

3271. **Wauters, A. J.** *Les Tatouages.* Congo illus., **1**, no. 20, 1892, s.p., ill.

3272. ——*L'Ivoire.* Congo. illus., **2**, no. 6, 1893, 42–43, ill.

3273. ——*Les colliers.* Congo illus., **2**, no. 21, 1893, 162–3, ill.

3274. **Weibel, A. C.** *Embroidered cloth of equatorial Africa.* Detroit institute of art, Bull. 28, no. 2, 1949, 41–43.

ROCK ART

3275. **Bevel, M. L.** *Muurschilderingen bij de Basonges.* Conseiller congolais, **14**, 11, 1941, 80.

3276. **Breuil, Henri.** 1952. *Les figures incisées et ponctuées de la grotte de Kiantapo* (*Katanga*). Pp. 32, ill. Tervueren: Musée royal du Congo Belge. (Annales du Musée royal du Congo Belge, Sér. in 8. Sciences de l'Homme. Préhistoire, vol. 1.)

3277. **de Munck, J.,** and **Others.** *Gravures et peintures dans la grotte de Mvangi.* Brousse, **12**, 1959, 8–23, ill.

3278. **Mortelmans, G.,** and **R. Monteyne.** *La grotte peinte de Mbafu, témoignage iconographique de la première évangélisation du Bas-Congo.* Actes 4ᵉ Congrès Panafricain de Préhistoire . . . (ed. G. Mortelmans and J. Nenquin), sect. 3, 1962, 457–86.

3279. **Vanden Bossche, J.** *Étude morphologique des gravures et peintures de la grotte de Mvangi.* Brousse, **12**, 1959, 13–18, ill.

3280. **Van Moorsel, Hendrik.** *Étude comparative des dessins des grottes du Bas-Congo.* Brousse, **12**, 1959, 19–21, ill.

TECHNIQUES

3281. **Bergmans, Lieven.** *La calebasse chez les Wanandes.* Afr. ardente (Bruxelles), **19**, 86, mai–juin 1955, 13–17, ill.

3282. **Bittremieux, L.** *Teekning motieven op Mayombsche matjes.* Brousse, **2**, 1940, 4–14.

3283. **Bogaerts, H.** *Het spel in onze koloniale scholen.* Aequatoria, **13**, 4, 1950, 121–6.

3284. **Brasseur, Com.** *Coutumes bizarres accompagnant l'extraction et la mode de traitement du minerai de cuivre au Katanga.* Bull. soc. géog. (Nancy), **18**, 1897, 290–1.

3285. **Brousse.** *Corporation des Ebénistes de Buta.* Brousse, **3**, 1939, 39–41.

3286. **Coart, E.** 1907. *La céramique.* Pp. 193, ill. (21 col. pl.). Brussels: Musée du Congo Belge. (Annales du Musée du Congo Belge, Tome 2, fasc. 1.)

3287. —— 1926. *Vannerie et tissage (les arts congolais).* Pp. 34 (6), 64 pl. in a portfolio. Brussels: Éditions de la Renaissance d'Occident.

3288. —— 1927. *Les nattes.* Tervueren: Annales du Musée du Congo Belge. (D. Anthropologie et Ethnographie, Série III, **2**, 2.)

3289. **Coppée, R. P.** *Nattes Yombe; la veillée funèbre.* Brousse, N.S. 9, 1956, 25–26, ill.

3290. **de Heinzelin, J.** *Metallurgie primitive du fer dans la région de la Passe-Semliki.* Bull. séances, acad. belge. sci. O.-M., **5**, 3, 1959, 673–98, bibl., ill., map.

3291. **de Hemptinne, J.** *Les mangeurs de cuivre du Katanga.* Congo, I, 1926, 371–403.

3292. **de Rode, Ph.** *Notes sur la fonte du fer.* Aequatoria, **3**, 4, 1940, 103.

3293. **de Rop, A.** *Nota's over de smidse der Nkundo.* Aequatoria, **17**, 1, 1954, 1–6.

3294. **de Sousberghe, L.** *Forgerons et fondeurs de fer chez les Ba-Pende et leurs voisins.* Zaïre, **9**, 1, janv. 1955, 25–31.

3295. **Detourbet, A. Masson.** *Le tissage du Raphia chez les Batéké* (*Moyen Congo*). J. soc. africanistes, **27**, 1957, 67–79, ill.

3296. **Emilienne, M.** *Raphia-Vlechtwerk in Bondombe.* Aequatoria, 5, 1940, 132–4.

3297. **François.** *Note sur la poterie 'Wembo nyama'.* Brousse, **3**, 1940, 16.

3298. **Gaurichon, Joseph.** *Céramique congolaise.* Bull. soc. préhist. fr., 1928, 198–9.

3299. **Hasse, G.** *Notes sur une forge primitive au Congo Belge.* Bull. soc. roy. belge anthrop. et préhist., **58**, 1947, 335–6.

3300. **Jacobs, J.** *La vannerie, la poterie et le tissage dans les proverbes Tetela.* Kongo-Overzee, **21** (3–4), 1955, 272–88, ill.

3301. **Joyce, T. A.** *Note on the pigment-blocks of the Bushongo, Kasai District, Belgian Congo.* Man, **10**, 46, 81–82, ill.; **61**, 1910, 106.

3302. ——*Babunda weaving.* Ipek, **1**, 1925, 105–10, ill.

3303. **Kaoze, St.** *Le métier à tisser chez les Batabwa* (*Mavungu*). Congo, I, 4, 1928, 515–19, ill.

3304. **Ladame, J.** *Le droit des indigènes sur les mines de cuivre du Katanga.* Congo, **2**, 5, 1921, 685–91.

3305. **Lefebure, P. L.** *Een weastervend bedrijf, het kopergieten bij de negers in Katanga.* Congo, **2**, 3, 1930, 359–67.

3306. **Loir, Hélène.** 1935. *Le Tissage du Raphia au Congo Belge.* Annales du Musée du Congo belge, Tome 3, fasc. 1. Pp. 66, bibl., ill., maps. Brussels: Musée du Congo Belge.

3307. **Maes, J.** *Métier à tisser des Ababua.* Rev. cong., ill., **2**, 1911–12, 393–5.

3308. —— *Les métiers à tisser du lac Léopold II.* Rev. cong., **4**, 1913, 111–13, ill.

3309. —— *Métiers à tisser des Batempa, des Bena Lulua et des Baluba.* Rev. cong., **4**, 1913–14, 113–16.

3310. —— *Le métallurgie au lac Léopold II et dans la Lukenie.* Rev. quest. sci., avr. 1920.

3311. —— *Le tissage chez les populations du lac Léopold II.* Anthropos, **25**, 3/4, 1930, 393–408, 12 Abb.

3312. —— La métallurgie chez les populations du lac Léopold II. Ethnologica, 4, 1930, 68–101, ill.

3313. —— 1936. Vannerie au lac Léopold II (Artes Africanae). Pp. 33, ill. Bruxelles: Commission pour la protection des arts et métiers indigènes.

3314. —— 1937. Poterie au lac Léopold II (Artes Africanae). Pp. 24, ill. Bruxelles: Commission pour la protection des arts et métiers indigènes.

3315. **Mahieu, A.** L'Exploitation du cuivre par les indigènes au Katanga. Congo, 2, 1, 1925, 107–29.

3316. **Manker, E.** Das Hakenkreuz in der majombe-basundischen Flechtswerkornamentik. Z. f. Ethnol., 63, 315–21.

3317. **Maquet, M.** La poterie marbrée au Bas-Congo. Quelques centres de fabrication. Arts et métiers indig., 7, 1938, 6–9.

3318. —— Note sur la vannerie au Bas-Fleuve et au Mayumbe. Brousse, 4, 1939, 16.

3319. **Maquet-Tombu, J.** La vannerie dans la région de Tumba. Arts et métiers indig., 4, 1938, 6–7.

3320. **Masui, Lieut.** Une forge à l'équateur. Congo illus., 1, no. 21, 1892, s.p., ill.

3321. **Moorsel, H. van.** Une industrie céramique ancienne dans la pleine de Léopoldville. Brousse, 3–4, 1948, 17–35, ill.

3322. **Nauwelaert, P.,** and **M. Maquet.** Les poteries Kakongo. Brousse, 2, 1939, 22–23.

3323. **Nenquin, Jacques.** Dimple-based pots from Kasai, Belgian Congo. Man, 59, 242, Sept. 1959, 153–4.

3324. —— Un importante contribution du Musée à la connaissance des cultures protohistoriques du Congo. Congo-Tervueren, 5, 1, 1959, 1–5, ill.

3325. —— Protohistorische metaaltechniek in Katanga. Africa-Tervueren, 7 (4), 1961, 97–101, ill.

3326. —— Notes on some early pottery cultures in Northern Katanga. J. Afr. hist., 4, 1, 1963, 19–32, ill.

3327. **Nsiesie, T.** La poterie dans la région de Mbanza-Nsundi (nord). Arts et métiers indig., 7, 1938, 12–13.

3328. **Plessers, K.** Op het matje. Nieuw Afr., 67, 2, 1951, 89–93, ill.

3329. **Vanden Bossche, Jean.** La poterie chez les Ba-Teke de Kingabwa. Brousse, N.S. 4, 1953, 11–16, ill.

3330. **van Hoeck, J.** Notes sur l'industrie de la poterie 'Mongo'. Brousse, 4, 1939, 15.

3331. **van Moorsel, H.** Une industrie céramique ancienne dans la plaine de Léopoldville. Brousse, 3/4, 1948, 17–39, ill., map.

3332. **Wannyn, Robert L.** 1961. L'art ancien du metal au Bas-Congo. (Les vieilles civilisations Ouest-Africaines.) Pp. 96, bibl., ill., map. Wavre (Belgium); Editions du Vieux Planquesaule.

3333. **Wauters, A. J.** La Vannérie. Congo illus., 3, no. 9, 1893, 66–70, ill.

UTENSILS, TOOLS AND WEAPONS; MISCELLANEOUS

3334. **Biebuyck, D.** La monnaie musanga des Balega. Zaïre, 7, 1953, 675–86, ill.

3335. **Kochnitzky, Léon.** Un sculpteur d'amulettes au Kwango. Brousse (Léopoldville), N.S. 3, 1953, 9–13, ill.

3336. **Wauters, A. J.** Le tabac et les pipes. Congo illus., 1, no. 16, 1892, s.p., ill.

AFRICAN ART TODAY

3337. **Africa.** École d'Art indigène de Katako-Kombi (Lusambo, B.C.). (Note in Africa, 19, 1949, 65.)

3338. **Arts Populaires.** 1930. Les arts populaires en Afrique; peintures indigènes congolaises. Geneva.

3339. **Art News.** Negro painting from the Belgian Congo at Carlebach gallery. Art news, 50, 1951, 48.

3340. —— Four Congo styles at Segy gallery. Art news, 52, 1953, 44.

3341. **Artes Africanae.** Publication de la commission pour la protection des arts et métiers indigènes. Brussels: Imprimerie Typ'art.

3342. **Belgium; Commission pour la protection des arts et métiers indigènes auprès du ministère des colonies de Belgique.** 1950. L'Art nègre du Congo Belge. Pp. 199, bibl., ill. Gand: Commission pour la Protection des Arts et Métiers Indigènes.

3343. **Bodart, Roger.** 1952. Dialogues africains (ornés par des artistes congolais de l'atelier d'Élisabethville). Pp. 120, ill. Bruxelles: Éd. des Artistes.

3344. **Bolamba, A. R.** Le peintre Albert Nkusu. Voix du congolais, 8, 1952.

3345. **Charlier, H.** Art et mission. Bull. miss., 13, 1937, 22. (Abbaye de Saint André.)

3346. **Charles.** L'Art indigène. Congo, 11, i, 1929, 5.

3347. **Cordemans, E. L.** La vie esthétique chez les Mbelo et les Okongo. Arts et métiers indig., 2, 1937, 3–7.

3348. **Dellepiane, G.** L'Art congolais au service du culte. Artisan liturgique, 10e ann., 43, 1936, 888–91.

3348a. **Desfossés, P. R.** Atelier de l'art indigène àt Elisabethville. See also Vanden Bossche, Louis. 1951. Peintures du Katanga. Pp. 6, ill. Bruges: Abbaye de Saint-André-lez-Bruges.

3349. **Gillès de Pélichy, Alexandre.** L'Église et la protection des arts indigènes au Congo Belge. Bull. miss., 15, 1936, 168.

3350. —— Vers une culture africaine chrétienne. Bull. miss., 24 (1), 1950, 60–67.

3351. **Hulstaert, G.** Note sur l'enseignement des arts et métiers indigènes dans les écoles du Vicariat Apostolique de Coquilhatville. Brousse, 3/4, 1947, 11–16.

3352. **Italiaander, Rolf.** 1959. Kongo; Bilder und Verse. Pp. 22, ill. Gütersloh: C. Bertelsmann Verlag.

3353. **Jadot, J. M.** Les tendances actuelles des arts plastiques indigènes au Congo Belge. Probl. Afr. centr., 44, 1959, 110–31, ill.

3354. **Life.** New native art; painters present gay views of Congo. Life, 34, 1953, 106–7, ill. (col.).

3355. **Maquet-Tombu, J.** 1935. La protection des arts plastiques indigènes par l'enseignement. Pp. 15. Éd. Léopoldville.

3356. —— Le sculpteur Mayele. Interview de Madame Daco. Brousse, 4, 1939, 25–28.

3357. —— Nos artistes congolais; Madya, graveur de calebasses. Brousse, 2, 1939, 27–29, ill.

3358. **Maquet-Tombu, Mme.** La protection des arts et métiers indigènes du Congo Belge. Vét. col., 19, 8, août 1947, 3–12, ill.

3359. **Mortier, F.** Enquête relative à la recherche et à l'étude de dessins de jeunes primitifs du Congo Belge. Vét. col., 19, 1947, 3–9, bibl., ill.

3360. **Périer, Gaston Denys.** Le blanc et le noir, curiosités congolaises. N.D. Pp. 45. Anvers: Éditions de l'essor Colonial.

3361. —— Le surréalisme de l'art Congolais. Grand artistique, 2, 1926, 30–36.

3362. —— 1936. L'Art vivant des noirs du Congo Belge (Artes Africanae). Pp. 13, ill. Bruxelles: Commission pour la protection des arts et métiers indigènes.

3363. —— Le dessin et la peinture nègre. Congo-Nile, 1937.

3364. —— Regards sur l'art graphique indigène au Congo Belge. Vét. col., 19, 7, 1947, 3–13.

3365. —— L'Art moderne chez les noirs. Rev. col. Belge, 1947, 646–8, ill.

3366. —— Rapport du Secrétaire de la Commission pour la protection des arts et métiers indigènes sur son voyage à Élisabethville. Zaïre, 4, 10, déc. 1950, 1093–1105.

3367. —— and **J. M. Jadot.** 1939. Native arts and craftsmanship in Belgian Congo. Pp. 32, ill. Brussels: .

3368. **Pittard, E.** Les arts populaires en Afrique. Peintures indigènes congolaises. Arch. suisses anthrop. générale, 5 (2), 1928–9.

3369. **Reynaert, L.** Les arts dans la région de Bolobo. Arts et métiers indig., 3, 1937, 4–7.

3371. **Rousseau, Madeleine,** and **Olivier le Corneur.** Quels sont les styles de l'art nègre? Musée vivant, 12, 36–37, nov. 1948, 23–29.

3372. **Scohy, André.** *Les nouveaux centres d'art indigène du Bas-Congo.* Rev. nat., **20**, 1948.

3373. —— *Les peintres Congolais du Stanley-Pool.* Vét. col., **20** (4), 1948, 5.

3374. —— *L'École Saint-Luc de Léopoldville et le destin des arts congolais.* Congopresse (Léopoldville), **70**, août 1950, 1392–3.

3375. **Stevens, G. A.** *The aesthetic education of the Negro.* Oversea education, **1**, 3, 1929–30, 88–94.

3375a. —— *The future of African art.* Africa, **3**, 2, 1930, 150–60.

3375b. —— *African art—the next phase.* Oversea education, **10**, 1939, 171–6.

3376. —— *Teaching and examining in art.* Oversea education, **13**, 1, Oct. 1941, 227–30.

3377. **Storms, D. A.** *Contemporary Christian art in the Belgian Congo.* Pp. 64–73.

3378. **Valroff, Nicolas.** *Art et artisanat indigènes.* Jalons, **14**, oct. 1942, 45–49.

3379. **Vanden Bossche, Adr.** *Le premier atelier congolais de céramique au Congo Belge.* Brousse, 3/4, 1949, 7–10, ill.

3380. **Vanden Bossche, Jean.** 1955. *Madya; Graveur de calebasses.* Pp. 47 + 10 pl. Bruxelles: A.R.S.C., Classe sci. mor. et pol., Mém. in-8°, N.S. 6.

3381. **van den Bossche, Louis.** *Possibilités chrétiennes de l'Art nègre.* Bull. Miss., **14**, 1935, 153. (Abbaye de Saint-André.)

3382. —— 1950. *Peintures du Katanga (avec commentaires).* Pp. 6 + 12 pl. Bull. Miss. Abbaye de Saint-André-lez-Bruges (Belgique).

3383. **Vanden Bossche, Jean.** *Pierre Romain Desfossés et son Académie d'Art Populaire.* Brousse, N.S. 6, 1955, 17–25, ill.

3384. **van Herrewege, P. R.** *Desfossés l'homme, son oeuvre et sa pensée.* Brousse, 1952 (2), 12.

3385. **Vidi, K.** *L'École d'art indigène de Katako-Kombe.* Brousse, 1948, 15–17.

3386. **Waldecker, Burkhart.** *Introduction à l'art décoratif congolais.* Congo illus., juil., août, oct. 1947, 13–51; 3–6; 8–14, ill.

ANGOLA

3387. **Almeida, A. de.** *Tipos de vestuário e adornos de Alguns Povos Bantos de Angola.* Garcia de Orta, **3**, 2, 1955, 213–16, ill. (Fotografias da Missão Antropobiológica de Angola.)

3388. **Barns, T. Alexander.** *Angolan sketches.* Pp. xi + 206, ill., maps. London: Methuen.

3389. **Bastin, Marie-Louise.** *Art décoratif tchokwe.* Comp. Diamantes Angola (Lisbon), **55**, 1961, 11–267.

3390. **Baumann, Hermann.** 1935. *Lunda; bei Bauern und Jägern in Inner-Angola.* Pp. 299, ill. Berlin: Würfel-Verlag.

3391. —— *Angola.* Encyclopaedia of world art, vol. **1**, 1959, 463–6, bibl., map.

3392. **Bruel, C.** *Les Mbaka Mombé.* L'Ethnographie, 1934, 63–72.

3393. **Cabrita, Carlos L. Antunes.** 1954. *Em terras de Luenas.* Pp. 195, ill. Lisbon: Agencia Geral do Ultramar.

3394. **Capello, H.,** and **R. Ivens.** 1882. *From Benguella to the territory of Yacca . . . in 1877–1880.* 2 vols. Vol. 1, pp. lii + 395, ill., maps. Vol. 2, pp. xv + 350, ill. London: Sampson Low.

3395. **Cardoso, Carlos Lopes.** *A arte mbali do distrito de Moçâmedes.* Colóquio (Lisboa), **25**, Oct. 1963, 20–24.

3396. **Castro Júnior, Augusto C. S.** *Aspectos da arte negra nos Luchazes.* Bol. inst. Angola (Luanda), **11**, July–Dec. 1958, 149–74, ill.

3397. **Correia, P. J.** *Une étude de l'ethnographie d'Angola.* Anthropos, **20**, 1925, 325–31.

3398. **da Silva, Afonso Dias.** *Algo açerca dos povos dos Luchazes.* Mensário admin., 24/25, 1949, 35–42.

3399. **de Cerqueira, Ivo.** 1947. *Vida social indigena na colónia de Angola (Usos e costumes).* Pp. 96, ill. Lisbon: Agência Geral das Cólonias.

3400. **Delachaux, Théodore,** and **Ch. E. Thiebaud.** 1936. *Land und Völker von Angola.* Pp. 143, ill., map. Neuchâtel: Verlagsanstalt Viktor Attinger.

3401. **Dos Santos, Eduardo.** 1962. *Sobre a religião dos Quiocos.* Pp. 160, bibl., ill., map. Lisbon: Junta de Investigações do Ultramar.

3402. **Estermann, Carlos.** *Etnografia e linguística.* Portugal em Afr., **5**, 1948, 219–25.

3403. —— *A investigação etnográfica em Angola.* Portugal em Afr., **15**, no. 89, 1958, 261–72.

3404. —— 1956–61. *Etnografia do Sudoeste de Angola.* (1) Os Povos Não-Bantos e O grupo étnico dos Ambós. (2) Grupo étnico Nhaneca-Humbe. Pp. 266, 299, bibl., ill., maps. (Junta de Investigações do Ultramar: Memórias Série Antropólogica e Etnológica, 4–5.)

3405. —— 1961. *O grupo étnico Herero.* Pp. 251, ill., bibl. Lisbon: Memórias da Junta de Investigações do Ultramar, no. 30 (2nd series). Etnografia do Sudoeste de Angola, vol. 3.

3406. **Freyberg, H.** *Urwald Kunst in Angola.* Weltkunst, Berlin s.D.

3407. **Gersdorff, Ralph von.** 1960. *Angola, Portugiesisch-Guinea, São Tomé und Príncipe, Kap-Verde-Inseln, Spanische-Guinea.* Pp. 165, map. Bonn: Kurt Schroeder.

3408. **Hambly, Wilfrid D.** 1934. *The Ovimbundu of Angola.* Pp. 87–362, bibl., ill., map. Chicago: Field Museum of Natural History. (Field Museum of Natural History: Anthropological Publications, 21 (2).)

3409. **Homburger, Lilias.** *Angola et Rhodesia, mission Rohan-Chabot.* Paris, 1925.

3410. **Jaspert, Fritz** and **Willem.** 1930. *Die Völkerstämme Mittel-Angolas.* Pp. xv + 155, bibl., ill., maps. Frankfurt am Main: Joseph Baer. (Veröffentlichungen aus dem Städtischen Völker-Museum, Frankfurt am Main, V.)

3411. **Lux, A. E.** 1880. *Von Loanda nach Kimbundu.* Pp. viii + 219, ill., maps. Vienna: Eduard Holzel.

3412. **McCulloch, Merran.** 1952. *The Ovimbundu of Angola.* Pp. 50, bibl., map. London: Int. Afr. Inst. (Ethnographic Survey of Africa: West Central Africa, part 2.)

3413. **Maesen, A. A. M.** *Les Holo du Kwango.* Reflets du monde, no. 9, 1956, 31–44, ill., map.

3414. —— *Art of the Holo of Kwango.* (Art in its context series: Studies in Ethno-Aesthetics.)

3415. **Marques, Alberto Ferreira.** *Contribuição para o estudo da etnográfia dos povos da Lunda.* Mensário admin., 26/27, 1949, 77–85; 28, 1949, 13–20.

3416. **Martins, João Vicente.** 1951. *Subsidios etnográficos para a historia dos Povos de Angola.* Pp. 200, ill. Lisbon: Agencia Geral do Ultramar.

3417. **Martins, Joaquim.** *O simbolismo entre os pretos do distrito de Cabinda.* Bol. inst. Angola, **15**, Jan.–Dec. 1961. (Repr., pp. 25, ill.)

3418. **Milheiros, Mário.** *Registo etnográfico e social sobre a tribo dos Maiacas.* Mensário admin., 67/68, 1953, 5–127, ill., maps.

3419. **Monteiro, J. J.** 1875. *Angola and the River Congo.* 2 vols. Vol. 1, pp. viii + 305, ill., map. Vol. 2, pp. iv + 340, ill. London: Macmillan.

3420. **Pechuël-Loesche, E.** 1907. *Volkskunde von Loango.* Pp. (6) + 482, ill., map. Stuttgart: Strecker u. Schroeder Verlag.

3421. **Pires, Antonio Emilio.** *'Ofundula'; festa cuanhama da puberdade feminina.* Mensário admin., 20/21, 1949, 45–52, ill.

3422. **Proyart, P.** 1819. *Histoire de Loanga, Kakongo et autres royaumes d'Afrique.* Pp. 295. Paris: Méquignon.

3423. **Redinha, José.** 1953. *Paredes Pintadas da Lunda.* Pp. 16 + 55 col. pl., ill., map. Lisbon: Companhia de Diamantes de Angola. (Museu do Dundo: Subsídios para a História, Arqueologia e Etnográfia dos Povos da Lunda.)

3424. —— 1953–5. *Campanha etnográfica ao Tchiboco (Alto-Tchicapa).* 2 vols. Vol. 1, pp. 171, ill., map. (Notas de Viagem.) Vol. 2, pp. 211, ill., maps. (Anotações e Documentação Grafica.) Lisbon: Museu do Dundo.

3425. —— *Alguns elementos de arte indígena.* Bol. cultural mus. Angola, **1**, 1960, 61–66, ill.

3426. **Sarmento, Alexandre.** 1945. *O negro de Menongue (notas antropológicas e etnográficas).* Pp. 88, ill. Lisbon: Divisão de Publicações e Biblioteca, Agência Geral das Colonias. (Art, p. 45.)

3427. **Schachtzabel, Alfred.** 1923. *Im Hochland von Angola.* Pp. 192, ill., maps. Dresden: Deutsche Buchwerkstätten.

3428. —— 1926. *Angola.* Pp. 224, ill., map. Berlin: Die Buchgemeinde.

3429. **Verly, R.** *Le 'roi divin' chez les Ovimbundu et Kimbundu de l'Angola.* Zaïre, **9** (7), 1955, 675–703, ill.

FIGURES AND MASKS

3430. **Bastian, Adolf.** 1874–5. *Die deutsche Expedition an der Loango-Küste.* 2 vols. Vol. 1, pp. xx + 374, ill., map. Vol. 2, pp. xv + 353, ill. Jena: Hermann Costenoble.

3431. **Bastin, M. L.** *Un masque en cuivre martelé des Kongo du nord-est de l'Angola.* Africa-Tervueren, **7**, 2, 1961, 29–40, ill., map.

3432. **Baumann, Hermann.** *Die Mannbarkeitsfeiern bei den Tsokwe und ihren nachbarn.* Baessler-Archiv, **15** (1), 1932, 1–54, ill.

3433. —— *Die Frage der Steinbauten und Steingräber in Angola.* Paiduma, **6**, 1956, 118–51, ill., map.

3434. **Delachaux, Th.** *Méthodes et instruments de divination en Angola.* Acta tropica, **3** (1 and 2), 1946, 41–72, 138–49, ill.

3435. **de Sousberghe, L.** *Noms donnés aux Pygmées et souvenirs laissés par eux chez les Pende et Lunda de la Loango.* Congo-Tervueren, **6**, 3, 1960, 84–86, ill.

3436. **Dyboski, Jean.** 1893. *La route du Tchad. Du Loango au Chari.* Pp. 381, ill., maps. Paris: Firmin-Didot.

3437. **Goncalves de Melo, António A.** *Arte indígena Angolana; esculturas dos 'Quiocos' do Minnungo.* Mensário admin., 69/70, 1953, 45–48, ill.

3438. **Joest, Wilhelm.** *Eine Holzfigur von der Loango-Küste und ein Anito-Bild aus Luzon.* Bastian, Adolf (Festschrift) zu seinem 70 Geburtstage, 1896, 117–27, ill.

3439. **Lima, Mesquitela.** 1964. *Exposição etnográfica de instrumentos musicais e máscaras dos povos de Angola.* Pp. 34, ill. Luanda: Instituto de Investigação científica de Angola e Museu de Angola.

3440. **Monard, A.** *Notes sur les collections ethnographiques de la mission scientifique Suisse en Angola, 1928–1929.* Bull. soc. Neuchâteloise. géog., **39**, 1930, 100–22, ill.

3441. **Redinha, José.** *Cabacas Gravadas.* Mensário admin., no. 7, 1948, 23–24, ill.

3442. —— 1956. *Máscaras de Madeira da Lunda e Alto Zambeze.* Pp. 37 + 28 col. pl. + 69 pp. Lisbon: Companhia de Diamantes de Angola.

BUILDINGS AND FURNITURE

3443. **Burkitt, M. C.** *House paintings in Angola.* (Subsidios para a historia, arqueologia e etnográphia dos povos da Lunda, by J. Redinha.) Nature, **173**, 1954, 229.

CLOTHING AND ADORNMENT

3444. **de Almeida, António.** *Tipos de vestuário e adornos de alguns povos Bantos de Angola; Fotografias da Missão antropobiológica de Angola* (1950). Garcia de Orta (Lisboa), **3**, 2, 1955, 213 + 10 pl.

3445. **Estermann, Carlos.** 1960. *Álbum de Penteados de Sudoeste de Angola.* Pp. 37, ill. Lisbon: Junta de Investigações do Ultramar.

3446. **Lampreia, José D.** *Iconografia étnica do ultramar português* (*Angola*). Garcia de Orta, **7**, 3, 1959, 583–4 + 12 pl.

3447. **Lima, Mesquitela.** 1956. *Tatuagens da Lunda.* Pp. 70 + 44, ill., map. Luanda: Museu de Angola.

3448. **Martins de Meireles, Artur.** 1960. *Mutilações étnicas dos Manjacos.* Pp. 172, bibl., map. Bissau: Centro de Estudos da Guiné Portuguesa, no. 22.

3449. **Redinha, J.** *Costumes religiosos e feiticistas dos Kiokos de Angola.* Bol. soc. geog. (Lisbon), **67** (ser. 3–4), 1949, 131–68, ill.

3450. **Sarmento, Alexandre.** *Mutilaçoes étnicas nos indigenas de Angola.* Mensário admin. (Angola), **1**, 1947, 21–26, ill.

ROCK ART

3451. **Baumann, Hermann.** *Vorläufiger Bericht über neue Felsbilder-Funde in Sud-Angola.* Paideuma, **6**, 1, Nov. 1954, 41–45, ill.

3452. **Breuil, Henri,** and **J. Janmart.** 1950. *Les limons et graviers de l'Angola du nord-est et leur contenu archéologique.* Pp. 58, ill., map. Lisbon: Companhia de Diamantes de Angola: Publicações Culturais, no. 3.

3453. —— and **António de Almeida.** *Sur les gravures et les peintures rupestres du désert de Mozamedes (Angola).* Actes 4e Congrès Pan-africain de Préhistoire . . . (ed. G. Mortelmans and J. Nenquin), sect. 3, 1962, 451–6, ill.

3454. **Camarate França, J.** *As gravuras rupestres do Tchitundo-Hulo (deserto de Moçâmedes).* Mensário admin. (Angola), 65/66, Jan.-Fev. 1953, 5–44, ill., map.

3455. **dos Santos Júnior, Joaquim N.,** and **L. dos Santos.** *Nota sôbre o 'muzimo' do abrigo com pinturas rupestres da Mavinga.* 13 congr. Luso-Espanhol para o progresso das Ciências, Lisboa, 1950, 4ª sec., vol. 5, 1950, 589–602, ill.

3456. **Redinha, J.** *Wall paintings among the Kioko (Chokwe) of Lunda.* Mensário admin. (Luanda), 6, 1948, 19–22, ill.

3457. —— *As gravuras rupestres de Alto-Zambeze e primeira tentativa da sua interpretação.* Publ. cult. comp. diamantes, Angola (Lisbon), **2**, 1948, 65–92.

TECHNIQUES

3458. **Almeida, M.a E. de Castro e.** *Contribuição para o estudo dos teares na Lunda (Angola).* Garcia de Orta, **9**, 4, 1961, 669–76, bibl., ill.

3459. **Fontinha, Mário,** and **Acácio Videira.** *Cabaças gravadas da Lunda.* Publ. cult. comp. diamantes, Angola, **57**, 1963, 12–94, ill. (In Portuguese, French and English.)

3460. **Hauenstein, A.** *La poterie chez les Ovimbundu (Angola).* Acta tropica, **21**, 1, 1964, 48–81, bibl., ill.

3461. **Leakey, M. D.** and **L. S. B.** 1949. *Some string figures from North-East Angola.* Pp. 24, ill. Lisbon: Museu do Dundo (Publ. Cult. separata).

3462. **Read, Frank W.** *Iron-smelting and native black-smithing in Ondulu country, South-East Angola.* J.R.A.S., **2**, 5, Oct. 1902, 44–49.

3463. **Redinha, J.** *Cerâmica indígena.* Mensário admin. (Angola), 5, Jan. 1948, 19–22, ill.

3464. **Wainwright, G. A.** *The Jaga and their name for iron.* Man, **55**, 62, Apr. 1955, 52–57, map.

SPANISH GUINEA

3465. **Bonelli, Y. R.** and **Juan D.** 1944–5. *Notas sobre la geografía humana de los territorios españoles del Golfo de Guinea.* Pp. 43, ill. Madrid: Dirección General de Marruesos y Colonias.

3466. **Buaki, José.** *Unidad del arte negro.* Guinea espãn., **56**, no. 1534, 1960, 203–5.

3467. —— *Tendencias del arte negro.* Guinea espãn., **56**, no. 1536, 1960, 265–7.

3468. —— *El arte negro. Formación de los centros de estilo.* Guinea espãn., **56**, 1537, 1960, 302–5.

3469. —— *Arte de los Bakota y de los Batéké.* Guinea espãn., **57**, 1540, Jan. 1961, 11–13.

3470. **Crespo Gil-Delgado, Carlos.** 1949. *Notas para un estudio antropologico y etnologico del Bubi de Fernando Poo.* Pp. xi + 290, bibl., ill. Madrid: Institutos de Estudios Africanos y Bernardino de Sahagun de Antropologia y Etnologia.

3471. **de Unzueta y Yuste, Abelardo.** 1944. *Guinea continental española.* Pp. 394, bibl., ill., maps. Madrid: Instituto de Estudios Politicos. (Pp. 337–40, Manifestaciones artisticas.)

3472. **Great Britain: Admiralty: Naval Staff Intelligence Reports.** N.D. 1919. *Spanish Guinea.* Pp. 39. Spanish possessions in the Gulf of Guinea: Fernando Po, pp. 4–16. Muni River Settlement (Fang), pp. 17–36. Annobon Island, pp. 37–39.

3473. **Ibarrola Monasterio, Ricardo.** *El arte de los pueblos pamues.* Archivos del instituto de estudios Africanos, **10** (41), 1957, 51–60.

3474. **Perramón, Ramón.** *Hallazgos prehistoricos en la region del Muni.* Guinea españ., **60**, 1573, Oct. 1963, 259–64, ill.

3475. —— *Manifestaciones artisticas entre los Fang.* Guinea españ., **61**, 1581, June 1964, 180–4, ill.

3476. —— *Notas sobre el arte fang; principales centros estilísticos.* Guinea españ., **61**, 1586, Dec. 1964, 336–9, ill.

3477. **Ramón Álvarez, Heriberto.** *Artes y oficios artísticos indigenas en Guinea.* Africa (Madrid), **12**, 157, Enero 1955, 12–14, ill.

FIGURES AND MASKS

3478. **Panyella, Augusto.** 1959. *Esquema de etnología de los Fang Ntumu de la Guinea española.* Pp. 77 + (14), bibl., ill., map. Madrid: Instituto de Estudios Africanos.

CLOTHING AND ADORNMENT

3479. **de Larrea y Palacín, Arcadio.** 1953. *Peinados bujebas; Iniciación al estudio del tacado de los pueblos de la Guinea española.* Pp. 50 (65 pl.). Madrid: Instituto de Estudios Africanos.

TECHNIQUES

3480. **Gonzalez Echegaray, Carlos.** *Un yacimiento de cerámica en el norte de Fernando Poo.* Africa (Madrid), **15**, 204, Dec. 1958, 14–16.

3481. **Ligero, Armando.** *Pequeña aclaración sobre terminologia bubi referente a cerámica.* Guinea españ., 1515, Mar. 1959, 69–70.

3482. **Martín del Molino, Amador.** *La cerámica del neolítico bubi.* Africa (Madrid), **13**, 169, En. 1956, 15–17, ill.

3483. —— *La cerámica antigua de Fernando Poo.* Guinea españ., **53**, 1957, 1481, 289–92; 1483, 321–4.

3484. —— *Tipología de la cerámica de Fernando Poo.* Guinea españ., **6**, 1538, Nov. 1960, 325–60, ill. (Reprint, pp. 36.)

3485. **Panyella, Augusto,** and **Jorge Sabater.** 1955. *Proceso técnico de la cerámica fang.* Pp. 95, ill., map. Madrid: Instituto de Estudios Africanos.

SÃO TOMÉ

3486. **Tenreiro, Françisco.** 1961. *A ilha de São Tomé.* Pp. 292, bibl. ill. Lisbon. (Memorias da Junta de Investigações do Ultramar, 24.)

EAST AFRICA

3487. **Ankermann, Bernhard.** *Vorlage von Negerzeichnungen aus Ostafrika und Kamerun (Landschaft Bondei).* Z. f. Ethnol., **45**, 1913, 632–6, ill.

3488. **Baumann, Oscar.** 1891. *Usambara und seine nachbargebiete.* Pp. xi + 375, map. Berlin: Reimer.

3489. —— 1894. *Durch Massailand zur Nilquelle.* Pp. xiii + 385, ill., maps. Berlin: Reimer.

3490. —— 1900. *Afrikanische Skizzen.* Pp. 119, ill. Berlin.

3491. **Beresford-Stooke, G.** *An Akamba fortune-telling ceremony (divination by throwing seeds).* Man, **28**, no. 137, 1928, 189.

3492. **Cole, Sonia.** 1954. *The prehistory of East Africa.* Pp. 301, ill., maps. London: Penguin Books. (Chapter on primitive artists.)

3493. **Desfossés, P. R.** *Over indo-nilotische sporen in de negerkunst van Oost-Afrika.* Band (Léopoldville), **9**, 12, 1950, 23–31.

3494. **Eichorn, August.** *Beiträge zur Kenntnis der Waschamba, I.* Baessler-Archiv, **I** (4/5), 1911, 155–222, ill.

3494a. —— *Beiträge zur Kenntnis der Waschamba, III.* Baessler-Archiv, N.F. 7, 1918–22, 60–80, ill.

3495. **Flatz, Josef.** 1936. *Die Kulturen Ostafrikas.* Pp. 216, bibl., map. Linz: Verlage des Verfassers.

3496. **Fox, Douglas C.** *British East Africa.* Encyclopaedia of world art, vol. 1, 1958, 47–50, map.

3497. **Gillman, C.** *An annotated list of ancient and modern indigenous stone structures in Eastern Africa.* Tanganyika notes and records, 1944, 44–55, maps.

3498. **Hobley, C. W.** 1910. *Ethnology of A-Kamba and other East African tribes.* Pp. xvi + 172, ill., map. Cambridge: Univ. Press.

3499. **Hollis, Sir A. C.** 1909. *The Nandi.* Pp. xl + 328, ill., map. Oxford: Clarendon Press.

3500. **Kollmann, Paul.** 1898. *Der Nordwesten unserer Ostafrikanischen Kolonie.* Pp. viii + 191, ill., map. Berlin: Alfred Schall.

3501. —— 1899. *The Victoria Nyanza.* Pp. ix + 254, ill., map. London: Swan Sonnenschein.

3502. **Kroll, Hubert.** *Plastische Menschendarstellungen von der Insel Ukerewe in Viktoria-See.* Ethnol. Anz., **3**, 3, 1933, 142–4, 1 Taf. m. 6 Abb.

3503. **Lindblom, Gerhard.** 1920. *The Akamba in British East Africa.* Pp. xii + 607, bibl., ill. Uppsala: Archives d'Etudes Orientales, 17. (2nd ed.)

3504. **Lutten, Eric.** *Les Wasamba et leur usage dans la circoncision.* Minotaure (Paris), **11**, 1933, 13–17, ill.

3505. **Merker, M.** 1904. *Die Masai.* Pp. xvi + 421, ill., map. Berlin: Reimer.

3506. **Meyer, Hans.** *The first ascent of Kilimanjaro.* Pp. xiii + 397, bibl., ill., maps. London: G. Philip.

3507. **Monneret de Villard, Ugo.** *Note sulle influenze asiatiche nell' Africa orientale.* Riv. studi. orient., **17**, 1938, 303–9, bibl.

3508. **Ntiro, Sam.** *East African art.* Tanganyika notes and records, **61**, 1963, 121–34, ill. (Reprinted from J. royal society of arts, May 1963, no. 5082, vol. CXI.)

3509. **Passarge, Siegfried.** *Ostafrika und Kamerun.* Meyer, Hans, Das deutsche Kolonialreich, 1909, 419–650, ill., maps.

3510. **Reche, Otto.** 1914. *Zur Ethnographie des abflusslosen Gebietes Deutsch-Ostafrikas.* Pp. xii + 130, ill., map. Hamburg: Friederichsen. (Abh. Hamburg. Kolonialinst., 17.)

3511. **Reckling, Walter.** *Handwerk und Kunst der Wazaramo.* Kol. Rund., **33**, 1942, 31–37.

3512. **Raum, J.** *Über angebliche Götzen am Kilimandscharo.* Globus, **85**, 1904, 101–5.

3513. **Schoeller, Max.** 1901–4. *Mitteilungen über meine Reise nach Äquatorial-Ost-Afrika und Uganda, 1896–1897.* 3 vols. Vol. 1, pp. viii + 237, ill. Vol. 2, pp. 329 (3) + 102 pl. + 33 pp. Vol. 3, maps. Berlin: Reimer.

3514. **Sharpe, A. A.** *Carved stool and other objects from British East Africa.* Man, **1**, 1901, 49.

3515. **Sheldon, M. French.** 1892. *Sultan to sultan; adventures among the Masai and other tribes of East Africa.* Pp. (8), 435, ill. Boston: Arena Pub.

3516. **Sheppard, T.** *A Mweso board from Mombasa.* Man, **31**, no. 243, 1931, 245, ill.

3517. **Stuhlmann, Franz.** 1894. *Mit Emin Pascha ins Herz von Afrika.* Pp. xxiv + 901, ill., maps. Berlin: Reimer.

3518. —— 1909. *Beiträge zur Kulturgeschichte von Ostafrika (Deutsch-Ostafrika).* Pp. xxiii + 907, maps. Berlin: Reimer.

3519. **Tate, H. R.** *Notes on the Kikuyu and Kamba tribes of British East Africa.* J. anthrop. inst., **34**, 1904, 130–48, 255–65, ill., map.

3520. **Vajda, L.** *Human and animal plastic figures from the Kilimanjaro region.* Néprajzi értesitö (Budapest), **37**, 1955, 181–90.

3521. **Velten, C. von.** 1903. *Sitten und Gebräuche der Suaheli.* Pp. xl + 423. Göttingen: Vandehoeck & Ruprecht.

3522. **von Luschan, F.** *Beiträge zur Ethnographie des abflusslosen Gebiets in Deutsch-Ostafrika.* ((1) Die Wassandaui.) Waldemar, Werther C., Die Mittleren Hochländer des nördlichen Deutsch-Ostafrika, part 5, 1898.

3523. **Weiss, Max.** 1910. *Die Völkerstämme im Norden Deutsch-Ostafrikas.* Pp. xx + 455, ill., maps. Berlin: Verlag von Carl Marschner.

3524. **Werth, E.** 1915. *Das Deutsch-Ostafrikanische Küstenland und die vorgelagerten Inseln.* 2 vols. Vol. 1, xvi + 334, ill. Vol. 2, vii + 265, ill., maps. Berlin: .

3525. **Weule, Karl.** 1908. *Wissenschaftliche Ergebnisse meiner ethno-graphischen Forschungsreise in den Südosten Deutsch-Ostafrikas.* Pp. x + 150, ill., maps. Berlin: Ernst Siegfried Mittler + Sohn.

3526. —— 1908. *Negerleben in Ostafrika; Ergebnisse einer Ethno-logischen Forschungsreise.* Pp. 524, ill., map. Leipzig: Brockhaus.

3527. —— 1909. *Native life in East Africa.* Pp. xxiv + 431, ill., map. London: Pitman.

3528. —— *Ostafrikanische Eingeborenen-Zeichnungen.* Ipek: Jb. f. Prähist. u. ethnogr. Kunst (Leipzig), **1**, 1926, 87–127, ill.

3529. **Widenmann, A.** *Die Kilimandscharo-Bevölkerung; Anthropo-logisches und Ethnographisches aus dem Dschaggalande.* Petermanns Mitteilungen: Ergänzungsheft, no. 129, 1899, ix + 104, ill.

FIGURES AND MASKS

3530. **Chubb, E. C.** *East African masks and an Ovambo sheathed knife.* Man, **24**, no. 110, 1924, 145–6, ill.

3531. **Routledge, W. S.** and **K.** *An Akikuyu image.* Man, **6**, 1, 1906, 1–3, ill. (Brief description of anthropomorphic clay image.)

BUILDINGS AND FURNITURE

3532. **Bisgaard, Agnete.** *House-types of the Banyakyusa.* Folk, **4**, 1962, 47–63, ill.

3533. **Fry, E. M.** *East Africa (architecture).* Arch. rev., **128**, 1960, 21–30, ill., map.
See also 3497.

CLOTHING AND ADORNMENT

3534. **Driberg, J. H.** *Note on hairdressing among the Lango.* Man, **19**, no. 38, 1919, 73–75.

3535. **Elliott, H. F. I.** *The coiffeur of the Masai warrior.* Tanganyika notes and records, **26**, Dec. 1948, 80–82, ill.

3536. **Kakoza, J.** 1949. *Abakomazi (bark-cloth making).* Kampala: East African Literature Bureau.

3537. **M. Anna, Sister.** *Bark-cloth making among the Baganda of East Africa.* Primitive man, **9**, 1, 1936, 12–14.

ROCK ART

3538. **Adamson, Joy.** *Rock engravings near Lake Rudolf.* J.E. Afr. nat. hist. soc., **19**, 1/2 (85/86), June 1946, 70–71.

3539. **Fischer, H.** *Eine gräko-ägyptische Figur in Ostafrika.* 50. Jahresber. Württ. Ver. f. Handelsgeog., 145–50.

3540. **Kohl-Larsen, Ludwig** and **Margit.** 1938. *Felsmalereien in Innerafrika.* Pp. 93, ill., maps. Stuttgart: Strecker u. Schröder. (Deutsche-Afrika-Expedition, 1934–6.)

3541. —— —— 1960. *Die Bilderstrasse Ostafrikas. Felsbilder in Tangan-yika.* Pp. 142, ill., maps. Eisenach: E. Röth. (2nd ed.)

3542. **Meyer, Hans.** 1909–10. *Das Deutsche Kolonialreich.* 2 vols. Vol. 1, Ostafrika u. Kamerun; pp. xii + 600, bibl., ill., maps. Vol. 2, Togo, Südwestafrika, etc., pp. xiii + 575, bibl., ill., maps. Leipzig and Vienna: Bibliographisches Institut.

3543. —— 1916. *Die Barundi.* Pp. xiv + 205, ill., map. Leipzig: Otto Spamer. (Kön. Sächs Forschungsinstitut in Leipzig: Institut für Völkerkunde.)

TECHNIQUES

3544. **Glover, J.,** and **Goldstucker.** September 1944. *Small scale pottery manufacture.* Pp. 15. Nairobi, Kenya: East African Standard, Ltd. (Technical pamphlet no. 10.)

3545. **Holý, Ladislav.** *Získávání a zpracovávání zeleza u vychodo-africkych Bantu* (Iron extraction and working among the East African Bantu). Československa ethnografie (Praha), 5 6, 1957–8, 273–395. (Summary in German.)

3546. **Posnansky, Merrick.** *Pottery types from archaeological sites in East Africa.* J. Afr. hist., **2**, 2, 1961, 177–98, ill., map.

3547. **Smolla, Günter.** *Prähistorische Keramik aus Ostafrika.* Tribus, N.F. 6, 1956 (1957), 35–64, ill., map.

3548. **Stuhlmann, Franz.** 1910. *Handwerk und Industrie in Ostafrika. Kulturgeschichtliche Betrachtungen, nebst einem Anhang. Die Gewinnung des Eisens bei den Nyamwezi.* Pp. xiv + 163, ill., maps. Hamburg: Friederichsen. (Abh. Hamburg. Kolonial-inst., 1.)

3549. **Wainwright, G. A.** *The diffusion of -uma as a name for iron.* Uganda J., **18**, 2, Sept. 1954, 113–36, map.
See also 3536, 3537.

AFRICAN ART TODAY

3550. **Behn, Fritz.** 1924 (orig. publ. 1918). *'Haizuru'. Ein Bildhauer in Afrika.* Pp. 267. 100 figs. on pl., 16 text figs. München: Georg Müller. (Generally on the East African negro, pictures of Masai, Ndorobo and Shashi.)

3551. **Elkan, Walter.** *The East African trade in woodcarvings.* Africa, **28**, 1958, 314–23.

3552. **Earl, E. R.** *African enterprise (Kamba woodcarvers).* East African annual, 1958–9, 145–7, ill.

3553. **Ntiro, Sam.** *East African art.* Tanganyika notes and records, no. 61, 1963, 121–34, ill.

3554. **Trowell, Margaret.** *Suggestions for the treatment of handwork in training of Teachers for work in Africa (with some notes on Mrs. Trowell's proposals, by Dr. W. B. Mumford).* Oversea Education, **7**, 2, 1936, 79–86.

3555. —— *Modern African art in East Africa.* Man, **47**, 1, Jan. 1947, 1–7, ill.

3556. **Trowell, K. M.** 1951. *Art teaching in African schools.* Book 1. Design. Book 2. Materials. Pp. 44, 40 ill. London: Longmans.

BURUNDI

3557. **Bourgeois, R.** 1957. *Banyarwanda et Barundi.* Tome 1. Pp. 792, bibl., ill., maps. Brussels.

3558. **Zuure, Bernard.** *Barundi Kunst.* Nieuw Afrika, **53**, 1936–7, 412–15.

TECHNIQUES

3559. **Goffin, J.** *La vannerie en Urundi.* Servir, no. 3, 1940, 4–10: Rev. Brousse (Brussels), no. 3, 1940, 14–15.

3560. **Jean-Marie, Soeur** (Chrysostome, M. J.). *Fabrication de poteries en Urundi.* Trait d'union, **21**, 3/4, 1953, 5, ill.

3561. —— *De klei-industrie in Urundi.* Nieuw Afrika, **69**, 5, 1953, 214–18.

3562. **Smets, G.** *La trompe du bronze, Eschyle et les Barundi.* Acad. R. belge, bull. classe lettres et sci. mor., **35** (5), 1949, 141–58.

KENYA

3563. **Browne, G. St. J. Orde.** 1925. *The vanishing tribes of Kenya.* Pp. 284, ill., maps. London: Seeley Service.

3564. **French-Sheldon, M.** 1892. *Sultan to sultan.* Pp. (8) + 435, ill. London: Saxon & Co.

3565. **Leakey, M. D.** *Report on the excavations at Hyrax Hill, Nakuru, Kenya Colony, 1937–38.* Trans. R. soc. S. Afr., **30** (4), 1945, 271–409, ill.

3566. **Leakey, M. D.** and **L. S. B.** 1950. *Excavations at the Njoro river cave.* Pp. vi + 78, ill., map. Oxford: Clarendon Press.

3567. **Schneider, Harold K.** *The interpretation of Pakot visual art.* Man, **56**, 108, Aug. 1956, 103–6.

FIGURES AND MASKS

3568. **Adamson, Joy.** *Kaya und Grabfiguren der Küstenbantu in Kenya.* Paideuma, **6**, 1957, 251–6, ill.

3569. **Lindblom, K. G.** 1950. *Carved initiation sticks and bows from Taveta, Kenya Colony.* Pp. 30, ill. Stockholm: Statens Ethnog. Museum. (Smärre Meddelanden, 23.)

BUILDINGS AND FURNITURE

3570. **Massam, J. A.** 1927. *The cliff dwellers of Kenya.* Pp. (6), 268, ill., maps. London: Seeley Service.

CLOTHING AND ADORNMENT

3571. **Adamson, Joy.** *Headdresses (of Kenya witch-doctors and dancers).* East African annual, 1951–2, 54–55, ill.

3572. **Arkell-Hardwick, A.** 1903. *An ivory trader in North Kenya.* Pp. xvi + 368, ill., map. London: Longmans, Green.

3573. **Elliott, H. F. I.** *The coiffeur of the Masai warrior.* Tanganyika notes and records, **26**, 1948, 80–82, ill.

3574. **Orde Browneg, G. St. J.** *An African shell ornament known as 'Kibangwa'.* J. Afr. soc., **29**, 115, Apr. 1930, 285–9.

ROCK ART

3575. **Fosbrooke, H. A.,** and **Petro I. Marealle.** *The engraved rocks of Kilimanjaro.* Man, **52**, 244, Nov., 161–2, 263, Dec. 1952, 179–81, ill.

3576. **Wright, R.** *A painted rock shelter on Mt. Elgon, Kenya.* Proc. prehist. soc., N.S. 27, 1961, 28–34, ill.

TECHNIQUES

3577. **Galloway, A.** *A note on the iron smelting methods of the Elgeyo Masai.* S. Afr. J. sci., **31**, 1934, 500–4, ill.

3578. **Kirkman, James.** *Potters' masks from medieval Arab sites in Kenya.* S. Afr. archaeol. bull., **13**, 52, Dec. 1958, 156–9.

3579. **Leakey, M. D.,** and **Others.** *Dimple-based pottery from central Kavirondo, Kenya colony.* Pp. 43, ill., map. Nairobi: Coryndon Memorial Museum (Occ. Papers, 2).

3580. **Smith, Mrs. D. Gregory.** *Hand-spinning and weaving in Nyanza Province, Kenya.* East African annual, **10**, 2, Oct. 1944, 92.

AFRICAN ART TODAY

3581. **Tracey, Andrew.** *Kamba carvers.* Afr. music, **2**, 3, 1960, 55–58.

UGANDA

3582. **Ingrams, Harold.** 1960. *Uganda.* Pp. xvi + 365, bibl., ill., maps. London: H.M.S.O.

3583. **Lanning, E. C.** *The Munsa earthworks.* Uganda J., **19**, 1955, 177–82, map.

3584. —— *Archaeology in Uganda.* Corona, **8**, 1956, 298–301.

3585. **Lawrence, J. C. D.** 1957. *The Iteso.* Pp. xx + 280, bibl., ill., map. London: Oxford Univ. Press.

3586. **Meldon, J. A.** *Notes on the Bahima of Ankole (2).* J. Afr. soc., **6**, 1906–7, 235–9, ill.

3587. **Roscoe, John.** 1911. *The Baganda.* Pp. xix + 547, ill., map. London: Macmillan.

3588. —— 1923. *The Banyankole.* Pp. xii + 176, ill., map. Cambridge: Univ. Press.

3588a. **Shinnie, P. L.** *Excavations at Bigo, Uganda.* Plans, diagrams. Antiquity, **33**, 54, 1959, 7.

3589. **Stigler, Robert.** *Ethnographische und Anthropologische Mitteilungen über einige wenigbekannte Volksstämme Ugandas.* Mitt. anthrop. gesell. (Wien), **52/53**, 1923, 113–261, ill., map.

FIGURES AND MASKS

3590. **Poznansky, Merrick.** *A stone carving from Angolom, Uganda.* Man, **63**, 177, Sept. 1963, 148–9, ill.

3591. **Roscoe, John.** *Kibuka; the war god of the Baganda.* Man, **7**, 95, 1907, 161–6, ill.

BUILDINGS AND FURNITURE

3592. **Kmunke, Rudolf.** 1913. *Quer durch Uganda . . . in 1911–1912.* Pp. xiii + 186, ill., maps. Berlin: Reimer.

3593. **Sekenti, C. M.,** and **K. P. Wachsmann.** 1956. *Wall patterns in Hima huts.* Pp. 10, ill. Kampala: Uganda Museum (Occ. Pap. 1).

CLOTHING AND ADORNMENT

3594. **A., D. F. T.** *Bark cloth making in Buganda.* Uganda J., **1**, no. 1, 1934, 17–21.

3595. **Chanell, J. W.** *Bark cloth makers of Buganda.* Corona, **14**, 4, Apr. 1962, 153–4, ill.

3596. **Lanning, E. C.** *The bone bark-cloth hammers from Mubende, Uganda.* Man, **57**, no. 37, 1957, 40–41, ill.

3597. —— *Bark-cloth hammers.* Uganda J., **23**, 1, Mar. 1959, 79–83, ill.

3598. **Meldon, J. A.** *Notes on the Bahima of Ankole, (1) 'Wig'.* J. Afr. soc., **6**, 1906–7, 143, ill.

3599. **Ntiro, Sarah.** *The basuti (traditional Ganda dress).* Crane (issued by the Uganda Development Corporation, Kampala), 1961, 7–8, ill.

3600. **Simons, F. J.** *A rain cape common to South Asia and Africa.* Uganda J., **23**, 1, Mar. 1959, 84–85, ill.

3601. **Thompson, A. D. F.** *Bark-cloth making in Buganda.* Uganda J., **1**, 1, Jan. 1934, 17–21.

ROCK ART

3602. **Lawrence, J. C. D.** *Rock paintings in Teso.* Uganda J., **17** (1), 1953, 8–13, ill.

3603. —— *Notes on rock paintings in Teso.* Uganda J., **19** (1), 1955, 90, ill.

3604. —— *Rock paintings in Teso and Bukedi.* Uganda J., **22**, 1958, 39–42, ill.

3605. **Posnansky, M.** *Rock paintings on Lolui island, Lake Victoria.* Uganda J., **25**, 1, Mar. 1961, 105–11, ill., maps.

TECHNIQUES

3606. **Birch, J. P.** *Madi blacksmiths.* Uganda J., **5**, 1, July 1937, 48–49.

3607. **Lanning, E. C.** *Some vessels and beakers from Mubende Hill, Uganda.* Man, **53**, 283, Dec. 1953, 181–2, ill.

3608. —— *Genital symbols on the smiths' bellows in Uganda.* Man, **54**, 262, Nov. 1954, 167–9, ill.

3609. **O'Brien, T. P.,** and **S. Hastings.** *Pottery making among the Bakonjo.* Man, **33**, 202, 1933, 189–91, ill.

3610. **Posnansky, Merrick.** *Dimple-based pottery from Uganda.* Man, **61**, 168, Aug. 1961, 141–2, ill., map.
See also 3594–7, 3601.

UTENSILS, TOOLS AND WEAPONS; MISCELLANEOUS

3611. **Braunholtz, H. J.** *The game of Mweso in Uganda.* Man, **31**, no. 131, 1931, 121–2, ill.

3612. **Shackell, R. S.** *Mweso—the board game.* Uganda J., **2**, no. 1, 1934, 14–20, ill.

3613. **Wayland, E. J.** *Notes on the board game known as Mweso in Uganda.* Uganda J., **4** (1), 1936, 84–89, ill.

AFRICAN ART TODAY

3614. **Trowell, Margaret.** *Development of art and indigenous crafts in Uganda.* Uganda teachers' journal, **2**, 2, May 1940, 76–81.

3615. —— *Some royal craftsmen of Buganda.* Uganda J., **8**, 2, Jan. 1941, 47–64, ill.

3616. —— and **K. P. Wachsmann.** 1953. *Tribal crafts of Uganda.* Part 1, Domestic and cultural. Part 2, The sound instruments. Pp. 423, ill., map. London: Oxford Univ. Press.

3617. —— *African arts and crafts.* J. roy. soc. arts, **86**, 354–5.

3618. —— 1960. *African design.* Pp. 78, pl. 1–76, map. London: Faber & Faber.

3619. —— 1957. *African tapestry.* (The author describes her life and art teaching in Uganda.) Pp. 164, ill. London: Faber.

3620. —— 1937. *African arts and crafts, their development in the school.* Pp. 202. London: Longmans.

RWANDA

3621. **de Cleene, N.** 1957. *Introduction à l'ethnographie du Congo Belge et du Rwanda-Burundi.* Pp. viii + 159, bibl., ill., map. Anvers: Editions de Sikkel.

3622. **Jadot, J. M.** *Popular arts in the Belgian Congo and in Ruanda-Urundi.* Unesco occasional papers in education (Paris), **8**, 1950, 7–13.

3623. **Kagame, Alexis.** 1956. *La Philosophie bantu-rwandaise de l'être.* Pp. 448. Brussels: A.R.S.C., 12.

3624. **Kandt, G.** *Gewerbe in Ruanda.* Z. f. Ethnol., **36**, 1904, 42–55, 62–75.

3625. **Maquet, Jacques J.** 1957. *Ruanda.* Pp. ix + 192, ill., maps. Brussels: Elsevier.

3626. **Pauwels, Marcel Le R. P.** *Les couleurs et les dessins au Ruanda.* Anthropos, **47**, 3/4, 1952, 474–82, ill.

3627. —— *La magie au Ruanda.* Ann. Lat., **17**, 1953, 83–155, ill.

3628. —— *Les métiers et les objets en usage au Rwanda.* (1) Les objets en argile, 195–9, ill. (2) Les Calebasses, 199–209, ill. (3) Travail du Bois, 209–16, ill. (5) La Vannerie, 227–35, ill. (6) La Corderie, 235–40, ill. (7) Les couleurs et les dessins, 240–51, ill. (8) Des objets garnis de perles de verroterie et de porcelaine ou de cauris, 251–4, ill. (9) Le travail du Fer, 254–67, ill. (11) Des cornes et des Os, 272–5, ill. (13) Les objets faits de peaux, 280–4, ill. Ann. Lat., **19**, 1955, 195–284, ill.

3629. —— *Le symbolisme du tabouret Munya-rwanda.* Kongo-Overzee (Antwerpen), **21**, 2, 1955, 144–56, ill.

3630. **Sasserath, Jules Simon.** 1948. *Le Ruanda-Urundi.* Pp. 77 (2), ill., map. Brussels: Editions Germinal.

3631. **Wannijn, R. L.** *Insignes religieux anciens au Bas-Congo.* Les arts au Congo Belge et au Ruanda-Urundi, 1950, 40–54. Brussels.

CLOTHING AND ADORNMENT

3632. **Leemans, J.** *Haartooi en modegrillen in midden-Afrika.* Nieuw Afrika, **54**, 11, 1937–8, 489–91. (Arrangement des cheveux chez les Tutsi.)

3633. **Schumacher, P.** *Die Tracht in Ruanda (Deutsch-Ostafrika).* Anthropos, **10/11**, 5/6, Sept.–Dez. 1915–16, 789–98, ill.

TECHNIQUES

3633a. **Durand-Decollogny, R.** *L'Art de la vannerie au Ruanda.* Bull. union femmes colon., **26**, 1955, 32–34, ill.

3634. **Hiernaux, Jean,** and **J. Maquet.** *Cultures préhistoriques de l'âge des métaux au Ruanda-Urundi at au Kivu (Congo Belge).* Acad. R. des sciences d'outre-mer: Mém. in 8. N.S. Tome 10, 1960, 102, ill.

3635. **Maquet, Emma.** *Au Ruanda; Une vannerie spiralée à brins roulés et montants verticaux passifs.* L'Anthropologie (Paris), **58**, 1954.

3636. —— *La pelleterie dans le Ruanda ancien.* Congo-Tervueren, **1**, 4, oct. 1955, 144–6.

3637. —— and **Robert Thys.** *Le tréfilage du cuivre et les bracelets en fil de cuivre au Ruanda et au Buhunde (Kivu, Congo Belge).* Anthropos, **50**, 1/3, 1955, 434–7, ill.

3638. *See* 3633a.

UTENSILS, TOOLS AND WEAPONS; MISCELLANEOUS

3639. **Merriam, Alan P.** *The game of Kubuguza among the Abatutsi of North-East Ruanda.* Man, **53**, no. 262, 1953, 169–72, ill.

3640. **Pauwels, Marcel Le R. P.** *Jeux et divertissements au Rwanda.* Ann. Lat., **24**, 1960, 219–363, ill.

AFRICAN ART TODAY

3641. **Maquet, Marcel.** *A propos de quelques métiers et ateliers d'art indigène du Ruanda et du Congo.* Brousse, **3/4**, 1948, 13–16.

TANZANIA
(Formerly Tanganyika and Zanzibar)

3642. **Blohm, B. W.** 1931. *Die Nyamwezi.* Pp. xii + 182, ill., maps. Hamburg: De Gruyter.

3643. **Lechaptois, Mgr.** 1913. *Aux rives du Tanganyika; étude ethnographique.* Pp. xii + 282, ill., map. Alger: Maison Carrée. (Art, pp. 221–2.)

3644. **Mathew, G.** *Mediaeval Islamic kingdom of the Tanganyika coast; new discoveries.* I.L.N., **219**, 1951, 591–93, ill.

3645. **Dempwolff, Otto.** 1916. *Die Sandawe.* Pp. 180, ill. Hamburg: Friederichsen. (Abh. Hamburg. Kolonialinst, 34.)

3646. **Noul, L.** *Le Mbulenga.* Les Musées de Genève, no. 8, 1960, 2–3, ill.

3647. **Swann, Alfred J.** 1910. *Fighting the slave-hunters in Central Africa.* Pp. xvi + 359, ill., map. London: Seeley Service.

3648. **Wilson, M.** *Traditional art among the Nyakyusa.* S. Afr. archaeol. bull., **19**, 75, 1964, 57–63, bibl., ill.

FIGURES AND MASKS

3649. **Bon, Irmgard.** *Masken und Plastiken der Makonde in Tanganyika.* Neues Afr., **3**, 11, Nov. 1961, 435–7, ill.

3650. **Cory, H.** *Figurines used in the initiation ceremonies of the Nguu of Tanganyika Territory.* Africa, **14**, 8, Oct. 1944, 459–64, ill.

3651. —— 1956. *African figurines; their ceremonial use in puberty rites in Tanganyika (Sambaa, Zigua, Nguu, Pare).* Pp. 176, ill. London: Faber.

3652. —— *Sumbwa birth figurines.* J. roy. anthrop. inst., **91** (1), 1961, 67–76, ill.

3653. **Gulliver, P. H.** *A tribal map of Tanganyika.* Tanganyika notes and records, **52**, 1959, 61–64, map.

3654. **Harding, J. R.** *'Mwali' dolls of the Wazaramo.* Man, **61**, no. 83, 1961, 72–73, ill.

3655. **Verneau, R.** *Trois statuettes stéatopyges.* l'Anthropologie (Wasukuma), **35**, 1925, 351.

BUILDINGS AND FURNITURE

3656. **Barton, F. R.** *Zanzibar doors.* Man, **24**, 63, 1924, 81–83, 1 pl., 2 figs.

3657. **Beidelman, T. O.** *A note on Baraguyu house-types and Baraguyu economy.* Tanganyika notes and records, **56**, 1961, 56–66, ill.

3658. **Cory, Hans.** 1953. *Wall-paintings by snake charmers in Tanganyika.* Pp. 99, ill. London: Faber.

3659. **Gray, R. F.** *Notes on Iranga houses.* Tanganyika notes and records, **35**, 1953, 45–52, ill.

3660. **Robinson, Arthur E.** *Notes on saucer and bowl decorations on houses, mosques and tombs.* Tanganyika notes and records, **10**, 1940, 79–87.

CLOTHING AND ADORNMENT

3661. **Bowie, D. F.** *The lip plug or 'Ndonya' among the tribes of the Southern Province.* Tanganyika notes and records, **27**, 1949, 75–77, ill.

3662. **Kimwani, Edward G.** *A pictorial description of the manufacture of bark-cloth in the Bukoba district.* Tanganyika notes and records, 30, Jan.–June 1951, 85–98.

3663. **Tripe, W. B.** *The tribal insignia of Heru.* Part 3, The Drums. Tanganyika notes and records, **16**, 1943, 5–6, ill.

ROCK ART

3663a. **Arundell, R. D. H.** *Rock paintings in Bukola District.* J. roy. anthrop. inst., 66, 1937, 113–16, ill.

3664. **Bagshawe, F. J.** *Rock paintings of the Kangeju Bushmen, Tanganyika Territory.* Man, **23**, 92, 1923, 146–7.

3665. **Culwick, A. T.** *Some rock paintings in Central Tanganyika.* J. roy. anthrop. inst., **61**, Dec. 1931, 443–53, ill.

3666. —— *Ritual use of rock paintings at Bahi, Tanganyika Territory.* Man, **31**, no. 41, 1931, 33–36, ill.

3667. —— *Rock paintings in Central Tanganyika.* Man, **31**, no. 69, 1931, 69–70.

3668. **Dar es Salaam. Tanganyika Travel Committee.** *Tanganyika rock paintings; a guide and record.* Pp. 64, bibl., ill., map. Dar es Salaam: Tanganyika Travel Committee. (Reproduced from Tanganyika Notes and Records, no. 29.)

3669. **Fosbrooke, H. A., and Others.** *Tanganyika rock paintings; a guide and record.* Tanganyika notes and records, no. 29, 1950, 1–61, bibl., ill., map.

3670. —— *Further light on rock engravings in Northern Tanganyika.* Man, **54**, 157, July 1954, 101–2, ill.

3671. **Fozzard, P. M. H.** *Some rock paintings in South and South-West Kondoa-Irangi District, Central Province.* Tanganyika notes and records, 52, 1959, 94–110, ill., map.

3672. **Nash, T. A. M.** *Note on the discovery of some rock paintings near Kondoa, Irangi, in Tanganyika Territory.* J. roy. anthrop. inst., **59**, 1929, 199–206, ill.

3673. **Inskeep, R.** *The age of the Kondoa rock paintings in the light of recent excavations at Kisese rock shelter.* Actes du IVe congrès panafricain de préhistoire, 1962, 249–56, ill.

3674. **Robinson, A. E.** *Rock pictures.* J. Afr. soc., **33**, 1934, 353–60, ill.

3675. **Tanner, R. E. S.** *A series of rock paintings near Mwanza.* Tanganyika notes and records, **34**, Jan. 1953, 62–67, ill., map.

3676. **Whiteley, W. H.** *Southern Province rock paintings.* Tanganyika notes and records, **31**, July 1951, 58–60.

TECHNIQUES

3677. **Beidelman, T. O.** *Ironworking in Ukaguru.* Tanganyika notes and records, **58/59**, Mar.–Sept. 1962, 288–9.

3678. **Crosse-Upcott, A. R. W.** *Barikiwa pottery.* Tanganyika notes and records, **40**, Sept. 1955, 24–29, ill.

3679. **Culwick, G. M.** *Pottery among the Wabena of Ulanga, Tanganyika Territory.* Man, **35**, 185, Nov. 1935, 165–9, ill.

3680. **Dorman, M. H.** *Pottery among the Wangoni and Wandendehule, Southern Tanganyika.* Man, **38**, 102, 1938, 97–102, ill., map.

3681. **Freyvogel, Thierry.** *Eine Sammlung geflochtener Matten aus dem Ulanga-Distrikt Tanganyikas.* Acta tropica, **16**, 4, 1959, 289–301, ill.

3682. —— *A collection of plaited mats from the Ulanga district of Tanganyika.* Tanganyika notes and records, **57**, 1961, 139–48, ill.

3683. **Greig, R. C. H.** *Iron smelting in Fipa.* Tanganyika notes and records, **4**, 1937, 77–81, ill.

3684. **Gutmann, Bruno.** *Der Schmied und seine Kunst im animistischen Denken (Dschaggastamm).* Z. f. Ethnol., **44**, 1912, 81–93.

3685. **Hall, R. de Z.** *Pottery in Bugufi, Tanganyika Territory.* Man, **39**, no. 132, 1939, 143–4, ill.

3686. **Rosemond, C. C. de.** *Iron smelting in the Kahama District.* Tanganyika notes and records, **16**, 1943, 79–84, ill.

3687. **Tanner, R. E. S.** *Some Chinese pottery found at Kilwa Kisiwani.* Tanganyika notes and records, **32**, Jan. 1952, 83–84.

3688. **Wise, R.** *Iron smelting in Ufipa.* Tanganyika notes and records, **50**, 1958, 106–11, ill. (Supplementary notes to those of R. C. H. Greig, 'Iron smelting in Fipa', Tanganyika notes and records, **4**, 1937, 77–81.)

3689. —— *Some rituals of iron-making in Ufipa.* Tanganyika notes and records, **51**, Dec. 1958, 232–8.

3690. **Wyckaert, R. P.** *Forgerons païens et forgerons chrétiens au Tanganika.* Anthropos, **9**, 1914, 371–80, ill.

SOUTH-EAST CENTRAL AFRICA

3691. **Frobenius, Leo.** 1931. *Erythräa; Länder und Zeiten des heiligen Konigsmordes.* Pp. 368 + vii, ill., map. Berlin Zürich: Atlantis Verlag.

ZAMBIA

3692. **Barnes, J. Albert.** *The material culture of the Fort Jameson Ngoni.* Occasional Papers of the Rhodes-Livingstone Museum No 1. 1948, 14, ill.

3693. **Brelsford, W. V.** *Some reflections on Bemba geometric art.* Bantu studies, **11**, 1, Mar. 1937, 37–45.

3694. —— 1957. *The tribes of Northern Rhodesia.* Pp. 128, bibl., ill., map. Salisbury: Rhodes-Livingstone Museum.

3695. **Burnier, Th.** *Notes d'ethnographie zambésienne.* Arch. Suisses anthrop. générale, **12**, 1946, 92.

3696–3697. *See* 3739a, 3739b.

3698. **Fagg, B.** *Archaeological notes from Northern Rhodesia.* Man, **46**, no. 48, 1946, 49–55, ill., maps.

3699. **Gibbons, Alfred St. Hill.** 1898. *Exploration and hunting in Central Africa, 1895–1896.* Pp. xi + 408. London: Methuen.

3700. **Gouldsbury, Cullen,** and **Hubert Sheane.** 1911. *The great plateau of Northern Rhodesia.* Pp. xxiii + 360, ill., map. London: Edward Arnold.

3701. **Holz, P.** *A visit to the Ndebele; vigorous art of a primitive people.* African world, 1957, 13–14, ill.

3702. **Maugham, Reginald Charles Fulke.** 1910. *Zambezia.* Pp. xiv + 408, ill., map. London: John Murray.

3703. **Melland, Frank H.** *Some ethnographical notes on the Awemba . . . of North-Eastern Rhodesia.* J. Afr. soc., **3**, 1903–4, 247–56, ill.

3704. **Moffat, Robert.** 1945. *The Matabele journals of Robert Moffat, 1829–60.* 2 vols. Vol. 1, pp. xv + 382, ill., maps. Vol. 2, pp. 295, ill., maps. London: Chatto & Windus.

3705. **Smith, Edwin W.,** and **Andrew Murray Dale.** 1920. *The Ila-speaking peoples of Northern Rhodesia.* 2 vols. Vol. 1, pp. xxiv + 423, ill., map. Vol. 2, pp. xiv + 433, ill. London: Macmillan.

3706. **Turner, V. W.** *Lunda rites and ceremonies.* Occ. Papers of the Rhodes-Livingstone Museum, no. 10, 1953, 1–56.

3707. **White, C. M. N.** 1948. *The material culture of the Lunda-Lovale peoples.* Pp. 3–15, ill. Livingstone: Rhodes-Livingstone Museum. (Occasional Papers of the Rhodes-Livingstone Museum, no. 3.)

3708. —— *A note on the 'Makishi'.* N. Rhodesia J., **4**, Dec. 1951, 67–70, ill.

FIGURES AND MASKS

3709. **Culwick, A. T.** and **G. M.** *Treatment of fits by the Wambunga.* Man, **34**, no. 156, 1934, 136, ill. (Figure of wooden female image.)

3710. **Joyce, T. A.** *On a ceremonial mask and dress from the Upper Zambesi.* Man, **3**, 38, 1903, 75, ill.

3711. **Richards, A. I.** *Pottery images or Mbusa used at the Chisungu ceremony of the Bemba people of North-Eastern Rhodesia.* S. Afr. J. sci., **41**, Feb. 1945, 444–58, ill.

BUILDINGS AND FURNITURE

3712. **Life.** *Painted village; Ndebele adorn homes.* Life, **34**, 1953, 173, ill. (pt. col.).

CLOTHING AND ADORNMENT

3713. **Oates, Frank.** 1889. *Matabele Land and the Victoria Falls.* Pp. xlix + 433, ill., maps. London: K. Paul. (2nd ed. Appendix 1. Ethnology by G. Rolleston.)

ROCK ART

3714. **Cooke, C. K.** *The prehistoric artist of Southern Matabeleland; his materials and technique as a basis for dating.* Third Pan-African congress on prehistory (Livingstone), 1955, 282–94, bibl., ill.

3715. **Fagg, B. E. B.** *The cave painting and rock gongs of Birnin Kudu.* Third Pan-African congress on prehistory (Livingstone), 1955, 306–12, ill., map.

3716. **Quick, G.** *Rock engravings from Northern Rhodesia.* Man, **31**, no. 241, 1931, 237, ill.

3717. **van Riet Lowe, Clarence.** *Prehistoric rock paintings in Northern Rhodesia.* S. Afr. J. sci., **34**, Nov. 1937, 399–412, ill.

3718. —— *Pinturas rupestres e a cultura do Zimbaué.* Bol. soc. est. coln. (Mocambique), **17**, 57/58, Abr.–Set. 1948, 3–16, ill.

3719. —— *Rock paintings and the Zimbabwe culture.* S. Afr. J. sci. (Cape Town), **45**, 1949, 141–2.

TECHNIQUES

3720. **Barnes, H. B.** *Iron smelting among the Ba-Ushi.* J. roy. anthrop. inst., **56**, 1926, 189–94, ill.

3721. **Campbell, A. C.** *Chimombe (Makorekore idol).* Nada, **34**, 1957, 31–37, ill.

3722. **Chaplin, J. H.** *Notes on traditional smelting in Northern Rhodesia (Lunda and Kaonde).* S. Afr. archaeol. bull., **16**, 62, June 1961, 53–60.

3723. **Clark, J. Desmond.** 1950. *The stone age cultures of Northern Rhodesia.* Pp. 157, ill., maps. Cape Town: S. African Archaeological Association.

3724. —— *A note on the pre-Bantu inhabitants of Northern Rhodesia and Nyasaland.* N. Rhodes. J., **1** (2), 1951, 42–52, ill.

3725. **Cooper, G.** *Village crafts in Barotseland.* Human probl. Brit. central Afr., **11**, 1951, 47–60.

3726. **Dart, R. A.,** and **N. del Grande.** *The ancient iron-smelting cavern at Mumbwa.* Trans. R. soc. S. Afr., **19**, 1931.

3727. **Fagan, Brian M.** *A note on potmaking among the Lungu of Northern Rhodesia.* Man, **61**, 104, May 1961, 87–88, ill.

3728. —— *Pre-European ironworking in Central Africa with special reference to Northern Rhodesia (Zambia).* J. Afr. hist., **2**, 1961, 199–210.

3729. —— *A collection of nineteenth-century Soli ironwork from the Lusaka area of Northern Rhodesia.* J. roy. anthrop. inst., **91** (2), 1961, 228–43, bibl., ill.

3730. —— *Two channel-decorated pottery sites from Northern Rhodesia.* Man, **64**, 8, Jan.–Feb. 1964, 15–18, ill., map.

3731. **Gluckman, Max.** *Barotse ironworkers.* Iscor magazine (Pretoria), 1946.

3732. **Housden, John,** and **Murray Armor.** *Indigenous iron smelters at Kalabo.* N. Rhodes. J., **4** (2), 1959, 135–8, ill.

3733. **Holý, L.** *Die Eisenerzeugung in Nordrhodesien und den benachbarten Gebieten.* Česk. Etnogr., **9/4**, 1961, 374–92, ill.

3734. **Kay, G.,** and **D. M. Wright.** *Aspects of the Ushi iron industry.* N. Rhodes. J., **5**, 1, 1962, 28–38, ill., map.

3735. **McAdams, L. J. B.,** and **Roger Howman.** *Notes on the hand-spinning and weaving of cotton.* Nada, **17**, 1940, 96–100, ill.

3736. **Silavwe, Newton.** 1962. *Bashimicelo.* (An account of iron-smelting in the old days and the traditional rituals associated with it.) Pp. 19. Lusaka: Northern Rhodesia Publ. Bureau.

3737. **van Riet Lowe, C.** *An unusual snake vessel from South-Central Africa.* Man, **40**, 140, Aug. 1940, 113–14.

3738. **Wells, L. H.** *A study of the ceramics from the deeper levels of the Mumbwa Cave, Northern Rhodesia.* Man, **39**, no. 63, 1939, 65–69, ill.

UTENSILS, TOOLS AND WEAPONS; MISCELLANEOUS

3739. **Brelsford, W. V.** *Notes on some Northern Rhodesian bow stands.* Man, **40**, no. 47, 1940, 35–41, ill.

3739a. **Chaplin, J. H.** *On the making of a chitumwa; a Northern Rhodesian protection amulet.* Man, **57**, no. 184, 1957, 148–9, ill.

3739b. —— *A note on mancala games in Northern Rhodesia* Man. **56**, no. 193, 1956, 168–70, ill.

AFRICAN ART TODAY

3740. **Brelsford, V.** *The teaching of art in North-Eastern Rhodesia.* Oversea education, **6**, 4, 1934, 174–8.

3741. **Chaplin, J. H.** *Some aspects of folk art in Northern Rhodesia.* Man, **63**, no. 81, 1963, 69–72, ill.

3742. **Wilson, G. H.** *The teaching of art in North-Eastern Rhodesia.* Oversea education, **7**, 3, April 1936, 125–9.

S. RHODESIA

3743. **Bart, H.** *Great Zimbabwe.* Unesco courier, **12** (10), Oct. 1959, 10–11, ill.

3744. **Bullock, C.** *Bushman paintings; Zimbabwe and romanticists.* Nada, **26**, 1949, 50–53.

3745. **Caton-Thompson, Gertrude.** 1931. *The Zimbabwe culture.* Pp. xxiv + 299, bibl., ill., map. Oxford: Clarendon Press.

3746. —— *Mapungubwe.* Antiquity, **13**, 1939, 324–41.

3747. **Dart, R. A.** *Foreign influences of Zimbabwe and pre-Zimbabwe eras.* Nada, **32**, 1955, 19–30.

3748. **Hall, R. N.** 1907. *Great Zimbabwe, Mashonaland, Rhodesia.* Pp. xliii + 460, ill. London: Methuen.

3749. *See* 3786a.

3750. **Holland, M.** *Zimbabwe and its secrets.* African world, July 1958, 13–14, ill.

3751. **Huntingford, G. W. B.** *The founders of the Zimbabwe civilisation.* Man, **52**, no. 117, 1952, 79–80, map.

3752. **Jensen, A. E.** *Simbabwe und die Megalithen Kultur.* Paiduma, **1** (3), 1938–40.

3753. **Jones, N.** 1949. *The prehistory of Southern Rhodesia.* Pp. 78, ill. Cambridge: Univ. Press.

3754. **Kearney, J. M.** *The ruins at Bumbusi.* Proc. Rhod. sci. ass., **7**, 1907, 59–62, ill.

3755. **Offe, Hans.** *Alte Kulturstätten Afrikas (Simbabwe).* Der Türmer, **45**, 1943, 413–18, ill.

3756. **Paver, B. G.** 1950. *Zimbabwe cavalcade.* Pp. 217, ill., maps. London: Cassell.

3757. **Roberts, J. G.** *Totemism, Zimbabwe and the Barozwi.* Nada, **24**, 1947, 48–51.

3758. **Robinson, K. R.** 1947–55. *Khami ruins.* Pp. xv + 178, bibl. Cambridge: Univ. Press. (App. pots, beads, metals, ivory and bone.)

3759. **Schebesta, P.** *Die Zimbabwe-Kultur in Afrika.* Anthropos, **21**, 1926, 484–522.

3760. **Schofield, J. F.** *Zimbabwe; a critical examination of the building methods employed.* S. Afr. J. sci., vol. xxiii, 1926.

3761. **Sicard, Harald von.** *The bird in the Zimbabwe culture.* Ethnos (Stockholm), **8**, 1943, 104–14.

3762. **Stevens, P. M.** 1950. *Zimbabwe culture.* Pp. 47. Cape Town: Univ. of Cape Town School of Librarianship: Bibliographical Series.

3763. **Summers, R.,** and **Others.** 1958. *Inyanga; prehistoric settlements in Southern Rhodesia.* Pp. 336, ill., maps. Cambridge: Univ. Press.

3764. **Trevor, T. G.** *Some observations on the relics of the pre-European culture in Rhodesia and South Africa.* J. roy. anthrop. inst., **60**, 1930, 389–400.

3765. **Wainwright, G. A.** *The founders of the Zimbabwe civilisation.* Man, **49**, no. 80, 1949, 62–66.

FIGURES AND MASKS

3766. **Roumeguère, Pierre,** and **Jacqueline Roumeguère-Eberhardt.** *Poupées de fertilité et figurines d'Argile.* J. soc. africanistes, **30**, 1960, 205–21, ill.

3767. **Summers, R.** *Human figures in clay and stone from Southern Rhodesia and adjoining territories.* Occ. Pap. Nat. Mus. S. Rhod., **3** (no. 21A), 61–75.

CLOTHING AND ADORNMENT

3768. **Gelfand, Michael.** *The charm and the bead in African practice.* Nada, **29**, 1952, 18–25, ill.

3769. —— and **Yvonne Swart.** *The Nyora (tattooing).* Nada, **30**, 1953, 5–11, ill.

3770. **Jeffreys, M. D. W.** *Brass disk pendants or beyops from Rhodesia.* Occ. Pap. Nat. Mus. S. Rhod., **19**, 1954, 729–31, ill.

3771. **Laidler, P. W.** *Beads in Africa south of the Zambezi (part II).* Transactions of the Rhodesia scientific association, **35**, 35–48.

3772. **Martin, C.** *Manyika beads of the XIX century.* Nada, **17**, 1940, 18–26, ill.

ROCK ART

3773. **Bleek, Dorothea F.** *The Ndanga rock paintings.* Nada, **5**, Dec. 1927, 79–80.

3774. —— and **George William Stow.** 1931. *Rock paintings in South Africa.* Pp. xxviii + 144, ill., map. London: Methuen.

3775. **Cooke, C. K.** *The occurrence of circle and dot in Southern Rhodesian rock art.* S. Afr. archaeol. bull., **12**, 1957, 62.

3776. **Cripps, L.** *Rock paintings of Southern Rhodesia.* Nada, **18**, 1941, 25–35, ill.

3777. —— *Rock paintings in Southern Rhodesia.* Proc. Rhod. sci. ass., **39**, Jan. 1942, 99–102.

3778. **Dart, R.** *Rhodesian engravers, painters and pigment miners of the fifth millennium B.C.* S. Afr. archaeol. bull., **8**, no. 32.

3779. **Frobenius, Leo.** *Prehistoric art in South Africa; 'The King's Monuments'; a unique series of rock drawings recently discovered in South Rhodesia.* I.L.N., **176**, 1930, 338, ill.

3780. —— *Dessins rupestres du sud de la Rhodésie.* Documents, **4**, 1930, 185–8, ill.

3781. **Goodall, Elizabeth.** *Domestic animals in rock art.* Rhod. sci. ass. proc. and trans., **41**, Apr. 1946, 57–62, ill.

3781a. —— *Some observations on rock paintings illustrating burial rites.* Rhod. sci. ass. proc. and trans., **41**, Apr. 1946, 63–73, ill.

3782. —— *Pictorial documents of prehistoric people.* Nada, **24**, 1947, 23–28, ill.

3783. —— (1) *Styles in rock paintings.* (2) *The geometric motif in rock art.* Third Pan-African Congress on Prehistory, Livingstone, 1955, 295–9, ill.; 300–3, ill.

3784. —— and **Others.** 1959. *Prehistoric rock art of the Federation of Rhodesia and Nyasaland.* Pp. xix + 267, ill., maps. London: Chatto & Windus for National Publications Trust.

3785. —— *A distinctive mythical figure appearing in the rock paintings of Southern Rhodesia.* Actes du IVe congrès panafricain de préhistoire, 1962, 399–406, ill.

3786. **Goodwin, A. J. H.** *Metal age or iron age?* S. Afr. archaeol. bull., **7**, 1952, 80–82.

3786a. **Hall, R. N.** 1911. *Bushman paintings at Maates jemshlope and Hillside, Southern Rhodesia.* Pp. 6, ill. Bulawayo.

3787. —— *Bushman paintings in the Ma-Dobo range (Matopos), Southern Rhodesia.* Geog. J., **3**, June 1912, 10–12, ill.

3788. —— *The Bushmen, the first human occupiers of Rhodesia, with special reference to paintings recently discovered in the Ma-Dobo (Matopos).* Proc. Rhod. sci. ass., **11**, 1912, 140–54, ill.

3789. —— *Bushman discoveries in the Matopo Hills, Rhodesia.* Weekly Cape times, 6 and 20 Nov. 1914.

3790. **Jeffreys, M. D. W.** *Doodling: Forest Vale (nr. Bulawayo) and Redan (nr. Vereeininging).* S. Afr. archaeol. bull. (Cape Town), **8**, 29, Mar. 1953, 15–19.

3791. **Maufe, H. B.** *The pigments of the Bushman rock paintings.* Proc. Rhod. sci. ass., **29**, 1930, 10–11.

3792. **Mochi, Aldobrandino.** *Pitture rupestri scoperte della spedizione Gatti nella Rhodesia meridionale.* B.R. soc. geog. Ital., ser, VI, 6, 1929, 676–84, ill.

3793. **Paterson, Edward.** 1949. *The Bantu as artist; notes on the possible contribution by the Bantu to the rock paintings and petroglyphs of Southern Africa.* Pp. 13 + 15, ill. (Cyclostyled.) Bulawayo, Bag P. 130.

3794. **Stebbing, E. P.** *Rock carvings at Bumbuzi.* Occ. Pap. Nat. Mus. S. Rhod., no. 16, 1951, 8.

3795. **Summers, Roger.** *Rock carvings at Bumbuzi (Bulawayo).* Occ. Pap. Nat. Mus. S. Rhod., no. 16, 1951, 343–51, bibl., ill.

3796. —— (ed.). 1959. *Prehistoric rock art of . . . Rhodesia and Nyasaland.* Pp. xix + 267, ill., maps. Salisbury (S.R.): National Publications Trust.

3797. **White, Franklin.** *Some rock paintings and stone implements near World's View, Matapos.* Proc. Rhod. sci. ass., 5, 1905, 7–11, ill. (See also J. Afr. soc., 1905–6, 213–14.)

TECHNIQUES

3798. **Bernhard, F. O.** *The Ziwa ware of Inyanga.* Nada, 38, 1961, 84–92, ill.

3799. **Cooke, C. K.** *An iron-smelting site in the Matopo hills, Southern Rhodesia.* S. Afr. archaeol. bull., 14, 55, Sept. 1959, 118–20.

3800. **Franklin, H.** *The native ironworkers of Enkeldoorn district and their art.* Nada, 22, 1945, 5–10.

3801. **Goodall, E.** *Rhodesian pots with moulded decorations.* Nada, 23, 1946, 37–49, ill.

3802. **Martin, C.** *Manyika pottery.* S. Afr. J. sci., 37, 1941, 350–60, ill.

3803. **Robinson, K. R.** *An early smelting site near Khami Ruins.* Occ. Pap. Nat. Mus. S. Rhod., 2, 1953, 508–17.

3804. —— *A note on hollow-based pottery from Southern Rhodesia.* Man, 61, 105, May 1961, p. 88, ill.

3805. **Schofield, J. F.** 1937. *Work done in 1934—Pottery.* Appendices: (1) Schedule of pottery. (2) Dating of Zimbabwe pottery. (3) Modern Bavenda pottery. Fouché, Leo, Mapungwe, pp. 32–102, ill.

3806. **Shropshire, Denys.** *The making of Hari (clay pots), Watewe tribe.* Man, 36, no. 182, 1936, 136–7, ill.

3807. **Stapleton, P.,** and **J. F. Schofield.** *Pottery from the Salisbury district, Southern Rhodesia.* Trans. R. Soc. S. Africa, 26, 1938, 321–40.

3808. **Stead, W. H.** *Notes on the types of clay pots found in the Inyanga District, 1945, identified from specimens collected for the purpose by native messengers at office of Native Commissioner, Inyanga.* Nada, 24, 1947, 100–2, ill.

3809. **Thompson, Louis C.** *Ingots of native manufacture.* Nada, 26, 1949, 7–19, ill.

3810. **Weber, M.,** and **Others.** 1937. *Notes on gold ornaments,* by M. Weber. *Gold from Mapungwe,* by R. Pearson. *Mapungwe metallurgical material,* by G. H. Stanley. Fouché, Leo, Mapungwe, pp. 114–18, ill.

AFRICAN ART TODAY

3811. **Lombard, S.** *Cyrene.* Jeune Afr., 5 (15), 1951–2.

3812. **McEwen, Frank.** 1963. *New art from Rhodesia.* s.p., ill. London: Commonwealth Institute. (An exhibition at the Commonwealth Institute, 21 Feb. 1963–15 Apr. 1963.

3813. **Paterson, Edward.** *Cyrene art.* Nada, 26, 1949, 45–50, ill.

MALAWI

3814. **Emslie, W. A.** 1901. *Among the wild Ngoni.* Pp. 319, ill., map. Edinburgh: Anderson & Ferrier. (2nd ed.)

3815. **Fülleborn, F.** 1906. *Das Deutsche Nyassa- und Ruwumagebiet.* Pp. xx + 636, bibl., ill., maps + atlas of pl. Berlin: Reimer.

3816. **Johnston, Sir Harry Hamilton.** 1897. *British Central Africa.* Pp. xix + 544, ill., maps. London: Methuen.

3817. **Mackenzie, Duncan R.** 1925. *The spirit-ridden Konde.* Pp. xvi + 318, ill., map. London: Seeley Service.

3818. **Rankin, Daniel J.** 1893. *The Zambesi basin and Nyassaland.* Pp. vii + 277, ill., maps. Edinburgh: Blackwood.

3819. **Sanderson, G. M.** *The use of tail-switches in magic.* Nyasaland J., 8 (1), 1955, 39–56, ill.

3820. —— *Inyago; the picture-models of the Yao initiation ceremonies.* Nyasaland J., 8 (2), 1955, 36–57, ill.

3821. **Stannus, H. S.** *The Wayao of Nyasaland.* Harvard African studies, Varia Africana, III, 1922, 229–372, ill.

3822. **Werner, Alice.** 1906. *The natives of British Central Africa.* Pp. xii + 303, bibl., ill., map. London: Constable.

FIGURES AND MASKS

3823. **Metcalfe, Margaret.** *Notes on a Nyasaland dance mask.* S. Afr. J. sci., 29, 1932, 687–9, ill.

CLOTHING AND ADORNMENT

3824. **Marett, R. R.** *Manganja headdresses.* Man, 14, no. 73, 1914, 145, ill.

3825. **Werner, A.** *Hairdressing and other customs in Angoniland.* Cape illustrated magazine, 6, 1895, 105–9, ill.

3826. *see 3847a.*

ROCK ART

3827. *see 3863a.*

3828. **Metcalfe, Margaret.** *Some rock paintings in Nyasaland.* Nyasaland J., 9, 1, Jan. 1956, 58–70, ill.

TECHNIQUES

3829. **Rangeley, W. H. J.** *Ancient iron working on the Nyika Plateau.* Nyasaland J., 13, 1, Jan. 1960, 18–20.

3830. **Stannus, H. S.** *Nyasaland Ngoni smelting furnace.* Man, 14, 65, 1914, 131–2.

3831. **Young, T. Cullen.** *A note on iron objects of unknown origin from Northern Nyasaland.* Man, 29, no. 147, 1929, 189–90, ill.

AFRICAN ART TODAY

3832. **Stannus, Hugh S.** *Native paintings in Nyasaland.* J. Afr. soc., 9, 1909–10, 184–7, ill.

3833. —— *Note on drawings by a native of Nyasaland.* Man, 24, 117, 1924, 160.

3834. **Werner, Alice.** *A native painting from Nyasa.* J. Afr. soc., 8, 1909, 190–2.

3835. —— *Note on drawings by a native of Nyasaland.* Man, 24, 87, 1924, 116–17, ill.

MOZAMBIQUE

3836. **Cabral, Augusto Antonio A Pereira.** 1925. *Raças, usos e costumes dos indigenas da provincia de Moçambique.* Pp. 95, ill. Lourenço Marques: Imprensa Nacional.

3837. **de Campos, Octavio Rodrigues.** *A Arte Negra de Moçambique.* Portugal em Afr., 13, no. 78, 1956, 337–56, ill.

3838. **de Castro, Soares.** *Artes plásticas no norte de Moçambique.* Bol. museu Nampula, 2, 1961, 115–29.

3839. **de Lima, Fernando de Castro Pires.** *Contribuição para o estudo da arte indígena em Moçambique.* Actos 1º Congr. de Antrop. Colonia, Porto, 1934, da 1º Exp. Colon. port. Comp de Moçambique. (1936 (new ed.).)

3840. **de Oliveira, J. N. Nunes.** *Arte gentilica em Moçambique (sumário duma crítica).* Documents Moçambique, 3, 1935.

3841. **Diaz de Villegas, José.** 1961. *Africa septentrional.* Pp. 28. Madrid: Instituto de Estudios Africanos.

3842. **Junod, Henri Alexandre.** 1911. *Zidji; Étude de moeurs sud-africains.* Pp. vi + 333. Sainte Blaise: Foyer Solidariste.

3843. **Monteiro, Rose.** 1891. *Delagoa Bay.* Pp. xi (1) + 274, ill. London: George Philip.

3844. **Pires de Lima, Americo.** 1943. *Explorações em Moçambique.* Pp. viii + 327, ill. Lisbon: Agência Geral das Colonias.

A.A.–F

3845. **Rita-Ferreita, A.** *Os 'Azimba'* (monografia etnografica). Bol. soc. est. coln. (Moçambique), **24** (84), 1954, 47–140: (85), 1954, 3–116.

3846. —— 1958. *Agrupamento e caracterização étnica dos indigenas de Moçambique.* Pp. 133, bibl., ill., maps. Lisbon: Ministério do Ultramar: Junta de investigações do Ultramar.

3847. **Silva, João Augusto.** *Arte; considerações varias.* Moçambique, **13**, Mar. 1938, 79–90.

3847a.**Worsfold, E. Basil.** 1899. *Portuguese Nyassaland.* Pp. (x) + 295, ill., maps. London: Sampson Low.

FIGURES AND MASKS

3848. **Bennet-Clark, M. A.** *A mask from the Makonde tribe in the British Museum.* Man, **57**, 117, July 1957, 97–98, ill.

3849. **Boléo, Oliveira.** *Moçambique.* Pp. 562, ill., maps. Lisbon: Agência Geral do Ultramar.

3850. **Earthy, E. Dora.** *Note on the decorations on carved wooden food-bowls from south Chopiland.* Ann. Transvaal mus., **11** (2), 1925, 118–24, ill.

3851. **Ferreirinha, Felisberto.** *A estatuaria dos Macondes.* Bol. soc. est. coln. (Moçambique), **19**, 1949, 19–33.

3852. **Gérard, Pe.** *Màhimo macuas.* Moçambique, **26**, Jun. 1941, 5–22, ill.

3853. **Lang, Werner.** *Makondemasken in der völkerkundlichen Sammlung der Universität Göttingen.* Z. f. Ethnol., **85**, 1, 1960, 28–36, bibl., ill.

3854. **Lourenço Marques, Moçambique.** Instituto de Investigação Científica. 1963. *Wood sculptures of the Maconde people; album . . . to celebrate the fiftieth anniversary of the Museum Dr. Alvaro de Castro.* Pp. 5 + 41 pl.

CLOTHING AND ADORNMENT

3855. **Alberto, Manuel Simões.** *Tatuagens e mutilações etnicas entre os negros de Moçambique.* Império (Laurenço Marques), **3**, Jul. 1951, p. 17.

3856. —— 1955. *Mutilações étnicais entre os negros de Moçambique* (Ethnical mutilations among the negroes of Mozambique). Bol. soc. est. coln. (Moçambique), **90**, 1955, 35–49, ill.

3857. **Earthy, E. Dora.** *On the significance of the body markings of some natives of Portuguese East Africa.* S. Afr. J. sci., **21**, 1924, 573–87, ill.

3858. **Gérard, Pe.** *Costumes dos Macua do Médo; Região de Namuno, circunscrição de Montepuez.* Moçambique, 1941, 5–20, ill.

3859. **Junod, Henri M.** 1927. *The life of a South African tribe.* 2 vols. Vol. 1, Social life, pp. 559, ill. Vol. 2, Mental life, pp. 660, ill. London: Macmillan. (1962. The life of a South African tribe. 2 vols. Reprint of above by University Books Inc. of New York.)

3860. **Lorenz, A.** *Etwas vom Lippenflocknegervolk (Makonde) in Ostafrika.* Jambo, **2**, 1925, 137–40.

3861. **Schulien, M. P.** *Kleidung und Schmuck bei den Atchwabo in Portugiesisch-Ostafrika.* Anthropos (Mödling), **21**, 1926, 870–920, ill.

3862. **Viana, Miguel J.** *Da tatuagem nembo entre os Wa-Yao.* Bol. ag. ger. colon., **23**, 270, Dez. 1947, 11–29, ill.

ROCK ART

3863. **Brásio, António.** *As pinturas rupestres em Moçambique.* Bol. ag. ger. colon. (Lisboa), **26**, 297, Mar. 1950, 7–11.

3863a.**de Castro, Soares.** *Pinturas rupestres do Niassa.* Bol. soc. est. Moçambique, **26**, 98, Maio–Jun. 1956, 29–39, ill.

3864. **de Oliveira, Octávio R.** *Pinturas rupestres do contraforte da Serra Vumba, Monte Chinhamapere (Vila de Manica).* Bol. soc. est. coln.(Moçambique), **32**, 136, July–Sept. 1963, 21–38, ill.

3865. **Santos Junior.** 1952. *Les peintures rupestres du Mozambique.* Actes du congrès Panafricain de préhistoire, 20 sess., Alger, 1952, communication no. 81, 747–58, ill.

3866. **Staudinger, P.** *Funde und Abbildungen von Felszeichnungen aus den alten Goldgebieten von Portugiesisch-Südostafrika.* Z. f. Ethnol. **1**, 1911, 140–6, ill.

TECHNIQUES

3867. **Dias, Margot.** *Makonde Töpferei.* Baessler-Archiv, **9**, N.F., 1961, 95–126, ill.

3868. ——*Aspectos técnicos e sociais da olaria dos Chopes.* Garcia de orta, **8**, 4, 1960, 779–85, ill.

3869. **de Oliveira, Octávio Roza.** *A cerámica changa.* Bol. soc. est. coln. (Moçambique), **32**, 134, Jan.–Mar. 1963, 32–35, ill.

3870. **de Castro, Soares.** *A cerámica gentílica no norte de Moçambique.* Bol. museu Nampula, **2**, 1961, 63–92.

UTENSILS, TOOLS AND WEAPONS: MISCELLANEOUS

3871. **Collings, H. D.** *Notes on the Makonde tribe of Portuguese East Africa.* Man, **29**, no. 17, 1929, 25–28, ill.

MADAGASCAR

3872. **Brousse.** *L'Art malgache.* Brousse, **2**, 1939, 31–32.

3873. **Danielli, M.** *The witches of Madagascar.* Folklore, **58**, 1947, 261–77.

3874. **Decary, R.** *L'Industrie chez les Antandroy de Madagascar.* Rev. ethnog. trad. pop., **7**, no. 25, 1926, 38–52, bibl., ill.

3875. —— *Deux amulettes malgaches.* Rev. ethnog. trad. pop., **9**, nos. 34/36, 1928, 176–8, ill.

3876. **Dubois, Henri M.** 1938. *Monographie des Betsileo (Madagascar).* Pp. xviii + 1510, ill., maps. Paris: Institut d'Ethnologie. (Travaux et mémoires de l'Institut d'Ethnologie, 34. L'Art, pp. 1127–48, ill.

3877. **Faublée-Urbain, Marcelle.** 1963. *L'Art malgache.* Pp. vii + 141, bibl., ill., maps. Paris: Presses Univ.

3878. **le Barbier, M. C.** *Contribution à l'étude des Bara-Imamono de Madagascar.* L'Anthropologie, **31**, 1921, 69–93, 495–517, ill.

3879. **Leblond, Marius-Ary.** *L'Art a Madagascar.* Revue de l'Art (Paris), 1907, 1–16.

3880. **Linton, Ralph.** *The Tanala; a hill tribe of Madagascar.* Field museum of natural history, Anthropological series, **22**, 1933, 1–334, bibl., ill., map.

3881. **Lormian, Henri.** 1934. *L'Art malgache.* Pp. 51, ill. Paris: E. de Boccard.

3882. **Mattei, M.** *Note sur les sculptures de la région d'Antalaha.* Bull. acad. malgache, N.S., **12**, 1929, 13.

3883. **Poirier, Charles.** *Ethnographie malgache; 1. Sorcellerie médicale, magie, art. 2. Aperçu sur la représentation de la femme et du boeuf.* Pp. 23, ill. Tananarive: Académie Malgache (Mém. 38).

3884. **Rabemanajara, J.-I.** 1947. *Les dieux malgaches.* Pp. 164. Gap. Ophrys ed.

3885. **Thiout, Michel.** 1961. *Madagascar.* Pp. 157, ill., map. Paris: Horizons de France.

3886. **You, André.** *Les populations de Madagascar.* L'Ethnographie, no. 25, 1932, 91–105, ill.

FIGURES AND MASKS

3887. **Camponé, P.** *Aperçu sur les malgaches et leurs conceptions d'art sculptural.* Anthropos, **23**, 1928, 1–18, ill.

3888. **Decary, R.** *La sculpture chez les Antandroy de Madagascar.* Bull. et mém. soc. anthrop. de Paris, ser. 7, tome 1, 1920, 30.

3889. —— and **Urbain Faurec**. 1941. *Les sites et monuments naturels de Madagascar*. Pp. 204, ill. Tananarive: Imp. Officielle.

3890. —— *L'Art des tombeaux à Madagascar*. Tropiques, **55**, 400, nov. 1957, 48–53, ill.

3891. **Dominjoud, M.** *Les fétiches malgaches. Les 'Ody'*. Les Musées de Genève, **10**, 1953, 3, ill.

3892. **Molet, L.** *Les statuettes bara de Iakora*. Naturaliste malgache, **6** (1–2), 1954, 109–20, ill.

3893. —— *La sculpture malgache*. Rev. Madag. (Tananarive), N.S., **1**, 1958, 35–38, ill.

3894. —— *Marques de propriété sur les animaux domestiques*. Rev. Madag., N.S., **4**, 1958, 23–26.

3895. **Sibree, James.** *Decorative carvings on wood, especially on the burial memorials, by the Bètsilèo Malagasy*. J. anthrop. inst., **21**, 1892, 230–44, ill.

3896. **Vernier, Elie.** *Bambous gravès malgaches (Collection Ch. Poirier)*. Objets et mondes, **3**, 4, hiver 1963, 293–8, ill.

3897. **Waterlot, Em. G.** *La sculpture sur bois à Madagascar*. L' Anthropologie, **35**, 1925, 133 f.

BUILDINGS AND FURNITURE

3898. **Decary, Raymond.** 1958. *L'Habitat à Madagascar*. Pp. 80, ill. Pau: Imprimerie Marrimpouey.

CLOTHING AND ADORNMENT

3899. **Millot, J.** *Considérations sur le commerce dans l'Océan Indien au Moyen âge et au pré-Moyen âge, à propos des perles de Zanaga*. Mém. inst. sci. (Madagascar), **1**, 2, 1952, 159–66.

3900. **Bernard-Thierry, S.** *Perles magiques à Madagascar*. J. soc. africanistes, **29**, 1959, 33–90, bibl., ill.

3901. **Decary, Raymond.** *Les tatouages Antandroy*. Rev. Madag., 1933, 37–54, ill.

3902. —— *Les tatouages chez les indigènes de Madagascar*. J. soc. africanistes, **5**, 1, 1935, 1–39, ill.

3903. —— *Les tatouages malgaches*. Rev. Madag., **19**, 1954, 41–48, ill.

3904. **Faublée, Marcelle et Jacques.** *Le costume à Madagascar, hier et aujourd'hui*. Tropiques, déc. 1953, 66–73, ill.

3905. **Leblond, Marius-Ary.** *La coiffure féminine à Madagascar*. Le monde moderne (Paris), 1907, 533–8, ill.

3906. **Molet, L.** *Métiers à tisser Betsimisaraka*. Mém. inst. sci. (Madagascar), **1**, 2, 1952, 196–208.

3907. **Radaody-Ralarosy, Mme E. Paul.** *Le costume malgache; le lamba*. Rythmes du monde, **4**, nov.–déc. 1946, 41–50, ill.

3908. —— *Terre des lambas*. Rev. Madag., **27**, oct. 1946–janv. 1947, 35–39.

3909. **Thierry, S.** *Les vakana malgaches ou perles de la chance*. Rev. Madag., N.S., **1**, 1958, 15–22.

TECHNIQUES

3910. **Decary, Raymond.** *Les anciennes industries du metal de Madagascar*. Communautés et continents: Nouv. rev. franc. O.-M., **54**, N.S., 14, avr.–juin 1962, 31–36, ill.

3911. **Faublée, Jacques.** *L'Ethnographie de Madagascar*. Pp. 171, ill., map. Paris: Bibliothèque d'Outre-Mer. (Les industries, pp. 37–50.)

3912. **Poirier, Ch.** *Réflexions sur les ruines de Maïlaka et de Vohémar; Oeuvre de céramistes persans*. Bull. acad. malgache, **28**, 1947–8, 97–107.

3913. **Ravelonanosy, Victoire.** *De la céramique à Madagascar*. Présence africaine, **31**, avr.–mai 1960, 90–95.

SOUTHERN AFRICA

REPUBLIC OF SOUTH AFRICA

3914. **Battiss, W. W.** *Primitive art of S. Africa*. London Studio, **18** (Studio 118), 156–61.

3915. **Bouman, A. C.** 1938. *Kuns in Suid-Afrika*. Pp. 135, ill. Cape Town: H.A.U.M.

3916. **Burchell, William J.** 1822. *Travels in the interior of Southern Africa*. 2 vols. Vol. 1, pp. viii (iii) + 582, ill., map. Vol. 2, pp. vi + 648, ill. London: Longmans.

3917. **Christol, F. I.** 1897. *Au sud de l'Afrique*. Pp. xli + 308, ill. Paris.

3918. —— *À propos d'une peinture de Busmen*. Bull. soc. Neuchât. de géog., **17**, 1906, 324–7, ill.

3919. —— 1911. *L'art dans l'Afrique australe*. Pp. xxi + 144, ill. Paris: Berger-Levrault. (Pictorial and decorative art of Bushmen and S. Sotho in particular.—Schapera, I., bibl., 1941.)

3920. **Chaplin, J. H.** *A preliminary note on the rainbow in Africa south of the Sahara*. Ethnos, **24**, 1959, 151–71, bibl., ill.

3921. **Clark, J. Desmond.** 1959. *The prehistory of Southern Africa*. Pp. xxv + 341, bibl., ill., maps. London: Penguin Books.

3922. **Duggan-Cronin, A. M.** 1942. *The Bushman tribes of Southern Africa*. Pp. 14, ill. Kimberley: Alexander McGregor Memorial Museum.

3923. **Dunn, E. J.** 1931. *The Bushman*. Pp. xii + 130, ill. London: Charles Griffin.

3924. **Fritsch, Gustav.** 1872. *Die Eingeborenen Süd-Afrikas*. Pp. xxiv + 528, bibl., ill., maps + atlas of 30 pl. Breslau: Ferdinand Hirt.

3925. **Hirschberg, Walter.** 1936. *Völkerkundliche Ergebnisse der südafrikanischen Reisen Rudolf Pöchs in den Jahren 1907–1909*. Pp. viii + 64, ill., maps. Vienna: Anthrop. Gesellschaft. (Rudolf Pöchs Nachlass, Ser. B. 1.)

3926. **Holub, Emil.** 1881. *Seven years in South Africa*. 2 vols. Vol. 1, xi + 426, ill., maps. Vol. 2, xi + 479, ill. London: Sampson Low.

3927. **Kidd, Dudley.** 1904. *The essential kafir*. Pp. xv + 436, bibl., ill., map. London: Black.

3928. **Maesen, Albert.** 1958. *Bantu culture*. Enciclopedia universale dell'Arte, vol. 2. (English edition, *Bantu Culture*. E.W.A., vol. 2, 1960, 211–52, bibl., ill., map.)

3929. **Müller, Hendrik P. N.,** and **Joh. F. Snelleman.** 1893. *Industrie des Cafres du Sud-Est de l'Afrique*. Pp. vi + 50, ill. (some in col.). Leiden: Brill.

3930. **Roberts, Noel.** *Bantu methods of divination*. S. Afr. J. sci., **13**, 1916, 406–8. (Ritual drums.)

3931. **Schapera, I.** 1930. *The Khoisan peoples of South Africa. Bushmen and Hottentots*. Pp. xi + 450, bibl., ill., maps. London: George Routledge.

3932. —— 1933. *The early Cape Hottentots*. Pp. xv + 309, ill. Cape Town: Van Riebeek Society. (Publication no. 14.)

3933. **Segal, B.** *A possible base for Bushman paint*. Bantu studies, **9**, 1935.

3934. **Spillmann, Joseph.** 1882. *Vom Cap zum Sambesi*. Freiburg i.B.: Herder.

3935. **Stopa, Roman.** 1949. *Hotentoci Kultura, Jezyk, Bajki, Piesni*. Pp. 103, ill. (inc. music). Cracow: T. Zapior.

3936. **Stow, George W.** 1905. *The native races of South Africa*. Pp. xvi + 618, ill. London.

3937. **Thurnwald, R.** *Psychologie des primitiven menschen Süd-Afrikas*. Kafka, Verg. Psychologie, **1**, 147–320, ill.

3938. **Theal, George McCall.** 1896. *The Portuguese in South Africa*. Pp. xvi + 324, maps. London.

3939. —— 1910. *The yellow and dark-skinned people of Africa south of the Zambesi*. Pp. xvi + 395, ill. London: Swan, Sonnenschein.

3940. **Walton, James.** *Some forms of Bushman art*. Afr. mus. soc., **1**, 4, 1957, 27–32, ill.

3941. **Werner, Alice.** *Bushman paintings.* J. Afr. soc., **7**, 1907–8, 387–93.

3942. —— *Bushman art.* Anthropos (Wien), **4**, 1909, 500–4, ill.

3943. **Zelizko, J. V.** 1904. *O nasténnych rytindch a kresbách jeskynnich palaeolithického člověka . . .* Pp. 24, ill. Olomouci.

3944. —— *Vorläufiger Bericht über Felsengravierungen der Buschmänner auf Grund vom Afrikaforscher Dr. E. Holub gesammelten Materiales.* Mitt. anthrop. gesell. (Wien), **39**, 1909, 34–35.

3945. —— 1925. *Felsgravierungen der südafrikanischen Buschmänner. Auf grund der von Dr. Emil Holub mitgebrachten Originale und Kopien.* Pp. 28, ill. Leipzig: Brockhaus.

FIGURES AND MASKS

3946. **Shaw, E. M.** *Fertility dolls in Southern Africa.* Nada, **25**, 1948, 63–68.

BUILDINGS AND FURNITURE

3947. **Walton, James.** *South African peasant architecture.* Afr. stud., **19** (2), 1949, 70–79, ill.

3947a.—— *Mural art of the Bantu.* S. African Panorama **10** (4), 1965, 30–37, ill.

CLOTHING AND ADORNMENT

3948. **Cohn, J. C.** *The bead collection of the archaeological survey, Johannesburg.* S. Afr. archaeol. bull., **14**, 54, 1959, 75–77.

3949. **Lagercrantz, Sture.** *Ethnographical reflections on 'Hottentot Aprons'.* Ethnos, **2**, 1937, 145–74, bibl.

3950. **Lieberman, H.** *Ornamentation of South African natives.* Empire review, 445, Feb. 1938, 111–14.

3951. **Schönland, S.** *On some implements and ornaments of South African native races made of stone and bone.* Graham's town, Rec., Albany mus., **2**, 1907, 18–23, ill.

ROCK ART

3951a.**Battiss, Walter W.** *Paintings in South African rock shelters.* Studio, **129**, May 1945, 151–4.

3952. —— *South African Bushman paintings.* Studio, **136**, 668, Nov. 1948, 144–7, ill.

3953. —— 1948. *The artists of the rocks.* Pp. 243, ill. (some col.). Pretoria: Red Fawn Press.

3954. —— *Bushman art.* Pp. 13, ill. Pretoria: Red Fawn Press.

3955. —— *Last Bushman artists.* Studio, **154**, Aug. 1957, 33–37.

3956. —— *Bushman paintings.* Commonwealth calling, Feb. 1958, 34–35.

3957. —— and **Others.** 1958. *The art of Africa.* (Edited and arranged by J. W. Grossert.) Pp. 140, bibl., ill., maps. Pietermaritzburg: Shuter & Shooter.

3958. **Bleek, Dorothea F.** *A survey of our present knowledge of rock-paintings in South Africa.* S. Afr. J. sci., **29**, 1932, 72–83, ill.

3959. —— 1940. *More rock paintings in South Africa.* Pp. xx + 28 pl. with descriptive text. London: Methuen.

3960. —— 1953. *Cave artists of South Africa.* Pp. 80, ill. 48 unpublished reproductions. Cape Town: A. A. Balkema.

3961. **Breuil, Abbé Henri.** *The palaeolithic art of North-Eastern Spain and the art of the Bushmen—a comparison.* Man, **30**, no. 121, 1930, 149–51, ill.

3962. —— *L'Afrique préhistorique.* Cah. d'art, **5**, 1930, 449–500, ill.

3963. —— *Rock paintings in South Africa* (Review of Stow and Bleek's book). Nature, **127**, 1931, 695–8.

3964. —— *Les roches peintes de l'Afrique du Sud.* France abroad, **3** (9), 1945.

3965. —— *The so-called Bushman art; paintings and engravings on rock in South Africa and the problems they suggest.* Man, **46**, no. 73, July–Aug. 1946, 84.

3966. —— *South African races in the rock paintings.* Robert Broom Commemorative Volume, 1948.

3967. —— 1949. *Des Cavernes peintes d'Aquitaine aux fresques rocheuses de l'Afrique australe.* Pp. 382–93. Acad, des Inscriptions et Belles-Lettres, Paris. C.R. des séances de . . . 1949. (Reprimé dans les publications . . . de l'Institut de France, no. 14, 1949, 14.)

3968. —— *Some foreigners in the frescoes on rocks in Southern Africa.* S. Afr. archaeol. bull., **4**, 14, 1949.

3969. —— *Rock paintings of South Africa.* Anthrop. Q., **27**, 1954, 31–42.

3970. —— *Les roches peintes d'Afrique australe.* Mém. acad. inscriptions et belles-lettres (Paris), **44**, 1954, 1–25, ill.

3971. —— and **Others.** 1959. *L'Homme avant l'écriture.* Ill. Paris: Colin.

3972. **Bushman paintings.** 1906. *Return showing the districts in the Attorney-General's Ministerial Division and as far as possible the places within them in which Bushman paintings are known to exist.* Pp. 4. Cape Town: Cape Parliamentary Paper. (Further return. Pp. 3. Cape Town: Cape Parliamentary Paper.)

3973. **Burkitt, M. C.** *Rock paintings in South Africa.* Antiquity, 1927, 226–8, ill.

3974. —— 1928. *South Africa's past in stone and paint.* Pp. xiv + 183, ill., map. Cambridge: Univ. Press.

3975. —— *'Bushman art' in South Africa.* Ipek, **4**, 1929, 89–95, ill.

3976. —— *Animals in art 2. South African rock paintings.* Geog. mag., **20**, 1947–8, 59–64, ill.

3977. **Castro Júnior, Augusto.** *As pinturas rupestres dos bosquimanos.* Mensário admin., 43/44, Mar.–Abr. 1951, 47–90, ill.

3978. **Craig, B. J.** 1947. *Rock paintings and petroglyphs of South and Central Africa; Bibliography of prehistoric art.* Biblio. Ser. Univ. of Cape Town School of Librarianship.

3979. **Dart, R. A.** *Rock engravings in Southern Africa and some clue to their significance and age.* S. Afr. J. sci., **28**, 1931, 475–86, ill.

3980. **Frobenius, Leo.** *. . . Katalog der Südafrikanischen Felsbilder-kopien der D.I.A.F.E., 1928–30.* Pp. 90, ill.

3981. —— *Südafrikanische Felsbilder.* Atlantis (Berlin), 1929, 308–13, ill.

3982. —— *Mystery of South Africa's prehistoric art; newly discovered rock drawings of divergent style.* I.L.N., **175**, 1929, 333, ill.

3983. —— *Les fresques rupestres découvertes en Afrique du Sud.* Les beaux-arts (Paris), **26**, 1930, 12, ill.

3984. —— *Allgemeines über die Felsbilder Südafrikas.* Mitt., Forschungsinst., Kultur-morph., 1930, 88–95. (Engravings, p. 89.)

3985. —— *L'Art de la silhouette.* Cahiers d'art, 4, 1930–1(?), 397–401, ill.

3986. —— 1931. *Madsimu Dsangara; Südafrikanische Felsbilderchronik.* 2 vols. Vol. 1, pp. 34, ill. Vol. 2, pp. 36, ill. Berlin: Atlantis.

3987. **Brown, Alfred Gordon.** 1952. *Pictorial art in South Africa during three centuries to 1875.* Pp. i–viii + 9–172, bibl., ill. London: Charles E. Sawyer.

3988. **Holm, Erik.** *Das Alter der südafrikanischen Felskunst.* Paideuma, **6**, 5, Aug. 1957, 297–300, ill.

3989. **Holz, P.** *Cave painting in South Africa.* Contemporary review, **192**, 1957, 162–5.

3990. **Hutchinson, Mark.** *Collection of facsimile Bushman drawings.* J. anthrop. inst., **12**, 1883, 464–5.

3991. **Impey, S. P.** 1926. *Origin of the Bushmen and the rock paintings of South Africa.* Pp. iv + 104, ill. Cape Town: Juta & Co.

3992. **Lang, H.** *A white rhinoceros pictured by a man of the Stone Age.* I.L.N., 14 July 1928, 72–73, ill.

3993. —— *A black rhinoceros tossing a 'Boskop' boy . . .* I.L.N., 6 Oct. 1928, 599, ill.

3994. —— *A mystery of Stone Age masters; South Africa's rock carved pictures—what is their meaning?* I.L.N., 6 Apr. 1929, 568–70, 598, 600, ill.

3995. —— *South Africa as the cradle of art; the Stone Age petroglyphs of the Transvaal.* I.L.N., 13 Apr. 1929, 613–15, 648, ill.

3996. —— *Wonderful South African Stone Age sculptures of mastodons.* (With note by A. W. Rogers.) I.L.N., 13 July 1929, 70–73, 100, ill.

3997. **Johnson, J. P.** *Aboriginal rock chippings on the farm 'Blauw-boschdrift Herbert, South Africa.'* Man, **7**, 88, 1907, 145, ill.

3998. **Jorgensen, B.** and **V.** *Ancient Bushman brushwork.* Nat. hist., **58**, 1949, 56–63, ill.

3999. **McMillan, Elsie,** and **R. E. G. Armattoe.** *Bushman rock paintings; early civilizations in parts of Africa.* W.A.R., **17**, 227, Aug. 1946, 913–15, ill.

4000. **Mannsfeld, E.** *Katalog der Felsbilder-Kopien der Expedition, 1928–30.* Mitt. Forschungsinst. Kultur-morph., Frankfurt a.M., 1930, 96–170, ill. (Engravings, p. 153.)

4001. **Nelson, N. C.** *South African rock pictures.* Pp. 12, ill.

4002. **Peringuey, L.** *On rock engravings of animals and the human figure, the work of South African aborigines, and their relation to similar ones found in Northern Africa.* Trans. S. A. phil. soc., **16**, 1905–7, 401–2, ill.

4003. —— *On rock engravings of animals and the human figure, found in South Africa.* Trans. S.A. phil. soc., **18**, 1907–9, 401–19, ill.

4004. **Rosenthal, Eric,** and **A. J. H. Goodwin.** 1953. *Cave artists of South Africa.* Pp. 80, ill. Cape Town: A. A. Balkema.

4005. **Rudner, I.** and **J.** *Who were the artists?* S. Afr. archaeol. bull., **14**, 55, Sept. 1959, 106–8.

4006. **Schapera, Isaac.** 1925. *Some stylistic affinities of Bushman art.* S. Afr. J. sci., **22**, 504–15. (*Rev.*: Anthropos, **22**, 625.)

4007. **Schofield, J. F.** *The age of the rock paintings of South Africa.* S. Afr. archaeol. bull., **3**, no. 12, 1948, 79–88.

4008. —— *L'âge des peintures rupestres du sud del 'Afrique.* L'Anthropo-logie, **53**, 1/2, avr. 1949, 20–32.

4009. **South Africa: Dept. of the Interior: Bureau of Archaeology.** 1936. *Prehistoric rock paintings and engravings; recorded sites to August 1936.* Pretoria: Central Mapping Office.

4010. **South African Archaeological Society.** 1961. *Rock paintings in Africa.* s.p., 66 col. pl., bibl. Cape Town: S. African Archaeo-logical Society.

4011. **Stow, G. W.,** and **Dorothea F. Bleek.** 1930. *Rock paintings in South Africa.* Pp. xxviii, ill., map. London: Methuen. (72 col. pl. copied by Stow in 1867 and sent to Cape by him in 1874 and finally purchased after Stow's death by Miss L. C. Lloyd in 1882. Most of the paintings from between Aliwal North and Mafeteng, but others from north and south of this area.)

4012. **Tongue, Helen M.** 1909. *Bushman paintings.* Pp. 47, ill. Oxford: Clarendon Press.

4013. **van Riet Lowe, Clarence.** 1936. *Prehistoric rock paintings and engravings (in South Africa).* Official Year-Book of the Union of South Africa, no. 17, 1934–5. Pp. 34–38, 9 figs. Pretoria: Government Printer.

4014. —— *Prehistoric rock paintings.* S. Afr. J. sci., 1937, 13.

4015. —— 1938. *Conventionalised human forms and related figures in the early art of Africa.* Pp. 16, ill. Pretoria: Bureau of Archaeology, Archaeological Series, no. 1.

4016. —— *Prehistoric art in South Africa.* Bureau of Archaeology, Union of South Africa, 1941, Archaeological Series, no. 5.

4017. —— *Colour in prehistoric rock paintings.* S. Afr. archaeol. bull., **1**, no. 1, 1945, 13–18. (Contains Breuil's classification of the principal colours in prehistoric rock paintings.)

4018. —— *The possible dawn of art in South Africa.* S. Afr. J. sci., 1946, 6.

4019. —— *Shields in South African rock paintings.* S. Afr. archaeol. bull., **1**, part 2, 1946.

4020. —— *Rock paintings of marine animals in the interior of South Africa.* S. Afr. archaeol. bull., **2**, no. 6, 1947.

4021. —— *L'âge et l'origine des peintures rupestres d'Afrique du Sud.* L'Anthropologie, **54**, 1950, 5–6, 421–31.

4022. —— 1952. *The distribution of prehistoric rock engravings and paint-ings in South Africa.* Union of South Africa: Dept. of Education, Arts and Science, Archaeological Survey, Archaeological Series 7.

4023. —— *Prehistoric art in South Africa; an explanation of a map and index of sites.* Pp. 38, map. Pretoria: Government Printer.

4024. —— *The cave of hearts.* S. Afr. archaeol. bull., Mar. 1954.

4025. **Willcox, A. R.** *Stone cultures and prehistoric art in South Africa.* S. Afr. J. Sci., **53**, 68–71.

4026. —— *The shaded polychrome paintings of South Africa, their distribu-tion, origin and age.* S. Afr. archaeol. bull. (Cape Town), **10**, 37, Mar. 1955, 10–14, ill., map.

4027. —— *The classification of rock paintings.* S. Afr. J. sci., **53** (16), Nov. 1957, 417–19.

4028. —— *Australian and South African rock art compared.* S. Afr. archaeol. bull., **14**, 55, Sept. 1959, 97–98.

4029. —— 1963. *The rock art of South Africa.* Pp. 96, ill. Johannes-burg: Nelson.

4030. **Woldmann, Käthe.** *Felsmalereien der Buschmänner in Südafrika.* Gäa Sophia. Jahrbuch der naturwissenschaften Sektion der freien Hochschule für Geisteswissenschaften am Goetheaneum (Dornach), **2**, 1927, 1–22.

TECHNIQUES

4031. **Anderson, Andrew Arthur.** 1887. *Twenty-five years in a wagon in the gold regions of Africa.* 2 vols. Vol. 1, pp. vi + 253, ill. Vol. 2, pp. x + 307, ill. London: Chapman & Hall.

4032. **Balfour, Henry.** *Flint-engraved pottery from the ruins at Khami and Dholo Dholo.* Man, **6**, 80, 1906, 17–19.

4033. **Hewitt, J. J.** *Pottery from the Eastern Province.* S. Afr. archaeol. bull., **9**, 34, June 1954, 38.

4034. **Laidler, P. W.** *Hottentot and Bushman pottery of South Africa.* S. Afr. J. sci., **26**, 1929, 758–86, pl.

4035. —— *Localized developments in the potter's art of the pre-Bantu races of South Africa.* S. Afr. J. sci., **28**, 1931, 512–20, ill.

4036. —— *The Bantu potting industry and its impacts on other native potting industries in South Africa.* S. Afr. J. sci., **29**, 1932, 778–91, ill.

4037. —— *South African native ceramics; their characteristics and classifi-cation.* Trans. R. soc. S. Africa, **26**, 2, 1938, 93–172.

4038. **Schofield, J. F.** *Pottery from Natal, Zululand, Bechuanaland and South-West Africa.* S. Afr. J. sci., **35**, 1938, 382–95.

4039. —— *A preliminary study of the pottery of the Bantu tribes of the Union of South Africa.* S. Afr. J. sci., **39**, Jan. 1943, 256–81.

4040. —— 1948. *Primitive pottery; an introduction to South African ceramics, prehistoric and protohistoric.* Pp. 220. Claremont C.P.: South African Archaeological Society.

4041. **Stanley, G. H.** *Some products of native iron smelting.* S. Afr. J. sci., **28** (1931), 131–4, ill.

4042. —— *The composition of some prehistoric South African Bronzes with notes on the methods of analysis.* S. Afr. J. sci., **26**, 1929, 44–49.

4043. —— *Primitive metallurgy in South Africa; Some products and their significance.* S. Afr. J. sci., **26**, 1929, 732–48, ill.

4044. **Thompson, Louis C.** *The Mu-Tsuku.* S. Afr. J. sci., **35**, 1938, 396–8, ill. (Copper ingots.)

4045. **Wainwright, G. A.** *The coming of iron to some African peoples.* Man, **42**, 61, Sept.–Oct. 1942, 103–8; **43**, 67, July–Aug. 1943, p. 88; **43**, 87, Sept.–Oct. 1943, 114–16. (Basuto, Bergdama, Ovambo, Ondulu.)

UTENSILS, TOOLS AND WEAPONS; MISCELLANEOUS

4046. **Shaw, E. M.** *South African native snuff-boxes.* Ann. S. Afr. mus., **24** (5), 32, ill.

4047. —— *Native pipes and smoking in South Africa.* Ann. S. Afr. mus., 1938, 24, ill.

AFRICAN ART TODAY

4048. **Anon.** *Illustrated article on an exhibition of African art.* South African Panorama, 1963, 19–21, ill.

4049. **Battiss, Walter.** *New art and old art in South Africa.* Studio (London), **144**, 714, Sept. 1952, 66–75, ill.

4050. **Schönland, S.** *Arts and crafts of the natives of South Africa.* Addresses, Brit. and S.A. Ass.(Johannesburg), **3**, 1905, 130–46.

4051. **Shaw, E. M.** *South African Bantu art and crafts.* Hellmann, E., and L. Abrahams, Handbook on race relations in South Africa', chap. XXX, 1949, 628–45.

4052. **Walton, James.** 1949. *Craftwork for African schools.* Pp. 32, ill. Cape Town: Juta.

TRANSVAAL

4053. **Fouché, Leo.** 1937. *Mapungwe; ancient Bantu civilisation on the Limpopo.* Pp. xiv + 183, ill., maps.

4054. **van Riet Lowe, Clarence.** *The Vaal river chronology; an up-to-date summary.* S. Afr. Archaeol. bull., **7**, 88, 13.

4055. —— *Mapungubwe; first report on excavations in Northern Transvaal.* Antiquity, Sept. 1936, 10.

FIGURES AND MASKS

4056. **Braunholtz, H. J.** *Divining bowl from the Bavenda, South Africa.* B.M.Q., **17**, 1952, 20–21, ill.

4057. **Junod, H. A.** *La divination au moyen de tablettes d'Ivoire chez les Pédis du Sud de l'Afrique.* Bull. Schweiz. Ges. f. Anthrop. and Ethnol., 1924–5, 11–12.

BUILDINGS AND FURNITURE

4058. **Walton, James.** *Carved wooden doors of the Bavenda.* Man, **54**, 58, Mar. 1954, 43–46, ill.

CLOTHING AND ADORNMENT

4059. **Bartels, M.** *Über die kostbaren Perlen der Kasutho in Transvaal.* Verh. Gesell. Anthrop. (Berlin), 1891, 399–401.

4060. **Beck, H. C.** 1937. *Report on beads.* Fouché, Leo, Mapungwe, pp. 103–13, ill.

ROCK ART

4061. **Holm, E.** *Felsbilder im Transvaal-Gebiet, Süd-Afrika.* Ipek, **19**, 1954–9, 77–84, ill.

4062. **Hübner, A.** *Eingrabungen von Thiergestalten in Schiefer auf 'Gestoppte Fontein' Farm von van Zijl bei Hartebeestfontein in Transvaal.* Z. f. Ethnol., **3**, 1871, 51–53, ill.

4063. **Johannesburg; The Star.** *Footmarks in the rock.* (In the N'Gelele valley, Northern Transvaal.) The Star, 1 Oct. 1928.

4064. **Pijper, C.** *Some engraved stones of the Lydenburg district . . . the occurrence of 'cup-and-ring' markings in South Africa.* Rep. S.A. ass. adv. sci., **15**, 1918, 416–17, ill.

4065. —— *A prehistoric rock sculpture from the north-eastern Transvaal.* Trans. R. soc. S.A., **9**, 1921, 195, ill.

4066. **Transvaal—Rock Paintings.** *Rock paintings of the Northern Transvaal.* By Rev. Noel Roberts. Rept. 14th annual meeting, South African ass., Maritzburg, 1916 (1917), 568–74, ill.

4067. **Slack, Lina M.** 1962. *Rock engravings from Driekops Eiland and other sites south-west of Johannesburg.* Compiled by P. A. Bennett: with an introductory paper by C. van Riet Lowe. Pp. 103, bibl., ill., map. London: Centaur Press.

4068. **Swierstra, C. J.** *Note on four rock engravings found in the Transvaal.* Ann. Trans. mus., **1**, 1908–9, 65–70, ill.

4069. **van Riet Lowe, Clarence.** *Prehistoric rock engravings in the Vaal river basin.* Trans. R. soc. of S. Africa, **24**, part 3, 1937, 8, ill.

4070. —— *The Makapan caves; an archaeological note.* S. Afr. J. sci., 1938, 11.

4071. —— *Further notes on the Makapan caves.* S. Afr. J. of sci., 1943, 6.

4072. —— *Prehistoric rock engravings in the Krugersdorp-Rustenburg area of the Transvaal.* S. Afr. J. sci., **41**, Feb. 1945, 329–44, ill.

4073. —— 1948. *Cave breccias in the Makapan valley.* Robert Broom Communications. Pp. 4, ill.

TECHNIQUES

4074. **Giesekke, E. D.** *Die Eisenindustrie der Bavenda.* Brücke, **7**, 4, 1930, 5–9.

4075. **Paver, F. R.** *Trade and mining in the pre-European Transvaal.* S. Afr. J. sci., **30**, 1933, 603–11.

4076. **Van der Lith, A. A.** *Die keramiek van die Venda.* J. social res., **13**, Dec. 1962, 71–82, bibl.

4077. **van Warmelo, J.** *Multi-mouthed pots from the Northern Transvaal.* Nada, **21**, 1944, 45–47, ill.

4077a. **Wagner, P.,** and **H. S. Gordon.** *Further notes on ancient bronze smelters in the Waterberg District, Transvaal.* S. Afr. J. sci., **26**, 1929, 563–74, ill.

ORANGE FREE STATE

See also 4145.

ROCK ART

4078. **Breuil, Henri.** *Sea animals amongst the prehistoric rock paintings of Ladybrand* (with addendum on 'Prehistoric fishing scenes' by Walter W. Battiss). S. Afr. J. sci., **41**, Feb. 1945, 353–60, ill.

4079. **Bushman Paintings Committee.** Report of the Committee. 1909. Pp. 9. MS. in possession of R. B. Young.

4079a. —— Report of the Bushman Paintings Committee of the Transvaal on the Bushman paintings and petroglyphs in the Orange Free State. December 1910. Pp. 18. MS. in possession of R. B. Young.

4080. **Leslie, T. N.** *The stone-age industry of Vereeniging.* (Pictographs of animals or geometric figures on sandstone, crudely pecked, the former mostly in outline.) S. Afr. J. sci., **23**, 1926, 867–8, ill.

4081. **Pöch, R.** *Buschmanns Gravierungen auf Vereeniging.* Anz. Akad. Wiss. (Wien), 1909, 130.

4082. **Wells, L. H.** *Marine animals in a rock painting near Fouriesberg, O.F.S.* S. Afr. J. sci., **42**, 1946.

NATAL

4083. **Mayr, Le R. P. Fr.** *The Zulu Kafirs of Natal.* Anthropos, **2**, 1907, 633–45, ill.

4084. **Snegirev, I. L.** (Trans.). *Zulu folktales 'Izinganekwane'.* Trans. into Russian by I. L. Snegirev. Illustrated by N. A. Ushin. Pp. 246, ill. Leningrad and Moscow: U.S.S.R. Academy of Sciences (Series Languages and Literature of Africa).

4085. **Vélcich, G.** *Pipes the Xhosa smoke.* baNtu, **9**, 11, Nov. 1962, 670–2, ill.

4086. **von Luschan, F.** *Über Buschmann-Malereien in den Drakensbergen.* Z. f. Ethnol. (heft 5), 1908, 20, ill.

CLOTHING AND ADORNMENT

4087. **Chubb, E. C.** *The Zulu brass armlet 'Ingxota'; a badge of distinction.* Man, **36**, no. 251, 1936, 185, ill.

4088. **Malan, B. D.** *Perforated stone disks from Natal.* S. Afr. J. sci., **53**, 1956, 89–94.

4089. **Mayr, F.** *Language of colours among the Zulus expressed by their bead-work ornaments, and notes on their personal adornment and clothing.* Ann. Natal Mus., **1**, 1907, 159–65, ill.

ROCK ART

4090. **Chubb, E. C.,** and **J. F. Schofield.** *Rock engravings at Otto's Bluff, Natal.* S. Afr. J. sci., **29**, 1932, 678–80, ill.

4091. **Malan, B. D.** *Zulu rock engravings in Natal.* S. Afr. archaeol. bull. (Cape Town), **10**, 39, 1955, 67–72.

4092. —— *Old and new rock engravings in Natal, South Africa; a Zulu game.* Antiquity, **31**, 1957, 153–4, ill.

4093. **Mason, A. Y.** *Rock paintings in the Cathkin Park Area.* Natal Bantu studies, **7**, 1933, 131–58, ill.

4094. **van der Riet, Joyce** and **Mollie.** 1940. *More rock paintings in South Africa from the coastal belt between Albany and Piquetberg.* Pp. xx + 56, ill., map. London: Methuen.

4095. **van Riet Lowe, Clarence.** *Rock paintings near Cathedral Peak.* S. Afr. archaeol. bull., **4**, 13, 1949.

4096. **Willcox, A. R.** 1956. *Rock paintings of the Drakensberg, Natal and Griqualand East.* Pp. 96, ill. London: Parrish.

CAPE PROVINCE

4097. **Kolben, Peter.** 1731. *The present state of the Cape of Good Hope.* Pp. xviii + 365, ill. London: Innys.

4098. **le Vaillant, François.** 1790. *Travels from the Cape of Good Hope into the interior parts of Africa.* 2 vols. Vol. 1, pp. 429–30. Vol. 2, pp. 122–30. London: Lane.

FIGURES AND MASKS

4099. **Power, J. H.** *Two sculptured heads in the McGregor Museum, Kimberley.* S. Afr. archaeol. bull., **6** (no. 22), 1951, 54–55, ill.

ROCK ART

4100. **Bartels, M.** *Copien von Felszeichnungen der Buschmänner.* (Copies made at Pniel.) Z. f. Ethnol., **24**, 1892, 26–27, ill.

4101. **Fredoux, J.** *Native sculptures on the Hart River.* Cape monthly magazine, **8**, 1860, 48–50.

4102. **Goodwin, A. J. H.** *Vosburg; its petroglyphs.* Ann. S. Afr. mus., 1936, 163–210, ill.

4103. **Hewitt, J.** *Discoveries in a Bushman cave at Tafelberg Hall.* Trans. R. soc. S. Africa, **19**, 1931, 185–96, ill.

4104. —— *Artefacts from Melkhoutboom.* S. Afr. J. sci., **28**, 1931, 540–8, ill.

4105. —— and **P. Stapleton.** *On paintings and artefacts in rock shelters near Cala.* Records of the Albany Museum, Grahamstown, **4**, 1931, 1–63, ill.

4106. **Huss, B.,** and **Otto.** 1925. *The origin of the Bushmen paintings at the Kei-River.* S. Afr. J. sci., **22**, 496–503, ill.

4107. **Rogers, A. W.** *Rock carvings at Inchwanin.* Rep. geol. com. (Cape Town), **12**, 1907, 72–73. (*Vide* Lang, V., Wonderful South African Stone Age sculptures of mastodons.)

4108. **Schweiger, Albert.** *Neu entdeckte Buschmannmalereien in der Cape-Provinz, Südostafrika.* Anthropos, **8**, 1913, 652–69, 1010–25, ill.

4109. **Sharples, W. G.** *Rock engravings near Beaufort West.* Trans. R. soc. of S. Africa, **24** (4), 1937, 2, ill.

4110. **Tredgold, M. A.** *Bushman paintings in the Citrusdal area and in the Cold Bokkeveld.* S. Afr. archaeol. bull., **10**, 1955, 124–5, ill.

AFRICAN ART TODAY

4111. **Lewis, David.** *Cape Malay art and crafts.* E. Hellmann, and L. Abrahams, Handbook on race relations in South Africa, chap. xxxi, 1949, 646–50.

BRITISH PROTECTORATES

BECHUANALAND

4112. **Brown, John Tom.** 1926. *Among the Bantu nomads.* Pp. 272, ill., map. London: Seeley Service.

4113. **Meiring, A. J. D.** *MaSarwa engraved egg-shell.* S. Afr. J. sci., **40**, 1943, 328–9, ill.

4114. —— *The significance of the engravings on MaSarwa egg-shells (Kalahari).* Fort Hare Papers, **1**, 1, June 1945, 3–8, and **5**, Feb. 1951, 255–6, ill.

4115. —— *Some more egg-shell engravings (Bechuanaland).* Fort Hare Papers, **1** (5), 1951, 255–6, ill.

4116. **Schofield, J. F.** *Pottery from Bechuanaland and Rhodesia.* Trans. R. soc. S. Africa, **30**, 1, 1943, 1–16.

4117. **Walton, James.** *The material culture of the Southern Sotho.* Afr. music soc., Newsletter, **1** (3), 1950, 28–29.

ROCK ART

4118. **Arnold, G.,** and **Neville Jones.** *Notes on the Bushman cave at Bambata, Matopos.* Proc. Rhod. sci. ass., **17**, part 1, June 1918–19.

4119. **Balsan, F.** *Découverte d'une oeuvre très ancienne dans Part Bushman à l'intérieur du Mont Tsodillo-Femelle au désert du Kalahari.* J. Soc. africanistes, **23**, 1/2, 1953, 139–43, ill., map.

4120. **Dornan, S. S.** 1925. *Pygmies and bushmen of the Kalahari.* Pp. 318, ill., map. London: Seeley Service.

4121. **Jones, John David Rheinalt,** and **C. M. Doke.** 1937. *Bushmen of the Southern Kalahari.* Pp. vii + 283, bibl., ill. Johannesburg: Univ. of Witwatersrand.

4122. **Maudit, Jacques.** 1954. *Kalahari; La vie des Bochimans.* Pp. 87, map. Paris: F. Nathan.

4123. **Molyneux, A. J. C.** *Note on rock gravings at Metsang, Bechuanaland Protectorate.* Rep. S.A. ass. adv. sci., **17**, 1920, 206.

4124. **Pöch, R.** *Bushman carvings in rock (at Metsing) in the Bechuanaland Protectorate.* Mafeking mail, 13 Apr., 1909.

4125. —— *Buschmannsgravierungen (Fussspuren) von Machen bei Mochudi . . .* Anz. Akad. Wiss. (Wien), 1909, 245–8.

4126. —— *Buschmannsgravierungen von Fourteen-Streams. Versuch die sogenannten 'geometrischen Figuren' zu erklären.* Anz. Akad. Wiss. (Wien), 1909, 249.

4127. **Schönland, S.** *On some supposed Bushman inscriptions and rock-carvings found in Bechuanaland.* Trans. S.A. phil. soc. (Cape Town), **9**, 1895–7, xix–xx.

4128. **Stow, G. W.** *The Bushmen* (sculptors of Griqualand West). The Athenaeum, 4 Aug. 1877, 151–2.

4129. **van Riet Lowe, Clarence.** *A preliminary account of the Wonderwerk Cave; Kuruman District.* S. Afr. J. sci., 1940, 13.

4130. **Wilman, M.** *The engraved rock of Loë, Bechuanaland Protectorate.* Rep. S.A. ass. adv. sci., **15**, 1918, 531–4, ill.

4131. —— *The engraved rock of Kopong and Loë, Bechuanaland Protectorate.* Rep. S.A. ass. adv. sci., **16**, 1919, 443–6, ill.

4132. —— 1933. *The rock engravings of Griqualand West and Bechuanaland, S. Africa.* xii + 77 and 70 pp. of pl., map. Cambridge: Deighton Bell & Co. Kimberley: Alex. MacGregor Museum. (Reviewed in *Africa*, vol. VII, no. 4, 1934.)

BASUTOLAND

4133. **How, Marion Walsham.** 1962. *The mountain Bushmen of Basutoland.* Pp. 63, ill. Pretoria: J. L. van Schaik.

4134. **Lagden, Sir Godfrey Yeatman.** 1909. *The Basutos.* 2 vols. Vol. 1, pp. xvi + 337, ill., maps. Vol. 2, pp. xii + 339–690, ill., maps. London: Hutchinson.

BUILDINGS AND FURNITURE

4135. **Walton, James.** 1956. *African village.* Pp. xii + 170, bibl., ill. Pretoria: J. L. van Schaik.

4136. —— *Patterned walling in African folk building.* J. Afr. hist., **1** (1), 1960, 19–30.

See also 3947a.

ROCK ART

4137. **Ellenberger, Victor.** *Peintures rupestres du Basutoland (Afrique du Sud).* C.R. sommaires séances inst. franç. anthrop., **3**, janv. 1947–déc. 1949, 31–33.

4138. **Cawston, F. G.** *A consideration of the Bushmen's paintings at Quthing.* S. Afr. J. sci., **28**, 1932, 470–1, ill.

4139. **Orpen, J. M.** *A glimpse into the mythology of the Maluti Bushman.* (With remarks by W. H. I. Bleek on the paintings at Mango-long.) Cape monthly magazine, **9**, 1874, 1–13.

4140. **Walton, James.** *Early Ba-Fokeng rock shelter dwellings at Ntlo-Kholo.* Afr. Stud., **10**, 1951, 83–86, ill.

4141. —— *Cave painting techniques in Basutoland.* Africana notes and news (Johannesburg), **11**, 1, Dec. 1953, 19–20.

4142. —— *The rock paintings of Basutoland.* Third Pan-African congress on prehistory, Livingstone, 1955, 277–81, bibl., ill.

4143. **Westphal, E. O. J.** *Notes about some rock paintings from Peka, Basutoland.* Rev. Inst. Super. Estudos Ultramar. (Lisbon), **6**, nos. 1–3, 1956, 111–16, ill.

4144. **Wilman, M.** *Notes on some Bushman paintings in the Thaba Bosigo district, Basutoland.* Rep. S. Afr. ass. adv. sci., **7**, 1910, 417–21.

UTENSILS, TOOLS AND WEAPONS; MISCELLANEOUS

4145. **Walton, James.** *Pestles, mullers and querns from the Orange Free State and Basutoland.* S. Afr. archaeol. bull., **8**, 1953, 32–39, ill.

AFRICAN ART TODAY

4146. **Damant, C. G.** 1951. *Samuel Makoanyane (Suto clay-modeller).* Pp. 35, ill. Morija Sesuto Book Depot.

4147. —— *A Basuto sculptor (Note on Samuel Makoanyane).* Africa **22**, 1952, 79.

SWAZILAND

4148. **Marwick, B. A.** *The Swazi; an ethnographic account.* Cambridge, 1940.

4149. **Myburgh, A. C.** 1949. *The tribes of the Barberton District.* Pp. 146, ill., map. Pretoria: Government Printer. (Union of S. Africa: Dept. of Native Affairs: Ethnological publications, no. 25.)

CLOTHING AND ADORNMENT

4150. **Twala, Regina G.** *Beads as regulating the social life of the Zulu and Swazi.* Afr. stud., **10**, 1951, 113–23, ill.

4151. —— *Umhlanga (reed) ceremony of the Swazi maidens.* Afr. stud., **11**, 3, Sept. 1952, 93–104.

SOUTH-WEST AFRICA

4152. **Bjerre, Jens.** 1960. *Kalahari.* Pp. 226, ill. London: Michael Joseph.

4153. **Delachaux, Th.** *Ethnographie de la région du Cunène.* Bull. soc. Neuchâtel. géogr., **44** (2), 1936, 1–108, ill.

4154. **Lebzelter, Viktor.** 1934. *Eingeborenen Kulturen in Südwest-und Südafrika.* Pp. x + 306, ill. Leipzig: Hiersemann. (Wiss. Ergebnisse einer Forschungsreise nach Süd-und Südwestafrika in . . . 1926–1928.)

4155. **Schultze, Leonhard.** 1907. *Aus Namaland und Kalahari.* Pp. xiv + 752, bibl., ill., maps. Jena: Gustav Fischer.

4156. **Schwarz, E. H. L.** 1928. *The Kalahari and its native races.* Pp. 244, ill., maps. London: Witherby.

FIGURES AND MASKS

4157. **Mullen, Ben H.** *Fetishes from Landana, South-West Africa.* Man, **5**, no. 59, 1905, 102–4, ill.

4158. **Péringuey, L.** *Bushman sticks decorated on intaglio and poker-work, a note on the decorative skill of the Bush people and other aborigines.* Trans. R. soc. S. Afr., **3**, 1913, xv–xvi.

CLOTHING AND ADORNMENT

4159. **Lehmann, F. Rudolf.** *Die Herkunft der heutigen Kopftracht der Herero-Frauen.* Sociologus (Berlin), N.F., **4**, 2, 1954, 170–3.

ROCK ART

4160. **Bauer, E.** *Auf der Suche nach Buschmannzeichnungen.* Monats Magazin (Windhuk), **1** (4), 1930, 150–7.

4161. **Breuil, Henri.** *Carbon testing and South-West African paintings.* S. Afr. archaeol. bull., **9**, 34.

4162. —— *Remains of large animal paintings in South-West Africa, older than all the other frescoes.* S. Afr. archaeol. bull. (Cape Town), **4**, 13, 1949.

4163. —— *Les roches peintes d'Afrique australe, leurs auteurs et leur âge.* L'Anthropologie, **53**, 5/6, janv. 1950, 377–406.

4164. —— *The age and the authors of the painted rocks of Austral Africa.* S. Afr. archaeol. bull., **4**, 13, 1949.

4165. —— Rock paintings of Southern Africa. Vol. 1. 1955. *The white lady of the Brandberg.* Pp. 31, ill. London: Trianon Press.

4166. —— Vol. 2. 1957. *Philipp Cave.* Pp. 21, ill. London: Trianon Press.

4167. —— Vol. 3. 1959. *The Tsisab ravine.* Pp. 53, ill., maps. London: Trianon Press.

4168. —— Vol. 4. 1960. *Anibib and Omandumba and other Eronga sites.* Pp. 39, ill., maps. London: Trianon Press.

4169. **Drews.** *Erkundung der Hunsberge. (Buschmannzeichnungen bei Arib.)* Mitt. Schutz., **23**, 1910, 161–3, ill., map.

4170. **Eckenbrecher, M. von.** 1909. *Was Afrika mir gab und nahm.* Pp. x + 242, ill., map. Berlin. (Engraved spoors of animals at Brandberg, p. 180. Edition V.)

4171. **Flaskamp.** *Zwischen Otawi und Grootfontein.* 11. Busch-mannzeichnungen bei Ghaub-Nabis. D. Kolonialblatt, **19**, 1908, 289–91. Windhuk, Windhuker Nachrichten, 16 Mai 1908.

4172. **Halbach, Axel J.** *Auf den Spuren vergangener Kulturen in Südwest-Afrika.* Neues Afr., **6**, 10, Oct. 1964, 346–8, ill.

4173. **Hoesch, Walter.** *Aus der Steinzeitkunst Südwestafrikas.* Ipek, **14**, 1940, 206–7, ill.

4174. **Jochmann, H.** *Die Buschmannzeichnungen in Deutsch Südwest-afrika.* Die Woche, **12**, 1910, 113–16, ill.

4175. **Johnson, Townley,** and **Others.** 1959. *Rock paintings of the South-West Cape.* Pp. 38, ill., map. Cape Town: Nasionale Boekhandel.

4176. **Link, Q.** *Buschmanzeichnungen und Tropfsteinhöhle bei Farm Ghaub in S. W. Afrika.* Jambo, **7**, 1927.

4177. **Mason, Revil.** *Stone Age art in South Africa . . . paintings in the Brandberg and Waterberg.* Pp. (12), ill., map. (Archaeological Survey of the Union of South Africa, Dept. of Education.)

4178. —— s.d. *New prehistoric paintings in the Brandberg, South West Africa and the Waterberg, Northern Transvaal.* s.p., ill. (some col.).

4179. **Moszeik, Otto.** 1910. *Die Malereien der Buschmänner in Südafrika.* Pp. 100, ill. Berlin: Dietrich Reimer.

4180. **Obermaier, H.,** and **H. Kühn.** 1930. *Buschmannkunst. Felsmalereien aus Südwest-Afrika. Nach den Aufnahmen von Richard Maack.* Pp. xii + 70–78. Berlin: Brandsche Verlagsbuch-handlung. (Oxford Univ. Press: English version.)

4181. **Passarge, S.** 1907. *Die Buschmanner der Kalahari.* Pp. 144, ill., map. Berlin: E. Vohsen. (Skulpturen und Malereien, p. 94; paintings at Tschorilobergen, pl. 2.)

4182. **Péringuey, L.** *Casts of rock gravings.* Rep. S.A. mus., 1909, 6.

4182a.—— *Rock gravings from the South-West Protectorate.* Rep. S.A. mus., 1918, 4.

4182b.—— *Rock gravings (casts) from Ghaub, South-West Africa.* Rep. S.A. mus., 1919, 16, ill.

4183. —— *Casts of petroglyphs (rock gravings) taken in the neighbourhood of Gobabis, South-West Africa.* Rep. S.A. mus., 1922, 6.

4184. **'Phagocyte.'** *Bushman paintings.* The State, Dec. 1909, 6.

4185. **Pöch, R.** *Buschmanns-Gravierungen auf Stampried bei'Oas.* Anz. Akad. Wiss. (Wien), 1908, 320–3.

4186. —— *Über die Kunst der Buschmänner.* Mitt. anthrop. gesell. (Wien) (1911/12), 1912, 13–16.

4186a.—— *Über die Kunst der Buschmänner.* KorrBl. deuts. gesell. Anthrop., **42**, 1911, 67–71.

4187. —— *Abklatsche alter Petroglyphen aus (Stampried) Südafrika.* Mitt. anthrop. gesell. (Wien), **47**, 1917, Sitzber. (54–56), ill.

4188. **Squire, W. A.** *The Bushmen and their art.* A paper read before the British Assoc. for the Advancement of Science. Aug. 1905, 4.

4189. **Staudinger, P.** *Einige kurze Bemerkungen über Buschmann-malereien und Felseinritzungen.* (Reviews Luschan's papers.) Z. f. Ethnol., **58**, 1926, 58–61.

4190. **Steyn, W.** and **S.** *The hunter paints; some biological considerations regarding prehistoric art and people.* Cimbebasia (Windhoek), **3**, Dec. 1962, 15–30, bibl., ill.

4191. **Viereck, Albert.** N.D. *South-West African rock paintings-Südwest-Afrikanische Felsmalereien.* Pp. 80, ill. Windhoek: South-West Africa Scientific Society.

4192. **von Luschan, Felix.** *Bildende Kunst bei den Buschmännern.* Die Umschau, **11**, 1907, 4–9, ill.

4193. —— *Peintures sur rochers des Boschimans.* L'Homme préhist., **7**, 1909, no. 2., ill.

4194. —— 1923. *Buschmann-Einritzungen auf Strausseneiern.* Z. f. Ethnol., **55**, S. 31–40.

4195. **von Sydow, Eckart.** *Probleme der Buschmannmalereien.* Arch. f. Anthrop., **53**, N.F. **25**, 1939, 101–11.

4196. **Walton, James.** *South-West Africa rock paintings and the triple-curved bow.* S. Afr. archaeol. bull., **9**, 36, Dec. 1954, 131–4.

4197. **Weyersberg, M.** *Buschmann Malereien in Südwest.* Journal S.-W. African Scientific Society, **5**, 1929–31, 46–54, ill.; 55–63, English translation.

UTENSILS, TOOLS AND WEAPONS; MISCELLANEOUS

4198. **Shaw, E. M.** *Ovambo knives.* Ann. South African museum, 1938, 24, ill.

CATALOGUES AND GUIDES TO MUSEUMS, EXHIBITIONS AND COLLECTIONS

GENERAL

4199. **Adandé, Alexandre.** *L'Impérieuse nécessité des musées africains.* Diop, A., 1951, 194–8.

4200. **Fagg, William B.** *International congress of African culture, Salisbury, 1–12 August 1962.* J. modern Afr. stud., **1**, 1, Mar. 1963, 105–7.

4201. **Jones, Neville,** and **Others.** *Symposium; The colonial museum.* Rhodes-Livingstone J., **4**, Dec. 1945, 33–84.

4202. **Kirk-Greene, Anthony H. M.** *Africa through the eyes of some museums in the United States.* Curator (Amer. mus. nat. hist.), **3**, 3, 1960, 242–6.

4203. **Lem, F. H.** *Pour un musée d'art africain.* Ann. col., 16 Sept. 1938. Paris.

4204. **Monod, Th.** *Autour de l'Institut d'Afrique. Un musée; ce qu'il est, ce qu'il n'est pas.* Jalons, **16**, déc. 1942, 27–32.

4205. —— *L'Académie africaine des arts plastiques.* Notes afr. I.F.A.N., 1950, 100.

4206. **Museums Assoc.: Africa: Ciroma, Hallam L.** *Formation of the Museums Association of tropical Africa.* Man, **61**, 171, Aug. 1961, 142–3.

4207. **Olbrechts, F. M.** *Kleine musea, en hoe ze te beheeren.* Kongo-Overzee, **4**, 4, 1938, 185–202.

4208. **Rivière, Georges H.** *Recherches et musées d'ethnographie française depuis 1939.* Man, **47**, 2, Jan. 1947, 7–11.

4209. **von Sydow, Eckart.** *Negerkunst in europäischem Privatbesitz.* Atlantis (Berlin), 1932, **2**, S. 113–28, ill.

4210. **Wescott, Joan.** 1958. *Yoruba art in German and Swiss museums.* Pp. 43, ill. Ibadan: Ditchling Press.

4211. **West African Review.** *New era in British West Africa; the Institute of West African Arts, Industries and Social Science (at Achimota).* W.A.R., **14**, 194, Nov. 1943, 18–23.

4212. —— *Nigeria's first museum.* W.A.R., **23**, 299, Aug. 1952, 802–5, ill.

4213. **West Africa.** *Murray's monument (the new museum in Lagos).* West Afr., 4 June 1955, p. 509, ill.

4214. **West African Review.** *Preserving Nigeria's heritage; new Nigerian museum of antiquities at Lagos.* W.A.R., **28**, 355, Apr. 1957, 368–71, ill.

4215. —— *Ghana's art in museum collections.* W.A.R., **28**, 363, Dec. 1957, 1183–5, ill.

4216. —— *Preserving Ashanti culture; cultural centre at Kumasi.* W.A.R., **31**, 395, Oct. 1960, 43–45, ill.

AFRICA

4217. **African Collections: Italiaander.** (ITALIAANDER, ROLF.) *Contemporary negro painting and graphic art from Central Africa; the collection of Rolf Italiaander.* Pp. 12, ill.

4218. **African Museums.** UNESCO: *African museums (musées africains).* Museum, **16** (3), 1963, 204, ill.

4219. **Algeria: Museums.** *Algeria; Museums. Musées et collections archéologiques de l'Algerie et de la Tunisie.* 2nd series.

4220. **Angola: Museums: Museu de Angola.** (REDINHA, J.) 1955. *Museu de Angola; collecção etnografica.* Pp. xvi + 101, ill. Luanda: Imprensa Nacional.

4221. —— **Museu de Angola.** (COIMBRE, CARLOS.) *O muséu de Angola.* Bol. cultural mus. (Angola), **1**, 1960, 17–27, ill.

4222. —— **Luanda: Museu de Angola.** 1964. *Exposição etnografica de instrumentos musicais e mascaras dos povos de Angola.* Pp. 34. Luanda: Museu de Angola: Instituto de Investigação Científica de Angola.

4223. —— **Dundo Museum.** (OSÒRIO DE OLIVEIRA, J.) *Le musée d'une culture africaine (musée de Dundo).* Congo-Tervueren, **2**, 1956, 55–59, ill.

4223a. —— 1959. *Angola, Companhia de Diamantes de.* A short note on the Dundo Museum. Pp. 30, ill. Lisbon.

4224. —— **Museu do Dundo.** *Le musée du Dundo.* Rev. Cong. ill., **31**, 1959, 22–24, ill.

4225. —— **Inst. de Investigação Científica.** (SANTOS, ANA DE SOUSA.) 1963. *Catálogo da exposição de miniaturas angolanas.* Pp. 84 + 7 pl., bibl. Luanda: Instituto de Investigação Científica de Angola.

4226. **Cameroons: Museums.** (E. MESLÉ.) *Les musées de l'I.F.A.N. au Cameroun.* Ét. cam., no. spécial, 52, 1956, 53, ill.

4227. —— (ROBERT D. READ.) *Museum for Southern Cameroons.* W.A.R., **31**, 1960, 41–46, ill.

4228. **Central Africa: Museums.** (KOCHNITZKY, L.) 1952. *Shrines of Wonder.* A survey of ethnological and folk-art museums in Central Africa. Pp. 60, ill. New York: Clar & Fritts.

4229. **Congolese Republic: Coquilhatville: Nkundo Art.** (BOELAERT, E.) *Exposition d'Art Nkundo à Coquilhatville.* Brousse, 1940, 7–9.

4230. **Congo: Kingoy Museum.** (STENSTRÖM, OSCAR.) *Le musée de la mission de Kingoy.* Brousse, **4**, 1940, 10–18, ill.

4231. **Congo Belge: Léopoldville Exhibition.** (TONNOIR, R., and J. MAQUET-TOMBU.) 1935. *Catalogue de l'exposition d'art indigène de Léopoldville, July 1935.* Pp. 72. Brussels: (Includes note of makers' prices.)

4232. **Congo Belge: Museum Léopold II, Elisabethville.** 1950. *Guide provisoire du Musée Léopold II à Elisabethville.*

4233. **Dahomey: Abomey Palaces.** (MEYEROWITZ, EVA L. R.) *The museum in the royal palaces at Abomey, Dahomey.* The Burlington magazine, **84**, 495, June 1944, 147–51, ill.

4234. **Dahomey: Museum d'Abomey.** *Bulletin Information et Renseignement.* Le musée d'Abomey. bull. information et rénseignement (Dakar), 216, 1939, 192–4.

4235. —— (PAUL MERCIER.) 1952. *Les ase du Musée d'Abomey.* Pp. 98, ill. Dakar: I.F.A.N. cat. no. 7.

4236. —— (LOMBARD, J.) *Le musée historique d'Abomey.* Museum (Paris), **I** (I), 1956 (UNESCO).

4237. —— (LOMBARD, J., and P. MERCIER.) 1959. *Guide du Musée d'Abomey.* Pp. 60, ill. Porto Novo: I.F.A.N.

4238. —— (GALLOTTI, J.) *Au musée d'ethnographie; les bas-reliefs d'Abomey.* Art et décoration, **62**, 1933, 189–92.

4239. **East Africa: Museums.** (OAKLEY, K. P.) *Notes on East African museums.* Mus. J. (London), **47**, 7, 1947, 131.

4240. **Gold Coast: National Museum of the Gold Coast.** (LAWRENCE, A. W.) *The national museum of the Gold Coast.* Universitas, **I** (2), 1954, 10–12.

4241. **Guinea: Museums.** (GONÇALVES, JOSÉ J.) *O museu do ultramar e a protecção das artes plásticas negro-africanas.* Bol. cultural Guiné portug., **12**, 47, July 1957, 347–53.

4242. **Guinea: Museu da Guiné Portuguesa.** (LAMPREIA, JOSÉ D.) 1962. *Catálogo-inventário da secção de etnografia do Museu da Guiné Portuguesa.* Pp. 91 + 17, ill. Lisbon: Junta de Investigações do Ultramar.

4243. **Ivory Coast: Musée d'Abidjan.** (HOLAS, B.) 1952. *Portes sculptées du musée d'Abidjan.* Pp. 71, ill. Dakar: I.F.A.N.

4244. —— (ROBERT, H.) *A propos d'une exposition Sénoufo.* Notes afr. I.F.A.N., **79**, 1958, 83–85, ill.

4245. **Libya: Tripoli Museum.** (NARDUCCI, GUGLIELMO.) *La sezione etnografica del Museo Libico di Storia Naturale di Tripoli.* Centro di Studi Col. Ist. Col. Fascista: Atti del 3 Congresso di Studi Col. **6**, 5, Aprile 1937, 160–7, ill. (P. 167, Bibliography.)

4246. **Madagascar.** *Ethnographie malgache; arts et techniques.* (Exhibition catalogue.) Rev. de Madagascar, **24**, 1955, 9–18, ill.

4247. **Madagascar: L'Institut des hautes études de Tananarivo. Bibliothèque.** 1960. *Madagasikara; Regards vers le passé exposition 10–20 Nov. 1960.* (Catalogue.) Pp. xiv + 163, ill., map. Tananarive: Imprimérie Nationale.

4248. **Madagascar.** (MILLOT, JACQUES.) *Dépôt d'une collection malgache choisie.* Objets et mondes, **4**, 1, printemps 1964, 47–72, bibl., ill., map.

4249. —— (PETIT, GEORGES.) *Sur une collection ethnographique provenant de Madagascar.* L'Anthropologie, **33**, 1923, 357–69, ill.

4250. **Natal: Bantu Zulu Museum.** *Bantu; Zululand's growing historical museum.* Bantu, **9**, 1962, 304–6, ill.

4251. **Niger: Musée du Niger.** (TOUCET, P.) *Le musée du Niger à Niamey et le 'village nigérien'.* Notes afr. I.F.A.N., 87, 1960, 100–1, ill.

4253. **Nigeria: Museums.** *Need for a museum in Nigeria; official neglect and the dangers.* Museums journal, **40**, 1940, 174–6.

4254. —— (MURRAY, K. C.) *Nigeria's first exhibition of antiquities.* Nigeria, **26**, 1947, 401–7, ill.

4255. —— *Museum of Nigerian antiquities, traditional art and ethnography.* Museums journal, **57**, 1957, 9–14.

4256. —— (MURRAY, K. C.) *An exhibition of masks and headdresses of Nigeria at the Zwemmer Gallery, London, 21st June to 16th July, 1949.* Nigerian field, **15**, 1, Jan. 1950, 26–39, ill.

4257. —— (FAGG, B.) 1952. *Nigeria's new museum.* Times British Colonies rev., **7**, Autumn, 29, ill.

4258. **Nigeria: Antiquities Service.** *Annual report of the Antiquities Service.* Lagos.

4259. **Nigeria: Dept. of Antiquities.** (MURRAY, K. C.) S.D. *Our art treasures.* Pp. 16, ill. Lagos: Public Relations Dept.

4260. **Nigeria: Nigerian Museum: Lagos.** 1955. *The art of Ife.* Pp. 28, ill. Lagos: Public Relations Dept.

4261. —— (MURRAY, K. C.) 1959. *Preserving the past; the Nigerian Museum and its art treasures.* Pp. 32, ill. Lagos: Dept. of Antiquities.

4262. —— (MILLOT, JACQUES.) *Le Nigerian Museum de Lagos.* Objets et mondes, **1** (2), 1961, 3–16, ill., map.

4263. **Nigeria: Mbari, Ibadan.** *Nigerian folk art.* Pp. (5), ill. Ibadan: Mbari, Ibadan. (Exhibition catalogue, 16 May 1962–2 June 1962.)

4264. **Nigeria: Udi Museum.** (CHADWICK, E. R.) *A divisional museum (Udi).* Nigerian field, **17**, 1952, 84–89, ill.

4265. **Nigeria: Western Region.** 1956. *Catalogue of an exhibition of Nigerian arts and crafts* (Feb. 1956). S.P.

4266. **Northern Rhodesia: Livingstone Memorial Museum.** (CLARK, J. D.) *The inception and aim of the David Livingstone Memorial Museum, Livingstone, Northern Rhodesia.* J. Livingstone Mem. Museum, **39**, 1931, 13–17.

4267. —— 1951. *The national museum of Northern Rhodesia—The Rhodes-Livingstone Museum, 1934–51.* Pp. 44, ill. Livingstone: Gov. Printer, Lusaka.

4268. **National Museum: Southern Rhodesia.** (JONES, N.) *The Codrington collection in the National Museum.* Occ. Papers, **1**, 7, 1938, 1–6, ill.

4269. **Rhodesia Int. Congress of African Culture, Rhodes National Gallery, Salisbury, Southern Rhodesia.** *First International Congress of African culture. Held at the National Gallery, Salisbury, Southern Rhodesia, 1 August to 30 September, 1962.* S.P. Ill., map. Salisbury: Rhodes National Gallery.

4270. **Ruanda: Musée Historique et Folklorique.** 1946. *Petit séminaire; Guide du musée historique et folklorique du Ruanda.* Pp. 68, ill. Kabgayi: L. Deprimoz.

4271. **Sahara: Exhibition.** (EYDOUX, HENRI-PAUL, and OTHERS.) *L'Exposition du Sahara.* La Renaissance, **17**, 7/9, 1934, 135/79, ill.

4272. **Senegal: Dakar, I.F.A.N.** (BARDON, P.) 1948. *Collection des masques d'or Baoulé de l'I.F.A.N.* Pp. 22, ill. Dakar: I.F.A.N. cat. no. 4.

4273. **Senegal: Musée Historique de l'A.O.F. à Gorée.** 1955. *Guide du musee historique de l'A.O.F. à Goree.* Pp. 33, ill. Dakar: I.F.A.N. cat. no. 13.

4274. **Senegal: Dakar Museum.** (MOULIN, RAOUL-JEAN.) *À propos d'une exposition d'art baoulé.* Notes afr. I.F.A.N., 70, 1956, 43–46, ill.

4275. —— *Le musée dynamique de Dakar.* Afrique (Paris), no. 35, 1964, 51–53, ill.

4276. **Somalia: Garessa Museum.** (LEWIS, I. M.) *The Garessa Museum, Mogadishu.* Africa, **27**, 1957, 288.

4277. **South Africa: F. S. Malan Museum.** (LOUW, JULIET.) 1964. *Catalogue of the Estelle Hamilton-Welsh collection (housed in the F. S. Malan Museum).* Pp. x + 147. Fort Hare Univ. Press.

4278. —— **Kimberley Museum.** (DUGGAN-CRONIN, A. M.) S.D. *Bantu Gallery; catalogue of the permanent collection of native studies.* Kimberley.

4279. —— **Africana Museum: Public Library, Johannesburg.** *The A. A. Jacques collection of native head-rests.* Afr. music soc. newsletter, **1**, 4, 1951, 26–28, ill.

4280. —— (GOODWIN, A. J. H.) *Prehistoric art in South Africa.* Pamphlet introducing an exhibition, 1946.

4281. —— **Cape Town: The South African Museum.** 1955. *South African Museum, 1855–1955.* Pp. 23, ill. Cape Town: South African Museum.

4282. —— **Durban-Africana Collection.** (CAMPBELL, MISS.) *Africana collection at Durban.* Afr. stud., **2** (2), 1943, 114–15.

4283. **Sudan Collection from the Upper Nile.** (HIRSCHBERG, WALTER.) *Eine alte, fast in Vergessenheit geratene Sammlung aus dem Oberen Nilgebiet.* Weltkreis (Berlin), **3** (1), 1932.

4284. **Sudan: Khartoum.** (BALFOUR-PAUL, H. G.) 1955. *History and antiquities of Darfur.* Pp. 28, ill., maps. Khartoum: Sudan Antiquities Service.

4285. **Sudan: Leipzig Museum.** (DROST, DIETRICH.) *Die Sonderausstellung 'Völker der Republik Sudan' 1959/60.* Jb. Mus. Völkerkde. (Leipzig), **18**, 1961, 113–38, ill.

4286. **Tanganyika: King George V Museum, Dar es Salaam.** (MNTAMBO, PETRO CH.) *Founding of King George V Memorial Museum, Dar es Salaam.* T.N.R., **12**, 1941, 20–22.

4287. **Tanganyika: Bweranyange Museum.** (HALL, R. DE Z.) *A tribal museum at Bweranyange, Bukoba District.* Tanganyika notes and records, **5**, 1938, 1–4.

4288. **Tunisia: Museums.** *Tunisia; Museums. Musées et collections archéologiques de l'Algérie et de la Tunisie.* 2nd series.

4289. **Tunisia and Morocco: Exhibition.** (LINDBLOM, G.) *Ethnographical exhibition from Tunisia and Morocco.* Ethnos, **9**, 1944, 46–48, ill.

4290. **Tunisia: Bardo Museum.** 1962. (DRISS, ABDELAZIZ.) *Trésors du musée national du Bardo.* Pp. 114, ill. Bardo: S.N.E.D.

4291. **Uganda: Museums and Libraries.** (TROWELL, K. MARGARET.) 1957. *A handbook of the museums and libraries of Uganda.* Pp. 16. Kampala: Uganda Museum (Occ. Pap. 3).

AUSTRIA

4292. **Linz.** *Kunst und Kultur in Afrika.* Introd. by A. Schweeger-Hefel.

4293. **Vienna: Naturhistorischen Museum.** (LANG, KARL, and RUDOLF OLDENBURG.) *Zur Sonderausstellung der Sammlung Oldenburgs im Wiener Naturhistorischen Museum.* Völkerkunde Wien), **1**, 1925, 118–22, ill. (Westl. Kamerun, Bamum, Tikar.)

4294. **Vienna: Museum für Völkerkunde.** 1955. *Masken und Schauspiele bei fremden Völkern.* Pp. 56, ill. Vienna: Museum für Völkerkunde. (Führer durch die Sonderausstellung.)

4295. —— (BECKER-DONNER, ETTA, and OTHERS.) 1956. *Textilien aus aller Welt.* Pp. 39, ill. Vienna: Museum für Völkerkunde. (Führer durch die Sonderausstellung.)

4296. —— (SCHWEEGER-HEFEL, A.) 1960. *Kunst und Kultur in Afrika. Ausstellungs Katalog.* Pp. 32, ill. Vienna: Museum.

AMERICA (U.S.A.)

4297. **Baltimore Museum of Art.** (LOCKE, A.) 1946. *The significance of African Art.* Pp. 44, bibl., ill. Baltimore: Museum of Art. (Exhibition catalogue, 1–24 Nov.)

4298. —— 1954. *The Alan Wurtzburger collection of African sculpture* (with an essay on African negro sculpture by P. S. Wingert). Pp. 30, bibl., ill., map. Baltimore: Museum of Art.

4299. **Binghampton: Harpur College.** (HOROWITZ AND LINDSAY.) 1962. *Primitivism, folk and the primitive.* Pp. 62, ill. Binghampton, N.Y.: Harpur College. (Essays and exhibition catalogue, Harpur College, New York, 29 Mar.–18 Apr. 1962.)

4300. **Boston: Museum of Fine Art.** 1958. *Masterpieces of primitive art.* s.p., ill. Boston: Museum of Fine Art. (Exhibition, 16 Oct.–23 Nov. 1958.)

4301. *See* 4302.

4302. **Brooklyn: The Brooklyn Museum, New York.** (CULIN, STEWART.) 1923. *Primitive negro art in the Brooklyn Museum.* s.p., ill. Brooklyn: Brooklyn Museum. (Exhibition catalogue.)

4303. —— 1954. *Masterpieces of African art. Catalogue of an exhibition held at the . . . Museum, 21/10/54–2/1/55.* Pp. 54, ill. New York: Brooklyn Museum.

4304. —— (TENENBAUM, F., and E. BRYANT.) 1958. *African sculpture in the Brooklyn Museum.* Pp. 24, ill., map. Brooklyn: Brooklyn Museum.

4305. **Buffalo (Albright Art Gallery): Buffalo Fine Arts Academy.** N.D. *Catalogue of the permanent collection.*

4306. **Buffalo.** 1937. *Master bronzes selected from museums and collections in America.*

4307. —— *Buffalo; loan exhibit of African gold.* Art news, **39**, 1941, 23.

4308. —— (CLAWSON, H. P.) *By their works.* Buffalo, 1941.

4309. **Cambridge (Mass.): Peabody Museum.** 1917. *Benin antiquities in the Peabody Museum.* Harvard African Studies, 1. Pp. 130–46, ill. Cambridge, Mass.: Peabody Museum.

4310. **Chicago: Art Institute.** 1952. *Exhibition of African (sculpture) from the collection of E. Elisofon.*

4311. —— 1957. *African art; collection of Mr. and Mrs. Raymond Wielgus.* Pp. (12), ill. Chicago: Art Institute. (Exhibition catalogue, 13 Apr.–16 June 1957.)

4312. —— 1960. *Primitive art from Chicago collections.* s.p., ill.

4313. **Chicago: Field Museum of Natural History.** 1924. *General guide.* ill.

4314. **Chicago: Natural History Museum.** (PLASS, M.) 1956. *The king's day.* Pp. 24, ill. Chicago: Natural History Museum.

4315. —— (DARK, PHILIP J. C.) 1962. *The art of Benin; a catalogue of an exhibition of the A. W. F. Fuller and Chicago Natural History Museum collections of antiquities from Benin, Nigeria.* Pp. 111 + 74, ill. Chicago: Natural History Museum.

4316. **Cincinnati: Art Museum.** S.D. *Guide to the Cincinnati Art Museum.* Pp. 82, ill., plan. Cincinnati: Art Museum.

4317. **Cleveland: Museum of Art.** (PLASS, MARGARET, and OTHERS.) 1959. *Seven metals of Africa. A travelling exhibition.* Cleveland Museum of Art, City Art Museum of St. Louis, University Museum, Philadelphia. Pp. 36, ill.

4318. —— 1925 and 1958. *Handbook, Cleveland Museum of Art.* Bulletin of the . . . Museum, no. 9, 1958.

4319. **Denver: Denver Art Museum.** *Denver Art Museum; exploring Africa's art.* Art news, **43**, 1945, 17. (Exhibition catalogue.)

4320. **Iowa: Iowa University: School of Fine Arts.** 1956. *African sculpture; 18th annual fine arts festival (12 June–31 July).* Pp. 7 + 10, ill. Iowa: State Univ.

4321. —— 1959. *Nigerian Arts; 21st Annual Fine Arts Festival, 15 June–12 Aug. 1959.* Pp. 4 + catalogue by R. Sieber of 8 pp., ill. Iowa City: Univ. School of Fine Arts.

4322. **Jefferson City, Miss.: Lincoln University.** N.D. *The Susan Reynolds Underhill African collection.* Pp. 16, ill. Jefferson City, Miss.: Lincoln Univ. (Exhibition catalogue.)

4323. **Kansas City (Miss.): Nelson Gallery and Atkins Museum.** *The imagination of primitive man; a survey of the arts of the non-literate peoples of the world.* Bull. Nelson Gallery and Atkins Museum, **4**, no. 1, 1962, 9–137, ill. (Catalogue compiled by Ralph T. Coe.)

4324. **Los Angeles: Dickson Art Center, University of California.** (ALTMAN, RALPH.) *Balega and other tribal arts from the Congo (Exhibition, Sept.–Oct. 1963, from collection of Jean-Pierre Hallet).* Pp. 28, ill. Los Angeles: Dickson Art Center, Univ. of California.

4325. **Merion: Barnes Foundation Collection.** (GUILLAUME, P., and T. MUNRO.) 1926. *Primitive negro sculpture.* (Members of the staff of Barnes Foundation.)

4326. **Michigan: State University.** (LANSING, E.) *Africa emergent. Centennial review of arts and science (College of Science and Art, Michigan State University),* **4**, no. 4, 1960, 409–519.

4327. **Milwaukee: Milwaukee Public Museum.** (BASCOM, WILLIAM R., and PAUL GEBAUER.) 1953. *Handbook of West African art.* Pp. 83, bibl., ill., map. Milwaukee: Public Museum.

4328. **Milwaukee: Layton School of Art.** 1957. *African sculpture.* Pp. (16), ill. Milwaukee: Layton School of Art. (Exhibition catalogue, 3 Jan.–9 Feb. 1957. Mr. and Mrs. Raymond Wielgus collection.)

4329. **Minneapolis: Minneapolis Institute of Arts.** *African ceremonial mask.* Bull. Minneapolis inst. of arts, **43**, 1954, 17–23.

4329a. —— (M. L. FRIEDMAN.) *Three African masks.* Bull. Minneapolis inst. of arts, **48**, 1959, 3–11.

4330. **Montclair, N. J.: Montclair Art Museum.** 1954. *Rites and Revelry.* Pp. 16, ill. Montclair, N.J.: Montclair Art Museum. (Catalogue: An exhibition of masks, 8 Mar.–18 Apr. 1954.)

4331. **Newark: Newark Museum.** (WINGERT, P. S.) *African art.* Newark museum, **6**, no. 4, 1954, 1–20, bibl., ill., map.

4332. —— 1959. The Museum Quarterly. Vol. 11, nos. 1–4, 1959, *A survey; 50 years of the Newark Museum.* (Illustrations of African and Oriental Material.)

4333. **New Haven: Yale University Art Gallery.** (LINTON, RALPH.) 1954. *The Linton collection of African sculpture.* Pp. 32, ill. New Haven: Yale Univ. Art Gallery. (*See:* Man, **54**, 85, Apr. 1954, p. 63.)

4334. **New York.** 1941. *African bronzes from Ife and Benin.* (Catalogue illustrated.)

4335. —— (BOULTON, LAURA C.) 1935. *Bronze artists of West Africa.* (Catalogue.)

4336. **New York: Blondian Theatre of Arts.** (LOCKE, ALAN.) 1927. *Introduction to the catalogue of the Blondian Theatre of Arts. Collection of primitive African arts.* Pp. 24, ill. New York: Blondian Theatre. (Exhibition: 7 Feb.–5 Mar. 1927.)

4337. **New York** and **Minneapolis: Duveen-Graham Gallery.** 1957–8. *Classical art of negro Africa.* Pp. 20, ill. New York–Minneapolis: Duveen-Graham Gallery. (Exhibition catalogue.)

4338. *See* 4299.

4339. **New York: Museum of Modern Art.** (SWEENEY, J. J.) 1935. *African negro art.* Pp. 58, ill. New York: Museum of Modern Art. (Exhibition catalogue.)

4340. —— (FROBENIUS, LEO, and DOUGLAS FOX.) 1937. *Prehistoric rock pictures in Europe and Africa from materials in the Archives of the Research Institute for the Morphology of Civilisation, Frankfurt-A.M.* Pp. 9 + 79, ill., map. New York: Museum of Modern Art.

4341. —— 1952. *Understanding African negro sculpture.* (Circulating exhibition catalogue.)

4342. **New York: Museum of primitive art.** 1958. *African sculpture lent by New York collectors.* Pp. 8, ill. New York: Museum of Primitive Art. (Exhibition catalogue.)

4343. —— 1957. *Selected works from the collection.* 1st Catalogue of permanent exhibits, Spring 1957. 2nd Catalogue, Summer 1957. 3rd Catalogue, October 1957. Pp. 32, ill. New York: Museum of Primitive Art. (Colour in sculptures and ceramics.)

4344. —— 1958. *The latest Ife finds.* (Introduction by William Fagg.) Pp. 5, ill. New York: Museum of Primitive Art.

4345. —— 1959. *Sculptures from three African tribes; Senufo, Baga and Dogon.* Pp. 32, ill. New York: Museum of Primitive Art.

4346. —— 1960. *Primitive art from the Lipchitz Collection.* (Introduction by Jacques Lipchitz.) Pp. 34, ill. New York: Museum of Primitive Art.

4347. —— (GOLDWATER, R.) 1960. *Bambara sculpture from the Western Sudan.* Pp. 64, ill. New York: Museum of Primitive Art.

4348. —— 1961. *Traditional art of the African nations.* Pp. 8. ill. (some col.), map. New York: Univ. Pubns. Inc. (Catalogue of the exhibition, 17 May–10 Sept.)

4349. —— 1962. *The Dominique collection (of primitive art).* Pp. 71, ill. New York: Museum of Primitive Art.

4350. —— 1963. *The Robert and Lisa Sainsbury collection (of primitive art).* Pp. 40, ill. New York: Museum of Primitive Art.

4351. —— 1963. *Sculpture from Africa in the collection of the museum.* Pp. 32, ill. New York: Museum of Primitive Art.

4352. **Oberlin, Ohio: Oberlin College: Allen Memorial Art Museum.** (FAGG, WILLIAM.) 1955–6. *The study of African art.* Exhibition of African Art, 6 Feb.–6 Mar. 1956. Bulletin, **13**, no. 2, 1955–6, 43–156, ill. Oberlin, Ohio: Dept. of Fine Arts of Oberlin College.

4353. **Philadelphia: University of Pennsylvania Museum.** (ANON.) 1912. *The Art of Great Benin.* Museum J., **2** (4), 1912.

4354. —— (TORDAY, E.) *The new Congo collection.* Museum J., **4** (1), 1913.

4355. —— (HALL, H. U.) 1922. *Handbook of Africa and the South Seas.* Philadelphia: Univ. Museum.

4356. —— Museum Bulletin: 1. (1) *Two new collections of African Art.* 1930, 2, ill. (2) *A Baule mask in the . . . collections.* 1930, 1, ill. (4) *An Ivory Coast Door.* 1930, 2, ill. 2. (2) *Two new West African sculptures.* 1930, 2, ill. (5) *A Batetela image.* 1931, 2, ill. 3. (6) *African collections.* 1932, 16, ill., map. 4. (1) *The African galleries.* 1932, 2, ill. (3) *An African wood carving (Lower Congo).* 1933, 1, ill.

4357. —— (HALL, H. U.) *Bushman collection.* Museum J., **2**, 1931, 128–31.

4358. —— (HALL, H. U.) *The West African Expedition, Nov. 1936 to Jun. 1937.* Museum J., 1937, 7, ill. (Univ. Museum bull., **7** (1), 1937. Sierra Leone. Univ. Museum bull., **6**, 1937, 6.)

4359. *See 4362.*

4360. —— (PLASS, MARGARET.) 1956. *African tribal sculpture.* Pp. 57, bibl., ill., map. Philadelphia: Univ. of Pennsylvania Museum. (Contains list of exhibits shown at the University Museum exhibition of African tribal sculpture, Apr. to Sept. 1956.)

4361. —— (1) *African negro sculpture.* (Introduction by C. S. Coon.) (2) *A walk through the gallery,* by M. Plass. Univ. Museum bull., **21**, 1957, 4.

4362. —— (WIESCHOFF, H. A.) *The African collections of the University Museum.* Univ. Museum bull., **11**, 1–2, 1945, 1–24, ill. (Handbook.)

4363. —— *Masks.* Univ. Museum bull., **13** (1), 1947, 1–32, ill.

4364. —— 1959. *Bulletin of African tribal sculpture.*

4365. **Philadelphia: Exhibition.** 1959. *Copper—silver—gold. Seven metals of Africa; a travelling exhibition.* ill. Philadelphia.

4366. **Philadelphia: Commercial Museum.** 1906. *Notes on the Madagascar collection.*

4367. —— (GUNN, HAROLD D.) 1960. *A handbook of the African collections of the Commercial Museum, Philadelphia.* Pp. 78, ill., maps. Philadelphia: Commercial Museum.

4368. **St. Louis: City Art Museum.** 1953. *Handbook of the collections.* St. Louis: City Art Museum.

4369. **San Francisco: M. H. de Young Memorial Museum.** (WINGERT, PAUL S.) 1948. *African negro sculpture; a loan exhibition.* Pp. 5 + 26 + 118 pl., map. New York: Columbia Univ. Press. (Exhibition held at the M. H. de Young Memorial Museum, San Francisco, 24 Sept.–19 Nov. 1948.)

4370. —— 1950. *Illustrations of selected works.* (From the M. H. de Young Memorial Museum).

4371. **Toledo, Ohio: Museum of Art.** 1959. (A new selection of tribal art.) *The African image (Exhibition).* Introduction and catalogue by Margaret Plass. Pp. 36, bibl., ill., maps. Toledo: Museum of Art. (Exhibition catalogue, 1–20 Feb. 1959.)

4372. **Washington: Howard University Gallery of Art.** 1953. *African negro art.* Pp. 24, ill. Washington: Howard Univ. Gallery of Art. (Exhibition catalogue, 6–31 May 1953.)

4373. —— 1957. *A collection of African negro sculpture and handicrafts from the estate of Alain le Roy Locke.* Pp. 6, ill. (Exhibition catalogue, Feb.–Mar. 1957.)

4374. **Washington: Smithsonian Institute: Herbert Ward Collection.** 1924. *The Herbert Ward African collection.* Pp. 49, ill. Washington: U.S. National Museum.

4375. **Washington: U.S. National Museum.** (ABBOTT, W. L.) *Ethnological collections in the . . . Museum from Kilimanjaro, East Africa.* Report U.S. National mus., part 3, no. 2, 1891, 381–428, ill. Washington: U.S. National Museum.

BELGIUM

4376. **Antwerp: Exposition Internationale.** 1930–3. *Angola, Portugal Agençia Geral dos Colonias. Exposition Int. d'Anvers.* 1930. (Rep. and ill., Lisbon, 1933.)

4377. **Antwerp: Propagandaweken.** 1938. *Kongo Kunst.* Tentoonstelung Antwerpsche Propagandaweken, 24 Dec. 1937–16 Jan. 1938. Antwerp: Stadsfeestzaal.

4379. **Antwerp: Art.** 1949. *Tentoonstelling van Hedendaagse Koloniale Kunst.* Pp. 54, ill. Antwerp. (Aboriginal art also included.)

4380. **Antwerp: Museum Vleeshuis.** 1955. *Fetisj, Totem en Taboe.* (Introduction by F. Smekens.) Pp. 40, ill. Antwerp: Museum Vleeshuis. (Exhibition catalogue, 15 Oct. 1955–15 Jan. 1956.)

4381. **Antwerp: Royal Museum of Fine Arts.** 1956. *Het Masker—catalogus.* Pp. 72, ill., maps. Antwerp: Royal Museum of Fine Arts. (Exhibition, 'The Mask', City of Antwerp, Royal Museum of Fine Arts, 16 Sept.–15 Nov. 1956.)

4382. **Antwerp: Museum für Völkskunde.** 1958. *Führer durch das Museum für Völkskunde Antwerpen.* Pp. 32, ill. Antwerp.

4383. **Antwerp: Tentoonstelling West-Zuid-Oost.** 1960. *Kunst buiten Europa. Uit de Verzamelingen van het Etnografisch Museum,* 23 Juli–25 Sept. 1960. Pp. 64, ill. Antwerp: Etnografisch Museum. (Africa, pp. 23–38.)

4384. **Brussels: Brussels-Tervueren Exhibition.** 1897. *Guide de la section de l'etat independent du Congo à l'exposition de Bruxelles-Tervueren en 1897.* Pp. 523, ill., map. Brussels.

4385. **Brussels: Palais des Beaux-Arts.** (MAES, J., and H. LAVACHERY.) 1930. *Art nègre; l'art nègre à l'exposition du Palais des Beaux-Arts.* Pp. 31, ill. Brussels: Palais des Beaux-Arts.

4386. **Brussels: Vatican Exhibition.** 1950. *Vatikaans tentoonstelling; de kunst in Belgisch-Congo en Ruanda-Urundi.* Pp. 95, ill. Brussels: Edited by Centre d'Information et de Documentation Congo Belge et Ruanda-Urundi.

4387. **Brussels: African Art Musea voor Kunst en Geschiedenis.** (WEYNS, J.). 1956. *Afrikaanse Kunst uit de koninklijke Musea voor Kunst en Geschiedenis.* Pp. 46, 30 ill., + separate catalogue (18 pp.). Brussels.

4388. **Brussels: Universal and International Exhibition, 1958.** Art in the Congo (Brussels Universal Exhibition, 1958). Belgian Congo and Ruanda-Urundi Section, Groups II–III: *Art and its means of expression.* Pp. 40, ill. Brussels: V.T.K., Antwerp.

4389. —— 1958. Exposition Universelle et Internationale de Bruxelles, 1958. Section du Congo belge et du Ruanda-Urundi: *Art in the Congo*. v.p., ill. Brussels.

4390. —— 1958. Art traditionnel: Section Congo Belge et Ruanda-Urundi, Groupe 2/3: *Les arts et leurs moyens d'expression*. s.p., ill. Brussels. (Liste des 423 objets.)

4391. **Brussels: Exposition Universelle et Internationale de Bruxelles en 1910.** 1958. *Le Congo Belge à l'Exposition de Bruxelles en 1910*. Brussels.

4392. **Brussels: Musées Royaux.** 1958. *Musées royaux d'Art et d'Histoire, Bruxelles. Antiquité, Ethnographie*. Pp. 116. Brussels.

4393. **Brussels: Collection van Geluwe.** (KERELS, HENRI.) *L'Art nègre dans la collection van Geluwe*. Rev. cong. ill., 28, 9, 1956, 19–21, ill.

4394. **Gand.** 1950. *Ars Exotica. Musée des Beaux-Arts*. (Introduction by F. Olbrechts.) Pp. 32, ill. Gand.

4395. **Liège: Musée des Beaux-Arts.** 1949. *Exposition d'art primitif*.

4396. **Malines.** 1956. *Primitieve kunst. Verzameling J. van der Straete*. Pp. 34, ill. Mechelen: De Zalm. (6 Oct.–11 Nov. 1956.)

4397. **Morlanwelz, Hainaut: Musée de Mariemont.** (FAIDER-THOMAS, TH.) *Quelques objets d'Afrique centrale conservés au Musée de Mariemont*. Africa Tervueren, 9, 1963, 95–104, ill.

4398. **Tervueren: Musée du Congo Belge.** (MASUI, TH.) 1899. *Les collections ethnographiques du Musée du Congo Belge*. Ann. Mus. Congo, Apr. 1899. Tervueren: Musée du Congo Belge.

4399. —— (DE HAULLEVILLE.) 1910. *Le Musée du Congo Belge à Tervueren*. Brussels: Musée du Congo Belge.

4400. —— (MAES, J.) 1922. *Völkenkundige gids van het Kongo Museum*. Brussels.

4401. —— (MAES, J.) 1925. *Le Musée du Congo Belge à Tervueren; Guide illustré du visiteur*. Pp. 148, ill. Anvers: De Sikkel.

4402. **Tervueren: Congo Art Exhibition.** (MAESEN, A.) *Kunststijlen in Kongo*. Tentoonstelling van Kongo-kunst, 1937, 15–17.

4403. **Tervueren: Musée du Congo Belge.** (DUCHESNE, FL.) 1948. *La section économique du Musée du Congo Belge*. Pp. 260. Tervueren: Musée du Congo Belge.

4404. **Tervueren: Musée Royal de l'Afrique Centrale.** *Musée du Congo belge à Tervueren. Guide illustré*. ill. Brussels: Musée Royal de l'Afrique Centrale.

4405. —— (OLBRECHTS, F. M.) 1952. *Some masterpieces of African art*. (24 reproductions from the Museum collections.)

4406. **Tervueren: Musée du Congo Belge.** (LAUDE, J.) *Le Musée du Congo Belge à Tervueren*. L'Oeil, 13, 1956, 32–39, ill.

4407. —— 1960. *Musée du Congo Belge—Umbangu; Art du Congo au Musée royale du Congo Belge*. Pp. 27, col. pl., map. Brussels: Cultura.

4408. **Tervueren: Musée Royal de l'Afrique Centrale.** (VAN GELUWE, H.) 1960–1. *La maternité dans l'art de l'Afrique centrale*. Pp. (1) 8. Tervueren: Musée Royal de l'Afrique Centrale. (Exhibition catalogue, 10 Dec. 1960–12 Feb. 1961.)

4409. —— 1961. *Collection André Ryckmans*. Pp. 37, ill., map. Tervueren: Musée Royal de l'Afrique Centrale.

4410. —— *Exposition sur le Tibesti, Dec. 1961–Feb. 1962*. (Catalogue.) Pp. 14. Tervueren: Musée Royal de l'Afrique Centrale.

4411. —— (LUWEL, M., and OTHERS.) *Musée royal du Congo Belge à Tervueren; 50ᵉ anniversaire de l'inauguration du palais actuel, 1910–1960*. Congo-Tervueren, 6, 2, 1960, 30–72, ill.

4412. ——*Art d'Afrique dans les collections belges*. (Exhibition: 29 June–30 Oct. 1963.) Tervueren, 1963, 134, map. (Catalogue by A. Maesen and H. van Geluwe.)

4413. —— 1963. *Exposition arts d'Afrique dans les collections belges, June–Sept. 1963*. (Catalogue.) Pp. xi, ill., map. Brussels: Palais des Beaux-Arts.

4414. —— 1963. *Kunst van Afrika uit Belgisch bezit*. Pp. 120. Tervueren: Musée Royal de l'Afrique Centrale.

CANADA

4415. **Toronto: Royal Ontario Museum.** 1952. *Catalogue of museum special exhibition 'East and West'*. Bull. Royal Ontario Museum of Archaeology, no. 19, 1952; 21, 1953.

4416. —— 1959. *Masks; the many faces of man*. An exhibition presented by the Division of Art and Archaeology.

4417. —— Division of Art and Archaeology list of publications, and index to Bulletin.

DENMARK

4418. **Copenhagen: National Museum.** (BIRKET-SMITH.) *Die neue Einrichtung des dänischen Nationalmuseums mit besonderer Berücksichtigung der völkerkundlichen Abteilung*. Ethnol. Anzeiger, 4, 6, 1940, 303–6, ill.

4419. —— 1940. *Den etnografiske samling. Tropiske naturfolk*. Pp. 112. Copenhagen: National Museum.

4420. —— Guides to the various departments in the museum.

4421. —— Anniversary volume (150th), 1957. ill. (Photographs of primitive art.)

4422. —— (YDE, I.) 1945. *Etnografisk Samlings Taletrommer (Africa)*. Nationalmuseets Arbeydmark, pp. 18–24. Copenhagen: Nordisk Forlag.

FINLAND

4423. **Helsinki: Lähetysmuseon.** N.D. *Opas*. (Catalogue of African and other objects in the museum.) Pp. 88, ill. (Museum of the Finnish Mission Society.)

FRANCE

4424. **Angoulême: Musée Municipal d'Angoulême.** (DELANGE, JACQUELINE.) 1950. *Collections ethnographiques. Collections . . . de l'Afrique noire*. Pp. 13–41, ill. Angoulême: Coquemard.

4425. **Arles: Musée Reattu.** 1954. *Art Afrique noire*. Pp. 45, ill. Arles: Musée Reattu. (Exhibition catalogue, 10 Apr.–30 Sept. 1954.)

4426. **Besançon: Festival Artistique.** 1958. *L'Art de l'Afrique noire*. Pp. 70, bibl., ill. Besancon: Palais Granvelle. (Exhibition catalogue, 12 July–5 Oct. 1958.)

4427. **Cabrerets, Lot: Musée Lebaudy.** (LEBEUF, J. P.) *Les collections Sao du Musée Lebaudy (Cabrerets, Lot)*. J. soc. africanistes, 13, 1943, 183–6.

4428. **Cannes: Palais Miramar.** 1957. *Première exposition retrospective internationale des arts d'Afrique et d'Océanie (6 July–29 Sept. 1957)*. (Edited by Hélène and Henri Kamer.) Pp. 42, ill. Cannes: Palais Miramar.

4429. **Lyons: Musée des Missions Africaines.** 1956. *Un coin d'art africain*. Pp. 20, ill. Lyon: Heliogravure M. Lescuyer et Fils.

4430. **Musée de Mariemont.** Illustrated guide to the museum.

4431. **Marseilles: Merwart Collection.** (MERWART, GOUVERNEUR.) 1922. *L'Art dahoméen; collection du Gouverneur Merwart (Exposition coloniale de Marseille, 1922. Palais de l'Afrique Occidentale Française)*. Pp. 24. Marseille: Moulot.

4432. **Nancy: Musée des Beaux-Arts.** (REVAULT, J.) *L'Exposition d'arts tunisiens au Musée des Beaux-Arts de Nancy*. Bull. Econom. Tunisie, no. 54, 1953, 89–97, ill.

4433. **Paris: Bibliothèque Nationale.** 1931. *Quatres siècles de colonisation française. Exposition d'oeuvres du XVe au XVIIe siècle*. Pp. 153, ill., maps. Paris: Bibliothèque Nationale.

4434. **Paris: Breton Collection.** 1931. *Sculptures d'Afrique, d'Amerique, d'Océanie*. (Collection André Breton and Paul Elouard.) Pp. 55, ill. Paris.

4435. **Paris: Bronzes et Terres Cuites du Tchad.** S.D. *Exposition de bronzes et de terres cuites du Tchad*. Paris.

4436. **Paris: Musée Cernuschi.** 1958. *Orient-occident. Rencontres et influences durant cinquante siècles d'art.* Pp. xvi + 122, ill. Paris: Edition des Musées Nationaux.

4437. **Paris: Hôtel Drouot: de Miré Collection.** (MIRÉ, G. DE.) 1931. *Sculptures anciennes d'Afrique et d'Amérique . . . Hôtel Drouot, 16 Dec. 1931.* Pp. viii + 29, ill. Paris: Hôtel Drouot.

4438. ——**Hôtel Drouot: Rupalley Collection.** (PORTIER, ANDRÉ.) 1930. *Catalogue de la vente de la collection Paul Rupalley, 17–18 May 1930.* ill., Paris: Hôtel Drouot.

4439. ——**Hôtel Drouot Sale Catalogue.** (BELLIER, ALPHONSE.) 1931. *Vente de sculptures d'Afrique et d'Océanie . . . Hôtel Drouot, 7 May 1931.* Pp. ii + 30, ill. Paris: Hôtel Drouot.

4440. ——**Hôtel Drouot: Fénéon Collection.** (RATTON, CH., and A. and G. PORTIER.) 1947. *Catalogue de la vente de la collection Fénéon, Hôtel Drouot, 11–13 June 1947.* Paris: Hôtel Drouot.

4441. ——**Hôtel Drouot.** 1955. *Objets de haute curiosite; arts primitifs.* (Catalogue.) ill. Paris.

4442. **Paris: Galerie Arnaud.** 1957. *Analogies, expressions nègres et peinture actuelle. Exposition prés. par O. Le Corneur.* Pp. 26 (3), ill. Paris: Galerie Arnaud O. Le Corneur.

4443. ——**Galerie Devambez.** 1919. *Exposition d'art nègre et d'art océanien.* Paris.

4444. ——**Galerie de la France d'Outremer.** 1951. *Collection Sâo du Tchad.*

4445. ——**Galerie Palmes.** 1948. *Exposition d'art nègre.*

4446. ——**Galerie Pigalle.** (FELS, F.) *Arts sauvages à la Galerie Pigalle.* L'Art vivant, **6**, 1930, 228–32.

4447. ——1938. *Exposition d'art africain et d'art océanien.*

4448. ——(EINSTEIN, CARL.) *A propos de l'exposition de la Galerie Pigalle.* Documents, **2**, 1930, 104–12.

4449. **Paris: Labouret Collection.** (HELFENBEIN, B.) *L'art au Cameroun (l'exposition Labouret).* Rev. d'Afrique, **13**, 1935, 12–15.

4450. ——(LAVACHERY, H. A.) *L'Exposition d'art africain et d'art océanien à Paris.* Cahiers de Belgique (Brussels), **3**, 1930, 4.

4450a. **Paris: Lebeuf Collection.** (LEBEUF, JEAN-PAUL.) *Collections Saô rapportés du Tchad par A. Masson-Detourbet and J. P. Lebeuf.* (Article and catalogue.) Cahiers d'arts, no. 2, 1951.

4451. ——(LELEU, J.) 1951. *Collection d'art nègre de F. H. Lem.* Paris: J. Leleu.

4452. ——(LELEU, J.) 1952. *Collection d'art nègre de P. Vérité.* Paris: J. Leleu.

4453. **Paris: Mosquée de Paris.** (GALLOTTI, JEAN.) *La renaissance des arts indigènes au Maroc. Une exposition d'art marocain à la mosquée de Paris.* Vu, 1930, 751, ill.

4454. **Paris: Musée des Arts Décoratifs.** 1925. *L'Art des colonies françaises et du Congo Belge.* (Exhibition catalogue.)

4455. ——(BREUIL, H.) 1957–8. *Peintures préhistoriques du Sahara.* Pp. 66, ill. Paris: Musée des Arts Décoratifs. (Exhibition catalogue: 'Mission L'hote au Tassili'.)

4456. **Paris: Musée Nat. d'Histoire Naturelle.** (LEBEUF, J. P.) *Les collections archéologiques du Tchad au Musée.* Bull. Musée Nat. d'Histoire Naturelle, **14** (2), 1942, 100–5.

4458. **Paris: Musée Pédagogique.** (COUSTILLAC, L.) *L'Exposition d'arts tunisiens au Musée Pédagogique à Paris.* Bull. econ. and social de la Tunisie, 1952.

4459. **Paris: Palais du Louvre: Pavillon de Marsan.** 1926. *Exposition de la croisière noire.* Pp. 40, ill. Paris: The Louvre. (Exhibition catalogue.)

4460. **Paris: Portique.** (EINSTEIN, CARL.) 1925. *Exposition au Portique.* ill. Paris.

4461. **Paris: Trocadéro Museum.** (LABOURET, HENRI.) 1935. *Catalogue de l'exposition de la Mission au Cameroun de M. H. Labouret, 9 mars–31 oct. 1934.* Pp. 56, ill. Paris: Musée du Trocadéro.

4462. ——1932. *Exposition de bronzes et ivoirerie du royaume de Bénin, 15 June–15 July 1932.* Pp. 32, ill. Paris: Palais du Trocadéro.

4463. ——(DE LAPIERRE, SUZANNE.) *Exposition de l'Afrique noire au Trocadéro.* La Vie (Paris), mars 1940, 61–62.

4464. **Paris: Musée de l'Homme.** (LEBEUF, JEAN-PAUL.) 1942. *Les collections du Tchad, guide pour leur exposition.* Pp. 24, ill. Paris: Muséum National d'Histoire Naturelle, au Musée de l'Homme.

4465. ——**Musée de l'Homme, Collections de l'Aurès.** 1943. *Catalogue des collections de l'Aurès.* Paris: Musée de l'Homme.

4466. ——**Musée de l'Homme.** (CUNARD, NANCY.) *The Musée de l'Homme.* Burlington mag., Mar. 1945, 66–71.

4467. ——1960. *La vie du Sahara.* Pp. xxiii + 84, bibl., ill., maps. Paris: Musée de l'Homme (exhibition guide.)

4468. ——1961. *Guide du musée.* Pp. 17, ill. Paris: Musée de l'Homme.

4469. ——(DELANGE, JACQUELINE.) *Les arts anciens de la plaine du Tchad (Exposition au Musée de l'Homme).* Objets et mondes, **2**, 3, automne 1962, 135–48, bibl., ill., map.

4470. ——(PAULME, D.) *Les collections d'Afrique Noire depuis 1945 (Musée de l'Homme)* Objets et mondes, **1** (1), 1961, 41–46, ill.

4471. ——(SCHAEFFNER, D.) *Un voyage au Musée de l'Homme.* Monde colonial illustré. Jan. 1940, 10–11.

4472. ——(RIVIÈRE, G.) *Recherches et musées d'Ethnographie française depuis 1939.* Man, **47**, no. 2, 1947, 7–11.

4472a. ——1965. *Chefs-d'oeuvre du Musée de l'homme.* Pp. 232, ill. Paris: Musée de l'homme.

4473. **Paris: Sahara (Exhibition).** *L'Exposition du Sahara, 1934.* La Renaissance, xvii année (nos. 7, 8, 9), 1934, v.p., ill.

4474. **Paris: Ville-Fabra Collection.** (CID, C.) *La Coleccion Ville-Fabra de Arte Negro en Paris.* Estudios, Seminario de Estudios Arqueologicos y Ethnologicos, no. 1, 1950, 8–10, ill.

4475. **Paris: Vlaminck Collection.** 1937. *Collection M. Maurice de Vlaminck; sculptures africaines et océaniennes; tableaux modernes.* Paris.

4476. **Paris: Cercle Volney.** *Les arts africains.* (Catalogue de l'Exposition, June–July 1955.) Pp. 72, ill., map. Paris.

4477. **Pau: Musée des Beaux-Arts.** *Exposition; 'Sculptures de l'Afrique Noire'.* Dec. 1961–Jan. 1962. (Catalogue by Françoise Debaisieux.) Pp. 54, ill. Pau: Impr. Marrimpouey.

4478. **Saint-Étienne: Musée d'Art et d'Industrie.** (ALLEMAND, MAURICE.) 1956. *L'Art de l'Afrique noire.* Pp. 32, ill., map. Saint-Étienne: Musée d'Art et d'Industrie.

GERMANY

GENERAL

4479. **General.** 1958. *Jahrbuch der Deutsches Museums und Kunst Instituts.* Pp. 240. (Guide to all museums, etc.)

4480. **German and Swiss Museums.** (WESCOTT, J.) *Yoruba art in German and Swiss museums.* Yoruba Historical Research Scheme, Ibadan, Nigeria, 1958, 43, ill.

4480a. **Westcott, J.** *Yoruba Collections in Germany and Switzerland.* Man, 57, no. 161, 1957, 133–5.

4481. **Klein, H.** *Die deutschen Afrika-expeditionen seit dem letzten Weltkrieg.* Afrika Heute Jb., 1957, 119–23.

4482. **Bastin, M. L.** *Quelques oeuvres Tshokwe de musées et collections d'Allemagne et de Scandinavie.* Africa-Tervueren, **7**, 4, 1961, 101–5, ill.

4483. **Berlin: Museum für Völkerkunde.** (LUSCHAN, F. VON.) 1919. *Die Altertümer von Benin.* 3 vols.

4484. ——1947. *Haus und Hausrat exotischer Völker.* Pp. 32, ill. Berlin: Gebr. Mann. (Exhibition catalogue and museum guide.)

4485. ——(MENZEL, B.) 1963. *Textil-Handwerk in Nord-Nigeria.* Pp. 8, ill. Berlin: Museum f. Völkerkunde. (Sonderausstellung.)

4486. **Berlin: Deutscher Kunstrat.** 1960. *Kunst aus Zentralafrika.* Eine Ausstellung des Deutschen Kunstrates, 1960–1: Berlin, Bremen, Dortmund, Darmstadt (essays by various authors). Pp. 58, ill. Opladen: F. Middelhauve.

4487. **Berlin: Collection von der Heydt.** (VON SYDOW, ECKART.) *1932. Kunst der Naturvölker; Sammlung Eduard von der Heydt.* Vol. 1, pp. 213, ill., maps. Vol. 2, Katalog der Sammlung Baron von der Heydt. Berlin: B. Cassirer.

4488. **Berlin: Völkerkunde Museum: Masks.** (KRIEGER, K. and G. KUTSCHER.) *1960. Westafrikanische Masken.* (Museum catalogue.) Pp. 93, ill. Berlin: Museum f. Völkerkunde. (Veröfftl. Museum f. Völkerkunde, N.F., 1, abt. Afrika 1.)

4489. **Brunswick: Exhibition Catalogue.** *1955. Götter, Ahnen und Dämonen.* (Kunst der Naturvölker im stadtischen Museum Braunschweig—June–Oct. 1955.) S.P., ill. Brunswick: Waisenhaus-Buchdruckerei.

4490. **Coburg Museum.** (AUMANN, G.) *1959. Kunst und Kunsthandwerk d. Naturvölker.* S.P., ill. Coburg: Jahresausstellung des Coburger Kunstvereins, 26 Apr.–24 May 1959.

4491. **Cologne: Rautenstrauch-Joest-Museum.** (HEYDRICH, M., and W. FRÖHLICH.) *1954. Plastik der Primitiven aus dem Besitz des Rautenstrauch-Joest-Museum der Stadt Köln.* Pp. 64, ill. Stuttgart: Die Schönen Bücher. (Pp. 49–64, Africa.)

4492. **Frankfurt a/M.** *1957. Ferne Völker, frühe Zeiten.* (Ausstellung des Museums für Völkerkunde und des Frobenius-Institutes an der Johann Wolfgang Goethe Universität Frankfurt am Main, 5 May–30 June 1957.) Pp. 74, ill. Frankfurt am Main: L. C. Wittich.

4493. **Göttingen: Sammlung der Universität.** (LANG, W.) *1960. Makondemasken in der Völkerkundlichen Sammlung der Universität Göttingen.* Zeit. f. Ethnol., 85, 1960, 28–36, bibl., ill.

4494. **Hagen: Folkwang Museum.** *1912. "Die Sammlung" Karl Ernst Ostham.* (Exhibition catalogue.)

4495. **Hamburg; Museum für Kunst und Gewerbe.** (MEYER, ERIC.) *Studien zu Werken in den Sammlungen des Museums für Kunst u. Gewerbe.* Festschrift für Eric Meyer, 1957, and published Hamburg, 1959.

4496. **Hamburg: Museum für Völkerkunde.** (DANZEL, TH. W.) *1936. Einführung in die Sonderausstellung 'Die Maske im Leben der Völker' im Museum für Völkerkunde, Hamburg.* Pp. 11. Hamburg: Museum für Völkerkunde.

4497. —— (HAGEN, CARL.) *1900–18. Altertümer von Benin in Museum für Völkerkunde zu Hamburg.* 2 vols. Hamburg: Museum f. Völkerkunde.

4498. —— (HERMANN, A.) *1954. Die Welt der Fellachen.* Wegweiser zur Völkerkunde, Heft 2: 'Führer durch Hamburgisches Museum für Völkerkunde und Vorgeschichte'. Pp. 39.

4499. —— *1956. Kunstwerk aus Indien, Siam, Die Sammlung Kurt Stavenhagen; Mexiko, Persien, Kolumbien, Afrika, aus verschiedenem Besitz.* Freiburg, 2 Dec. 1960: Hamburg, 1956.

4500. **Hanover: Niedersächsisches Landesmuseum.** Autumn *1958. Ferne Welten Fremder Geist.* (Exhibition catalogue.) Pp. 64, ill. Hanover: Museum. (Guide catalogue to the African and Pacific art collections.)

4501. **Hermannstadt: Sammlung Franz Binder.** (HIRSCHBERG, WALTER.) *1931–2. Die Sammlung Franz Binder in Hermannstadt und Mühlbach.* Pp. 15, ill. Hermannstadt: Verhandlungen u. Mitteilungen des Siebenbürgischen Vereins f. Naturwissenschaften.

4502. **Hermannstadt: Sudan Collections.** (HIRSCHBERG, WALTER.) *Eine der ältesten ethnographischen Sammlungen aus dem Oberen Nilgebiet.* Siebenbürgisch-Deutsches Tagebl. Hermannstadt, 18 Aug. 1932.

4503. **Hermannstadt: Sudan (Upper Nile Area).** (HIRSCHBERG, WALTER.) *Eine alte, fast in Vergessenheit geratene Sammlung aus dem Oberen Nilgebiet.* Weltkreis (Berlin), 3, 1, 1932.

4504. **Leipzig: S. Mus. Völkerkunde.** Jahrbuch . . . Vol. 1– 1960–.

4505. —— *1912–13. Führer durch das Museum.* Pp. 204, ill.

4506. —— *1948. Kunst und Kunsthandwerk in Afrika.* 9 May–31 July 1948. (Exhibition catalogue.)

4507. **Linz: Stadt Linz Wolfgang Gurlitt Museum.** 1960. (W.G.) Museum, Neue Galerie: und Wiener Museum für Völkerkunde. *Kunst und Kultur in Afrika.* Pp. 32, ill., map. Linz: W.G. Museum. (Exhibition catalogue.)

4508. **Mannheim: Reiss-Museum.** (PFAFF-GIESBERG, R.) *1957. Die Völkerkundlichen Sammlungen der Stadt Mannheim im Reiss-Museum.* Pp. 7–12, ill. (West African dance mask.)

4509. **Munich: Staatliches Museum für Völkerkunde.** *1953. Afrikanische Kunst. Ausstellung im Amerika-Haus.* Pp. 42, ill. Munich: Amerika-Haus.

4510. **Munich: Kunsthalle.** (FAGG, WILLIAM.) *1961. Nigeria; 2000 Jahre Plastik.* (Catalogue of an exhibition at the Städtische Galerie, Munich.) Munich: Städtische Galerie.

4511. —— *1962. Nigeria; 2000 Jahre Plastik.* (Catalogue of an exhibition at the Kunsthalle, Basle.) Basle: Kunsthalle.

4511a. **Offenbach: Ledermuseum.** *1956. Das deutsche Ledermuseum.* (Museum catalogue and guide: introduction by Eberhardt.) Pp. 163, ill. Offenbach a.M.: Ledermuseum.

4512. **Recklinghausen: Kunsthalle.** *1957. Negerkunst und Christentum.* (Exhibition catalogue, Mar.–Apr. 1957. Einführung F. von Trigt.)

4513. **Stuttgart: Knorrsche Collection.** (LUSCHAN, FELIX VON.) *1901. Die Karl Knorrsche Sammlung von Benin.* Stuttgart: Linden-Museums.

4514. **Stuttgart: Linden-Museum.** (GLÜCK, JULIUS F., and FRITZ JÄGER (Ed.).) *1951. Jahrbuch des Linden-Museums.* Museum für Länder- und Völkerkunde, N.F., 1. Pp. 259, ill. Heidelberg: K. Vowinckel Verlag.

4515. —— *1932. Zur chronologie der Benin-Platten.* Pp. 121–8.

4516. **Stuttgart: Museum für Länder-und Völkerkunde.** *Westafrika in seiner Kunst aus den Sammlungen des Museums.* (Sonderausstellung.) Pp. 19, ill. Stuttgart.

4517. **Stuttgart.** *1956. Aussereuropäische Kunst; China, Persien, Peru; Kunst der Naturvölker.* (Auktion Katalog, Stuttgart, p. 134, pl. 78.)

4518. **Stuttgart: Linden-Museum.** *1957. Katalog der Neuerwerbungen.* Pp. 21, ill. Stuttgart: Linden Museum.

4519. **Stuttgarter Kunstkabinett.** *1957. Kunst der Naturvölker; Afrika, Südsee, Amerika.* Pp. 48, ill. (27 Auktion, 3 May 1957.) Stuttgart: Theodor Körner.

4520. **Stuttgart: Linden-Museum.** (ZWERNEMANN, J.) *1961. Kongo und Benin—Höhepunkte afrikanischer Kunst; eine Einführung in die Sammlungen des Linden-Museums.* Pp. 24, ill. Stuttgart: Linden Museum.

4521. **Ulm: Museum.** (ANDRÉE, RICHARD.) *Seltene Ethnographica des städt. Gewerbe-Museums zu Ulm.* Objekte aus Afrika, p. 34. Baessler-Archiv, 4 (1), 1913, 29–38, ill. (Benin spoons.)

4522. **Winterthur: H. Coray Collection.** *1931. Ausstellung afrikanische Negerkunst.* Sammlung H. Coray, Lugano. Pp. 11, ill. Winterthur: Gewerbemuseum.

4523. **Wescott, J. A.** *Yoruba collections in Germany and Switzerland.* Man, 57, no. 161, 1957, 133–5.

GREAT BRITAIN

4524. **Aberdeen: Marischal College.** *1912. Museum catalogue.* Pp. 299–339, ill.

4525. **Arundel: Totem Museum.** S.D. *The Hooper collection of primitive art.* Pp. 12, ill. Chippenham, Wilts. (Private museum catalogue.)

4526. **Bicester.** (WEBSTER, W. D.) *Illustrated catalogue of ethnographic specimens.* Nos. 1–10, Bicester, c.1895. Nos. 23–31, Bicester, c.1899–1901.

4527. **Birchington, Kent: Powell-Cotton Museum.** (COOKE, H. B. S.) *1957. The Powell-Cotton Museum of African fauna and ethnology.* S.A. museum assoc. bull., Sept. 1957, 7, ill.

4528. **Bournemouth: Russell-Cotes Museum.** *African idols.* Bull. R.C. museum, 10, 1931, 58–59, ill.

4529. ——*Ashanti gold weights.* Bull. R.C. museum, **10**, 1931, 21–22, ill.

4530. **Farnham, Dorset: Pitt-Rivers Museum.** (PITT-RIVERS, A. H. LANE FOX.) 1900. *Antique works of art from Benin.* (Illustrated catalogue of Benin Collection.)

4531. **Edinburgh University: Department of Social Anthropology.** 1962. *An exhibition of African art held at the Royal Scottish Museum, 24 Feb.–24 Mar. 1962.* Pp. 38, ill., map. Edinburgh: Royal Scottish Museum.

4532. **Liverpool: Public Museums.** 1898 and 1900. *Bulletin of Liverpool museums.* Vols. 1 and 2, ill. (Benin bronzes.)

4533. —— 1931. *Handbook and guide to the African collection.* Pp. 32, ill., map. Liverpool: Public Museums.

4534. —— *The Liverpool Libraries, Museums and Arts Committee.* Bulletin, **7** (1), 1958, 28, ill.

4535. **London.** 1949. *Exhibition of African Art. See:* Africa, **19**, 1949, 160. (Place of meeting not stated.)

4536. **London: Arcade Gallery.** *A small anthology of the human figure.* S.P., ill. London: Arcade Gallery. (Exhibition catalogue, 26 Jan.–20 Feb. 1960.)

4537. **London: Arts Council.** (ARCHER, W. G.) 40,000 *years of modern art.* ill. London: Arts Council. (Bound with catalogue of exhibition entitled 'The art of primitive peoples', pp. 48–54.)

4538. —— 1960. *The Epstein collection of tribal and exotic sculpture.* (Introduction by W. Fagg.) Pp. 42, ill. London: Arts Council.

4539. —— (JONES, G. I.) *The exhibition of Nigerian tribal art.* Africa, **31** (1), 1961, 83–84.

4540. **London: Benin Collection.** (NEVILLE, G. W.) 1897. *A catalogue of the . . . bronzes, ivory and wood carvings from the walled city of Benin.* Pp. 16, ill. London: Foster.

4541. **London: Berkeley Galleries.** 1945. *Exhibition of the art of primitive peoples.* S.P. (16), ill., maps. London: Berkeley Galleries.

4542. —— 1947. *Exhibition of primitive art.* (Foreword to catalogue by F. M. Olbrechts.) London: Berkeley Galleries.

4543. —— (FAGG, W.) 1947. *Art of primitive peoples.* London: Berkeley Galleries.

4544. —— *Exhibition of the art of ancient Nigeria, 8 Jan.–3 Feb* (195–).

4545. —— *Nigerian pottery shown a* t*he Berkeley Galleries; new techniques based on traditional West African methods.* Museums Journal, **57**, 1958, 291.

4546. **London: British Museum: Ethnographical Department.** *Collection of illustrations of African art and African peoples, classified geographically.* (Permission to inspect must be sought from the Keeper.)

4547. **London: British Museum.** (READ, SIR C. H., and O. M. DALTON.) 1899. *Antiquities from the city of Benin, and from other parts of West Africa.* Pp. vi + 61, ill. London: British Museum.

4548. —— (JOYCE, T. A., and H. J. BRAUNHOLTZ.) 1925. *Handbook to the ethnographical collections.* ill. London: British Museum. (2nd ed.)

4549. —— (FAGG, WILLIAM.) 1953. *Webster Plass collection of African art.* (Catalogue of pieces in the King Edward VII Gallery.) Pp. 45, ill. London: British Museum.

4550. —— (GRIGSON, R.) 1957. *Art treasures of the British Museum.* Pp. 210, ill. London.

4551. **London: Colonial and Indian Exhibition.** 1886. *Catalogue of the exhibits of the Colony of the Cape of Good Hope.* Pp. 134. London.

4552. **London: Commonwealth Institute.** (McEWEN, FRANK.) 1963. *New art from Rhodesia.* Pp. 5, ill. London. (Catalogue of an exhibition held at the Commonwealth Institute, 21 Feb.–15 Apr. 1963.)

4553. **London: Collection: Curtis Moffat.** (LEDERER, P.) *Primitive Art of Africa . . . in the collection of Curtis Moffat.* Connoisseur, **95**, 1935, 205–10.

4554. **London: Hanover Gallery.** (LEIRIS, M., and J. DAMASE.) 1959. *Sculpture of the Tellem and the Dogon (Sculptures . . . found in the high cliffs of Bandiagara).* (Partly in French.) Pp. 56, ill. London: Graphis Press. (Exhibition catalogue.)

4555. **London: Hulbert, Charles.** 1826. *Museum Africanum or select antiquities, curiosities, beauties and varieties of nature and art in Africa.* Pp. 234, ill., map. London: G. & W. B. Whittaker.

4556. **London: Imperial Institute** (afterwards **Royal Commonwealth Institute**). 1951. *Traditional sculpture from the Colonies. An illustrated handbook . . . May to Sept. 1951.* (Introduction by W. Fagg.) Pp. 7, ill. London: H.M.S.O.

4557. **London: Institute of Contemporary Arts.** (PLASS, MARGARET.) 1957. *Metal casting on the Guinea coast.* S.P. (12), map. London: Institute of Contemporary Arts. (Exhibition catalogue.)

4558. —— (PLASS, WEBSTER.) 1957. *Lost wax (metal casting on the Guinea coast.)* (Introduction by W. Fagg.) Pp. 12, map as endpaper. London: Institute of Contemporary Arts.

4559. **London: Knoedler Galleries.** 1935. *Bronzes and ivories from the old kingdom of Benin.* Pp. 36. (Exhibition catalogue, 25 Nov.–14 Dec. 1935.)

4560. **London: Lefevre Galleries.** 1933. *Primitive African sculpture.* Pp. 32, ill., map. London: Lefevre Galleries.

4561. **London: Royal Anthropological Institute.** (TONGUE, HELEN M.) *Bushman paintings; catalogue of the facsimiles of Bushman paintings, and chippings . . . on view at the Royal Anthropological Institute.* Pp. 8. London: Spottiswoode.

4562. —— (FAGG, WILLIAM.) 1949. *Traditional art of the British Colonies exhibition, 21 June–20 July 1949.* (Catalogue.) Pp. v (1), 18, ill. London: Royal Anthropological Institute.

4563. —— (FAGG, BERNARD.) *New discoveries from Ife on exhibition at the Royal Anthropological Institute.* Man, **49**, no. 79, 1949, 61, ill.

4564. **London: Sotheby Sale: Allman Collection.** (FAGG, WILLIAM.) *The Allman collection of Benin antiquities.* Man, **53**, 261, Nov. 1953, 165–9, ill.

4565. **London: Sotheby & Co. Sale Catalogue.** 1959. *Catalogue of fine African sculpture, American and oceanic art.* Pp. 40, ill. London: Sotheby & Co.

4566. **London: Victoria and Albert Museum.** (WACE, A. J. B.) 1935. *Catalogue of Algerian embroideries.* London: Victoria and Albert Museum.

4566a. **London: Whitechapel Art Gallery.** *Painting and environment; Nigeria, Uganda.* Pp. 12, maps. London: Whitechapel Art Gallery. (Exhibition catalogue, 12 May–25 July 1964.)

4566b. **London: Zwemmer .** (MURRAY, K. C.) *Nigerian masks and head-dresses; a London exhibition.* Man, **49**, no. 147, 1949, 114–15, ill., and Nigerian Field, **15**, 1950, 26–39, ill.

4567. **Manchester: Museum.** (SEWTER, A. C., and F. WILLETT.) 1952. *Primitive art from the Manchester Museum, 7 May–2 June 1952.* (Introduction by A. C. Sewter and catalogue by Frank Willett.) Pp. 20, ill. Manchester: Manchester Museum.

4568. —— (WILLETT, FRANK.) 1958. *Manchester Museum; Ethnology.* (Guide.) Pp. 16, ill., map. Manchester: Manchester Museum.

4569. **Swansea.** 1957. *Traditional African sculpture.* (Introduction by W. Fagg.) Pp. 24, ill., map. County Borough of Swansea. (Exhibition catalogue.)

4570. **Wakefield: City Council.** 1950. *Art in South Africa; prehistoric rock engravings and rock painting, Bantu arts and crafts.* Pp. 24, ill. Wakefield: City Art Gallery. (Exhibition catalogue.)

4571–2. See 4566a, 4566b.

HOLLAND

4573. **Amsterdam: Stedelijk Museum.** 1955. *Moderne Kunst, niuew en oud.* 37 photographs. Amsterdam: Stedelijk Museum.

4574. **Amsterdam: Koloniaal Instituut. Afdeeling Völkenkunde.** 1940. *Kameroen en Kongo; Kunst en Cultuur en Afrika.* Pp. 63, bibl., ill. Arnhem: Van Loghum Slaterus.

4575. **Amsterdam: Tropen Museum.** (BERGMAN, R. A. M.) *Marokko.* (Exhibition, 14 Oct. 1955–1 Mar. 1956.) Pp. 12, ill. Amsterdam: N. V. Drukkerij Sigfried.

4576. —— 1952. *Rotstekeningen Afrika* (Wall paintings in Basuto-land.) Feb.–Mar. 1952. Pp. 20, ill., map. Amsterdam: Tropen Museum.

4577. —— 1957–8. *Arts en Medicijnman.* Dec. 1957–Apr. 1958. Pp. 20, ill. Amsterdam: Tropen Museum.

4578. —— Summer 1959. *Congolese contrasts.* ill. Amsterdam: Tropen Museum.

4579. **Delft Etnografisch Museum.** 1960. *Van Niger tot Limpopo; Negerkunst uit Afrika.* 28 May–3 Sept. 1960. (Text, J. Den Hoog: Catalogue no. 2.)

4580. **Groningen: Groninger Museum voor Stad en Lander.** 1962. *Kunst van verre Landen.* S.P., ill. Groningen: Museum. (Catalogue of an exhibition.)

4581. **Leiden: Reichsmuseum.** (MARQUART, J.) 1913. *Die Benin-sammlung des Reichsmuseums für Völkerkunde iu Leiden.* 16 + ccclxvii, 132, ill. Leiden: Brill.

4582. **Leiden: Rijksmuseum voor Volkenkunde.** 1947. *Afrikaanse Kunst in Nederland.* (Catalogue.) Pp. 119 (3), ill. Leiden: Museum voor Volkenkunde.

4583. **Otterlo: Rijksmuseum Kroeller-Mueller.** 1960. *Vorm en Kleur; Beeldhouwwerken (Uit) Africa . . . de Kunst der . . . Kongo.* Pp. 8, ill. Otterlo: Museum. (Exhibition, July–Sept. 1960. List of exhibits in separate pamphlet, p. 26.)

4584. **Rotterdam: Museum voor Land-en Volkenkunde.** 1956. *Negerkunst.* Pp. 26 (2), ill. Rotterdam: Museum voor Land-en Volkenkunde.

4585. —— 1958. *Orientatic in het Museum . . . Primitive Kunst.* Pp. 39, ill. Rotterdam: Museum voor Land-en Volkenkunde.

4586. —— 1961. *Mythen, maskers, magie bij het Volk van de Dogon.* Pp. 36, ill. Rotterdam: Museum voor Land-en Volkenkunde.

ISRAEL

4587. **Jerusalem: National Museum.** 1953. *Masks of primitive peoples from the collection of Alex Rafaeli.* Pp. 32, ill. (Catalogue of exhibition, Feb.–Mar. 1953.)

4588. **Tel Aviv: Museum.** 1960. *African art; collection Samuel Dubiner.* Pp. 28, ill. Jerusalem: Bezalel National Museum. (Exhibition, 7 Aug.–7 Oct. 1960: 'The Traditional Sculpture of Negro Africa'.)

ITALY

4589. **Museums.** (RUGIU, GIULIO.) *Sui materiali etnografici procurati al nostro Paese dalla R. Societa Geografica Italiana.* Roy. Ist. Superiore di Scienze Sociali e Politiche 'Cesare Alfieri', Centro di Studi Col.: atti del 1 Congresso di Studi Col., **4**, 3, Apr. 1931, 64–67.

4590. **Florence: Museo Nazionale d'Antropologia.** (MOCHI.) 1901. *Gli oggetti etnografici delle popolazione etiopiche posseduti dal Museo Nazionale d'Antropologia in Firenze.* Florence.

4591. **Naples: Arts du Cameroon.** (TRUITARD, SUZANNE, and OTHERS.) 1934. *Arts du Cameroun à l'exposition d'art colonial de Naples,* 1934. Pp. 35, ill. Paris: Agence Economique des Colonies Autonomes et des Territoires Africains sous Mandat.

4592. **Rome: Fratelli-Palombi.** 1931. *Mostra Internazionale d'Arte Coloniale; Catalogo.* Pp. 406, ill.

4593. **Rome: Museo 'Luigi Pigorini'.** (BAROCELLI, P.) 1939. *Il Museo preistorico ed etnografico 'Luigi Pigorini'.* Pp. 30, ill. Rome: Ist. Studi Romani.

4594. **Rome: Missionary Exhibition of Primitive Art.** 1950. *The arts in Belgian Congo and Ruanda-Urundi.* Pp. 82, bibl., ill. Rome.

4595. **Rome: Palazzo Venezia.** (MAESEN, A.) 1959. *Arte del Congo.* Pp. 86, bibl., ill., pl. 1–63, map. Rome: De Luca Editore. (Exhibition at the Palazzo Venezia, Nov. 1959.)

4596. **Rome: Galleria Cichi: Via del Greci.** 1960. *Sculture dell' Africa Nera.*

4597. **Turin.** (SCOTTI, P.) *La collezione etnografica delle Missione Salesiana in Torino.* Riv. biologia coloniale, **4** (4–5), 1941, 193–214.

4598. **Vatican City.** (MAESEN, A.) 1950. *Traditional sculpture in the Belgian Congo.* Pp. 9–34. (Vatican exhibition catalogue, 1950.)

4599. —— (MAESEN, A., and OTHERS.) 1950. *Les arts au Congo Belge et au Ruanda-Urundi.* Pp. 89, ill. Brussels: Centre d'Information et de Documentation. (Exposition Vaticane.)

4600. —— 1950. *Le Arti nel Congo Belga e nel Ruanda-Urundi.* Pp. 84 + 98 pl. Brussels: Centre d'Informazione. (Vatican exhibition.)

NORWAY

4601. **Bergen: Bergens Kunstforening.** S.D. *Eksotisk Kunst* (Exhibition). Pp. 44, ill. Bergen: Bergens Kunstforening.

4602. **Oslo: Kunstindustrimuseet.** 1956. *Kongokunst; Kunst og Kunstindustri fra Belgisk Kongo.* Pp. 33, ill., map. Oslo: Kunstindustrimuseet.

4603. —— 1959. *Hulemalerier fra Sahara* (Henri L'hotes ekspedisjon til Tassili, 4–27 Sept. 1959). (Foreword by G. Gjersing; text by Henri L'hote.) Pp. 31, ill. Oslo: O. Andersens Boktrykkeri.

POLAND

4604. **Warsaw: Musée de la Culture et de l'Art Populaire.** (SZYFELBEJN-SOKOLEWICZ, Z.) *Exposition Ethnographique; 'L'Afrique Inconnue'.* (Catalogue.) Pp. 40, ill. Warsaw: Editions Polonia.

PORTUGAL

4605. **Lisbon: Maconde of Mozambique.** (DIAS, ANTÓNIO JORGE.) 1959. *Vida e arte do povo Maconde.* Pp. 7. Lisboa: Exposição . . . Junta de Investigações do Ultramar.

4606. **Lisbon: Museu Escola do Ultramar.** *Noticias de Portugal.* No. 688, Ano. 14, 1960. O Museu Escola do Ultramar, 8–10, ill.

4607. **Anon.** *Musées ethnographiques du Portugal.* Objets et mondes, **3** (4), 1963, 331–2, ill.

4608. **Pessanha, D. S.** *Museus Etnograficos.* Actas Congr. Etnograf-folclore, **1**, 1963, 177–81.

4609. **Coimbra: Museu de Etnografia do Ultramar.** 1955. *Catálogo-Inventario do M.E.U. do Instituto de Antropologia da Universidade de Coimbra.* Junta de Investigações do Ultramar, Anais 10 (1), 1955, 581, ill. Lisbon. (Africa, pp. 1–495.)

4610. **Lisbon: Exposição de Arte Sacra Missionaria.** 1951–2. *Exposição de Arte Sacra Missionaria.* Pp. 101, ill. Lisbon: Agência Geral do Ultramar.

4611. **Luanda: Museu de Angola.** (REDINHA, JOSÉ.) 1955. *Colecção etnográfica.* Pp. xvii + 101 (1) (1) (1), ill. Luanda: The Museum.

RUSSIA

4612. **Olderogge, D. A.** 1958. *Iskustvo narodov zapadnoi Afriki v Muzeyakh U.S.S.R.—L'art de l'Afrique occidentale représenté dans les musées de l'URSS.* Pp. 93 + xlvii pl., bibl. Moscow: 'Iskustvo' (State art publishing house).

4613. **Yablochkov, L. D.** 1958. *Afrikanski etnograficheski sbornik* II (African ethnographic collection, 1 and II). No. 2, pp. 270, maps. Moscow: Akademia Nauk, U.S.S.R.

SPAIN

4614. **Barcelona: Museo Etnologico y Colonial.** (PANYELLA, AUGUSTO.) 1952. *El Museo Etnologico y Colonial.* Pp. 200, ill. Barcelona: Museo Etnologico y Colonial.

4615. —— (HUERA, CARMEN.) *Catálogo del Arte negro africano del Museo Etnologico de Barcelona.*

4616. **Madrid: Museo Arqueologico Nacional.** 1883. *Catalogo del Museo Arqueologico Nacional.* Pp. 356, ill. Madrid.

4617. —— *Catalogo sumario del Museo Arqueológico Nacional; Antiguedades prehistoricas.* Pp. 78, ill.

4618. **Madrid: Museo Etnológico.** (BARBERAN, CECILIO.) *El Tema Arabe en el Museo Etnológico de Madrid.* Africa (Madrid), nos. 56/57, 1946, 426–7, ill.

4619. **Madrid.** (GAYA NUÑO, JUAN ANTONIO.) 1955. *Historia y Guia de los Museos de España.* Pp. 917, ill. Madrid: Espasa-Calpe.

4620. **Madrid: Museo Etnológico.** 1947. *Guia del Museo Etnológico.* Pp. 158, ill. 1957. Cuadernos del Museo Etnológico, vol. I.

4621. **Madrid.** *Exposición de Pintores de Africa.* (1) Pp. 114 + 14 pl. 1951. (2) Pp. 148 + 9 pl. 1952. (3) Pp. 144 + 12 pl. 1952. (4) Pp. 112 + 9 pl. 1953. (5) Pp. 192 + 14 pl. 1953.

SWEDEN

4622. **Göteborg (Gothenburg): Etnografiska Museet.** 1955–6. *Arstryck.* Pp. 94, ill. (Annual report in progress.)

4623. **Stockholm: National Museum.** 1953. *Negerkonst.* Pp. 128, ill., map. Stockholm: National Museum. (Exhibition catalogue, Mar.–Apr. 1953.)

4624. **Stockholm: Statens Etnografiska Museet.** (RUDNER, I. and J.) 1957. *A. Sparrman's ethnographical collection from S. Africa.* Pp. 28, ill. Stockholm: Statens Etnografiska Museet. (Smarre Meddelanden, 25.)

SWITZERLAND

4625. **Basler Museum für Völkerkunde.** 1912. *Bericht über das Basler Museum für Völkerkunde,* 1911. (In continuation.)

4626. —— 1939. *Einführung in das Museum für Völkerkunde.* Pp. 96. Basle: Museum f. Völkerkunde.

4627. —— 1953. *Führer durch das Museum für Völkerkunde und Schweizerische Museum für Volkskunde. Primitive Stoffmusterungen.* Pp. 23, ill. Basle: Museum f. Völkerkunde. (Special exhibition catalogue, 6 Sept.–31 Dec. 1953.)

4628. —— 1954. *Negerschmiede; Metalltechnik Exotischer Völker.* Pp. 11. Basle: Museum f. Völkerkunde. (Exhibition catalogue, 31 Jan.–28 Mar. 1954.)

4629. —— 1957. *Beduinen aus Nordost-Afrika (Burckhardt Sammlung).* Pp. 24, bibl., ill., maps. Basle: Museum f. Völkerkunde. (Exhibition catalogue, 12 Apr.–30 Sept. 1957.)

4630. —— 1959. *Mensch und Handwerk; 'Die Töpferei'.* (Catalogue.) Pp. 27, ill. Basle: Museum f. Völkerkunde.

4631. —— (REICHSTEIN, R.) 1961. *Geldformen und Zierperlen der Naturvölker. Führer durch das Museum f. Völkerkunde . . . Sonderausstellung,* 6 May–29 Oct. 1961. Pp. 39, ill. Basle: Museum f. Völkerkunde.

4632. —— 1962. *Die Maske; Gestalt und Sinn.* Pp. 40, ill. Basle: Museum f. Völkerkunde.

4633. —— 1963. *Technologie Frühzeitlicher Waffen.* Pp. 82, bibl., ill. Basle: Museum f. Völkerkunde. (Exhibition guide, 1 June–31 Dec. 1963.)

4634. **Basle: Sammlung Nord-Kamerun Expedition.** (HINDERLING, PAUL.) *Die Ethnographische Sammlung von Nordkamerun der Expedition Gari-Hinderling,* 1953. Verh. Naturf. Ges. (Basel), **65,** 1954, 106–22, ill.

4635. **Basle: Galerie Beyeler.** 1958. *L'Art nègre; negerplastik (mainly Dogon).* Pp. 32, ill. Basle: Galerie Beyeler. (Catalogue de l'Exposition . . . Feb. 1958.)

4636. **Basle: Kunsthalle.** 1962. *Nigeria; 2000 Jahre Plastik.* (Introduction by W. B. Fagg.) Pp. 56, bibl., ill., map. Basle: Kunsthalle. (Exhibition catalogue, 20 Jan.–18 Feb. 1962.)

4637. **Bern: Bernisches Historisches Museum.** (VON DER HEYDT, E.) 1947. *Kunst der Naturvölker.* Wiss. Beilagen zum Jb. des Bernischen Historischen Museums Ethnog. Abt.

4638. **Bern: Kunsthalle.** 1953. *Kunst der Neger.* Pp. 23, ill., map. Bern: Kunsthalle. (Exhibition catalogue.)

4639. **Geneva: Musée d'Ethnographie.** (LOBSIGER-DELLENBACH, M.) 1944. *Les masques dans le monde. La fabrication des masques à la Côte d'Ivoire.* Les Musées de Genève, **1,** 4, 1944, 3, ill. (Catalogue of an exhibition of the masks open until 31 Oct. 1944.)

4640. **Geneva.** (MONTANDON, GEORGES.) *Catalogue raisonné des Instruments de Musique du Musée ethnographique de Genève (Au parc Mon-Repos).* Archives Suisses d'anthropologie générale, 3 mars 1919, 95–118, ill.

4641. **Neuchâtel: Musée d'Ethnographie.** (VAN GENNEP, A.) 1914. *Guide sommaire du Musée d'Ethnographie de Neuchâtel.*

4642. —— 1957. *Sahara 57.* Pp. 180, ill. Neuchâtel: Musée d'Ethnographie. (Collection of essays to accompany an exhibition.)

4643. —— 1961. *Exposition; 'Parures et Bijoux dans le Monde'* (18 June–31 Dec. 1961). (Catalogue.) Pp. 102, ill. Neuchâtel: Le Musée.

4644. **Zürich: Kunstgewerbemuseum.** 1931. *Prähistorische Felsbilder Sudafrikas* (Leo Frobenius). *Negerkunst* (H. Koray). Zürich: Kunstgewerbemuseum. (Exhibition, 2–30 Aug. 1931.)

4645. —— (ITTEN, JOHANNES.) *Wegleiter 166. Ausstellung. Afrikanische Kunst aus Schweizer Sammlungen* (24 June–2 Sept. 1945). Pp. 31, ill. Zürich: Kunstgewerbemuseum.

4646. —— (VON SYDOW, E.) 1952. *Bildwerke aus Afrika, etc.* Pp. 3, ill. Zürich: Kunstgewerbemuseum. (Sonder ausstellung Sammlung von der Heydt.)

4647. **Zürich: Sammlung für Völkerkunde der Univ. Zürich.** (HINTERMANN, H.) 1932. *Eine Führung durch die Sammlung für Völkerkunde der Universität, Zürich. Abt. Afrika und Südsee.* Pp. 168, ill., map. Zürich: Grethlein and Co.

4648. —— (STEINMANN, ALFRED.) 1943. *Die Sammlung für Völkerkunde der Univ. Zürich.* Mitt. d. Geogr.-Ethnogr. Ges. Zürich, Bd. 41, 1941–3, 25–84.

4649. —— (STEINMANN, ALFRED.) 1956. *Einführing in die Sammlung f. Völkerkunde der Universität Zürich.* Pp. 26 + xxiv, ill.

4650. —— (LEUZINGER, E.) *Afrikanische Plastik in der Sammlung fur Völkerkunde, Zürich.* Mitt. Geogr.-Ethnogr. Ges. Zürich, 1935–6, 165–83.

4651. —— 1956. *Basler Forscher bei fremden Völkern.* S.P., ill. Zürich. (Ausstellung, 9 June–30 Sept. 1956.)

4652. **Zürich: Sammlung von der Heydt.** 1935. *Führer durch die Leihgaben primitiver Kunst aus der Sammlung von der Heydt im Züricher Museum für Kunstgewerbe.* Zürich: Museum f. Kunstgewerbe.

4653. **Zürich: Rietberg Museum.** (LEUZINGER, ELSY.) 1962. *Guide to the Rietberg Museum (von der Heydt Collection).* Pp. 133, bibl., ill. Zürich: Rietberg Museum.

4654. —— (LEUZINGER, ELSY.) *Afrikanische Skulpturen; Beschreibender Katalog (Widmung zum 80 Geburtstag von Dr. Eduard von der Heydt).* Pp. 326, bibl., ill., map. Zürich: Atlantis Verlag. (German and English in parallel columns.)

4655. **Zürich.** (ILG.) 1892. *Katalog der ethnographischen Sammlungen aus Abessinien.* Zürich.

U.S.A.

See America.

U.S.S.R.

See Russia.

YUGOSLAVIA

4656. **Zagreb: Musée des Arts Décoratifs.** 1957. *Musej za umjetnost i obrt u Zagrebu. Iz Afrike i Oceanije.* Pp. 44, ill. Zagreb: Musée des Arts Décoratifs.

4657. **Zagreb: Ethnographical Museum,** (GUŠIĆ MARIJANA.) 1955. *Commentary on the exhibited material.* Zagreb Ethnographical Museum.

BIBLIOGRAPHIES OF AFRICANA LIKELY TO BE OF USE TO THE STUDENT

AFRICA: GENERAL

(*See also* under Southern Africa, page 93)

4658. *African abstracts*, 1950–. In progress.

4659. *African studies bulletin*. African Studies Association, 409 West 107 Street, New York. Vol. 1, no. 1, Apr. 1958, 35.

4660. **Anon.** *A bibliography of African bibliographies covering territories south of the Sahara.* Cape Town. (3rd ed. rev. to August 1955.)

4661. **Atkins, Guy.** 1958. *Selected bibliography of African sculpture.* Pp. 8, ill. London: School of Oriental and African Studies.

4662. —— 1961. *An introduction to the literature on African sculpture with bibliography.* Legum, Colin, Africa: a handbook to the Continent, pp. 425–427.

4663. **Balandier, G., Middleton, J. F. M.,** and **Others.** *International bibliography of social and cultural anthropology.* Vol. 1 (1955), pub. 1958, 259. Vol. 2 (1956), pub. 1959, 391. Vol. 3 (1957), pub. 1959, 410. Paris: UNESCO.

4664. **Banks, A.** 1960. *An African book-list.* London.

4665. **Belgium: Ministère des Colonies.** 1913. *Catalogue de la bibliothèque; 1 Afrique.*

4666. **Breuil, Henri.** *Publications on Africa.* J. soc. africanistes, 32, 1962, 75–89, map.

4667. **Collison, R. L.** *Bibliographical services throughout the world* (Africa, pp. 8–19). 4th ann. rep., 1954/55, 145. Paris: UNESCO.

4668. —— 1950. *The cataloguing, arrangement and filing of special material in special libraries.* Pp. iv + 76. London: A.S.L.I.B.

4668a.**Conover, H. F.** 1957. *Africa south of the Sahara: a selected annotated list of writings,* 1951–56. Pp. 269. Washington: Library of Congress.

4669. —— 1960. *A list of references on libraries, archives and book production in Africa.* Pp. 54. Washington: Library of Congress.

4670. —— 1961. *Serials for African studies.* Pp. viii + 163. Washington: Library of Congress. (Introductory list of bibliographies, 1861, p. 7.)

4671. —— 1962. *African libraries, book production and archives.* Pp. vi + 64. Washington: Library of Congress.

4672. —— 1959. *The bibliography of newly developing areas.* Library trends (Urbana, Ill.), 8 (2), 1959, 322–41.

4673. **Dahlberg, Richard E.,** and **B. E. Thomas.** *An analysis and bibliography of recent African atlases.* Afr. Stud. Bull., 5, no. 3, 1962, 23–33.

4674. *Encyclopédie de l'Afrique française.* Algérie-Sahara (2 vols.). Tunisie. Maroc. *Afrique occidentale française* (2 vols.). Afrique équatoriale française. Cameroun-Togo, 1951. Madagascar-Reunion (2 vols.). (Ed. by d'Eugène Guernier.) Editions de l'Union Française. All with bibls.

4675. *Ethnographic survey of Africa.* (Ed. by C. D. Forde.)

4676. *Ethnologischer Anzeiger.* 1926–1944. (4 vols.).

4677. *Ethnology and sociology.* Quarterly list of ethnology (and) sociology. An international index of current books, monographs, brochures and separates. Vol. 2, no. 1. 1951.

4678. **Evanston: Northwestern University.** 1962. *Catalog of the African collection* (21,500 vols.) (2 vols.). Vol. 1, A–K, pp. 698. Vol. 2, L–Z, pp. 652. Boston, Mass.: G. K. Hall.

4679. **Fontán Lobé, Juan.** 1946. *Bibliografía colonial; contribución a un indice de publicaciones africanas.* Pp. 669. Madrid: Dirección general de Marruecos y Colonias.

4680. **Forde, C. D.** N.D. *Select annotated bibliography of tropical Africa.* Pp. 504. London: Int. African Inst. 20th Century Fund, New York.

4681. **Fraser, Douglas.** *African architecture (bibliography).* Afr. Stud. Bull., 5, no. 2, 1962, 47–49.

4682. **Freer, P.** (*ed.*). 1952. *Catalogue of Union periodicals.* Vol. 2, The humanities. Pp. 806. Pretoria: National Council of Social Research.

4683. **Frobenius, Leo.** *Das wissenschaftliche Schrifttum von L. Frobenius.* Paiduma, 4, 1950.

4684. **Geiger, P.,** and **R. Wildhaber.** 1949, 1950. *Bibliographie internationale des arts et des traditions populaires,* 1939–41, 1942–47. Pp. 273, 482. Paris: Commission Int. des Arts et Traditions Populaires (C.I.A.P.).

4685. **Gray, T.** 1875. *Bibliographie des ouvrages relatifs à l'Afrique et à l'Arabie; catalogue méthodique de tous les ouvrages français et des principaux en langues étrangères traitant de la géographie, de l'histoire, du commerce, des lettres et des arts de l'Afrique et de l'Arabie.* San Remo, Paris.

4686. **Haden, J. W.** 1958. *Bibliographical contributions.* No. 16, Africa. Pp. 97. Geneva: Int. Labour Office.

4687. **Hambly, Wilfrid D.** 1937. *Source book for African anthropology.* Pp. 404, 953, 292, bibl., ill., maps. Pt. 2, 728–866. Chicago: Field Museum of Natural History (Anthropological Series), vol. 26. (Supplement in Fieldiana (anthropology), 37, 1952, 155–292.)

4688. **Hewitt, A. R.** 1958. *Guide to resources for Commonwealth studies in London.* Pp. 219. London: Athlone Press.

4689. **Holdsworth, Mary.** *Afrikakunde in der Sovjetunion.* Osteuropa (Stuttgart), 7–8, 1959, 442–51.

4690. **Hodgkin, Thomas.** *Soviet Africanists.* West Afr., 2209, 1959, 801; 2210, 1959, 829–30; 2211, 1959, 857–8.

4691. **Hughes, H. G. A.** *The bibliography of British Africa and the co-ordination of African studies.* Afr. affairs, 48 (190), 1949, 63–72.

4692. **Hutson, J. B.** *African materials in the Schomburg collection of negro literature and history.* Afr. stud. bull., 3, no. 11, 1960, 1–4.

4693. **Italiaander, Rolf.** 1961. *Africana; selected bibliography of readings in African history and civilisation.* Pp. 6 + 103. Hope College, Holland, Michigan.

4694. **Jolly, D.** *Bibliography and the arts of Africa.* Afr. stud. bull., 3 (1), 1960, 4–9.

4694a.**Johnson, A. F.** 1964. *A bibliography of Ghana.* Pp. xiii + 210. London: Longmans.

4695. **Keesing, F. M.** 1953. *Culture change; an analysis and bibliography of anthropological sources.* Pp. ix + 242. Stanford, Calif.: Stanford Univ. Press.

4695a.**Kelley, Douglas C.** 1960. *Africa in Paperbacks . . . in print,* May, 1960. Pp. 37. East Lansing: Michigan State Univ.

4696. **King, P. S.,** and **P. L. Theimer.** 1956. *Tropical Africa; administrative division (map and list).* Pp. 5. Stanford, Calif.: Stanford Univ. Press. (Stanford University Ford Research Institute, California, U.S.A.)

4697. **Klein, H.** *Afrika südlich der Sahara.* Ethnol. Veröff., 1945–50. Paiduma, 5, 1951, 138–50.

4698. **Lavanoux, Maurice.** *A selected, annotated bibliography on Africa.* Liturgical arts (N.Y.), 26, 3/4 (suppl.), Apr. 1959, 3–39.

4699. **Levi-Strauss, C.** 1956. *French bibliographical digest; Anthropology 1—Physical anthropology and prehistoric archaeology; 2—Ethnology and social anthropology.* Pp. 63 and 88, ill. New York: Cultural Division of the French Embassy.

4700. **London: Central Office of Information.** 1954. *Commonwealth book list.* Pp. 43 and map. London: Central Office of Information.

4701. **McKay, V.,** and **Others.** *American library resources for African studies.* Afr. Stud. Bull. (N.Y.), 2 (1), 1959, 21.

4702. **Michigan State University.** 1958. *Michigan State University; Institute of Research and Overseas programmes. The international progress of American universities; an inventory and analysis.*

4703. **Mylius, Norbert.** 1952. *Afrika bibliographie, 1943–1951.* Pp. vi + 237. Vienna: Museum für Völkerkunde.

4704. **New York: Metropolitan Museum of Art.** 1960. *Library catalog.* Vols. 1–25, A–Z. Boston: G. K. Hall.

4704a. **Pan-African Touring Club.** *Principal tribes of sub-equatorial Africa.* Map. Johannesburg: The Club.

4705. **Paris: Comité du Film.** *Ethnographique catalogue des filmes ethnographiques français.* UNESCO: Cah. Centr. Documen., 15, 1955, 72.

4706. **Paulitschke, P.** 1882. *Die Afrika-literatur in der Zeit von 1500 bis 1750 B.C.* Pp. v + 122. Vienna.

4707. **Porter, D. P.** (ed.). 1958. *A catalogue of the African collection in the Moorland Foundation, Howard University Library.* Pp. 398. Washington: Howard Univ. Press.

4708. **Ragatz, L. J.** 1943. *A bibliography for the study of African history in the 19th and 20th centuries.* Pp. 47. Washington: Paul Pearlman.

4709. **Robinson, A. M. L.** 1955. *A bibliography of African bibliographies.* Pp. 169. Cape Town: S. African Library. (Grey bibliographies, no. 6.)

4710. **Royal Anthropological Institute, London.** 1953. *Anthropological and monograph series . . . in the libraries of Great Britain.* Pp. 24. London: Royal Anthrop. Inst.

4711. —— *List of periodical and monograph series.* J. roy. anthrop. inst., 76, 1946, 189–210.

4711a. —— 1957. *Survey of anthropological journals and monograph series in libraries in the United Kingdom.* Pp. 17. London: Royal Anthrop. Inst.

4711b. —— *Index to current periodicals received 1962.* (In progress.) London: Royal Anthrop. Inst.

4712. **Scientific Council of Africa, South of the Sahara.** 1955. *List of scientific societies.* Pp. 32. London. 1955. *Maps of Africa south of the Sahara.* Pp. 70. London. 1957. *Mapping and surveying Africa south of the Sahara.* P. 58.

4713. **Sieber, Roy.** *African art (bibliography).* Afr. Stud. Bull., 5, no. 2, 1962, 40–44.

4714. **Spain.** 1947. *Exposicion de libros españoles sobre historia de Africa.* Pp. 100.

4715. **Standing Conference on Library Materials on Africa.** 1963. *The SCOLMA directory of libraries and special collections on Africa.* Pp. 18. London.

4716. **Streit, P. Robert,** and **P. Johannes Dindinger.** 1951–4. *Bibliotheca Missionum* (6 vols.). (Afrikansiche Missionsliteratur.) Band 15, 1053–1599, nos. 1–2217. Band 16, 1600–99, nos. 2218–5151. Band 17, 1700–1879, nos. 5152–7723. Band 18, 1880–1909, nos. 7724–9753. Band 19, 1910–40, nos. 9754–9843. Band 20, 1910–40, nos. 9844–10818. Freiburg: Herder.

4717. **Tenri Central Library: Tenri, Japan.** 1960. *Catalogue of books relating to Africa.* Tenri Central Library, series no. 24. Pp. 431, ill.

4718. **Ternaux-Comparus, H.** 1841. (–2). *Bibliothèque asiatique et africaine ou catalogue des ouvrages relatifs à l'Asie et à l'Afrique qui ont parus depuis la découverte de l'imprimerie jusqu'en 1700.* Paris.

4719. **University of London: School of Oriental and African Studies.** 1963. *Library catalogue.* Vol. 15, Subject catalogue Africa. Pp. 618. Boston, Mass.: G. K. Hall.

4720. **U.S.A. Dept. of State: Office of Intelligence.** *Africa.* External research list no. 13.6. April 1956, 12.

4721. **Valle, Rafael Heliodoro.** *Para la Bibliografia Afroamericana.* Ortiz, Fernando, Miscelanea de Estudios dedicados a Fernando Ortiz, vol. 3, 1957, 1427–65.

4721a. **Van den Berghe, L.** and **L. de Heusch.** *Rencontres internationales; le cinéma et l'Afrique au Sud du Sahara.* Expos. Univ. et Internat, Brussels, 24–26 July, 1958, 130.

4721b. **Van Warmelo, N. J.** 1952. *Language map of Africa.* Pp. 20, map. Pretoria: Dept. of Native Affairs. (Ethnol. pubn. no. 27.)

4721c. **Von Luschan.** *Die bibliographie Felix von Luschan.* Z.f. Ethnol. 83, 1958, 285–95, ill.

4722. **Washington: Library of Congress (European Affairs Division).** 1952. *Introduction to Africa; a select guide to background reading.* Pp. x + 237. Washington: Univ. Press.

4723. **Washington: Library of Congress.** 1952. *Introduction to Africa; a selective guide to background reading.* (Prepared by the Library of Congress European Affairs Division.) Washington.

4724. **Wieschoff, H. A.** 1948. *Anthropological bibliography of negro Africa (up to 1942).* Pp. xi + 461. New Haven, Conn.: Amer. Orient. Soc. Amer. Orient Series, vol. 23.

4725. **Work, Monroe Nathan.** 1928. *A bibliography of the negro in Africa and America.* Pp. 21, 698. New York: H. W. Wilson.

4725a. **Worthington, E. B.** ed. 1954. *Recherches relatives aux sciences humaines en Afrique au Sud du Sahara.* Pp. 75. Bukavu, Congo Belge: C.S.A., 5175 (pubn. no. 7.)

NORTH AFRICA

4726. **Bauer, Y.,** and **Ignacio Landauer.** 1922. *Apuntes para una bibliografia de Marruecos.* Pp. xvi + 1023. Madrid: Editorial Ibero-Africano-Americana.

4727. **Blaudin de Thé, Bernard.** 1960. *Essai de bibliographie du Sahara français et des régions avoisinantes.* Pp. 258. Paris: Arts et métiers graphiques. (Addresses of some of the French periodicals mentioned in the bibliography.)

4728. **Conover, H. F.** 1957. *North and North-East Africa; a selected, annotated list of writings 1951–57.* Pp. 182. Washington: Library of Congress.

4729. **C.O.W.A. Surveys and Bibliographies.** *North-West Africa,* no. 1. 1958. Cambridge, Mass.: Council for Old World Archaeology.

4730. **Creswell, K. A. C.** 1961. *A bibliography of archaeology, arts and crafts of Islam.* Pp. 480, ill. London.

4731. **de Cenival, Pierre,** and **Others.** N.D. *Bibliographie marocaine, 1923–1933.* Pp. 606. Paris: Larose.

4732. **Evans-Pritchard, E. E.** *A select bibliography of writings on Cyrenaica.* Afr. stud., 4, 1945, 146–80; 5, 1946, 189–94.

4733. **Funck-Brentano, Chr.** *Études, notes et documents sur le Sahara occidental.* VIIe Congrès de l'Institut des Hautes-Études Marocaines, 1930, 203–96.

4734. **Hill, R. W.** 1959. *A bibliography of Libya.* Pp. 100. Durham: Durham Colleges in the University of Durham: Dept. of Geography, Research papers series no. 1.

4735. **Huard, P.** *Répertoire des stations rupestres du Sahara oriental français (confins-Nigéro-Tchadiens, Tibesti, Borkou, Ennedi).* J. soc. africanistes, 23, 1953, 43–76, maps. (Contains an index bibliographique, pp. 74–76.)

4736. **Ibrahim Hilmi, Prince.** *The literature of Egypt and the Soudan from the earliest times to . . . 1885* (2 vols.).

4737. **Jones, Ruth.** 1959. *North-East Africa.* Pp. iii + 51. London: Int. African Inst. (Africa bibliography series.)

4738. **Lacoste, Camille.** 1962. *Bibliographie ethnologique de la Grande Kabylie.* Pp. 103. Paris and The Hague: Mouton & Co.

4739. **Lhote, Henri.** *Inventaire et référénces bibliographiques des peintures rupestres de l'Afrique nord-équatoriale.* Actes du Congrès de Préhistoire, 2nd session, Alger, 1952.

4740. **Monod, Th.** *Notes bibliographiques sur le Sahara occidental.* J. soc. africanistes, 3 (1), 1933, 129–96. Supplément, 1, Tome 3, 1933, 335–40. Supplément, 2, Tome 5, 1935, 117–24.

4741. **el Nasri, Abdel Rahman.** 1962. *A bibliography of the Sudan, 1938–58.* Pp. x + 171. London: Oxford Univ. Press.

4742. **Pearson, J. D.** 1958. *Index Islamicus, 1906–55.* Pp. xxxvi + 897. Cambridge: Heffer.

4743. —— 1962. *Supplement to Index Islamicus, 1956–60.* Pp. xxviii + 316. Cambridge: Heffer.

4744. **Rabat: Institut des Hautes Études Marocaines.** *Publications de l'institut des hautes études marocaines, 1915–35.* Tables et Index-supplément à 'Hespéris', 1936, p. 81. Rochfort-sur-Mer: Institut des Hautes Études Marocaines.

4745. **Tetuán: Bibliotheca General del Protectorado.** 1946. *Catálogo de Autores.* Pp. 677, ill. Tetuán: Librería Escola.

CENTRAL AFRICA

4746. **Baxter, J. W.** *The preservation of archives with particular reference to Central Africa.* Human problems, British Central Africa, 8, 1949, 57–66.

4746a. **Carpenter, Olive.** 1946. *The development of Southern Rhodesia . . . to 1900.* S.P. Cape Town: University School of Librarianship.

4746b. **Jones, Ruth.** 1961. *South-East Central Africa and Madagascar.* Pp. III + 53. London: Intern. African Institute.

4746c. **Salisbury.** *First biennial International Congress of African Culture.* Rhodes National Gallery, Aug.–Sept., 1962.

4747. **Santandrea, S.** 1948. *Bibliografia di studi africani della missione dell' Africa Centrale (Verona Mission).* Pp. xxviii + 167, map. Verona: Istituto Missioni Africani. (Museum Combonianum, no. 1.)

4748. **University of Sydney: Anthrop. Dept.** *Ethnography of Central Africa. Select bibliography revised to February 1958.* 1958, 16.

4749. **Urvoy, Captain.** *Essai de bibliographie des populations du Soudan central.* Bull. com. études A.O.F., 1936, 243–333.

CONGO

4750. **Belgium.** 1957. *Office de l'information pour le Congo Belge et le Ruanda-Urundi. Liste des sociétés et institutions coloniales.* Pp. 80.

4751. **Berlage, J.** 1955. *Répertoire de la presse du Congo Belge (1884–1954) et du Ruanda-Urundi (1920–1954).* Pp. 64. Brussels: Min Colonies (Bibl. Belgica, 10).

4752. **Boone, Olga.** *Carte ethnique du Congo Belge et du Ruanda-Urundi.* Congo-Tervueren, 1, 1955, 6, map.

4753. —— *Bibliographie ethnographique du Congo Belge et des regions avoisinantes.* 1945. (In progress (1963).)

4754. **C.E.P.S.I.** *Centre d'Études des Problèmes Sociaux Indigènes.* 1948. *Catalogue de la bibliothèque.* Pp. 103. Elisabethville: C.E.P.S.I.

4755. **de Rop, E. P. A.** 1956. *Bibliografie over de Mongo.* Pp. 101, map. Brussels: Acad. roy. des Sci. Col. Classe des Sci. Mor. & Polit. Mem. in 80, N.S., tome 8, fasc. 2.

4756. **Heyse, Théodore.** 1948. *Bibliographie du Congo Belge et du Ruanda-Urundi (1939–47).* Pp. 32. Brussels: Cahiers Belges et Congolais, no. 6.

4757. —— 1950. *Bibliographie du Congo Belge et du Ruanda-Urundi, 1939–1949.* Pp. 46, ill. Brussels: Cahiers Belges et Congolais, no. 11.

4758. —— 1951. *Bibliographie du Congo Belge et du Ruanda-Urundi (1939–50).* Pp. 51. Brussels: G. van Campenhout.

4759. **Kellermann, L.** 1953. *Catalogue de la bibliothèque de l'I.E.C.* (*Suppl. no. 1.*) Pp. 234. Brazzaville: Inst. d'études Centrafricaines.

4760. **Lambert, J.** 1951. *Catalogue de la bibliotheque de l'I.E.C.* (*matières, auteurs et périodiques*). Pp. 153. Brazzaville: Institut d'études Centrafricaines (Mém. no. 4).

4761. **Maes, J.,** and **Olga Boone.** 1935. *Les peuplades du Congo Belge; nom et situation géographique.* Pp. iv + 379, maps. Brussels: Imprimerie Veuve Monnom.

4762. **Perrier, G. D.,** and **J. Leyder.** *Essai de bibliographie chronologique sur le graphisme et l'expression graphique au Congo Belge et dans les régions avoisinantes (1900–1947).* Vét. col., 12, 1947, 3–7; 1, 33–48, 1948, 2, 39–47.

4763. **Simar, Th.** 1912. *Bibliographie congolaise de 1895 à 1910.* Brussels.

4764. **Walraet, M.** *Bibliographie du Katanga.* Fasc. 1, 1824–. Fasc. 2, 1900–24. Fasc. 3, 1925–9. A.R.S.C. (sciences morales), 32, 14 and 23, 1954–60, 136, 234, 280, maps.

4765. **Wauters, A. J.** 1895. *Bibliographie du Congo, 1880–1895. Catalogue méthodique de 3800 ouvrages et brochures relatifs au Congo.* Brussels, 354.

4766. **Wauters, G.** 1949. *L'Esoterie des noirs devoilée.* Pp. 384, ill. Brussels: Editions Européennes.

EAST AFRICA

4767. **Brantschen, Anastas.** *Die ethnographische Literatur über den Ulaga-Distrikt, Tanganyika Territorium.* Acta Tropica: Separatum, vol. 10, no. 2, 1953, 150–85.

4767a. **Costa, Mário.** 1946. *Bibliografia geral de Moçambique.* Pp. 359. Lisbon: Agência geral das Colonias.

4768. **C.O.W.A. Surveys and Bibliographies.** *East Africa,* no. 1. 1958. Cambridge, Mass.: Council for Old World Archaeology.

4768a. **de Almeida de Eca, F. G.** 1949. *Bibliografia de Moçambique.* Pp. 134. Lisbon: Agência geral das Colónias.

4769. **Fosbrooke, H. A.** *Tanganyika rock paintings; a guide and record.* Tanganyika notes and records, no. 29, 1950, 1–61, bibl., ill., map.

4770. **Gillman, C.** *A bibliography of Kilimanjaro.* Tanganyika notes and records, 18, 1944, 60–68.

4771. **Jones, Ruth.** 1960. *East Africa.* Pp. iii + 62. London: Int. African Inst. (Africa bibliography series.)

4771a. **Rita-Ferreira, A.** 1962. *Bibliografia Etnologica de Moçambique (Das origens a 1954).* Pp. xiii + 254. Lisbon: Junta de Investigacões do Ultramar.

4772. **Whiteley, W. H.,** and **A. E. Gutkind.** 1954. *A linguistic bibliography of East Africa.* Pp. 61. Kampala: Government Printer.

MADAGASCAR

4772a. **Grandidier, G.** and **W.** 1904–28. *Ethnographique de Madagascar.* Tom. i, 2, and 3 (1908–17), ill., maps.

4772b. **Grandidier, G.** and **E. Joucla.** 1935 and 1957. *Bibliographie de Madagascar, 1904–33. Bibliographie de Madagascar, 1934–35.* Pp. viii + 1350; viii + 1351–1910, ill. Paris: Société des Editions Géographiques, Maritimes et Coloniales. Tananarive: Institut de recherche scientifique de Madagascar. *See also* 4746b.

WEST AFRICA

4773. **Brasseur, Paule.** *Bibliographie générale du Mali (Anciens Soudan français et Haut-Sénégal-Niger.* Pp. 461, map. Dakar: I.F.A.N. (Catalogues et documents, no. 16.)

4774. **Bruel, Georges.** 1914. *Bibliographie de l'Afrique équatoriale française.* Pp. iv + 326. Paris: E. Larose.

4775. **Cardinall, A. W.** 1932. *A bibliography of the Gold Coast.* Pp. 384. Accra: Government Printing Office.

4776. **Clozel, M.** 1891. *Bibliographie des ouvrages relatifs à la Sénégambie et au Soudan occidental.* Pp. 60. Paris: Institut Géographique de Paris. (Ex. La revue de géographie.)

4777. **Cole, Herbert M.,** and **R. F. Thompson.** 1964. *Bibliography of Yoruba sculpture.* Pp. 11. New York: Museum of Primitive Art. (Primitive art bibliographies, no. 3.)

4778. **Conover, H. F.** 1959. *Nigerian official publications, 1869–1959: a guide.* Pp. xi + 153. Washington: Library of Congress.

4779. —— 1960. *Official publications of French West Africa, 1946–58; a guide.* Pp. 88. Washington: Library of Congress.

4780. **C.O.W.A. Surveys and Bibliographies.** *Equatorial Africa,* no. 1–, 1958–. Cambridge, Mass.: Council for Old World Archaeology.

4781. —— *West Africa*, no. 1–99. 1958–59. Cambridge, Mass.: Council for Old World Archaeology.

4782. **Estermann, Carlos.** 1961. *Bibliografia do Etnólogo.* Pp. 15. Luanda: Instituto de Angola.

4783. **Gamble, David Percy.** 1958. *Bibliography of the Gambia.* Pp. 36. London: Colonial Office Research Department.

4784. **Harris, J.** 1959. *Books about Nigeria; a select reading list.* Pp. 39. Ibadan: Univ. Press.

4785. **Jones, Ruth.** 1958. *West Africa.* Pp. v + 116. London: Int. African Inst. (African bibliography series).

4786. **Joucla, E.,** and **Others.** 1937. *Bibliographie de l'Afrique occidentale Française.* Pp. 704. Paris: Société d'Editions Géographiques, Maritimes et Coloniales. (2nd ed.)

4787. **Junta de Investigações do Ultramar.** *Centro de Documentação Cientifica Ultramarina.* Bibliografia Cientifica da Junta de Investigações do Ultramar. Vol. 1 (1958), pp. 371. Lisbon: Junta de Investigações do Ultramar.

4788. **Lebeuf, Jean-Paul.** *Bibliographie Saô et Kotoko (A.O.F.).* Bull. Études Cam., 1948.

4789. **Lopes Cardoso, Carlos.** *Contribuição para a Bibliografia dos Bochimanes de Angola.* Boletim do Instituto de Angola, no. 14, 1960, 21, map.

4790. **Luke, Harry Charles.** 1910. *A bibliography of Sierra Leone.* Pp. 144, maps. Oxford: Clarendon Press.

4791. **Pitcher, G. M.** 1960. *Bibliography of Ghana, 1957–1959.* Pp. 177. Kumasi: Kumasi College of Technology.

4792. **Portugal: Junta de Investigações do Ultramar.** 1959. *Periódicos Portugueses de interesse ultramarino (actualmente em publicação).* Pp. 89. Lisbon: Centro de Documentação Cientifica Ultramarina.

4793. **Sanner, P.** 1949. *Bibliographie ethnographique de l'Afrique équatoriale française, 1914–48.* Pp. 107. Paris: Imprimerie Nationale.

4794. **Schmeltz, J. P. E.** *Neue Literatur über Benin.* Int. archiv. ethnog., 16, 1903.

4795. **Schutze, J.** 1929. *Bibliographie der Canarischen, Madeirischen und Capverdischen Inseln (to 1920).* Graz.

SOUTHERN AFRICA

4796. **Boone, Olga** (*ed.*). 1962. *Bibliographie ethnographique de l'Afrique Sud-Saharienne to 1960.* Pp. (6) 444. Tervueren: Musée Royal de l'Afrique Centrale.

4797. **Brett, Edwin A.** N.D. *Tentative list of books and pamphlets on southern Africa, published in the U.S.A. and Canada.* Pp. iii + 48. Johannesburg: Public Library.

4798. **Brown, J. Cudd.** 1959. *A reading list on Africa south of the Sahara.* Pp. 21. Stanford, Calif.: Hoover Inst. on War, Revolution and Peace.

SOUTH AFRICA

4799. **Cape Town: South African Public Library.** 1948. *A bibliography of African bibliographies.* Grey bibliographies, no. 2. Pp. 52.

4800. —— 1951. *Classified list of South African annual publications as at March 1951.*

4801. —— 1951. *Handlist of South African periodicals current in December 1951.*

4802. —— 1952. *South Africa in print; catalogue of an exhibition of books atlases and maps in the . . . Library, 1 March to 5 April 1952.*

4803. —— *Africana Nova; a quarterly bibliography.* No. 1 (1958), 20. Cape Town: S.A. Public Library.

4807. **C.O.W.A. Surveys and Bibliographies.** *South Africa*, no. 1–, 1958–. Cambridge, Mass.: Council for Old World Archaeology.

4811. **Johannesburg: Public Library.** *African native tribes.* Pp. xxvii + 142. Johannesburg: Public Library.

4815. **Louw, H. A.** *South African sculpture, 1910–1959.* (A bibliography.) Pp. vi + 37. Cape Town: Univ. Press.

4816. **Mendelssohn, S.** 1910. *Mendelssohn's South African bibliography* (2 vols.). Vol. 1, lxxii + 1008. Vol. 2 (6) + 1139. London: Kegan Paul.

4817. **Musiker, R.** (*ed.*). 1958. *Guide to South African reference books.* Rondebosch, P.O. 59 for Univ. of Cape Town.

4820. **Rosenkranz, L.** 1958. *Rock paintings and petroglyphs of South and Central Africa, 1947–1958.* Pp. iii + 27, bibl. Cape Town: The University.

4821. **Schapera, Isaac.** 1941. *Select bibliography of South African native life and problems.* Pp. xii + 249. London: Oxford Univ. Press.

4822. —— 1950. *Supp. to above.* Pp. 32. Cape Town: University.

4823. **Sherlock, J.** 1963. *The Zambezi; a bibliography.* Pp. iv + 20. Cape Town: Univ. of Cape Town (School of Librarianship).

4824. **South Africa: University.** 1958. *List of dissertations and theses accepted by the University of South Africa 1919–1958.* Pp. 96. Pretoria: Communications of the University of S. Africa.

4825. **Spohr, O. H.** 1949. *Photographic service points in libraries, archives and museums in South Africa.* Pp. 18. Cape Town: Univ. Library.

4826. **Stevens, Pamela.** 1947. *Bibliography of Bechuanaland.* Cape Town.

4827. **Welch, Floretta J.** 1946. *South West Africa; a bibliography.* Pp. v + 88. Cape Town: University School of Librarianship.

SPECIAL NUMBERS OF PERIODICALS

4830. *Action*, Paris, **3**, 1920.
4831. *A.O.F. (magazine)*, Dakar, **14**, Jan., 1956.
4832. *Art et décoration*, Paris, **62**, 1933.
4833. *Art and Industry*, London, 1949.
4834. *Arts Plastiques*, Brussels, June–July, 1951.
4835. *Atlantic Monthly*, Boston, **203**, **4**, 1959.
4836. *Atlas*, **3**, 1930.
4837. *Beaux-Arts*, Brussels, 1952.
4838. —— 1955.
4839. —— **15**, 1956.
4840. *Belgique d'Outre-Mer*, Brussels, **28**, July, 1958.
4841. *Brousse*, Léopoldville, **1**, 1939.
4842. —— **4**, 1940.
4843. *Bulletin*, Allen Memorial Museum, Oberlin, **13** (2), Winter 1955–56.
4843a. *Cah. d'art*, Paris, **17**, 1932.
4844. *Cah. d'art*, Paris, **2**, 1951.
4845. *Études camerounaises*, Douala, **52**, 1956.
4846. *Études et information*, Paris, **148**, **6–7**, 1950.
4847. *Grands lacs*, Brussels, June–July, 1956.
4848. *Holiday*, London, April, 1959.
4849. *Das Kunstwerk*, Baden-Baden, Kunstwerkschriften, **17**, 1950.
4850. *Marg*, Bombay, **15** (3), June, 1962.
4851. *Le Maroc artistique*, 1917.
4852. *Minotaure*, Paris, **2**, 1933.

4853. *Museum Journal*, Philadelphia, **4** (1), 1913.
4854. *Le Musée vivant*, Paris, 1948.
4855. *Nada*, Salisbury, **24**, **23–28**, 1947.
4856. *Nervie*, Paris, **9–10**, 1926.
4857. *Nigerian Field*, Stroud, Glos., **17**, **84–89**, 1952.
4858. *Nigeria Magazine*, **66**, Oct., 1960.
4859. *Notes africaines*, I.F.A.N., Dakar, **47**, 1950.
4860. —— **79**, 1958.
4861. —— **82**, 1959.
4862. —— **87**, 1960.
4863. *Opportunity*, New York, May, 1926.
4864. *Présence africaine*, Paris, **10–11**, 1951.
4865. *Problèmes d'Afrique Centrale*, Paris, **13** (2), **44**, 1959.
4866. *Revue de Madagascar*, Tananarive, Dec., 1950.
4867. *Tanganyika notes and records*, Dar es Salaam, **5**, **1–4**, 1938.
4868. —— **12**, **20–22**, 1941.
4869. *Togo-Cameroun*, Paris, 1935.
4870. *Tropiques*, Paris, **357**, Dec., 1953.
4871. *UNESCO Courier*, Paris, **10**, Oct., 1959.
4872. —— **12**, **24–25**, 1959.
4873. *Variétés*, Brussels, **7**, 1928.
4874. *Weltkreis* (Berlin), **3** (1), 1932.
4875. *West African Review*, Liverpool, **14**, **194**, Nov., 1943.
4876. —— **28**, **363**, April, 1957.
4877. *Zeitschrift für Ethnologie*, Berlin, **88** (1), **86–97**, 1963.

PERIODICALS CONSULTED

Numbers in brackets refer to entries extracted from the periodicals consulted

A

4878. *Abbia* (Yaoundé) (2668), (2702), (2727).

4878a.*Abhandlungen und Berichte des Staatlichen Museums für Völker-kunde, Dresden* (1961–3).

4879. *Academie Royale des Sciences Coloniales* (Brussels) (3121), (3241), (3290). Mém: Section de sciences, morales et politiques (3077), (3380), (3634).

4880. *Acta Tropica* (Basle) (270), (546), (560), (715), (2441), (2451), (2467–8), (2475), (2517), (3215), (3434), (3460), (3681).

4881. *Action* (Paris) (256), (385).

4882. *Aequatoria* (Coquilhatville) (2969–70), (3283), (3292–3), (3296).

4883. *Africa* (London) (215), (384), (502), (611), (613), (773), (1458), (1484), (1507), (1573), (1624), (1689), (1742), (1836), (1858), (1861), (1945), (1947), (1960), (2016), (2113), (2122), (2158), (2175), (2204–5), (2259), (2405), (2534), (2592), (2872–3), (2886), (2896), (2995), (3009), (3175), (3227), (3551), (3650), (4147).

4884. *Africa* (Madrid) (247), (359), (505), (1004), (1043), (1706), (1708), (2878), (3477), (3480), (3482).

4884a.*Africa* (Milan) (1786).

4885. *Africa* (Rome).

4886. *Africa South* (Cape Town) (369), (531), (1428a), (1444), (1725), (1869), (2053).

4887. *Africa-Tervueren* (1430), (3135–6), (3140), (3219), (3226), (3325), (3431).

4888. *African Affairs* (London) (481), (2143).

4889. *African Missionary* (Cork) (266).

4890. *African Music Society Newsletter* (Johannesburg) (3940), (4117).

4891. *African Observer* (Bulawayo) (290).

4892. *African Studies* (Johannesburg) (1476), (1513), (1611), (1807), (1809), (2019), (2643), (3078), (3242), (3947), (4140), (4150), (4151).

4893. *African Studies Bulletin* (New York) (45), (575), (1843), (4140).

4894. *African Women* (London) (637).

4895. *African World* (London) (640), (668), (1634), (1972), (2105), (3153), (3701), (3750).

4896. *Africana Notes and News* (Johannesburg) (4141).

4897. *Africanae Fraternae Ephemerides Romanae* (Namur) (2186).

4898. *Afrika* (now *Neues Afrika* (Munich) (1917).

4899. *Afrika Heute* (Bonn) (471).

4899a.*Afrika* (München) (2593).

4900. *Afrika-Nachrichten* (663), (2612).

4901. *Afrika und Übersee* (Hamburg) (1237).

4902. *Afrique Ardente* (Brussels) (3281).

4903. *Afrique en Marche* (Paris) (2246), (2253a).

4904. *Afrique du Nord Illustré* (808).

4905. *L'Afrique Francaise. Renseignments de l'Office Coloniale* (Paris) (1065), (2436).

4906. *Afrique Occidentale Française* (Magazine).

4907. *American Anthropologist* (Menasha, Wis.) (22), (78), (162), (195), (687), (2245).

4908. *American Image* (557).

4909. *American Journal of Archaeology* (New York).

4910. *American Magazine of Art* (Washington) (246), (469), (1586), (2570).

4911. *Ampurias* (Barcelona) (1108).

4912. *Annales Coloniales* (Paris).

4913. *Annales du Musée (Royal) du Congo Belge* (Tervueren) (2934), (3005), (3014–15), (3074–5), (3173–4), (3178), (3182), (3276), (3286), (3288), (3306).

4914. *Annales d'Éthiopie* (Addis Ababa) (1305).

4915. *Annali dell' Africa Italiana* (Rome) (963).

4916. *Annali Istituto Universale Orientali* (Naples) (793), (1024).

4917. *Annali Lateranensi* (Vatican City) (647), (3106), (3627–8), (3640).

4918. *Annals of the Natal Museum* (Pietermaritzburg) (4089).

4919. *Annals of the Transvaal Museum* (Pretoria) (3850), (4068).

4920. *Annals of the South African Museum* (Cape Town) (4046–7), (4102), (4198).

4921. *l'Anthropologie* (Paris) (838), (867), (877), (893), (913), (956), (1008–9), (1111a), (1157), (1280), (1421), (2315), (2323), (2337), (2351), (2373), (2437), (2492), (2544), (2555), (2854–5), (3049), (3221), (3244), (3635), (3655), (3878), (3897), (4008), (4021), (4163).

4921a.*Anthropology Quarterly* (Washington) (3969).

4922. *Anthropos* (Freiburg) (600), (727), (1275), (1306), (1522), (1538), (1923), (2324), (2830), (2893), (2925), (3154), (3311), (3397), (3626), (3633), (3637), (3690), (3759), (3861), (3887), (3942), (4083), (4108).

4923. *Antiquity* (Gloucester) (787), (968), (971), (975), (1092), (1189), (1224), (1309), (1354a), (1367), (1482), (1552a), (1860), (3588a), (3746), (3973), (4055), (4092).

4924. *Anzeiger der Kais. Akademie der Wissenschaften* (Wien) (4081), (4125–6), (4185).

4925. *Apollo* (London) (343), (1215), (2887).

4925a.*Apollon* (Paris) (2183).

4926. *der Ararat* (607).

4927. *Architectural Review* (London) (1429), (3533).

4928. *Archiv fur Anthropologie* (Brunswick) (117), (248), (680), (1158), (4195).

4929. *Archiv für Ethnologie*.

4930. *Archiv für Religionswissenschaft* (Leipzig) (442).

4931. *Archiv für Völkerkunde* (Wien) (564), (1300), (1918–19), (2239), (2582), (2717).

4932. *Archives du Congo Belge*.

4933. *Archives de Sociologie des Religions* (Paris) (2261).

4933a.*Archives Suisses d'Anthropologie Générale* (Geneva) (1291), (2510), (2557), (3368), (3695).

4934. *Archivio per l'Antropologia e la Etnologia* (Florence) (1289), (1333), (1347).

4935. *Archivos del Instituto de Estudios Africanos* (Madrid) (2882), (3473).

4936. *Art and Archaeology* (Concord) (589).

4937. *Art et Décoration* (Paris) (319), (987), (1831), (2273), (2867), (3128).

4937a.*Arts and Decoration* (New York) (274).

4938. *Art de l'Industrie* (810).

4939. *Art in America* (250).

4940. *Art League News* (Milwaukee) (1357).

4941. *Art News Magazine* (New York) (258), (489), (1664–5).

4942. *l'Art Vivant* (Paris).

4943. *l'Art Sacré* (Paris) (3048).

4944. *Artibus Asiae* (Dresden) (1460), (2470).

4945. *Artisan Liturgique* (New York) (3348).

4946. *The Arts* (London) (119), (308), (405), (407), (626), (2292), (2562), (3000).

4947. *Art Digest* (London) (254–5), (1602), (3239).

4948. *Arts et Métiers Congolais* (Brussels) (3209), (3261).

4949. *Arts et Métiers Indigènes* (Leopoldville) (718), (3020), (3032), (3317), (3319), (3327), (3347), (3369).

4950. *Les Arts Plastiques* (Brussels) (709), (3200–1).

4950a.*Arts Review* (Leeds) (2148).

4951. *Atelier* (Paris) (573).

4952. *The Athenaeum* (London) (4128).

4953. *Athene* (Bedford) (1648).

4954. *Atlantic Monthly* (Boston, Mass.) (18), (325), (4835).

4955. *Atlantis* (Berlin, Zürich) (1388), (1944), (2670), (2714), (2752), (2773), (3981).

B

4956. *Baessler Archiv* (Berlin) (692), (700), (807), (823–4), (914), (1148), (1229), (1354), (1569), (1635), (1645), (1825), (2045), (2288a), (2431), (2518), (2618), (2635–6), (2678), (2741), (2888), (2902), (3432), (3494), (3867).

4957. *Band* (Léopoldville) (3025), (3225), (3493).

4958. *BaNtu* (Pretoria) (261), (4085).

4958a.*Bantu* (Johannesburg) *Studies* (2924), (3693), (3933), (4093).

4959. *Beaux-Arts* (Paris) (269), (285), (2976), (3983). (See also *Gazette des Beaux Arts*.)

4959a.*Beaux-Arts* (Brussels) (2987), (3040–1), (3179).

4960. *Beiträge zur Kolonial-Forschung* (Berlin) (363), (408), (1141).

4961. *Belgian Congo of Today* (Brussels) (3115–16), (3207).

4962. *Belgique d'Outremer* (Lèopoldville) (2984), (4840).

4962a.*Belvedere* (Vienna) (1685).

4963. *Berichte Berliner Museen.*

4964. *Bildende Kunst* (Berlin).

4965. *Black Orpheus* (Ibadan) (1678–9), (2130), (2133), (2471).

4966. *Boletim Cultural da Guiné Portuguesa* (Bissau) (1594), (2760), (2768–9), (2775), (2777), (2779).

4967. *Boletim Cultural Museu de Angola* (Luanda) (3425).

4968. *Boletim do Instituto de Angola* (Luanda) (3396), (3417).

4969. *Boletim da Sociedade de Estudos da Colonia de Moçambique* (Laurenço Marques) (3718), (3827), (3845), (3851), (3856), (3864), (3869).

4970. *Boletim da Sociedade Geografia de Lisboa* (3449).

4971. *Boletim Agencia Geral das Colonias* (Lisbon) (3862–3).

4972. *Boletim Museu Nampula* (3838), (3870).

4973. *Boletín Real Sociedad Geográfica* (Madrid) (1069).

4974. *Bolletino della Reale Società Geografica Italiana* (Rome) (962), (3792).

4975. *Bolletino Istituti di Studi Etiopici* (Asmara) (1313), (1316), (1343).

4976. *British Museum Quarterly* (1695), (1754–5), (1762), (2398), (2709), (3139), (4056).

4976a.*Brooklyn Museum Quarterly* (581).

4977. *Brousse* (Léopoldville) (244), (760), (2307), (2916), (2973), (3021), (3053), (3079), (3123), (3151–2), (3183), (3217), (3222–3), (3251), (3277), (3279–80), (3282), (3285), (3289), (3297), (3318), (3321–2), (3329–31), (3335), (3351), (3356–7), (3379), (3383–5), (3641), (3872).

4978. *Brücke.*

4979. *Bulletin des Séances de l'Académie Royal des Sciences d'Outre-Mer* (Brussels) (4879), (4980), (5188).

4980. *Bulletin des Séances de l'Académie Roy. de Belgique:* Classe des Sciences Colon. (Brussels) (2954), (3562). See also (4879), (5188).

4981. *Bulletin de l'Académie Malgache* (3882), (3912).

4982. *Bulletin of the Allen Memorial Art Museum, Oberlin College* (333–4), (4869).

4983. *Bulletin des Amis d'Art Indigène* (Katanga) (3037), (3191–2), (3260).

4984. *Bulletin de la Sociéte Roy. Belge d'Anthropologie de Bruxelles* (2508).

4985. *Bulletin et Mémoires de la Société d'Anthropologie de Paris* (754–5), (2408), (3888).

4986. *Bulletin de l'Institut des Études Centrafricaines* (Brazzaville) (2418), (2786), (2788), (2868), (2884).

4987. *Bulletin Chicago Art Institute* (476), (1840).

4988. *Bulletin of the Cleveland Museum* (1535), (1856), (2414), (2507).

4989. *Bulletin Institut Royal Coloniale Belge.* See (5122).

4990. *Bulletin du Comité d'Études Historiques et Scientifiques de l'A.O.F.* (Dakar) (915), (1129), (1447), (2241), (2342), (2344), (2356), (2394), (2401), (2450), (2543), (2730).

4991. *Bulletin de la Société des Recherches Congolaises* (Brazzaville) (1822), (2829), (2831–3), (2958), (2958a), (2968).

4992. *Bulletin Detroit Institute of Art* (3274).

4993. *Bulletin de l'Enseignement Publique du Maroc* (989).

4994. *Bulletin Musée d'Ethnographie du Trocadéro,* (Paris).

4995. *Bulletin d'Information et Renseignement* (Dakar) (2341).

4996. *Bulletin d'Information et de Documentation* (Brazzaville) (2845).

4997. *Bulletin de l'Institut Français d'Afrique Noire I.F.A.N.* (Dakar) (25), (630), (796), (880–1), (891), (895), (996), (1103–5), (1113), (117–18), (1126), (1132), (1143), (1438), (1454), (1469), (1795), (2210–11), (2221), (2225), (2234–5), (2238), (2244), (2285–6), (2340), (2345–6), (2350), (2361), (2367), (2370–2), (2411), (2463), (2469), (2478), (2498), (2577), (2587–8), (2595–7), (2657), (2706), (2782), (2811), (2863–4).

4998. *Bulletin of the International Committee on Urgent Anthropological Research* (Vienna) (3047).

4999. *Bulletin des Juridictions Indigènes et du Droit Coutumier Congolais* (Elizabethville) (2947), (3265).

5000. *Bulletin de Liaison Saharienne* (Alger) (876), (888), (1061), (1134).

5001. *Bulletin Liverpool Libraries, Museums and Arts Committee* (1686), (1781).

5001a.*Bulletin Militaire* (Léopoldville) (2927).

5001b.*Bulletin Minneapolis Institute.*

5001c.*Bulletin des Missions* (Paris) (259), (3250), (3349–50).

5002. *Bulletin des Missions, Abbaye de Saint André* (3345), (3381–2).

5003. *Bulletin des Musées Royaux (Belge) d'Art et d'Histoire* (Brussels) (1728), (1887), (2194), (2443–4), (2477), (3233–5).

5004. *Bulletin Museum of Modern Art* (New York) (265).

5005. *Bulletin of the Museum of Science and Art* (Philadelphia) (1911).

5006. *Bulletin des Naturalistes de Mons et du Borinage* (3258).

5007. *Bulletin de la Société Royale Belge d'Anthropologie et de la Préhistoire* (Brussels) (1449), (3131), (3229), (3299).

5008. *Bulletin Société d'Études Camerounaises* (Douala) (became *Études Camerounaises* with nos. 23/24 in 1948).

5009. *Bulletin de la Société de Géographique d'Alger de l'Afrique du Nord'* (Alger) (821), (859).

5010. *Bulletin de la Société Géographique de Nancy* (3284).

5011. *Bulletin de la Société Historique Algérienne.*

5012. *Bulletin de la Société de Géographie et d'Archéologie d'Oran* (849), (2217).

5013. *Bulletin de la Société Neuchâteloise de Géographie* (1066), (1290), (1561), (3440), (4153).

5014. *Bulletin de la Société Préhistorique Française* (Paris) (844), (1088), (2393), (2515), (2708), (2710), (3298).

5014a.*Bulletin de la Société des Recherches Soudanaises* (456).

5015. *Bulletin de la Société Suisse d'Anthropologie et d'Ethnologie* (Bein). See *Bulletin Schweizerische Gesellschaft für Anthropologie und Ethnologie.*

5016. *Bulletin St. Louis Museum* (1873), (1908).

5017. *Bulletin Schweizerische Gesellschaft für Anthropologie und Ethnologie* (sometimes found under French title *Bulletin de la Société Suisse d'Anthropologie et d'Ethnologie*) (1138), (2208), (4057).

5018. *Bulletin of the Transvaal Museum* (1565).

5019. *Bulletin de l'Union des Femmes Coloniales* (3633a).

5019a.*Burlington Magazine* (London) (291), (540), (1540), (1701), (1845), (1847–9), (1865), (1892).

C

5020. *Cahiers d'Art* (Paris) (29), (240), (295), (356), (447), (539), (1585), (1612), (1671), (1813), (1829), (1902), (2815), (3008), (3962), (3985).

5021. *Cahiers des Arts et Techniques d'Afrique du Nord* (1163).

5022. *Cahiers de Belgique* (Brussels) (342), (451), (3007), (3170), (3210).

5023. *Cah. d'Études Africaines* (569), (2378).

5024. *Cahiers de Saint-André* (St. André-lez-Bruges) (3027).

5025. *Cahiers de Tunisie* (Tunis) (805), (1154), (1156), (1160), (1164), (1169), (1172–3).

5026. *Canadian Art* (Ottawa) (574).

5027. *Cape Illustrated Magazine* (Johannesburg) (3825).

5028. *Cape Monthly Magazine* (Cape Town) (4101), (4139).

5029. *Cepsi; Création du Centre Interfacultaire d'Anthropologie et de Linguistique Africaine, l'Université Officielle du Congo Belge et du Ruanda-Urundi* (Elisabethville) (3249).
5030. *Československa Ethnografie* (Prague) (3545), (3733).
5031. *Chroniques d'Outre-Mer; Études et Information* (Paris) (2531).
5032. *Ciba Review* (Basle) (629), (643), (645), (667), (848).
5033. *Ciba—Rundschau* (Basle) (644), 646).
5033a. *Ciba Zeitschrift* (Basle) (583), (585).
5034. *der Cicerone* (Cologne) (2201).
5035. *Cimbebasia* (Windhoek) (4190).
5036. *Colóquio* (Lisbon) (3395).
5037. *Congo* (Brussels) (312), (2911–12), (2917), (3044), (3057), (3228), (3291), (3303–5), (3315), (3346).
5038. *Congo Illustré* (Brussels) (3102), (3232), (3259), (3271–3), (3320), (3333), (3336), (3386).
5039. *Congopresse* (Léopoldville) (3374).
5040. *Congo-Tervueren* (3124), (3205), (3218), (3246), (3257), (3324), (3435), (3636).
5041. *Connaissance du Monde.*
5042. *Connoisseur, The* (London) (1405), (1713), (1787), (1938).
5043. *Conseiller Congolaise* (2905), (3275).
5044. *Corona* (London) (1729), (1756), (1934), (3584), (3595).
5045. *Le Courrier d'Afrique* (Léopoldville) (2986), (3019).
5046. *Craft Horizons* (New York) (305–6), (534), (1448).
5047. *Crane* (Kampala) (3599).
5048. *Criticism* (571).
5049. *Critique* (Paris) (445).
5050. *Crown Colony* (London) (666).
5051. *Cuadernos Africanos y Orientales* (Madrid) (134).
5052. *Cuadernos de Historia Primitiva* (Madrid) (1707).
5053. *Current Anthropology* (Chicago) (392), (1238).

D

5054. *Decoration Ny.*
5055. *Dedalo* (Milan) (249).
5056. *Der Querschnitt* (262).
5057. *Der Türmer* (3755).
5058. *De Standaard* (Anvers) (3035).
5059. *Design* (London) (315), (1654).
5060. *Deutsche Koloniale Zeitung* (Berlin) (1731), (2659).
5061. *Die Woche* (Leipzig) (1319), (4174).
5062. *Diogène* (Paris) (572).
5063. *Discovery* (London) (1723).
5064. *Documents* (Paris) (346), (1739), (1941), (3137), (3780).
5065. *Documents* (Moçambique) (3840).

E

5066. *East African Annual* (Nairobi) (3552), (3571), (3580).
5067. *Echo des Missions Africaines de Lyon* (1591).
5068. *Education Africaine* (Gorée) (2425).
5069. *Education Ménagère* (2319).
5070. *Empire Review* (London) (3950).
5071. *Encyclopédie Mensuelle d'Outre-Mer* (Paris) (459), (1171), (1435), (1455), (2479), (2807).
5072. *En Terre Islam* (214), (1159).
5073. *Erdball* (Berlin) (355), (725), (738), (782), (1239), (1663), (2703).
5074. *Esso-Magazine* (London) (3076).
5075. *Ethiopie d'Aujourd'hui* (Addis Ababa).
5076. *l'Ethnographie* (Paris) (907), (2692), (2827–8), (3110), (3392), (3886).
5077. *Ethnologia Cranmorensis* (1656), (1785), (1855).
5078. *Ethnologica* (Cologne) (153), (357), (495), (654), (693), (753), (1401), (1406), (3312).
5079. *Ethnologischer Anzeiger* (Stuttgart) (439), (1942–3), (2202), (2453), (2493), (3502).
5079a. *Ethnologische Studien* (Leipzig) (437), (2749).

5080. *Ethnology* (Pittsburgh, Pa.).
5081. *Ethnos* (Stockholm) (47), (179–80), (190–1), (707), (1133), (1152), (1325), (1485), (1835), (1841), (2212), (2870), (3216), (3761), (3920), (3949).
5082. *Études Camerounaises* (Douala) (2624), (2642), (2667), (2683), (2690), (2704), (2715), (4858).
5083. *Études Dahoméennes* (Porto-Novo) (2522), (2528), (2539–41), (2559), (2561).
5084. *Études Guinéennes* (Conakry) (2412), (2438).
5085. *Études Marocaines* (1090).
5086. *Eurafrique* (Alger) (2512).

F

5087. *Farm and Forest* (Ibadan) (2066), (2108), (2173).
5088. *Feuer* (Weimar) (1784).
5089. *Folia Scientifica Africae Centralis* (Bukaru) (3093).
5090. *Folk* (Copenhagen) (1975), (3532).
5090a. *Folklore* (London) (3103), (3873).
5091. *Fortschungen und Fortschritte* (Berlin) (839–40), (960).
5092. *Fort Hare Papers* (4114–15).
5093. *France Abroad* (Paris) (3964).
5094. *France Illustrée* (55), (2247a), (2796a).
5095. *Frankfurter Zeitung* (329).

G

5096. *Gallery Magazine.*
5097. *Garcia de Orta* (Lisbon) (168), (311), (2762), (3387), (3444), (3446), (3458), (3868).
5098. *Gazette des Beaux-Arts* (Paris) (302), (2195).
5099. *Geographical Journal* (London) (1106), (1636), (2736), (2923), (3787).
5100. *Geographical Magazine* (London) (1698–9), (1816–17), (1973), (1976), (2800), (3976).
5101. *Geographical Review* (New York) (827).
5102. *La Géographie* (Paris) (814), (1084).
5103. *Geographische Zeitschrift* (Leipzig) (1073).
5104. *Ghana Bulletin of Theology* (Achimota).
5015. *Glasgow Art Review* (398).
5106. *Globus* (Brunswick) (522), (747), (944), (1390), (1408), (1422), (3512).
5107. *Gold Coast Review* (Accra) (1548–9).
5108. *Grand Artistique* (3361).
5109. *Grands Lacs* (Namur) (2977), (2981), (3063), (3254), (3269), (4838).
5110. *Graphic* (London) (1267).
5111. *Guinea Española* (Santa Isabel) (3466–9), (3474–6), (3481), (3483–4).

H

5112. *Hespéris* (Rabat) (afterwards *Hespéris Tamuda*) (789), (815), (926), (977), (981), (995), (997), (1000–1), (1007), (1012), (1016–17), (1019–23), (1026), (1029), (1032–3), (1044), (1047–8), (1050–2), (1054–8), (1067–8), (2360).
5113. *L'Homme* (Paris) (2266).
5113a. *L'Homme Préhistorique* (Paris) (4193).
5114. *Horizon* (Salisbury, Rhodesia).

I

5115. *Ibadan* (1662), (2177).
5116. *Illustrated London News* (London) (414–25), (768–9), (967), (1241), (1339), (1668), (1744), (1750), (1773), (2149), (2152), (2799), (3644), (3779), (3982), (3992–6).
5117. *Illustrated Studio* (484).
5118. *L'Illustration* (Paris) (2321), (2938).
5119. *Illustration Congolaise* (3016), (3180), (3185), (3195), (3262).

5120. *Illustrierte Deutsche Monatshefte* (580).
5121. *Initiations et Études Africaines*, I.F.A.N. (Dakar), (167), (1358), (1443), (2181).
5121a.*Institut des Belles-Lettres Arabes* (Tunis) (908), (1162), (1167).
5122. *Institut Royal Colonial Belge* (Brussels) (774), (3096), (3193), (3202). (Bull. séances (3267).)
5123. *Instituto Italiano d'Arti Grafiche.*
5123a.*Interiors* (578).
5224. *Internationales Archiv für Ethnographie* (Leiden) (664–5), (682), (731), (1228), (1422–3), (1913), (1924), (2600), (3119).
5125. *International Studio.*
5126. *Ipek* (Berlin) (59), (434), (519), (691), (834–5), (845), (1124), (1434), (3006), (3169), (3302), (3528), (3975), (4061), (4173).

J

5127. *Jahrbuch des Bernischen Historischen Museums* (300), (1298), (1315), (1480), (1489), (1564).
5128. *Jahrbuch des Städtischen Museums für Völkerkunde* (Leipzig) (659), (659a), (1006), (1312), (1353), (2385), (2686–7).
5129. *Jahresbericht der Geographischen Gesellschaft in Bern* (1297), (2682).
5130. *Jahresbericht des Württembergischen Vereins für Handelsgeographie* (Stuttgart) (1827), (3539).
5131. *Jalons* (3378).
5132. *Jambo* (3860), (4176).
5133. *Jeune Afrique* (Elizabethville) (1757), (2691), (2908), (3212), (3811).
5134. *Jewish Quarterly Review* (Philadelphia) (1823).
5135. *Jezuieten Missies* (3094–5), (3231).
5136. *Journal of Aesthetics* (London) (68), (297).
5137. *Journal of African History* (London) (3326), (3546), (3728), (4136).
5138. *Journal of the African Society* (London) (became *Royal* with vol. 33, 1934) (1231), (1396), (1457), (1499), (1528), (1532), (1545), (1626), (1716), (1740), (2005), (2037).
5139. *Journal of the Royal Asiatic Society* (London) (3462).
5140. *Journal of the East African Natural History Society* (Nairobi) (3538).
5141. *Journal of Egyptian Archaeology* (London) (2798).
5142. *Journal of Human Relations* (Wilberforce, Ohio) (559), (570).
5143. *Journal of Negro History* (Washington) (48).
5144. *Journal of the Historical Society of Nigeria* (Ibadan) (1440), (1587–8), (1692), (1749), (1842), (1922), (1979).
5145. *Journal de Psychologie Normale et Pathologique* (Paris) (2251).
5146. *Journal of the Royal Anthropological Institute* (London) (675), (724), (726), (734), (744), (922), (924), (1095), (1194), (1240), (1445), (1473), (1528), (1544), (1546), (1550), (1567), (1597), (1641), (1688), (1717), (1720), (1724), (1805), (1906), (1930), (1935), (2039), (2064), (2369), (2859), (2879), (3070–1), (3073), (3097), (3104), (3462), (3519), (3652), (3665), (3672), (3720), (3729), (3764), (3895), (3990).
5147. *Journal of the Royal Society of Arts* (London) (618), (3617).
5147a.*Journal of Social Research.*
5148. *Journal de la Société des Africanistes* (Paris) (204), (833), (868), (871), (875), (887), (890), (892), (957), (1027), (1040–1), (1112), (1282), (1318), (1442), (2118a), (2216), (2219), (2252), (2258), (2262), (2265), (2299), (2300), (2310), (2318), (2327), (2335–6), (2352), (2395), (2403), (2513), (2516), (2569), (2583–5), (2590), (2649), (2697), (2712), (2720), (2787), (2801), (2819), (2820), (2826), (2862), (2865a), (2869), (2871), (2890), (3001), (3295), (3766), (3900), (3902), (4119).
5149. *Journal of the South West African Scientific Society* (Windhoek).
5150. *Journal of World History* (89).

K

5151. *Koloniale Rundschau* (Leipzig) (632), (780), (1227), (1844), (2046), (3511).

5152. *Kongo-Overzee* (Anvers) (2448), (2748), (2915), (2919), (3034), (3122), (3240), (3263), (3300), (3629).
5153. *Konstrevy* (Stockholm) (465), (598), (1122).
5154. *Korrespondenzblatt der Deutschen Gesellschaft für Anthropologie, Ethnologie und Urgeschichte* (Berlin) (1697), (4186a).
5155. *Kruis en Wereld* (2956).
5156. *Kunst* (3010).
5157. *Kunstblatt der Jugend* (683).
5158. *Kunstchronik und Kunstmarkt.*
5159. *Die Kunstwelt* (354).
5160. *Das Kunstwerk* (Baden-Baden) (401–2), (473), (670).
5161. *Kush* (Khartoum) (976), (1216), (1245), (1252).

L

5162. *La Renaissance* (Paris) (988), (1087), (2185), (2928).
5163. *Latitude* (London).
5164. *Le Domaine Colonial Français* (Paris).
5165. *Le Magazine de l'Afrique du Nord.*
5167. *Le Monde Colonial Illustré* (979), (1136), (1828), (2836).
5168. *Le Sotho* (Maseru).
5169. *Liaison* (Brazzaville) (772), (2894), (3002).
5170. *Liberia Today* (2735), (2746–7).
5171. *Libia* (Alger) (969).
5172. *Libyca* (Alger) (869), (958).
5173. *Life* (Chicago) (464), (3354), (3712).
5174. *The Listener* (London) (292), (370), (763).
5175. *Liturgical Arts* (New York) (467), (518), (764), (2139), (2556).
5176. *Living Age* (273).
5177. *Lore* (Milwaukee) (2129).
5178. *Lovania* (Elizabethville) (2840).

M

5179. *Mafeking Mail* (4124).
5180. *Le Magasin Pittoresque.*
5181. *Magazine of Art* (1759), (2140).
5182. *Man* (London) (133), (163), (209), (211), (237), (347), (621), (743), (745), (749), (929), (941), (978), (1042), (1153), (1161), (1165), (1207), (1218–19), (1225), (1242), (1248), (1254–5), (1258), (1263), (1317), (1332), (1338), (1341), (1348), (1441), (1456), (1466–7), (1481), (1485a), (1493), (1510), (1517), (1519), (1520–1), (1524), (1531), (1537), (1539), (1547), (1551–2), (1646), (1657–60), (1666–7), (1693–4), (1718–19), (1745–7), (1752–3), (1758), (1761), (1765–8), (1772), (1774), (1777), (1788), (1794), (1804), (1810–12), (1815), (1819–21), (1833), (1846), (1850–1), (1871), (1891), (1894), (1904–5), (1921), (1931), (1946), (1952), (1954–6), (1959), (1978), (1982), (1994–7), (2004), (2014–15), (2020), (2023), (2032–3), (2036), (2038), (2040–3), (2049), (2058), (2062–3), (2068–9), (2087), (2089–90a), (2100), (2109–11), (2117–18), (2121), (2123), (2317), (2410), (2427–8), (2462), (2483), (2536), (2553), (2558), (2623), (2637), (2662), (2688–9), (2695), (2718), (2722–3), (2733), (2861), (3004), (3069), (3072), (3108), (3132), (3138), (3157–9), (3172), (3220), (3266), (3301), (3323), (3464), (3491), (3514), (3516), (3530–1), (3534), (3555), (3567), (3575), (3590–1), (3596), (3607–11), (3639), (3654), (3656), (3664), (3666–7), (3670), (3679–80), (3685), (3696–8), (3709–10), (3716), (3727), (3730), (3737–9), (3741), (3751), (3765), (3804), (3806), (3824), (3830–1), (3833), (3835), (3848), (3871), (3961), (3965), (3997), (4032), (4045), (4058), (4087), (4157).
5182a.*Marg* (Bombay) (4850).
5182b.*Maroc Artistique* (Casablanca) (4851).
5183. *Maroc Médical* (1011), (1013).
5184. *Le Masque* (2296).
5185. *Mededelingen van het Rijksmuseum voor Volkenkunde* (Leiden) (360), (2489), (2797).
5186. *Mélanges de Sociologie Nord-Africaine.*

5187. *Mémoires de l'Académie des Inscriptions et Belles-Lettres* (Paris) (3967), (3970).

5188. *Mémoires de l'Académie Royale de Belgique. Classe des Sciences; Science Coloniale* (Brussels).

5189. *Mémoires de l'Institut Scientifique de Madagascar* (Tananarive) (3899), (3906).

5190. *Memoirs and Proceedings of the Manchester Literary and Philosophical Society* (332), (1536), (2079).

5191. *Mensário Administravo* (Luanda) (187), (1715), (3398), (3415), (3418), (3421), (3437), (3441), (3450), (3454), (3456), (3463), (3977).

5192. *Mercure de France* (Paris) (267).

5193. *Messager de St. Joseph* (3054).

5194. *Midwest Journal* (777), (3213).

5195. *Minotaure* (Paris) (156), (1281), (1287), (1384), (2289), (2301), (2334), (2532), (3003), (3504), (4852).

5195a. *Miroir du Congo Belge* (3058).

5196. *Missions Belges, Cie. Jésus* (3125–6).

5196a. *Missions Pères Blancs.*

5197. *Mitteilungen der Anthropolischen Gesellschaft in Wien* (352), (628), (690), (729), (843), (1796), (1798), (2663), (3589), (3944), (4186–7).

5198. *Mitteilungen aus den Deutschen Schutzgebieten* (Berlin) (2639), (2895), (4169).

5199. *Mitteilungen der Geographischen Gesellschaft in Wien* (1797), (1799).

5200. *Mitteilungen Forschungsinst. Kultur-Morphologie* (Frankfurt a.M.) (3984), (4000).

5201. *Mitteilungen der Ostschweizerischen Geographisch-kommerziellen Gesellschaft in St. Gallen.*

5202. *Mitteilungen des Städtischen Museums für Völkerkunde* (Leipzig) (660).

5202a. *Moçambique* (Lourenço Marques) (3847), (3852), (3858).

5203. *Monats Magazin* (Windhuk) (4160).

5204. *Le Mois* (Paris).

5205. *Le Monde Colonial.*

5206. *Le Monde Moderne* (Paris) (3905).

5207. *Mouvement Sociologique International = Revue néo-Scolastique supplément* (Louvain).

5208. *Les Musées de Genève* (260), (279), (472), (514), (657), (1292), (1899), (2390), (2402), (2480), (2693), (3112), (3646), (3891).

5209. *Musée Vivant* (Paris) (288), (492), (535), (1915), (3371), (4862).

5210. *Museion* (Paris).

5211. *Museum Journal and Bulletin, University of Pennsylvania* (Philadelphia) (386), (517), (1403–4), (1790–3), (2142), (2198–9), (2383), (2891), (3145–50).

5212. *Museums Journal* (London) (697), (2086).

5213. *Muslim World* (Hartford, Conn.) (1100).

N

5214. *Nada* (Salisbury, S.R.) (775), (3721), (3735), (3744), (3747), (3757), (3768–9), (3772–3), (3776), (3782), (3798), (3800–1), (3808–9), (3813), (3946).

5214a. *Nagyvilág* (2990).

5215. *Nation* (London) (1872).

5216. *Natural History* (New York) (443), (1123), (1393), (2546), (3255), (3998).

5217. *Naturaliste Malgache* (3892).

5218. *La Nature* (Paris) (1111), (3130).

5218a. *Nature* (London) (3443), (3963).

5219. *Negro History Bulletin* (561), (2095).

5220. *Néprajzi Értesítö* (Budapest) (3520).

5221. *Nervie* (Paris) (3068), (4856).

5222. *Neues Afrika* (formerly *Afrika*) (Berlin) (2167), (3649), (4172).

5223. *Newsweek* (494).

5224. *Nieuw Afrika* (2946), (3080–1), (3328), (3558), (3561), (3632).

5225. *Nigeria* (afterwards *Nigerian Magazine*) (Lagos) (171), (350), (686), (756), (819), (1576), (1581), (1613), (1627), (1649), (1652–3), (1655), (1661), (1672–6), (1680), (1687), (1691), (1702), (1709–12), (1721–2), (1733–6), (1741), (1782–3), (1818), (1832), (1864), (1867), (1870), (1875–86), (1932), (1936a), (1964–6), (1968–70), (1974), (1977), (1981), (1985), (1987–93), (1999–2001), (2007–13), (2021), (2024–31), (2035), (2044), (2052), (2054–6), (2059–61), (2072), (2074), (2078), (2080), (2082–5), (2091–3), (2096–9), (2101–2), (2106), (2112), (2114), (2124–5), (2127–8), (2134–7), (2144–7), (2155–6), (2161), (2164), (2168–9), (2171–2), (2174), (2571), (2616), (2661), (2721), (4846–7), (4851), (4868).

5225a. *Nigeria Digest* (1743), (1863).

5226. *Nigerian Field* (Stroud, Glos.) (1553), (1603), (1803), (1806), (1814), (1854), (1859), (1862), (1866), (1971), (1983–4), (1998), (2017), (2065), (2067), (2070–1), (2081), (2088), (2094), (2104), (2119), (2711).

5227. *Nigerian Teacher* (1852–3), (2022), (2151).

5227a. *Nigrizia* (Verona) (1230), (1232).

5228. *North Africa.*

5229. *Northern Rhodesia Journal* (Livingstone) (3708), (3724), (3732), (3734).

5230. *Notes Africaines I.F.A.N.* (Dakar) (199), (243), (393), (722), (816), (894), (921), (1036), (1116), (1127), (1131), (1144), (1246), (1336), (1352), (1424–5), (1432–3), (1437), (1439), (1453), (1465), (1471), (1486–8), (1490), (1500), (1529), (1554), (1684), (1837), (1890), (2002), (2073), (2203), (2213–15), (2218), (2220), (2227), (2233), (2236–7), (2240), (2242–3), (2248), (2253), (2263), (2280), (2284), (2288), (2305), (2308–9), (2314), (2322), (2325–6), (2330), (2332–3), (2338–9), (2347), (2349), (2354), (2357), (2359), (2364), (2381), (2388), (2392), (2399), (2404), (2406), (2416), (2419–22), (2426), (2430), (2432–4), (2439–40), (2459–61), (2466), (2495–7), (2499–503), (2514), (2524), (2551), (2554), (2565), (2567), (2581), (2591), (2603–6), (2608), (2610–11), (2719), (2792), (2840a), (2865), (3196).

5231. *Notes et Documents, Institut des Hautes Études Marocaines.*

5232. *Nouvelle Revue Française d'Outre-Mer* (Paris) (3910).

5233. *Numismatist* (London) (226), (1464).

5234. *Nyasaland Journal* (Blantyre) (3819), (3820), (3828–9).

O

5235. *Objets et Mondes* (la Revue du Musée de l'Homme) (Paris) (713), (857), (864), (889), (909), (1125), (1145), (1301), (1398), (2232), (2257), (2396), (2552), (2694), (3896).

5236. *Occasional Papers of the National Museum of Southern Rhodesia* (Salisbury, S.R.) (3767), (3770), (3794–5), (3797), (3803).

5237. *Odu* (Ibadan) (1650), (1681), (1704–5), (1950), (1957), (1967), (1980), (2138), (2176), (2563).

5238. *L'Oeil* (Paris).

5239. *Opportunity* (New York) (263–4), (379–80), (468), (490), (4863).

5240. *Outre-mer* (Paris) (990).

5241. *Oversea Education* (London) (1592), (2153), (2159–60), (2163), (2170), (3375–6), (3554), (3740), (3742).

P

5242. *Paiduma* (Frankfurt a.M.) (529), (3187), (3433), (3451), (3568), (3988).

5243. *Parnassus* (365), (739), (1703).

5244. *Passat* (Hamburg) (970).

5245. *Petermanns Mitteilungen aus J. Perthes' Géographischer Anstalt.* (Gotha) (3529).

5246. *Phylon* (Atlanta) (272), (441), (555), (568), (776).

5247. *Portugal em Africa* (Lisbon) (3045), (3402–3), (3837).

5247a. *Préhistoire* (Paris) (2796).

5248. *Présence Africaine* (Paris) (245), (413), (458), (493), (509), (627), (757), (1562), (1763), (2391), (2423), (2652), (3913), (4864).

5249. *Primitive Man* (Washington) (3537).

5250. *Problèmes d'Afrique Centrale* (Brussels) (383), (3030), (3188–9), (3353), (4865).

5251. *Proceedings of the Prehistoric Society* (London) (1514), (3576).

5252. *Proceedings and Transactions of the Rhodesia Scientific Association* (Salisbury, S.R.) (3754), (3777), (3781), (3788), (3791), (4118).

5253. *Pro Medico* (Paris) (3168), (3171), (3176–7), (3184).

5253a.*Propos d'Atelier* (Paris) (541).

5254. *Psyché* (Paris) (558), (563).

R

5255. *Rassegna di Studi Ethiopici* (Rome) (1307–8), (1311), (1342), (1344–5).

5256. *Records of the Albany Museum* (Grahamstown) (4105).

5257. *Reflets du Monde* (Brussels) (3413).

5258. *Reliquary and Illustrated Archaeologist* (London) (1910).

5259. *Repertoire d'Art and d'Archéologie* (Paris).

5260. *Reports of the South African Association for the Advancement of Science* (Cape Town) (4066), (4123), (4130–1), (4144).

5260a.*Reports of the South African Museum* (Cape Town) (4182–3).

5261. *Review of General Semantics* (Chicago).

5262. *Revista do Gabinete de Estudos Ultramarinos* (Lisbon) (528), (2772).

5263. *Revista do Instituto Superior de Estudos Ultramarinos* (Lisbon) (4143).

5264. *Revue Africaine* (Alger) (790–1), (820), (900), (919), (1014), (1018), (1046), (1137), (3247).

5266. *Revue Anthropologique* (Paris) (2701).

5267. *Revue de l'Art* (Paris) (3879).

5268. *Revue Artes Africanae* (Brussels) (3013).

5269. *Revue Artisan and Arts Liturgiques* (Bruges) (3120).

5270. *Revue de l'Aucam* (Louvain) (512–13).

5271. *Revue Belge* (510).

5272. *Revue Coloniale Belge* (Brussels) (486), (3118), (3162), (3365).

5272a.*Revue Congo* (3099).

5272b.*Revue Congolaise* (Brussels) (3308–9).

5273. *Revue Congolaise Illustrée* (Brussels) (3144), (3253), (3268), (3270), (3307).

5274. *Revue d'Esthétique* (Paris) (444).

5275. *Revue d'Ethnographie* (Paris) (799), (1077).

5276. *Revue d'Ethnographie et des Traditions Populaires* (Paris) (822), (1007a), (1010), (2291), (2576), (2707), (2846a), (3023), (3874–5).

5276a.*Revue des Études d'Ethnographie et de Sociologie* (Paris) (801), (853), (933), (1080), (2377), (2397), (2509), (2572).

5277. *Revue Française de l'Élite* (Paris) (811), (3224).

5278. *Revue de Géographie humaine et d'Ethnologie* (Paris) (453), (650), (2883).

5279. *Revue de l'Histoire des Religions* (862), (2876).

5280. *Revue de Madagascar* (Tananarive) (3893–4), (3901), (3903), (3908–9), (4860).

5281. *Revue Missionaire* (3064), (3164).

5282. *Revue Missionnaire des Jésuites Belges* (2547).

5283. *Revue de Psychologie des Peuples* (Le Havre) (223), (565).

5283a.*Revue des Questions Scientifiques* (Brussels) (3310).

5284. *Revue des Sciences* (Paris) (206).

5285. *La Revue Sincère* (Paris).

5286. *Revue des Voyages* (479).

5287. *Rivista di Scienze Preistoriche* (Florence) (883), (923), (965), (966a), (974), (1115), (1349–51), (2817).

5288. *Rivista delle Colonie* ('Oltremare') (Bologna) (1322–3).

5288a.*Rivista delle Colonie Italiane* (Rome) (954).

5289. *Rivista di Studi Orientali* (Rome) (3507).

5290. *Rivista della Tripolitania* (Rome) (798).

5291. *Roho* (Makerere College School of Art).

5292. *Rhythmes du Monde* (Paris) (712), (3907).

S

5293. *Sabena Revue* (Brussels) (3204).

5294. *Sbornik Museia Antropologi i Etnografii* (Prague).

5294a. *School Arts Magazine.*

5295. *Sciences et Voyages* (Paris) (1140), (1436), (2293).

5296. *Scottish Art Review* (1727).

5297. *Scottish Geographical Magazine* (Edinburgh) (2699).

5298. *Sélection* (Paris).

5299. *Servir* (Brussels) (3559).

5300. *Sierra Leone Studies* (1495).

5301. *Sitzungsberichte der Kön. Preussischen Akademie der Wissenschaften zu Berlin* (12).

5302. *Societé Royale Belge de Géographie* (Brussels).

5303. *Sociologus* (Berlin) (4159).

5304. *Somali d'Oggi* (Mogadiscio) (1334).

5305. *South African Archaeological Bulletin* (Cape Town) (1953), (3578), (3648), (3722), (3775), (3778), (3786), (3790), (3799), (3948), (3968), (4005), (4007), (4017), (4019–20), (4024), (4026), (4028), (4033), (4054), (4091), (4095), (4099), (4110), (4145), (4161–2), (4164), (4196).

5306. *South African Journal of Science* (Johannesburg) (677–8), (1518), (3577), (3711), (3717), (3719), (3760), (3802), (3823), (3857), (3930), (3958), (3979), (4006), (4014), (4018), (4025), (4027), (4034–6), (4038–9), (4041–4), (4070–2), (4075), (4077a), (4078), (4080),(4082), (4088), (4090), (4104), (4106), (4113), (4129), (4138).

5307. *South African Museums Association Bulletin* (*SAMAB*) (Durban) (688), (2018), (2120).

5308. *South African Panorama* (Pretoria) (4048).

5309. *South Western Journal of Anthropology* (Albuquerque) (3024).

5310. *Southern Workman* (Hampton) (694–5).

5311. *Studi Materiali di delle religioni Storia* (Rome).

5312. *Studio* (New York) (554), (2154), (3031).

5312a. *Studio* (London) (1365), (1395), (1912), (1937), (2424), (3156), (3914), (3952), (3955), (4049).

5313. *Studium Generale* (Berlin) (208), (399), (402a), (586).

5314. *Sudan Notes and Records* (Khartoum) (748), (1212), (1223), (1226), (1233–4), (1244), (1247), (1249–51), (1253), (1257), (1259), (1261–2), (1264).

5315. *Sudan Society* (Khartoum) (1268).

5316. *Sunday Times* (878), (1190).

5317. *Synthèses* (Paris) (436).

T

5318. *Tanganyika Notes and Records* (Dar es Salaam) (3497), (3508), (3535), (3553), (3573), (3653), (3657), (3659–63), (3668–9), (3671), (3675–8), (3682–3), (3686–9).

5319. *Teachers' Monthly.*

5320. *Time* (Chicago) (778), (2150).

5321. *Togo-Cameroun* (Paris) (2601), (2645–6), (2700), (2710a), (4869).

5322. *Trait d'Union* (Anvers) (3560).

5323. *Transactions of the Lancashire and Cheshire Antiquarian Society* (711).

5324. *Transactions of the New York Academy of Sciences* (3107), (3237).

5325. *Transactions of the Rhodesia Scientific Association* (Bulawayo) (3771).

5326. *Transactions of the Royal Society of South Africa* (Cape Town) (3565), (3726), (3807), (4037), (4065), (4069), (4103), (4109), (4116), (4158).

5327. *Transactions of the South African Philosophical Society* (Cape Town) (4002–3), (4127).

5328. *Travaux de l'Institut des Recherches Sahariennes* (Alger) (873), (928), (1102), (1119), (1139), (2809).

5329. *Travaux et Mémoires de l'Institut d'Ethnologie* (Paris) (863), (2250), (2295), (2298), (2302), (2353), (2564), (2627), (3876).

5330. *Tribus* (Stuttgart) (400), (566), (671), (973), (1386), (1527), (2464), (2560), (2586), (2724), (3111).

5331. *Tropiques* (Paris) (457), (2651), (2806), (2874), (3890), (3904).

5332. *Tunisie* (Tunis) (1155).

U

5333. *The Uganda Journal* (Kampala) (596), (797), (3549), (3583), (3594), (3597), (3600–6), (3612–13), (3615).

5334. *Umschau* (Frankfurt a.M.) (633), (4192).

5335. *Unesco Courier* (Paris) (Occasional Papers in Education) (662), (685), (779), (1276), (1371), (1533), (1730), (1770), (2980), (3622), (3743), (4871–2).

5336. *United Asia* (Bombay) (1570).

5337. *United Empire* (London) (1374).

5338. *Universitas* (Achimota) (1397).

5339. *L'Universitaire Colonial* (3038).

5340. *L'Universo* (Florence) (1780), (2306).

V

5341. *Variétés* (Brussels) (296), (4873).

5342. *Verhandlungen der Gesellschaft für Anthropologie* (Berlin) (4059).

5343. *Veröffentlichungen aus dem Städtischen Völker-Museum Frankfurt am Main* (3410).

5343a. *Veröffentlichungen des Reichs museums für Völkerkunde in Leiden* (1841a).

5344. *Veröffentlichungen des Museums für Völkerkunde zu Leipzig* (403–4), (851), (2077), (2684).

5345. *Vétérans Coloniaux* (Tervuren) (2978), (2997), (3358–9), (3364), (3373).

5347. *Völkerkunde* (Vienna) (2725), (3208).

5348. *Voix du Congolaise* (Léopoldville) (3022), (3344).

W

5348a. *Weekly Cape Times* (3789).

5349. *Weltkunst.*

5350. *West Africa* (London) (169), (236), (1461–2), (1470), (1498), (1895), (1948–9), (1951), (2075).

5351. *West African Review* (Liverpool) (130), (307), (475), (703), (761), (1504), (1534), (1574–4a), (1596), (1629), (1700), (1748), (1808), (1920), (2048), (2051), (2126), (2131–2), (3999).

5352. *Westermanns Monatshefte* (Brunswick) (351), (770).

5353. *Wetenschappelijke Tijdingen* (Ghent) (3186), (3198).

5354. *Wiener Beiträge zür Kulturgeschichte und Linguistik* (74), (679).

5354a. *Wiener Völkerkundliche Mitteilungen* (639), (758–9).

Y

5355. *Ymer* (Stockholm) (705), (1410), (1800), (2268).

Z

5356. *Zaïre* (Brussels) (222), (562), (746), (2793), (2906–7), (2930), (2952), (2966), (2979), (2982), (3026), (3083), (3133–4), (3214), (3230), (3243), (3264), (3294), (3334), (3366), (3429).

5357. *Zeitschrift für Ästhetik und Kunstwissenschaft* (Stuttgart) (728).

5358. *Zeitschrift für Ethnologie* (Brunswick) (116), (118), (390–1), (638), (1220), (1243), (1256), (1834), (1925–6), (2107), (2465), (2575), (2613), (2638), (2841), (3017), (3316), (3487), (3624), (3684), (3853), (3866), (4062), (4086), (4100), (4189), (4194).

5359. *Zodiaque* (377).

ABBREVIATIONS

A

Abh. Hamburg. Kolonialinst. *Abhandlungen des Hamburgischen Kolonial-instituts.*

Abh. Sächs. Gesell. (Akad.) Wiss. *Abhandlungen der Kgl. Sächsischen Gesellschaft der Wissenschaften (Phil.-Hist. Kl.) (Leipzig).*

Abh. u. Ber. Staatl. Mus. Völkerkunde (Dresden). *Abhandlungen und Berichte des Staatlichen Museum für Völkerkunde (Dresden).*

A.R.S.C. *Académie Royale des Sciences Coloniales.*

Afr. affairs. *African Affairs.*

Afr. franc. rens. col. *L'Afrique Française; Renseignmentes de l'Office Coloniale.*

Afr. stud. *African Studies.*

Afr. stud. bull. *African Studies Bulletin* (New York).

Afr. u. Übersee. *Afrika und Übersee.*

Afr. Women. *African Women.*

Afr. world. *African World.*

Amer. Anthrop. *American Anthropologist.*

Amer. J. archaeol. *American Journal of Archaeology.*

Amer. mag. of art. *American Magazine of Art.*

Ann. Afr. Ital. *Annali dell'Africa Italiana.*

Ann. Ist. Univ. Orient. Napoli. *Annali del Istituto . . . Orientale di Napoli.*

Ann. Lat. *Annali Lateranensi.*

Ann. S. Afr. Mus. *Annals of the South African Museum.*

Ann. Trans. Mus. *Annals of the Transvaal Museum.*

Ann. Natal Mus. *Annals of the Natal Museum.*

Anz. Akad. Wiss (Wien). *Anzeiger der Kais. Akademie der Wissenschaften* (Wien).

Arch. rev. *Architectural Review.*

Archiv. f. Anthrop. *Archiv für Anthropologie.*

Arch. I. paleontol. hum. *Archives de l'Institut de Paléontologie Humaine.*

Arch. suisses anthrop. générale. *Archives Suisses d'Anthropologie Générale.*

Arch. sociol. relig. *Archives de Sociologie des Religions.*

Arch. f. Völkerkunde (Wien). *Archiv für Völkerkunde* (Wien).

Archivio antrop. e etnol. *Archivio per l'Antropologia e la Etnologia* (Florence).

Arts et métiers indig. *Arts et Métiers Indigènes.*

B

Beitr. z. Kol.-Forschung. *Beitrage zür Kolonial-Forschung.*

Bol. Ag. Ger. Colon. *Boletim Agencia Geral das Colonias.*

Bol. Inst. Angola. *Boletim do Instituto de Angola* (Luanda).

Bol. Cultural Mus. Angola. *Boletim Cultural Museu de Angola* (Luanda).

Bol. Cultural Guiné Portug. *Boletim Cultural da Guiné Portuguesa* (Bissau).

Bol. soc. geog. (Lisbon). *Boletim da Sociedade de Geographia de Lisboa.*

Bol. soc. est. coln. Moçambique. *Boletim da Sociedade de Estudios da Colónia de Moçambique.*

Bol. R. soc. geog. Madrid. *Boletín Real Sociedad Geográfica Madrid.*

B.R. soc. geog. Ital. *Bollettino della Reale Società Geografica Italiana.*

Boll. ist. studi Etiopici. *Bolletino Istitut Studi Etiopici* (Asmara).

B.M.Q. *British Museum Quarterly.*

B.S.E.C. *Bulletin de la Société d'Études Camerounaises* (afterwards *Études Camerounaises*).

Bull. (Séances) Acad. Belge Cl. Sci. Outre-Mer. *Bulletin (Séances) de l'Académie R. de Belgique, Classe des Sciences d'Outre-Mer.*

Bull. acad. Malgache. *Bulletin de l'Académie Malgache.*

Bull. amis art indig. (Katanga). *Bulletin des Amis d'Art Indigène.*

Bull. Chicago art inst. *Bulletin Chicago Art Institute.*

Bull. com. Études, A.O.F. *Bulletin du Comité d'Études Historiques et Scientifiques de l'Afrique Occidentale Française* (Paris).

Bull. enseign. pub. Maroc. *Bulletin de l'Enseignement Publique du Maroc.*

Bull. mus. ethnog. Troc. *Bulletin du Musée d'Ethnographie du Trocadéro.*

Bull. de l'I.F.A.N. *See* I.F.A.N.

Bull. inform. et docum. (Brazzaville). *Bulletin d'Information et de Documentation* (Brazzaville).

Bull. int. Ctee. urgent anthrop. research. *Bulletin of the International Committee on Urgent Anthropological Research.*

Bull. inst. ét. centrafricaines. *Bulletin de l'Institut d'Études Centrafricaines.*

Bull. jurid. indig. *Bulletin des Juridictions Indigènes et Droit Coutumier Congolais.*

Bull. liaison saharienne. *Bulletin de Liaison Saharienne* (Alger).

Bull. Militaire. *Bulletin Militaire* (Léopoldville).

Bull. des missions. *Bulletin des Missions.*

Bull. miss. Abbaye de Saint André. *Bulletin des Missions, Abbaye de Saint André.*

Bull. mus. roy. belge d'art. et d'hist. *Bulletin des Musées Royaux d'Art et d'Histoire.*

Bull. nat. Mons. *Bulletin des Naturalists de Mons et du Borinage.*

Bull. rech. Soudanaises. *Bulletin de la Société des Recherches Soudanaises.*

Bull. Schweiz. Ges. Anthrop. u. Ethnol. *Bulletin Schweizerisches Gesellschaft für Anthropologie und Ethnologie.*

Bull. soc. anthrop. Bruxelles. *Bulletin et Mémoires Société Anthropologie de Bruxelles.*

Bull. soc. anthrop. Paris. *Bulletin et Mémoires Société d'Anthropologie de Paris.*

Bull. soc. roy. belge d'anthrop & préhist. *Bulletin de la Société Royale Belge d'Anthropologie et de Préhistoire.*

Bull. soc. géog. d'Alger. *Bulletin de la Société de Géographie d'Alger.*

Bull. soc. géog. Nancy. *Bulletin de la Société Géographique de Nancy.*

Bull. soc. Neuchâteloise géog. *Bulletin de la Société Neuchâteloise de Géographie.*

Bull. soc. préhist. fr. *Bulletin de la Société Préhistorique Française.*

Bull. soc. rech. congol. *Bulletin de la Société des Recherches Congolaises.*

Bull. trim. géog. & d'archéol. d'Oran. *Bulletin Trimestriel de la Société de Géographie et d'Archéologie d'Oran.*

Bull. union femmes col. *Bulletin de l'Union des Femmes Coloniales.*

C

Cah. *Cahiers.*

Cah. d'art (Paris). *Cahiers d'Art* (Paris).

Cah. d'ét. Afr. *Cahiers d'Études Africaines.*

Cah. de St. André. *Cahiers de St. André.*

Cah. Belgique. *Cahiers de Belgique.*

Chron. d'outre-mer: ét. & inform. *Chroniques d'Outre-Mer; Études et Information.*

Ciba-Rdsch. *Ciba-Rundschau.*

Ciba rev. *Ciba Review.*

Cib. Z. *Ciba Zeitschrift.*

Comm. Communication or Communications.

C.R. *Compte-rendu.*

Congo illus. *Congo Illustré.*

Crown Col. Crown Colonies.

D

Deutsche Kolon. Ztg. *Deutsche Koloniale Zeitung.*

D.I.A.F.E. Deutsche Inner-Afrika Forschungs-Expedition. (Various dates: Leader Prof. Leo Frobenius.)

E

Éduc. ménagère. *L'Éducation Ménagère.*
Encycl. mens. O/M. *Encyclopédie Mensuel d'Outre-Mer.*
Ergän. *Ergänzungsheft.*
Est. Ultramar. *Estudos Ultramarinos.*
Ethnol. Anz. *Ethnologischer Anzeiger.*
Ethnol. Stud. *Ethnologische Studien.*
Études Cam. *Études Camerounaises* (formerly *Bulletin de la Société d'Études Camerounaises*).
Études Dah. *Études Dahoméennes.*
Études Guin. *Études Guinéennes.*
Études Ebur. *Études Eburnéennes.*

F

Forsch. u. Fortschritte. *Forschungen und Fortschritte.*
France illus. *France Illustrée.*
Frankfurter Zeit. *Frankfurter Zeitung.*

G

Geog. J. *Geographical Journal.*
Geog. mag. *Geographical Magazine.*
Geog. rev. (New York). *Geographical Review.*

I

I.B.L.A. *Institut des Belles-Lettres Arabes.*
I.F.A.N. *Institut Français d'Afrique Noire* (Bulletins and mémoires, etc.).
Illustr. congol. *Illustration Congolaise.*
I.L.N. *Illustrated London News.*
Illus. Deut. Monatshefte. *Illustrierte Deutsche Monatshefte.*
Illus. studio. *Illustrated Studio.*
Int. Archiv. Ethnog. *Internationales Archiv für Ethnographie.*
I.R.C.B. *Institut Royal Colonial Belge.*

J

Jb. bern hist. Mus. *Jahrbuch des Bernischen Historischen Museums.*
Jb. S. Mus. Völkerkunde (Leipzig). *Jahrbuch des Städtischen Museums für Völkerkunde* (Leipzig).
Jahresber. Geog. Gesell. Bern. *Jahresbericht der Geographischen Gesellschaft in Bern.*
Jahresber. Würt. ver. f. Handels Geog. *Jahresbericht des Württembergischen Vereins für Handelsgeographie.*
Jeune Afr. *Jeune Afrique.*
J. Aesthetics. *Journal of Aesthetics.*
J. Afr. soc. *Journal of the (Royal) African Society.*
J. Afr. hist. *Journal of African History.*
J. E. Afr. nat. hist soc. *Journal of the East African Natural History Society.*
J. Egypt. archaeol. *Journal of Egyptian Archaeology.*
J. negro history. *Journal of Negro History.*
J. hist. soc. Nigeria. *Journal of the Historical Society of Nigeria.*
J. psychol. norm. path. *Journal de Psychologie Normale et Pathologique.*
J. social res. *Journal of Social Research.*
J. soc. africanistes. *Journal de la Société des Africanistes.*

K

Kol. Forschung. *Koloniale Forschung.*
Kol. Rund. *Koloniale Rundschau.*
Korrbl. Deuts. Ges. Anthrop. *Korrespondenzblatt der Deutschen Gesellschaft für Anthropologie, Ethnologie und Urgeschichte.*

L

La G. *La Géographie.*

A.A.–H

M

Maroc méd. *Maroc Médical.*
Meded. Rijksmus. Volkenkunde (Leiden). *Mededelingen van het Rijksmuseum voor Volkenkunde* (Leiden).
Meded. Afr. Inst. (Leiden). *Mededelingen van het Afrika Instituut* (Leiden).
Mém. acad. inscriptions et belles-lettres (Paris). *Mémoires de l'Académie des Inscriptions et Belles-Lettres* (Paris).
Mém. acad. roy sci. colon. *Mémoires de l'Académie Royale Belgique Classe des Sciences, Science Colonial.*
Mém. inst. sci. Madagascar. *Mémoires de l'Institut Scientifique de Madagascar.*
Mensario admin. *Mensário Administrativo.*
Mitt. mus. Völkerkunde (Hamburg). *Mitteilungen Museum für Völkerkunde* (Hamburg).
Mitt. s. Mus. Völkerkunde (Leipzig). *Mitteilungen des Städtischen Museums für Völkerkunde* (Leipzig).
Mitt. Anthrop. Gesell. Wien. *Mitteilungen der Anthropologischen Gesellschaft in Wien.*
Mitt. Geog. Gesell (Wien). *Mitteilungen der Geographischen Gesellschaft in Wien.*
Mitt. Schutz. *Mitteilungen aus den Deutschen Schutzgebieten.*
Monde colon. *Le Monde Colonial.*

N

Nat. hist. *Natural History.*
Negro hist. bull. *Negro History Bulletin.*
N. Afr. *Nieuw Afrika.*
Neues Afr. *Neues Afrika.*
N. Rhodes. J. *Northern Rhodesia Journal.*
Notes Afr. I.F.A.N. *Notes Africaines, Institut Français d'Afrique Noire.*
Nouv. rev. franc. O.M. *Nouvelle Revue Française d'Outre-Mer.*

O

Occ. pap. Nat. Mus. S. Rhod. *Occasional Papers of the National Museum of Southern Rhodesia.*

P

Portugal em Afr. *Portugal em Africa.*
Probl. Afr. centr. *Problème d'Afrique Centrale.*
Proc. prehist. soc. *Proceedings of the Prehistoric Society.*
Proc. Rhod. sci. ass. *Proceedings Rhodesia Scientific Association and Transactions.*

R

Rass. Studi Etiopici. *Rassegna di Studi Etiopici.*
Rep. S.A. ass. adv. sci. *Reports of the South African Association for the Advancement of Science.*
Rev. afr. *Revue Africaine.*
Rev. col. belge. *Revue Coloniale Belge.*
Rev. cong. *Revue Congolaise.*
Rev. cong. ill. *Revue Congolaise Illustrée.*
Rev. économique française. *Revue Economique Française.*
Rev. d'esthétique. *Revue d'Esthétique.*
Rev. ethnog. *Revue d'Ethnographie.*
Rev. ethnog. trad. pop. *Revue d'Ethnographie et des Traditions Populaires.*
Rev. étud. ethnog. sociol. *Revue des Études Ethnographiques et Sociologiques* (Paris).
Rev. f. de l'élite. *Revue Française de l'Élite.*
Rev. Gabinete Est. Ultramar. *Revista do Gabinete de Estudos Ultramarinos.*

Rev. geogr. Americana (Buenos Aires). *Revista Geografica Americana* (Buenos Aires).

Rev. géogr. humaine et ethnol. *Revue de Géographie Humaine et d'Ethnologie.*

Rev. hist. rel. *Revue de l'Histoire des Religions.*

Rev. Inst. Super. Estudos Ultramar. *Revista do Instituto Superior de Estudos Ultramarinos.*

Rev. Madag. *Revue de Madagascar.*

Rev. nat. *Revue Nationale* (Belge).

Rev. quest. sci. *Revue des Questions Scientifiques* (Brussels).

Riv. col. Ital. *Rivista delle Colonie Italiane* ('Oltremare') (Bologna).

Riv. sci. Preist. *Rivista di Scienzi Preistoriche* (Florence).

Riv. stud. orient. *Rivista di Studi Orientali.*

S

S.A.M.A.B. *South African Museums Association Bulletin.*

Sci. et voyages. *Sciences et Voyages* (Paris).

Sb. Preuss. Akad. Wiss. *Sitzungsberichte der Kon. Preussischen Akademie der Wissenschaften zu Berlin.*

S. Afr. archaeol. bull. *South African Archaeological Bulletin.*

S. Afr. J. sci. *South African Journal of Science.*

T

Tanganyika notes. *Tanganyika Notes and Records.*

Trans. Lancs. & Cheshire antiq. soc. *Transactions of the Lancashire and Cheshire Antiquarian Society.*

Trans. New York acad. sci. *Transactions of the New York Academy of Sciences.*

Trans. S. Afr. philos. soc. *Transactions of the South African Philosophical Society.*

Trans. Rhodesia sci. assoc. *Transactions of the Rhodesia Scientific Association.*

Trans. R. Soc. S.A. *Transactions of the Royal Society of South Africa.*

Trav. inst. rech. sahariennes (Alger). *Travaux de l'Institut des Recherches Sahariennes.*

U

Uganda J. *Uganda Journal.*

U. Empire. *United Empire.*

V

Verhand. Gesell. Anthrop. (Berlin). *Verhandlungen der Gesellschaft für Anthropologie* (Berlin).

Veröff. Städt. Völkermus. (Frankfurt a/M). *Veröffentlichungen des Städtischen Völkermuseums* (Frankfurt a/M).

Veröff. Mus. Völkerk. Leipzig. *Veröffentlichungen des Museums für Völkerkunde zu Leipzig.*

Veröff. Reichsmus. Völkerkunde. *Veröffentlichungen des Reichsmuseums für Völkerkunde in Leiden.*

Vét. col. *Vétérans Coloniaux.*

W

W.A.R. *West African Review.*

Wetensch. Tijd. *Wetenschappelijke Tijdingen.*

Wien. Völkerk. Mitt. *Wiener Völkerkundliche Mitteilungen.*

Wiener Beitr. z. Kulturgesch. u. Linguistik. *Wiener Beiträge zur Kulturgeschichte und Linguistik.*

Wiss. Z. Fr.-Schiller-Univ. (Jena). *Wissenschaftliche Zeitschrift Friedrich-Schiller-Universität* (Jena).

Z

Z. f. Ästh. u. allg. Kunstwissenschaft. *Zeitschrift für Ästhetik und Allgemeine Kunstwissenschaft.*

Z. f. Ethnol. *Zeitschrift für Ethnologie.*

AUTHOR–INDEX

References to regional art, such as Benin, will be found in the Geographical and Ethnic Index.
For consistency English versions of the names of all countries have been given.
Spelling of vernacular names follows that used by the author of the book or paper concerned.

GEOGRAPHICAL AND ETHNIC INDEX

For consistency English versions of the names of all countries have been given.
Spelling of vernacular names follows that used by the author of the book or paper concerned.

SUBJECT-INDEX

For consistency English versions of the names of all countries have been given.
Spelling of vernacular names follows that used by the author of the book or paper concerned.